Sports Culture

Also by Ellis Cashmore from Routledge

Making Sense of Sports

The Black Culture Industry

... and there was television

Dictionary of Race and Ethnic Relations

Black Sportsmen

Out of Order: Policing Black People (with Eugene McLaughlin)

Sports Culture

An A–Z Guide

Ellis Cashmore

Routledge
Taylor & Francis Group

LONDON AND NEW YORK

First published 2000
by Routledge
11 New Fetter Lane, London EC4P 4EE

Simultaneously published in the USA and Canada
by Routledge
29 West 35th Street, New York, NY 10001

This edition first published 2002

Routledge is an imprint of the Taylor & Francis Group

© 2000, 2002 Routledge

Typeset in Ehrhardt by Taylor & Francis Books Ltd

Printed and bound in Great Britain by Biddles Ltd, Guildford and King's Lynn

British Library Cataloguing in Publication Data
A catalogue record for this book is available from the British Library

Library of Congress Cataloging in Publication Data
Cashmore, Ernest
Sports culture / Ellis Cashmore
p.cm.
includes bibliographical references (p.) and index.
1. Sports – Sociological aspects Encyclopedias.
2. Sports – Anthropological aspects Encyclopedias. I. Title.
GV706.5.C383 2000
306.4′83′03–dc21   99-16891

ISBN 0–415–18169–0 (hbk)
ISBN 0–415–28555–0 (pbk)

Contents

Editorial team   vi
Introduction   vii
Acknowledgments   xiii

Entries A–Z   **1**

Index   453

Editorial team

Editorial assistant

Erwin Bengry
School of Humanities and Social Sciences
Staffordshire University, England

Editorial consultant

Lawrence Wenner
Sports and Fitness Management Program
University of San Francisco, USA

Specialist contributors

Simon Gardiner
Sports Law Centre
Anglia Polytechnic University, England

Barrie Houlihan
Department of Sport Science, PE and
  Recreation Management
Loughborough University, England

David Jary
Graduate School
Staffordshire University, England

Oswald Jones
Aston Business School
Aston University, England

Marc Keech
Chelsea School
University of Brighton, England

Deborah Lupton
School of Social Sciences and Liberal
  Studies
Charles Sturt University, Australia

Dominic Malcolm
Centre for Research into Sport and Society
University of Leicester, England

Toby Miller
Department of Cinema Studies
New York University, USA

Steven J. Overman
Department of Health and Physical
  Education
Jackson State University, USA

George Paton
Aston Business School
Aston University, England

David Podmore
Aston Business School
Aston University, England

David Rowe
Department of Leisure and Tourism
  Studies
University of Newcastle, Australia

Amy I. Shepper
Social Science Reference Library
Florida Atlantic University, USA

Belinda Wheaton
Centre for Sport Development Research
Roehampton Institute, London, England

Introduction

What is sports culture?

Over the next four years, there will be soccer's World Cup finals, a Goodwill Games, the Rugby World Cup, a Commonwealth games, two Olympic games, winter and summer, two World Track and Field championships, four Formula One motor racing seasons, two Ryder Cups, four seasons of football, baseball, basketball and hockey, twenty tennis Grand Slam tournaments and over fifty international cricket matches. The reader will almost certainly witness some of these events "live" and many more on television. He or she will read of the competitions in the sports pages of newspapers and specialist magazines, log onto sports websites and listen to reports on radio. It will be difficult to dodge the gun-to-tape coverage of many international spectacles, especially the Summer Olympics, which seems to saturate our lives. It will be impossible to avoid buying merchandise associated with some of the events: burgers, for instance, will carry the endorsement of "official food of the ...". Even a trip to the supermarket will involve us in sports: count how many of the labels bear the logo of some sporting event.

Whether we like it or not, we live in a culture in which sports play an increasingly important role. Once, the impact of sport was segmental; it was an area distinct from many of the other, more important, domains of our lives. Now, sport is central. Following sports occupies more of our time, our money, our energies, even our braincells. Sport may once have been bracketed with leisure: now it is business. Some sports measure their annual turnovers in billions; their stars earn more in a week than many people earn in five years. People fight – and often die – in the pursuit of their sporting ambitions. The values and artifacts of sport surround us and permeate us. (I use "sports" when referring to the activities and organizations, "sport" for the general institution.)

In his survey "The world of sport," John Andrews concludes that "human society's premier ritual of competition," as he calls sport, is "as natural and enduring as the migration of birds, the locking of antlers or other rituals of the animal kindom" (*The Economist*, June 6, 1998). The urge to compete and perhaps even watch others compete may have its sources in the realms of nature. But, sports competitions themselves are not natural affairs; they are products of cultural endeavors, enterprises that have been manufactured in particular kinds of historical and social circumstances. Bound with rules and governed by organizations, sport became a social institution, though one, as Andrews points out, that may have origins in our genetic makeup.

In this book, I am less interested in the natural roots of sport, and more in the panoply of innovations, articles, qualities, peculiarities and other characteristics that we have developed around sport and the effects sport has had on us: the culture of sports. Culture has been defined in various ways. Back in 1871, the anthropologist Sir Edward Burnett Tylor described culture as: "That complex whole which includes knowledge, belief, art, law, morals, custom and other capabilities and habits acquired by man [*sic*] as a member of society." Tylor wanted to include the gamut of learned skills, habits, ways of communicating and beliefs that went into making a particular way of life.

"The learned part of human behavior," is how Harry Kerbo addresses culture in his *Sociology: Social Structure and Social Conflict* (Macmillan, 1989). Together, the two definitions provide us with a wide but serviceable remit for approaching sports culture: everything we learn and do that has sources in sports. So, the terrain of sports culture is not only the competitive events themselves, but the processes and issues that underlie and surround them. It includes the historical conditions under which sports emerged and matured, the changes that encouraged certain developments and discouraged others. Crucially, sports culture relates to the symbols, myths, language that are either part of or spin-offs of sports. Sports stars are interesting, but not in themselves. Sports culture identifies individuals as characters in a drama, representatives of forces, symbols of eras, signposts to new directions or embodiments of a combination of all these.

Sports culture's focus can be very wide, even when it at first appears to be narrow. For instance, in the entry on PATERNITY (I have avoided adding " . . . and sports" or ". . . in sports" throughout), it will be seen that sports-related paternity is not just about individual athletes getting single women pregnant. It incorporates a compound of cultural issues, including questions of race and ethnicity, masculinity, commodification and money. Like other elements of sports culture, it needs to be looked at in context.

This is exactly what this book aims to do: examine individual issues, people, events and organizations in their social and cultural contexts. Sports culture embraces everything apart from the competitive events themselves: the reader will not find many reports of famous games, fights, races and so on. But, he or she will discover something about the meanings of events, their place in history, the reactions to them, the institutions they actualized and the changes they either signaled or ushered in: in other words, the culture encircling the event. The image of circles is quite useful in understanding sports culture: if the event is at the center, then the affairs, episodes, circumstances, incidents, occurrences, situations and artifacts, all of which contribute to cultural activities, swirl around it. The latter define the subject matter of sports culture and, as such, are covered in this book.

Reading *Sports Culture*

Sports today have little of their previous innocence or simple romance; they have none of the idealism nor much of the heroism that once set them apart from other spheres of human activity. Sport is now a form of entertainment, what some writers call the new rock'n'roll. It has become a vast television studio, with every event taking place amid a deluge of cameras and pundits (a term which, interestingly, comes from the Hindu word *pandit*, meaning a learned expert and teacher). Sports stars often push showbusiness personalities to the sidelines. And it is not simply that sports performers have glamour, money and celebrity partners. More importantly, they have managers, agents, sponsors and television companies projecting them, and a fandom that has become decidedly curious about its favorites. Fans were once interested in what baseball players did in the diamond; now they want to know every detail about their private lives, including whom they are sleeping with. This curiosity is part of the process in which competitive sports have been changed into entertainment. And entertainment has become a central mode through which many of us live our lives.

Many of our reference points derive in some way from televised entertainment. We are disappointed if physicians do not live up to mental constructions we have derived from *ER*. Crime series were once based on true cases; now, it seems the reverse process is happening and aspiring criminals take their cues from cop shows. As we emerged into modernity, film at first and later television supplanted the old certainties that religion once delivered, helping to supply some measure of meaning to our lives. Writers on the postmodern condition have observed that, as society has become more complex and fragmented, so we have become more atomized, our identities splintering into multiples as we drift in and out of what Robert Bellah calls "lifestyle enclaves." Sports have become such lifestyle enclaves. Once they were competitive activities and were addressed mainly as such. Now, they are loaded with the symbolism, imagery, myths, rituals; in short, the meaning-making apparatus that we associate with any other area of cultural life.

Sports have traditionally not been self-conscious pursuits; enthusiasts either like them or they do not. If players or fans like them, they rarely reflect too deeply on why they like them, on the sources of their ardor, the consequences of their devotion or the way in which sports intersect with so many other aspects of their lives. Yet there are reasons for these things: we just need to look for them. So, to talk in terms of sports *culture* means an invitation to interrogate, to ask these kinds of questions and many more besides in an effort to discover the sources and effects of our fascination with sport, to determine how we educe meanings from it, to analyse the significance we attach to it and to examine the products we build from it. No human institution is immune from investigation, not even ones that provide so much pleasure, which is why there have been theories and studies of humor, of sex, of art and so on. Sport has been a little slow to catch on.

In many ways, sports practitioners and journalists have warned off those who bring too much intellect to what is, after all, a joyous human activity. Theoretical contemplation is all very well; but sports are for doers, not thinkers. If you intellectualize over an activity too much you lose sight of the fundamental reason why people like it: because it is fun. This was a stock response. Now it is changing. Sport as an institution is just too big economically, too important politically, too influential in shaping people's lives not to be taken seriously as a subject for academic inquiry. People kill in the name of sport; and, correspondingly, others die. Fans spend small fortunes in the pursuit of their sport. Bookies make and, occasionally, lose big fortunes. Corporations are built on what is now a sports industry. Elite sports performers can outgross many countries. This may have once been an exaggerated claim but, since the career of Michael Jordan, it is now literally true.

Jordan's effect on his sport was tangible. It was also measurable, according to a June 1998 edition of *Fortune* magazine, which added up sales of sports gear and shoes by Nike, his sponsor, and other companies, the sales growth of NBA-licensed apparel and the increased attendance at games, television and advertising revenue. It came up with the breathtaking figure $10 billion (£6 billion), which means that Jordan's persona was worth about as much to the US economy as Vermont, or, put another way, the gross national product of the European state of Luxembourg. Jordan's videos alone generated $80m retail up until his retirement in 1998.

Jordan was, of course, a phenomenon unto himself. There had never been a sports icon like him. It is trite to say that he transcended sports; but it is also true. He was a superb technical player, and his skill alone was probably enough to secure him his place in the sports pantheon. But he was also a product of a cultural construction. He came into professional sports at a time when a contract with television was a *sine qua non* of any successful sports operation and the NBA was busily negotiating its future. Jordan was its first videated star in the sense that his fans followed him through watching his image on their television screens rather than seeing him in the flesh. As viewer ratings for NBA games spiraled, so Jordan's fandom spread across the nation, and then across the world.

Jordan also distinguished himself as a player at the precise moment that Phil Knight was looking for a suitable endorser to push his products. Jordan's association with Knight's corporation Nike is renowned. As Nike surged to the position of market leader, burning off rivals like Reebok and Adidas, Jordan ascended to the position of the best-known athlete in the world. Nike and Jordan were almost synonymous. Both are assigned entries in this volume. I dwell on them only to make the point that Jordan the player, while of great interest in himself, is less important in this context that Jordan the cultural figure. The same goes for all the individual sports performers covered in this book. Some are champions, others are also-rans; but each in his or her own way merits interest. Some champions are obvious choices for inclusion; but the reader will also find less famous names, some from history, some from the present. All have in some way either instigated or reflected cultural change and have, perhaps in a minute way, contributed to the evolution of sports culture.

It is not possible to consider culture without scrutinizing its artifacts. Many would argue strongly that artifacts define a culture. Like other works of art, films have provoked new forms of awareness about sports. My selection of films, some well-known, others obscure, is not based on their box office success, but on their ability to (1) prompt understanding about facets of sports or (2) externalize features of sports that may otherwise have been concealed. Obviously, drama is an effective way of conveying motifs that are integral to sports but also have wider resonance. My choice of films has been guided by such considerations. So: the reader will find entries on blockbusters, but also on little-known movies. As with all other entries, the effort is to set films in their context and pull out their relevance: in this sense, the films that form the core of entries are devices to lead to wider issues.

The dark side of sports culture

Certain themes resurface again and again in this book and all relate to what we might call the "dark side of sports": drugs, racism and sexism. As the reader will discover, none of these can be extricated from the wider processes at work in sports, processes that have permitted or encouraged corporate interests to develop (some would say distort) sports into commodities or articles of trade. The incursions of business into sports have fortified the importance of winning at any cost. The competitive culture of contemporary sports affects its practitioners as well as its fans; their values are changed by ambition and, increasingly, money. No amount of drugs testing or condemnation will remove drugs from contemporary sports; at least, not while there is so much to win. Taking a banned substance in order to win seems much easier if those who are already winning are also thought to be using banned substances.

The drugs question has been one of the great debating points of recent years and will probably continue to command our attention in future. As such, the debate will remain a central feature in the landscape of sports culture. I have tried to disentangle facts from values by including two separate entries. The reader will find drug-related questions in several other entries, including those that deal with cheating and corruption.

Sports have tried to submerge racial barriers, yet, for much of the twentieth century, sports actually held these barriers in place, so much so that it is possible to tell the story of racism through sports. All the elements are there: exclusion, prejudice, stereotyping, exploitation and ideology, to name but a few. The reader will find racism in many of the historical entries as well as more contemporary ones. It is impossible to understand the development of sports culture without paying attention to the race issue which has occasionally split it asunder. At various times in history, racism has manifested itself in sport; at other times, sport has facilitated racist oppression. There have been key moments throughout history that have in some way contained the forces of racist conflict; and there have been key individuals who have served as needles on a compass pointing to the direction of cultural change. I have opted to capture the multiple issues connected with racism through an examination of the lives of people who have been involved in racist conflict, whether wittingly or not. There is also a generic entry on the concept of racism, its impact on sports and, of course, sport's impact on racism.

There is little doubt that the sporting boycott of South Africa contributed in some measure to the downfall of apartheid, but what of black soccer players in Britain? Or the African American domination of the NBA? Or, the likes of Tiger Woods and Venus Williams, who both excelled in traditionally "white" sports? The fact that some sports, like hockey, cricket and skiing, are overwhelmingly white is due to historical and cultural rather than legal or even natural factors. These issues will surface in several entries.

Ethnic minorities are not the only groups to have been affected by sports.

Historically, sports, particularly those that involve strenuous competition, have validated masculinity: by providing the kind of unmediated athletic challenge rarely encountered in working days, sports made possible a strong and assertive proclamation of men's strength, valor and, above all, superiority over women. Industrial society brought with it, among other things, a less physical life, one in which manual labor, while still essential in many spheres of work, was less dangerous and taxing than in pre-industrial times, The proliferation of organized sports toward the end of the nineteenth century is due in large part to the desire for an expression of canalized aggression to counteract what was becoming an increasingly sedentary lifestyle.

Sports had the added benefit of providing a sense of traditional masculinity which was in the process of erosion as the seas of industrial and urban change swept against it. As such, the deep impact made by women in contemporary sports has to be scrutinized and evaluated against this background. Sports were constructed as masculine institutions; they were strongboxes of sexism. Many of the entries in the book engage with the gendering of sport. Sexism manifests in several guises and will come to the fore not only in essays on masculinities/ feminities and the medical discourse about women and sports, but also in items relating to the body in history and in contemporary culture.

These are but three themes that appear throughout the volume. The reader will notice that they criss-cross in several of the entries. They are historically central and abiding issues in sports culture and are likely to provoke intellectually taxing discourses into the twenty-first century.

Particular sports are approached through the organizations which gave them shape and longevity. This is another device. By stressing the manner in which activities have been organized, I have been able to concentrate attention on the changing social conditions under which sports developed and progressed. The interest is less with the actual activities themselves, and more with the culture of which they were part and on which they, in turn, had an effect. I have been guided by popular norms in entitling: for example, Major League Baseball is preferred to the initials MLB, which are not often heard, while the abbreviation NBA is preferred to the longer National Basketball Association.

Three final observations on practices. Rather than use a cumbersome cross-referencing system, I have opted to employ small capitals in the text when a term or name crops up that occupies a full entry elsewhere in the book. I also included a guide to further study which typically includes three items – books, articles, videos etc. – after each entry. Where appropriate, I have converted US dollars to sterling and vice versa at the exchange rate applicable at the time in history.

There are 174 entries in the book, seventeen of which have been written by scholars who have specialist knowledge in particular aspects of sports culture. Their names and affiliations appear on a separate page. I thank them all for their contributions.

Sports culture is not a formally prescribed field of study and, as such, its boundaries are not set. This book is an attempt to map out a terrain in an area with few coordinates. As such, there will be many errors of omission and maybe some of inclusion. I will thank in advance all those readers who will write to me to point out how I might improve this book in future editions.

Acknowledgments

This book owes much to the research skills of a number of librarians, in particular Amy Shepper of Florida Atlantic University, Sheelagh Rowbottom of Staffordshire University, and Carole Daly of Aston University. I thank them for their endeavors. The book has benefited from an uncommonly great and valuable input from its commissioning editor, Fiona Cairns, and the head of Routledge's reference division, Anna Hodson.

Aaron, Hank

b. 1934, USA

Aaron will be remembered as the man who broke Babe Ruth's home run hitting record in 1974. Had the record fallen to a white player, the response would certainly have been euphoric. But, as an African American, Aaron had to accept congratulations and death threats in roughly equal measures.

About 500 hate letters arrived at Aaron's door in the aftermath of his feat. Far from being allowed to bask in triumphalism, crowds booed him and diminished his achievement in passing the Babe's 714 mark by pointing out that Aaron had taken longer to match the number of home runs. In fact, Aaron went on for several more years, becoming the most productive home run hitter with a career total of 755. In many ways Aaron's "sin" was as heinous as that of Jack JOHNSON, who in 1908 took the world heavyweight title from Tommy Burns. Both took possession of symbolic titles that whites had regarded as their own property.

The aggressive reactions to both revealed what the writer Aaron D. Gresson, in his *The Recovery of Race in America* (University of Minnesota Press, 1995) calls "the symbolic and substantive dimensions of racial reempowerment." The taunts, threats and haranguing were collective efforts to recover what many whites considered "moral losses."

Aaron was born in Alabama amid the poverty of the Great Depression. He learned his baseball in the segregated Negro Leagues, as they were known. The breakthrough of Jackie ROBINSON into MAJOR LEAGUE BASEBALL in 1947 opened the doors for many black players. Aaron's first club was the Milwaukee Braves, with which he signed in 1954 at the age of 20. Aaron experienced a relatively smooth transition with the midwestern club.

However, in 1966 the Braves relocated to Atlanta, Georgia, and ran into the type of southern hospitality reserved for African Americans. His competence as a first rate slugger and a decent right fielder failed to win over the Georgia crowds, and he became embittered. As he was to admit later: "People say I'm bitter, but haven't walked a mile in my shoes." Unlike his predecessor Robinson, who, in the 1950s, became quite vocal in his condemnation of racism, Aaron tended to keep his own counsel.

Lightly-regarded, Aaron gradually approached Ruth's record in the 1970s, largely thanks to perseverance. As many white baseball fans sensed that a historic record long held by a white favorite was in danger, they barracked Aaron. Ultimately, his moment of triumph turned into the start of an enduring nightmare that still stands as testimony to the racist sentiments in American sports.

At the time of his record-breaking home run, the first Civil Rights Act, of 1964, was ten years old. This had met with stern resistance in the south. The Act extended federal powers to eliminate discrimination in place of public accommodation (like baseball stadiums) and the desegregation of all public facilities maintained by public organizations. In addition, public education was desegregated and the Civil Rights Commission was granted increased powers. Discrimination on the grounds of "race, color, sex, or national origin" was made unlawful.

Ten years was insufficient time for the resistance to subside, and southern attitudes toward race had softened only slightly by the time of Aaron's deed. The event itself came seven years after a riot in Detroit seemed to signal the climax of a turbulent period of civil unrest across the whole of the United States. More violence was to come in 1980 when the Miami district of Liberty City exploded and angry blacks responded to the acquittal of four police officers who had been accused of beating a black male to death. The two instances of disorder suggested that the potential for urban rioting had been submerged rather than extinguished during Aaron's reign: blacks' discontent at the lack of progress after the civil rights legislation was as real as whites' reluctance to yield the privileges that had been conferred on them by the racist traditions of the old south.

Of related interest

Ashe, Arthur R. (1988) *A Hard Road to Glory: A History of the African-American Athlete Since 1946, Vol 3.*

Wiggins, David K. (1997) *Glory Bound: Black Athletes in a White America*, Syracuse University Press.

acceptability/nonacceptability

The proposition that there were certain types of sports in which it was "acceptable" for women to compete and others in which it was "categorically unacceptable" was introduced by Eleanor Metheny in her 1965 essay "Symbolic forms of movement: The feminine image in sports" (in Metheny 1965). Sports that emphasized aesthetics and grace (gymnastics, lawn tennis) as opposed to strength and speed were acceptable. For instance, in figure skating, spectators enjoy, as Ellyn Kestnbaum expresses it, "the fluid motion of stroking and gliding on ice, and find it more appropriate to watch on female rather than male bodies" (in "What Tonya means to me, or images of independent female power on ice" in Baugham (1995)).

Metheny's distinction was later employed in the context of a wider discussion of "The female athlete" by the sociologists Eldon Snyder and Elmer Spreitzer in their text *Social Aspects of Sport* (1983). "The 'appropriateness' of the type of sport continues to reflect the tenets of the Victorian ideal of femininity," they write, invoking Metheny's three basic categories: categorically unacceptable, generally not acceptable and generally acceptable.

Categorically unacceptable sports include combat sports, endurance events, some field events and many team sports. These sports involve bodily contact, sometimes violent collision and the application of bodily force to heavy objects; they also involve the projection of the body through space over long distances and face-to-face encounters.

Generally not acceptable for women, though perhaps not for minority group women, are field sports such as the shot put, discus, javelin and long jump. These sport require the application of bodily force to moderately heavy missiles or the projection of the body through space over distances; they also involve a display of strength in controlling bodily movements.

Generally acceptable competition involves women in projecting their bodies in aesthetically pleasing patterns, using a device to facilitate bodily movement, the application of force to move a light instrument, overcoming the resistance of a light object and the maintenance of a spatial barrier that prevents body contact with opponents. Examples of such sports would be swimming, diving, skiing, figure skating, gymnastics, golf, archery, fencing, badminton, squash, tennis, volleyball and bowling.

Snyder and Spreitzer employ these categories to suggest that the very activity of sports competition implicates women in contradictory role expectations: those of being a woman and those of being an athlete. The traits of the former include dependence, passivity, intuitiveness and submissiveness, while those of the latter include self-confidence, AGGRESSION, tough-mindedness and RISK-taking. The second group of role characteristics are more conventionally associated with males, according to Snyder and Spreitzer. This is why for many years, women who were conspicuously successful in sports that were "categorically" or "generally" not acceptable were subject to innuendo about their sexuality or sometimes openly accused of LESBIANISM.

While neither Metheny nor Snyder and Spreitzer make the point explicitly, Helen Lenskyj, in her *Out of Bounds: Women, sport and sexuality* (The Women's Press, 1986) writes: "Throughout the century of women's mass sporting participation, femininity and heterosexuality have been seen as incompatible with sporting excellence: either sport make women masculine, or sportswomen were masculine at the outset." Lensykj's book was published in 1986, five years after the scandal surrounding Billie Jean KING. But the King affair was one of a number of catalysts that effectively rendered the acceptability/nonacceptability distinctions archaic, though perhaps not obsolete.

In 1972, during the debate over TITLE IX, which eventually came into force in 1975, opponents of integrated sports (i.e. men and women competing together), argued that the idea of men and women physically colliding with each other was "offensive" to both participants and spectators. It was suggested that all team sports be designated contact sports. Ostensibly, this was to protect women from sex-specific injuries involving breasts and genitals, although, of course, men are also vulnerable to injuries during collision sports.

Lenskyj cites an Ontario, Canada, government report of 1982 that claimed that "contact with genital areas" in sports such as rugby or football constituted an offense against "public decency." Genital contact was acceptable for men, but not for women. When performed by men, hitting and grappling was seen as a form of male bonding; when performed by women, it was indecent and, perhaps, loaded with sexual innuendo.

Throughout the 1990s, more and more women challenged the male hegemony of sports by triumphing in areas traditionally defined as "unacceptable." Quite apart from the pathbreaking marathons of Greta Waitz, who broke the seemingly impossible 2:30 barrier, and the USA Eagles rugby team who became the first female world champions in 1991, women made significant advances in many of the sports considered categorically unacceptable; professional boxers were the most dramatic examples of women competing in a sport for long regarded not only as a male preserve, but an exclusive preserve at that (women were barred from even attending some boxing clubs). In 1998, England's Marylebone Cricket Club (MCC) voted to allow women cricketers to join the once exclusively male club.

Yet, amid the "progressive" movements that permitted or even encouraged women to cross the barriers of the old typology, there remained conservative tendencies. Kestbaum, in her discussion of contemporary figure skating, proposes that: "Men are expected to assert their individuality; women are expected only to be charming and beautiful. Men may be judged as artists, women as works of art." This proposition found support at the 1998 Volleyball World Champion-ships, held in Japan, where it was stipulated by tournament organizers that women competitors must wear shorts only half as long as their male counterparts. The shorter shorts should be "tight in the waist and length" and "cut in an upward angle towards the top of the leg." Traditional volleyball had been overshadowed in previous years by its more dazzling relative, beach volleyball. Introducing skimpier clothing for women was thought to make the game more attractive. Volleyball was a sport described by Snyder and Spreitzer as "generally acceptable" for women.

Of related interest

Baugham, Cynthia (1995) *Women on Ice: Feminist Essays on the Tonya Harding/ Nancy Kerrigan Spectacle*, Routledge.

Metheny, Eleanor (ed.) (1965) *Connotations of Movement in Sport and Dance*, William C. Brown.

Snyder, Eldon E. and Spreitzer, Elmer (1983) *Social Aspects of Sport*, 2nd edn, Prentice-Hall.

adrenaline rush

"Adrenaline rush" describes the sudden sensation of excitement or power that often occurs in response to a stressful situation. In sports, it typically occurs in the context of events that use natural conditions rather than synthetic environments. Long-distance swimming, orienteering, car rallying and rock climbing are examples of sports in which the performers' lives may occasionally be jeopardized. These create perfect conditions for an adrenaline rush.

Cus D'Amato, trainer of heavyweight champions Floyd Patterson and Mike TYSON, among others, was an exponent of fear as a positive force in sporting performance. In his book *Tyson* (Pan Books, 1990), Peter Heller writes of D'Amato's introductory talk to aspiring boxers:

> The first thing I'd do was talk to them about fear ... I would always use ... the same example of the deer crossing an open field and upon approaching the clearing suddenly instinct tells him danger is there and nature begins the survival process, which involves the body releasing adrenaline into the bloodstream, causing the heart to beat faster and enabling the deer to perform extraordinary feats of agility and strength ... fear is your friend.

But the person experiencing the rush may not always be the one sensing danger. Maxwell Rogers, a Florida mother weighing 123lbs (8st 11lbs), lifted a 3,600lbs station wagon under which her son was trapped. In normal circumstances the task would have been impossible, perhaps even for several weight-lifters twice her weight. Yet the life-threatening nature of the predicament precipitated a number of physiological changes that allowed her body to perform abnormally.

The surge of power and exhilaration she must have felt is difficult to reproduce artificially, although swimmers have been known to accelerate after sighting a shark fin. Cross-country runners could probably improve performance if chased by wolves, long jumpers could probably cover fantastic distances were sandpits replaced by a one-hundred-foot drop. Realistically, boxers sometimes describe unexpected feelings of power and resilience when under severe pressure, such as after being knocked down. Muhammad Ali once referred to the condition of being driven to the very brink of a knockout yet somehow finding an extra reserve which enabled him to fight his way out of what he called the "near room."

When dangerous situations threaten, the skeletal muscles might receive up to 70 per cent of the cardiac output, that is, the total blood pumped from the heart (under resting conditions, the liver, kidneys and brain receive 27, 27 and 14 per cent respectively). More blood is fed to muscles that need it at the expense of the viscera, especially the abdomen, where the needs are not urgent. Feelings of pain and tiredness are minimized and the body is prepared for extraordinary feats.

A release of large quantities of the hormone adrenaline is responsible for the emergency action. This action effectively mobilizes the whole body for either *fight* or *flight*. Adrenaline causes profound changes in all parts of the body by stimulating the release of glycogen (which serves to store carbohydrates in tissues) from the liver, the expansion of blood vessels in the heart, brain and limbs and the contraction of vessels in the abdomen. It diminishes fatigue, speeds blood coagulation and causes the spleen to release its stores of blood. The pupils of the eyes dilate. The increased adrenaline level ensures that more food and oxygen will reach the muscles ready for vigorous activity and that they will be cooled by the increased amount of sweat. One can easily see the value of adrenaline to the sports performer.

One of the properties of pseudoephedrene, which is found in many cold remedies and decongestants, is that it mimics the adrenaline rush; it is thus a banned substance. Five different types of the stimulant were found in the urine of Argentina's soccer star Diego Maradona when he was tested at (and subsequently banned from) the 1994 World Cup championships.

The street drug phencyclidine (PCP), better known as "angel dust," has been known to produce something similar. Although the mechanics of the drug are unclear, those who have taken it have been known to behave violently and exhibit remarkable physical power, sometimes requiring several people to subdue them. It has been suggested that sporting performances achieved with chemical enhancement can be replicated without it. Fear would seem to elicit the kind of changes in the body's natural chemistry that are perfectly suited to high-level performance.

Of related interest

Dunn, S (1996) "Thrills and chills" *Shape* vol 15, no 6.

Stanford, B. (1987) "The 'adrenaline rush'" *Physician and Sportsmedicine* vol 15, no 12.

Kendall, B. and Wheeler, M (1994) "Fight or flight? There are other ways to deal with conflict" *Perspective*, November.

age

Biological change ultimately lowers the human's or, indeed, any organism's ability to survive in its environment. Degenerative changes guarantee that a sports performer cannot endure past a certain age: aging increases the probability that a competitor will lose with more frequency or more emphatically as the performer's skill degrades or types of body cells die. The accumulated damage to the machinery of our cells, especially their powerhouses, the mitochondria, caused by exposure to natural toxins and the effects of generating energy in the cell will limit the career of any individual, in or out of sports.

Beyond this obvious statement of fact, there are few recognizable guidelines that hold good for all sports. Fu Mingxia was 12 years old when she won the world diving championship in 1991. Tara Lipinski, at 15, was the youngest gold medalist in winter Olympic games history in 1998. Björn BORG, Stephan Edberg and John McEnroe were all dominant tennis champions, but none won a Grand Slam title after the age of 25. Olga Korbut was considered old in gymnastic terms when she won the 1972 Olympic gold at the age of 17. At 21, she conceded: "My body was overworked, my inner fire died." Her career was effectively over.

Jack Nicklaus was 58 when he tied for sixth place in the 1998 US Masters – ahead of hot favorite Tiger WOODS. Miruts Yifter won two gold medals at the

1980 summer Olympic games at the (reputed) age of 43. 42-year-old Yekaterina Podkopayeva was the world's number one ranked female 1,500 meters runner in 1994. Up to the age of 25, Linford Christie was an indifferent sprinter; but, between 25 and 35, he won eleven major championship golds and, in the process, became the oldest man (33) to win an Olympic 100 meters title.

Wilfred Benitez, who had his first professional fight two months after his fifteenth birthday, won the first of three world titles at the age of 17. At the age of 23, he lost to Thomas Hearns and never recaptured his best form or his titles. At the same age, Archie Moore was barely into his stride: he was a professional boxer for an uninterrupted 28 years, and did not win his world light-heavyweight title until he was 39. He was almost 50 when he had his last fight, which he won on a third-round knockout.

Sports are full of such apparent anomalies. There are, of course, patterns in some sports. In tennis, players tend to mature at an earlier age and experience BURNOUT by their mid-twenties. The intensity and quantity of competition makes exceptional demands on the body. This, coupled with the fact that the rewards of professional tennis make it possible for even a moderately successful player to be a multimillionaire by his or her mid-twenties, has meant a relatively short career parabola for most players, quite unlike in 1969 when Rod Laver won the last of his four Wimbledon titles at 31. Martina Hingis won her first Wimbledon title (1997) in her sixteenth year.

Less physically demanding sports in which competition is less frequent, like sailing or golf, can accommodate a range of ages: witness Dennis Connors and Greg Norman, who competed at the highest levels in their forties. However, contact sports would seem to militate against senior competitors. Thus the case of George Foreman came as a surprise. Foreman turned professional in 1969 at the age of 20, won a world title at 23, another (after a 10-year retirement) at the age of 45 and fought his last fight at the age of 49. His success inspired a new generation of "come-backing" boxers, some of whom met with success.

It has been estimated that an adult human being produces 3–4 million cells per second; these replace a similar number of cells that have died. Some cells, such as muscle and nerve cells, do not undergo cell division at all in the adult being, while other cells, such as the cells in the bone marrow that produce red blood cells, may divide twice in each 24-hour period. Obviously, the muscle and nerve ending cells that are not replaced will cause a performer to decline physically, which makes Foreman's experience all the more remarkable. There is perhaps some truth in the adage "the last thing a fighter loses is his punch."

Never a mobile fighter, Foreman was virtually stationary in his forties. His reactions were also relatively slow, and no amount of training could improve them. His compensating attributes were his wide range of experience and a knockout punch. It is possible that muscle cell degeneration prevented Foreman from punching with the same power as he could in his twenties, but his experience enabled him to use timing, balance and leverage to good effect and these gave his punches enough velocity to finish off many opponents.

A professional sports lifespan of more than 28 years is exceptional for boxing, as it is for most other sports, all the more so when one considers the injuries that are habitually incurred in boxing. Single injuries or an accumulation of them often bring careers to an end. American football players rarely play professionally beyond five years. Quarterbacks are able to prolong active careers because they occupy the most protected position on the field. Joe Montana was sidelined several times during his career but played into his late thirties, and the 38-year-old John Elway led Denver Broncos to Super Bowl XXXIII in 1999.

It is amazing that a soccer player could last into his late forties, but England's Stanley Matthews, who won the first of his international representative honors in 1934 when aged 19, was still playing professionally at the age of 50. When Matthews did retire, it was not due to injury, but simply a loss of motivation.

Of course, motivation is a great antidote to aging. Younger competitors typically have more motivation in their quest for honors. Older performers who have won championships may lose the propulsion that fired their early careers. And competitors who have never won accolades may simply resign themselves to the fact that they never will.

Today, there is another great MOTIVATION, of course. Foreman himself made no secret of the fact that the lure of several million dollars per fight kept him fighting. Tennis, as mentioned earlier, has many rewards for younger players; so many that the burnout that was once so feared is no longer regarded as a problem: a player can have earned his or her fortune in a matter of five years.

Michael JORDAN's re-entry into basketball in 1995 at age 33, after "retiring" in 1993, may have had money somewhere in the motivational mix. But his annual earning for the years prior to his first departure were over $30m, making his personal fortune too great for him to want even more millions. Or maybe not: Evander Holyfield, whose personal worth was estimated to be $300m, continued to box at the age of 35, still managing to perform well enough to remain world heavyweight champion.

Of related interest

Baillie, Patrick and Danish, Steven (1992) "Understanding the career transition of athletes," *The Sport Psychologist* vol 6, no 1.

aggression

Definitions

In essence, aggression is primarily a learned behavior which is the result of an individual's interactions with his or her social environment over time ... Aggression occurs in sports where an athlete's generalized expectancies for reinforcement for aggressive behavior are high (e.g. receiving praise from parents, coaches, peers) and where the reward value outweighs punishment value (e.g. gaining a tactical and/or psychological advantage with a personal foul, yardage penalty in American football).

Gershon Tenenbaum *et al.* (1997) "Aggression and violence in sport: An ISSP position stand," *The Sport Psychologist* vol 11, no 1)

Tenenbaun *et al.* conclude that: "Behavior that inflicts harm upon another, either physical or psychological, and bears no direct relationship to the competitive goals of sport is unacceptable."

The problem with this pronouncement is that aggression is so central to many sports that it is difficult to determine when it "bears no direct relationship to the competitive goals." Intimidating opponents with illegal tactics may escape the condemnation of Tenenbaum *et al.* because it may result in a subdued or slightly repressed performance from an opponent and thus have a strategic yield. In boxing, headbutting an opponent in a disguised way may open a cut that impairs the opponent or even forces a stoppage. As for "psychological" harm, it would be naive to imagine any serious competitor missing an opportunity to hurt an opponent psychologically, and impossible not to see this as having a direct bearing on the outcome of a contest. So, while the authors' definition of aggression is accurate, their edict on its acceptability seems ingenuous.

Considered as a workplace, professional sport is more aggressive and hazardous than most others, save for the military and, historically, chemical and nuclear industries. Working as a miner, a steeple-jack or an oil-rigger carries with it attendant RISK of bodily harm, but not on such a regular basis as sports such as boxing, football and hockey, or even non-contact sports, like skiing or tennis. This is to be expected, considering the value placed on aggression, or, as sportscasters are wont to call it, "aggressiveness." Some measure of aggression is desirable in most sports and it is essential in contact or collision sports, perhaps in any sport in which an ADRENALINE RUSH proves valuable.

Historically, sports, or at least their precursors, were encouraged by some cultures as a way of preparing for war. Combative sports in particular were considered as training practices and competitions were miniature war zones. Competition was thought to reflect perfectly the values and attitudes germane to warrior cultures. A certain belligerence was thought essential to success in competition. This is a view still held dear by many coaches and trainers, especially those who approach their task in the give-no-quarter style of someone like Vince LOMBARDI. To such people, losing, as it is often said, is not an option.

As sports became organized into governed activities with rules and codes, as well as ethics, so they were thought to build character, discipline and the ability to overcome adversity. Accepting defeat was a regrettable yet valuable experience: in Rudyard Kipling's famous verse, both victory and defeat were "impostors," each to be dealt with nobly.

Aggression as catharsis

Neo-Freudians have little trouble in understanding aggression in sports: for them, sporting activity is in itself a form of VIOLENCE, albeit in a symbolic guise. The aggressive energy stored in the id part of the mind needs some form of expression, whether in fantasy or actuality. Aggressive sports are a catharsis of sorts, activities that can serve as a purgative release for both competitors or spectators, the latter releasing their energies vicariously; or, in the case of HOOLIGANISM, in reality.

While disagreeing about the sources of the aggressive energy, ethologists would share the general conclusion about sport's utility, as a type of valve that can be turned on and off to discharge aggression that might otherwise be vented in other contexts. Sport is a healthy option: it is better for people to be beating up on each other in a controlled arena, rather than in other environments where the damage may not be limited. Both perspectives incorporate an image of the human being as brimming with violent potential. Sporting activity is a relatively safe channel for converting this into harmless competition.

Frustration → aggression

While this has been a popular conception, it is not supported by evidence; quite the contrary, as Jeffrey Goldstein writes: "Research with high school and college athletes finds that they are more quick to anger than non-athletes and that those who participate in combative sports, such as hockey and football, respond to frustration with a greater degree of aggression when compared to athletes in non-contact sports and non-athletes" (in D. Stanley Eitzen (ed.) (1989) *Sport in Contemporary Society: An anthology*, 3rd edn, St Martin's Press).

Goldstein goes so far as to say that, far from providing a way of letting off steam, sports allow that steam to build up. By competing in sports, a performer is generating aggression that may well not be dissipated in the course of a competition. The sports contest may then become a kind of rehearsal for violent behavior in real life. This kind of view finds some agreement with a school of thought based on the work of John Dollard in the 1930s. Dollard, a Yale psychologist, theorized that frustration – defined as the thwarting of any goal-directed behavior – produces an aroused state in which the individual is driven to injure the source of the frustration.

Since virtually all sports by definition involve the attempted obstruction of goal-directed behavior, frustration and the aroused state it produces are inevitable. It has often been said that great sports performers are the ones that can control their frustration and remain FOCUSED on the job at hand. Epitomizing the phlegmatic performer would be Björn BORG, someone who gave the impression that an earthquake would not perturb him. By total contrast, John McEnroe was intolerant of even minor frustrations and allowed his aggression to boil over in practically every game. Somehow, he was able to convert what might otherwise have been wasted energy into competitive excellence: he played entire games in a high state of arousal.

The frustration–aggression theory has two contrasting applications in sports. First, observing sports competitions could spark violence among crowds: simply witnessing an act of violence. Several psychologists have documented a strong relationship between violence witnessed at sports events and violent behavior among fans. The theory underpinning this relationship derives from behaviorism or social learning. The premise of this is: humans learn through a basic stimulus–response mechanism and, if their response is rewarded, or at least goes unpunished, then they are likely to repeat it.

This is basically the view taken by Tenenbaun *et al*, and its application in sports is obvious. An overly aggressive approach may win few rewards from referees or umpires, but, if opponents are shaken up or physically impeded, then enraptured team mates, coaches and fans may compensate for the official disapproval. It has often been rumored that head coaches in the NFL have actually put bounties on particular quarterbacks.

It is this irremovable streak of aggression that runs through much of sport that leads many disapproving observers to conclude that the overt display of primitive, marauding masculinity is an occasion for men to exhibit their manhood. Even women's sports, for long a mere appendage to men's, began to take on an aggressive character in the 1990s: the women's National Basketball Association (NBA) and women's professional boxing were but two examples of sports that reflected their traditionally more bellicose male equivalents. Even women's tennis, a successor to the gentle game designed for Victorian ladies, grew more fierce and bad-tempered in the 1990s with the rise of physically powerful players such as Steffi GRAF and Monica Seles.

It is not an exaggeration to suggest that sports are often stages for both symbolic and actual aggression. As the attribute of aggression has traditionally been closely associated with (if not part of the definition of) masculinity – "What are you, a man or a mouse?" – sports have been arenas for the presentation of manhood and the bifurcation of MASCULINITIES/FEMININITIES. In this sense, we can see the sport as one of the few parts of society where men can generate, discharge and reveal their aggression with relative impunity. This is a view of sports as a legitimator of behavior that would be otherwise deemed intolerable. The players are part of a subculture in which uncouth and boorish behavior is not condemned, as it is elsewhere, but commended. Stories of SPOUSAL ABUSE, hard drinking, street fighting, reporter bashing and divers other uncivilities are legion in sports.

An Italian study by Lenzi et al. (1997) suggests that sports serve as a means of controlling the aggression of women and help the "psychosocial" development of men; in other words, sports participation enables men to conform to male stereotypes that portray the male as aggressive and the woman as gentle and submissive. In the chapter "Aggression in society" of his book *Sport in Society* (1998), J. Jay Coakley summarizes the research:

> Aggression originates in some combination of (1) frustration coupled with anger, opportunities, stimulus cues, and social support; (2) strategies used by athletes and encouraged by peers, parents, coaches, spectators, and sponsors; and (3) definitions of masculinity emphasizing violence as a basis for becoming a man and being superior to a woman.

Of related interest

Coakley, J. Jay (1998) *Sport in Society: Issues and Controversies*, 6th edn, McGraw-Hill.

Gruneau, Rick and Whitson, David (1993) *Hockey Night in Canada: Sport, Identity and Cultural Politics*, Garamond Press.

Lenzi, A., Bianco, I., Milazzo, V., Placidi, G. and Castrogiovanni, P. (1997) "Comparison of aggressive behavior between men and women in sport," *Perceptual and Motor Skills* vol 84, no 1.

Aids

The announcement by Earvin "Magic" JOHNSON that he had contracted the HIV virus and would retire immediately from professional basketball was major news around the world in November 1991. While there had been other sports performers who had tested HIV-positive in routine medical examinations (such as boxer Ruben Palacios), no one approaching Johnson's fame and stature had come forward and openly proclaimed that they had the virus. His disclosure of casual heterosexual liaisons was in the manner of a confession; but it also served as a caution against unprotected sex, and Johnson became involved in campaigns for Aids awareness.

The original source of the HIV-1 virus responsible for the bulk of the Aids epidemic was almost certainly a chimpanzee, from which closely related viruses were later isolated. The point at which Aids made its leap from ape to man was not known until the discovery of the virus in a blood sample taken from a man in Central Africa in 1959. How the HIV-1 got from the ape to man is not known. Close contact with blood – for example, while butchering a chimpanzee to eat – could have been the cause. Evidence revealed in 1999 suggested that the virus repeatedly passed from chimpanzees to humans for several thousand years.

Precisely how it turned into an epidemic and, later, a pandemic (i.e. prevalent all over the world) is unclear. It has been suggested that mass immunization campaigns in Africa by the World Health Organization helped to spread the disease. Epidemiological evidence linking the spread of Aids in each African country with the extent of the smallpox campaign was inconclusive, however. Another theory holds that the major social changes of the 1950s took the virus from the rural areas of Africa to urban centers and, as tribal customs changed, there was greater sexual contact. Increasing urbanization, breakdown of traditional lifestyles, population movements and sexual promiscuity all contributed to increases in sexually transmitted disease. According to this view, the virus may have existed in humans as far back as the 1940s, but did not spread until the urbanization of the 1950s. For HIV-2, the other Aids virus, the source was a sooty mangabey, another primate that occupies the forests of central western Africa. Both viruses were capable of generating an epidemic.

US deaths from Aids peaked in 1994–5 and then nose-dived in 1996. The fall accelerated in 1997. In the first half of 1997, 12,040 Americans died of Aids, compared with 21,460 in the first half of 1996. The drop benefited men and women, blacks and whites.

In 1997, 30.6 million people were living with HIV or full-blown Aids. In the previous year, there had been 5.8 new HIV infections and 2.3 million deaths due to HIV/Aids, bringing the cumulative number of deaths due to the virus to 11.7 million. Worldwide, 1.0 per cent of the population was living with Aids.

It was estimated that, even in the late 1990s, nine out of ten HIV-infected persons were unaware of their condition. In the developing world and especially in Africa the virus took an extraordinary toll: it was estimated that 2,300,000 people would die of an Aids-related illness in 1997–8, a 50 per cent increase on 1996–7. One in five of the victims were children, mostly infected from birth. A three-drug cocktail, including AZT plus one of the protease inhibitors, revolutionized Aids care. Typically, a person taking the cocktail as soon as infected could remain well and be able to function effectively. Johnson began actively pursuing a new career in boxing promotion six years after his disclosure.

Former WBO heavyweight champion Tommy Morrison was diagnosed HIV-positive on the eve of a fight in Las Vegas in February 1996, when aged 27. Unlike Johnson, who was able to continue an active interest in sports by using the protease inhibitor drug AZT, Morrison refused medication. Despite the diagnosis, Morrison fought in Japan in November 1996 and recorded a win over Marcus Rhode. Morrison believed he caught the virus either by sharing the needles he used to inject anabolic steroids, or through heterosexual sex.

Former world champion lightweight boxer Esteban de Jesus, who held the distinction of being the first man to defeat Roberto Duran, had slipped from the public gaze by the time he died of an Aids-related illness in 1989. Arthur Ashe was the first high-profile sports victim of Aids: he died after receiving a blood transfusion in a hospital, where he had just pulled through bypass surgery to treat a hereditary heart condition. Unlike Johnson, Ashe was a famously clean-cut family man who had dedicated much of his post-tennis career writing on the imbalance between black achievement in sports and failure in education. He eschewed publicity and concealed the fact that he was HIV-positive. When the news came out in 1992, he spent the remaining year of his life raising money for the Aids Foundation.

Neither Johnson or Ashe were among high-risk groups: statistically, those at most risk from HIV/Aids were – indeed, still are – active homosexuals and habitual drug users. Given the ethos of machismo that pervades much contemporary sports, GAYS have understandably been reluctant to come out during their active competitive careers. Olympic diver Greg Louganis's autobiography *Breaking the Surface: A Life* (Random House, 1995) was published after his retirement. In the book, Louganis revealed that six months before the 1988 summer Olympics, he had been diagnosed HIV-positive, yet kept his secret from fans and sports governing federations. The double gold medalist cut his head and spilled blood attempting a reverse two-and-a-half pike during a preliminary round. The poolside doctor who treated the wound did not wear protective gloves. While the chances of contracting Aids in the pool were extremely remote, one wonders how many of Louganis's rivals would have followed him into the water had they known of his condition beforehand.

Another Olympic champion, John Curry, died of an Aids-related illness in 1994, a year before Louganis's declaration. John Curry won the 1976 Olympic gold medal for figure skating in spite of arguments over his style, which some considered too delicate and lacking in the robustness expected of male skaters in the 1970s. In addition to the Olympic gold, Curry won the European and World championships. He then started his own figure skating company, performing at venues such as the Kennedy Center in Washington DC and London's Royal Albert Hall.

Of related interest

Dworkin, Shari Lee and Wachs, Faye (1998) "Disciplining the body: HIV-

positive male athletes, media surveillance and the policing of sexuality"
Sociology of Sport Journal vol 15, no 1.

Hums, M.A. (1994) "AIDs in the sports arena: After Magic Johnson, where do
we go from here?" *Journal of Legal Aspects of Sport*, vol 4, no 1.

Rowe, David (1994) "Accommodating bodies: Celebrities, sexuality and 'Tragic
Magic' " *Journal of Sport and Social Issues* vol 18, no 1.

Ali, Muhammad

b. 1942, USA

The fearsome warrior

On October 2, 1980, Muhammad Ali, then aged 38, and Larry Holmes, the
heavyweight champion of the world, entered a temporary arena built at Caesar's
Palace, Las Vegas. A gate of nearly 25,000 had paid $5,766,125, a record in its day.
Ali weighed 217lbs (15st 7lbs), his lightest since 1974, while the champion was
211lbs. Biographer Thomas Hauser summarizes the clash: "It wasn't a fight; it
was an execution" (1997).

After ten sickeningly one-sided rounds, Ali's trainer Angelo Dundee called
over the referee to signal Ali's retirement. Ali's aide and confidante Bundini
Brown pleaded: "One more round." But Dundee snapped back: "Fuck you! No!
... The ballgame's over."

In a way, he was right: one game had indeed finished. Ali fought only once
again, in a fight for which their was little public demand. His health had been
deteriorating for several years before the misbegotten Holmes fight, and the
savaging he took repulsed even his sternest critics. Ali the "fearsome warrior," as
Hauser calls him, would disappear. Yet, as Michael Oriard, in his essay
"Muhammad Ali: Hero in the age of mass media" reminds us: "There was not a
single Ali but many Alis in the public consciousness" (in Gorn 1995). Hauser
argues that he evolved into a "benevolent monarch and ultimately to a benign
venerated figure."

We might add that he had already been a symbol of black protest, a cipher for
the anti-Vietnam movement, a martyr (or traitor, depending on one's
perspective), a self-regarding braggart basking in a culture of NARCISSISM –
and many more things beside. While there have been several sporting ICONS, none
have approached Ali in terms of complexity, endowment and sheer potency.
Jeffrey Sammons suggests: "Perhaps no single person embodied the ethic of
protest and intersected with so many lives, ordinary and extraordinary" (in
"Rebel with a cause: Muhammad Ali as sixties protest symbol," in Gorn 1995).

Born in Louisville, Kentucky, in the segregated south, Cassius Clay, as he was
christened, was made forcibly aware of America's "two nations," one black, one
white. In his autobiography, he relates how, after the euphoria of winning a gold
medal at the Rome Olympics of 1960, he returned home to be refused service at a
restaurant. This kind of incident was to influence his later commitments. Clay's
amateur triumphs convinced a syndicate of white entrepreneurs to finance his
early professional career.

Basing his approach on that of Gorgeous George, a flamboyant and boastful wrestler, Clay both infuriated and fascinated audiences with his outrageous claims to be the greatest boxer of all time, his belittling of opponents, his poetry and his habit of predicting (often accurately) the round in which his fights would end. "It's hard to be modest when you're as great as I am," he once remarked.

An UNDERDOG going into his challenge for Sonny Liston's world title in 1964, he forced the champion into retirement and easily dismissed him in the rematch. Between the two fights, he had proclaimed his change of name to Muhammad Ali, reflecting his conversion to Islam. In fact, he had made public his membership of the Nation of Islam, sometimes known as the Black Muslims, prior to the first Liston fight, but the full ramifications came later.

The Nation of Islam was led by Elijah Muhammad, and had among its most famous followers Malcolm X, who kept company with Ali and who was to be assassinated in February 1965. Among the Nation of Islam's principles were (and are) that whites were "blue-eyed devils" who were intent on keeping black people in a state of subjugation and that integration was not only impossible, but undesirable. Blacks and whites should live separately, preferably by living in different states. The view was in stark distinction to North America's melting pot ideal.

Ali's camp comprised only one white man, Angelo Dundee. Cassius Clay, Sr. was violently opposed to Ali's affiliation, not on religious grounds but because he believed the entourage of Black Muslims he attracted were taking his money. But Ali's commitment deepened and the media, which had earlier warmed to his extravagance, turned against him. A rift occurred between Ali and Joe Louis, the former heavyweight champion who was once described as "a credit to his race." This presaged several other conflicts with other black boxers whom Ali believed had allowed themselves to become assimilated into white America and had failed to face themselves as true black people.

Ali saved his most ardent criticism for Floyd Patterson, whom he called an "Uncle Tom" and "the rabbit," after Patterson had refused to use his Islamic name. He seemed to delight in punishing Patterson in their fight in 1965. The almost malicious performance brought censure from sections of America, both black and white.

Martyrdom

The events that followed Ali's call-up by the military in February 1966 were dramatized by a background of growing resistance to the US involvement in the Vietnam war. Ali failed to meet the qualifying criteria in the mental aptitude tests at first, but, by 1966, with the war intensifying, the US Army lowered the required percentile, making him eligible for the draft. A legal request for a deferment from military service was denied. Ali's oft-quoted remark, "I ain't got no quarrel with them Vietcong," made headlines around the world and positioned him in the eyes of many as the most famous-ever draft dodger. However, he insisted that his conscience, not cowardice, guided his decision not to serve in the military, and so to many others he became a mighty symbol of pacifism.

Ali continued to defend his title, often traveling overseas in response to attempted boycotts of his fights. At the nadir of his popularity he fought Ernie Terrell, who, like Patterson, persisted in calling him "Clay." The fight in Houston had a grim subtext with Ali constantly taunting Terrell. "What's my name, Uncle Tom?" Ali asked Terrell as he administered a callous beating. The torment was prolonged by Ali until the fourteenth round. The phrase "What's my name?" became a slogan of defiance (it features on the Rolling Stones' "Sympathy for the devil"). Media reaction to the fight was wholly negative. Hauser quotes Jimmy Cannon, a boxing writer of the day: "It was a bad fight, nasty with the evil of religious fanaticism. This wasn't an athletic contest. It was a kind of lynching . . . [Ali] is a vicious propagandist for a spiteful mob that works the religious underworld."

In April 1967, Ali refused to be inducted into the armed forces. Despite claims that he deserved the same status as conscientious objectors from the Mennonite Church or other Christian groups, Ali was denied and found guilty of draft evasion. After a five-year legal struggle, during which time Ali was stripped of his title, a compromise was reached and Ali was set free. During his exile, Ali had angered the Nation of Islam by announcing his wish to return to boxing if this was ever possible. Elijah Muhammad, the supreme minister, denounced Ali for playing "the white man's games of civilization." Elijah had objected to sports for some time, believing them to be detrimental to the progress of black people.

Other critical evaluations of sport were gathering force. The black power inspired protests of John Carlos and Tommie Smith at the 1968 Olympics, combined with the anti-apartheid movement in South Africa, where people like Sam RAMSAMY were rallying against racism, had made clear that sport could be used to amplify the experiences of black people the world over. While Ali was a *bête noir* for many whites and indeed blacks, several civil rights leaders, sports performers and entertainers came out publicly in his defense. "Still others in American society viewed Ali as a genuine hero," writes David Wiggins in his *Glory Bound: Black Athletes in a White America* (Syracuse University Press, 1997). "Many people in the black community viewed Ali in this manner, considering him a champion of the black Civil Rights movement who bravely defied the norms and conventions of the dominant culture."

Ali's moves were monitored by government intelligence organizations: given the growing respect he was afforded, he was seen as an influential figure. Many of his conversations were wiretapped. He spent three and one-half years without his title, unable to earn a living. By the end of this time, cultural conditions had shifted so much that he was widely regarded as a martyr by the by-then formidable antiwar movement and practically anyone who felt affinity with civil rights.

Return from exile

Ali's first fight after exile was in October 1970. He beat Jerry Quarry at an Atlanta fight where the majority of fans were African Americans. Any prospect of a smooth transition back to the title was dashed March 1971 by Joe Frazier, who had taken the title in Ali's absence and defended it with unexpected tenacity in a contest that started one of the most celebrated RIVALRIES in sport. Ali had called

Frazier a "white man's champion," and declared: "Any black man who's for Joe Frazier is a traitor." Ali beat Frazier twice over the following years, every fight being viciously fought and punishing for both men.

Ali had to wait until 1974 before getting another chance at the world title. By this time, Frazier had been dethroned by George Foreman and Ali, at 32, was not favored; in fact, many feared for his well-being, especially as he had been given two tough fights by the unheralded Ken Norton (one win each; Ali won a third later, in 1976). The fight in Zaire was promoted by Don KING, at that stage building his way toward becoming one of the world's most powerful sports entrepreneurs. The circumstances surrounding what was known as "The Rumble in the Jungle" are the subject of Leon Gast's documentary film *WHEN WE WERE KINGS*. Ali's remarkable Phoenix-like victory re-established him as the world heavyweight champion.

The death of Elijah Muhammad in 1975 led to a split in the Nation of Islam, with Louis Farrakhan taking the movement in a fundamentalist direction while Elijah's son Wallace D. Muhammad founded the World Community of Al-Islam in the West, which dwelt less on past atrocities of blue-eyed devils and more on the future. Ali sided with Wallace.

In June 1979, having lost and regained the title against Leon Spinks and beaten Frazier once more, Ali announced his retirement from boxing. There were clear signs of decline in both Spinks fights and, at 37, Ali appeared to have made a graceful exit when he moved to Los Angeles with his third wife Veronica, whom he had married two years before. His first marriage lasted less than a year ending in 1966; Ali had married again in 1967.

Ali had also split with the business syndicate which handled his early affairs after joining the Nation of Islam. Herbert Muhammad became his manager. Hauser estimates Ali's career earnings to 1979 to be "tens of millions of dollars." The three Frazier fights alone brought Ali $11m; the 1976 Norton fight grossed him $6m; his purse for the Foreman fight was $5.45m; he earned $6.75m for the two Spinks fights. His lesser-paid fights were typically worth $2m each to Ali. Yet, on his retirement, Ali was not wealthy. His wife had an extravagant lifestyle and his business investments were poorly judged. He also gave generously to the Nation of Islam and to various causes.

Within fifteen months of his announced retirement, Ali returned to the ring, his principal MOTIVATION being money, though Ali himself reckoned it was the prospect of winning the world title for a record fourth time that drove him. While public sentiment seemed against a comeback at 38 against a peak-form Larry Holmes, who was employed as Ali's sparring partner between 1973–5, box office interest was strong enough to justify paying Ali $8m. Holmes, as champion, received less than $3m. It was the first fight in which Ali failed to last the full distance, and it seemed an inglorious, if lucrative end, to a grand career.

Ali's ill-fated business ventures took another bad turn when he became involved with Muhammad Ali Professional Sports, an organization headed by Harold Smith, which proved to be a fraudulent operation. A return to the ring appeared impossible after medical tests revealed all manner of complications, and Ali relinquished his boxing license to the Nevada State Athletic Commission. But, this still left him free to box elsewhere in the world and, in December, 1981, he fought once more in Nassau, the Bahamas. It ended in another resounding defeat, this time by Trevor Berbick. The fight was promoted by James Cornelius, who was a member of the Nation of Islam. As in the Holmes fight, there was plain evidence of Ali's acute deterioration and, although he lasted the ten rounds distance, he spent much of the fight against the ropes soaking up punishment. He was 39 and had fought 61 times, with a 56–5 record.

Further questionable business deals and an expensive divorce in 1986 followed. In 1984 he disappointed his supporters when he nominally supported Ronald Reagan's re-election bid. He also endorsed George Bush in 1988. The Republican Party's policies, particularly in regard to affirmative action programs, were widely seen as detrimental to the interests of African Americans and Ali's actions were, for many, tantamount to a betrayal.

Ali's public appearances gave substance to stories of his ill health. By 1987 he was the subject of much medical interest. Slurred speech and uncoordinated bodily movements gave rise to several theories about his condition, which was ultimately revealed as Parkinson's Syndrome. His public appearances became rarer and he became Hauser's "benign venerated figure."

Over a period of four decades, Ali excited a variety of responses: admiration and respect, of course, but also cynicism, anger and condemnation. At different points in his life, he drew the adulation of young people committed to civil rights, black power and peace. Yet, as Wiggins points out: "Members of the establishment were, moreover, infuriated by Ali because he exposed, for all the world to see, an America that was unwilling to honor its own precepts."

Ali engaged with the central issues that preoccupied America: race and war. But, it would be remiss to understand him as a symbol of social healing; much of his mission was to expose and, perhaps, to deepen divisions. He preached peace, yet aligned himself with a movement that sanctioned racial separation and the subordination of women. He accepted a role with the liberal Democratic administration of Jimmy Carter, yet later sided with reactionaries, Reagan and Bush. He preached black pride, yet disparaged and dehumanized fellow blacks. He preached the importance of self-determination, yet allowed himself to be sucked into so many doubtful business deals that he was forced to prolong his career to the point where his dignity was effaced. Like any towering symbol, he had very human contradictions.

Of related interest

Ali, Muhammad (1975) *The Greatest: My Own Story*, Random House.
Early, Gerald (ed.) (1998) *I'm a Little Special: A Muhammad Ali Reader*, Yellow Jersey Press.
Gorn, Elliott (ed.) (1995) *Muhammad Ali: The People's Champ*, University of Illinois Press.
Hauser, Thomas (1997) *Muhammad Ali: His Life and Times* Pan Books.

American Gladiators

It could be argued that *American Gladiators*, an indoor made-for-television competition that began in 1990, captured the spirit of contemporary sport more truly than many traditional sports. The contest had no existence independent of the television network, no audience apart from television viewers and no history beyond its first broadcast. And yet its popularity, as reflected in television ratings, ensured it a regular slot in the USA and gave rise to a sibling show in Britain called simply *Gladiators.*

While *American Gladiators* appeared to have leaped from the imagination of a television executive, it was in fact the progeny of several other competitive programs that were designed, coordinated and managed exclusively for television. The *Superstars* competitions were loosely based on decathlon-like multi-disciplinary contests in which well-known sports stars competed against each other in a variety of contrived competitions, some drawn from Olympic events (track, swimming and so on) and others devised specially for the program.

Another relation was wrestling, not the Greco-Roman variety, but the "Wrestlemania" and WWF style spectacles featuring highly theatrical contestants in settings that owed more to drama than to competitive sports. Despite the somewhat artificial nature of the event, television wrestling proved commercially successful on both sides of the Atlantic and gave rise to its own stars, like Hulk Hogan and BIG DADDY.

There were certainly also overlaps with the roller derby contests that were television staples in the 1960s, and which thrilled American audiences with their seemingly unfettered VIOLENCE. The contest allied roller skating to a gladiatorial chase and produced a winning formula that, interestingly, had even greater success when it was dramatized for the movies. Raquel Welch was the eponymous *Kansas City Bomber* in Jerrold Freedman's 1972 film about roller derby, which featured several long competitive sequences. Norman Jewison's futuristic *Rollerball* (1975) extended the format: in his film, the losers were maimed or killed.

As its name suggests, *American Gladiators* boasted a longer ancestry than earlier television shows: although it was a far cry from the Roman contests that were held either side of the beginning of the Christian era, the TELEVISION show retained the faint traces of trained human combat, albeit in safe environments. For example, contestants – who were nonprofessionals selected from the public after a series of elimination rounds – were made to go head-to-head with trained "Gladiators," who were employed by the television network. They may be required to sprint along a twenty-yard course while a Gladiator would try to halt them, or slam balls in a net that was protected by Gladiators. In a perennially popular contest called The Wall, contestants would be encouraged to scale an artificial rockface while pursued (after a ten-second delay) by a Gladiator who would try to drag them down. No harm would come to the contestants, who were held in harnesses in the event that they were displaced by the pursuant Gladiators, who were known to audiences by single metaphorical names, such as "Wolf," "Laser" or "Diamond."

While it was never made explicit, the influence of *The Running Man*, a 1987 movie directed by Paul Michael Glazer and starring Arnold Schwarzenegger, never seemed far from the surface. In this vision of a future society, a television sport involves plucking prisoners from their cells and pitching them against specialized gladiators with names like Buzzsaw, Dynamo and Subzero in contrived contests. Schwarzenegger's runner seems uncannily similar to the *American Gladiator* contestants who were also seeking to escape the clutches of specialists. The difference in the movie version is that the contestants are hunted to the death.

"Live" audiences would cheer for the contestants and hiss at the Gladiators while music blared. No trick of TECHNOLOGY would be missed as cameras zoomed in from all angles on the mock battle. Close-ups, slo-mos, reverse angles, replays and other devices learnt from years of televising "real" sports were used in the effort to create a competition that incorporated ideas from several other sports. Programs would be pre-recorded several weeks in advance. The US version was staged at Universal Studios, the British version at Birmingham's National Indoor Arena.

Robert Rinehart believes that there was a "sexist kitsch" that aided the show's appeal. By this he means that female contestants were usually asked questions of the kind "You're learning about yourself," "You're tiny in stature, quiet when you compete" and "Don't worry honey, you'll be a success." While for men: "It's more than a game for you – it's a cause" and "You take a beating, and keep on competing." According to Rinehart: "This sexist kitsch may serve to paradoxically [sic] deny empowerment for women."

The character and value of artifice, the unreal and all things synthetic has changed over the decades: once natural, real and genuine articles were prized over their counterfeit alternatives. A leather jacket was a treasured possession, while a plastic alternative had no value. Sports were played on real grass in preference to artificial turf. People enjoyed proper food, not the junk served in fast food chains. But, like the omnipresent fast food chains themselves, society has become what George Ritzer calls "McDonaldized." *American Gladiators* was the perfect sport for a McDonaldized world in which homogeneity, efficiency, predictability and a quick turnaround were the orders of the day.

Of related interest

Rinehart, Robert (1994) "Sport as kitsch: A case study of the *American Gladiators,*" *Journal of Popular Culture* vol 28, no 2.
Murphy, A (1991) "Gods and goddesses at play" *Sports Illustrated*, vol 75, no 24.
Ritzer, George (1998) *The McDonaldization Thesis: Explorations and Extensions,* Sage.

Angels With Dirty Faces Effect, the

Cultural goals and the various means to achieve them

The *Angels with Dirty Faces* Effect refers to the rehabilitative consequences of participating in sports for young offenders, or potential offenders. The term derives from the classic Michael Curtiz movie of 1938, in which two working-class youths from the urban slums pursue different career paths. James Cagney famously portrayed the youth who became a petty gangster (in those days, spelt with "er" rather than "a"), while Pat O'Brien played his friend who becomes a priest.

The well-meaning priest is committed to the beneficial effects of sports and encourages members of the street gangs in his neighborhood to train at his gym. The *Angels with Dirty Faces* Effect is that the youths are drawn away from their fatalistic resignation to a life of petty crime and assume charge of their own destinies. The morally and socially uplifting power of sports is underlined by the sense of purpose and achievement that seems to emerge from even the most limited success in sports.

A few tawdry trophies or medals may seem insufficient reward for hours of perseverance at the gym or on the training field, but they are enough to maintain dedication. A similar theme resurfaced in Shane Meadows's *TwentyFourSeven* (1998) in which a benevolent social worker uses boxing to woo drug dealers, skinheads and other disaffected youths from their errant ways.

Subscribers to this conception of sport believe that deviant behavior is the product of the enforced idleness that comes through unemployment combined with a general condition of social deprivation – which is why certain sports, like basketball and boxing, prosper among poor sections of the population. Provided with sports facilities, young people who might otherwise be liable to engage in criminal acts will be dissuaded from doing so. Instead, they will set themselves new targets and gain an ability to focus on achievable, legitimate goals.

Involvement in sports also inculcates young people in the discipline, especially self-discipline, that is needed to train effectively: going to bed early, maintaining a healthy diet, sticking to a strict regimen and so on. It may also drain them of the physical energy that might otherwise be channeled into fighting, stealing or other kinds of miscreant behavior conventionally associated with street gangs.

In the year of the film's release, the celebrated sociologist Robert K. Merton published a paper, "Social structure and anomie," in the *American Sociological Review* (vol 3, 1938) in which he set out "to discover how some social structures exert a definite pressure upon certain persons in the society to engage in non-conforming rather than conforming conduct." Merton's theory stated that "pressure" takes the form of a great emphasis on the successful attainment of cultural goals. Looking at American society in the 1930s, Merton concluded that the ultimate cultural goal was material success which was to be conspicuously displayed. The ability to consume was highly valued and people were encouraged through various media, such as schools and particularly advertising, to maximize this ability – within certain boundaries. Merton's view was that the boundaries defined the legitimate means through which people could realize their goals: in any society where there are moral guidelines, or norms, to remind people of the correct way to approach their goals. Hard work, RISK-taking and acting on initiative, for example, are considered well within boundaries.

Although many groups are equipped to achieve the prescribed goals through legitimate means, others – such as the street gang in the movie – live in the kind of circumstances that make it practically impossible. Merton believed that this gives rise to a situation of *anomie*, meaning that the members of the gangs still strive for the goal of material success, but simply do not have the opportunities to reach them; or at least, not legitimately. On this account, the Cagney character and his accomplices would have wanted all the material trappings that advertisements were constantly telling them were signs of success, yet they would have no access to such things as good education or vocational training and so had little chance of gaining them, unless they sought to gain them through illegitimate means: *ergo* crime.

Merton termed this response *innovation*: deprived social groups accepted the cultural goals, but not the means of gaining them. The clothes, the cars and the other items of conspicuous consumption were there to be had, and "pressure" to grab them grew intense as the youths grew up. Young people such as the "angels with dirty faces" stole either money to buy the goods, or the goods themselves. Inevitably, this brought them into contact with the law.

Merton's theory seems to chime well with the premise of the movie, which is that deprived young people want to achieve the same cultural goals as everybody else in society, and that they are prepared to break rules to do so. O'Brien's priest does his best to stop them and his best bet, as he sees it, is to involve them in sports. Merton himself did not investigate the reformative powers of sports, but later researchers became involved in a series of debates on the subject. Basically, the divisions developed over the relationship between participation in sports and (1) educational achievement; and (2) criminal behavior.

The educational benefits of sports

Four years before *Angels with Dirty Faces*, an interesting article by E. Davis and J. Cooper reviewed a total of forty-one studies and concluded that the school performance of non-athletes was consistently better than that of athletes, and that athletes tended to do better academically after the conclusion of the sports season ("Athletic ability and scholarship" *Research Quarterly*, vol 5, 1934). Twenty-seven years elapsed before this view was given enormous backing by James Coleman's influential work *The Adolescent Society* (Free Press, 1961), a comprehensive study in which was argued that the heavy emphasis placed on sport in high school diverted the energies of participants – and, for that matter, non-participants – away from academic studies. Coleman found that achievement in sports was valued more highly than academic achievements or social background by high school boys, the majority (44 per cent) expressing a wish to be remembered as an athletic star rather than a brilliant or popular student.

In 1968, however, two independent studies, one by Emile Bend (*The Impact of Athletic Participation on Academic and Career Aspiration and Achievement*, National Football Foundation and Hall of Fame, 1968), the other by Walter Schafer and J. Michael Armer, brought forth broadly similar results which suggested that, contrary to Coleman's findings, high school athletes achieved slightly better grades than non-athletes ("Athletes are not inferior students" *Trans-action* vol 5, 1968). Poor and disadvantaged students were actually helped academically by participating in sports. This set in motion a debate.

Schafer remained an active figure in the field and in another study, this time with Richard Rehberg, he found that for youths from disadvantaged backgrounds, there was an association between involvement in sports and high expectations of educational achievement ("Athletic participation, college aspirations and college encouragement" *Pacific Sociological Review* vol 13, 1970). Among those youths from better-off backgrounds, involvement in sports had no effect on their other aspirations, presumably because they were already predisposed toward high educational achievement by virtue of their upbringing.

H.G. Buhrmann took up this point in his 1972 study "Scholarship and athletics in junior high school." He too found that "athletics may be the most important means for these lower socioeconomic status students to gain social recognition and acceptance, and through it, greater academic aspirations and higher scholarship" (*International Review of Sport Sociology* vol 7, 1972). In their article "Residence and the athletic participation-aspiration hypothesis," Steven Picou and E.W. Curry expanded the relationship further by reporting that athletes from underprivileged backgrounds who received little or no encouragement from parents to do well in further education held higher aspirations educationaly than similarly-situated youths who had no involvement at all in sports (*Social Science Quarterly* vol 55, 1974). On the other side, William Spady argued that participation in sports could stimulate greater academic aspirations, but without helping develop the requisite scholastic skills. The result was that, if inflated aspirations were solely due to involvement in sports, then that involvement was dysfunctional in the sense that the students' reach exceeded his or her grasp ("Lament for the letterman" *American Journal of Sociology* vol 75, 1970).

More contemporary contributions to the debate have focused not so much on whether sports participation helps or hinders educational aspiration and attainment, but on mediating factors in the relationship. Examples include the emphasis given to sports by the educational institutions, the carry-over of achievement orientations from sports to school and then work, and the values of informal networks of contacts built up during a sports career. Most of the findings supported the idea that a positive relationship of some kind between sports and education existed, and that the relationship was most pronounced among groups from deprived backgrounds. In the USA, where sports scholarships are available, this can have an important effect in inclining working-class youths to stay in education, principally to pursue sporting goals; while in education, they can achieve academic qualifications.

Crime and sporting achievement

Evidence on the relationship between sports participation and criminality is no more conclusive. Intuitively, the concept of "keeping kids off the streets" is appealing. At its simplest level, it suggests that time spent practicing or competing cannot be spent committing acts of deviance. But, it also suggests that there is a deeper function for sport in curbing rule-breaking tendencies, or perhaps subordinating them to the greater goal of succeeding in sports.

Sport operates with a success ethic: no one seriously surrenders so much of their effort to the pursuit of sporting excellence if they believe they will fail. With the advent of professional sport, the cultural goal of material success written of by Merton has become a central MOTIVATION. Coaches have no need to offer athletic honors as an alternative or even an adjunct to material success: aspirant sports performers are typically aware of the riches that await the victors.

Sports history is full of stories of successful sports performers who either rehabilitate themselves through sport after an early life of youthful offending, or keep on the straight and narrow while their peers veer off the rails. Of course, there are those successful sports ICONS who seem never to leave their past completely behind. Mike TYSON was imprisoned for rape when already rich and successful.

Michael Trulson believes this is explicable in terms of the type of sport. In his study "Martial arts training: a novel 'cure' for juvenile delinquency," Trulson reported on a study of three groups of "delinquents," who had been split into a traditional taekwondo training class, an eclectic martial arts class and a multisport training class (*Human Relations*, vol 39, 1986). After six months, the taekwondo youths, who had been taught the philosophy and self-discipline associated with the sport, exhibited fewer delinquent tendencies, while the eclectic martial arts trainees were more aggressive. The third group showed no change, apart from an improvement in self-esteem.

Commenting on the study, J. Jay Coakley writes in his book *Sport in Society: Issues and Controversies*: "It appears that certain types of sport participation might indeed keep kids out of trouble." He concludes: "Simply getting kids off the street is just a beginning. If kids play a sport with an emphasis on hostility towards others, using aggression as a strategy and bodies as tools, dominating others, and letting referees and coaches make calls they should be making for themselves, we *cannot* expect rates of deviance to decrease" (McGraw-Hill, 1998).

Eldon Snyder's "Interpretations and explanations of deviance among college athletes: A case study" serves to undermine the *Angels With Dirty Faces* Effect. Snyder disclosed a bonding subculture among sports performers. This subculture promotes the kinds of attitudes and values that actually commission rule-breaking. Snyder reported burglaries by athletes, most of whom came from middle-class families. He concludes that, far from, deterring deviance, sport can actually develop the kinds of relationships and group dynamics that can lead to it, either during an athletic career or after. This ties in with research done by Jeffrey Benedict and Alan Klein, who examined SEX CRIMES either committed or allegedly committed by athletes and discovered that, while a disproportionate number of sports performers are accused of sexually related offenses, including rape, a disproportionately small number are ever convicted. Added to the high-profile cases of elite athletes who have been involved in similar cases, this leads to a tentative conclusion that being a sports performer may present opportunities for crime that are not available to non-athletes. While there is no empirical evidence to support the view, many commentators have suggested that sports stars who command mega-salaries and iconic status have come to regard themselves as above the law in some respects.

Of related interest

Angels with Dirty Faces, directed by Michael Curtiz, 1934.
Benedict, Jeffrey and Klein, Alan (1997) "Arrest and conviction rates for athletes accused of sexual assault," *Sociology of Sport Journal* vol 14, no 1.
Snyder, Eldon E. (1994) "Interpretations and explanations of deviance among college athletes: A case study," *Sociology of Sport Journal* vol 11.

animal racing

Ancient chariots

The domestication of animals, which probably began about 10,000 years ago, coincided with the cultivation of plants and the decline of hunter-gatherer modes of production. Animals were enclosed, bred, fostered and slaughtered. While there is no evidence of their being used for racing, it is at least possible that primitive competitions took place.

Certainly by the thirteenth century BC, Mycenaean Greece was holding quite sophisticated races featuring two-wheeled chariots drawn by HORSES. Homer's *Iliad* gives examples of chariot racing in the eighth century BC. Chariot racing became the first ever mass spectator sport in the fourth century AD, when crowds of up to 250,000 packed into Rome's Circus Maximus to watch charioteers compete for what were then huge sums of money and considerable fame throughout the Roman Empire. William Wyler's 1959 film *Ben Hur* includes a vivid and convincing recreation of a chariot race, which remains one of the most exhilarating film depictions of a sporting competition.

Dogs and horses

There is no lineal line of descent from the ancient chariots to today's equivalent, known as harness racing (trotting or pacing), which is very tame by comparison and is practiced mainly in Macau, the former Portuguese colony in southeast Asia, the southern and midwestern states of America and Canada. The colonial British introduced trotting to America and, after a surge of popularity in the mid-nineteenth century, its appeal diminished.

Dog racing has its origins in coursing, which was popular in eighteenth- and nineteenth-century England and involved highly bred and trained dogs which chased and (usually) killed a fleeing hare. The hare was given a start of over 200 yards (183 meters). One of the attractions of meetings was the opportunity to wager and drink convivially. Hoteliers and publicans would promote coursing meets. It became an organized sport in Britain, complete with its own organization in 1858, when a National Coursing Club was established. At around the same time, other sports, including ball sports and boxing, were developing governing associations.

As opposition to what was one of a number of blood sports prevalent at the time grew, coursing dispensed with living hares and substituted a mechanical equivalent. The fastest breed of dog was the greyhound, which pursues its prey by sight rather than scent. Experiments with mechanical hares took place in England over the last three decades of the nineteenth century, though the type used today was pioneered in South Dakota in the early years of the twentieth century. In 1919, an electric hare mounted on an oval rail sped away from a pack of pursuant hounds in the first precursor to today's dog racing, a sport which continued to attract regular crowds in Britain, Canada and the USA for the rest of the century. Massachusetts and Florida generated especially strong support for greyhound racing. The attraction of the dog track is gambling: in Britain, wagers are freely made on individual dogs and bookmakers on- and off-course set odds. It retains a distinct working class base of support. In the States, the norm is pari-mutuel betting, in which winners divide the losers' stakes, less an administrative charge.

In horse racing, steeplechasing grew out of foxhunting. Events were initially a means of training horses for the English hunts. There also developed contests after the completion of a hunt, when riders would race each other to an observable feature in the landscape, such as a church steeple, betting on their own horses to win. This type of event probably began informally in the early nineteenth century and, by the end, was more popular than the hunts themselves. The potential of such races as a spectator sport was not realized until 1847 when the course at Aintree, near Liverpool, began an annual race known as the Grand National.

Much later, in the 1920s, a course similar to Aintree was built in Tennessee. Steeplechasing had been practiced by American fox hunters possibly since the 1830s, but more organized races began after the formation of the National Steeplechase Association in 1895, although it has never rivaled flat racing in terms of national popularity. Flat racing was also a British export, though a much older one, probably dating back to the seventeenth century.

Britain's Jockey Club was created in 1750, while its American counterpart, the American Jockey Club did not come into existence until 1894. Both were designed to regulate a sport that had been – and remains – run by wealth-owning classes, but whose appeal widened to include the whole spectrum of classes. Its popularity lay not so much in the racing, but in the opportunities it held for betting. Owners of racehorse stables were traditionally drawn from the landed gentry who raced principally for prestige but also for prize money. The stables were those of England's Great Houses, owned by an aristocracy, many families of which had inherited wealth that had been handed down from the times of Henry VIII (with redistributions during Elizabethan times). Major sponsors of racing such as the Darleys and the Godolphins came on the scene very much later. Gentlemen-owners were the only group with sufficient funds to maintain stables and breed horses for the purpose of racing (rather than working).

Jockeys would have been livery boys or servants, though as the sport became more profitable it was possible to release them from their other duties and employ them full time as jockeys. The system of patronage, whereby jockeys are employed by owners, still holds, although a number of top jockeys are freelances or on retainer to a trainer rather than an owner.

Colonialism

As with steeplechasing, promoters exploited the spectator interest in flat racing by building enclosed courses and charging admission; this innovation began in the late nineteenth century, a time when most of what we now recognize as major sports were organizing themselves in such a way as to capitalize on industrial working-class enthusiasm. The series of races that became known as the Classics all began in a relatively short span: the St Leger in 1778, the Oaks in 1779, the Derby in 1780, and the 2000 Guineas in 1809. In the same period, British colonialists began America's most famous horse race, the Kentucky Derby, which was almost a microcosm of the master–slave relations that had been brought to a legal end only a decade before. In the first Kentucky Derby, fourteen of the fifteen jockeys were black; all the owners were white.

For gambling turnover, there are no rivals to Happy Valley racecourse in Hong Kong. Founded in 1846 specifically for the indulgence of the colonial British, the racecourse developed into a gambling mecca as the former colony became one of the commercial powerhouses of Asia. Officially, the totalizer (pari-mutuel) is the only form of gambling on the island, but there are countless illicit outlets provided by organized crime.

Flat racing, no less than the many other sports originating in England, served as a virtual metaphor for British IMPERIALISM. Racing started in Sydney, Australia in the first decade of the nineteenth century, with the stimulus again being the expatriate British. One of Australia's most celebrated horses was the subject of an eponymous 1983 film, *Phar Lap*. Simon Winder's movie showed how, in the 1930s, the underachieving thoroughbred was coaxed into becoming one of the country's outstanding horses.

The Australian experience also served to show how horse racing was absolutely dependent on gambling. In the 1880s, South Australia outlawed betting and horse racing was all but extinguished. The dependence has invited CORRUPTION, and horse racing has been beset by horse doping, ringing (switching horses) and a variety of scams, one of which is dramatized in Stephen Frear's *The Grifters* (1990).

Horse racing, whether flat or steeplechase, has mutated since its inception as a postscript to fox hunts, though there are several forms which still approximate the early pursuit. Eventing, also known as horse trials, began as a primarily military equestrian discipline, combining elements of the training needed for a cavalry horse. Showjumping's descent from foxhunting is shown in the outfits worn by the riders, which are typically those of a hunt follower. Working hunter classes still take place in an enclosure inside which natural brooks and obstacles are recreated.

Endurance rides take place outdoors, usually on rugged terrain. These events actually owe more to the American pioneers' push west than to the English foxhunters, but are now an international sport. Endurance riding's growth from the 1960s was part of a movement in which conventional definitions of endurance were challenged. The rise of long-distance swimming, ultramarathons and multisports, particularly triathlons, were products of a culture that had become sedentary with the decrease in manual jobs and the so-called managerial revolution. New challenges raised the threshold of expectations.

Endurance rides, some over 500 miles of rugged land, tested both horse and rider to extremes. This bears comparison with the astonishing Iditarod, a 1,180-mile race through Alaska featuring teams of huskies pulling a person in a sled. The original trail was forged by dogsleds carrying freight to miners and prospectors; the latter-day contest recreates the hunger and exhaustion of driving for eight days and nights at temperatures of −60°C.

Of related interest

Holt, Richard (1990) *Sport and the Working Class in Modern Britain*, Manchester University Press.
Paulsen, Gary (1994) *Winterdance: The Fine Madness of Alaskan Dog-Racing*, Gollancz.
Vamplew, Wray (1988) "Odds against: The punter's lot is not a happy one," *Sporting Traditions* vol 5, no 1.

Anquetil, Jacques

b. 1934, France; d. 1987

Anquetil's place in sports history is justified by his five TOUR DE FRANCE wins between 1957 and 1964. His place in sports *cultural* history is justified by his widely-known views on performance-enhancing DRUGS; views that earned him few plaudits from officials.

Ever a pragmatist, Normandy-born Anquetil confessed to taking stimulants prior to and during his races. Ten years after his first Tour de France win, he derided those who believed cyclists should be more stringently tested for dope. He sneered at the naivety of those who believed that professional racers could cycle 235 days a year in all weather conditions and across mountainous terrain without stimulants. Anquetil admitted that he had taken drugs.

The confession proved controversial, coming as it did in the same year as the DEATH of fellow cyclist Tommy Simpson. On July 13 1967, Simpson, then 29, collapsed and died on the thirteenth stage of the three-week long Tour de France. Simpson, a British rider, was lying seventh overall when the race set off from Marseilles. The temperature was well over 40°C (105°F). Simpson fell and remounted twice before falling for the final time. Three tubes were found in his pocket, one full of amphetamines and two empty. The British team's luggage was searched and more supplies of the pills were found.

The incident was something of a watershed. It started a debate on the uses of drugs in sports which eventually led to extensive dope-testing and heavy punishments for offenders. By the time of Anquetil's retirement in 1969 the debate had barely transferred to other sports, though it is commonly believed that track and field, American football and weightlifting were sports in which drug taking was rife. All were subject to close scrutiny over the following decades.

Cycling also came under surveillance but, as Anquetil's outbursts made clear, it was not a sport that could be purged of drugs and remain the same: the conditions under which cyclists perform were inhuman and, as he put it, only a "fool" would believe that cyclists could endure them unassisted. However, Anquetil's statements were forgotten in later years.

Despite his racing record, Anquetil was something of an outcast and his views on drugs reinforced this status. He won an Olympic bronze medal at the Helsinki summer games of 1952 and his first Tour de France title in 1957. He also won the Grand Prix de Nations title nine times. His close and bitterly-contested races against Raymond Poulidor created one of the great sports RIVALRIES. Anquetil died of cancer at age 53.

Of related interest

Fife, Graeme (1999) *Tour de France: The History, the Legend, the Riders*, Mainstream.
Voet, Willy (2000) *Breaking the Chain: How Drugs Destroyed a Sport*, Yellow Jersey.

Arledge, Roone

b. 1931, USA

As ABC television's producer of network sports, Arledge effectively redefined television's relationship with sports in the 1960s. In the process, he mapped out a new direction for TELEVISION. Instead of following sports events, television could lead the way: sports would either follow or perish.

Born in Forest Hills, New York, Arledge graduated from Columbia University, did military service in the army and completed an apprenticeship at NBC before moving to what was then a minor television company. When Arledge joined ABC in 1961, the television behemoths CBS and NBC dominated viewer ratings. These two had identified sports as of being of interest principally to men. US television, being driven by advertising revenues, tended to segment its potential audiences; thus advertisers of products bought by men, such as razor blades, beer, car tires and so on, were drawn to sports programs. CBS and NBC enjoyed a relatively peaceful co-existence, carving up the big sporting events between them.

Arledge had different ideas. He created the weekly *Wide World of Sports* with its globe-ranging, multi-camera celebration of events with a view to attracting a much wider audience than ever conceived by ABC's rivals. Instead of accepting that sporting occasions had a "natural" appeal that should be reflected in television coverage, Arledge created interest across the widest possible range of the population. He recognized no barriers set by class, gender or age. His premise was much the same as that of the advertisers on whose patronage ABC ultimately depended: if the demand is not there to begin with, build it. The way Arledge built demand was by taking obscure sports and adding something to them, something that only television could provide.

For example, ABC's cameras would venture to the top of cliffs, peer over the edge, then draw back to view a diver hurtling into the sea below, where another camera would join him or her in the water. Close-up action would convert the dive into drama. Only television cameras could catch the details of a facial expression that brought a new type of humanity to sports viewing. Minority sports and activities that were barely competitive sports at all attracted Arledge. Rodeos, demolition DERBY and even bizarre firefighters' bucket-filling contests were all fair game for ABC. Arledge vandalized established traditions in sports broadcasting by making an overt appeal to younger audiences who were not bound by the fidelities of their parents. ABC sought more women viewers on the sound assumption that women spent a considerable portion of a family's disposable income. Advertisers were obviously interested in this sector of the market.

Arledge's philosophies were shamelessly populist, projecting personalities, highlighting unusual features, reducing almost any activity to its most basic competitive elements. Frog-jumping contests, while not actually televised, would not have been out of place in ABC's sports panoply.

Gillette, traditionally one of North America's biggest sports sponsors, linked up with ABC to present a regular Friday night boxing show: boxing's crowds were already in steep decline, but its popularity with television viewers was steadfast. "How are you fixed for blades?" asked Gillette's trademark hyperactive parrot in the boxing show. Gillette's money helped Arledge to bid successfully for NCAA football in the 1960/61 season, and this proved to be the first of several coups.

As ABC went from strength to strength, professional football sprang to the fore as a major sport. Arledge had sensed the potential of football and helped commission a rival to the established National Football League. The American Football League was a second-rate outfit filled with players who could not make the grade with the rival league. However, it was very competitive and, as it was shown by ABC, very dramatic. No device or gimmick was spared in ABC's coverage. Its ratings were respectable enough for it to loosen ABC's apron strings and negotiate its own deal with NBC in 1965. By 1968, it had become such a threat that it was merged with its rival to become what we now recognize as the NFL.

Arledge's interest in football continued and, in 1970, he launched a new initiative: Monday Night Football, or MNF as it became abbreviated. This was to be Arledge's crucible. He used slow-motion, instant replays, close-ups, split-screens, diagrams and interviews to complement the knowledgeable play-by-play commentary. There were personality close-ups, emphasizing the "human" side of the players and coaches. The main commentator was Howard Cosell, an often disagreeable man who unfailingly provoked controversy.

The success of MNF was instant: ABC won a one-third share of the national audience. It had paid the NFL $8.5 million per year for thirteen games, and claimed this back by charging advertisers $65,000 per minute during the game. By 1980 it was regularly the eighth most watched program in the country, enabling ABC to charge $110,000 for a thirty-second commercial slot.

Arledge leased a satellite for "live" coverage of international events, including Le Mans, the Irish Sweepstakes and ten Olympic games. Its sports coverage raised ABC from a distant poor relation to CBS and NBC to an equal contender among the networks.

Arledge has often defended his network's use of synthetic sports, such as log-sawing and tree-climbing, by reminding critics that sports were not delivered by God, as rules inscribed on tablets of stone. They are completely artificial contests, designed purely to challenge human beings in what Arledge called "preconceived settings." Teams of firefighters competing over how many buckets of water they can carry from point A to point Z is no more or less of a pure sport than eleven men trying to move an inflated ball in the opposite direction to another eleven men. Purists tend to snicker at one, yet treat the other with gravity. Arledge's skill was in persuading viewers that, at any given moment, one type of competition can be as exciting as another.

While he did not openly acknowledge Arledge's influence, Rupert MURDOCH used sport to heighten interest in his various television channels in the 1990s, and often encouraged a re-formatting of sports in a manner similar to Arledge.

Of related interest

Klatell, David and Marcus, Norman (1988) *Sports for Sale: Television, Money and the Fans*, Oxford University Press.

Rader, Benjamin (1984) *In Its Own Image: How Televison has Transformed Sport*, Collier-Macmillan.

Wenner, Lawrence (ed.) (1998) *MediaSport*, Routledge.

Ashe, Arthur

b. 1943, USA; d. 1993

Ashe was an African American tennis player who exhorted young black people not to squander their energies on sports, but to channel it in academic and vocational studies. He vigorously advised young black Americans to spend more time in libraries than on playing fields. While he is now revered, his protests made him unpopular during the 1980s. Ashe contracted the HIV virus through a blood transfusion and died of AIDS in 1993, aged 50.

Mindful of the vagaries of RACISM, Ashe reflected on his own career and analyzed it in terms of the history of blacks in America. He chronicled his perceptions in books which were both factually informed and passionately written. Ashe's historical writing on the history of African Americans in sport spawned a multivolume, multimedia series, *A Hard Road to Glory*.

Ashe was never in doubt that his own success was a statistical aberration and that the realistic chances of young blacks in sports were extremely limited. The vast majority of African Americans in sports were effectively pursuing HOOP DREAMS.

Ashe's own career was exceptional. Born in Richmond, Virginia, he served in the United States army and had a good amateur career. When he turned professional in 1969, he was an African American in a sport completely dominated by whites. He signed with the PROSERV agency which also handled the affairs of Stan Smith and Bob Lutz, who played with Ashe in the US Davis Cup team. Between 1970 and 1980, Ashe won the Australian Open and Wimbledon, and doubles titles at the French Open and the Australian Open.

Heart problems necessitated open heart surgery in 1979 and, chastened by this, Ashe retired in the following year. In 1983, during a second bypass operation, it is likely he was given blood tainted human immunodeficiency (HIV-positive), which causes Aids. During his final years he maintained his profile, campaigning for racial equality in South Africa, Haiti and Aids research. Other black sports figures, most notably basketball player Harry Edwards, echoed Ashe's plea to black youth in the 1970s, but Ashe's position of prominence as a Grand Slam tournament champion gave his message a particular potency.

Of related interest

Ashe, Arthur R. (1993) *A Hard Road to Glory: A History of the African–American Athlete*, 3 vols, Amistad Warner.

Ashe, Arthur R. and Rampersad, Arnold (1994) *Days of Grace: A Memoir*, Ballantine.

B

bars and pubs

Bars and pubs the world over are sites for competitions, some new, others ancient. Many sports that have their origins in English pub games or North American bars have become mainstream competitive sports that have ultimately acquired an organizational structure and a wide audience (due mainly to television coverage). Darts is the most apparent example of this.

The original "darts" were probably weapons used in close combat during the medieval era, presumably as a convenient alternative to spears and arrows. A form of dart was used as a weapon by Roman armies. It is thought that the Pilgrims actually shipped some type of darts with them on their *Mayflower* voyage. A smaller variety came into use during the nineteenth century; these were blown through a pipe rather than thrown. The blowpipe is, of course, a weapon favored by some Amazonian tribes.

The game we recognize today as darts started life in the pubs of northern England in the late nineteenth century and became nationally popular in the early twentieth century, especially after a celebrated court case in 1918 which declared that it was not a game of chance (which were prohibited from licensed premises), but a game of skill. It was played as a pub game until the postwar period, when tournaments were organized and sponsored by newspapers. The National Darts Association of Great Britain was formed in 1953.

The nature of darts competition was typically pub *vs.* pub, and this continues to the present day. However, the individual-based competitions were more attractive from television's point of view. During the 1980s, TELEVISION recognized the potential of darts: the combination of pub ambiance and the human drama which could be captured in the tight close-ups of the players' faces made ideal – and relatively cheap – television. Potential advertisers and sponsors eventually grew uncomfortable with the continuous drinking and smoking of the crowd and asked the British Darts Organization (BDO) to instruct players and spectators to refrain from drinking and smoking. This was a major irony, but the BDO obliged. It was a sign of the sport's professionalization and of its break from its original *mise en scène*. Top players began to report yearly earnings in millions.

As television's interest waned in the 1990s, more money was sought from sponsors. The TOBACCO companies Benson & Hedges and Embassy obliged, only to find tobacco sponsorship of sport banned in May 1997. Of all the sports affected by this ban, professional darts suffered most.

Other competitive games that started at the pub or bar level but later became fully-fledged sports (i.e. with codified rules and governing organizations) include pool, arm-wrestling and dominoes. Pool started life as "pocket billiards," a miniature version of a game that has its origins in late fourteenth or fifteenth century Britain. It was an outdoor game, played on measured plots of ground, then later adapted for an indoor table game. The green baize that covers tables is meant to resemble the grass on which the game was once played. In the authoritative *William Hendrick's History of Billiards*, evidence is given that King Louis XI of France (1461–83) played a version of pool at his court.

Billiards and its derivative snooker became popular under IMPERIALISM: they were taken to South Asia by British colonizers in the late nineteenth century, eventually reaching all parts of the former Empire, but never caught on in the United States. Snooker, which is usually played on the same size or smaller table as billiards, became particularly popular in the twentieth century, leading to the growth of snooker halls in virtually every British city and the installation of snooker tables in many pubs. Its association with unemployment and dissipation led to playing excellence being jokingly regarded as a sign of a "mis-spent youth."

Snooker's popularity in Britain was never matched in the United States where a version of pocket billiards, in which balls are numbered, spawned three variations: straight ball, eight ball and nine ball. The first of these was at first adopted for tournaments, although from the 1980s nine ball, which encourages a much faster game, superseded it. Eight ball has the pace of nine ball and also allows for plenty of alternation of players; it is less technically demanding than the other two and, for all these reasons, became the most popular of all. By the end of the 1980s, few bars and taverns had not installed pool tables, most of them coin-operated.

Arm-wrestling became an organized sport in 1988 when the Yukon Jack World Arm-Wrestling Championships were held. One of its main ambitions was to render what was hitherto a macho response to a spontaneous challenge into a respectable sport. The World Armsport Federation became the principal governing body of the sport and although it secured television contracts, the sport remained localized and predominantly amateur.

In the 1980s, the sport, or at least contests, were featured in two FILMS. In David Cronenburg's 1986 remake of *The Fly*, an arm-wrestling contest results in the loser's radius and ulna being snapped and protruding through his flesh. And in Menahem Golan's 1986 *Over the Top*, Sylvester Stallone plays a trucker who is also a competitive arm-wrestler. Neither film did much to elevate the sport.

Of related interest

Finn, P.T. (1975) *Pub Games of England*, Queen Anne Press.
Jeffrey, E. (1977) *Armwrestling: How to Become a Champion*, Marc Sheldon.

Big Daddy

b. 1937, Britain; d. 1997

Big Daddy was the *nom de plume* of British wrestler Shirley Crabtree, who rose to fame on the successful Independent Television (ITV) program *World of Sport* in the 1970s and early 1980s. He became synonymous with the hybrid sport that we now associate with the World Wrestling Federation: half combat sport and half circus act, and totally showbusiness. While his fame as a television personality was short lived, his reputation as a wrestler lingered and only deteriorating health prevented him transferring to a children's television series, which would have made him into a prototype Hulk Hogan.

Born in Halifax in the north of England, Crabtree learnt to fight as a matter of self-preservation. Presumably, believing the wisdom of Johnny Cash's song "A Boy named Sue" (in which an absentee father christens his son with a girl's name on the assumption that he would be teased so relentlessly that he would quickly acquire the ability to defend himself), Crabtree's father was a professional wrestler who believed his son could also make a living in the ring.

Taunted as "Shirley Temple" at school, Crabtree did indeed learn to look after himself. In fact, he became too aggressive for Bradford Northern rugby club and spoiled what might otherwise have been a different sporting career with too much AGGRESSION. He turned to being a lifeguard and then to wrestling. As well as his real name, Crabtree used the names "The Blond Adonis," "Mr. Universe" and "The Battling Guardsman." In the 1950s, wrestling was not televised and professional wrestlers would need to fight several times a night, possibly in different guises, to make a living.

The idea for "Big Daddy" came from Burl Ives's patriarchal character in the 1958 Richard Brooks movie of Tennessee Williams's *Cat on a Hot Tin Roof*. The boxer Riddick Bowe later used the nickname. Crabtree's Big Daddy persona was his most successful to date; it was complemented by a fake leopardskin leotard emblazoned with the letter "D."

Wrestling at this stage had become less a competitive sport and more a staged mock conflict. The contestants would work out moves, holds and throws beforehand and take turns in winning. Many developed love–hate relationships with crowds, and would venture into the first few rows as if to attack spectators. Heroes and villains were soon established, with villains typically snarling and threatening at the braying crowds. It was as if the spectators suspended belief for the duration of a fight. Like people who read horoscopes in the full knowledge that they will not come true, wrestling fans in all probability knew that the matches were rehearsed and managed, but still enjoyed the spectacle.

Not that the wrestlers were devoid of skill or athleticism. The bouts were often carefully choreographed to the point where the competitors needed a high degree not only of basic fitness, but of technique. Crabtree, who weighed more than 360 pounds, specialized in a body throw which kept opponents pinned to the canvas. Escaping serious injury required expertise. In fact, one unfortunate opponent, Mal "King Kong" Kirk, died after a bout with Big Daddy in 1985.

The formula transferred to television with amazing smoothness. Britain's first commercial network, ITV, began in 1955; previously, the BBC had been the only service. ITV had sensed the ratings potential of sport and looked to the USA for examples. In particular, the network found a model in ABC, which specialized in making mundane events in flamboyant displays. The BBC had the advantage of experience in televising sports and, more importantly, the patronage of the national government, which believed that significant sports events like the FA Cup Final and Wimbledon should be shown by the BBC. The localized structure of ITV meant that it could not reach all areas of the country in its early years, so exclusive commercial coverage of events would have left some areas of the country without access.

Faced with this forbidding competition, ITV shrank from a fight with BBC over mainstream sports but tentatively experimented with the trashy populist wrestling that had become popular around the country. It was a massive success. In 1956, ITV gave only 5 per cent of its weekly programming over to sport. By 1966, this was up to 6.12 per cent; and, by 1976 – with wrestling in its ascendancy – 8.38 per cent. BBC regularly showed more sports than its competitor (between 12 and 16 per cent), but it was regularly beaten into second place in terms of numbers of Saturday afternoon viewers. ITV scheduled its wrestling in direct opposition to BBC Saturday flagship sports show *Grandstand*. ITV's *World of Sport* (based on Roone ARLEDGE's brainchild at ABC, *Wide World of Sports*) struggled to begin with, but wrestling was its secret weapon.

Chad Dell, in his essay " 'Lookit that hunk of a man!' " records much the same experience in the USA with television ratings for wrestling rising, mainly because of the popularity of the sport among women. Dell writes of the "transgressive" FANDOM: "These women could enjoy the pleasure of defiance – of shared public defiance – and, in the domestic context, the momentary pleasure of male disapproval and male inability to alter such behavior."

At the peak of Big Daddy's career he, like his American counterparts, was watched by an enthusiastic female television audience and a vociferous "live" audience. A hero rather than a villain, he wooed the crowds and greeted every victory with chants of "Easy, Easy." He supplemented his income with the usual celebrity functions, such as opening stores and endorsing products.

In the early 1980s, enthusiasm for wrestling waned and *World of Sport* ratings dropped. Compounding wrestling's problems, in 1985 a tabloid newspaper published an exposé detailing wrestling's by-then open secret. Of course everyone knew the sport was stage-managed, but no one liked being reminded of it. In 1986, ITV withdrew the ailing sport from its schedules. Crabtree continued to use the Big Daddy moniker for a while longer, but without television money the game became hard work for a man approaching 50. He retired to run a fitness center.

Years later, with the advent of cable and satellite television, wrestling returned to British television screens: American WWF followed very much the same format of Big Daddy and his peers of the 1970s, though with more glitz. Crabtree himself died in 1997.

Of related interest

Ball, M.R. (1990) *Professional Wrestling as Ritual Drama in American Culture*, Mellen Press.

Dell, Chad (1998) " 'Lookit that hunk of a man!': Subversive pleasures, female fandom, and professional wrestling," in Harris, Cheryl and Alexander, Alison (eds), *Theorizing Fandom: Fans, Subculture and Identity* Hampton Press.

blood doping

"Doping" in this context does not refer to the administration of drugs, but to the more correct use of the term, pertaining to a thick liquid used as a food or a lubricant. Blood doping involves a sports performer (or anyone else, for that matter) removing an amount of his or her own blood, storing it and then reintroducing into his/her system via transfusion. Typically, the extraction would take place while in intense training at altitude, and the transfusion would take place immediately prior to competition.

Training at altitude where the air is rare and oxygen less available produces systemic changes in the human organism. Greater quantities of the protein molecule hemoglobin, which is found in red blood cells, are naturally produced. As most oxygen in the blood is combined with hemoglobin rather than simply plasma, the more hemoglobin present in a red blood cell, the more oxygen it can transport to the muscles. Sports performers can benefit from having a plentiful supply of oxygen to react with glucose and release the energy stored in food. The advantage of training at altitude where oxygen is scarce is that the body compensates, producing more hemoglobin.

After a period of altitude training, the competitor has a quantity of hemoglobin-rich blood removed before descending to sea level (or wherever the competition is taking place). Each day spent at the lower level diminishes the benefit of altitude training: proliferation of hemoglobin ceases in the presence of available atmospheric oxygen. A return to normal is probable within ten weeks. However, one way to "capture" the benefits is to re-introduce the oxygenated blood to the circulatory system prior to the competition.

While the competitor is using no artificial stimulants, he or she is making use of medical technologies and the procedure is proscribed in the same way as using performance-enhancing DRUGS. Maarti Vainio lost a silver medal at the Los Angeles summer Olympics after anabolic steroid traces were discovered in his urine. The Finn had been careful enough to cease using steroids well before competition and so escape detection, but he blundered by having himself reinfused with blood that had been removed from his body early in 1984 when training at altitude. He neglected to take account of the fact that he had been on steroids during the time he spent at altitude and that the stored blood contained evidence of this.

Experimental work on blood doping took place in the 1940s, though it was not specifically applied to the improvement of sporting performance until the late 1960s. Research at the Institute of Physiology of Performance in Stockholm,

Sweden, suggested a definite relationship between increasing hemoglobin in the blood and enhanced athletic performance, especially in endurance events. While the process was known in sporting circles, no evidence of its specific application was uncovered. Rumor and innuendo surrounded the Finnish athlete Lasse Viren, who won an Olympic gold medal in 1972, then did nothing of note until the 1976 Olympics. He took another gold medal, prompting suspicions. Viren replied by stating that his "secret" for reaching peak performance at exactly the right time was no more mysterious than a regular imbibing of reindeer milk.

In his article "The development of sports medicine," Ivan Waddington cites several sources supporting the fact that members of a US cycling team that won a total of nine medals (including four golds) at the Los Angeles Olympics of 1984 had used blood doping. The USA had not won a cycling medal since 1912. The IOC immediately banned the procedure and began researching ways of testing for it.

Waddington points out that, in a relatively short period of time, blood doping changed from one of several science-assisted techniques of improving athletic performance to a form of cheating. One might add that its change in status reflects the acceleration in the MEDICALIZATION of sports in the postwar period. As recently as 1983 the process was discussed in terms of its efficacy and safety, rather than whether it conferred unfair advantages on the blood doper. Waddington is careful to note that ethical issue had been raised by some researchers in the late 1970s, though these concerned informed consent when using human subjects in experiments. After the 1984 games, however, debate began in earnest and, while blood doping did not involve the introduction of anything but a substance indigenous to the athlete's own body into a healthy circulatory system, the process was outlawed as if it were a performance-enhancing chemical.

One of the most interesting contributions to the debate came from Clifton Perry in his article, "Blood doping and athletic competition." Perry argued the case for and against blood doping. He offered the distinction between "performance enhancers" that do not cause lasting changes to the body of the user, and "capacity enhancers" that do have long-term effects. This means that anabolic steroids are ruled out, not on the grounds that they are capacity enhancers, but because they have deleterious effects (there is evidence that they elevate enzyme levels in the liver). Does this mean that blood doping should be allowed, as it enhances capacities without the deleterious consequences? Perry's answer is no: the body's response to coming off the enhancer is his reason. "There is a difference between the loss of performance output through the loss of a mere performance enhancer and the loss of a capacity through inactivity." After coming off an enhancer, the body returns to homeostasis: "There is nothing the athlete can do by way of performance to retain the former level of performance. This is not the case when a performer simply stops training." Perry was also concerned with the implications of blood doping. It could lead to the use of "artificial blood" or other people's blood, or even the supplement Fluosol-DA, which increases the oxygen-carrying capacity of blood. Perry's fears seemed to have been confirmed by the advent of perfluorocarbon (pfc), a synthetic blood-like substance that substantially increases the body's oxygen-carrying capacity and which was favored by endurance athletes in the late 1990s. Also popular at this time was EPO (ERYTHROPOIETIN).

Of related interest

Perry, Clifton (1983) "Blood doping and athletic competition," *International Journal of Applied Philosophy*, vol 1, no 3.
Voy, Robert (1991) *Drugs, Sport and Politics*, Leisure Press.
Waddington, Ivan (1996) "The development of sports medicine," *Sociology of Sport Journal*, vol 19.

blood sports

Eighteenth and nineteenth centuries

Recreational pursuits that involve inflicting harm on animals fall into three types, all very popular between 1780 and 1860 and modestly popular, though illegal, beyond that time. The period following the peak years of their popularity witnessed a decline in the overtly violent aspects of what we now regard as legitimate sports. Governing organizations developed rules and codes of practice designed to regulate activities and promote uniformity. And, while sports encouraged robustness and a physical "manliness," they also discouraged the outright aggression that had characterized earlier forms of competition.

The absence of prohibitions on what we now understand to be willful cruelty extended beyond animal sports: popular ball games and combat sports also permitted, if not encouraged a degree of physical brutality that would have been considered horrific by the end of the nineteenth century. By the end of the twentieth century, the kind of biting that would have been commonplace in the mid-1800s was the cause of universal furore (such as when Mike Tyson bit Evander Holyfield's ear in their 1997 WBA heavyweight title fight). In addition to biting, gouging, kicking and cudgeling were permitted in many types of contest.

While blood sports persist to the present day, our conceptions of them are fundamentally different from those prevalent during the seventeenth and eighteenth centuries and the thresholds of repugnance would have been far higher. For example, there is evidence of crowds gathering to watch the burning of a live cat for amusement. It is in this context that we have to understand the popularity and the acceptability of blood sports.

Baiting

Baiting involved chaining, tethering, or cornering an animal and setting trained dogs to torment or attack it. The fettered animals were usually badgers, bears or bulls. It was a favored recreation of the American and British plebeian, or working class, in the eighteenth century.

Typically, a bull would be brought by a butcher or farmer who would be paid to have it secured to a post while specially trained dogs were encouraged to snap at and bite it. The historian Richard Holt gives an account:

> Sometimes the dog seized the bull by the nose and 'pinned' him to the earth, so that the beast roared and bellowed again, and was brought down upon its knees ... The people then shouted 'Wind, wind!' that is, to let the bull have breath, and the parties rushed forward to take off the dog ... However, the bulls were sometimes pinned between the legs, causing [them] to roar and rave about in great agony.
>
> (from *Sport and the Working Class in Modern Britain*, Manchester University Press, 1990)

The enraged bull would do its best to shrug the dogs, but the dog that held the bull the longest would win the competition for its owner. The bull, having been ripped by the dogs, would be slaughtered and its meat sold; the baited bull's meat was considered to be of superior quality to most: indeed, this was a justification for continuing the practice.

The bear pit was the name given to a hole specially dug to accommodate a tethered bear. Again, dogs were prompted to attack the captive animal, though the bear was often preserved to fight repeatedly as it was expensive for its owner to rear and was thought of as an investment. Badgers, having strong jaws, could take chunks out of an aggressive dog, although the odds were still against them because they were tied to a stake. Dogs were sometimes released down a badger set. A fourth variant on baiting involved rats, which were placed in an enclosure with a small dog (usually a terrier) which would chase the rodents furiously, while onlookers timed how long it took before it killed all the rats

While not exactly the same as baiting, another sport involved bulls being made to run through the streets of many British cities, most famously through Birmingham and, of course, even today in Pamplona, Spain. Bull running ceased in England in 1825, a year after the founding of the Royal Society for the Prevention of Cruelty to Animals (RSPCA). The same organization campaigned successfully against cockfighting. The crucial piece of legislation was the 1835 Act Against Cruelty to Animals, which also affected animal fighting sports.

As with many other activities that were diffused and popularized throughout the British empire, animal baiting gained enthusiastic followings in South Asia. In the 1990s, investigations revealed that bear baiting persisted, indeed flourished, in certain parts. A 1997 World Society for the Protection of Animals report on "Bear-baiting in Pakistan," authored by John Joseph, detailed the rampancy of the practice in the state of Punjab (despite laws against it dating back to 1890).

Bullfighting

In terms of animal fatalities, there are few sports to rival bullfighting: every year, over 25,000 bulls are killed by matadors in Spain alone. The sport, known as *la corrida*, is also practiced in Mexico, southern France and parts of Central and South America where Hispanic influence is pronounced. In its present form, bullfighting began to take shape in the eighteenth century. The bull, for long a priapic symbol, has a special place in Latin cultures and to triumph over the beast was thought to confer prowess on the victor.

Matadors typically emerged from Spanish slums, their desire to escape poverty providing enough motivation to risk their lives in front of baying crowds. Great honor and *machismo* were the spoils of victory. Bullfighting codes developed: dress became more formal, rules of conduct were observed, styles were formulated. Even in defeat, a gored matador could take kudos should he show style and courage enough to suggest he possessed valor, a quality that fascinated Ernest Hemingway in his classic *Death in the Afternoon* (1932).

More contemporary matadors have risen to positions of great wealth and influence. El Cordobés is an outstanding example of a matador who became an icon in Spain, Mexico and Southern California (where there is a large Latino population). At time of writing, top matadors command up to £50,000 ($82,500) for an appearance. Like many sports which involve a gratuitous waste of life, there are objectors. Defenders of bullfighting point to its central place in Hispanic culture and its displacement value: it functions, they argue, as a vicarious form of AGGRESSION, an outlet.

Under a 1976 law, *la corrida* is banned in France, except in those areas where there is an "unbroken local tradition." In 1952, it was declared illegal to kill bulls in the public ring, except in 29 specified "traditional" towns. Controversy broke out in 1997 when the small town of Brêde, south of Bordeaux, introduced commercial bull fights; it had neither an unbroken nor a local tradition, but its Mayor, Michel Dufranc, was a known leader of the hunting and blood sports lobby and was instrumental in attracting the Spanish company which staged the fight.

Fighting

There seems to be an almost universal appeal to animal fighting. Cockfighting probably has its origins in ancient China and Persia. Greeks may have been aware of it after their victory over Persia at Salamis in 480 BC, and in turn introduced it to the Romans. For Greeks, the courage of fighting birds was regarded as exemplary: youths were encouraged to watch and emulate the birds' tenacity and valor in combat. Later, fighting became a mere source of entertainment, especially for gamblers. it first appeared in Britain in the twelfth century, though its popularity waxed and waned until the sixteenth century, when Henry VIII built a royal cockpit at his palace. In the eighteenth and nineteenth centuries, cocks were bought and sold, bred and trained in a more organized way.

Social historian Hugh Cunningham relates a Sunday morning meeting in London in 1816 at which several hundred people were assembled in a field adjoining a church yard. In the field, "they fight dogs, hunt ducks, gamble, enter into subscriptions to fee drovers for a bullock" (*Leisure in the Industrial Revolution*, Croom Helm, 1980). As well as birds, all manner of other animals were used to fight. Dogs especially were bred and trained specifically for this purpose.

Dog fighting persists to the present day. In the early 1990s, amid a panic over the number of ferocious breeds proliferating, the British banned the import of

American pit bulls (such animals are required to be registered in Britain under the Dangerous Dogs Act, 1991). There are occasional reminders that the human thirst for animal blood (for example, in 1995 in Durham in northeast England, fourteen dead cockerels and forty live birds were found, together with implements, including sharpened spurs, weighing machinery and a board that listed names, weights and betting odds on birds).

Hunting

Hunting animals for sustenance is a human adaptation originated in the hunter-gather modes, possibly two million years ago. Procuring food came at first through scavenging, which was later complemented by hunting. It is probable that the hunting acquired a division of labor, specially developed weapons and a degree of tactical organization. As recently as 10,000 years ago, *homo sapiens* devised a way of exploiting food supply which effectively removed the necessity of hunting and freed our predecessors from the burden of having to risk their lives in order to find food. The rise of agricultural modes of production, however, did not end the desire to hunt.

Recapturing the spirit of the hunt without any obvious practical benefit meant converting hunting into an autotelic activity (from the Greek *auto* , meaning for or by itself and *telos*, end, having or being a purpose in itself). Many of today's sports embody components of hunting, whether actual or symbolic (from darts to tennis).

Richard Mandell's book *Sport: A Cultural History* (Columbia University Press, 1984) describes Egyptian frescos dated to the fourteenth century BC, in which the Pharaoh Tutankhamun is shown hunting lions from his chariot. Amphibian Nile dwellers like crocodiles and hippopotamuses were also hunted. Crete had trade contacts with Egypt and some kind of cultural cross-fertilization is possible. Certainly Cretans were avid hunters, and their relics suggest they were combat enthusiasts as well; there is some evidence of a type of bull-fighting and cattle-wrestling as found at US rodeos.

The predominant variety of hunting in the modern era has its roots in England. At first stags were the most popular prey; then foxes, once thought of as vermin, were identified as quarry. This probably occurred in the early eighteenth century. Foxhunting was a pursuit of the wealthy classes. It is thought that Hugo Meynell introduced structure to the practice when he bought a pack of hounds and began breeding them for hunting at his land in the English Midlands. Hunting's "appeal" was captured by the nineteenth century writer R.S. Surtees, in his *Handley Cross* : "Hunting is the image of war but without its guilt and only five-and-twenty percent of its danger." The practice of organized hunting was taken to North America during the colonial era. Several prestigious hunting clubs were established in Canada and the United States in the first half of the nineteenth century, although the prey extended beyond foxes and included coyotes and bobcats. By the twentieth century, foxhunting clubs were abundant in New England and Virginia.

Contemporary foxhunting retains the format and affectations of the sport that took shape in Victorian England. The uniform, hierarchy and protocols have remained. It is still a pastime of the wealthy, indeed the very wealthy: during the 1990s, many hunts were abandoned due to the expense of breeding dogs specifically for the hunts.

Foxhunting has been under pressure from organized protest groups from at least 1950. Hunt saboteurs have appeared at virtually every English hunt. The advent of the animal rights movement from the 1970s added to the pressure to ban foxhunting and, by the mid-1990s, foxhunting was in danger of collapse, especially after Labour MP Michael Foster's Private Member's Bill to ban foxhunting. In the United States many hunting practices, particularly of big cats, were banned as a result of animal welfare groups' opposition.

Other forms of hunting for sport have also been the subject of animal welfare groups' scrutiny. There is a lobby that contends that fishing is cruel and unnecessary. (Fishing remains one of the most popular participant sports in the world.) Falconry, pigeon shooting and rodeo have all come under pressure during the postwar period.

Blood sports in general and foxhunting in particular are seen by Norbert Elias and his collaborator Eric Dunning as having central importance to our understanding of culture. The "civilizing" of society from the medieval era demanded greater personal self-control and a stricter constraint on violence; but the process of hunting or just observing allowed "all the pleasures and the excitement of the chase, as it were, mimetically in the form of wild play." While the passion and exhilaration associated with real hunting would be aroused, the actual risks to life and limb would be absent in the imagined versions (except for the animals, of course) and the effects of watching would be, according to Elias and Dunning, "liberating, cathartic." Blood sports, for these analysts, are peculiar testimonies to human transitions from barbarism to civilization. If this is the case, then vestigial barbarism is still found in many parts of the world. For example, the hunting of American black bear is still allowed in most parts of the USA, so much so that about 40,000 bears were killed in 1997 alone. There are also legal hunts of brown and polar bears in North America.

Of related interest

Carr, Raymond (1976) *English Foxhunting: A History*, Weidenfeld & Nicholson.
Dundes, Alan (1994) *The Cockfight: A Casebook*, University of Wisconsin Press.
Elias, Norbert and Dunning, Eric (1986) *Quest for Excitement*, Blackwell.

Blue Chips

Any sport, amateur or professional, is amenable to CORRUPTION. That is the message of William Friedkin's film *Blue Chips* (1994) in which successful college basketball coach Pete Bell, played by Nick Nolte, offers cash incentives to lure recruits to his university. The Bell character is headstrong, belligerent and prone to locker room explosions; it is possible that some features are drawn from the volatile Indiana University coach Bob Knight, whose exploits were covered in the book *A SEASON ON THE BRINK*.

The movie begins at the nadir of Bell's otherwise laurel-strewn career. His first losing season plunges him into a desperate soul-searching, in which he questions his ability to coach. He decides his technique is not the problem; talent *is*. His search then turns to young players. A fictional sports goods company, "Gazela," tips him off about several potential young players and he scours the country for them. Of the three young men he targets, two ask for gifts, such as a tractor for one's father (an Indiana farmer) or a new home for another's mother (a single parent in Chicago). The third asks for nothing, but receives a brand new Lexus anyway.

The Director of the Athletic Program at Western University in Los Angeles, where Bell works, turns a blind eye to the fact that a wealthy alumnus named Happy (J.T. Walsh) is prepared to underwrite the cost of recruiting the young men, despite this being an obvious violation of National College Recruiting Association rules. Bell despises Happy for his wealth, but is reminded that he is "owned." Bell is referred to a college championship game in 1991 in which one of the players was paid to shave points. On examining a tape of the game, Bell concludes that one of his most trusted players had indeed taken a bribe to throw the game.

Disillusioned, Bell, who has tried to distance himself from the illicit gifts, busies himself with his three new rookies, who make an immediate impact. Yet after a spectacular winning start to the new season, Bell is stricken by conscience and admits his complicity in the transgression at a press conference. "There are two words I thought I'd never say," he announces to the stunned press corps. "I quit." He ends his career coaching at a high school. The university is suspended from competition for four years.

The movie leaves the viewer ambivalent about Bell, a man driven by a vision of competitive yet untainted amateurism and, at the same time, so obsessed by winning that he is prepared to sacrifice all his lofty ideals in the pursuit of success. Is Bell simply following the logic of the success ethic that pervades all organized sport? Has he lost sight of the fundamental concept of amateurism, the love of competition rather than winning? Or did he really never understand the amateur sports ethos at all? "It's not about basketball," he confesses somewhat naively. "It's about money; and I bought into it big time."

In a sense, the young recruits and at least one of their parents show more awareness of the *realpolitik* of college sports. One of them shamelessly asks for a $30,000 (£18,000) sweetener to sign with the university. The mother of Butch McRae (played by Penny Hardaway) explains that she wants a new house before she lets her son move west. When Bell tells her that this would be a serious infringement of the rules, she replies: "A foul is not a foul unless the referee blows his whistle." When he gets homesick, he asks whether the home will be taken from his mother should he choose to leave the program. Bell confirms that it will be.

The third recruit, Neon Bordeaux (played by Shaquille O'Neal) is less motivated by money, but does not decline the Lexus all the same. While the coach is disgraced, the players continue, McRae and Bordeaux going on to NBA (National Basketball Association) careers (as we are told at the end of the movie).

There is no room for innocence in Bell's team. After realizing when watching the tape of the rigged 1991 game, Bell confronts the player he suspects, but is not met by remorse or penitence. The player fails to see the problem. "We won by eight," he reminds Bell. With SPREAD betting, it is of course possible to back the losing team as long as the losing margin is tighter than the points spread (in the game in question, the Western University team was favored to win by a wide margin). Only later does Bell recognize that his player's "betrayal" is more than matched by his own participation in offering inducements. He explains that the rules may not always be good ones, but they should still be obeyed.

While college basketball is ostensibly an amateur sport, it generates substantial revenue both for the NCAA and for the universities involved. In addition to the monies taken in admission to games and the prestige accruing to successful universities, television money has become a factor, especially since the 1970s. At one stage in the film, Western University's failure to recruit promising young players is explained by the attraction of East Coast universities that typically gain more television exposure. College basketball's televisual appeal was hurt by the rise of the NBA in the 1980s and, for a while, had to stave off the problem of becoming a cheap preparatory institution for the professional league.

It was feared that only the conspicuously successful universities would survive in the face of the media-friendly NBA. A successful team was a virtual necessity. Wealthy, enthusiastic patrons were only too willing to support the athletic programs financially through such schemes as the "Friends of the Program" featured in the film. This was the source of the funds that were eventually channeled to the players and their families. Bell's tacit agreement to endorse the payments highlights the extent to which all interested parties are willing to go in the pursuit of success.

Corruption in basketball has been a stock theme of the sport's history. As Alan Wykes points out, "American basketball has been more notorious than football for its fixing scandals of the 1950s when college stars or whole teams were being bribed to throw games." Like any other competitive sport, basketball is a natural, if unwitting, ally to GAMBLING. And history suggests that, where gambling is present, corruption is rarely far away.

Former Arizona State star Stevin Hedake Smith admitted helping a gambling ring by shaving points during his senior year as a way of relieving his own gambling debts. In one 1994 game, the Sun Devils were favored by 14 points, so Smith and his accomplices had to make sure their team won by six points because the bookie wanted a cushion. Late in the game Arizona State led 40–27, but Smith began to allow more space to the shooters he was meant to be guarding and the score narrowed to finish 88–82. Smith revealed to *Sports Illustrated* how he could adjust his game to accommodate the various spreads, usually by easing off . By holding a victory margin to a certain number of points, players could earn $20,000. Players sometimes bet on their own games.

Of related interest

Blue Chips, directed by William Friedkin, 1994.

Putnam, Douglas T. (1999) "Superstars for sale," in Douglas T. Putnam, *Controversies of the Sports World*, Greenwood Press.

Yaeger, Don (1996) *In Due Process: The NCAA's Injustice for All*, Sagamore.

—— (1998) "Confessions of a point shaver," *Sports Illustrated* vol 89, no 19.

body regulation

The cultural body

Because sporting activities typically take place in highly controlled environments complete with rules and codes of behavior, the human body must be subject to *regulation*: that is, it must be ordered, managed and coordinated with prevailing norms. Although engagement in sporting activities may sometimes involve transgressions of such norms, such as may be incited by bursts of emotion (excitement, anger, frustration and so on), the body is, for the most part, regulated. The way in which this is achieved is much more than a straightforward physical process, and implicates us in a sociocultural analysis.

The premise of such an analysis is that there is no such thing as a purely "natural" body: rather, the body is inevitably shaped through social, cultural, historical and political contexts, and it is impossible to think about or experience the human body outside of these contexts. In short, when we refer to the body, we are referring to more than a set of biological attributes.

In books such as *Discipline and Punish* (Vintage, 1979) and *The History of Sexuality, Volume One* (Allen Lane, 1979), the French philosopher Michel Foucault analysed the human body as the archetypal subject of power and political control. Bodies of citizens at both the individual level and as members of identified populations, or subgroups, are regulated through state and other apparatuses so as to conform to objectives. Such institutions as medicine and public health, the education system and the law serve to construct norms to which subjects are expected to conform and by which they are measured.

In modern Western cultures, power relations operate through and are inscribed on the body, often in subtle rather than violent or coercive ways. By the very fact of being involved in a discourse (i.e., a set of conventions or codes) that prescribes ranges of normality for the human body, subjects are inclined toward conformity. This is not to say that they cannot and do not resist what Foucault calls "discourses of embodiment" emerging from powerful institutions. Nonetheless, the subtlety of processes of regulation and, importantly, the focus of dominant body techniques on voluntarily-achieved human health and "happiness" is such that they can be difficult to resist. Positive values are attached to such notions as physical fitness, well-being and "being in shape."

While there is much that could be examined in relation to the concept of the regulated sporting body, of primary interest in the present discussion is the convergence between the notion of the sporting body and those of the healthy and attractive body, the historical underpinnings of this convergence and issues of gender and the regulated sporting body.

Technologies of the self

There is a strong link and overlap in discourses on the healthy body and that of the sporting body. In both the arenas of medicine and public health, and sport, there has been a focus on the controlled body, the body that is able to self-regulate and discipline itself. Both the ideal body of public health discourses and that of sporting discourses is lean, muscular, tight, devoid of fatness or flabbiness, free of physical disabilities, youthful and sportive. Overweight, disabled and aged bodies are marginalized and stigmatized.

The practices associated with achieving and maintaining good health are what Foucault has called "technologies of the self"; that is, they are individual acts directed at achieving the "best possible" self, a project that continues for the whole of an individual's lifespan. The process is elaborated by Foucault and others in the volume edited by L. Martin *et al.*, *Technologies of the Self: A Seminar with Michel Foucault* (Tavistock, 1988).

For the contemporary *self*, it is believed that the body conveys the thoughts and dispositions of its "owner." Given this inextricable link between self-identity and embodiment, the deportment and appearance of the body have become highly important. Good health and physical fitness have become viewed as personal achievements that require constant work and vigilance to accomplish because they do not come "naturally." Those who take up and maintain a regular physical exercise program, as recommended by health authorities, demonstrate to others their capacity for self-discipline and ability to overcome the temptation of the sins of the flesh. Physically fit, slim individuals are deemed to be superior in their capacity for self-control to those who are overweight, flabby and out of condition.

In medical and public health discourses, it is argued that regular sporting activities are important to achieving and maintaining good health, while in sporting discourses, good health is championed as important to excellence. To be "fit" is to be considered both "healthy" and "physically active." It is for this reason that sports stars who have a serious illness, or appear to be physically unfit, are anomalies in cultural representations. Thus, for example, when Magic JOHNSON revealed that he had tested positive for HIV/AIDS at a media conference in late 1991, there was widespread shock and disbelief voiced in the mainstream new media. How could such a sporting hero, who seemed so physically superior and bursting with good health and vitality, possibly carry the virus associated with a potentially fatal (and highly stigmatized) syndrome?

In the international test cricket season of 1996/7, the Australian spin bowler Shane Warne was subject to much ribbing in the media and by some members of opposing cricket teams concerning his acquisition of a rather noticeable paunch. Monica Seles's comeback appearance at Wimbledon in 1997 elicited often cruel jibes about her weight from the British media. In all cases, the suggestion was that elite athletes should not allow their bodies to "degenerate" to such an extent.

There is also a strong link between this ideal vision of the body and commodity culture's portrayals of the body. Particularly in advertisements for such products as "lite," low-fat," "low-sugar" or "low-salt" foods, vitamins, mineral water, sports drinks, sports equipment and apparel, the ideal body representing the consumption of such products is sporty, healthy and sexually attractive for both men and women. The sporting body is also often a highly commodified body: elite athletes are literally bought and sold, and they can command vast sums for their ENDORSEMENTS.

Elite sports performers are also frequently portrayed as objects of sexual desire, for the gaze of others. In Australia, for example, one glossy magazine regularly features nude photographs of the country's sporting stars shot in an aesthetic, erotic style. Elite sports performers have been featured nude or semi-nude in pin-up calendars. In sports such as body-building, gymnastics and synchronized swimming, the physical appearance and attractiveness of the contestants is particularly to the fore as part of the general performance of the sports. The stress on physical appearance is not unrelated to the high proportion of EATING DISORDERS in those sports.

Historical underpinnings

There are strong moral meanings that attach to the notion of the "civilized" or properly regulated body as opposed to the grotesque or uncontrolled body. The origins of this can be traced back to ancient times. For Greeks, particularly in the High Classical period, the muscular male athlete's body was considered to be the epitome of human perfection. For the ancient Greeks, as for individuals in contemporary Western societies, the notion of the "person" was intimately connected with that of the body: cultivation of body and mind were associated. Spiritual elevation was believed to be accomplished through fighting and mastering the distractions of the material world. The muscular athletic male body was considered to represent heroism, strength of will and the capacity for self-discipline (historical details of this can be found in K. Dutton's *The Perfectible Body: The Western Ideal of Physical Development*, Cassell/Allen & Unwin, 1995).

Christian doctrine built on the ancient Greek understanding of the body as the seat of unreason and chaos. It also concerned itself with the importance of the individual's capacity for mastery of the body in response to fleshly temptations, with hedonism associated with sinfulness and asceticism with godliness. In earlier eras, where religion held more sway, illness and particularly epidemic diseases were often considered to be God's punishment for individual sinners or debauched communities. These moral meanings are also evident in contemporary discourses on health and illness in Western societies, in which illness is often associated with loss of self-control. This is particularly the case with illnesses, or diseases that are associated with "lifestyle choices," such as HIV/Aids and other sexually transmissible diseases, heart disease and some forms of cancer (for example, lung cancer, which is linked to the now reviled practice of TOBACCO smoking). Although less direct reference is made in the modern, secularized world to religious principles, the central association of sin and social deviance remains in such cases.

The public health movement, as a modernist institution, intensified the focus on the regulated body in the interests of health. The beginnings of the modern public health movement emerged at a time in Western history, the age of the Enlightenment (beginning at the end of the seventeenth century), when there began to be a strong focus on rationalized techniques of controlling populations and the use of science rather than divine ordination as a means of achieving human progress. The public health movement built on these approaches, positioning good health as the outcome of careful surveillance and regulation of populations. From the early nineteenth century onwards, following large-scale changes such as industrialization and urbanization, the efforts of public health reformers were directed at the ideas of sanitation, hygiene and the self-regulation of individuals in protecting themselves against ill-health. The application of a medical model to such issues was only one aspect of a MEDICALIZATION process in which the influence of medicine was extended into areas of life that were considered non-medical.

Associated with the development of public health in the nineteenth century was a focus on physical education and sporting activities, especially for young people. The doctrine of *mens sana in corpore sano* (a healthy body in a healthy mind) had emerged as a tenet of organized physical and sporting activities by the middle of the nineteenth century. Engagement in such activities was seen to foster a morally appropriate and disciplined approach to life, through learning how to achieve self-mastery over the body, conforming to regimens of exercise and training and obeying the orders of others when participating in team sports. Individual responsibility for maintaining harmonious social order in sporting activities was fostered, as was the competitive spirit, the need to vanquish opponents and determination. Contemporary discourses on physical education and sport, both in the education system and elsewhere, have maintained this focus on the regulated body as the outcome of such activities.

Gender and the regulated sporting body

There are certain defined limits to the presentation of sporting bodies, including limits in relation to gender. Although female athletes are encouraged to present a sculpted, muscular, slim body – and, indeed, the presentation of such a body in form-fitting Lycra outfits has become a dominant sexualized image in contemporary culture – to "go too far" in developing muscles and losing body fat tends to be considered butch or non-feminine. The fate of bodybuilder Bev Francis is exemplary. In the 1980s, Francis, despite her superior muscular development, regularly lost to more "feminine" bodybuilders (those with smaller muscles, larger breasts and conventionally pretty faces). In their article "Women's bodybuilding: Feminist resistance or femininity's recuperation?" L. St. Martin and N. Gavey (*Body and Society* vol 2, no 4, 1996) indicate that, in efforts to conform to dominant notions of femininity, top female bodybuilders routinely engage in such activities as bleaching their hair blonde, undergoing surgical breast augmentation and wearing obvious makeup. In the same way, the female boxer is considered to step outside the boundaries of appropriate feminine behavior because this sport is so strongly associated with the masculine-coded meanings of aggression, VIOLENCE, virility and physical power, according to Jennifer Hargreaves ("Women's boxing and related activities: Introducing images and meanings" *Body and Society* vol 3, no 4, 1997).

As in ancient Greece, the ideal sporting body remains predominantly a masculine body with elite female athletes often portrayed as inappropriate aberrations, less worthy of attention or interest than their male counterparts. The distinction is underlined in the disparity between media coverage given to top-level female athletes compared with that afforded male equivalents. There are links here with broader cultural understandings related to the gendered body, in which women are considered to lack the capacity to properly regulate and discipline their bodies. Femininity has historically been deemed an inferior form of humanity, with women being portrayed as being far more at the mercy of their bodies and less able to exert rational control over them than men. A contemporary example is the constant association of female "irrationality" with female hormones, as in discourses on pre-menstrual syndrome and menopause. In medical discourses, women have also been continually portrayed as physically inferior to men, as weaker and more susceptible to illness (see D. Lupton, *Medicine as Culture: Illness, Disease and the Body in Western Societies* Sage, 1994).

It is because of the negative meanings associated with the out-of-control female body that many of the women who engage in sporting or exercise activities often find their participation exhilarating, as a means of resistance to these meanings. To pare down one's "womanly" flesh to a thinner silhouette, to increase muscularity and physical strength (but only to a certain level) is to transcend the stereotyped meanings of the passive, enfeebled and undisciplined feminine body. In a context in which femininity remains less valued than masculinity, achieving the ideal of the regulated body can be experienced by women as empowering. As this suggests, engaging in the technologies of the regulated body may be experienced as a positive exercise of autonomy and self-expression.

Of related interest

Lupton, Deborah (1995) *The Imperative of Health: Public Health and the Regulated Body*, Sage.
Rail, G. and Harvey, J. (1995) "Body at work: Michel Foucault and the sociology of sport," *Sociology of Sport Journal* vol 12.
Shilling, Chris (1993) *The Body and Social Theory*, Sage.
Turner, Bryan (1996) *The Body and Society: Explorations in Social Theory*, 2nd edn, Sage.

DEBORAH LUPTON

Bogotá Affair, the

While most British sports fans would typically associate "The Bogotá Affair" with a famous incident in 1970 when the English soccer team captain Bobby Moore was arrested on suspicion of stealing a bracelet, historian Tony Mason discloses a different, arguably more important meaning for the phrase. In 1950, seven British professional soccer players broke their contracts with British clubs and fled to Colombia where they were offered more lucrative salaries to play. They were not the first sports performers to travel in search of better conditions of work: indeed, the migration of soccer players had begun before even the 1939–45 war.

Following the Second World War, British soccer experienced a boom. Crowds began to grow in numbers and the maximum wage was raised to £12 during the season and £10 during the summer. With the sport itself already a full-time professional activity and the promise of extra revenues from the then initiatory television, the prospect of more money flowing into soccer whetted the appetites of professionals.

Neil Franklin was a player for Stoke City. He requested a transfer, but was denied. News of this reached Luis Robledo, the owner of Colombian club Santa Fé, who had been educated at Cambridge. Robledo approached Franklin with a view to enticing him to his club. Robledo also offered Franklin's colleague George Mountford the chance to play in South America. While the British transfer system of the time was not nearly as limiting as, for example, baseball's reserve clause, it still kept power with the club. FREE AGENCY was a distant prospect for players, who were traded to other teams only if their clubs agreed. Franklin and Mountford were still contractually tied to Stoke City when they left for Colombia; they told their club that they were going only to coach during the summer break.

Five other players, including the outstanding Manchester United goalkeeper Charlie Mitten, were recruited for Colombian teams around the same time. He and Mountford both stayed in Bogotá for one year. Their salaries were higher than average British wages, although the cost of living was also higher. Mitten claimed to have netted £3,500 for his year with Santa Fé, as opposed to the £600–800 he earned with Manchester United. His bonuses were £25 for a win and £8 for a draw, plus a seasonal bonus of £750, meaning that he earned more in one year than in his previous fourteen in Manchester.

The Colombian league's ability to recruit overseas players by inducing them to break contracts was based, according to Mason, on an internal power struggle: "The Colombian Football Association *was* affiliated to FIFA but was in dispute with the Division Mayor del Futbol professional de Bogotá (the Colombian league) which was not." This meant that Colombian clubs could sign maverick professionals from around the world without have to answer to FIFA, the world's governing federation. As well as Santa Fé, the other Bogotá club, Millionarios, was able to take advantage of this situation, employing the Argentinean Alfredo DI STEFANO, who went on to become a key player in the Real Madrid team that won the first five European Cups. Millionarios was one of the world's leading clubs in the early 1950s.

None of the seven British players completely settled in South America, and their returns to Britain were greeted mostly with condemnation. Franklin actually broke a second contract, hastily leaving Bogotá after a mix-up over his hotel bookings. Apparently aggrieved that the club had no made adequate arrangements for his wife's return to Britain to have a baby, he fled back to Stoke only to find himself fined and suspended. All the others were similarly punished.

The affair served to highlight the disaffection in British soccer. In the early phases of the relative affluence that came in the postwar years, professional players sensed their own exploitation. The salary cap was not removed until 1961, and even then not until fierce campaigning from the Players' Union. The bribery cases of Tony Kay, Peter Swan and David Layne suggested that players in the 1950s and 1960s were willing to augment their incomes through illicit means. Even in the more prosperous 1980s and 1990s, soccer players, coaches and managers, it seems, have been wont to seek alternative incomes, as the "BUNG" INQUIRY indicated.

The movement of Franklin *et al.* was a very small-scale affair compared to mass migrations that surrounded the BOSMAN CASE, which effectively made players free agents at the end of their contracts. While the longer term contract and the constant renewals maintained transfer fees, the input of television monies into European soccer enabled the wealthier western European clubs to attract players from Eastern Europe and South America. Indeed, Colombia became a notable exporter of soccer talent in the 1990s, Faustino Asprilla moving to England's Newcastle United and Carlos Valderrama moving to the North American MAJOR LEAGUE SOCCER.

Of related interest

Mason, Tony (1994) "The Bogotá affair," in Bale, John and Maguire, Joseph, *The Global Arena: Athletic Talent Migration in the Interdependent World*, Frank Cass.

Borg, Björn

b. 1956, Sweden

The adjective "enigmatic" is often misused to describe sports performers, but in the case of Borg it seems perfectly appropriate. A Wimbledon champion at the age of 20, he went on to defend the title for four consecutive years before being relieved of his title by John McEnroe in 1981. In the same year he was the French Open champion and a United States Open finalist. In 1981, he earned more than $4 million from endorsements, more than any other sports performer of the day, and in 1982, despite a reduced playing schedule, he earned $3m from advertising. Then, with lucrative contracts with, among others, Fila and Donnay rackets amounting to about $4m, and a lucrative season on the ATP circuit ahead, Borg inexplicably announced his retirement. It was 1983; Borg was then 26.

No explanation was forthcoming. Borg's form had wavered, but he was still ranked in the top ten as a player and was far from used up. His agent, Peter Worth, tried to dissuade him from leaving a sport he had dominated in the late 1970s. Worth reminded him that he would probably command a ranking for another four years. But Borg was adamant and refused to disclose his reasons, though it was thought that he found it hard to suffer the indignities of having to pre-qualify for certain tournaments (because of his refusal to commit himself to the required number of tour events in 1982).

Five years later and only months before he was due to marry, Borg was rushed to a Milan hospital, where he had his stomach pumped. His own account of the situation was that he had suffered food poisoning and taken a few sleeping pills. Other reports suggested a barbiturate overdose.

In 1991, Borg, by then 34, made a comeback on the tennis tour. His insistence on using a wooden racket at a time when all the world's top players were playing with synthetic fiber models hardly helped his efforts. He was quickly dispatched back into retirement. Borg's second wife, Loredana Berte, attempted suicide in 1989 and the couple were divorced in 1993. Borg's domestic disasters were paralleled in his business career; it was thought that his abortive comeback might have been motivated by lack of money. His prize money revenue alone exceeded £3.6m when he first retired.

Borg was tennis's first contemporary ICON. Teenage women afforded him a status comparable with that of a rock star: they camped outside stadiums before his games, screaming at first sight of him; they interrupted his games shrieking and crying and sometimes throwing underwear on court. His face adorned posters, tee-shirts and other merchandise, making him the most marketable tennis player in history. His commercial affairs were handled by Mark McCORMACK's International Management Group.

Right-hander Borg was surprisingly suspended for six months by the Swedish Tennis Association as a junior following an undisciplined incident. Thereafter he developed into one of the world's most FOCUSED sports performers, showing a cool implacability in the face of the most adverse conditions. Technically, his game was based on a topspin forehand that has arguably been bettered only by Pete Sampras. The shot was perfected under the tutelage of his coach, Lennart Bergelin.

Borg began playing at the age of nine and was the number one ranked junior by the time he was 14. He won his first major title, the Italian, and the first of six French Open titles in 1974 at the age of 18. The following year he lost to Arthur ASHE in the Wimbledon quarter-finals. After that game he remained undefeated at Wimbledon for five years (41 matches) until the four-set defeat by McEnroe in the 1981 final. His stumbling block was the US Open: he lost in the finals six times. He won a total of eleven Grand Slam singles titles and, between 1976 and 1981, enjoyed hegemony over the male game.

While Borg's reign never had the edge that comes with great RIVALRIES, Jimmy Connors once vowed to trail the Swede to the ends of the earth in what was ultimately a vain attempt to break his grip of the world's game. The American pushed Borg to the fifth set of the 1978 Wimbledon final, but never again threatened his nemesis. In 1980, Borg delayed the ascendancy of McEnroe when he narrowly defeated him in a five-set thriller in the 1980 Wimbledon final. But the following year saw the start of McEnroe's domination, and Borg's apparently premature retirement ensured that the two would not reprise their two combative matches.

Borg's success proved a catalyst for Swedish tennis. He was replaced as his country's number one by Mats Wilander and then Stephan Edberg. The momentum has been carried on by the likes of Jonas Bjorkman and Magnus Larsson.

Of related interest

Kennedy, J., Rotfeld, B. and Rotfeld, S. *The Legend of Bjorn Borg* (videocassette), Sports Legends Inc.
Kirkpatrick, C. (1991) "UnBjorn: After myriad setbacks, a changed Bjorn Borg made a sad return to tennis" *Sports Illustrated* vol 74, no 17.
Skarke, Lars (1993) *Winner Loses All*, Blake Publishing.

Bosman case

The ruling in the case of Jean-Marc Bosman effectively ended the necessity for transfer fees in soccer and opened the way for freedom of employment. Players were permitted to move from club to club as soon as their contracts had expired: prior to the ruling, clubs had the right to withhold a player's registration and, if so desired, could demand a fee before transferring that registration.

Until 1991, Belgian soccer operated a system not unlike that in early baseball. If, at the end of a contract, a professional player did not wish to re-sign with his existing club on the terms offered by that club and no other club wished to employ him, the player would be suspended and could not play at all. Bosman opposed this tradition: as a player for the Belgian club, FC Liege, he was denied the opportunity to move to another club when Liege insisted on a prohibitive transfer fee. As a result of the case *Bosman v. FC Liege and URBSFA*, the Belgian Football Association came into line with other European Community countries by taking into consideration the wishes of the players involved. The transfer fee demanded for Bosman was still too high for other clubs to take interest. The player argued that this was in violation of the Treaty of Rome, which allowed freedom of contract for citizens of nations belonging to the European Community (EC). Bosman's club was intransigent, so he took his case to the European Court of Justice in 1995.

In finding in his favor, the court brought the contracts of employment in soccer into alignment with those of any other industry. Transfer fees were traditionally sums of money paid by one club to another for the unused portion of a player's contract. The precise length of the unexpired portion did not typically affect the fee, which was based on the evaluation of the player's skills and possible benefit to the club. Typically, a player could expect to receive the equivalent of 10 per cent of the fee. Post-Bosman, a player was free to move to any club with whom he could agree personal terms.

Many of Europe's smaller clubs feared extinction as a result of the case: it was argued that the survival of clubs in lower divisions depended on their ability to scout potentially good players, develop their skills, enhance their competitive experience and then transfer them to a bigger club for a fee. Without such fees, it was possible for players simply to wait out their contracts and then sign lucrative contracts with wealthier clubs. In 1997 UEFA, European soccer's governing body, established a fund (from television revenues) to provide compensation to small clubs which lost valuable players.

In the two years following the Bosman decision, the initial fears for the smaller clubs' survival appeared to be unfounded. In the 1996/7 season, clubs in the English Premiership spent a record £105m ($172m) on transfer fees, receiving only £55m in return for players sold. But, of the net outflow of £50m, only £2.5m went to the second division and £800,000 to the third, while the first division actually had a deficit with the Premiership. The net flows represented an average subsidy of £104,000 per second division club and a mere £33,000 per third division club; marginal at best to their overall finances and far less than they received from television revenue. Most of the net outflow from Premiership clubs went to overseas clubs.

Two other consequences flowed from the Bosman decision. First, clubs began to extend contracts, especially for bankable players. For example, a team signing a player may insist on an eight- to ten-year deal, ensuring that he would remain in contract during his peak years and that, should another club wish to sign him, the contract holders could legally demand some form of compensation, whether through player exchanges or money. Clubs would rarely allow a valuable player's contract to wind down: more likely would be the offer of improved terms at least twelve months before the end of the contract. If a player's stature increased during his time with a club, then the club would try to ensure that (a) he stayed at the club, or (b) at least signed a deal that allowed the club to demand a fee for his contract.

Condition (b) had the effect of maintaining a transfer fee system. Within months of the Bosman ruling, English club Newcastle United paid Blackburn Rovers, also from England, a record fee of £15 million ($25m) for the unused portion of Alan Shearer's contract; Shearer received a percentage of the fee plus £3million ($5 million) per year in salary. And, in 1997, the Brazilian player Ronaldo tried to renegotiate his contract with Spanish club Barcelona, but failed to agree terms. At a cost of £16.5m ($27m), Ronaldo attempted to buy his way out of his contract with Barcelona so that he could join the Internazionale club in Italy. Barcelona objected to this on the grounds that FIFA rules state that individual players could not buy their way out of contract for the purposes of obtaining an international transfer to another club. FIFA confirmed this in its "Circular 616."

In July 1997, the European Commission declared that this constituted "an unjustified obstacle to the free movement of workers." It alleged that FIFA's circular appeared to maintain a system that had been ruled illegal by the European Court of Justice in its Bosman verdict, and which also appeared to contravene European Union regulations. Effectively, Internazionale paid the £16.5m to the player to enable him to buy his way out of his contract.

This differed from another transfer that followed within two months, this time involving the Brazilian club São Paulo which received a then world record fee of £22m from Real Betis, of Seville, for the services of the striker Denilson for eleven years. The most surprising aspect of the arrangement was the insertion of a buyout clause into the contract. Mindful of the Ronaldo transfer, Betis stipulated that a prohibitive £260m – far beyond the means of all but a handful of clubs – should be paid if the player wished to move within the eleven-year period. This dwarfed the £91m clause set by Real Madrid for its Dutch player Clarence Seedorf.

It is no small irony that Bosman himself benefited hardly at all from the ruling which precipitated huge salary increases for many players, as well as FREE AGENCY movement between clubs. His playing career nearing an end, Bosman found himself without a club within three years of the court decision.

Of related interest

Katz, P. (1994) "A history of free agency in the United States and Great Britain," *Comparative Labor Law* vol 15, no 3.

Miller, Fiona and Redhead, Steve (1994) "Do markets make footballers free?" in Bale, John and Maguire, Joseph, *The Global Sports Arena: Athletic Talent Migration in an Interdependent World*, Frank Cass.

"bung" inquiry, the

In British sports vernacular, a "bung" is an improper payment made to a club's manager, coach or official in exchange for favors in trading or transferring players. (The word *bung* is Old English for a purse.) In 1995, after a widely publicized series of stories alleging misconduct of this kind, soccer's official Premier League inquiry was set up under the leadership of Robert Reid, a prominent lawyer, Rick Parry, then the chief executive of the Premier League (later replaced by his successor Peter Leaver) and Steve Coppell, then head of the League Managers' Association. In September 1997, the inquiry submitted its report.

The submission was based on interviews with sixty-six witnesses in person and twenty-four by telephone: it was 300 pages long, with almost half of its content focusing on the transfer of player Teddy Sheringham from Nottingham Forest to Tottenham Hotspur in 1994. It concluded that bungs had been offered and received in this particular transaction, but that the sport itself was not "corrupt."

The incident that precipitated the inquiry involved a Norwegian sports agent, Rune Hauge, who gave £400,000 ($650,000) in "gifts" to manager George Graham. The disclosure cost Graham his job as the manager of the Arsenal club in North London and a one-year ban from the Football Association. Hauge was suspended from acting as a professional sports agent. Prior to the BOSMAN CASE, the transfer of players from club to club typically involved a fee paid by the receiving club for the unused portion of the player's contract and registration. The clubs' managers and players' agents often agreed on the amount of the transfer fee, and the owners or directors would usually accept the amount. Were managers dishonestly inclined, they might inflate the price so as to favor both the agent, whose commission would be greater, and the selling club, which would receive more money. Either might then clandestinely return the favor with a secret "gift."

Hauge also featured in the "bungs" inquiry; the former Nottingham Forest coach Ronnie Fenton admitted that he received money from Hauge. Earlier, he had told a British tabloid newspaper that a check for £45,000 "came out of the blue" and that Hauge had told him that it was a reward for service over a period of six or seven years. Fenton had advised Hauge on a number of Scandinavian players whom he believed had potential. By the time of the inquiry, Fenton had moved to a coaching position in Malta. The Sheringham move was said to have involved a meeting at a motorway (intercity highway) service station and a handover of cash that was not reported. Present at the meeting were the player, his agent and Fenton.

Perhaps the most remarkable episode reported was the transfer that is alleged to have concluded with the payment of £45,000 brought in a fishing boat by an Icelandic trawler for a rendezvous in Hull in the north of England. It concerned the move made by Thorvaldur Orlygsson from the Iceland club Akureyrar to Nottingham Forest in December 1989. The inquiry was told that the trade did not involve agents or intermediaries, and that all Nottingham's negotiations were conducted by their manager at the time, Brian Clough, and his colleague, Fenton. When the deal was first set up in October 1989, the fee proposed was £150,000, but by the time the details had been finalized, the figure had increased to £174,000, a fee paid on December 5. (The player himself agreed to terms of £25,000 per year, later rising to £35,000). Fenton flew to Iceland to, in his words, "finish the deal." The report stated that Fenton "was unable to explain why the money had been transferred before the deal was finished. He was adamant he had not brought any money back with him: he told us he only brought back two artificial Christmas trees."

Fenton said that it was while he was in Iceland that the asking price was increased and that, having called Clough, the club agreed to the new fee. The suggestion that Fenton received £45,000 in "a fishing box off a trawler in Hull" was made by Allan Clarke, a member of Nottingham Forest's backroom staff. The mode of payment – on board a trawler – although not the exact amount, was supported by two other members of Forest's staff.

Disclosures of improper payments in British soccer began shortly after the professional game began to attract genuinely mass crowds. In 1921, several players were involved in accusations of taking bribes to "throw" games. The timing of the allegations and subsequent scandal was interesting, coming shortly after grumbling players had threatened to organize into a union to press for better salaries. The maximum wage arrangement ensured players were low-paid servants of their clubs. Its removal in the late 1950s preceded a second major corruption scandal. The *cause célèbre* involved three professional players and a former player whose career had been cut short by injury and who were thought to have been involved in a national betting syndicate. Players at clubs all over England were alleged to have been paid to throw games, while the betting syndicate took advantage of long odds by betting on the UNDERDOG.

The players, Peter Swan and David "Bronco" Layne of Sheffield Wednesday and Tony Kay, formerly of Wednesday, but later of Everton, were all imprisoned for four months and banned from professional soccer, while the ex-player, Jimmy Gauld, was sentenced to four years. The three players were all outstanding, high-profile players, Kay being the most highly valued player in the country in 1963 when the fix was discovered. It is possible that many other players were involved and that the big name players were made scapegoats; and, it is at least conceivable that the media-driven investigation into the corruption was assisted by the English Football Association (FA), which was at the time concerned about the probable effects of what was then called "player power." The removal of the salary cap in 1961 gave players unprecedented power to negotiate their own contracts, thus undermining the authority of the FA. Johnny Haynes was England's highest paid professional with an annual salary of £5,000, about eight times the national average. Kay's salary was slightly less at the time of the scandal.

It is perhaps significant that the "bungs" inquiry followed the widely-publicized trial of three players who were accused of throwing games in the interests of an East Asian betting cartel. The players, John Fashanu, Bruce Grobelaar and Hans Segers, were not convicted and the latter two continued to play professionally. Shortly before, in 1995, the Bosman case had released players from their dependence on particular clubs by making it possible for them to move freely from club to club at the end of their contracts. The case paved the way for players to negotiate previously unheard-of salaries. As before, the scandals served to undermine players at a stage when they were poised to assume new powers.

Of related interest

Sharpe, Graham (1997) *Gambling on Goals: A Century of Football Betting*, Mainstream Publishing.

Wallace, B. (1995) "The tabloid season: English soccer's year of living scandalously," *Maclean's* vol 108, no 23.

burnout

Meaning

Burnout is "a psychological, emotional, and physical withdrawal from a formerly pursued and enjoyable sport as a result of excessive stress which acts on the athlete over time." This is the definition favored by Daniel Gould *et al.* (1996): "It is the manifestation or consequence of the situational, cognitive, physiologic, and behavioral components of excessive stress."

The condition typically affects teenage sports performers whose rise is sudden, if not meteoric, but whose decline is premature and abrupt. Young tennis prodigies such as Tracy Austin and Jennifer Capriati were exemplars of burnout, both being top-class professionals in their teens and seeming to be destined for long reigns at the top. Both were prolific achievers on the professional circuit, but neither fulfilled their early promise, Austin retiring after injuries and exhaustion, Capriati losing form after becoming involved in youthful misdemeanors that seemed to suggest her success had deprived her of an "ordinary" adolescence. The majority of those who withdraw from sport because of excessive long-term stress are unlikely ever to reach the headlines, of course.

Capriati and Austin were well-publicized figures. There are countless others who burn out before even approaching their potential. At the time of the 1996 Summer Olympics at Atlanta, a report was published that claimed that the rigors of competitive gymnastics amounted to child abuse. According to the report's authors, over-ambitious parents were pushing their children to succeed in sports out of selfish reasons. "Achievement by proxy" is how Tofler *at al.* described the manner in which parents drove their offspring toward an almost certain burnout ("Physical and emotional problems of elite female gymnasts," *New England Journal of Medicine*, vol 335, no 4, 1996).

Similar conclusions were reached by Joan Ryan in her book *Little Girls in Pretty Boxes: The Making and Breaking of Élite Gymnasts and Figure Skaters* (1998). She chronicles the short-lived careers of Betty Okikino, practicing and competing with a broken neck, wearing a brace when resting; Kelly Garrison, pounding her ankle while waiting her turn until the pain of the stress fracture was numbed; Julissa Gomez, fatally snapping her neck in Tokyo; Chrysty Henrich, who should have made the 1992 Olympics but died instead two years later, weighing less than 50 lbs. A combination of parental pressure and coaching tyranny contrived to bring a premature halt to many promising sporting careers.

Theories

There are several theories that purport to account for burnout. In his article "Toward a cognitive-affective model of athletic burnout" (*Journal of Sport Psychology* vol 8, 1986), Smith argues that there is a progression to burnout, with the child being placed under pressure to train and develop competitive approaches by significant others, including parents and coaches. The young athlete then begins to see the demand placed on her or him differently, some finding the situation threatening, others not so. If the demand is perceived as threatening, the youth enters a third stage in which there is a physiological response, such as fatigue or insomnia. Finally, in a fourth state, the physiological response leads to some type of coping strategy: this might manifest itself in decreased levels of competitive performance, interpersonal problems or complete withdrawal from the sport.

For Smith, the four stages of the burnout process are influenced by personality and motivational factors. The player's sense of self-esteem, ambition and personal anxiety are all factors, so it is difficult to generalize from his theory. Some young sports performers might react positively, whereas others will feel the pressure.

J.M. Silva identified "training stress" as the determinant in the burnout process ("An analysis of the training stress syndrome in competitive athletics," *Journal of Sport Psychology* vol 8, 1990). This is a physical characteristic: sometimes the body becomes overloaded with the burden of training and competition; but, at other times, the young body becomes stronger and adapts to the rigors associated with higher levels of competition. The young competitors who are prone to burnout experience a "psychophysiological malfunction" after their body's failure to respond positively to training. Their mental orientation is then affected and they become incapable of meeting the demands placed on their bodies. Again, emphasis on how individuals respond limits the applicability of the theory.

Lindsey MacDonald was a 16-year-old schoolgirl from Scotland when she reached the final of the 400 meters at the Moscow Summer Olympics of 1980. Although she was well beaten, she recovered three days later and helped the British team to bronze in the relay. The surprise performance spurred her to great ambitions, and she set herself a challenging and draining training schedule. Injuries and illness beset the rest of her career and the promise shown in her teens was never fulfilled. She competed only until the AGE of 25.

Perhaps the most fruitful model is that of Jay Coakely. In his "Burnout among adolescent athletes: A personal failure or social problem?" (*Sociology of Sport Journal* vol 9, 1992), Coakley argues that the intensity of competitive professional sports and the time demands it places on promising young players denies the young person the opportunity to develop a normal multi-faceted personality. The youth is encouraged to focus totally on success in their sport and to exclude other experiences in their social life. The Capriati case would fit perfectly with this model. A young girl from Florida urged to play tennis at a very early age and provided with every manner of top class coaching and facility, Capriati reached the final of her first tournament on the women's professional tour when she was only 13. Capriati later resumed her tennis career.

Two months later, in her first Grand Slam event, she progressed to the semi-finals of the French Open. In 1990 she became the youngest player in history to win a match at Wimbledon. Two years later, at the Barcelona summer Olympics, she took gold, beating the overwhelming favorite Steffi Graf. It was a peak moment in her short career: a year later, still only 17, she was out of sport. Capriati was never allowed to indulge in the kind of youthful exuberances of her peers. Once she glimpsed the possibility of experiencing aspects of a "normal life," she took it, but as a result ended up in trouble with the police for marijuana possession.

Coakley contends that a young phenom's ability to make decisions that affect her or his life are taken away, or minimized to the point where they feel powerless to influence the direction of their own lives. It is this sense of inability or disempowerment that creates the burnout.

Gould has conducted empirical studies into burnout, and pinpoints the importance of "perfectionism" in the burnout process. Frequent worry about others' evaluations, uncertainty regarding one's own abilities and competitive state anxiety are all factors affecting young athletes striving and being encouraged to reach ever-improving level of performance. "Some youngsters have an 'at-risk' perfectionist personality that may predispose them to burnout," Gould and his colleagues conclude in their article "Burnout in competitive junior tennis players: II. Qualitative analysis." They also believe that many of those mistakenly identified as burnout cases in fact drop out not because of any stress but simply because their interests and ambitions change.

Burnout is a far from inevitable experience for precocious sports performers. Steve Cauthen, for example, was already the US champion jockey and rider of the Kentucky Derby winner of 1978 by the time he was 18. Cauthen moved to England and enjoyed a laurel-strewn career until 1993. A shorter but equally successful career was that of Puerto Rico's Wilfred Benitez, who had his first professional fight two months after his fifteenth birthday and won the first of three world titles at the age of 17. Benitez's six years as a world champion ended in 1982. Still only 23, he lost to Thomas Hearns and his star waned thereafter.

It is also possible to see burnout where in fact there has been a natural cycle of progression. In some sports – gymnastics being an obvious example – athletes reach their peak at a relatively early age and have a plateau period no shorter than many other athletes in other sports. Signs of decline may show when the athlete is still very young. At the time of her figure skating gold medal win at the Nagano winter Olympics of 1998, Tara Lipinski was 15, 60 days younger than Sonja Heine was when she won the same title in 1928. Her contest with Michelle Kwan was portrayed by the media as one of the most bitter RIVALRIES since HARDING *VS* KERRIGAN. Kwan, at 16, had been deposed by Lipinski as world champion the previous year. A year on and with another defeat, the 17-year-old Kwan was having to come to terms with the fact that her peak years might have passed.

Of related interest

Gould, D., Udry, E., Tuffey, S. and Loehr, J. (1996) "Burnout in competitive junior tennis players: I. A quantitative psychological assessment," and "Burnout in competitive junior tennis players: II. Qualitative psychological assessment," *The Sport Psychologist* vol 10, no 4.

Martens, R., Vealey, R. and Burton, D. (1990) *Competitive Anxiety in Sport*, Human Kinetics.

Ryan, Joan (1998) *Little Girls in Pretty Boxes: The Making and Breaking of Élite Gymnasts and Figure Skaters*, Women's Press.

C

Cantona, Eric

b. 1966, France

The tempestuous, often nihilistic soccer maverick Cantona was widely acknowledged as the most gifted player in Britain, where he played for five years between 1992 and 1997 before unexpectedly announcing his retirement at the age of 31. A self-styled philosopher and lover of poetry, Cantona was one of the most celebrated players of the 1990s and the harbinger of a significant change in English soccer.

During the final phase of his competitive career, Cantona won five championships, one with Leeds United and the others with Manchester United, was fined and suspended three times – for a miscellany of offenses, including spitting and fighting with fans and police officers – and was voted the Footballer of the Year by the British Football Writers' Association, in 1996.

Born in Paris, Cantona was raised in Marseilles and played professionally first for Auxerre and then for Marseilles. He played forty-three times for the French national side, but in 1988 was banned from international games for one year after swearing at the national coach, Henri Michel. It was one of several confrontations for which Cantona was punished; others included a fine for punching a team mate, a suspension for throwing his shirt at a referee, a ban for smashing his boots into the face of a team mate and a suspension for throwing a ball at a referee. At the disciplinary hearing for this offense in 1991, Cantona walked up to each committee member and said "Idiot" – for which his ban was extended to two months. After this Cantona announced his first retirement, only to return to soccer the following year, this time with Leeds United in northern England.

Leeds won the championship in Cantona's first season with the club, but he was unsettled and moved to Manchester United after one year, the transfer fee being what seems in retrospect a bargain at £1.2 million ($2 million). Over subsequent years he was a key figure in Manchester's four championship wins and was widely acknowledged as one of the best, if not *the* best, player in Britain. Yet, the fire and fury that contributed helpfully to his competitive play also assisted an almost self-destructive tendency. For example, in January 1995 he was ejected from a game for foul play and, while walking from the field, leapt into the crowd and attacked a fan who was mocking him. He was banned until September 30 of that year and fined £10,000 ($16,000). A two-week prison sentence for the offense was varied on appeal to 120 hours of community service. It was after this incident that Cantona demonstrated his penchant for homespun philosophy. "When the seagulls follow the trawler, it is because they think that sardines will be thrown into the sea," he told the media. In a *pensée* on sport as art, he once wrote: "An artist, in my eyes, is someone who can lighten up a dark room. I have never and will never, find any difference between the pass from Pelé to Carlos Alberto in the final of the World Cup in 1970 and the poetry of the young Rimbaud. There is, in each of these human manifestations, an expression of beauty which touches us and gives us a feeling of eternity."

Ever unpredictable, Cantona announced his retirement for the second time in May 1997, at the age of 31 and with a year of his contract with Manchester United still to run. His reason were ostensibly to pursue other interests outside soccer, though sports critics noted that he had seemed slower in thought and movement in the period immediately prior to the announcement.

Cantona presaged a significant change in the composition of English soccer, one that stirred parochial fears. In the mid-1990s, Manchester United and a handful of other clubs formed an elite group with money enough to tempt well-paid players from Italy and Germany. The formation of the Premiership and, more pertinently, a television agreement with the Rupert MURDOCH-owned BSkyB subscription channel made more money available to the clubs. The first contract was worth £304 million ($495m); on renewal, this was increased to £670m for the 1996–2000 period. While most clubs promised to spend their share of the television largesse on stadium improvements, it soon became clear that they were intent on using it as bait for high-profile players from continental Europe. The first players to arrive in the wake of Cantona, already playing for the Manchester club at the time of the BSkyB deal, were aging stars seeking lucrative pastures in which to play out their final few seasons. Ruud Gullit of Holland joined Chelsea, played for two seasons, then converted to team coach. Germany's Jürgen Klinsmann restricted his stay with Tottenham Hotspur, of London, to one year and left amid acrimony.

But after poor omens, many continental Europeans relocated to England and some to Scotland in return for favorable salaries. In 1996, for example, Fabrizio Ravanelli transferred from Juventus to Middlesbrough for an annual salary of £2 million ($3.3m). The expected effects of the BOSMAN CASE did not materialize: it was thought that transfer fees (the compensation for the unexpired portion of a player's contract paid by one club to another) would disappear to be replaced by inflated salaries. In fact, the transfer fees remained when players traded, but in addition, salaries also rose sharply. In the 1995/6 season, English clubs spent almost £93m in transfer fees to import foreign players, three times the previous year's total. Salaries multiplied by three times from the previous year.

Despite the appearance of unfettered prosperity, only seven of the twenty Premiership clubs were profitable in 1997, according to company records (reported in the *Financial Times*, August 8 1997). Newcastle United, which had spent heavily on both transfer fees and salaries, lost £23.6m on turnover of

£42.2m; the club's annual salary bill was £19.7m (this compared with the £31.4m in salaries paid by AC Milan of Italy in 1996). By contrast, Cantona's own club, Manchester United, reported sales of £53m in the season he "retired," making it far and away the most profitable club in Britain.

Of related interest

Cantona, Eric and Flynn, Alex (1996) *Cantona on Cantona*, Deutsch.
Cantona, Eric and Scanlon, George (1995) *Cantona* Headline Books.
(1997) "Hanging it up: Eric Cantona retires" *Sports Illustrated* vol 86, no 21.

Chariots of Fire

Hugh Hudson's Oscar-winning film *Chariots of Fire* (1981) recalls Corinthian days, when the joy of sport was in the competing rather than winning, when the meaning of the word amateur – from the Latin *amorosus*, pertaining to love – was fresh in the mind and when good losers earned as much respect as winners.

The film is set in the twilight of the Empire and has no plot to speak of: it simply traces the build-up to the 1924 Summer Olympics through the experiences of two real British track athletes. Harold Abrahams was a well-heeled Jewish university student at Oxford. Eric Liddell was a Scottish working-class Christian who ran because he believed it was for the greater glory of God. In a sense, both were outsiders.

A third competitor, Lord Andrew Lindsay, presents an interesting portrait of the English gentleman competitor of the 1920s: he places champagne flutes on the edge of his hurdles during practice runs to deter him from clipping them and spilling his favorite tipple. After training (and, occasionally, before) he partakes in a few glasses of champagne. He is the complete gentleman-amateur, with no trace of the single-mindedness, less still the ruthlessness, that gradually takes hold of his fellow student Abrahams.

At Oxford, the Master of Trinity College senses Abraham's potential and urges him to set his sights on the Olympics. The conception of sports as a way of solidifying character was popular among Britain's elite universities and public (independent) schools. Abrahams, played by Ben Cross, straddles the old and fading world of amateurism and the newer beckoning world of professional values, if not money: he engages a professional coach, Sam Mussabini, who is not even allowed into the Olympic stadium and listens to his charge's progress on radio from a nearby hotel.

In Abrahams, we see the emergence of a new kind of athlete, committed to amateur principles but manifesting ambitions that seem much more familiar than those of his fellow Oxford scholars. Abrahams openly defied the amateur ethos of the day when he declared: "I don't run to take beatings. If I can't win, I won't run."

Liddell, played by Ian Charleson, has few counterparts today; Britain's triple jumper Jonathan Edwards is one of a tiny minority of athletes whose religious convictions structure their approach to competition. Charleson's Liddell trains in his Scottish rural community, the life of which revolves around the church. When faced with the prospect of having to run his Olympic final on a Sunday, he withdraws (as did Edwards in the 1990s), only to find Lord Lindsay amenable to a swap.

Both Abrahams and Liddell emerge triumphant in the face of their American competitors, Charley Paddock and Jackson Schultz. The film's climax is predictably triumphalist. Yet the early realism makes the film an interesting historical document allowing the viewer to glimpse the passing away of amateur MOTIVATION.

Of related interest

Chariots of Fire, directed by Hugh Hudson, 1981.

The Fastest Men in the World, video directed by B. Greenspan and C.P. Greenspan, CIC Videos, 1980.

Keddie, J.W. (1977) "The Eric Liddell story," 3 parts, *Athletics Weekly* vol 31, nos. 3, 4 & 6, January 15 – February 5.

Watman, Mel (1978) "Legendary Harold Abrahams," *Athletics Weekly* vol 32, no 4, January 28.

cheating

Instrumentalism and players

It might plausibly be argued that the cheat epitomizes contemporary sports more dependably than the fair player. The sports performer who is prepared to risk disqualification and the defeat, shame and abject humiliation that often follow embodies the very qualities that define competitive sports in the late twentieth century.

To cheat is to act fraudulently, to deceive, swindle or flout rules designed to maintain conditions of fairness. In the context of sports, fairness may be defined as in accordance with specified rules. In his book *Leftist Theories of Sport*, William Morgan argues that the institution of sport has corrupted the actual practice of sport. From the middle of the twentieth century, business interests have introduced an instrumental rationality into all sports that have shown the potential to yield profit. Slipping economic clauses and incentives into professional players' contracts have put sporting practices on a par with business transactions, and this has openly encouraged the co-optation of sports by the "instrumental logic of the market."

Instrumental qualities such as prudence and calculation have seeped into sports and one effect of this has been the loss of the abandon with which competitors once pursued their goals, which were gratuitous before the onset of professionalization. The underpinnings of sport have been destroyed, says Morgan. Market norms have come to prevail: sports "practitioners," as Morgan calls them, have no compelling reason to value or engage in competitive challenges save for extrinsic rewards, or money. They are provided "with no reason not to cheat and every reason to cheat in order to obtain the external goods they desire."

For Morgan, rules have become little more than technical directives that enable practitioners to acquire the external goods they seek. Any moral power the rules of sports once had has disappeared. So, sports performers break every rule they can get away with and comply with every rule they cannot. If a player gets caught, he or she is rightly accused of not being clever or adept enough, or even being plain stupid. This is either a technical infraction or a miscalculation. Morality does not enter into it.

A soccer player may handle the ball in such a disguised way that it appears that he or she has not made contact. If the ball goes into the goal, a professional player is unlikely to own up to the REFEREE and have the "goal" disallowed. Similarly in American football, a wide receiver may look to have caught cleanly a low pass in the end zone, while in fact the ball may have touched the ground. It is probable that neither player would feel much compunction about their infractions. Morgan believes that the institutional imperatives of professional sports "underwrite and legitimate such rule breaking."

Only by making the costs of committing such infractions prohibitive could we expect to minimize them. In soccer, hand-balls may today be penalized with a red card, meaning the player is ejected from the game. In American football, however, there is no penalty for trying to fool game officials in this way. "The technical measures institutions adopt to stem deliberate rule breaking come out of the same technical logic that excites such disdain for the rules in the first place," states Morgan.

This explains why track and field athletics found itself in the somewhat precarious position in the 1990s of discouraging the use of performance enhancing DRUGS, an action which itself was encouraged by what Morgan would call the "displacement of the logic and goods internal to sporting practices." In other words, after track and field became professionalized, promoters, television companies and an assortment of other interested parties sought to impose a new type of economic logic. Athletes began competing for very high stakes as the prizes for success rose sharply. Many were prepared to take banned substances in the all-out effort to win at any cost, so much so that taking drugs became almost synonymous with cheating in the 1990s.

Owners, managers and coaches

Cheating is not confined to competitors. Owners, managers and coaches want to win just as fiercely as those who play under their supposed guidance. For much of 1993, French sport was gripped by a scandal involving Bernard Tapie, director of the soccer club Olympique Marseilles, whose attempt to bribe members of the Valenciennes team faced by his club in a championship game may be less of an aberration than we wish to believe.

Tall stories of cornermen slipping horseshoes into their boxers' gloves may be laughable, but the most famous yet unproven case of tampering with gloves came in 1963, when Henry Cooper was poised at the brink of an upset victory over a dazed Cassius Clay (later Muhammad ALI). Clay clung on until the end of the round, at which point his cornerman Angelo Dundee claimed that a tear in his charge's glove occasioned a replacement. In the several minutes it took to change the glove, Clay's head cleared and he went on to defeat Cooper. It was widely suspected that the tear was Dundee's own handiwork, posing the question: was this the action of a brilliant, quick-thinking strategist, or a scummy cheat? Or both?

Even coaches, so often depicted as the underappreciated, underpaid sentinels of amateur values and Corinthian virtues, have become susceptible to commercial imperatives. Willie John McBride's revelation about the British Lions touring rugby team is a telling illustration of how the pragmatism typically associated with coaches can become wholesale cheating. Players were told to strike members of the opposing teams whenever they heard a coded instruction from the sideline. The foul tactic was rationalized as a defense against referees, who favored the home sides. The discovery of vials of somatotropin, the HUMAN GROWTH HORMONE, in the luggage of a member of the Chinese team at the 1998 World Swimming Championships cast doubt on the integrity of coaches who, it was thought, packed the drugs either with or without the consent of Yuan Yuan, the swimmer concerned. The quantity of somatotropin involved indicated that this was not the swimmer's personal supply; it was more likely to be that of the whole team.

It is difficult to imagine an instance when a coach would not condone cheating if there was a guarantee that it would go undetected. In 1997, during a soccer match between two English teams, Liverpool player Robbie Fowler was awarded a penalty after the referee ruled that he had been fouled by Arsenal's goalkeeper, David Seaman. Fowler risked censure by insisting to the referee that he had not been fouled by Seaman. The referee was adamant that the penalty stood, and Fowler duly took it. While Fowler's spot kick was saved and driven home on the rebound, one wonders what might have happened had the player remained true to his original confession and deliberately sliced the ball wide of the goal. It strains credibility to believe that Liverpool's head coach would have commended him on his uprightness. More likely, he would have been disciplined for failing to act in the best interests of his team.

Sports scholars have tried to formalize this type of question. The work of Bredemier *et al.* in particular has highlighted how team norms influence individuals' propensity to teach. Cheating can be expected to occur when there is a widespread belief that the coach sanctions rule-breaking if necessary to win games ("Leadership, cohesion and team norms regarding cheating and aggression," *Sociology of Sport Journal* vol 12, no 3, 1995). However, this does not necessarily work in reverse: in 1999, Arsène Wenger, the head coach of the Arsenal soccer team in England, offered to play opponents Sheffield United again, despite the fact that his team had already won the match 2–1. Arsenal's second goal had been scored after a misunderstanding in which the team took advantage of a "sportsmanlike" gesture by the Sheffield team. Despite Wenger's magnanimity, however, his team had a poor disciplinary record over the whole season.

Cheating on a more organized scale leads to CORRUPTION in sports, which usually takes the form of bribing individual players or officials to predetermine or "fix" a result. In this way, the very incalculability that defines competitive sport is subverted. Rules governing actual contests are but one set of regulations in sport. There are also rules that specify appropriate courses of action in, for example, trading players or negotiating contracts. Suspicions of the subversion of the former in European soccer led to what became known as the "BUNG" INQUIRY. In recent decades, sports' governance has become enmeshed in legal considerations and the LAW has played an increasingly prominent role in the enforcement of rules.

Of related interest

McIntosh, Peter (1980) *Fair Play*, Heinemann Educational.
Morgan, William J. (1994) *Leftist Theories of Sport*, University of Illinois Press.
Leaman, Oliver (1988) "Cheating and fair play in sport," in Morgan, William J. and Meier, Klaus V. (eds), *Philosophic Inquiry in Sport*, Human Kinetics.

China Football Association

Liberalization

The economic changes that swept through China in the 1980s and 1990s were reflected in the country's sports, especially soccer. As with most other major sports, television worked as a catalyst. In 1993, China's soccer federation was approached by the International Management Group (IMG), headed by Mark McCORMACK. IMG had brokered a deal with the Philip Morris TOBACCO company, which was prepared to sponsor a new league, known as the Marlboro League. China had lax anti-smoking laws which permitted the use of brand names, but not specific products (such as cigarettes). Sponsors rushed to attach their names to individual clubs; players wore shirts adorned with such names as Kenwood, Ford and Motorola.

Players' salaries rose as new sources of revenue opened up. In ten years, top players' salaries increased tenfold, so that a figure of 1 million yuan ($115,000 or £71,000) was not unusual by the late 1990s. Hao Hai Dong commanded a Chinese record transfer fee of £172,000 when he left the Army club August First for Dalian Wanda. Hao was the leading scorer as China advanced through the first stage in the campaign to reach the 1998 World Cup championship finals in France.

Most advertising and sponsorship revenue went to the China Football Association and the clubs' proportion of the monies grew accordingly, especially with the advent of the kind of merchandising popular everywhere soccer is played. This was no doubt helped by China's policy of one-child families: parents were prepared to indulge their only children and buy them replica shirts, season tickets and so on.

The Chinese left soccer's world governing organization FIFA in 1958 in protest over teams from Taiwan and Hong Kong being allowed to play under the name of China. There was already a strong tradition of soccer; indeed, China took part in the first international game on Asian soil against the Philippines, in Manila in 1913. After 1958, however, North Korea assumed the position of the leading East

Asian soccer nation, going on to beat Italy in the 1966 World Cup championships. By the time of China's readmission to FIFA in 1979, North Korea had been joined by Japan as an emerging force in East Asian soccer.

The sources of China's sporting rebirth lie in the early 1970s. In 1971, "ping pong diplomacy" heralded the end of China's political isolation. Intercontinental table tennis competitions symbolized the passing of an age in which China's communist system was all but impermeable to outsiders. Mao Zedong's invitation to the US team to visit China for a friendly exhibition paved the way for the opening of business links between North America and China.

The process was very gradual, however, and China revealed its champions only at major events; and even then only in specific events. In addition to table tennis, China excelled at weightlifting, volleyball, swimming, diving and badminton. Then in the late 1980s, economic liberalization took off and sports were exposed to the kinds of commercial influences that had transformed sports in most other parts of the world. By 1997, soccer had become the country's most popular sport, attracting a total of 3.2 million spectators to its premier league games – 50 per cent more than in 1995 – and an average weekly television viewing audience of 40m. China's total population is 1.25 billion. Admission to soccer games was about $4, or 4 per cent of an average weekly wage.

The economic reform that began in China in the late 1978 under Deng Xiaoping, saw the rise of a private and collective sector. "Socialism with Chinese characteristics" was the phrase used at the 1992 Communist Party Congress to enshrine the policy that market forces had a central role to play in Chinese socialism; and to justify the fact that some citizens were getting richer faster than others. Under President Jiang Zemin, the People's Republic of China initiated a program of further liberalization that would effectively merge, lease out or sell off more than 300,000 previously state-owned enterprises by the early years of the twenty-first century. Only 3,000 strategic large and medium-sized companies were to remain in state hands.

Sponsorship

Marlboro was the sponsor of the China National Soccer League, the most widely followed sports competition in China. Sports, like cigarette production, was completely state-run on the mainland and the decision to choose Marlboro was made by a government department. In 1996, the China National Tobacco Corporation (CNTC) produced and sold 1.7 trillion cigarettes, about one-third of the world market, or about the same number as the three largest multinational tobacco companies combined. The CNTC employs ten million Chinese workers in the industry, and three million retailers. CNTC is also becoming a leading exporter of tobacco. According to the World Health Organisation, Chinese export revenue from tobacco was $600m in 1995. Further economic benefits come from domestic tax revenues from tobacco, the largest single source for government. Tobacco taxes raised 83 billion yuan (£6.4bn) in 1996, compared with 14.5 billion yuan a decade earlier. Despite this, the government officially opposed cigarette advertising in sports and welcomed the decision of many cities to ban advertisements for cigarettes. According to projections in the late 1990s,

100 million Chinese males under the age of thirty were destined to die from tobacco-related diseases.

In 1999, the soft drinks manufacturer Pepsi bought the sponsorship of China's premier league and renamed it the "Pepsi League" for the relatively small price of 90 million yuan ($11m; £6.7m).

Of related interest

Knutten, Howard, Qiwei, M.A. and Wu Zhongyuan, B.L. (eds) (1990) *Sport in China*, Human Kinetics.

choking

In sports, anxiety is usually situation-specific. Some performers experience stress before competition and may even manifest symptoms of this, such as vomiting. It is not unusual for such athletes to perform well once the competition starts. Others simply choke: that is, they either freeze on the big occasion, become tense when things start going against them during competition, or, most dramatically, begin to make crass errors when victory is within their grasp.

Historically, the event that became known as The Choke involved Steffi Graf and Jana Novotna, who was the anxious loser of a Wimbledon tennis match that she looked to have almost won. Leading 4–1 in games and 40–0 with serve in the third set of the 1993 singles final, Novotna "tightened" and lost the game. Up to that point, Novotna had looked composed, organized and in complete control of her game; yet the prospect of winning the final introduced anxiety into her play which disintegrated in the face of Graf's consistency.

Novotna, a technically able player, later choked again, this time in the French Open when leading 5–0 and 40–30 with serve against Chanda Rubin, in 1995. Her opponent survived nine match points. Some pointed to Novotna's lack of a "killer instinct," though there are other factors to be considered. First, there is the character of the sport itself: tennis is a game that has to be won. Choking can be disguised in some sports in which an individual or team can build up a lead and then become anxious, but not to the extent where their opponent overhauls that lead. Often winners are made to "cling on" in the dying moments of a competition.

Second, tennis is a sport requiring high levels of complex skills. Other sports, such as weightlifting or running, require judgment and technique but not the intricate skills of tennis. Some high level weightlifters and runners may feel anxious and produce inexplicably mediocre performances, but it is unlikely that their behavior will be interpreted as choking.

Psychologists have advanced several suggested ways of understanding the onset of anxiety that causes choking. Some degree of arousal is necessary to complete a successful sporting performance; all athletes need to be psyched, though through different means. The conventional account of how arousal functions is known as the inverted-U theory, and this states that small incremental increases in arousal result in small incremental increases or decreases in performance *and* moderate arousal results in optimal performance. Each sport has its own optimal level of arousal. A golfer or darts player who is highly aroused – hyped – would not produce optimal performance. A sprinter or wrestler, on the other hand, may benefit from much more arousal.

Apart from the difficulties in testing this (most of the experiments were done using mice!), the theory suggests a smoothly-shaped relationship between arousal and performance. Graphically, the classic choke looks more like a cliff-face than a bell curve. Richard Cox (1998) gives the example of Greg Norman in the 1996 Masters golf tournament: after three rounds, Norman held a six-shot lead over his nearest competitor with one round (eighteen holes) remaining. During the fourth round there came the most "catastrophic" four holes in Norman's career. On the ninth through twelfth holes he surrendered his six-stroke lead to Nick Faldo, then went on to lose the trophy by five strokes.

Cox uses this as an illustration of an alternative to the catastrophe model. In this, "cognitive anxiety" is the crucial factor in determining the relationship between arousal and performance. If a competitor has low cognitive anxiety, the U-shaped relationship between arousal and performance will occur. But, when cognitive anxiety is high, a catastrophe will interrupt and, at this point, every small increase in physiological arousal will result in a very large and abrupt decrease in performance: in other words, a choke.

Using archival baseball data as the basis for their article, "The 'championship choke' revisited," Heaton and Sigall analyzed the "fear of failing" as a factor in "performance decrements under pressure" (*Journal of Applied Social Psychology* vol 19, 1989). But, in contrast to explanations that rest on situational factors, Grant in his *The Psychology of Sport: Facing One's True Opponent* (McFarland Jefferson, 1988), believes that upbringing, athletic history and interactions with coaches and others come together to affect a competitor's propensity to choke. Leith concludes that just talking about the possibility of choking before a competition may contribute to the probability of its happening ("Choking in sports: Are we our own worst enemies?" *International Journal of Sport Psychology* vol 19, no 1, 1988).

The sources of cognitive anxiety are diverse, as are the conditions under which it occurs and the type of performer it is likely to affect. So-called "clutch" players actually become more FOCUSED and raise their performance to unprecedented levels when faced with daunting situations. It could be argued that The Choke matchup tells us more about Graf's singular clutch play than Novotna's propensity to choke.

Of related interest

Baumeister, R.F. and Showers, C.J. (1986) "A review of paradoxical performance effects: Choking under pressure in sports and mental tests," *European Journal of Social Psychology* vol 16, no 4.

Cox, Richard H. (1998) *Sport Psychology: Concepts and applications*, 4th edn, McGraw-Hill.

Jones, J.G. and Hardy, L. (1989) "Stress and cognitive functioning in sport," *Journal of Sport Sciences* vol 7, 1989.

Combat 18

Combat 18, or C18, was a neo-nazi organization formed in the 1990s which quickly attracted the soccer hooligan elements of the Right, mainly from around London and southeast England. Initially numbering just a few dozen members, the group grew rapidly as it went on the offensive, attacking left-wing bookstores, gay bars and anti-apartheid activists. It began enlisting support from around British soccer stadiums.

C18 took its name from the numerical position of Adolf Hitler's initials in the alphabet: 1 and 8. It originally provided security for the British National Party (BNP), the principal far right organization of the early 1990s, but it branched off into its own ventures. While accepting the BNP's basic racist philosophy that whites were the superior "race" and that only after a cataclysmic confrontation would whites be restored to their historical supremacy, C18 eschewed its policy of trying to win elections.

C18 operated strictly outside conventional party politics, and found almost natural partners in soccer hooligans (though HOOLIGANISM was in decline in the late 1980s). The alliance with C18 gave the residual hardcore a political cause and an organization through which to advance it. This brought it into conflict with some elements of soccer's FANDOM. For example, the editor of the *Chelsea Independent* fanzine criticized C18 and remarked that racism had no place in soccer. He was attacked on several occasions, once after a Chelsea game in Prague, in the Czech Republic. Despite the hostility of some soccer fans, however, the older "firms" which were vestiges of the 1970s and 1980s were enthusiastic about C18, which provided a "legitimacy" for their VIOLENCE.

The organization came to public prominence in 1995 when the media reported that it had initiated riots at a soccer game in Dublin featuring the Republic of Ireland and England. The game was abandoned amid crowd violence, and C18 claimed a victory of sorts. Its notoriety stimulated interest across continental Europe and even in the USA. It forged links with Loyalist paramilitary groups in Northern Ireland. In 1993, one follower was arrested with six handguns in his car, and a year later a C18 member was arrested trying to deliver submachine guns and a rocket launcher to the Ulster Defence Association (UDA). The links with the UDA led some to suggest that the entire Combat 18 concept was actually dreamed up by Britain's secret service, MI5, as a way of infiltrating the Loyalist terrorist groups in Northern Ireland. Security sources repudiated this. Beyond dispute, however, was C18's connections with neo-nazi movements in Denmark, France, Sweden and elsewhere.

Apart from its violent actions at soccer stadiums, C18's infamy was also based on its music. Many racist "white power" bands recorded on labels owned and run by C18. In fact, some record companies such as ISD Records reaped the benefits of the boom in independent labels in the 1990s. ISD produced an average of 10,000 CDs per year, yielding over £200,000 ($320,000) for C18 in the mid-1990s. As the decade drew to a close, the organization foundered and its influence waned.

Of related interest

"Exposed – C18," special Issue of *Searchlight: The Anti-Fascist Monthly*, no 214 (April), 1993.

Ryan, Nick (1998) "Memoirs of a street-fighting man" *Independent on Sunday*, Sunday Review section, February 1.

coming out

The number of gay sports performers who have either openly declared their sexual preferences, or been forcibly "outed" by others, is relatively small. Some of those who have opted to come out have suffered financially. Tennis player Billie Jean KING, whose lesbian relationship with her former secretary became known in 1981, lost many of her endorsement deals as a result and was virtually forced into making a comeback.

After King's experience, gay athletes, female and male, grew cautious about disclosing details of their private lives. Martina Navratilova was outed by the *New York Post* in 1981, but refused to discuss her personal life with the media, presumably because she was mindful of King's experience. But, like King, she was at the center of a palimony suit, hers brought by her one-time companion Judy Nelson, and this brought her sexuality into focus. After this, she became more open about her LESBIANISM and played an active role in gay causes.

Women's tennis became something of a safe haven for lesbian players, the circuit providing a comfortable environment in which GAYS and straight players had a peaceful coexistence. This encouraged several women players to come out, although in 1999 the French player Amélie Mauresmo became involved in a dispute when her opponent in the final of the Australian Open, Martina Hingis, was quoted as saying: "She is half a man." An earlier opponent, Lindsay Davenport, had previously made similarly derogatory comments. Mauresmo, then 19, had made known her lesbian relationship with a woman with whom she cohabited.

Golf is another sport in which a significant number of lesbians compete. This was something of an open secret for many years before Muffin Spencer-Devlin's announcement that she was gay in 1996. She chose to do so through the pages of *Sports Illustrated*. At the time, she was not financially well-off. In the aftermath of the magazine's revelation, other golfers and officials acknowledged that there were other lesbians on the women's tour.

Mariah Burton Nelson was – and is – one of the most effective advocates of gay pride in sport. A basketball player-turned-writer, Nelson became a self-styled role model for lesbians and encouraged gay players in all sports to declare their sexual preferences.

Gay men who chose to come out typically did so either late in or after the end of their athletic careers. Tom Waddell, the Olympic decathlete from the 1968 Mexico Olympics, was one of the founders of the Gay Games in 1982. He became involved in a legal case with the US Olympic Committee, which refused to let him use the word "Olympics" to describe the gay tournament. Waddell died of AIDS in 1987, aged 49.

Glenn Burke, who also died of Aids, was the first MAJOR LEAGUE BASEBALL player to declare his homosexuality. After playing in the Los Angeles Dodgers World Series-winning team in 1977, Burke refused to take part in a marriage of convenience to allay rumors of his homosexuality and was traded to Oakland Athletics. He later competed at the Gay Games, winning sprint medals, and later turned to basketball. Burke died in 1995. American football star Dave Kopay came out in the 1960s toward the end of his playing career, but his decision made it impossible for him to gain coaching positions and he was forced out of the sport.

Other men have come out after facing the probability that they would be exposed by others. Diver Greg Louganis's public declaration of his homosexuality came through the publication of his autobiography *Breaking the Surface: A Life*, which was published in 1995 and contained details of his HIV positive diagnosis. Louganis revealed how, in the 1988 Summer Olympics, he cut his head and spilled blood into the pool when attempting a reverse two-and-half pike. The doctor who treated Louganis's wound did not wear protective gloves. Louganis's disclosure came after an acrimonious split with his former partner Tom Barrett, who threatened to reveal details of Louganis's medical condition. Louganis' came to a court settlement with Barrett and preempted any disclosure with his book.

Australian rugby league player Ian Roberts faced a similar situation. Confronted by the prospect of being outed without his consent, he chose to forestall the news by declaring himself to be gay through the publication *New Weekly*. British soccer player Justin Fashanu also chose to come out via a news story in the *Sun*, a sensationalist daily owned by Rupert MURDOCH. Fashanu also claimed he had slept with a Tory party politician. His playing contract was terminated by his club and he moved to several others, including a club in the USA. He committed suicide in London in 1998 after fleeing the United States, where he had allegedly assaulted a teenage male.

In 1998, two Canadian Olympians came out within months of each other. Stung by the cancellation of a contract as a motivational speaker on the grounds that he was "too openly gay," Mark Tewksbury, the gold medal-winning swimmer from the 1992 Olympics, who set seven world records in his athletic career, came out voluntarily in a television interview. Tewksbury, like other gay athletes before him, suffered financially. Figure skater Brian Orser claimed his career would also be "irreparably harmed" if his homosexuality were made public; involved in a palimony suit with his former partner, Orser requested to an Ontario Court Justice that records of the case be sealed. When the request was denied, Orser was effectively outed. One immediate consequence was that he lost his job as a TELEVISION commentator.

Of related interest

Cahn, Susan K. (1995) *Coming On Strong: Gender and Sexuality in Twentieth Century Women's Sport*, Harvard University Press.

Cashmore, Ellis (1999) "Why sport isn't glad to be gay," *Sunday Tribune* (Ireland) vol 20, no 6 (February 7).

Louganis, Greg (1995) *Breaking the Surface: A Life*, Random House.

Constantine, Lord Learie

b. 1902, Trinidad; d. 1971

Constantine was an explosive and (in the words of cricket commentator John Arlott) "spontaneous" cricketer, whose impact off the field of play came to be as profound as that on it. He played international Test cricket for the West Indies as an all-rounder (batsman and bowler) between 1929 and 1939, touring England in 1923, 1928, 1933 and 1939. During the 1930s, Constantine made his living as a professional cricket player for the Nelson club in the Lancashire League, in the north of England, outside the first-class game. Nelson won the highly competitive Lancashire League competition eight times in the ten years Constantine played for the club.

Constantine's first-class and Test career statistics are not outstanding, but contemporary accounts stress his tremendous athleticism (the cricket writer Neville Cardus saw him as "a sort of elemental, instinctive force"), explosive fast bowling, unorthodox hard-hitting batting and brilliant fielding. West Indies cricket went on to contribute many comparable talents to world cricket, but Constantine's uniqueness was in his role as a champion of black people.

The Caribbean writer C.L.R. James commented that Constantine "revolted against the contrast between his first class status as a cricketer and his third class status as a man." In the first quarter of the century, a number of English cricketers had reacted (to little avail) against the class prejudice inherent in first-class cricket. Constantine was the first sports performer to speak and act against the English color bar and the racism in British society. He did so in a low-key, non-confrontational style, but speak out he did.

Much of Constantine's adult life, from the late 1920s onward, was spent in England. He had reached almost the end of his cricket career when war came in 1939, and he chose to remain in Britain throughout the Second World War, working as an industrial welfare officer mainly with West Indian workers. He faced – and fought – the low-level "taken-for-granted" racial discrimination that was endemic in employment, housing and virtually all aspects of everyday life. His work to improve the status of black people culminated in a high-profile civil case which he fought and won in 1944.

The case, *Constantine v. Imperial London Hotels*, was heard on June 19, 21 and 28, 1944. Represented by the redoubtable advocates Sir Patrick Hastings and Miss Rose Heilborn, Constantine claimed damages on the grounds that the defendants "refused to receive and lodge him" at the Imperial Hotel in London. Constantine, together with his wife and daughter, had arrived in London in July 1943 to play in a charity cricket match at Lords, the home of the MCC (Marylebone Cricket Club). Constantine had been given special leave of absence by his employers, the Ministry of Labour in Liverpool. He had booked the hotel in advance for four nights and his downpayment had been accepted. At the hotel lobby desk, the Constantines were told that they could stay for one night only and must leave the following day. The management, they were told, "did not want to have niggers in the hotel." After some delay, Constantine was able to call to the hotel desk his chief at the Ministry of Labour. This witness gave evidence that the hotel manageress had reiterated that: "We are not going to have these niggers in our hotel."

Evidence was given by other witnesses to the effect that the Constantine family had remained quiet and dignified throughout the incident. The family decided to leave the premises and they found accommodation in the nearby Bedford Hotel. Cross-examination of the Imperial Hotel staff elicited the reply that they believed that the Constantines' presence in the Hotel would give offense to the many American and Commonwealth soldiers who were staying there. After reserving judgment, Mr. Justice Birkett found for Constantine and awarded damages and costs against Imperial London Hotels. The ruling was major news in its day. Britain lacked a significant ethnic minority population and had no legislation forbidding discrimination. The first law outlawing racial discrimination did not arrive until twenty-one years later (in 1965), by which time the ethnic composition of the nation had changed dramatically.

After the war, Constantine continued to make his home in England and worked as a cricket coach, writer and broadcaster, at the same time studying law. Called to the bar (i.e. to become a practicing barrister) in 1954 (at the age of 52), he later returned to his native Trinidad to begin a career in politics. He became a Minister of Parliament in the post-independence era, returning to Britain as Trinidad and Tobago's High Commissioner. He later became a member of the British Race Relations Board. Constantine was knighted in 1962 and created life peer in 1969 (the first black member of the House of Lords). He died in London in 1971.

Of related interest

Arlott, John (1972) "Lord Constantine," *Wisden*, Sporting Handbooks.
Blake, Lord and Nicholls, C.S (eds) (1986) "Lord Constantine," in *The Dictionary of National Biography, 1971–80*, Oxford University Press.
Cardus, Neville (1963) "Learie Constantine," in *The Playfair Cardus*, Dickens Press.

DAVID PODMORE

corruption

There is one obvious condition that either permits or encourages dishonesty and venality in sports: the possibility of financial gain. It follows that corruption is an almost inevitable consequence of professionalization. Corruption occurs in every other known commercial sphere; it is unreasonable not to expect that it will continue to exist in sports. Some form of deception or fraud has probably been present in all organized sports.

Even amateur sports in which competitors officially receive no money are vulnerable: GAMBLING has been integral to the sports experience and, while there are observers willing to wager on the outcome of a contest, the probability that they will try to control, manipulate or determine the desired outcome will persist.

In horse racing, this has been achieved through administering DRUGS to the horses, a tactic known as NOBBLING. The HORSES are debilitated to the point where they cannot race effectively. The most usual way of managing a result in a human sport is by bribing competitors, a practice that was exposed in English soccer by the "BUNG" INQUIRY.

English soccer was also embarrassed by the case of Bruce Grobelaar, Hans Segers and John Fashanu (brother of Justin FASHANU) who were alleged to have been involved with a Malaysian gambling syndicate which passed cash to players in return for helping fix game results. The case was unproved, but the possibility of a Malaysian gambling interest in soccer remained and, in 1999, featured in another series of incidents that resulted bizarrely in floodlight failure at several soccer stadiums.

Gambling syndicates also figured in a well-publicized cricket calumny involving Australian players Shane Warne and Mark Waugh, who were fined after accepting payments from an Indian bookmaker in return for information about the state of the GRASS and the weather during an Australian tour of Sri Lanka in 1994. It seemed an unlikely exchange, if only because the information seemed of little value. Previously, Australian players had been censured for betting on games involving themselves.

Even well-paid athletes, it seems, have been prepared to risk humiliation, shame and disqualification from their sport for dishonestly earned cash. This suggests an instrumentalism among players that many doubt existed in eras when "sportsmanship" animated competitors and the joy was meant to lie in participating rather than winning. This transition to a success orientation has affected the character and ethos of sport and virtually commissioned illicit incentives to "throw" contests. Yet there are examples from history that suggest that corruption has been an unwanted presence for the entire twentieth century. The infamous world heavyweight title fight between Jack JOHNSON and Jess Willard in Havana in 1916 was never proved to be fixed, though suspicions about it persisted. Johnson was knocked down in the twenty-sixth round and made no attempt to regain his feet. It is doubtful if money was the source of Johnson's lax performance: he was wanted by the police in the USA, and it was thought the promoter, Jack Curley had negotiated a pardon for him on the condition that he lost to Willard, a white fighter.

The "Black Sox Scandal" of 1919 involved several Chicago White Sox baseball players who were bribed by a gambling syndicate to throw a World Series against the UNDERDOG Cincinnati Reds. Money was at the root of this instance of corruption, which was chronicled by John Sayles in his movie *EIGHT MEN OUT*. The players were poorly paid and exploited by MAJOR LEAGUE BASEBALL long before the advent of FREE AGENCY. The film, and the Elliot Asinof book of the same title on which it is based, depicts the players sympathetically, being in some senses cheated by their employers.

Boxers, baseball players and competitors in many other sports today compete for high stakes, and the incentives for winning are higher than at any time in history. Increases in the use of performance-enhancing drugs are not unrelated to this. Over the final two decades of the twentieth century, drugs were proscribed in virtually every sport. Inducements to win were a factor in the tendency of many competitors to use dope. In this sense, commercialism was, again, the source of what some regarded as the most insidious form of corruption in contemporary sports.

However, while officials, particularly those of the International Olympic Committee (IOC) have pontificated over cheating by athletes, the SALT LAKE CITY SCANDAL of 1999 disclosed evidence of widespread corruption among official guardians of the Olympic movement, which had for long been regarded as the embodiment of all that was wholesome and virtuous in sports. Members of the IOC were asked to resign after revelations that they had accepted "gifts" from the organizers of the Salt Lake City bid for the Winter Olympic games. Reporting the scandal for *Sports Illustrated*, E.M. Swift concluded: "In the last two decades, virtually every election to choose an Olympic host city has been marked by backroom political deals and questionable gifts to IOC members or their pet causes." Swift described "a culture of unchecked corruption and greed within the IOC." To reinforce his point, he cited various "gifts" that had been given to assist the election of several host cities in past Olympics, including Seoul (1988), Albertville (1992), Atlanta (1996) and Sydney (2000).

A *cause célèbre* of the 1990s involved the French tycoon and former owner of Adidas sportswear, Bernard Tapie, who was tried for match rigging. The prosecution argued that the soccer club he owned, Olympique Marseilles, became involved in a bribery scandal shortly before its European Cup Final with AC Milan in May 1993. For Tapie, a member of France's Socialist Party, the accusation was one of a long line of legal difficulties that left him bankrupt and ineligible for public office. His club was found guilty of attempting to bribe members of the Valenciennes team, against whom Olympique Marseilles played in a French championship game days before the AC Milan encounter. The Marseilles club was suspended from European competition.

William Morgan argues that sport itself as an activity has been corrupted by the rise of corporate interests. In his book *Leftist Theories of Sport*, Morgan maintains that, from the middle of the twentieth century, business interests have introduced an instrumental rationality into all sports that have shown the potential to yield profit. Slipping economic clauses and incentives into professional players' contracts has put sporting practices on a par with business transactions, argues Morgan, and this has openly encouraged the co-optation of sports by the "instrumental logic of the market."

For Morgan, rules have become little more than technical directives that enable practitioners to acquire the external goods they seek. Any moral power the rules of sports once had has disappeared. In other words, sports today are *intrinsically* corrupt, and we should perhaps regard occasional scandals less as aberrations and more as typical occurrences, most of which remain concealed.

Of related interest

Jennings, Andrew (1996) *The New Lords of the Rings: Olympics, Corruption and How to Buy Gold Medals*, Pocket Books.
Morgan, William J. (1994) *Leftist Theories of Sport*, University of Illinois Press.
Simson, Vyv and Jennings, Andrew (1992) *The Lords of the Rings: Power, Money and Drugs in the Modern Olympics*, Simon & Schuster.
Swift, E.M. (1999) "Breaking point," *Sports Illustrated* vol 90, no 4 (February 1).

D

death

The vocabulary of sports is full of grim hyperbole: "disasters" occur, "tragedies" happen, competitions come down to "sudden death." It is only after genuine loss of life that a sense of perspective is regained. Sports contain risks; many are dangerous, and competitors actually die.

Accidents occurring during the process of competition are the most prevalent and publicized forms of death. However, deaths also occur as the result of training and preparation, athletes pushing their bodies beyond the limits of endurance or perhaps taking substances that take a toll on them. Some deaths are related to the lifestyles of professional athletes: earning a living in what is often a glamorous and high-profile occupation may bring a performer into contact with the kinds of risks many others avoid.

In almost any sport, a death presents an occasion not only for mourning, but for painful reflection on the acceptability of the risks that are habitually taken in the pursuit of sporting excellence. In boxing, death is invariably followed by demands for a total ban on the sport, with American and British medical associations typically advancing evidence to suggest that boxing is one of the few sports in which the actual objective is to inflict physical punishment on opponents.

Statistically, however, deaths occur in greater volume and at greater rates in several other sports. Air sports and motor sports have far more victims than others, with accidents claiming the lives of competitors in what are clearly high-risk endeavors involving elaborate pieces of technology. Research by Mueller and Cantu indicated that American football, ice hockey, gymnastics and wrestling were sports in which competitors were at greatest RISK. Less obviously dangerous sports include running and cycling. In these sports, athletes are typically killed in road accidents while training, or by over-training when in middle age.

Boxing typically ranks about seventh or eighth in terms of annual mortalities, but, as critics point out, the whole purpose of boxing is to strike an opponent as hard and as often as possible. Deaths in boxing are usually the direct result of serious brain damage incurred during a contest. Hemorrhaging is precipitated by the jolts to the skull.

Motor racing and horse racing are the only two sports in which the participants are routinely followed by ambulances. Drivers' deaths are dramatically recorded by the media. Yet, the "carnage," as animal rights activists call it, of horse racing rarely makes the news. Steeplechasing is the most dangerous sport in the ANIMAL RACING portfolio: fatalities average less than one per cent, though some events, such as the British Grand National are notoriously fraught with risk to both horse and rider. The event attracts 450 million TELEVISION viewers from 150 countries, and it is this kind of audience that persuades many owners to enter horses that have little hope of completing one of the most taxing courses in horse racing. It is not unusual for 75 per cent of thirty or more starters to fall or refuse, and for as many as three horses to be "humanely destroyed," to use the vernacular.

Apart from accidents, there are other types of dangers unconnected to the actual performance of sports: even preparing for some sports can end fatally. Anabolic steroids have been cited as killers in some sports, particularly bodybuilding. In 1987, Britain's Keith Singh died with liver tumors after a period of using the drug. Joanne Amies-Winter died in her sleep in 1998 amid rumors that she had been preparing for bodybuilding and triathlon competitions by taking anabolic steroids. In 1994 Zoe Warrick, a former European bodybuilding champion, killed herself, blaming the effects of the DRUGS she took when competing in the late 1980s.

The most bizarre sports-related death was that of Andres Escobar, a Colombian soccer player who had represented his country at the 1995 World Cup in the USA. During the game between Colombia and the United States, Escobar scored an own goal which effectively eliminated his country from the tournament. Having returned to South America in disgrace, Escobar was taken out in a Medellin parking lot and shot dead, the murderer mimicking soccer commentators by shouting "*Gol!*" after each of the twelve bullets pierced Escobar's body.

The man who killed Escobar was Humberto Muñoz Castro, who was sentenced to forty-three years imprisonment. While this might have given the impression that his act was that of an obsessional fan – like the murderous character of the movie *THE FAN* – there was a widely held theory that Escobar was killed by members of a Medellin drug cartel, who had lost heavily after GAMBLING. Colombia was one of the pre-competition favorites to win the World Cup. Death threats had been issued to a number of other players in the Colombian squad. The drug baron Pablo Escobar (no relation) was filmed in the company of players prior to the tournament.

Being a professional athlete has lifestyle implications. Escobar could hardly avoid the "bad company" in which Colombian players sometimes find themselves. However, there are also less obvious dangers for unprotected sports stars. It is known that, in times when sports performers enjoy the adulation once afforded only showbusiness entertainers, congeries of female fans have become sports groupies.

During the 1990s, a number of high-profile sports performers died as a result of AIDS-related illness. These included Arthur Ashe, who died after a blood transfusion, and Esteban de Jesus, who was believed to have used unclean syringes. John Curry, the former ice skater, also died of Aids. Some sports stars, like Magic JOHNSON and Tommy Morrison, on their own accounts, contracted the HIV virus through heterosexual sex.

There have been several mass deaths of sports performers. The disasters at Turin in 1949, Chile in 1961, the Andes in 1969, the Pacific ocean and Parmaribo in 1989 and the Atlantic in 1993 are grisly reminders that whole teams can sometimes be destroyed in a single airplane catastrophe. The MUNICH DISASTER of 1958 remains the most memorable tragedy of this kind.

Fans are sometimes at risk too. Deaths in European soccer became an unwanted feature of the late 1980s and early 1990s. Mass casualties at Brussels, in Belgium, and at Bradford and HILLSBOROUGH in the north of England were caused by HOOLIGANISM, stadium fires or deficiencies in policing.

Of related interest

Leviton, D. (1997)"Some reactions toward death among danger-defying sports-men," in Kenyon, Gerald and Grogg, Tom (eds.) *Proceedings of the Second Congress of the International Society of Sports Psychology*, Chicago Athletic Institute.

Mueller, F.O. and Cantu, R.C. (1990) "Catastrophic injuries in high school and college sports," *Medicine and Science in Sports and Exercise* vol 22, no 6.

Slusher, H.S. (1985) "Sport and death," in David, L. and Wertz, Spencer (eds), *Sport Inside Out*, Texas Christian University Press.

Deep Blue

Deep Blue was the name of the IBM supercomputer that defeated world chess champion Garry Kasparov in May 1997 and so became the first machine to beat Kasparov in organized competition. The concept of staging sporting events that pitch humans against nonhumans is probably as old as the competitive impulse itself. If ethologists such as Desmond Morris are to be believed, the activities we now recognize as sports have their roots deep in hunter-gatherer modes of existence when the challenge was, in its rawest form, human versus beast. Bear wrestling and mock boxing matches featuring kangaroos are vestigial reminders that such challenges have not been completely removed by the growth of contemporary sports. In his late career, Jesse Owens ran against horses and motorcycles and boxer Jack Johnson was similarly reduced to circus-like contests against bulls.

The introduction of time-pieces provided for another form of challenge: runner (or rider) against the clock. The clock, of course, facilitated the quantification that became central to a great many sports and timed competition (for example, twenty-four-hour road races) are still common. The rapid growth of TECHNOLOGY in the post-Enlightenment period alerted humanity to the prospect that machines could be created that not only duplicated human endeavor, but actually improved on them. The factory system indicated that automation was full of utility in sports. Machines that served tennis balls or retrieved golf balls were rudimentary applications. However, the logical extension of this concept was a machine with intelligence: the computer was, of course, a machine created by humans in such a way as it could think for itself. It could be programmed with human thoughts, and summon them with a seemingly matchless alacrity.

Chess seemed a perfect sport to test the concept of man (and the original contestants *were* male) against machine. As International Grandmaster Yasser Seirawan asks in his foreword to Monty Newborn's *Kasparov versus Deep Blue*: "What sterner test of 'thinking' is there than a game of chess? ... After all, what on earth are we doing when we play a game of chess if not thinking? Surely, if machines could best man, what more proof need we have that machines indeed can and do think?"

Human chess players use intuition, judgment, anticipation and experience in making their moves, all of which are uniquely human facilities. They also suffer from fatigue, distraction and changes of temperament The chess-playing machine could not hope to mimic human processes. But, it was hoped that by making its operation dependent on fast-searching and many fundamental algorithmic methods, an equivalence could be reached. In other words, the machine would reach similar ends through entirely different means. While a human would be thinking judiciously and imaginatively about one or two positions per second, a computer would be searching several positions per second using a search and evaluation function. And of course, the computer does not need to be FOCUSED: it is programmed to perform.

The origins of chess-playing computers lie in the research of two men: Claude Shannon, a scientist at the Bell Telephone laboratories in New Jersey, and Alan Turing, of Manchester University, who was a trailblazer of computer science and was known for cracking German coded messages in the Second World War. In an influential article "Programming a computer for playing chess" (published in *Philosophical Magazine* vol 41, 1950), Shannon laid the foundations for a fast-searching machine capable of playing chess, although his ultimate aim was not simply to create a machine that could play humans. As he wrote: "the investigation of the chess-playing problem is intended to develop techniques that can be used for more practical applications."

The Massachusetts Institute of Technology's Institute of Theoretical and Experimental Physics (ITEP) built on Shannon's work to produce a computer called Kaissa, which became universally recognized as the most efficient chess-playing computer. The Association for Computing Machinery, later changed to Association for Computing (ACM), capitalized on the developing interest in competitive chess-playing computers by introducing a championship in tournament in 1970. By this time, Northwestern University had introduced its model, Belle, which went on to dominate competitive chess. Belle, which was eventually beaten by CrayBlitz in 1983, was developed by Ken Thompson and had specially built circuitry which could generate chess positions at a rate of 120,000 per second. These matches were between computers, although the concept of pitting a computer against a human player had been explored by Richard Greenblatt. In 1967, Greenblatt launched his Mac Hack, the first computer to use a facility that could sort chess positions as they were encountered and retrieve them for later use.

IBM began conceptualizing a computer with the ability to play chess in the 1950s, although its first ventures were with machines that played checkers. The corporation was cautious about its approaches to chess playing, and it was not until 1988 a team of Carnegie-Mellon graduate students, including Feng-Hsuing Hsu and Murray Campbell, created the original of Deep Thought. The basic version of Deep Thought's chess engine contained 250 chips and two processors on a single circuit board, and was capable of analyzing 750,000 positions per second or 10 half-moves ahead, which equates to an international performance rating of 2450; this placed it in the lower ranks of the world's grandmasters. Computers' rating points are determined by a combination of speed and knowledge.

Deep Thought's successor, Deep Blue, was launched in 1985. It was purpose-built for playing chess at the level of human grandmasters and had a processing speed a thousand times faster than the original Deep Thought. In addition, the Deep Blue team gave the computer even greater resources from which to draw by collecting an opening game database, which provides the system with grandmaster games played over a 100-year period leading up to its games. Alongside the opening database was an endgame database which was activated when only five chess pieces remained on the board. This database provided literally billions of endgame scenarios.

In 1988, Deep Thought become the first computer to defeat a grandmaster in a tournament. The following year, an experimental version of Deep Blue, capable of searching more than two million positions per second, was beaten by Kasparov in a two-game exhibition. David Levy, who had taunted the computer developers for two decades by throwing out challenges and beating every machine, lined up but was unexpectedly beaten by Deep Thought. In 1990 the IBM computer was put back in its place by the former world champion, Anatoly Karpov. In August 1993, Deep Blue conquered the world's top female player and youngest grandmaster ever, Judit Polgar. The computer again won the title of International Computer Chess Champion in June 1994.

Kasparov won the world championship in 1985 when he was 22, beating Karpov. Born in Baku and the based in Moscow, Kasparov was the youngest person ever to win the world championship. His early mentor was Mikhail Botvinnik, world champion for over a decade beginning in 1948 and the engineer who pioneered Russian computer chess. Kasparov had for long insisted that human skill would not be overcome by a machine. "Chess gives us a chance to compare brute force with our abilities," he once said. "In serious, classical chess, computers do not have a chance in this century. I will personally take any challenge."

Kasparov won a $400,000 prize by beating Deep Blue in 1996 in a game that was watched closely by the world's media. The 1,000 spectators who attended watched the moves on a giant board. Those who followed the game on the Internet (at a rate of 1,200 hits per minute on the second day) increased the "live" and virtual audience to about eight million. The rematch created the greatest worldwide interest in chess since the days of Bobby Fischer. Stung by his unexpected loss, Kasparov issued a challenge for a $1.5 million (£938,000) rubber match. IBM Research turned down the offer, preferring to concentrate on other applications for the machine, such as air traffic control or weather forecasting. Instead, IBM Research toured the USA with a less powerful version of its chess-playing computer, called Deep Blue Junior.

Attempts to build chess-playing computers were less successful than versions that took advantage of the machine's simple but rapid search functions. Rather than try to build imagination, tactical awareness and intuitive decision-making into a program, designers opted for depth-first searching. This employs what is called "iterative-deepening," which means that the computer carries out a sequence of deeper and deeper searches for as long as competition time permits in the attempt to decide on the appropriate move. Newborn draws the analogy with a person searching for a valuable ring that has been lost. The person proceeds by searching the room in which the ring was kept, then the house, then the surrounding areas, before calling the police. It would make little sense calling the police first, before completing the initial search. On the other hand, if clues are found that suggest a burglary, then the police might be informed and told of any clues.

Of related interest

Atkinson, George (1993) *Chess and Machine Intuition*, Ablex Publishing.
Newborn, Monty (1996) *Kasparov versus Deep Blue: Computer Chess Comes of Age*, Springer-Verlag.
Pandolfini, Bruce (1998) *Kasparov and Deep Blue: The Historic Chess Match between Man and Machine*, Simon & Schuster.

derby

The Derby is the name given to the annual horse race at Epsom Downs, England, and the Kentucky Derby, which takes place every year in Louisville, Kentucky. Over time, the term "derby" has been used to describe any sporting competition which attracted great interest and, later, to denote soccer games between proximate rivals, or "local derbies," as they were called.

The original race took place in 1790 at the instigation of Edward Stanley, the 12th Earl of Derby. The race was for three-year-old colts and fillies only. The word "Derby" was shorthand for the race and, eventually, similar races also became known as derbies.

In pre-industrial times, folk football in English villages took place in streets, meadows, fields or on common ground; there were no arenas. Goals were often several miles apart, and there were few rules of competition. In the nineteenth century, when factories and churches took over the game from the upper-class public (independent) schools, teams would often compete regularly on "home" soil. Local crowds would gather to watch their nearest team play and, over time, loyalties grew.

Most, though not all, teams clustered in the cities, which is where most of the factories were. Often several teams would operate within relatively small areas with small populations. For example, the West Midlands area that surrounds the city of Birmingham produced six teams within a twenty-mile radius. Games between these teams generated local interest.

Although the distances between the home stadiums were not great by today's standards, fans would often arrive by foot, bicycle or steam train. Often they had to stand in the rain and with little protection from the winter winds, but, as Desmond Morris writes in his *The Soccer Tribe* (1981), "the passion for the game was so intense that few complained." He goes on: "Attending the match became a shared 'ordeal by climate,' almost a test of manhood."

Morris sees the game of soccer itself as a vast tribal ceremony in which fans congregate and enact sometimes elaborate rituals, such as chanting, dressing in the local team's colors and carrying flags, banners and the once-popular rattles. Local rivalries took on an especially intense character with bragging rights going to fans of winners and humiliation to followers of losers; at least, until the next contest. Such was the importance attached to these games that they took on status comparable in importance to that of the Derby horse race. In time, the name itself was adopted and then, as soccer expanded across the world, exported; the local derby became a feature of the sport.

Other competitions have given rise to games between local teams. Basketball games between the Los Angeles teams, Lakers and Clippers, and football games between the New York clubs, Jets and Giants (whose stadium is actually in New Jersey) generate rivalries. But the soccer derby has a particular asperity, perhaps because of soccer's own violent history and its roots in working-class communities, where neighborhood status was often tied to that of the local team.

Another reason for the virulence of soccer derbies is the origins of clubs. Historically, teams have evolved from churches, factories, the initiatives of colonial British and, in some cases, ethnic communities. These cleavages are represented in the clubs and manifest themselves at games. For example the Flamengo club of Rio de Janeiro, Brazil, is traditionally a peasant team that has had many players of dark complexion. In Brazilian culture, lighter skin accrues more prestige and Flamengo players have been subject to racist ridicule by fans of its Rio rivals, Fluminese.

Religious conflict has been played out in games between the two major Glasgow teams, Rangers – representative of Protestants – and Celtic, which is a traditionally Roman Catholic club. The same sectarian rivalry colors games between Liverpool and Everton in England.

A class conflict underlies games between Real Madrid and Atletico Madrid, the former being soccer's equivalents of royalty, its opulent Bernebeu stadium being in one of the city's wealthiest districts and its history being studded with every prize in world soccer. Atleticos play near a prison and has won few trophies.

In Sofia, Bulgaria, the CSKA club started life as the team of the Communist Army. Its rivals, Levski Sofia has traditionally drawn its base of support from the city's police force, giving games between the two an army *vs* police dimension.

According to sports writer Piers Newbery, one of the few city derbies in soccer "that does not breed overwhelming animosity" is that of America *vs* Unam

(Pumas) of Mexico City. The reason for this is that both sets of fans are united in their hatred of a third club, Guadalajara (*The Independent*, October 17, 1998).

Of related interest

Bowden, M. (1995) "Soccer," in Raitz, K.B. (ed.). *The Theater of Sport*. Johns Hopkins University Press.
Lever, Janet (1983) *Soccer Madness*, University of Chicago Press.
Morris, Desmond (1981) *The Soccer Tribe*, Cape.

Di Stefano, Alfredo

b. 1926, Argentina

Di Stefano was the first universally recognized soccer superstar. Playing for the invincible Real Madrid club that won the first five European Cups, Di Stefano established himself as the most valuable player in the world, rivaled only by his team mate Ferenc Puskas. Born in Buenos Aires, Di Stefano claims to have been a competitor in road races before signing for the Argentinian club River Plate. He represented Argentina in international games seven times, and was then tempted to the Millionarios club of Bogota, Colombia. Like many other professionals from around the world, Di Stefano was attracted to Colombia by the prospect of high earnings. An internal dispute in Colombia meant that its league was disaffiliated from soccer's world governing organization FIFA (Fédération Internationale de Football Associations). Seven British players made the transition in what became known as the BOGOTÁ AFFAIR.

Di Stefano left Millionarios in 1953 and moved to Spain, where he became a naturalized citizen, thus enabling him to represent Spain in international games. Between 1956–60, Real was the peerless world leader in soccer: in addition to five consecutive European championships, the team won the World Club championship. During this period, Di Stefano was the most prolific attacker in the world, scoring a record-breaking 49 goals in European competition and finishing as top striker in the Spanish league for five straight seasons. His record for Spain was also outstanding: 23 goals in 31 appearances.

Di Stefano was fêted by the sports world as a universal star. Coming to the fore as interest in international competition was increasing and television was becoming available, Di Stefano became what we would today recognize as one of the world's leading sports ICONS. Once his glittering playing career was over, he managed and coached the Real Madrid, Valencia, Español, Elsche and Boca Juniors teams, but without matching his playing success.

Of related interest

Challis, Drummond. and Millichope, Ray (1989) *Greatest Players, Volume One* (videocassette), British Soccer Week.

Didrikson, Mildred "Babe"

b. 1913, USA; d. 1956

During the 1930s and 1940s, Didrikson flouted conventional definitions of femininity by excelling at javelin, shotput and other field events conventionally regarded as the domain of men. She was also adept at baseball, swimming and golf. As such, she transgressed the boundaries that established "acceptable" events for women. Didrikson's body, which was hard and muscular, defied traditional images of the svelte and frail women and attracted widespread suspicions over her sexual status. In her *Strong Women, Deep Closets: Lesbians and Homophobia in Sport* (1998), Pat Griffin notes how Didrikson, like Martina Navratilova in the 1970s, was thought to have an "unfair advantage" over her rivals. She was not regarded as a "real woman."

Born in Port Arthur, Texas, Didrikson represented the USA at the 1932 Summer Olympics at Los Angeles, where she won and set records in the javelin and the 80 meters hurdles. Her undoubted athleticism was regarded with some suspicion at a time when any woman who could approximate the sporting accomplishments of men was the subject of debate.

Later in her athletic career, Didrikson tired of the innuendo and made a conscious attempt to redefine her image in a way that suited traditional conceptions of femininity. In the late 1930s, she began to wear makeup and skirts, something she had never previously done. She also styled her hair differently. Commenting on the sports writers who were astonished at her transformation, Didrikson said: "Their idea is that I used to be all tomboy, with none of the usual girls' interests, and then all of a sudden I switched over to being feminine."

In 1938, as if to underline the fact that she was really "feminine," she married a wrestler, George "The Weeping Greek" Zaharias. On reflection, the marriage may have been one of convenience, designed to deflect criticism and improve her marketability. Didrikson even turned her attentions to golf, a sport considered "generally acceptable competition" in Metheny's typology of ACCEPTABILITY/ NONACCEPTABILITY. It was not until the publication of her biography by Susan Cayleff in 1995 that the nature and extent of her relationship with her companion Betty Dodds became clear.

Donald Mrozek's essay "The 'Amazon' and the American 'Lady': Sexual fears of women as athletes" (1987) analyzes the reasons why Didrikson and other women who dared to dispute conventional definitions of "womanhood" provoked so much consternation. "To the extent that woman challenged the stereotype of a 'ladylike manner' in sport and physical leisure, they fell prey to such fear, partly by appearing to encroach upon the competitive, confrontational, shameless character which men supposedly brought to sporting events by virtue of their masculinity," writes Mrozek.

Didrikson competed in an era when the dominant medical discourse warned of the dangers of athletics to women, particularly to their reproductive capacities. Women's inherent fragility equipped them poorly to engage in physical pursuits. But, as Mrozek points out: "Didrikson proved to be among the most troubling – and troublesome – cases for those who believed women to be psychologically and physiologically weaker than men and so saw highly competitive sport to be properly restricted to males."

Didrikson's controversial career underwent another twist when she fought the American Athletics Union (AAU), which had stripped her of her amateur status after she allowed her image to be used in ENDORSEMENTS for cars. The AAU offered her reinstatement, but Didrikson refused, explaining later that she had merely wanted to expose the AAU's excessive rules and regulations governing the conduct of athletes.

A mooted exhibition boxing match against Babe Ruth prefigured the "Battle of the Sexes" between Billie Jean KING and Bobby Riggs. The match never materialized, though Didrikson expressed an interest in the fight and told the media that she trained by punching a heavy bag. Comedian Bob Hope added to the aura that seemed to surround Didrikson when he observed of her golf "she hits it [the ball] like a man."

At a time when fears of virilism – that women's participation in sports can lead to their acquisition of male characteristics – were rife, Didrikson both prompted controversy and fueled fears about the purported effects of physical competition. While Didrikson's peers, including the likes of Eleanor Egg, Eleanora Randolph Sears, Gertrude Ederle and Eleanor Holm, showed abilities that defied orthodox expectations of women, none deviated so sharply from accepted notions of femininity as Didrikson herself (though Sears favored men's clothes). Didrikson prefigured athletes like Billie Jean King, Martina Navratilova, Nancy LOPEZ and Florence GRIFFITH JOYNER all of whom in their own way, forced a re-examination of femininity and its meaning in the context of sports.

Of related interest

Cayleff, Susan (1995) *Babe: The life and legend of Babe Didrikson Zaharias*, University of Illinois Press.

Griffin, Pat (1998) *Strong Women, Deep Closets: Lesbians and Homophobia in Sport*, Human Kinetics.

Mrozek, Donald J. (1987) "The 'Amazon' and the American 'Lady': Sexual fears of women as athletes," in Mangan, J.A. and Park, Roberta J. (eds), *From "Fair Sex" to Feminism: Sport and the Socialization of Women in the Industrial and Post-Industrial Eras*, Frank Cass.

disability

Sports for persons with disabilities, whether physical or mental, were conceived in a spirit of rehabilitation rather than competition. In 1944, Ludwig Guttmann set up the spinal injuries unit at England's Stoke Mandeville Hospital. Four years later, Guttmann experimented with an organized sports meeting involving patients from different rehabilitative centers. At first the meets were informal, but hospitals from around the world were attracted by the idea and regular competition led to more structure.

The program of activities was gradually widened in scope. In addition to track and field events designed for wheelchair users, bowling and table tennis (ping pong) and, later, weightlifting, fencing and swimming were included. Guttman made contact with Benjamin Lipton, director of the Joseph Bulova School of Watchmaking, which encouraged persons with disabilities to train as watch-makers. Lipton was especially keen on getting involved in sports for wheelchair users, and was responsible for starting the National Wheechair Games in the USA in 1958.

By 1960, the tournaments had a wide enough constituency of support and participation to justify the establishment of a governing association, the British Sports Association for the Disabled (BSAD), which began coordinating with what became the Paralympic movement. The spread of interest made it possible to hold Olympiads, specifically for disabled competitors; these coincided with Olympic games on all but two occasions after 1962 (Mexico in 1966 and Moscow 1980). Countries hosting Olympic games also hosted international events for the blind and partially sighted, paraplegics, tetraplegics and amputees.

In 1968, Eunice Kennedy Shriver helped kickstart another kind of tournament geared to the requirements of performers with mental disabilities. Called the Special Olympics, the games also offered a year-round program of training. Ultimately, this was the only program or event allowed to use the term "Olympics": the International Olympic Committee (IOC) in 1981 restricted the use of the term. Hence Paralympics became the accepted description of the major tournament for disabled performers.

Perhaps the most significant tournament for the Paralympic movement was the Atlanta games of 1996, which were held just after the summer Olympics, themselves marred by a bomb explosion. Almost 4,000 paralympians from all over the world attended, representing over 100 nations. The spectrum of events was the most expansive ever, incorporating rugby, fencing and soccer. It was debated whether the Paralympics had outgrown its status as a marginal tournament and deserved a full integration into the Olympic games proper.

We can understand the growth of sports for disabled persons as part of what some call the "rightsism" of the 1980s and 1990s. Groups, many of which were minorities – either in terms of actual numbers or political power – began to claim what they believed to be their entitlements. Such entitlements included both privileges to engage in activities from which they were previously excluded and immunity from treatment that contributed toward their inferior status. The first wave of feminism in the 1960s, itself part of a more general cultural re-evaluation, was important in several respects, not least of which was the *demand* rather than request for protection of women from discrimination that had historically denied them full participation in society. Legislation to prohibit sex discrimination and promote equality in the workplace was enacted in the 1970s on both sides of the Atlantic, although laws that permitted legal abortion were arguably as, if not more, influential in "liberating" women.

Laws prohibiting racial discrimination have also been part of the same movement. In the United States, the civil rights movement issued notice that the decades, even centuries, of legal segregation and the open denial of civil rights to African Americans were drawing to a close. By 1965, two crucial pieces of legislation had paved the way for what became known as equality of opportunity.

Of course, in neither case did legislation end discrimination either against women or ethnic minority groups: they signaled the direction of cultural change, rather than catalyzing the change itself.

Disabled groups have in a sense been the "forgotten minority": not until the 1990s did the demand for rights reach receptive ears. In the United States, President George Bush's Republican administration enacted the landmark American with Disabilities Act (ADA), a tough piece of legislation that made it impossible to discriminate against people with disability in any area of society.

But, while sports specifically for persons with disabilities have developed, some individual competitors have opted for other routes. College basketball player Eddie Shannon, for example, underwent an operation in 1998 to have an eye removed; his vision had deteriorated since he was a child, and by the end of 1997 he had glaucoma. After having the operation, Shannon resumed his career with the Florida Gators.

Of related interest

De Pauw, Karen P. and Gavron, Susan (1995) *Disability and Sport*, Human Kinetics.

Guttmann, Sir Ludwig (1976) *Textbook of Sport for the Disabled*, H & M Publishers.

Miller, Patricia D. (ed.) (1995) *Fitness Programming and Physical Disability*, Human Kinetics.

drugs: facts

Taking supplements as a way of improving physical or mental performance in sports is arguably as old as sports themselves. Competitors in the ancient Greco-Roman games were known to eat animals' parts, such as horns or the secretions of testes, which they thought would confer the strength of bulls, for example. It is probably that Greeks habitually used plants and mushrooms with chemically active derivatives either to aid performance or accelerate the healing process.

In the modern era, as sports became professionalized, evidence of the systematic application of stimulants arrived initially through the six-day cycle races in Europe. Riders in the late nineteenth century favored ether and caffeine to delay the onset of fatigue sensations. Sprint cyclists preferred nitroglycerin, a chemical later used in conjunction with heroin, cocaine, strychnine and others.

If there was a turning point in attitudes toward the use of drugs in sport, it came on July 13, 1967, when cyclist Tommy Simpson, then 29, collapsed and died on the thirteenth stage of the three-week-long Tour de France. Simpson, a British rider, was lying seventh overall when the race set off from Marseilles. The temperature was well over 40°C (105°F). Simpson fell and remounted twice before falling for the final time. Three tubes were found in his pocket, one full of amphetamines and the other two empty. The British team's luggage was searched and more supplies of the pills were found. At the time, the drugs element did not cause the sensation that might be expected today: the death itself was of most concern. In continental Europe, there was substantial and open advocacy of the use of such pills to alleviate the strain of long-distance cycling. There is little doubt that many of the leading contenders in the 1967 and other tours were taking amphetamines. Seven years before, in a less publicized tragedy, another cyclist, Knut Jensen, died at the Olympics after taking nonicol, a blood dilatory.

An attempt in the previous year to introduce drug testing was opposed by leading cyclists, including the five-times Tour winner Jacques ANQUETIL, who told the newspaper *France-Dimanche*: "Yes, I dope myself. You would be a fool to imagine that a professional cyclist who rides 235 days a year in all temperatures and conditions can hold up without a stimulant." Interestingly, Simpson was not denounced as a cheat at the time; his death opened up a rather different discourse about the perils of drug taking rather than the morality of it. The Tour de France was at the center of a huge doping scandal in 1998 when the whole Festina team was disqualified and copious amounts of drugs were discovered.

The IOC had actually set up a Medical Commission in 1950, mainly to investigate the medical effects of the use of stimulants, especially amphetamines, to increase endurance. Simpson's death prompted the introduction of testing, which came into force in 1968. Systematic, full-scale drug testing was introduced at the 1972 Summer Olympics and carried out at all subsequent games with increasing rigor and sophistication. The first athlete to be disqualified from a major competition was Eduard Noorlander, of Holland, who had finished sixth in the European decathlon championship.

Unquestionably, the case that converted drug use in sports from concern to hysteria was the ejection of Canadian sprinter Ben Johnson from the 1988 Seoul Olympics after he had won the 100 meters in a world record 9.79 seconds. Stanozolol, an anabolic steroid, was detected in Johnson's urine sample; he was stripped of his gold medal and his time expunged from the records. Overnight, Johnson went from the "world's fastest man" to the "world's fastest cheat." While he was the thirty-first competitor to be disqualified for drug use since the IOC instituted its testing, Johnson's stature in world sport ensured that his case would make news everywhere and that he as an individual would carry the sins of all. As well as his medal and record, he instantly lost (at the most conservative estimate) $2 million in performance-related product endorsement fees.

Following the Johnson case, the use of drugs to improve athletic performance was universally condemned by sporting authorities. Lists of prohibited substances lengthened so that many prescription drugs and perfectly legal products that could be purchased at drug stores were banned. Alexander Watson, an Australian pentathlete, was disqualified from the same Olympics as Johnson for having an excessive level of caffeine in his system.

The IOC's policy on drug use was adopted, usually with only minor changes, by other sports federations. It grouped prohibited substances in six classes, as follows:

Anabolic steroids are synthetically produced substances that produce an effect similar to that of the male sex hormone testosterone. Their use is thought to permit a more demanding training schedule and allows an increase in muscle bulk and strength. Production of the synthetic form began in 1935, although a French physiologist, Charles Brown-Sequard, was experimenting with secretions from the testes of dogs and guinea pigs in the 1880s, and another physiologist, Oskar Zoth, published a paper in 1896 which concluded that extracts from bulls' testes when injected into athletes led to improvements in muscular strength and "neuromuscular apparatus."

Experiments continued, many of them recounted in an influential book by Paul de Kruif, *The Male Hormone*. The book, published in 1945, was seized on as a sort of manual by bodybuilders on the USA's West Coast and, through the 1950s, influenced the training regimes of other strength-reliant performers such as field eventers and football players. In 1971 Jack Scott, in his book *The Athletic Revolution* (Free Press), reported that more than one college football team had used steroids. While estimates about the extent of steroid use in sports are inevitably flawed, it is at least suggestive that, twelve years after Scott's information was published, an article in *Sports Illustrated* stated that NFL steroid users accounted for between 40 and 90 per cent of all players (May 13, 1983). The Players' Association rejected this claim.

In 1984, the director of sports medicine research at the Chicago Osteopathic Medicine Center attributed the death of six sports performers to steroid use and three years later, British bodybuilder Keith Singh died with liver tumors after a period of using steroids. In addition to these consequences, anabolic steroids were linked with psychological changes, particularly aggression, known as "roid rage," and infertility in men; and the acquisition of male characteristics in women. It is, however, worth noting that the doses of anabolic steroid taken by Ben Johnson was allegedly lower than what the World Health Organization subsequently found safe to administer as a male contraceptive.

Beta blockers are typically prescribed for the treatment of angina, cardiac arrhythmia, high blood pressure, migraine, overactive thyroid and the physical symptoms of anxiety. They slow down the heart rate and lower blood pressure by controlling the release of adrenaline, thus making exertion more difficult and sometimes constricting airways. Performers in sports that require steadiness, such as shooting, archery and snooker, have found utility in beta blockers. In the 1980s, the Canadian snooker player Bill WERBENIUK became well-known for his consumption of large quantities of lager, which was thought to steady his nerves. This in itself was not a problem – from a technical viewpoint at least. Werbeniuk was also a habitual user of inderal, a beta blocker which helped counteract the effects of an hereditary nervous disorder.

After criticism from the British Minister for Sport, the World Professional Billiards and Snooker Association (WPBSA) reviewed its drugs policy and included inderal on its list of banned substances. Unable to find an alternative, Werbeniuk admitted to the WPBSA that he intended to continue using the drug and was eventually banned from tournaments.

Diuretics are commonly used therapeutically as an aid to short-term weight loss and as a treatment for heart failure and high blood pressure. Their effect is to excite the kidneys to produce more urea and, basically, speed up a perfectly natural waste disposal process. They inhibit the secretion of the antidiuretic hormone which serves as a chemical messenger, carrying information from the brain to the kidneys. Diuretics are found in alcoholic drinks and caffeine.

In sports, they have two functions: to control body weight in sports that require weigh-ins, such as boxing or weightlifting, and to flush out of the body traces of other banned substances. Kerrith Brown lost his Olympic bronze medal for judo despite pleading that the diuretic furosemide found in his urine was introduced into his system by a medical officer who gave him an anti-inflammatory substance containing the chemical to reduce a knee swelling.

Stimulants inhibit the sensations of fatigue; they have also been used to reduce appetite. Their attraction to sports competitors is obvious. Endurance performers such as long-distance cyclists, who probably pioneered their use in sports, risk an increase in blood pressure, cardiac arrhythmia and heatstroke. Coffee, tea and a variety of sodas contain caffeine which is, of course, a stimulant.

A group of stimulants are known as sympathomimetic amine drugs and these act directly on the nerves affecting organs, rather than on the brain. Ephedrine is commonly used as a decongestant and is bought off the shelf; it is also prescribed for asthma patients. Sports performers are encouraged to read the labels of the products they use as many products contain ephedrine.

Painkillers can also be bought legally in stores, and are habitually used in sport to mask pain and enable performers to carry on training. Strong narcotic analgesics, such as morphine and codeine, have been prohibited, along with anti-inflammatory ones.

Peptide hormones include HUMAN GROWTH HORMONE (hGH), or somatotropin, which is naturally secreted in the pituitary gland. For a while in the early 1990s, it was rumored that hGH was being taken from aborted foetuses and sold illegally to athletes. A synthetic version of the hormone, somatonorm, is prescribed to stimulate body growth and development in people who naturally do not produce enough and have a condition once known as dwarfism. This is an expensive treatment, but one which has been adapted by those athletes who can afford it. Allied to a training program, human growth hormone can stimulate dramatic increases in body size and muscle development. Because it is a naturally-occurring chemical, hGH is difficult to detect. It is thought that prolonged use can lead to muscular or skeletal abnormalities.

Another way of mimicking nature is BLOOD DOPING, which involves training at altitude for a sustained period: the lack of oxygen in the atmosphere encourages the production of haemoglobin in the blood. This protein molecule is found in red blood cells and has a remarkable ability to form associations with oxygen, which can be transported to the muscles and is of great service to middle-distance runners in particular. One such runner was Martti Vainio, who lost his silver medal for the 10,000 meters at the Los Angeles Olympics following disqualification. Britain's Mike McLeod was upgraded to second after Vainio's positive test. The idea behind blood doping is to "capture" the oxygen-rich blood produced when training intensely at altitude, then reintroduce it into the circulatory system just prior to a competition, thus gaining the advantage of extra haemoglobin. Perfluorocarbon (PFC) is essentially artificial blood that performs a similar function, increasing the oxygen-carrying capacity of the body.

Erythropoietin (EPO) achieves much the same results as blood doping, but without the tell-tale needle tracks in flesh. Nor is it easily detectable in urinalysis. Basically, it facilitates the production of extra red blood cells, which absorb oxygen. In the 1990s, a number of professional cyclists underwent surgery to widen the iliac artery (in the hip), claiming it was "corrective surgery" since the artery gets constricted by the posture on the saddle of a cycle. The alternative view was that the artery becomes damaged by viscous blood caused by the taking of EPO. The TOUR DE FRANCE of 1998 confirmed suspicions that this drug was widely used by cyclists.

Miscellaneous other substances that have been banned include corticosteroids, which enhance the circulation of natural hormones, and illicit recreational drugs.

Most debates on drugs in sport center on doping human beings. However, in horse racing, several CORRUPTION cases have revealed extensive drug use on animals. The most commonly used drugs are used habitually for veterinary purposes, such as shoeing and clipping. Acetylpromazine (ACP) is administered prior to such procedures; it has the effect of sedating the horse. Given either as a paste, tablet or injection, it can be given to a horse prior to a race in amounts small enough to escape detection, but sufficient to slow down the horse. (Other drugs favored by veterinarians include Detomidine, Romifidine and Xylazine.) The process of slowing the horse is known as NOBBLING.

A horse's performance can be enhanced by giving it Phenylbutazone, known as "bute," which is an anti-inflammatory drug, and Lasix, which prevents blood vessels breaking. These are permitted on some American tracks, though controversially: bute is opposed by many because it works as a painkiller and allows the horses to run even when injured, while Lasix dilates airwaves and aids breathing. Horses are also known to have been given clenbuterol, an anabolic steroid that has been used by humans.

Of related interest

Hoberman, J. and Yesalis, C. (1995) "The history of synthetic testosterone," *Scientific American* vol 272, no 2.

Yesalis, Charles (1993) *Anabolic Steroids in Sport and Exercise*, Human Kinetics.

Yesalis, Charles and Coward, Virginia (1998) *The Steroids Game: An Expert's Look at Anabolic Steroid Use in Sports*, Human Kinetics.

drugs: values

Harsh denunciations of sports performers found to be taking drugs began to appear from the 1980s. The deaths of cyclists Knut Jensen and Tommy Simpson in the 1960s drew sympathetic responses, quite unlike the virtual demonization of Ben Johnson in 1988. For ten years after the Johnson discovery, every competitor found guilty of drugs violations was accused of cheating and incurred penalties, ranging from fines to life suspensions. Media opinion became unanimous: drug users were roundly condemned, though the stigmata did not always stick. The early career misdemeanors of Michael Johnson, for example, were ignored as he was fêted as the world's greatest athlete in the mid-1990s. By contrast, the otherwise glittering career of Argentinian soccer star Diego Maradona was forever tarnished by his experience at the World Cup championships of 1994, when he was disqualified after a positive dope test.

During the 1980s and 1990s there was little disagreement over the use of performance enhancing substances and recreational drugs in sports: it was wrong and should be eliminated. This position became axiomatic. Statements such as "drug-taking in sports is wrong" did not invite argument; rather, they seemed to state fact. Yet this did little to stem the amount of drug taking in sports, and few major track and field championships (where dope testing apparatus is most sophisticated) failed to expose drug users. To understand the censure that unerringly meets drug-using sports performers, we need to examine how the modern world has cultivated a wish for us to control ourselves.

The civilizing process, as Norbert Elias calls it, is a historical trend beginning in the Middle Ages (c.900–1600) that has drawn us away from barbarism by bringing social pressures on people to exercise self-control. At one level, this meant increasing our conscience as a means of regulating our behavior toward others. At another, it meant becoming enmeshed in a network of often subtle, invisible constraints that compelled us to lead ordered lives. One important result of this was the decrease in the use of direct force: violence was brought under control and the state became the only legitimate user of physical violence – outside of combat sports, of course (and these were subject to progressively strict regulation).

The civilizing process implicated humans in some form of control over their bodies. Elias focused mainly on the restraint in using physical violence, but notes the simultaneous trend for people to subdue bodily functions and control their physical being. The physical body became subordinated to the rational mind. While Elias did not discuss this, we might point to the literary fascination with the potential of science to complete this process. Mary Shelley's *Frankenstein* tells of a scientist obsessed by the possibility of reconstructing a total human being. In *Dr Jekyll and Mr Hyde*, Robert Louis Stevenson imagined another man of science experimenting with his own mind and body. These and other works of fiction suggest a fascination with trying to reshape the body in accordance with the imperatives of the mind.

Pharmacological advances in the twentieth century hastened the probability that the body could be brought under complete control. Not only could maladies be kept at bay, or even vanquished, but moods could be altered and physical well-being could be promoted. The early efforts of Charles Brown-Sequard at the end of the nineteenth century were aimed at finding a rejuvenating therapy for body and mind; his work presaged the development of anabolic steroids. Any initial suspicions about introducing chemicals into the body faded with two world wars in which colossal and often horrific injuries were treated or palliated with medicines.

The desire for good health that followed the end of the 1939–45 war was complemented by the availability of drugs for the treatment of practically every complaint. A visit to the doctor was incomplete without a prescription, if only for antibiotics. An expanding range of over-the-counter remedies often made the visit unnecessary. The impact of drugs on people's self-evaluations was that ill-health, pain or even mild discomfort became less and less tolerable. The good life, which seemed to beckon in the postwar period, offered both freedom from suffering and access to well-being. The latter became accessible through a variety of non-medicinal options, including supplements, dieting and exercise, all of which combined in a culture of NARCISSISM.

It was perhaps inevitable that sports performers, themselves embracing aspirations to self-fulfillment through control of the body, would turn to drugs. Many kinds of substances have been used historically to promote performance, though rarely so effectively. One did not need to be a pharmacist to spot how the effects of, for example, amphetamines or anabolic steroids might be of use to a competitor specializing in speed or power.

The unanticipated, often tragic consequences of pharmacological products were not confined to sports. Thalidomide was prescribed for pregnant women in Australia, Britain and Germany in the 1960s as treatment for morning sickness and caused thousands of deformities in their children. The deaths of cyclists Knut Jensen and Tommy Simpson, also in the 1960s, alerted the world to the perils of ingesting chemical substances to affect changes in the body's condition. Yet ironically, the imposition of controls by the IOC in the 1970s probably enhanced the appeal of many substances. As the criminologist David Matza once reasoned, banning something immediately makes it more attractive than it would otherwise be (*Becoming Deviant*, Prentice-Hall, 1969).

As the importance of victory became more pronounced and professionalization made the rewards more extravagant, the value placed on winning replaced that of merely competing. A win-at-all-cost ethic came to pervade sports, making cost-benefit calculations simpler: the benefits of winning seemed greater than the risk of being found out, for many. Anti-drugs policies changed emphasis accordingly. Whereas early controls were protective in approach, designed to prevent athletes harming themselves, later policies became more expansive, their intention being to stop competitors gaining an unfair advantage. Drug taking became equated with cheating.

The concept of cheating has always to be defined in relation to rules of fair play. If the rules of a sport dictate that drug taking is disallowed, then there is no ambiguity. Historically, other features of contemporary sports have been defined as cheating: using spikes, for example, or even training, which was once said to confer an unfair advantage on the English working class when facing their gentleman opponents (who considered training to be against amateur ideals). Cheating is not a fixed principle but a changing process; although few people noticed this when the Ben Johnson story broke in 1988. This event, more than any other, cemented the connection between drug taking and cheating.

Other forms of assistance to performance were available and in use at the time of the Johnson case, including acupuncture, hypnosis, neuromuscular stimulation and altitude training, to name a few. Yet, performance-enhancing substances provoked an uncritical disapproval that escaped the others, all of which are thought to provide an advantage to the user. There is always another, far more obvious way in which some competitors gain advantages. Some are born into wealthy families that accord them every conceivable facility to train under expert supervision since an early age (Jennifer Capriati is one of many examples). Others are born at high altitude where the rarefied atmosphere promotes high haemoglobin counts and the oxygenated blood so useful in endurance events (as any number of Kenyan middle- and long-distance runners will attest to).

Drugs have been singled out for special treatment. The reasons for this may lie in the fact that they are still seen as dangerous to the users. But, this explanation is offset by the fact that the intense training required for today's competitions is potentially damaging to the athlete's health; yet few question it. There is also the powerful argument that many sports themselves are dangerous, making competing in itself a hazardous affair: air and motor sports, in particular, have casualties on a regular basis.

Another possible, though barely mentioned, explanation concerns the commercial demands made of sport to keep its image clean. The very word "drugs" has the kind of emotive connotation that evokes images of moral disintegration, physical dissipation and mental dissolution. All are totally antithetical to images carefully fostered by sports. Through the 1980s and 1990s, all major sports and an increasing number of minor ones recruited or attracted sponsors. The 1984 Summer Olympics at Los Angeles is, to date, the event that best epitomizes this. Lampooned as the "Hamburger Olympics," the games were widely thought to be a travesty: the IOC negotiated with six multinational companies, which were able to gain television exposure in markets around the world and to use the five-ring symbol as a logo. The biggest sponsor paid $14m (then £9m). Since then, every national and international sports event, every league, every club and several thousand individual players have struck lucrative deals with corporations eager to have their product associated with an activity as virtuous and beneficent as sport.

Every positive dope test in some way defiles the image so central to sport. Sports performers who test positive invariably lose their sponsors as well as their eligibility to compete. The impact of a drugs "shock" on sports is incalculable. It is worth pondering how history might have been different had steroids, amphetamines and other controlled but not illicit substances not been called "drugs," but something less dramatic, like nutritives or assistants. Stressing the substance's use as a performance aid might have had the effect of dissociating it from products that are typically used for recreational purposes.

Whatever the reasons for sport's anathematization of performance-enhancing substances, there is little doubt about the negative value it continues to attach to them. Equally, there were signs in the late 1990s that positions were softening. After the debacles of the Reynolds and Modahl cases (when the suspended athletes were cleared and compensated) and the possibility that professional athletes may be moved to take legal action against sports governing federations for restraint of trade, the International Amateur Athletics Federation (IAAF) in 1997 reduced its four-year suspensions to two years.

Of related interest

Cashmore, Ellis (2000) *Making Sense of Sports*, 3rd edn, Routledge.
Downes, S. and Mackay, D. (1996) *Running Scared: How Athletics Lost its Innocence*, Mainstream.
Hoberman, John (1992) *Mortal Engines: Human Engineering and the Transformation of Sport*, Free Press.

Dubin Inquiry, the

The Dubin Inquiry was set up in the wake of Ben Johnson's disqualification from the 1988 Seoul Olympics, to investigate the extent of drug use among athletes in Canada. The official committee was headed by Charles Dubin and its results were published as *Commission of Inquiry into the Use of Drugs and Banned Practices Intended to Increase Athletic Performance* (Ministry of Supply and Services, 1990).

The background to the inquiry was that Johnson, a Jamaican-born member of the Canadian team, won the Olympic men's 100 meters final in a world record breaking time of 9.79 seconds. The mandatory post-race dope test showed positive and Johnson was found to have taken stanozolol, an anabolic steroid, which was a banned substance. He was stripped of his gold medal and his record was expunged.

Prior to the games, there had been widely circulated rumors that performance enhancing DRUGS were taken quite freely by elite athletes. David Jenkins, himself an Olympic silver medalist and convicted trader in drugs for athletes, estimated that 50 per cent of all athletes had used drugs. Canada accepted the IOC's list of banned substances but, prior to the early 1980s, failed to devise a domestic policy or testing procedure. In 1983, Sport Canada (the country's governing sports body) published an anti-doping policy in which possession of drugs was an offense; this extended the IOC mandate concerning positive tests. This was spurred by the positive testing of two Canadian competitors at the 1983 Pan-American Games, at Caracas. In addition, a group of Canadian wrestlers returning from a tournament in Eastern Europe was found in possession of anabolic steroids.

Sport Canada's response was to commit its government to punishing athletes found guilty of taking dope. Between the publication of the statement in 1983 and 1989, twenty-five Canadian athletes tested positive for breaches of anti-drugs rules, fifteen of whom were weightlifters. Among the others was Johnson, who was in many ways a high-profile scapegoat. Johnson was by far the best known and the most prestigious athlete in the Canadian squad; he was also the most famous athlete to date to test positive and, in this sense, he was an ideal case for exemplary treatment.

The Dubin inquiry heard testimony from Johnson's physician Dr. Jamie Astaphan, who referred to the "brotherhood of the needle" in describing the circle of athletes who habitually took performance-enhancing substances. Dr. Robert Kerr, of San Gabriel, California, testified that he had prescribed anabolic substances to approximately twenty medalists at the 1984 Summer Olympics. The inquiry disclosed drug taking on a scale never suspected and that, even coaches who did not encourage drug taking, tacitly accepted it by ignoring its prevalence. Richard Pound, IOC vice-president and the highest-ranking Canadian official, claimed that while there were rumors regarding drug taking among Canadians (including Johnson), he, as a lawyer, believed he was "better off not knowing" about it. Johnson's coach Charlie Francis, of York University in Ontario, was also heard.

The Dubin Inquiry instituted new procedures for policy development, and also recommended granting the Sports Medicine Council of Canada an autonomous role in the control of drugs in sports. In 1992 a completely new organization, the Canadian Centre for Drug-Free Sport, was created to take responsibility for a national drug-testing program. This was able to manage out-of-competition testing, which was seen as vital to the whole program. Dubin suggested unambiguous punishments for offenders; a four-year ban for a first offense, followed by a life ban for a second.

The Dubin Inquiry was something of a symbolic purgation. Sport was seen to be owning up to what many regarded as its seamier side. While drug taking was known to occur, Dubin indicated that its proportions had been underestimated. Not until the Moabit trials of 1998 was there such a significant legal event related to the drugs issue in sport.

Of related interest

Dubin, Charles (1990) *Commission of Inquiry into the Use of Drugs and Banned Practices Intended to Increase Athletic Performance*, Ministry of Supply and Services.

Houlihan, Barrie (1997) *Sport, Policy and Politics: A Comparative Analysis*, Routledge.

E

eating disorders

Anorexia nervosa and bulimia

Research has shown that eating disorders, particularly anorexia nervosa and bulimia, are more prevalent in certain sports than in the general population. Sports that emphasize the importance of physical appearance, such as gymnastics, ice dancing and synchronized swimming, harbor more eating disorders and competitors have been encouraged by coaches and trainers to restrict food intake, use purgatives or induce vomiting in an effort to maintain a nymph-like body.

While it may contradict popular expectations of healthy young people with, one assumes, a keener sense of their own bodies than most, several studies in Europe and the USA have indicated that young athletes are more rather than less prone to eating disorders. Since the early 1980s, researchers have reported an increase in clinically diagnosed eating disorders and eating disordered tendencies (like faddish dieting, diuretics abuse and overdosing on diet pills). The rates have varied between 1–4 per cent in the general population, with an increase in anorexia occurring primarily in white females between the ages of 15–24 years. In 1983, Puglise *et al*. ("Fear of obesity," *New England Journal of Medicine* vol 309) coined the term *anorexia athletica* to indicate the particular eating disorder that affects competitive sports performers. Estimates of the prevalence of eating disorders in the female sporting population vary between 4–22 per cent, with gymnasts, long-distance runners and synchronised swimmers being most affected.

Monitoring weight is normal in most sports, and in some, leanness is considered of paramount importance. Sports that are subject to judge's evaluation, like gymnastics, diving and figure skating, encourage participants to take care of all aspects of their appearance. About 35 per cent of competitors have eating disorders, and half practice what researchers term "pathogenic weight control." In some sports, looking young and slender is considered such an advantage that competitors actively try to stave off the onset of menstruation and the development of secondary sexual characteristics, or to counterbalance the weight gain that typically accompanies puberty. Menstrual dysfunctions, such as amenorrhoea and oligomenorrhoea, frequently result from anorexia.

In endurance events, excess weight is generally believed to impair performance. Athletes reduce body fat to increase strength, speed and endurance, though they risk bone mineral deficiencies, dehydration and a decrease in maximum oxygen uptake (VO_{2max}). The Norwegian biologist Jorunn Sundgot-Borgen suggests that the training load typically carried by endurance athletes may induce a calorific deprivation which, in turn, elicits "certain biological and social reinforcement leading to the development of eating disorders" ("Eating disorders in female athletes," *Sports Medicine* vol 17, no 3, 1994). However, the prevalence of bulimia is more difficult to explain.

Sundgot-Borgen also argues that competitors most at risk tend to be characterized by "high self-expectation, perfectionism, persistence and independence." In other words, the qualities that enable them to achieve in sports make them vulnerable to eating disorders. The same researcher reports that a change of coach can trigger an eating disorder, as can an injury that prevents the athlete training at usual levels.

A further finding of Sundgot-Borgen and several other scholars is that coaches actually recommend the use of pathogenic control methods, including vomiting, laxatives and diuretics. Coaches and trainers in weight-sensitive sports need to keep an eye on their charges' eating habits in preparation for competitions. For example, lightweight rowers and jockeys must meet weight restrictions before competition. In their article "Weight concerns, weight control techniques, and eating disorders among adolescent competitive swimmers," Diane Taub and Rose Benson write that: "Excess body fat and body weight in both males and females are widely considered by coaches, parents and participants to hinder performance" (*Sociology of Sport Journal* vol 9, no 2, 1992).

Stories of boxers, "drying-out" (as they call it) were legion before the 1990s. Instead of swallowing liquid, they gargled to quench their thirsts and spent dangerously long periods in saunas to keep their body weight down. Such procedures are now condemned by boxing's governing associations and weigh-ins take place the day before a fight so that boxers have time to replenish themselves before a contest. There was evidence that rapid weight loss exposed boxers to serious injury by lowering their resistance to punishment.

Body dissatisfaction

There have been recent studies of what used to be called "reverse anorexia nervosa," now called MUSCLE DYSMORPHIA. There is a symmetry between this and anorexia: sufferers of both conditions believe their bodies to be so deficient that that are driven to extreme measures. In the case of anorexics, the individual regards her (only a very small minority of cases involve men) body as too fat while others see her as emaciated. No amount of persuasion convinces the anorexic that she is not in fact fat. The muscle dysmorphic will typically have a well-vasculated body hewn from hours of steadfast work on the weights. Yet he (it is predominantly a male syndrome) regards himself as wimpish. Both anorexics and dysmorphics tend to conceal their bodies by wearing loose-fitting clothes. Their conditions often lead to tensions in domestic relationships.

One of the complex of factors that lead to eating disorders is what J.D. Marshall and V.J. Harder call "Body dissatisfaction and drive for thinness in high-performance field hockey athletes" (*International Journal of Sports Medicine* vol 17, no 7, 1996). The research uncovered, perhaps surprisingly, that concern for body shape and size was a greater issue than preoccupation with height among hockey players, who exhibited the kind of behavior associated with eating disorders. Body dissatisfaction is not the preserve of sports performers, of course, and to understand the high degrees of eating disorders in sports, it is necessary to open out the context.

Feminists have for long argued that big women have been erased from history, men preferring notable women to be small and, by implication, fragile. Large, warrior-like women, such as Boudicca or the Amazons are regarded as exceptional. In the late twentieth century, images of attractive women were typically frail, the continuity between Twiggy, in the 1960s, to Kate Moss, in the 1990s, is apparent. Critics interpret this as a patriarchal strategy to encourage women toward debilitating conditions brought about by crash dieting, diet pills and, of course, anorexia and bulimia. Women striving to correct a body that they define as deficient is a self-disempowering act: a large part of their dwindling energies are diverted inwardly towards making their bodies smaller and weaker.

Paradoxically, anorexic and bulimic women themselves might be seen as exercising a form of power over their own bodies. Women suffering from eating disorders are usually not high-achieving and financially independent professionals; they have few resources apart from the ability to control their own bodies. But in this respect, they have total sovereignty.

The reason many woman (only a tiny minority of men experience eating disorders) become anorexic or bulimic is that they, like others, are members of a culture of NARCISSISM that rewards a close attention to one's own body and its regulation. The body has become central to contemporary culture; yet, there is irony. As we are induced, via our television screens, to gorge on such things as candy, ice cream and chocolate, we are also urged to aspire to the kind of lean bodies paraded before us by gaunt models and the like. (In 1996, cK cologne models were singled out for criticism for promoting what was called "heroin chic.")

Of related interest

Chapman, Gwen E. (1997) "Making weight: Lightweight rowing, technologies of power, and technologies of the self," *Sociology of Sport Journal* vol 14, no 3.

Petrie, Trent A. (1996) "Differences between male and female college lean sport athletes, nonlean sports athletes, and non-athletes on behavioral and psychological indices of eating disorders," *Journal of Applied Sport Psychology* vol 8 , no 2.

Sundgot-Borgen, Jorunn (1994) "Risk and trigger factors the development of eating disorders in female elite athletes," *Medicine and Science in Sports and Exercise* vol 26, no 4.

Eight Men Out

The Black Sox Scandal

John Sayle's film *Eight Men Out* (1988), based on the book by Elliot Asinof, is a sympathetic account of the famous 1919 baseball scandal in which members of the Chicago White Sox allegedly threw the World Series. Sayle's sympathy lies with the players, who are seen little more than factory fodder, dutifully turning out to play for a pittance, locked into contracts that allow legal exploitation and cheated out of bonuses by the club's owner, Charles Comiskey, for whom the club is a bauble.

The White Sox had enjoyed a stunningly good season and were prohibitive 3-to-1 on favorites to take the series, many believing a sweep was the only possible result. (Asked if the Sox was the best team he had ever seen, an African American answers: "Yeah .... well, the best *white* team, anyway": segregation prevented blacks and whites playing together and there were "Negro Leagues" that ran their own competitions.

Much of the adulation afforded the players in the early years of the century masked the fact that they were paid meager salaries and denied basic workers' rights, such as the ability to withdraw their labor. In an early scene, we see pitcher Eddie Cicotte (played by actor David Strathairn) reminding Comiskey that he had been promised $10,000 if he won thirty games. Comiskey (played by Clifton James) asks his assistant to check the records and finds Cicotte is one short. "29 is not 30, Eddie," says Comiskey solemnly, to which Cicotte responds that he was benched after his 29th win even though there were three weeks to go until the end of the regular season. Cicotte leaves Comiskey's office without his money or even a hope of getting it.

Earlier, it had been determined by the gamblers trying to fix the series that Cicotte's co-operation would be crucial but the pitcher himself was not interested. After the meeting with Comiskey, he changes his mind and agrees to the fix. His decision proves crucial to the outcome of the series.

America's penchant for GAMBLING on sports was at the root of the CORRUPTION. The fix was made possible because of the heavy betting on the in-form Chicago team. A couple of small-time gamblers saw the potential in trying to bribe a few team members to throw games, while they themselves bet on the Cincinnati Reds, who were rank outsiders. If the Reds won games their odds would shorten, so it was necessary to bet with large stakes, especially in the opening games. In the film, the players are tentatively approached via Chick Gandl (played by Michael Rooker) and those who show interest are promised $10,000 each. Needing substantial up-front money, the gamblers venture to ask wealthier sources and, through various brokers, reach high roller Arnold Rothstein (played by Michael Lerner) who effectively bankrolls the project.

One of Rothstein's minions is Abe Attell, a Jewish former pro featherweight boxer from San Francisco, who held the world title between 1904 and 1912 – and who crops up in A.J Liebling's best-selling chronicle *The SWEET SCIENCE*. Attell was a renowned gambler and once won $40,000 (a fortune in those days) betting against his opponent Harry Forbes, whom he beat in five rounds. In the movie, he talks casually about the number of times he threw fights in his boxing days, as if it were part and parcel of professional sports (other movies, such as *SOMEBODY UP THERE LIKES ME*, have dramatized this aspect of boxing).

Sayles depicts the emergence of a new illicit gambling hierarchy symmetrical with that of baseball's internal hierarchy: Rothstein is shown to be as acquisitive, avaricious and callous as Comiskey. Each character in the chain of command is opportunistically searching for a chance to earn extra money. The players are at the lowest order of both hierarchies. When it comes to getting paid, they discover that the majority of their bribe money has been laid out by gamblers on bets. At 1–4 down and only one game away from defeat in the best of nine series, some of the eight are seen changing heart: they play to their mettle and pull back the next game in style, only to be warned that they are in too deep to renege on the arrangement. Lefty Williams is told that his wife will die if the Sox do not lose the series.

But the sudden, inexplicable contrasts in form alert at least some to the fact that a fix has gone in and Hugh Fullerton, a Chicago sports writer, played in the movie by writer/broadcaster Studs Terkel, starts an investigation that eventually results in a series of "confessions." These are later mysteriously lost.

The players are punished in triplicate, losing not only the World Series, but their livelihood and the money they should have received from the gamblers; not to mention the honor typically afforded baseball players in the first decades of the century. As competitors in America's national sport, their status was on par with that of Jack Dempsey, who had won the world's heavyweight championship only a few months before the World Series of 1919. Baseball's Babe Ruth and Ty Cobb were certainly revered in the same way as Dempsey.

The White Sox scandal in many ways destroyed the American ideal of sport and ushered in a new understanding of a profession that was just as corrupt, vile and rotten as any other area of society. "Say it ain't so, Joe," was the assurance asked for by a young fan as Shoeless Joe Jackson (played by D.B. Sweeney) left the courtroom where the trial of the eight was taking place. In the film, Jackson walks away sheepishly, humbled by the boy's ingenuous request. Much of North America's population wanted the same confirmation.

Gambling and corruption in American sports

The case was unique in the sense that it became enshrined in American sports history, but it is also possible that fixing games may have been a regular feature of baseball in the context of what was effectively a power struggle. MAJOR LEAGUE BASEBALL had been troubled by the presence of the once minor but now growing Federal League, which had begun life in 1913 and was attracting Major League players by having no reserve clause and offering long-term contracts. The several hundred Major League players who crossed over saw their salaries more than double.

This precipitated a reaction from the Major League, which began to pay more in an effort to keep its star players. Having lifted its salaries, the Major League sensed ruinous problems ahead should a salary war escalate: both leagues lost money over the two years from 1913. By 1915, the Major League found it more expedient to negotiate an agreement with the Federal League, which effectively put the latter out of business and restored the legal monopoly enjoyed by the Major League.

Its supremacy regained – and officially mandated by the Supreme Court – the Major League tightened up on players' wages. Chicago was known to have the meanest salary structure in the league. For example, Jackson – shown in the film to be an illiterate, naive and reluctant participant in the fix – had been traded from Cleveland for $65,000. He was paid less than $6,000 in 1918 and 1919, despite batting .408, .395 and .372 in the three previous seasons. The underplayed players were ripe for bribing.

During the First World War (1914–18), the USA's racecourses were closed down, thus depriving professional gamblers from a source of income. Baseball presented itself as a logical alternative. It was well known that gambling was rife, whether at the stadiums or at the bookies. In fact, the eventual ruling on the eight White Sox players was seen as a victory in baseball's war against the gamblers. The severe sentences – eight life suspensions – were meant to have the symbolic effect of a purgative. While the eight players involved were cleared of a felony, baseball club owners feared a loss of credibility: fans might stay away if they suspected not all games were "on the level."

Comiskey was instrumental in appointing a new baseball Commissioner, Kenesaw Mountain Landis, who earned an annual salary of $50,000, almost nine times that of Joe Jackson, whose career was ended by Landis's ruling. The inimical effects of professional gamblers seemed slight compared to those of the salaried official and profiteering owners. It is no coincidence that the 1920s were years of unprecedented economic success for professional baseball, though precious few of the players saw much improvement in their conditions; the aforementioned Babe Ruth and Ty Cobb were exceptions.

Of the eight men suspended from the sport for life, Buck Weaver (played by John Cusack) continued to plead innocence and attempted to have his name cleared right up to his death. The other "Black Sox," as they became known, Cicotte, Jackson, Gandl, Williams, Swede Risberg, Oscar Felsch and Fred McMullin, faded into folklore, never reappearing in Major League Baseball.

Of related interest

Asinof, Elliot (1963) *Eight Men Out: The Black Sox and the 1919 World Series*, Holt, Rinehart & Winston.

Devine, J.R. (1994) "Baseball's labor wars in historical context," *Marquette Sports Law Journal*, vol 5, no 1.

Eight Men Out, directed by John Sayles, 1988.

Nathan, D.A. (1995) "Anti-semitism and the Black Sox scandal," *Nine: A Journal of Baseball History and Social Policy Perspectives* vol 4, no 1.

Elias, Norbert

b. 1897, Germany; d. 1990

The civilizing process

Elias was among the first social theorists to focus on the central importance of sports in modern culture. "What kind of societies are they," asked Elias, "where people in great numbers and almost world wide enjoy, as actors or spectators, physical contests between individual people or teams of people and the tensions, the excitement engendered by these contests under conditions where no blood flows, no serious harm is done to each other by contestants?"

Elias's book with his one-time student Eric Dunning, *Quest for Excitement* (Blackwell, 1988), supplies an answer. In the book, sport is described as: "One of the great social inventions which human beings have made without planning to make them. It offers people the liberating excitement of a struggle involving physical exertion and skill while limiting to a minimum the chance that anyone will get seriously hurt."

Elias left Germany in the Hitler era, and worked first in England and later in Ghana and Holland before returning to Germany. His pioneering work on sport was undertaken at Leicester University, England. The central motif of Elias's theory is that sport is associated with the increasing pacification of external social control – or coercion – and the parallel development of internal constraints, or self-control. In other words, the amount of violence used to maintain control and regulation in society decreases and the individuals take more responsibility for their own conduct. Both processes are linked to the rise of the modern state.

Sport arose as a substitute for previously violent and exciting behavior. Activities such as public torture, bare-knuckle fighting, bear baiting or other BLOOD SPORTS were gradually replaced by more controlled forms of activity that we have come to recognize as sports. The replacement took place amid what Elias called in the title of one of his books *The Civilizing Process* (Blackwell, vol 1, 1978; vol 2, original German, 1939). Comparison of ancient and modern sports shows that the forms of sport and leisure characteristic of modern societies reflect a requirement for greater emotional restraint and the control of VIOLENCE in societies generally. At the same time, the function of modern leisure, whether sport, game or rock concert, is to act as a "counter-measure against stress-tensions." The stress-tensions are themselves the result of the constant need for self-restraint.

Elias wrote that the "mimetic fear or pleasure, sadness and joys" presented in "play" form "momentarily lift the burden of risks and threats ... surrounding human existence." Far from being peripheral activities, sports are absolutely central to the process whereby human *configurations* move away from barbarism.

A *configuration*, sometimes abbreviated to figuration, is "a nexus of interdependencies between people," the "chains of functions" and "axes of tensions" (both of cooperation and conflict) which can be identified in any social context. The figuration conjures up the image of a vast web of relationships, though Elias himself favored more mobile models, such as a dance or a game.

In *The Civilizing Process*, Elias used the concept of the figuration to demonstrate how changes in individual patterns of behavior, personality, morality and self-control were connected with the formation of European states. *The Court Society* (Blackwell, 1969) deals with related themes: Elias showed how what he called "the structures of affects" that are now regarded as "civilized" involved profound redefinitions of previously "proper" behavior, such as spitting and breaking wind in public. New standards of decorum and repugnance came into being in western society, occurring first in court society and later spread by a process of social emulation.

As stated earlier, the tensions generated by the emphasis of the civilizing process on self-control and BODY REGULATION were managed by means of sports: Elias's empirical work on fox hunting, soccer and rugby showed how mimetic activities – resembling more harmful and repugnant activities – were not only containable within the civilizing process, but actually satisfied the "quest" for the *frisson* that became a feature of modern figurations.

In a series of articles, some co-written with collaborators from Leicester, Elias set out a program for the sociological study of sport and identified specific features of contemporary sport. For example, he noted the destruction of the "play" element and the rise of "achievement striving" as sport acquired a new seriousness and greater significance as a source of meaning and personal identity. The article "Sport as a male preserve," as its title indicates, suggested that gender equalizations arising from the civilizing process had led to re-construction of sport as a proving ground for the construction of male identity, a point developed by later writers on the facilities of sport in the production of MASCULINITIES/ FEMININITIES. This point was later disputed by writers such as Jennifer Hargreaves (in "Where's the virtue? Where's the grace? A discussion of the social production of gender relations in and through sport," *Theory, Culture and Society* vol 3, no 1, 1986).

Elias, with Dunning, also analyzed the symbolic role of sport in providing significant representations of nation and community in modern society. The suggestion was that the "collective effervescence" (as the classical social theorist Emile Durkheim called it) generated in religious rituals can be transferred *mutatis mutandis* to modern sporting events. The relevance of sport to NATIONALISM is evident.

Sportization

"Sportization" is a term chosen by Elias to capture the process by which industrialization and modernization have revolutionized games and pastimes. In many senses the codified forms of older activities reflected features of newly industrialized societies. For instance, "functional democratization" and equality were central to the civilizing process and these were embodied in sport's conceptions of "fairness" and "fair contests" (equal numbers in teams, impartial referees and so on). Elias in fact located the process of sportization earlier than industrialization, seeing it as initiated by the English landed classes and gentry at a point in English history when "enclosures had broken the back of free English peasantry," class conflicts were under control and the upper classes shared in an increasingly unified and "gentlemanly" lifestyle.

The construction of a democratic government – what Elias called "parliamentarization" – enabled political differences to be settled by non-violent means. Sportization allowed what might previously have been violent pastimes to be settled similarly. This is contrary to the more usual thesis that the development of institutional sports, replete with codes and governing organizations, *begins* with industrialization; for Elias, the process precedes industrialization.

In an "Essay on sport and violence," English fox hunting is presented by Elias as exemplifying the new type of pastimes which the onset of modern sport introduced. The hunting of foxes no longer occurred with the objective of eating the quarry, but purely for the pleasure of the "fine run," the tension and the excitement of the chase.

Rick Gruneau, in his *Class, Sports and Social Development* (University of Massachusetts Press, 1983) offers an alternative conflictual account to the one offered by the figurational approach. For Gruneau, the history of sport "is a history of cultural struggle to define the dominant forms and meaning of sports practices and 'the legitimate' uses of time and the body."

The power of Elias' theory is in situating the growth of what we now recognize as sport in the wider historical and cultural context of the civilizing process. Despite this, his theories are contentious. Often, the symmetry between sports and the civilizing process appears to be too neat. When actual developments do not seem to fit – for example, the rise of violence with soccer HOOLIGANISM – Elias invokes clauses such as the "reverse gear" to explain that the civilizing process does not only proceed in one direction and that there can be reversals to older forms of social solidarity. However, Elias resists "testing" this; it remains an assertion.

Of related interest

Dunning, Eric and Rojek, Chris (eds.) (1992) *Sport and Leisure in the Civilizing Process*, Macmillan.

Horne, John and Jary, David (1987) "The figurational sociology of sport and leisure of Elias and Dunning: An exposition and a critique," in Horne, John, Jary, David and Tomlinson, Alan (eds), *Sport, Leisure and Social Relations*, Routledge & Kegan Paul.

Mennell, Stephen (1989) *Norbert Elias: Civilization and the Human Self-Image*, Blackwell.

DAVID JARY

endorsements

In sports, endorsements refer to a performer's public declaration of his or her approval of a commercial product, or range of products; this declaration is then used in advertising and marketing campaigns as a way of both enhancing recognition of the product(s) and heightening its appeal to consumers who may identify or respect the performer. It typically (though not always) involves a commercial transaction, the sports figure being paid an amount commensurate with the estimated value of his or her approval.

Whether or not the endorser actually uses, let alone likes, the product(s) is of little relevance to advertisers: Jackie Robinson, the baseball player famed for breaking the "color line," endorsed Chesterfield cigarettes, even though he did not smoke. He also appeared in advertisements for bread and breakfast cereal. Interestingly, General Foods (GF), the company that signed Robinson to endorse its Wheaties product, revived his image fifty years after he made his Major League debut, plastering his face across the products' packets in a commemorative gesture. GF was involved in one of twenty-one licensing deals linked to Robinson in 1997, highlighting the commercial power of sports personalities even after their death. In Britain, Denis Compton, the Middlesex cricketer, became known as the "Brycreem Boy" after endorsing the men's hair preparation in the 1940s. It was during the 1970s that commercial companies realized that no one had truly exploited the potential of the sports marketing strategy. Phil Knight, the founder of NIKE, paid tennis player Ilie Nastase $3,000 to endorse his Cortez sports shoe in 1972. Knight also used Steve Prefontaine and Dan Fouts in an exercise that ranks as the most successful symbiotic marketing strategy in history. The arrangements were all mutually advantageous: the sports stars gained exposure through a series of stylish advertising campaigns, while the product gained the credibility of being favored by top athletes.

Knight's most influential signing was Michael JORDAN. His rise to the status of one of the best-known ICONS ever was due in no small part to the meticulously choreographed television commercials in which he was seen wearing Nike shoes and apparel. In the 1990s, Jordan regularly grossed over $20 million (£12.5m) from endorsement deals alone. Several of his contemporaries could match or exceed their salaries with endorsement income.

The potency of the sports star as a selling aide increased during a period of transition for sports. As TELEVISION took more interest in broadcasting sport events, so more fans, both committed and casual, were made aware of the personalities. In the United States, the challenging innovations of Roone ARLEDGE of ABC humanized sports performers by featuring them in close-up shots and providing their background details.

In Britain, a soccer player like George Best was able to command the status of a pop star not just because he was an exceptional player with good looks, but because he was fêted by the media and lauded in a way typically reserved for great artists. Fans with little knowledge of soccer flocked to watch Best play. The fact that he was invited to endorse only a few products – and even these were soccer-related, like football boots – indicates how companies had not yet woken up to the idea of linking products with stars in the 1960s.

Misdemeanors beset Best's career and possibly deterred commercial companies from offering contracts to a celebrity prone to bouts of drunkenness. Thirty years on, companies were not always so cautious. Controversial and somewhat infamous characters like Dennis Rodman and Eric CANTONA were rarely short of offers to endorse products. But, companies tend to exercise caution in some respects and tend to target "safe" celebrities. Jack Nicklaus and Arnold Palmer, both represented by Mark McCORMACK, consistently featured among the best-paid endorsers between 1970–80. Of course, they were both white males who seemed to embrace family values.

A more self-consciously transgressive character like Andre Agassi may have seemed riskier, were it not for the fact that he too, was a white heterosexual male and his rebellion was conducted strictly at the level of hair style and clothing. Robinson had beaten a path for other ethnic minority sports stars like Jordan and Tiger Woods, both of whom were rendered "color-free" by advertisers. Like other holders of lucrative endorsement contracts, they both avoided becoming involved in affairs that might have been seen as political. Because the market that advertisers usually address is dominated by whites, black athletes who might be seen as dangerous or "threatening" were rarely the beneficiaries of large contracts. Nor were GAYS: despite her obvious supremacy in women's tennis, Martina Navratilova was never "safe" enough for advertisers.

Yet even "safe" bets can go wrong. Ben Johnson's shame after testing positive for DRUGS at the Seoul Olympics reflected on the brands he endorsed, including Diadora sports equipment. Magic JOHNSON had a portfolio of contracts at the time of his declaration that he was HIV-positive. The dilemma faced by the companies he worked with was whether to appear heartless in releasing him, or risk associations with the specter of Aids. One cringes to think what Mike TYSON's business colleagues thought after he was convicted of rape.

Outside sports, Madonna was involved in various endorsement projects when she was denounced by the Vatican for her "Like a prayer" single. Michael Jackson's fall from grace resulted in companies such as Pepsi removing him from their roster of endorsers. It is usual for companies to write into contracts with celebrities a "get-out" clause that enables them to negate the arrangement in the event of scandals or contretemps like the above.

Do endorsements work? The amount of money spent by advertisers on public figures suggests they do. But, in his book *Advertising and Popular Culture*, Jib Fowles quotes a study conducted shortly after the 1991 Super Bowl. An impressive 70 per cent of a sample of the television audience interviewed recalled that Joe Montana had appeared in a commercial during the telecast; but only 18 per cent remembered that the product he endorsed was Diet Pepsi.

Of related interest

Cashmore, Ellis (2000) *Making Sense of Sports*, 3rd edn, Routledge.
Coakley, Jay J. (1998) *Sport in Society: Issues and Controversies*, 6th edn, McGraw-Hill.
Fowles, Jib (1996) *Advertising and Popular Culture*, Sage.

EPO

Erythropoietin (EPO) facilitates the production of extra red blood cells which absorb oxygen and leaves the user with no tell-tale needle tracks. EPO was originally produced for kidney dialysis patients. As EPO does not show up in urinalysis, inspection is possible only by blood tests before and after competition.

As well as being more convenient than transfusion, EPO has the advantage of being undetectable in competitors who object to invasive testing techniques on religious or ethical grounds. As with the other favored performance enhancer of the late 1990s, HUMAN GROWTH HORMONE (hGH), blood doping and EPO copied the body's natural processes and demanded extra vigilant testing procedures at competitions.

While EPO was thought to be popular among professional cyclists, only one, Eddy Planckaert of Belgium, the winner of the 1988 TOUR DE FRANCE, admitted using it. Hein Verbruggen, the president of the International Cycling Union (ICU), once said of EPO: "It's a very efficient doping product. I think it's the only one that really works." The discoveries during the 1998 Tour suggested EPO was an extremely popular enhancer among cyclists.

In an attempt to stem its use, the ICU introduced a test that checked cyclists' blood: if their red cell count exceeded 50 per cent, cyclists were prevented from racing for fifteen days. Riders Javier Ochoa, of Spain, and Italian Nicola Loda were among those excluded from the competition; a random test registered the Giro d'Italia leader Marco Pantini 2 per cent over the level and cost the Italian a triumph.

Interestingly, the cyclists were not banned or fined, suggesting a difference between the ICU policy and that of most of the world's governing associations. The deaths of eighteen cyclists in Belgium and Holland in the period 1987–90 were linked with possible EPO use.

Of related interest

Voy, Robert (1991) *Drugs, Sport and Politics*, Leisure Press.
Waddington, Ivan (1996) "The development of sports medicine," *Sociology of Sport Journal*, vol 19.

eroticism

Inherent sexuality

Sport objectifies the human body. However much we know about the personalities of the performers, fans remain interested because they enjoy and appreciate what athletes can do with their bodies in appropriate contexts. Participants are driven by all sorts of MOTIVATION, but all share the goal of exhibiting their skills in front of appreciative fans. While fans and athletes alike would deny any sexual component to their interest in sports, some writers have theorized that eroticism is implicit and occasionally explicit in sports. This is not a new development: indeed, the presence of eroticism in sports dates back to antiquity.

In his book *The Erotic in Sports* (1996), the historian Allen Guttmann writes: "I am inclined to believe that there is an *inherent* erotic element in doing and watching sports." Sporting activity involves BODY REGULATION, training the body, controlling it and employing it in ways that might be described as unusual; competition may mean coming into close contact with the bodies of others in ways that, in other contexts, might be regarded as intimate, even sensual.

Guttmann chronicles how in ancient Greek societies, the confluence of the military and athleticism guaranteed that masculinity was equated with physicality and that the athletic male body was a cultural ideal. Homosexual relations were rife and the gymnasium provided opportunities for selecting and meeting sexual partners. Guttmann writes of the "erotic ambiance of the gymnasium," though without noticing the relevance of his phrase to today's gyms.

In the Roman societies, the gladiator was an "erotically charged figure" either willing or coerced to RISK his life in armed combat. His physical presence excited women; even his title was derived for the word *gladius* (sword) which was slang for penis. While it is impossible to know the motives behind female spectators at sites of contests, there is at least inferential evidence that many were drawn by the sexual overtones of the spectacles. It is possible that men were similarly aroused. In 295 BC, brothels were built in the Circus Maximus for the convenience of male spectators excited by the gladiatorial contests.

The visual art depicting sports performers and events evokes strong comparisons with erotic art. The poetry and songs about athletics are often ambiguous enough to suggest more than one interpretation. It has been acknowledged by several contemporary scholars that sports have played central parts in constructing definitions of MASCULINITIES/FEMININITIES.

All of these indicate that there is some substance to Guttmann's claim. The traditional male-centeredness of sport has ensured that it has been a site for bonding, the assertion of macho identities and the construction of male physicality. In the collection of essays, *Making Men: Rugby and the Masculine Identity*, edited by John Nauright and Timothy Chandler (1996), it is argued that the sport of rugby was vital in the promotion of a particular version of masculinity that incorporated virility, aggression and a boisterous physicality.

The opportunities for close bodily contact between men were – indeed are – rife. "This not to say that the game was latently homosexual," writes Jock Phillips, in his chapter on what he calls "the formation of male identity in New Zealand." "It is simply to claim that most human beings need the affirmation of touching other people, that colonial men often could not obtain that affection from women and turned for support and intense fellowship to other men, and that rugby provided one place in which the tensions of their situation could be relieved."

Guttmann is more certain that homosexuality is latent in much of male-dominated sports, some of it experienced vicariously. "There is a homosexual component in the heterosexual's response to athletes of his or her own sex," writes Guttmann. "The frenzy of the mostly male spectators at a boxing match must be more than the excitement occasioned by the demonstration of the manly art of self-defense."

In his book *Mike Tyson: Money, Myth and Betrayal* (Grafton, 1991), Montieth Illingworth writes of the "confusing signals" boxer Mike TYSON must have received from his management team early in his career. D'Amato set the tone, according to Illingworth: in a 1985 interview for CBS television, D'Amato described his feelings when he first saw the 13-year-old prospect in action: "I got excited. I see a fighter, you know, physically I get excited just like a guy who's no longer capable of any sexual involvement and then all of a sudden he becomes sexually interested again."

Guttmann interprets the ecstatic responses of mostly female spectators at women's figure skating competitions in similar terms; and while he does not refer to it, the argument between the sports goods company Reebok and members of the American Basketball League (ABL) is relevant to Guttmann's argument. In 1995, the all-female basketball ABL was launched. Some of its better-known players were contracted to appear in a commercial for Reebok; they made it very clear that they objected to the amount of cosmetics they were expected to wear. Apparently, the basketball players wanted to appear as exactly that: players. Instead, they felt they were made to conform with traditional – i.e. male – notions of femininity.

Sexuality has not always been sublimated: in eighteenth- and nineteenth-century England, women's foot races and pugilism attracted fans with what Guttmann calls "voyeuristic motives." While he does not acknowledge it, Guttmann would presumably argue that male spectators at today's female boxing contests are similarly motivated.

While some of these claims may seem exaggerated, the objectification of the human body brought about by the growth of spectator sports provides at least the potential for eroticization. The development of organized sports at the end of the nineteenth century was accompanied by the growth of a physical culture, what Guttmann calls "the gospel of muscular hedonism." Interest in the body, how it could be reshaped, controlled, disciplined, presented and visualized artistically, continued through the twentieth century, particularly after the NARCISSISM that began in the 1970s.

The aesthetic of bodybuilding

Perhaps the ultimate in narcissistic and, indeed, erotic sports is bodybuilding. This is a competitive sport in which performance is subordinated to aesthetic beauty: while the successful entrant must be able to pose effectively, he or she will be judged on appearance. The physical body is the object to be evaluated: the competitor's strength is irrelevant, and only balanced muscular development, symmetry and skin and muscle tone are to be judged. A bodybuilding contest is an exhibition of muscular beauty.

While the first organized bodybuilding contests were held in the early years of the twentieth century (the first recorded contest took place in 1903), it was not until the 1940s that the sport gained recognition as a legitimate competition rather than an excuse for lewdness. The coexistence between the athletic and the erotic was plain to see as skimpily-clad, anatomically perfect bodies paraded and flexed in an ambiguous pageant. Even in today's highly organized and professionally run contests, the pleasures derived from competing and spectating may not be purely athletic.

It is also possible to discern the ways in which cultural archetypes of male sexuality have derived from bodybuilding models. This was commercially exploited by Charles Atlas who – under his real name, Angelo Siciliano – was a regular winner of bodybuilding contests in the 1920s before marketing his bodybuilding system mail order. His advertising addressed the issue of sexuality in featuring a storyboard of a skinny man on the beach spurned by an attractive woman who favors the company of a hulking bodybuilder-type. After taking a course of the Charles Atlas "dynamic tension" system, the puny man returns to the beach, now with bulging muscles and a trim waist. This time, he gets the woman. Today, there are gyms instead of mail order programs and cosmetic surgery for those without time or inclination to emulate bodybuilders.

The influence of women bodybuilders was not so clearly discernible until the 1990s. The unwitting *ur*-postfeminists who paraded their well-vasculated bodies in the 1984 movie *Pumping Iron II: The Women* (directed by George Butler) drew disapproving responses from men, who saw them as either steroid-loaded dykes or freaks (or both) and possibly asexual. Women who excelled in this sport were seen as transgressively masculine. But, by the time of James Cameron's *Terminator 2: Judgement Day* in 1991, sexual dimorphism had morphed some more: actor Linda Hamilton's widely-publicized quest for muscle involved her in a Procrustean training program. Guttmann believes that Hamilton's combination of good looks and muscular torso inspired a new "look" for women. Broad shoulders, big biceps and a rippling "sixpack" abdomen were *de rigueur* for the sexy body of the 1990s.

Of related interest

Guttmann, Allen (1996) *The Erotic in Sports*, Columbia University Press.
Nauright, John and Chandler, Timothy J.L. (eds) (1996) *Making Man: Rugby and the Masculine Identity*, Frank Cass.
Pumping Iron II: The Women, directed by George Butler, 1984.

ESPN

ESPN (Entertainment and Programming Sports Network) was the world's first television network dedicated exclusively to sports. It offered a mixture of "live" events, taped highlights, analysis and news. At its official launch in 1980, an executive announced: "We believe the appetite for sports in this country [the USA] is 'insatiable' " (quoted in McChesney 1989). His confidence seemed well-founded: by 1998, ESPN was taken by about 70 per cent of all US television-owning households, and ESPN broadcast 23 per cent of all televised sports. In addition, the network's reach extended to 160 different countries around the world and it provided services in 19 languages. In 1996 it set up a second ESPN channel specializing in news items; and, to complement its extensive television coverage, started ESPN Radio.

The channel was the creation of Bill Rasmussen, who in the 1970s dreamed up an original idea for a regional network of radio stations to broadcast the University of Massachusetts's football games. Cable broadcasting was then in its infancy and Rasmussen was able to buy time on a communications satellite (transponder) inexpensively. He filled the time with small-scale sports commentary, interviews and analysis. The Entertainment Sports Programming Network operated out of Plainville, Connecticut, and gained permission from the Federal Communications Commission to begin broadcasting in September 1979. Getty Oil sensed the potential of the enterprise and invested heavily; in fact, it assumed effective control and sold out to Texaco, which in turn sold the network to ABC television. ABC's interest transformed ESPN from a local operation to a national network, reaching 34 million homes by 1984. This was the year David Stern became the new NBA commissioner and Michael JORDAN made his debut for the Chicago Bulls. ESPN had held a contract with the NBA for the previous two years, and had shown NCAA games from the start of 1979.

ESPN developed out of the early cable television initiatives, themselves a product of the geographical problems of broadcasting in the United States. In 1949, only 2 per cent of US households owned television sets. Broadcast television was available, but remote and shielded areas could not get reception. Two separate initiatives in Landsford, Pennsylvania and Astoria, Oregon led to an embryonic cable television service: in both places, individuals tapped into signals on master antennas which distributed them to local houses via coaxial cables hung on poles. The initiators of both systems (Robert Tarlton in Landsford and Ed Parsons in Astoria) then charged customers for rebroadcasting the shows to their homes.

The concept was a simple but workable solution to the problems faced in remote areas, and it soon caught on. By 1961 there were 700 maverick cable systems, and in 1962 there were 1,325, with 1.2 million subscribers yielding $40 million. Subscribers had become inured to paying for their television. But the money went to the cable operators rather than the originators of the programs. Court cases ensued, with cable operators winning several key cases which allowed them to continue operating, but the Federal Communications Commission also had minor but significant, successes. One of these ruled against a firm that wished to use a community antenna to import distant signals into Wyoming on the grounds that it would virtually put paid to the local stations (those within sixty miles of the cable headquarters). It confined cable to local rebroadcasting and, in 1972, brought operators into its fold by requiring them to get an FCC certificate of compliance for which they paid a fee based on their size. At that time, there were 2,750 systems serving six million homes, unevenly distributed across the USA.

In another notable development in 1972, Time Inc.'s Home Box Office (HBO) began its then unique service to 365 cable subscribers. The idea behind it was to charge an extra fee above the basic cable subscription in exchange for full-length feature FILMS and "live" sport uninterrupted by commercials. The TECHNOLOGY that permitted this was demonstrated in the 1940s when Hollywood tried to stem the popular growth of television by essaying a scrambled signal which could be unscrambled in the form of a film for those who wished to pay.

While it used the cable system, HBO was essentially a different organization. It offered original programs and distributed them nationally by bouncing them off satellites to local cable operators. HBO struggled at first, but then turned its fortunes around. If any event signaled the upturn, it was the Muhammad ALI–Joe Frazier heavyweight title fight which was beamed "live" from Manila, Philippines in 1975 by HBO. Over the following decade, new satellite–cable linked networks proliferated over the states, some offering esoteric services, like the Home Shopping Channel and the Weather Channel.

HBO and other premium operators drew income from subscriptions, while the others generated theirs from advertisers and local cable operators. ESPN was – and is – in the latter group. It specialized in high quality production, knowledgeable commentary/analysis and up-to-the-minute news. While its format has been copied by other cables, ESPN's experiences has generally given it an edge and its has managed to stay ahead of the market.

ESPN's owner Cap Cities/ABC's sale to Disney for $19 billion meant that the sports cable became nested in the Disney group of media and entertainment companies. Disney has extensive interests in sports through its franchises (Anaheim Mighty Ducks, Anaheim Angels), both of which are located near Disneyland. It is also able to promote interest in these franchises with movies like *The Mighty Ducks* (released as *Champions* in Britain), which was directed by Stephen Herek and released in 1992. Thus ESPN was a further valuable addition to Disney's sports portfolio.

As a sports-only television service, ESPN's global span is surpassed only by Rupert MURDOCH's complex of channels, many of which specialize in sports and have interests in Asia with Star Television. ESPN has production facilities in Singapore.

Of related interest

Barnouw, Eric (1990) *Tube of Plenty*, 2nd edn, Oxford University Press.
McChesney, R. (1989) "Media made sport," in Wenner, Lawrence A. (ed.), *Media, Sports and Society*, Sage.
"Steve Risser: The vice-president of programming for ESPN and ESPN2 discusses how sports events are chosen for broadcast and why his networks are moving toward more event ownership" (1997) *Sports Travel* vol 1, no 3.

F

Fan, The

Although its reception by the media was, at best, tepid, Tony Scott's film *The Fan* (1996) was a fascinating account of a baseball fan's obsessive and ultimately tragic devotion to his team. The viewer never doubts that baseball's FANDOM – and those of most other major sports – comprises a substantial element of fixated followers, perhaps stymied by their own lack of ability but no less firm in their commitments. Robert De Niro's fan gets his spiritual nourishment only by following MAJOR LEAGUE BASEBALL: his job as a knife salesman holds no interest for him and he is prepared to sacrifice it in order to pursue his real love.

His beliefs in the primacy of the team over the individual and the higher ideals embodied in America's national game are unshakable, if ultimately destructive. Scott's film is a study in sports monomania: the interest in baseball is so overpowering that there is little time for anything but the most perfunctory of interests in other matters, even those that threaten family and work.

The thriller plot of *The Fan* is not out of the ordinary: it involves the dramatic disillusionment of a fan who realizes that his own values are not shared by a player he reveres. Stunned when he recognizes that the player, far from being committed to baseball, is basically in the game for the money and adulation, his respect turns to malice and he kidnaps the player's child. His experience is like that of a religious zealot confronted by verifiable evidence that God does not exist.

However, the plot is less important than the characters. De Niro's fan organizes his life around baseball: he calls his local radio phone-in show to fulminate when driving to work, he cuts out important sales meetings in order to catch games, he antagonizes his estranged ex-wife by keeping his son too late at the ball game. Wesley Snipe's star player is a much less lovable mercenary than his counterpart character in the film *Jerry Maguire* (released shortly after *The Fan*) whose shameless extrinsic attachment to sport actually endeared him to audiences ("show me the money!"). In their face-to-face encounter, Snipes is surprised at the naivety of his supporter, but never sympathetic: as a professional, he earns his money, however indirectly, from fans and in his view of the world they are a necessary irritation. His attitude shuttles between disdain and barely veiled contempt. The player–fan attachment may be unbreakable, but it is stretched to its limits when one's idealism confronts the other's pragmatism.

Of related interest

Eastman, S.T. and Riggs, K.E. (1994) "Televised sports and ritual: Fan experiences," *Sociology of Sport Journal* vol 11, no 3.
Hornby, Nick (1992) *Fever Pitch*, Gollancz.
The Fan, directed by Tony Scott, 1996.

fandom

The term "fan" is a shortened version of "fanatic," a person filled with excessive and often unreasonable enthusiasm. The Latin root is *fanum*, a temple. Some sports have attracted a following of devoted support that fully justifies "fandom" ("dom" meaning a collectivity, or ways, as in "kingdom" or "officialdom").

Fandoms are not restricted to sports: pop music, soap operas, some TELEVI-SION shows (like *Star Trek* and *The X-Files*) develop followings of devotees, who exhibit occasionally obsessional interest in their chosen genres or ICONS. The behavior of fans has been interpreted variously as escapism, compensation, wish-fulfillment and fantasy. While fandoms were in evidence in the 1940s and perhaps even before the Hollywood star system existed, the advent of global mass media and multimedia have added significantly to the ability of fans to communicate and organize, both of which enhance the group identities of fandoms.

Some sports clubs have generated genuinely global fandoms. Manchester United, of the English soccer Premiership, for example, has fan clubs in virtually every Commonwealth and European country, as well as Japan, South Africa and the USA. It even has a branch on the Indian Ocean island of Mauritius. Its fans are dispersed across England and frequently travel to continental Europe for away games. In the USA, the National Football League's Oakland Raiders used to have its apparel and merchandise sold everywhere in the world and, for a while, was arguably, the most followed American football team. In the 1990s the mantle shifted to Dallas Cowboys, whose lone star motif signifies allegiance all over the world.

In his book *Textual Poachers*, Henry Jenkins (Routledge, 1992) argues that fans are often treated as having immoderate tastes and abnormal likings. This, he argues, justifies elitist and disrespectful beliefs about common life. Fans, in this conception, are "others" unlike "us" in their beliefs and activities; they are also seen as dangerous (as in Tony Scott's movie *The FAN*, in which Robert De Niro plays a knife salesman with a grudge against the baseball star he once idolized) or pathological (as with the British hooligans that gathered weekly at stadiums with the intent of wreaking havoc rather than watching the game). Reinforcing this outsider status is the fact that fans are typically associated with cultural forms that are often denigrated: sports, pop music, television, romance novels and comic books, for example.

In her essay "Fandom as pathology" (in Lisa A. Lewis (ed.) *The Adoring Audience*, Routledge, 1992), Jenson suggests two popular images: the obsessed loner, and the hysterical crowd. The first has come under the media's influence and developed an intense fantasy relationship with a particular figure; while the second is susceptible to the effects of crowds and is easily swept away by the frenzy of large gatherings at stadiums, airports or other venues. Both have destructive tendencies. Each conveys a symptom of social dysfunction: the former expressing the isolation or atomization of mass culture, the latter a vulnerable victim of mass persuasion.

There may be truth concealed in both images, although the majority of fans are less exaggerated: they structure part of their often mundane lives around the more celebrated lives of individuals or teams of individuals. Up to the late 1970s, the celebrities themselves were remote, glamorous figures, and fandom was based on mystery and ignorance. In recent decades, the mass media have demystified the stars: secrets are shared with magazines, close-up interviews are featured on television, biographies spare no detail of personal lives. Videos have made it possible for fans to capture moments of an individual's or a team's life for their own delectation. There is now an entire industry geared to selling proximity to VIDEATED celebrities.

This has occasionally created the illusion of intimacy, with fans gaining such an expertise in the personal lives of subjects that they experience feelings of closeness that are at once real and yet artificially induced. Unwittingly, the unresponsive subject can become the target of attacks or unwelcome attention. Tennis player Steffi GRAF was harassed by a stalker; in 1993, her rival Monica Seles was stabbed in an attempt to prevent her from ousting Graf from the number one spot in women's tennis. The attacker kept a shrine to Graf in his aunt's attic.

Less well known is the case of multiple world snooker champion Stephen Hendry. A female fan became fixated on the Scottish player and wrote him a series of letters which grew progressively abusive. In 1991, she threatened to shoot him, later claiming that her threat afforded her "power over people's lives … to know that you can cause such harm to people by doing something as simple as writing a letter" (quoted in *The Sunday Times*, September 29, 1996). While this is an extreme statement of the sense of empowerment that accompanies fandom, it signals the powerlessness that is in some way negated by following the exploits of others and perhaps displacing one's own perceived inadequacies in the process.

In his *Post-Fandom and the Millenial Blues: The Transformation of Soccer Culture* (Routledge, 1997), Steve Redhead uses the term "post-fandom" in preference to just plain fandom. This term, he believes, shifts the focus away from the obsessive fans and toward the general sports culture which "has become both privatized and marketed (or, for some critics 'Americanized') on the one hand, yet ever more legally 'governed' and regulated on the other." "Post-fans" do not have to leave the home or the bar to see the object of their gaze because TELEVISION and the other elements of the mass and multimedia have made possible a vicarious sharing of experience. The post-fans' intensity of emotion or sense of empowerment is not diminished by the fact that they may rarely leave their television or home computer screen.

Of related interest

Brown, Adam (ed.) (1998) *Fanatics: Power, Identity and Fandom in Football*, Routledge.

Harris, Cheryl and Alexander, Alison (eds.) (1998) *Theorizing Fandom: Fans, Subculture and Identity*, Hampton Press.

Lewis, Lisa A. (ed.) (1992) *The Adoring Audience: Fan Culture and Popular Media*, Routledge.

fanzines

Beginning life in the mid-1970s as inexpensively produced and informally sold chronicles of life as told by ordinary fans, fanzines were originally based on the mimeographed publications that were circulated among UFO (unidentified flying object) spotters and science fiction devotees in the 1940s and which helped bind sci-fi followers into a cult. Sightings of weird crafts and accounts of alien abduction were exchanged through the medium of stenciled papers.

Revived in 1976 amid the efflorescence of punk, fanzines, later abbreviated to just 'zines, became popular with rock fans of all persuasions, many of whom were also sports followers. The original punk fanzine *Sniffin' Glue* became something of a blueprint for soccer 'zine editors. Seemingly thrown together, the farrago of concert reviews, interviews and street news lacked anything resembling editorial direction, less still control. The hotchpotch style – or lack thereof – was perfectly suited to a period when many young people empathized with the iconoclastic Sex Pistols when they sang: "Don't know what I want, but I know how to get it. I wanna destroy!" (from *Anarchy in the UK*, Virgin Music, 1977).

In contrast to glossier mainstream publications in which fans had their say usually via a letters column, the soccer fanzines allowed fans to vent their thoughts and feelings, often comically. Owners, managers and coaches were frequently satirized, players mocked and other clubs' fans derided, sometimes caustically, by the amateur writers. An informal condition of writing for a fanzine was that the contributor (including editor) was not a professional writer or journalist. Like their punk predecessors, the soccer 'zines often used jumbled ransom note typefaces, as if to emphasize their distance from mainstream publications such as *World Soccer* or *Football Monthly*.

In 1972, Cambridge University graduates began producing a humorous publication that parodied serious soccer publications of the time, many of which bore exclamatory titles such as *Shoot!* and *Goal*. The Cambridge alternative was entitled *Foul* and was intended to be a spoof. It bore little resemblance to the original sci-fi cult publications, but indicated that a market could be found among soccer fans. The publication was later taken over by the owners of the satirical magazine *Private Eye*, and folded in 1976 after a libel action.

The aims of the first spate of soccer fanzines appear to have been rather different from those of the Cambridge publication in that, while humor was an element, the main concern was to provide a forum for soccer fans. They expressed the views of working-class fans who might approach querulously the "big issues" of the day, like escalating salaries and transfer fees, admission prices, facilities at stadiums and HOOLIGANISM, which continued to dominate discourses on soccer until the late 1980s.

The fanzines were at pains to establish an alternative agenda. In particular, a Liverpool fanzine called *The End*, which began life in 1981 and eventually achieved a circulation of 4,500 nationwide, challenged mainstream views at every opportunity. *The End* was started by members of a band called The Farm, and prided itself on speaking for working-class fans, often against those who owned and ran the sport. "Yet *The End* despite its originality was a solitary profane voice from the terraces, until what can be considered to be the political watershed of 1985, with regard to fans' active participation in the politics of the game," writes Richard Haynes in his *The Football Imagination* (1995).

After the disasters at Bradford and Brussels, soccer fanzines began to flourish. In contrast to the official versions of events, the fanzines issued fresh perspectives on such issues as the causes of the disasters, the desirability of stadium improvements or the future of sport. The publications were driven by what Haynes calls "a creative spirit which exposed and cast into doubt the workings of the football industry and related issues of policing and media influence."

Of the 1980s fanzines, David Jary *et al.* (1991) identify six common features: (1) they were produced *by* fans *for* fans; (2) they were not affiliated in any official sense to a club and so remained independent (this sometimes led to acrimony: Brighton actually sued a fanzine produced by its own fans); (3) they opposed trends in the sport which led to, among other things, its being run in the interests of business and commerce; (4) fans of smaller clubs were seeking to compensate for the media attention afforded by larger, more fashionable clubs; (5) they sought to combat the misrepresentation of the majority of soccer fans by the mass media – such stereotyping was blamed for the spiral of media amplification that assisted the continuation of hooliganism and led to a degeneration of the spectating experience; and (6) they opposed what many fans regarded as excessive police presence, indiscriminate police action, crowd segregation, the replacement of traditional terracing (where fans stood) by seats and other measures taken to control soccer fans. This final point was given added importance in the wake of the HILLSBOROUGH tragedy of 1989.

Hillsborough followed four years after a comparable soccer stadium disaster at Heysel, Belgium. In the intervening period, an organization known as the Football Supporters Association (FSA) had sprung up. This was intended as a pressure group for articulating the views of grassroots fans. Jary *at al.* believe that the FSA's "fortunes appear in some ways coterminous with the flowering of football fanzine culture" and that "the main proliferation in the numbers of football fanzines in Britain has occurred in the period since 1985."

Haynes believes that much of the effort of fanzines in the late 1980s and 1990s was directed at opposing the "bourgeoisification" of a sport which has strong working class links. One "symbolic" development was the luxury suite. As Haynes notes: "The executive box, designed for corporate entertainment, was the football industry's form of gentrification." This was regarded by most fanzines as soccer's attempt to subordinate its "true" grassroots fans. While many came and went, a few, such as *When Saturday Comes* and *Off the Ball*, secured distribution deals with national outlets and continued to prosper into the late 1990s. They also spawned anthologies and were instrumental in instigating a series of books authored by fans. Among these were *The Red Army Years* (Hodder Headline, 1998) and *If the Reds Should Play in Rome or Mandalay* (Juma, 1998) both written by followers of Manchester United. Related to these were other fanzine-influenced accounts either by or about fans, all published by mainstream publishing houses. These included John King's novel *The Football Factory* (Cape, 1996) and *Awaydays* (Cape, 1998) by Kevin Sampson, one of the founders of *The End*. Former fanzine writer Nick Hornby's FEVER PITCH (Gollancz, 1992) became one of the publishing successes of the 1990s.

Of related interest

Haynes, Richard (1995) *The Football Imagination*, Arena.

Jary, David, Horne, John and Bucke, Tom (1991) "Football fanzines and football culture: A case of successful 'cultural contestation'," *Sociological Review* vol 39, no 3.

Redhead, Steve (1997) *Post-Fandom and the Millennial Blues: The Transformation of Soccer Culture*, Routledge.

Fashanu, Justin

b. 1961, England; d. 1998

Fashanu was an acknowledged GAY soccer player, whose life ended as a fugitive from American justice following allegations of sexual assault arising from an incident with a teenage boy in Maryland. Fashanu was found hanged in a garage, a verdict of suicide being recorded. His picaresque sports career included a brief but illustrious spell as one of Britain's most valuable soccer players, a conversion to Christianity, a scandalous outing followed by a near-ostracism, and several attempts to revive his career in the USA, Canada and New Zealand.

The son of a Nigerian lawyer, Fashanu was abandoned as a child and raised, with his younger brother John (who also became a soccer pro), by foster parents, who were white. A decent heavyweight amateur boxer, he considered turning professional but opted for soccer instead. After playing for the Norwich City club from 1978–80, he moved to Nottingham Forest for the then extravagant transfer fee of £1 million. He was the leading light of a small number of black players who were breaking through to the highest levels of British soccer.

Fashanu's conflicts with his manager, Brian Clough, were legion. In his autobiography, the homophobic Clough recalled with some arrogance how he responded to rumors of Fashanu's sexuality. He asked the player where he would go if he wanted a loaf, to which Fashanu answered, "baker's." Clough barked: "So why do you keep going to that bloody poof's club?"

Clough's sentiments were probably typical of the aggressively macho sports culture of the 1970s. Indeed, this situation remains: no soccer players after Fashanu proclaimed their homosexuality. Fashanu's symbolic expulsion from the macho ranks of soccer served as a warning. Fashanu himself struggled for ten years after he left Forest before COMING OUT. In the interim, gossip and innuendo were rife and his career went into freefall.

Turning to religion, he became involved in Charismatic and Pentecostal assemblies, believing that some sort of divine intervention would prove his salvation. In fact, the church deepened his sense of inner conflict, as homosexuality was strictly proscribed. His sojourns to the United States and Canada amounted to little and he returned to England in 1989, still only 28. Presumably believing that the more enlightened England of the 1990s would prove a more accommodating environment, he chose to volunteer the truth of his sexual preferences and start afresh. The decision prompted his brother John, by then a celebrated player with Wimbledon, to repudiate him. He played for several lesser clubs, including the Scottish team Heart of Midlothian, of Edinburgh, from which he was dismissed in 1993 for "conduct unbecoming a professional." The incident that precipitated this was bizarre: Fashanu tried to sell stories of alleged sexual encounters with Conservative Party politicians to the tabloids.

After moving to the United States where his reputation was not so great, he worked with several youth projects in Atlanta, then with the Atlanta Ruckus soccer club and, finally, the Maryland Mania, for which he worked as a coach. It was during his employment in Maryland that he became involved in a purported offense that preceded his suicide. A 17-year-old male alleged that he had been to Fashanu's house in Ellicot City, with five others. They had all consumed alcohol and DRUGS. The youth claimed that he slept on the sofa and awoke the following morning to find Fashanu making forcible sexual contact. Fashanu voluntarily gave himself up for questioning about the incident (there were two specific allegations).

Of related interest

Cashmore, Ellis (1999) "Why sport isn't glad to be gay," *Sunday Tribune* (Ireland) vol 20, no 6 (February 7).

Pronger, Brian (1990) *The Arena of Masculinity: Sports, Homosexuality and the Meaning of Sex*, St. Martins Press.

Fever Pitch

"One thing I know for sure about being a fan is this: it is not a vicarious pleasure, despite all appearances to the contrary, and those who say that they would rather do than watch are missing the point." The disclosure is from Nick Hornby's *Fever Pitch*, a diary-style account of twenty-four years of obsessive FANDOM, which was first published in 1992 and later became the basis of a television movie and a play. The book itself stands as one of the best-selling sports books ever, vying with A.J. Liebling's *THE SWEET SCIENCE* and John Feinstein's *A SEASON ON THE BRINK*.

Hornby's semi-autobiographical book charts the passage into adulthood of a fan of Arsenal, the North London soccer club. As a child, the first-person author is possessed of the kind of fanaticism that typically dissolves in maturity. Not for Hornby: the ardor, fervor and passion stay with him, often overwhelming more practical concerns. "The point" referred to in the above quotation is that: "Football is a context in which watching *becomes* doing ... I am a part of the club, just as the club is a part of me."

The players are "our representatives," as Hornby puts it. The "organic connection" he feels with Arsenal is both stronger and more durable than anything players can ever feel. His is a "sweeter appreciation" of what it means to be an integral part of a football club. This perception lies at the heart of the American film *THE FAN*, in which the title character is unhinged by the professional indifference of a high-paid baseball player at "his" club and attempts to kill him.

Yet, Hornby is reflective enough to acknowledge that "the club exploits me, disregards my views, and treats me shoddily on occasions." He observes the manner in which British soccer moved from its nadir in the 1980s when HOOLIGANISM was rife and stadium disasters threatened the entire sport. Yet, its efforts to rehabilitate itself often came at the expense of genuine fans whose wishes were subordinated to those of TELEVISION.

Hornby knows this, and deconstructs this apparent contradiction. "*For alarmingly large chunks of an average day, I am a moron*," he emphasizes. "There is no analysis, or self-awareness, or mental rigour going on at all, because obsessives are denied any kind of perspective on their own passion." It is Hornby's ability to stand outside his own position, coupled with his obsessive one-eyedness that makes his work a potent mixture of personal reminiscences and sly observations on the changing character of contemporary sports. The book is, as the author claims, "about the consumption of football, rather than football itself."

Hornby's fan's childhood is broken up by a move from inner London to the suburbs. He moans at stories of urban deprivation: for him, being removed from his favorite club is a case of *sub*urban deprivation. Coming from a working-class background, he takes some pride in retaining his inner city accent and mannerisms, even while his more upwardly mobile sister begins to speak "like the Duchess of Devonshire."

Having his first serious relationship with a woman and going to a university both promise to supplant his fixation with Arsenal. But, even as he approaches 20, he remains as "stupidly optimistic for the club and as hungry to see a game" as he had been years before "when my obsession had been at fever pitch." Soccer gives him all his main reference points: "Football *was* life, and I am not speaking metaphorically."

The observations on the soccer violence that surfaced habitually in Europe through the 1970s and 1980s are free of moral evaluation. He describes how it was possible to be drawn into the hooligan body without making any conscious decision. At the height of hooliganism, analysts bemoaned the mob psychology and the contagion effect of disorders at soccer stadiums. Yet Hornby writes: "Those who mumble about the loss of identity football fans must endure miss the point: this loss of identity can be a paradoxically enriching process. Who wants to be stuck with who they are the whole time?" This kind of perception also informed the movie *I.D.*, in which an undercover police officer becomes immersed in a hooligan gang and finds what he believes to be his true self among the gang; compared to the excitement he finds with the hooligans, his former life as a police officer and family man seem dull, tedious and leaden.

With hooliganism a stable feature of British soccer in the 1970s, Hornby recalls how traveling to away games was something of a military exercise. "Football Specials" were dilapidated trains, the corridors of which were patrolled by police with guard dogs. The journeys usually took place in darkness as most of the light bulbs on the trains had been smashed by vandals. Some of the fans would signal their affiliations by dressing in uniforms, a stained white butcher's coat being popular apparel.

Hornby recounts the bizarre SUPERSTITIONS held dearly by fans. Bizarre liturgies, as he calls them, are observed meticulously until the overwhelming evidence of Arsenal's poor results convinces them that they do not work. He also recollects the grim aftermath of the HILLSBOROUGH disaster and the incursions of RACISM directed by fans at black players.

One of the abiding themes of *Fever Pitch* is that of masculinity: Hornby writes about male feelings in a way that both sexes can identify. As a fatherless boy, Hornby self-reflects that his fan's obsession with Arsenal was something to do with the fact that "it gave me a quick way to fill a previously empty trolley in the Masculinity Supermarket." He believes that to admit being a soccer fan to a "thinking woman" is to invite a sobering glimpse of the female conception of the male.

It is probable that much of the success of the book derived from Hornby's ability to write about the MASCULINITIES/FEMININITIES distinction in a way that male sports fans could recognize without feeling abandoned as pathetic creatures. At the same time, the book may have appealed to women, whose disgust at men's sports fixations would have been confirmed. Yet there was also the raw material for understanding such fixations for those who wanted to find it.

If there is a question that lurks in Hornby's book, it is: what does a young man do when he finds that the sports fanaticism he thought would disappear with the onset of maturity stubbornly remains? Yesterday's "Golden Age" of youth meets its nemesis, not to say apocalypse in the 1990s' crassly commercialized, commodified and merchandised version of soccer. Yet Hornby can despise this unwelcome development and still retain his fixation with the club that *belongs* to him. Without this widely-felt sense of belonging, Hornby believes "football would fail as a business." There are those who doubt his conclusions, pointing to the decreasing relevance of attending fans who travel the length and breadth of the country and the increasing relevance of the armchair fans who simply pay their cable/satellite television subscriptions.

The peculiar status of *Fever Pitch* as a kind of autobiography-cum-diary that feels like fiction enabled Hornby's publishers to promote his second book, *High Fidelity* (Gollancz, 1995) as his first novel. It was also about an obsessive, this time a record store owner whose world revolved around music. Hornby's third book *About a Boy* continued his attempt to explore young men who are the products of dysfunctional families and have interests that make it hard for them to relate to, less still understand, women.

Of related interest

Hornby, Nick (1992) *Fever Pitch*, Indigo; television film *Fever Pitch* directed by
    David Evans, 1996.
Hornby, Nick (1998) *About a Boy*, Gollancz.

Field of Dreams

Baseball has an inclusive and democratic quality that separates it from all other
sports. It has a curiously positive and uplifting effect on Americans, not least on
writers and film directors. The movie *Field of Dreams* (1989) tells of an Iowa
farmer tormented by a discordant relationship with his dead father, itself a
microcosm of the generational conflict that affected the Western world in the
1960s. Baseball is his form of redemption, and he sacrifices almost everything in
the pursuit of it.

Written and directed by Phil Alden Robinson from W.P. Kinsella's novel
Shoeless Joe Jackson Comes to Iowa, *Field of Dreams* was a commercially successful
film, featuring Kevin Costner as 36-year-old Ray Kinsella who hears a Voice
whispering to him: "If you build it, he will come." No one else hears the voice,
but Kinsella believes he must raze an acre of cornfield to make a baseball field. It
is the kind of irrational, spontaneous action his father studiously avoided, and
Kinsella hated his father for it. In his rebellious youth, he argued with his father
and refused even to play a game of catch with him. "The sonofabitch died before
I had time to apologize," he reflects in his maturity. Building the baseball field is
his "penance."

The field built, Kinsella waits and, in time, the ghost of Shoeless Joe Jackson
(played by Ray Liotta) appears, as do those of the seven other Chicago White Sox
players who were involved in the notorious 1919 World Series, itself the subject of
another movie *EIGHT MEN OUT*. The mysterious voice returns, instructing
Kinsella to "ease his pain," and somehow he interprets this to mean that he must
visit Terence Mann (played by James Earl Jones), an African American Pulitzer
Prize-winner and former 1960s idealist, who is wrenched from oblivion in his
Boston apartment to join Kinsella in his quest for deliverance. In the novel,
Kinsella sets off for New Hampshire with a plan to kidnap J.D. Salinger and take
him to a baseball game.

The Salinger-type Mann , we are told, coined the expression "Make love, not
war," and has exiled himself, silenced himself as a public persona and traded
creative writing for writing computer programs. A third message, "Go the
distance," motivates Kinsella and Mann to travel to Minnesota where they find
the home of Archibald "Moonlight" Graham, a little-known baseball player of
the early 1920s who became a doctor and died in 1972. Graham appears to
Kinsella, first as an old man (Burt Lancaster), then as an aspiring youth filled
with baseball ambitions.

Returning to Iowa, Kinsella and Mann find foreclosure looming. His project
has all but bankrupted his farm and he is under pressure to sell. His hard-nosed
brother-in-law questions his sanity as Kinsella, his family and Mann sit and

watch the players, swathed in legend: he cannot see them. All but one leave the field and Kinsella recognizes his father as a young man, a baseball player who never made it out of the minor leagues.

In the film, the generation of the 19-teens jousts with that of the 1980s for proprietorship of the American dream. Kinsella tries to recreate a bygone America. His obsession is less mania, more nostalgia, and in many respects expresses something obdurately retro in the American psyche: evidence of this is to be found all over the States, but no more so than in Celebration, Disney's faux-Rockwell recreation of small-town USA at the turn of the century. Despite his reckless idealism, commercial possibilities like this are not lost on Kinsella and he hits on the idea of opening his baseball field to the public. Mann assures him that people will pay $20 admission without blinking. "It'll be as if they'd been dipped in magic waters," says Mann. "The one constant in all these years is baseball ... it reminds them of all that was once good and can be good again. People will come." Of course, they do – in their droves.

Sentiment and fantasy apart, the film has much to say about the genuine meaning of baseball in American history and culture. The honesty and integrity of the sport, the meritocracy it promotes, the family values it embodies, the bonding it encourages, the glory it allows and the traditions with which it links yesterday to today are all features of a sport that remains a model for American society. By resurrecting the suspended Sox players and rehabilitating them, the story erases any remaining doubts about the sport. Kinsella confides to Mann how he hurt his father, whose hero was Joe Jackson. "I told him I could never respect a man whose hero was a criminal." Mann reminds him that "Jackson wasn't a criminal," and Kinsella confirms that he knew that all along. Perhaps the film's success at the American box office – it took $60million in 1989, the year of its release – was attributable to its restoration of baseball as a pillar of stability in America's otherwise shaky cultural architecture.

Of related interest

Altherr, T. and Fong, B. (1993) "The magic cocktail: the enduring appeal of *Field of Dreams*," *Aethlon: The Journal of Sport Literature*, vol 11, no 1.
Field of Dreams, directed by Phil Alden Robinson, 1989.
Joffe, L.S. (1992) "Praise baseball: American religious metaphors in Shoeless Joe and *Field of Dreams*," *Aethlon: The Journal of Sport Literature*, vol 9, no 2.

FIFA

Origins

Created in 1904 with seven member nations, FIFA (Fédération Internationale de Football Associations) is the international governing body of soccer, the most widely watched and played game in the world, and the organizer of the largest global sports tournament, the World Cup, which takes place every four years. In many ways, its development follows that of sport itself. At the start of the century it was primitive in its organization, loose in its structure and recognized in only a few countries. By the time of its championships in 1998, FIFA had affiliations in all six continents (over 170 member states and growing) and could legitimately claim to be the largest (in terms of span and financial turnover) sports organization in the world.

At the time of FIFA's formation, soccer as a sport had gained a following in several countries, largely because of British settlers. Since the 1850s, a number of clubs, mostly in southern England, specialized in the sport we now recognize as soccer – as opposed to rugby, with which it was mixed in some areas. The formal distinction between the two sports came in 1863 with the creation of the Rugby Football Union and the Football Association (FA), the latter being the governing federation for English soccer. One of the FA's most pressing tasks was to codify a set of rules that would be commonly recognized.

By the turn of the century there was a virtual soccer diaspora, with the sport being scattered across the world. It became *Fußball* in Germany, *fútbol* in Spanish, *voetbal* in Holland and similar sounding names in a variety of other places. Like the sorceror's apprentice, the "natives" were good learners and virtually every country the English taught to play, in time, bettered them. Nowhere was this more so than Brazil, where the game was known as *Futebol*. Charles Miller was the Brazilian-born son of English parents responsible for introducing the sport to São Paulo, where he organized a soccer section of a local athletics club. By 1901 a regional league was up and running. The game was played mostly by white European colonialists up to the 1920s, when enthusiasm among the working class caused a shift in the composition of league teams. By the 1950s, the Brazilian national team had assumed a position of world leadership, a position it surrendered only occasionally over the next half-century.

FIFA's original membership had no South American affiliates, even though Argentina and Uruguay as well as Brazil were playing soccer at an organized level, while three of FIFA's members – France, Spain and Sweden – had no organized leagues at all. The other members, Belgium, Denmark, Holland and Switzerland, were hardly as advanced as England, although the parent nation expressed no interest in the fledgling organization. England's imperious attitude was that it gave birth to the sport and had no need to align itself with lesser nations. This quickly changed when England spotted the potential of international competition, which it believed it would dominate as completely as it had its own empire.

At the fourth modern Olympic games in 1908, the IOC invited only European teams to its tournament, which was won, to the satisfaction of the FA, by England. FIFA's first president, Jules Rimet and Henri Delauney, general secretary of the French football association, were struck by the Olympic concept of bringing representative teams together over a short period to compete in a *tornoi* – a shorter version of the kinds of competition that many nations spread over a full season (typically lasting eight months). As most of the European soccer leagues professionalized, so their eligibility for the amateur Olympics was nullified, making Rimet's idea more of a necessity than a choice.

By 1930, FIFA was in a position to be able to mount a serious attempt at a global competition, attracting thirteen nations to Uruguay for the first World Cup championship, which was duly won by the hosts. By the 1998 World Cup, staged in France, there were 112 entries. England, despite its pretensions to supremacy, did not enter the Uruguay championship, having withdrawn its membership of FIFA first in 1920, after a dispute over a game against Germany, a First World War enemy, and again in 1928, after rejoining briefly in 1924. England did not win a World Cup championship until 1966.

The first World Cup was, of course, an extremely different affair to the type of colossal production we witness today – and it *is* witnessed by virtually every nation, via television. Yet, the historical conditions that were eventually to lead to the multimedia extravaganza of the 1990s were established. In 1923, Vladimir Zworykin patented his "iconoscope," a device in which he activated photoelectric cells in a cathode ray tube; but domestic television (which is what the device became) was still more than twenty years away. Still, mass communications was in its ascendancy thanks to technology made necessity by the First World War effort. Wireless transmissions through radio waves were used during 1914–18 and this stimulated both technical improvements and the mass production of components. Amateur enthusiasts began building their own "radio sets," as they were called. The general interest in radio was not lost on the British government nor on North American commercial companies. By the mid-1920s, a network of radio broadcasting stretched over Britain, Europe and some parts of the United States, providing the matrix of what we now call the mass media. A fast national and, later, international system of communications in which entire populations could be embraced by a single voice, or sound, was something entirely new. The new medium was anonymous and remote, yet at the same time personal and near. It was perfect for relaying sports events.

One of FIFA's premises when it staged the first World Cup was that there was sufficient interest to sustain a one-sport competition over a period of weeks. The indications were that several mainstream sports had undergone changes in the 1920s, developing an audience that was – and again the word arises – mass. The idea of people either congregating together or sharing an experience because of sports was not new, but it certainly took on added dimensions in the 1920s. A record-setting 120,000 people huddled into New York's Yankee Stadium in 1926 to watch the Gene Tunney–Jack Dempsey fight. Three years before in London, 200,000 fans had packed into Wembley Stadium for the FA Cup Final.

Interest in sports had grown steadily since the 1890s, so much so that many soccer and baseball clubs were able to professionalize and charge admissions. But the appeal of major events in the 1920s was an indication that the industrial working class had taken sports to heart in a huge way and was prepared to part with hard-earned cash, again in a huge way. Not since the ancient Roman tournaments, when 80,000 or more would wait feverishly for the kill in the Coliseum, had sports – in the broadest sense of the term – attracted such crowds on a regular basis.

The global game

100,000 people attended the final World Cup game between Uruguay and Argentina, two countries which share a border in South America. As the game was held in Montevideo, it attracted traveling Argentinean fans. This alerted

FIFA to a new element that was entering sports: nationalism. The idea of having teams representing an entire nation was not new, but, even in Olympics, its full value had not been exploited to the full. Soccer was the first sport to be able to do this, thanks principally to its established internationally federated structure and its willingness to export its wares. (This is still the case, of course: desperate to stake a presence in the hugely lucrative US market, FIFA agreed to let the States host the 1994 World Cup only on the explicit condition that a national league was to follow. The result was MAJOR LEAGUE SOCCER.)

The complementarity of an embryonic mass media and mass spectatorship meant that the World Cup competitions could be staged at four-yearly intervals *pace* the Olympics. And, in a manner similar to the early English colonizers, FIFA proceeded to cast its net ever more widely, trawling in Asian and African as well as South and North American nations. Television performed the same function for soccer as it did for most other major sports, except that in soccer's case it did so on a global scale.

Britain's BBC television network sensed that the World Cup was ripe for international consumption in 1966, the year in which the tournament was staged in England. BBC beamed many of the games "live" quite literally to the world. This was a case of soccer showcasing its most prestigious event on a global scale, and in this sense the event functioned as a massive advertisement. Previously, games had been listened to via radio or watched days after they had occurred. The Telstar telecommunications satellite, which went into orbit in 1962 and made it possible to bounce transmissions around the world, changed all that.

BBC introduced viewers to arguably its most ingenious and significant piece of technology as far as sports are concerned: the instant replay. What the naked eye missed, the camera caught, then replayed, then slowed down, then froze, then showed over and over again. In the final game, an incident seemed to have been sent gift wrapped when England scored a controversial goal, which the entire German team (and many others beside) disputed. Television was able to capture the moment and show it not only in the immediate aftermath, but for decades after. It signaled the beginning of a long and prosperous relationship between FIFA and television. Some idea of soccer's universal appeal can be gained from the fact that 500 million television viewers worldwide watched the European Champions' League Final between Borussia Dortmund and Juventus in May 1997 (compared to 56m Americans who watched the record-breaking coming-out episode of *Ellen* a month before).

While the globalizing medium of television helped FIFA penetrate markets all of the world, it met with resistance in the USA. The obvious reason for this is that the United States is well served with mainstream sports and has little need for another. The USA also tends to opt for sports played only on a limited scale elsewhere: American football, baseball and basketball are unassailably American and international competition is relatively meaningless. But, there is also the particular problem soccer presents for television, which is driven by advertising revenue in the USA. Soccer is a flowing game divided into two 45-minute halves with no time-outs or structured stoppages. The failed North American Soccer League of the late 1960s–1970s experimented with artificial delays in play to accommodate television commercials, but the result was unsatisfactory.

In countries where soccer is played, commercial television companies have to content themselves with commercials before and after the action and at half-time.

The unqualified success of FIFA's women's 1999 World Cup in the USA prompted the organization's president Sepp Blatter to predict that "the future of football is female." Compared to the desultory MLS, women's soccer in the USA was spectacularly successful, suggesting that perhaps, if an integration of the men's and women's sport happens anywhere, it will be in the States.

Virtually everywhere else, FIFA has managed to find a formula that works with local television. Its supple federated structure has enabled it to work with entire federations, not only of countries but of whole continents. For example, the Union des Associans Européenes de Football (UEFA) was formed in 1956 to oversee a European-wide club competition and became affiliated to FIFA. In the following year, the Confédération Africaine de Football was set up to organize a competition between African nations. More recently, FIFA has supported the Japanese J-League in advance of Japan's and South Korea's initiative in staging a World Cup championship.

Compared to the other global sports federation, the IOC, it has led a trouble-free existence, experiencing few of the boycotts, deaths or explosions that have marred Olympic games. The exception was in 1966, when sixteen African nations withdrew from World Cup.

Of related interest

Dauncey, Hugh and Hare, Geoff (1999) *France and the 1998 World Cup: The National Impact of a World Sporting Event*, Frank Cass.
Glanville, Brian (1997) *The Story of the World Cup*, Faber.
Sugden, John and Tomlinson, Alan (1998) *Fifa and the Contest for World Football: Who Rules the People's Game?*, Polity Press.

films

Of all the art forms, film has arguably been the most vivid and enriching interpretive medium of sport. Films that have used sports themes as their plot dynamic have become a virtual genre in themselves. The drama of sports action has a naturalism well suited to film: like movies themselves, sports have the same kind of narrative structure, of course, they usually end with a climactic triumph or disaster. It is hardly an accident that so many sports movies have been internationally lauded. *ROCKY* and *CHARIOTS OF FIRE* won Academy Awards for Best Picture in 1976 and 1981 respectively.

We can identify three sub-genres of sports films: dramatic/biographical, comedy/fantasy, and documentary. These are discussed in turn below.

Dramatic/biographical

John G. Avildsen's *Rocky* (1976) and Hugh Hudson's *Chariots of Fire* (1981) were both biographical dramas, the first fictional, the second based on real characters. Films inspired by real lives have been the most enduringly popular. The whole *Rocky* series was an exaggerated compilation of every fighter who battered his way to a world title and the riches it entailed. The "pride goeth before a fall" apothegm runs through all four films in the series; and, while the film is hardly typical of sports movies, it embodies themes that recur throughout the sub-genre. It tells of endurance, of impossible odds and of improbable success. (Stallone reprised the role, though in a different guise, in 1986, when he played a competitive arm-wrestler in Menaghem Golan's virtually ignored *Over the Top*.)

In many respects the antithesis of *Rocky*, another boxing film, RAGING BULL , manages to contain the same themes albeit in a completely different structure. The monochrome story of former world middleweight champion Jake LaMotta was an often harrowing experience, lacking all the sentimentality that made the *Rocky* movies (or at least the first two) so appealing. Like all sports movies, both films included sports action, *Rocky* opting for rather clownish knockabouts, *Raging Bull* attempting a visceral hyper-realism by taking the camera in the ring and showing how a boxer might see his opponent.

Boxing has been a fertile terrain for film-makers, who have often probed into the dirtier aspects of the fight game: *Kid Galahad*, directed by Michael Curtiz and released in 1937, did exactly this. Robert Wise's *The Set -Up* (1948) was a noirish look at an aging boxer's last fight; Robert Ryan, who had boxed at college, played the lead. Mark Robson's 1949 film *Champion* changed Kirk Douglas' career: he played a ruthless fighter, Midge Kelly, who has a DISABLED brother.

In the late 1950s and early 1960s, SOMEBODY UP THERE LIKES ME (1956), *The Harder They Fall* (1956) and *Requiem for a Heavyweight* (*Blood Money* in Britain, 1962) showed how effectively boxing could work as a background for larger human drama. John Huston's *Fat City* (1972) was a piercingly miserable exploration of the lives of two losers who have both spent too much time inside rat-infested gyms. Mixing sporting, political and romantic themes, Jim Sheridan's *The Boxer* (1998) cast Daniel Day Lewis as an ex-IRA prisoner trying to resurrect a career as a pro middleweight amid the conflict of Northern Ireland.

Chariots of Fire apart, track and field athletics have not captured the interest of too many directors. Tony Richardson's film adaptation of Alan Sillitoe's short story *The Loneliness of the Long Distance Runner* (1962) used running as a simile for a young British working class offender's gutsy clamber out of hopelessness. Similarly, Michael Mann's *The Jericho Mile* (1979), also set in a prison context, offered the concept of track success as redemption.

In *Personal Best* (1982), director Robert Towne cast Mariel Hemingway and Patrice Donnelly as two pentathletes who become involved in a lesbian relationship in the run-up to the Olympics. A more straightforward account was D.S. Everett's *Running Brave* (1983), which was a biopic of Olympic middle-distance runner Billy Mills, who left a Sioux reservation on a University of Kansas athletics scholarship only to run into all manner of racial hatred. Mill's moment of glory came in the 10,000 meters final of the 1964 Olympics.

In the 1980s and 1990s, baseball became a source for several historical and biographical dramas. Screen biographies of real baseball stars, Babe Ruth (Arthur Hiller's *The Babe*, 1991), Ty Cobb (Ron Shelton's *Cobb*, 1994) and fictional ones, like *Bull Durham* (also directed by Shelton, 1988) were commercial successes, as was the earlier adaptation of Bernard Malamud's story *The Natural* (1984) in which director Barry Levinson turned a baseball bat into an Excalibur-type weapon.

John Sayle's astringent re-telling of the scandalous 1919 World Series, *Eight Men Out* (1988) highlights the exploitative nature of the sport in the early years of MAJOR LEAGUE BASEBALL. The poorly paid and virtually indentured Chicago White Sox players are depicted as fodder for greedy gamblers looking to make a killing by betting on the Cincinnati Reds. Sayles makes the corruption of something as sacred as baseball comprehensible, indeed logical. His film contrasts markedly with early innocent baseball films, like Harmon Jones's *The Pride of St Louis* (1952), which tells the story of hillbilly pitcher Dizzy Dean of the St. Louis Cardinals.

Roy Campanella's drama *Quiet Victory: The Charlie Wedemeyer Story* (1988) was about the one-time football star who developed muscular dystrophy in 1977 when aged 30 and went on to become a victorious high school coach – and was still teaching in 1988, although unable to speak and using a wheelchair. The film closely resembled the 1973 John Hancock film *Bang the Drum Slowly*, in which a baseball player (played by Robert De Niro) is dying from Hodgkins Disease. Perhaps the most memorable film of this kind is Sam Woods's *The Pride of the Yankees* (1942) which featured Gary Cooper as Lou Gehrig, who was stricken with MS.

Steven Kampmann and Will Aldiss combined to direct *Stealing Home* (1988), which follows a washed-up baseball player going home to recover the ashes of a childhood sweetheart who has committed suicide. *THE FAN* (1996) featured Robert De Niro as a knife salesman turning on a baseball star who seems to have sacrificed sports values for money. Tony Scott's film was a study in how contemporary sports are able to destroy the very things they build, like devotion, loyalty and hero worship.

Football has a less distinguished cinematic tradition than baseball, though Ted Kotcheff's *NORTH DALLAS FORTY* (1979) is arguably one of the boldest attempts to show the side of American football rarely disclosed: players pumped with pain-killing and recreational drugs, often carrying serious injuries onto the field of play. Taylor Hackford's *Against All Odds* (1984) was an updated remake of the film noir classic *Out of the Past*, in which an injured pro at a loose end agrees to help a disreputable friend find a missing young woman who has fled to Mexico. But complications arise when the athlete becomes involved with his quarry. Jane Greer played the female in the original; in this remake, she played her mother. Less celebrated was Michael Chapman's *All the Right Moves* (1983), featuring a young Tom Cruise as a football player wannabe.

Soccer has been at the nucleus of a few, usually nondescript films, the exception being Bill Forsyth's *Gregory's Girl* (1980) a low-budget affair set in Scotland, organized around a young man's pursuit of a young woman who is more proficient at soccer than he. Soccer's filmic nadir was plumbed in 1981 by John Huston's embarrassing *Escape to Victory*, in which Michael Caine and a motley crew of actors and soccer players teamed up in a Second World War prisoner of war camp. Sylvester Stallone was never less plausible than when he donned the goalkeeper's shirt.

While not exactly a sport-themed film, Wim Wender's acclaimed *The Goalkeeper's Fear of the Penalty* (*Die Angst des Tormanns beim Elfmeter*, 1971) at least lent some respectability to soccer dramas: the fleeing murderer at the story's heart is a German goalie. Neil Leifer's *Yesterday's Hero* (1979) and Maria Giese's *When Saturday Comes* (1995) were two British attempts to dramatize the private lives of professional soccer players. In *I.D.* (1994), director Philip Davis turned his camera away from the players and to the fans, tracking the progress of an undercover police officer who has assumed the guise of a hooligan.

Rugby league football is the central metaphor in Lindsay Anderson's THIS SPORTING LIFE (1963), set in the North of England. Richard Harris' mud-spattered struggle on the rugby field parallels the rest of his life and, in many senses, that of the northern working class in the 1960s: the hero (as he describes himself) embraces sterile aspirations to self-fulfillment in a culture that is halfway to affluence, half-stuck in postwar depression. Perhaps one of the most neglected and underrated football dramas is Bruce Beresford's *The Club* (1980), which tells of the travails of an Australian Rules club owner who buys a star player only to find his man has undergone a conversion and despises the competitive machismo of contemporary sports.

Dynastic imbroglios lie at the heart of the pair of "Fast Eddie" pool movies, THE HUSTLER/THE COLOR OF MONEY, the first directed by Robert Rossen and released in 1961, its sequel directed by Martin Scorsese and released twenty-five years later in 1986. In both, the elder sports master is challenged by a younger contender to his position. Paul Newman played "Fast Eddie" Felson in both movies and matures from challenger to challenged. The two films offer a scope on the changes in pool as it moves from the dark and dingy poolhalls of the 1960s to the garish Atlantic City ballrooms of the 1980s. A similar motif appeared in Norman Jewison's *The Cincinnati Kid* (1965), in which Steve McQueen played a young hot-shot poker player in the 1930s, trying to depose the king of the game, "The Man," played by Edward G. Robinson.

Cycling has served at least two films quite well. Peter Yates' celebrated *Breaking Away* (1979) told of class antagonisms in small-town America, and John Badham's *American Flyers* (1985) featured two brothers in a fraternal rivalry.

Given the life and death element of motor sports, it is hardly surprising that they have provided the background to several dramas, though few of them have been well-received. *Le Mans* (1971), directed by Lee H. Katzin, was little more than an underpowered vehicle for car enthusiast Steve McQueen to show how adept he was at maneuvering his way around the famed circuit. Tony Scott's *Days of Thunder* (1990) was another star vehicle, this time with Tom Cruise taking the wheel of a stock car. Jonathan Kaplan's *Heart Like a Wheel* (1983) centers on drag racing and, unusually, follows the fortunes of a woman driver trying to break into the male-dominated race circuit. James Goldstone's 1969 film *Winning* featured Paul Newman racing at the Indianapolis 500.

Michael Ritchie's *Downhill Racer* (1969) is a win-at-all costs skiing movie, Robert Redford being the ambitious maverick racer who spurns the advice of his coach, Gene Hackman. The snow and ice landscapes have made good locations for ski movies, though few have gained much recognition. Larry Peerce's *The Other Side of the Mountain* (*A Window in the Sky*, 1975) focuses on the plight of a young skier who is paralyzed on the eve of her selection for the US Olympic team. *The Ski Bum* (1971) is director Bruce Clark's rendering of Romain Gary's novel, though this is only tenuously connected to competitive skiing.

The horse racing track has been the site for a number of films. Outstanding among these is Stephen Frear's *The Grifters* (1979), which revolves around a racetrack scam. Similarly, Stanley Kubrick's *The Killing* (1956) focuses on a heist at a racetrack. In complete contrast, *Champions* (1983), directed by John Irwin, examined real-life jockey Bob Champion's successful fight against cancer.

From today's vantage point, it is difficult to know whether to cover the 1970s wave of martial arts films in this sub-genre or the next: certainly, the original intention seems to have been that they were serious dramas, but on reflection, they seem agreeably comical. Hong Kong studios churned out literally hundreds of kung fu movies, a few of which did good box-office business in the United States and Britain. Lo Wei's *The Big Boss* (1971) and *Fist of Fury* (1972), for example, were both successful, and paved the way for their star Bruce Lee to direct his own films, the most notable of which was *The Way of the Dragon* (1973). Lee went to the USA to make Robert Clouse's *Enter the Dragon* (1973). A biopic, *Dragon: The Bruce Lee Story*, directed by Rob Cohen, was released in 1993.

For a short period in the late 1960s and early 1970s, the television-driven sport of roller derby rose in popularity. It inspired an undistinguished film entitled *Kansas City Bomber* (1972), directed by Jerrod Freedman and starring Raquel Welch as the bomber herself. The film's importance lies not so much in its own qualities as in its influence on another, more acclaimed work that seemed to portend the future of professional sports. Norman Jewison's *Rollerball* (1975) suggested that sports of the future would lose their symbolic qualities and be won or lost as ancient contests once were: by death. Players competed in a lethal form of roller derby, the losers being carried off in body bags.

Rollerball was not the only speculative fiction film that depicted sports as kill-or-be-killed competitions: Paul Bartel's *Death Race 2000* (1975) and *Deathsport* (1978), directed by Henry Suso and Allan Arkush, both followed similar lines. Paul Michael Glazer's *The Running Man* (1985), with Arnold Schwarzenegger playing prey to predators with names like Buzzsaw and Fireball, was probably the inspiration behind television's AMERICAN GLADIATORS (in Britain, *Gladiators*), although in the film the gladiators killed the contestants rather than beat them with foam-padded clubs. Glazer also directed *The Cutting Edge*, a 1992 ice skating melodrama in which an injury-retired hockey star teams up with a skater and heads for Olympic glory.

Comedy/fantasy

Film-makers have found ready-made material in the comedy and fantasy that are essential to the appeal of sports. The most seminal sports fantasy is *Here Comes Mr Jordan* (1941), directed by Alexander Hall and featuring Robert Montgomery as a boxer prematurely called to heaven due to a clerical error; returned to earth as an angel, the boxer seeks out his incredulous manager and tries to resume his ring career. The plot was updated in 1978 and the boxer was replaced by a football player for *Heaven Can Wait*, directed by Buck Henry and Warren Beatty, who also played the deceased sports star. Much the same theme was reprised again in 1997 with *The Sixth Man*, this time the sports star being a basketball player.

Basketball has provided the setting for one of the most successful sports comedies of the 1990s, Ron Shelton's *White Men Can't Jump* (1992) in which the old con tricks shown in *The Hustler* are transposed to the municipal courts of Los Angeles. Although not ostensibly a fantasy, David Anspaugh's *Hoosiers* (in Britain, *Best Shot*, 1986) told of a white high school basketball team of the 1950s which finds victory as their grizzled coach (played by Gene Hackman) finds redemption for his past misdeeds. Similar themes are present in Paul Michael Glaser's *The Air Up There* (1993) – in which a basketball scout assembles a team of Kenyans – and Jeff Pollack's *Above the Rim* (1994), in which ghetto kids overcome adversity in street basketball tournament. A not dissimilar film about adversity was Jon Turteltaub's *Cool Runnings* (1993) about the tribulations of a team of Jamaicans searching for Olympic glory in the bobsled competition of the Seoul Olympics.

Shelton specialized in sports films: his *Cobb* and *Bull Durham* (mentioned earlier) were both based on baseball heroes. One of the most commercially successful baseball movies was the gently fantastic *FIELD OF DREAMS*, directed by Phil Alden Robinson and released in 1989. Hearing the mandate, "if you build it, they will come," from beyond the grave, farmer Kevin Costner clears a section of his land in Iowa and builds a baseball diamond. Sure enough, "they" – the ghosts of baseball greats – do appear.

A brace of comedies (rather than fantasies) directed by David S. Ward brought manic humor to the baseball field. *Major League* (1989) and *Major League II* (1994) featured the adventures of a team of misfits who somehow contrived to win the occasional game. Another pair of baseball films were based on the real All American Girls' Professional Baseball League, which was formed in 1943 to fill the void left by the male baseball players who were involved in the war effort. Penny Marshall's *A League of Their Own* (1992) was a minor triumph, spawning a less successful sequel.

Fred Schepisi's 1993 big budget flop *Mr Baseball* featured Tom Selleck as a slightly past his best baseball player who is traded to Japan. "Comic" moments result from his attempts to readjust to life in Japan, where the approach to baseball is highly regimented and total loyalty to one's coach is assumed.

The Longest Yard (also known as *The Mean Machine*) featured Burt Reynolds as a professional football player who winds up in prison and leads a team of inmates against a team of guards. Directed by Robert Aldrich, the 1974 film counterpoints the comedy action with many moments of stark brutality. Stan Dragoti's *Necessary Roughness* (1991) was a somewhat formulaic fantasy: over-the-hill football star makes comeback and inspires mediocre team to victory. Like the earlier football-oriented *The Best of Time*, directed by Roger Spottiswoode and released in 1986, the movie limped to poor reviews. By contrast, the Oscar nominated *Jerry Maguire*, written and directed by Cameron Crow and released in 1997, drew rave reviews. A satirical-sentimental comedy starring Tom Cruise as a sports agent who acquires a conscience, the film's subtext involves a relationship between the agent and his sole client, a football-playing braggart played by Cuba Gooding Jr.

Golf movies have been either airy feelgood affairs or outright farces. Harold Ramis's *Caddyshack* (1980) is the well-known vulgar comedy starring Rodney Dangerfield. *Happly Gilmore*, directed by Dennis Dugan and released in 1996, was part of the "dumbing-down" (i.e. imbeciles-at-large) process that affected American cinema in the mid-1990s. Having established his sports credentials with *Bull Durham*, *White Men Can't Jump* and *Cobb*, Ron Shelton sliced into the commercial rough with *Tin Cup* (1996), although, in artistic terms, the film was a minor triumph, featuring Kevin Costner as a golf pro trying to woo his client, a female psychoanalyst played by Rene Russo.

In George Roy Hill's *Slap Shot* (1977), Paul Newman plays an ice hockey manager desperately trying to revive the fortunes of his team by recruiting three newcomers who specialize in violent play. *Rage on Ice* (1986), directed by Jean-Claude Lord, was a deep-frozen ice hockey yarn.

While violence may be an essential ingredient of boxing, not too much of it crept into Phil Carlson's *Kid Galahad* (1962). This was ostensibly a remake of Michael Curtiz's 1937 movie featuring Edward G. Robinson and Humphrey Bogart. However, the 1960s version was a limp musical starring Elvis Presley in the title role.

Documentaries

Leni Riefenstahl's 1938 *Olympiad* (or *Olympische Spiele*) is the mother of all sports documentaries. Ostensibly a record of the 1936 Berlin Olympics, the film contrives to be an exercise, indeed a brilliant exercise, in propaganda: its glorification of Aryan ideals, particularly physical ideals of beauty, made it the perfect ideological tool of Nazi Germany. The Olympic games themselves were intended to showcase the sublimity of Aryanism and Riefenstahl's uncritical lens complements this so much so that, at times, one senses Hitler himself is at the shoulder of the cinematographer. Fascist iconography is everywhere the camera points. It is a kind of overtly political sports documentary seldom seen in contemporary cinema.

The Munich Olympics of 1972 was the focus for *Visions of Eight* (1973) which brought together eight noted directors from around the world, each concentrating on a particular event or athlete. Only John Schlesinger's portion integrated the Palestinian terrorist hostage deaths into a sports story, this one telling of British marathon runner Ron Hill. Other directors included the Arthur Penn (of *Bonnie and Clyde* fame) who looked at the pole vault; Mai Zetterling, who dwelled on weightlifting; and Kon Ichikawa, whose segment analyzed the men's 100-meter sprint.

Pumping Iron (1976), directed by George Butler and Robert Fiore, was effectively a documentary held together by a wispy storyline about competitors in a bodybuilding competition. Butler was the co-author (with Charles Gaines) of the book of the same name, which inspired the movie. Jealousy, love and a manic narcissism are all ingredients in a film that took the sport of bodybuilding to its widest ever audience and bequeathed Arnold Schwarzenegger to Hollywood.

In the 1980s, competitive bodybuilding was no longer the exclusive terrain of men: George Butler's *Pumping Iron II: The Women* (1984) was more of a straightforward documentary than its precursor, but it also challenged male conceptions of womanhood: the film paraded well-vasculated, ripped-up women, competing in ruthless yet sisterly way for the 1983 Caesar's Cup in LA.

HOOP DREAMS (1994) directed by Steve James, Fred Marx and Peter Gilbert, began as a small-scale project but developed into a long (2 hours 50 minutes) film involving the study of two young ghetto residents in Chicago, both convinced they can make it to the National Basketball Association. Their progress is tracked over four years. The viewer is left wondering if the two aspirants are wooing their own oblivion, and if they are but two of countless other young blacks for whom sports is their only escape.

Joe Louis – For All Time, directed by Peter Tatum and released in 1984, also tempers sport's triumphalism with sadness. It tells the story of a heavyweight champion once described as "a credit to his race": footage of Louis' early fights are interposed with images of his decline in later years. Leon Gast's *WHEN WE WERE KINGS* (1997) highlights another heavyweight champion, albeit in only one fight. Muhammad Ali's upset win over George Foreman in Kinshasa in 1974 is showcased in a way that enriches the viewer's appreciation of the wider issues surrounding the fight.

This resumé is by no means exhaustive and there are dozens of other films, some of them more recent releases made for television. Summaries of early minor movies can be found in the volumes below.

Of related interest

Bergan, Ronald (1982) *Sports in the Movies*, Proteus Books.
Davidson, Judith (ed.) and Adler, Daryl (compiler) (1993) *Sport on Film and Video: The North American Society for Sport History Guide*, Scarecrow Press.
Zucker, Harvey M. and Babich, Lawrence J. (1976) *Sports Films: A Complete Reference*, HM & M Publishers.

flow

Athletes occasionally reflect on an outstanding sports performance for which they have no logical explanation. They may have trained exactly as they have done for other events, observed the same regimen of food and sleep, even taken heed of the same SUPERSTITIONS. Yet, for no rational reason, they achieve a singular performance that defies causal analysis. The performers report a state in which every feature of their performance is working perfectly without any undue effort from themselves: they do not try harder, nor concentrate on any detail; everything quite simply *flows*.

Historically, David Moorcroft's world record-breaking 5,000 meters run in 1982 is an illustration of flow. Moorcroft, who had never approached the 13:00.41 mark before (nor indeed after), looked back on the race and recounted how he felt almost carried along effortlessly. After his record-breaking long jump of 29 feet 2 inches (8.90 meters) at the 1968 Mexico Olympics, Bob Beamon had no explanation, but reported a sensation of unprecedented power as he soared through the air. These were one-off performances; some other competitors find flow occasionally and others on a regular basis.

Tennis player Andre Agassi was, at times, unsurpassable, such was his uncanny anticipation and unconstrained returns on both forehand and backhand sides. Once into his rhythm, Agassi was impossible to beat; yet he could find it only sporadically. On the other hand, Caribbean cricketer Brian Lara exhibited a flow-like quality in his batting on a regular basis.

Sport psychologist Susan Jackson (1996) adopted the theories of Mihaly Csikszentmihalyi on the state of flow. She writes of the concept's employment in sports: "Flow is a state of optimal experiencing involving total absorption in a task, and creating a state of consciousness where optimal levels of functioning often occur." Csikszentmihalyi (1990) had referred to flow as offering a totally autotelic experience; in other words, done for no end, only for itself. This does not square with the concept's application to sports, where there is invariably a goal or end to which all endeavor is directed. It is possible to watch tapes of basketball player Michael JORDAN in the 1990s and understand his often exquisite performances as completely autotelic, as if he were involved in a display of skill rather than a contest. Of course, the point about Jordan's frequent flow-like performances is that they were made possible precisely because they were organized around achieving a prescribed objective. It is the concept of a challenge that elicits the flow performance from a competitor.

Despite a wealth of theories on motivation in sport and studies of how best to encourage competitors to become FOCUSED, the understanding of how flow can be achieved or replicated is scant. Jackson's research formalizes rather than adds to the knowledge of flow, which seems by all accounts to arrive unexpectedly, often spontaneously, and is repeated rarely, if at all. The status of the likes of Jordan and Lara was built on their ability to function at optimal levels seemingly at will, while many others' places in sports history are based on the production of a single flow performance.

Of related interest

Csikszentmihalyi, Mihaly (1990) *Flow: The Psychology of Optimal Experience*, Harper & Row.
Jackson, Susan (1996) "Toward a conceptual understanding of the flow experience in elite athletes," *Research Quarterly for Exercise and Sport* vol 67.

focused

The term "focused" describes the condition of sports performers when their consciousness is fixed on the immediate objective and their bodies respond effectively yet seemingly effortlessly. Some competitors are able to induce in themselves what they later describe as an altered state of awareness; others can focus only under specific conditions, and still others seem unable to get focused at all in tense situations.

Japanese martial arts competitors refer to the concept of *mushin* ("no mind") which equates with being focused. All feelings of negativity vanish, the idea of losing disappears and the fighter is able to think only of winning his or her fight. In the West, sports performers try to reach similar states through careful preparation prior to an event. One of the most popular methods is by cultivating an inner calm or mental relaxation which releases tension and enables the performer to align body and mind on the proximate assignment.

Some accounts suggest that the state of being focused involves neural functions, principally the assembly of alpha brain waves. These are measurements of electrical activity in the brain and their graphic presentations as recorded on an electroencephalograph (EEG) shows multiple patterns reacting to sensory information which is fed through our senses. When the various brain waves emit synchronously, an alpha rhythm, or alpha state, is said to occur. This indicates that the subject's consciousness is directed toward the relevant task and that other distracting stimuli are shut out. This is the perfect condition for getting focused.

Perhaps the first star performer to practice the achievement of a focused condition was the tennis player Arthur ASHE, who often used the break when players changed ends by closing his eyes and appearing to meditate for a minute or so. The sprinter Linford Christie also closed his eyes in the period immediately prior to a race: while his rivals warmed up by stretching and bouncing, Christie remained motionless, opening his eyes and approaching his blocks only on the starter's orders. He talked of the "tunnel vision" he attained, limiting his peripheral vision and excluding thoughts of his competitors. Boxer Steve Collins used to sit in his corner with a towel draped over his head listening to a Walkman stereo while the ring announcer went through the preliminaries.

Dwight Stones, the Olympic high jump gold medalist of 1976, employed a technique that approximates what many today call positive visualization. Stones would pace his run up in slow motion, raising his elbows at his intended takeoff point. He would then return to his mark and trace his steps, nodding his head to establish the cadence of his runup. Stones was in fact imagining himself in action, as if rehearsing a successful jump. Many competitors use a mantra-like method, repeating key phrases to themselves over and over again as they approach their event.

The accounts of these and other performers suggest a FLOW-like state in which the performer experiences no pressure and can react with total concentration. Not that being focused is the same as concentration: it is perfectly possible for a competitor to concentrate on winning to the point where he or she actually imposes stress on themselves and cannot produce a telling performance. To focus effectively, the athlete needs to remain calm in the face of any amount of pressure. It has been speculated that only highly skilled performers can do this because, having mastered technique to a high degree, the athlete can produce efficient performance almost without thinking.

For example, more than fifty muscles are used to make a simple forward movement of a leg in walking. The sequence and strength of the contractions must be intricately organized if the foot is to go where we want it to. Yet we can easily walk and do other things, such as talking, or thinking about something else. The activity of walking is under the unconscious control of the cerebellum, which is the organ at the back of the brain that is responsible for the fine coordination of movements. In sports, the coordination of movements needs to be precise and especial. In other words, it requires skill.

What actually happens is that in the process of skill acquisition, information about force, distance, velocity and so on enters the central nervous system via eyes, ears and limbs. This immediate feedback enables often highly complex tasks to be completed as if instinctively. Skill is far from instinctual: its repetition enables the performer to produce it without constantly attending to it. The movement of limbs in sports, or any other type of activity, requires a continuous stream of motor nerve implses out to the muscles and another stream of sensory nerve impulses that feed back instructions about their exact position to the spinal cord and cerebellum. This information is constantly modified as the activity takes place, taking into account the external environment.

Once skill production has been surrendered to the cerebellum, the cortex, which controls intelligence and learning, is released to function in different areas, such as working out tactics or analysing situations, or even just relaxing in a way that allows the competitor actually to enjoy performing. It is as if the skill component is part of a system that has a life of its own. Baseball catchers or cricket wicketkeepers need to analyze situations and communicate quickly with pitchers and bowlers respectively; but once the ball has been released, their reactions need to be almost instantaneous and it is in this phase of their game that the cerebellum takes over.

In A.J. Liebling's classic book on boxing, THE SWEET SCIENCE, Charlie Goldman, who trained Rocky Marciano, makes exactly the same point when he expresses regret about not being able to train Marciano from the outset of his active career. "He would have learned to do things right without thinking," says Goldman. "Then all he would have to think about is what he wanted to do."

In highly focused states, the performer's cerebellum assumes priority and the athlete can perform without any apparent distraction. Occasionally, conditions permit a competitor to produce a high-level performance that he or she can never again approach. In 1982, David Moorcroft broke the world 5,000 meters track record under peculiar conditions at Oslo's Bislett Stadium. Sensing he had gone off too fast in early phases, the rest of the field allowed him to forge ahead. The strategy effectively removed pressure from Moorcroft and he was able to relax. He later reflected how his whole body seemed to course forward in a completely unfettered way, taking him to a time of 13:00.41.

Buster Douglas produced one of the biggest upsets in boxing's history when he soundly beat the then unbeaten Mike Tyson in Tokyo in 1990. There was nothing in Douglas's previous form to indicate that he had the remotest chance against the world heavyweight champion. Such thoughts must have affected his approach, which suggested none of the usual inhibitions of fighters facing a fighter considered unconquerable at the time. Neither Moorcroft nor Douglas was ever able to reproduce anything resembling their singular feats. Similarly, Bob Beamon never approached his wondrous long jump at Mexico in 1968, although he remained a world class athlete for many more years.

Some competitors are able to summon the power to get focused seemingly at will, while others completely lose the ability in stressful situations. Those who can are the "clutch players"; those who cannot are "chokers." Examples of the former are American football quarterback Joe Montana, who regularly remained calm even in near-impossible situations, bringing his brain's higher functions to bear on tactical issues and letting his unerring skill in throwing the football take care of other business. Basketball player Michael JORDAN was another unflappable competitor who would never panic at the prospect of defeat and could usually produced brilliant play at the appropriate moment.

Chokers typically lose focus in high-pressure situations, often when victory is in their grasp. Tennis player Jana Novotna crumbled at the 1995 French Open when leading Chandra Ruben 5–0 and 40–0 in the final set. Occasionally CHOKING affects entire teams, the most memorable instance being the American football team, the Houston Oilers, who ran up what seemed an unassailable 32-point third quarter lead against the Buffalo Bills in the 1992 NFL playoffs only to lose 41–38. The Oilers contrived to play a nervous, tentative spell full of crass errors, and handed the Bills a near-unbelievable win.

Of related interest

Cohn, Patrick J. (1994) *The Mental Game of Golf: A Guide to Peak Performance*, Diamond Communications.

Kendall, G., Hrycaiko, D., Martin G. and Kendall, T. (1990) "The effects of an imagery rehearsal, relaxation, and self-talk package on basketball game performance," *Journal of Sport and Exercise Psychology* vol 12.

Taylor, Jim (1994) *The Mental Edge for Competitive Sports*, 3rd edn, Alpine-Taylor.

Fosbury Flop

The high jump technique known as the Fosbury Flop was devised by American athlete Dick Fosbury, who revolutionized the discipline. The irony is that Fosbury himself never held the world record. However, his triumph at the Mexico summer Olympics of 1968 inspired countless others to emulate his style.

A native of Oregon, Fosbury was born in 1946 and went to Oregon State University. He won the Olympic gold in his international debut at age 21, using an odd-looking method that some believed was based on a careful study of physics and engineering. Fosbury himself claimed it was the product of pure intuition.

Prior to Fosbury, high jumpers used one of two techniques. The most popular was "the straddle," which involved a front-leg-first take-off, the athlete passing over the bar face-down and the back leg straddling, as the name suggests. Athletes using "the scissors" technique took off with their backs facing the bar, their heads crossing the bar with their front leg extended. The legs would open like scissors as they passed over.

Fosbury's style was to approach the bar in a curve, accelerating sharply in the final few strides. At the point of take-off, he would rotate his body so that he leapt backwards, his head passing the bar with his face toward the sky. As his back arched, he kicked his legs clear of the bar as his head and shoulders descended. The impression was that of dolphin jumping through a hoop backwards.

Fosbury had begun experimenting with the propulsion technique at the age of 16 when at high school. He unveiled an early version of the "flop" at the Rotary Invitation at Grants Pass, Oregon, in 1963, and officials needed to check the rules before permitting his jump. In 1968 he cleared 6.13m at an indoor meeting at Oakeville, California. It was here the technique was christened when a local newspaper captioned a picture of the jumper: "Fosbury flops over the bar."

Fosbury won the Olympic gold medal by 2 cm from fellow American Ed Carruthers. He never jumped 2.24m (in 1968, an Olympic record) again, but his technique was widely copied. Changes in surfaces permitted faster run-ups and inflatable landing surfaces eliminated the dangers of landing on one's head or neck. Many thought Fosbury risked serious injury landing backwards. The flop soon became the favored technique of all world-class high jumpers. Once his technique had been copied and perfected by others, the progress of high jumping accelerated exponentially. Between 1895 and 1968, the world high jump record increased from 1.97m (achieved by USA's John Sweeney) to 2.28m (USSR's Valery Brumel). After Fosbury's Olympic-winning leap of 2.24m, the record improved to 2.30m (USA's Dwight Stones), 2.36m (GDR's Gerd Wessig), 2.40m (USSR's Rudolf Povarnitsyn) then 2.45m (Cuba's Javier Sotomayor).

Of related interest

Conrad, Derek and Smith, Marc (1984) *The Olympics: The First 90 Years* (videocassette), Conrad Film Associates.

Track and Field News (1986) *Video Images of the High Jump: The Men* (videocassette), Track and Field News.

free agency

"Free agency" refers to the ability of sports performers to negotiate their own contracts with clubs without being subject to trade restrictions, such as baseball's famous reserve clause. The dissolution of this clause in 1976 effectively enabled players to demand salaries proportionate with their market value and usher in the era of the sports multimillionaire. Agents came to occupy key roles in the negotiation of performer's contracts. Similarly, European soccer's transfer system was modified in 1995 introducing freedom of movement between clubs for out-of-contract players.

Before the 1970s, players in North America's four principal team sports, baseball, basketball, ice hockey and football, were obligated to play for one club until the club voluntarily decided to trade them to another club (possibly in exchange for draft picks or other players) or released them from their contracts. Historically, baseball had the most restrictive covenant in its notorious reserve clause, which had been challenged periodically but survived until 1976. Baseball's reserve clause has its origins in a meeting held on September 30, 1879 in Buffalo, New York and called by Arthur Soden, the owner of the Boston Red Stockings.

Soden, who was known to make players' wives pay admission to games and oblige the players themselves to work on turnstiles before the games, proposed to reserve five players per team.

The players were prevented from transferring to another club by the clause that reserved to the team the right unilaterally to impose a new contract on a player whose contract had expired. With the core of players secured, the clause enabled clubs to curb the growth of salaries and shore up profits. While the concept of contracting the services of players exclusively to particular clubs went against the grain of open commercial competition, baseball's owners insisted that it was necessary: without it, there would be freedom of movement between clubs and richer clubs would attract better players with higher salaries.

The system of servitude ensured that players stayed with one club or moved outside the league. MAJOR LEAGUE BASEBALL saw off competitors either by absorbing them or merging with them. But, it was the protest of one player that precipitated the system's downfall. In 1969, Curt Flood, an outfielder for St. Louis Cardinals, was traded to Philadelphia Phillies. Flood objected to the move and refused to report for training. After having his request to negotiate his own deal with National League teams turned down, he filed suit under the Sherman Act, which prohibited restraint on competitive practices . In 1971 his contract was traded to the Washington Senators. Flood played a handful of games, then retired from competitive baseball. His legal action looked like foundering when it was ruled that two pieces of legislation – *Federal Baseball Club of Baltimore, Inc. vs. National League of Professional Baseball* (1922) and *Toolson vs New York Yankees* (1953) – exempted the sport from antitrust laws. The ruling stated that professional baseball was a business and engaged in interstate commerce, and that, while other sports that operated interstate were subject to antitrust laws, the reserve system made baseball an exception, indeed, an anomaly. The court accepted that, if there was "inconsistency" and "illogic" in baseball's uniqueness, they were so long-standing that they needed remedying by Congress rather than the courts.

James Quirk and Rodney Fort quote a *New York Times* editorial on the Flood ruling: "The only basis for a judge-made monopoly status of baseball is that the Supreme Court made a mistake the first time it considered the case fifty years ago [*Toolson*] and now feels obligated to keep on making the same mistake because Congress does not act to repeal the exemption it never ordered" (in *Pay Dirt*, Princeton University Press, 1992). By the 1970s, the convenience of this argument for owners was transparent and other methods of ensuring a competitive balance between clubs – like sharing gate receipts, television revenues – were seen as preferable. Players' demands increased pressure on baseball club owners to modify what was seen, by then, as an archaic institution.

Discontent among players grew: in 1972, a dispute over players' pension funds erupted and a thirteen-day strike resulted in eighty-six lost games, which delayed the start of the World Series. The threat of STRIKES in the following year also alerted baseball's owners to the sense of injustice felt by players. Quirk and Fort suggest that: "In handing down the *Flood* decision, the Supreme Court had suggested the labor-management negotiations might settle the issue of player contract terms, and bargaining over free agency occurred during the 1972 season."

A new arrangement was settled in 1973, but the reserve clause remained and the players' union was becoming more militantly opposed to it. They were encouraged by a decision in favor of Jim "Catfish" Hunter, who was granted free agent status after he successfully claimed that Oakland A's owner Charlie Finley had violated his contract. The case was heard by a three-man arbitration panel. This was soon followed by action from two pitchers, Dave McNally of the Montreal Expos and Andy Messersmith of the Los Angeles Dodgers, who refused to sign contracts offered to them in 1975. Baseball's standard contract provided for automatic renewal for one year at the club's discretion. The two played out the season, but without signing their contracts. They insisted that the reserve clause was simply a one-year option clause (such as those that operated in basketball and football) and that playing for a year without signing a contract fulfilled their obligation. Once the season was over, they were no longer under contract and wished to continue as free agents.

In December 1975, an independent arbitrator agreed that McNally and Messersmith were indeed free to negotiate their own contracts in future. The arbitrator was dismissed and his ruling appealed; but the ruling was upheld twice and the club owners accepted the inevitable. Any player refusing to sign his 1976 contract would be required to play out the season, after which they would become free agents. After 1977, a player with six years of Major League service could become a free agent simply by notifying the club after the season was over and any player with five years under his belt could demand a trade (subject to some limitations).

The decision opened up a completely new market in baseball, and trades became commonplace. Salaries more than doubled in the three years following 1976, when the average salary was $44,700 (£27,000), as clubs held out cash incentives to players wishing to trade. By 1985, the average salary was $371,200. By the early 1990s it was approaching $1m. The NBA salary structure also altered dramatically following the case of Oscar Robertson, who, in the mid-1970s, played for a Cincinnati-based NBA team called the Royals. He sat out whole games while pressing for more money and eventually initiated an antitrust suit against the league. The ruling held that the player draft, uniform contract and reserve clause were in violation of federal antitrust law and handed players the right to free agency. Football and ice hockey followed the example, though much later: football players became free agency in 1993 and hockey players in 1995. In both cases, salaries soared.

The move to free agency changed the character of the relations between clubs. Previously, they had worked in tandem, as complementary members of a well-organized club. Free agency meant that the clubby friendship was replaced by a more competitive relationship: players were often prepared to sacrifice loyalty and sign for whichever club offered them the best terms. Clubs responded, sometimes leading to acrimony, such as between football's San Francisco 49ers and Dallas Cowboys, both of whom vied for the services of Deion Sanders in 1995 (he eventually signed for Dallas).

While the term "free agency" is rarely used in European soccer, the BOSMAN

CASE introduced a situation that closely paralleled the North American condition, with players being released from the prohibitive transfer fees demanded by clubs trading players to other clubs. Players had for long protested against the constrictions of the transfer system. In 1959, George Eastham approached his club, Newcastle United, and asked to leave. The club turned down his request and suspended his salary. Eastham challenged the club through the courts and, after a four-year legal process, won his case. It was declared that the rules that permitted his club to cease paying him *and* refuse him a transfer – reminiscent of baseball's reserve clause – were illegal restraints of players' ability to ply their trade. The ruling did not lead to free agency, but it established that soccer clubs should extend to players, as employees, the same kinds of rights and freedoms that would be recognized in other forms of work. The difference was that clubs regarded players not only as employees but as capital assets, and the transfer system guaranteed them compensation for players when they moved to different clubs. So, while clubs continued to retain players' contracts, they had to pay them; when out of contract, they could either release them on a "free transfer" or continue to pay them until they agreed a fee with another club.

The Bosman ruling decreed that, once players were out of contract, they were completely free to sign for whichever club they believed offered them the best deal. One of the responses of soccer clubs was to re-sign players on improved terms at least one year before the expiry of their contracts. By retaining players under contract, the clubs could effectively keep the transfer system intact by demanding compensation for the unused portion of the player's contract. Transfer fees continued, and indeed spiraled, as did players' salaries. One effect of the decision was the gravitation of players from Eastern European clubs to the much richer clubs of England, France, Germany, Italy and Spain, which could offer higher salaries.

Of related interest

Gorman, Jerry and Calhoun, Kirk (1994) *The Name of the Game: The Business of Sports*, John Wiley & Sons.

Quirk, James and Fort, Rodney (1992) *Pay Dirt: The Business of Professional Team Sports*, Princeton University Press.

Sanderson, Allen and Siegfried, John (1997) "The implications of athlete freedom to contract: Lessons from North America," *Economic Affairs* vol 17, no 3.

gambling

The motive behind gambling

Playing games of chance for money or staking wagers on the outcome of events, human or otherwise, probably dates back to antiquity. Two great minds of the seventeenth century, Isaac Newton and Gottfried Wilhelm Leibniz, inadvertently contributed to our understanding of gambling when they independently formulated a new mathematics of instantaneous motion. We think of time as a natural element in the description of nature. This was not always the case: prior to the theories of Newton and Leibniz, the flux of time, or what Newton called *fluxions*, was not a component of human thought on nature. After, the laws of nature became more properly understood as laws of motion and nature itself became not a series of static frames but an ever-moving process.

Both Newton and Leibniz, like Einstein who followed them, were committed to a view of the world as ordered mechanically and moving according to definable principles with potentially predictable outcomes. Nature moves, but not in an indeterminate manner. The *primum mobil* for Leibniz was God, and this provided for a rational, structured passage of time and nature. As with all Enlightenment thinkers, reason and rationality lay behind all earthly affairs. As Galileo had shown in his *Starry Messenger*, first published in 1610, forces that work to render the sky predictable are also at work on earth.

Chance has no place in this ordered universe. Ignorance is merely imperfect knowledge. Everything is potentially knowable; and, of course, Newton and Leibniz were prominent in the advancement of both theoretical and practical science. Given greater knowledge, we could apply the infinitesimal calculus, a method of calculating or reasoning about the changing world. The seeming vagaries of nature could be comprehended and subordinated to the rational, calculating mind.

Gambling is guided by such reasoning. Admittedly, the conscious thought that lies behind rolling dice or drawing lots is hardly likely to resemble any kind of calculation; these are games of chance, played with the intention of winning money. But, the motive behind gambling on sports is very much influenced by a more rational style of thinking: that it is possible to predict the outcome of an event by the employment of a calculus of probability. No one wagers money on a sporting event without at least some inkling that they are privy to a special knowledge about how a competition will end. A suspicion, a taste, a fancy, a "feel"; all these add to the calculus at work in the mind of even the most casual of gamblers when he or she stakes money on a competition.

Orientations of gamblers differ widely: some always feel a tingle whether it is in watching a horse romp home or dice roll, others observe from a position of detachment, their interest resting on only the result. The sports gambler bets with head as well as heart; the reward is both in the winning and in the satisfaction that he or she has divined a correct result from the unmanageable flux of a competitive event. In his book *Gambling* (Spring Books, 1964), Alan Wykes gives weight to the role of gambling in supplying a sexual compensation to the gambler. Intellects as great as Freud and Dostoevski have theorized on the sexual dimensions of the gambling impulse.

Gambling on sports

The seventeenth-century philosophers' concerns were not with gambling, though in fact they may well have observed the surge in popularity in games of chance in the pre-Enlightenment period. Nicholas Rescher locates a surge in popularity in wagering on contests of skill and chance during the English Civil War (1641–5) and the Thirty Years War in continental Europe (1618–48). Starved of entertainment, soldiers and sailors killed time by wagering on virtually any activity. Rescher cites a seventeenth-century soldier's remembrance of betting on a race between lice. Returning to civilian society, the militia brought with them their habits and the enthusiasm for gambling diffused, aligning itself quite naturally with the games of skill that were growing in popularity in England.

The 1665 Gaming Act was the first piece of dedicated legislation to outlaw gambling, principally to restrict the debts that were being incurred as a result of the growing stakes. Some activities had attracted gambling for decades, perhaps centuries. Swordplay, for example, was a pursuit that was viscerally thrilling to watch and stimulated the human passion for prediction. As the military use of swords declined, so the contests continued simply for recreation and entertainment. Engaging in competitive contests simply for the satisfaction they afforded the competitor and observer was exactly the kind of wasteful and sinful behavior despised by Puritans.

Gambling was actually the basis of many early sports, especially BLOOD SPORTS, in which the *frisson* of watching animals fight or be ravaged was complemented by a wager. Apart from swordplay, pugilism was another combat sport that attracted what was known as a "fancy" or following of ardent spectators who would pit their forecasting skills against each other. Sponsors of pugilists were extravagant backers of their charges. In one famous bet, the Duke of Cumberland, patron of prize fighter Jack Broughton, lost £10,000 on his man. The influence of gambling on prize fighting became malign and CORRUPTION was rife.

Boxing and gambling have gone hand in hand ever since, though there were other less probable sports that attracted betters. Cricket, for example, in the early nineteenth century had its hardcore spectators who were prone not only to gambling but to drinking and rowdiness. Gambling regulations remained in the laws of the game until the 1880s, and betting was still very much part of the sport until at least mid-century. Lords, the home ground of the MCC, banned gambling in the 1820s and, according to Dennis Brailsford (1997), in his *British Sport: A Social History*, "at least one player was banned for allegedly throwing a match."

Brailsford estimates that the money staked on boxing was rivaled "and sometimes exceeded" by that involved in pedestrianism, the period's form of track. Pedestrianism defined a miscellany of races and events, sometimes head-to-heads or against the clock, often involving both men and women. There were wheelbarrow races and hopping contests as well as such unusual challenges as picking up potatoes. The appeal of pedestrianism was that it was possible to wager on practically anything.

Opposition to working-class gambling on sports bore fruit in the form of two pieces of legislation in 1853 and 1906, which were ostensibly framed to forbid off-course betting. ANIMAL RACING, from its outset, was fair game for gaming. Rome's notorious chariot races in the third century AD were ferociously contested for high stakes. In their modern forms, horse racing and dog racing proved the most attractive to gamblers. Dog racing has its origins in eighteenth century coursing (and involved highly bred and trained dogs which chased and – usually – killed a fleeing hare). The hare was given a start of over 200 yards (183 meters). One of the attractions of meetings was the opportunity to wager and drink convivially. Hoteliers and publicans would promote coursing meets. It became an organized sport, complete with its own organization in 1858, when a National Coursing Club was established.

As opposition mounted to what was obviously one of a number of blood sports prevalent at the time, coursing dispensed with living hares and substituted a mechanical equivalent. The electric hare was first used in 1919 and came into popular use at the end of the 1920s. In the United States, the betting norm became *pari-mutuel* (from the French, meaning "mutual stake".) This type of betting had been introduced in New Zealand as far back as 1880. In the 1930s this also took off in on-course British horse racing, where it was known as totalizer, or simply "tote," betting in which winners divide the losers' stakes, less an administrative charge.

A new form of gambling on soccer posed threats to both greyhound and horse racing. Known as the pools, it appeared in the early 1930s and captured the British public's imagination almost immediately. Newspapers had been publishing their own versions of pools for many years, but the practice was declared illegal in 1928. Brailsford notes how the £20 million staked in the 1934–5 season doubled within two years. The outlay was usually no more than a few pence, and the bets were typically collected from one's home. The aim of pools was to select a requisite number of drawn games, so it was classified not as a game of chance but as one of skill, thus escaping the regulation of gaming legislation. By the outbreak of war, there were ten million gamblers on the pools. The popularity the pools enjoyed with working-class betters stayed intact until the introduction of the national lottery (modeled on the US state lotteries) in the early 1990s.

In the 1990s, betting on the SPREAD became one of the most popular gambling forms. The better could wager not only on the result of a contest but on any facet of it: for example, the number of times Dan Marino licked his fingertips, or how often Mark McGwire spat, or the total number of positive drug tests at an Olympic games.

Of related interest

Brailsford, Dennis (1997) *British Sport: A Social History*, Lutterworth Press.
Rendall, Jonathan (1999) *Twelve Grand: The Gambler as Hero*, Yellow Jersey Press.
Rescher, Nicholas (1995) *Luck: The Brilliant Randomness of Everyday Life*, Farrar Straus Giroux.
Shaffer, Howard J. (ed.) (1984–) *Journal of Gambling Studies*, Human Sciences Press.
Wykes, Alan (1964) *Gambling*, Spring Books.

gays

Homophobia/homoeroticism

There can be little doubt that, of all the fields of popular culture, sport has been one of the most effective in the making and sustaining of "supremacist" forms of masculinity. Playing, talking about and claiming command over sport has been extraordinarily important for boys and men. From the playground humiliations of "weakling" boys to the consummate sporting insult of "playing like a girl," sport has provided a reliable mechanism for sorting males into dominant and subordinate types, and for differentiating a certain heterosexual image of manliness from the compromising threat of "femininity." For women, sport is a much more dangerous place, one where femininity is brought into question. Being "too physical" or "tough" casts doubt on one's heterosexuality. High sporting achievement in an all-female environment routinely generates moral panics, often about LESBIANISM.

Despite the coding of male sport as undeniably "straight," it is a *homosocial* cultural institution in which men are licenced to touch intimately, to kiss and openly admire each others' bodies, to spend concentrated time together in showers and bedrooms, and so on. Some women have viewed male attachment to sport as a sign of general latent homosexuality, a charge that seems to be mirrored by the "protesteth-too-much" arrant homophobia of much male sports culture. Hence, as in the case of the military, sports organizations and male sports performers have tried to negate the well-documented incidence of homosexuality in the general population by asserting that the essential sportsman's values of aggression, toughness and so on are inherently antithetical to homosexual desire and conduct. It is not so much a policy of "don't ask, don't tell" as "it couldn't happen in *my* sport." Yet, in his *The Arena of Masculinity* (1990), Pronger claims that the very basis of sport is "a covert world of homoeroticism." He does not suggest that all sportsmen are gay, but that sporting segregation by gender is about the intense separation of men from women that requires them to form their most intimate bonds with the same sex.

Despite the pink dollar market and other emergent late capitalist commercial phenomena, there are enormous barriers confronting gay sports performers. The US Olympic Committee sued the Gay Games over ownership of the Olympic name in the Supreme Court in 1987 and placed the home of founder Tom Waddell – a decathlete from the 1968 Mexico Olympics – under lien as he was in the last stages of dying. It did not take such actions against the Police, Diaper or Dog Olympics. At the same time, this obstruction may have encouraged the inclusive Gay Games *ethos*: you don't have to be gay to participate, and there is no minimum level of competence required. The notion is of a contest with one's own record as much as against others, and the idea is to meet as much as to defeat. The media have hardly been friendly to the Gay Games: when heterosexual North American ABC telecaster Dick Schaap wrote an obituary on Waddell for *Sports Illustrated*, the editors deleted a reference to his kissing the decathlete farewell.

Coming out

What is the response when a sports star "comes out"? It is very rare for retired elite sports performers to declare that they are gay, still more uncommon for one in the twilight of their careers, and almost unprecedented in the case of an athlete in their early or peak sporting life. So, on a kind of personal revelatory sliding scale, it is more likely that a retired sportsman like Olympic diver Greg Louganis or American football player David Kopay will come out than one in late career like British soccer player Justin FASHANU, who committed suicide in 1998 when being pursued by US police in connection with an alleged sexual assault on a teenage male.

Kopay came out in the hope that it would improve matters for others, but claims that many onfield brawls still result from players being called "fag," a sign of continued intolerance. Kopay was out to many team-mates, finding particular solace and support from African Americans, whose knowledge of straight white male bigotry made them excellent confidants. He says that obstacles lie with franchise owners, who believe that having openly gay players on their teams would cause them to lose money from sponsorship and television audiences.

Kopay called for football associations and players' unions to issue a civil rights statement of support for gay athletes and to provide assistance to high school and college players, where suicide rates were – and are – high. In the period immediately after he came out, only two other major US team sportsmen followed: retired baseballer Glenn Burke and footballer Roy Simmons. The noted gay magazine *The Advocate* ran a 1996 cover story entitled "Inside the NFL Closet: Why pro football players can't come out." It quoted major media commentators explaining that gay and lesbian football fans may have to wait longer still to claim an out footballer like rugby league's Ian Roberts. It was felt that life on and off the field, plus endorsement issues, made such a bold move impractical. But rumors about players were and remain intense.

Troy Aikman, the quarterback star of the dominant Dallas Cowboys team of the mid-1990s, was subject to rampant innuendo. In his book *Hell Bent* (HarperCollins, 1996), Skip Bayless writes that he had heard rumors about Aikman from 1991. Aikman himself maintained he was not gay. Bayless suggests that some high-profile athletes are provided with images of "most eligible bachelor" in order to maximize their chances of making millions from endorsements. Media stories of affairs with well-known women are encouraged. It is probable that clauses are inserted into the contracts of some athletes, detailing acceptable public behavior and prohibiting attendance at gay bars.

Clearly, many homosexual, bisexual or queer sports performers opt to leave their legend uncomplicated; the economic penalties for COMING OUT, especially with regard to product endorsement and individual corporate sponsorship, are considerable. For example, when in 1991 the African American basketballer Magic JOHNSON announced that he was HIV-positive – while also declaring that "I have never had a homosexual experience" – market analysts immediately canvassed the devaluation of his stock in the corporate celebrity marketplace on the grounds of a widespread, negative association between AIDS or HIV status and homosexuality. Of course, Martina Navratilova and Billie Jean KING have long been out, but where are their endorsements and opportunities to comment on major television networks? Another key lesbian sports icon, Babe DIDRIKSON, was forced to marry to hide her secret. At the organizational level, the old professional league of women's basketball banned LESBIANISM, requiring women to be straight, while the Gay Games saw a Canadian national female hockey player having to hide the fact she was coaching lest the media find out. The position of openly gay men is similar.

When the multiple Olympic gold-medal winning diver Greg Louganis came out, it appeared to cost him a media position "calling" the Atlanta Games. It also led to a Florida State Senator trying to prevent him speaking at the University of Southern Florida on the grounds that he would "promote homosexuality" and "moral decadence," not to mention the female colleagues who once stuffed a gerbil with its legs tied together in his sportsbag at a competition, or male competitors from the "Beat The Faggot Club" – displays of homophobia on a par with Arsenio Hall's talkshow remark that: "If we can put a man on the moon, why can't we get one on Martina Navratilova?" Instead, we hear from players who never made it to the Top Ten or were one-off successes. Louganis's successor as US number one, David Pichler, ran into bizarre abuse after announcing his homosexuality, to the point of his ex-coach seeking restraint orders on the diver's male partner to keep him away from the coach and his son. But the sport now sees a lot of people coming out, despite taunts from straights. The only gold-medal swimmer on the list so far is Bruce Hayes. In skating, Rudy Galindo, 1996 US national champion, is publicly gay, as is Gene Kuffel, Mr USA International 1997; while Bob Paris, a former Mr America, was married to his boyfriend during his tenure, suffering jibes from other competitors as a result.

Ambiguities and "otherness"

Renowned in the late 1980s as one of the bad boys who hustled and bumped the Detroit Pistons to championships, and for his obsessive exercising after games, Denis Rodman was known not just for his peerless rebounding but also for dressing in boas, frequenting gay bars, sleeping with Madonna (and telling), and *imagining* sex with other men. Rodman was also notable for his rejection of comfortable pigeonholing by gay politicians: he says he is not in the closet, he just has not as yet wanted to sleep with men. This refusal asks us to think again about tight definitions of personhood in terms of sex practices.

Rodman might have sex with a man, or he might not; but he would still be the best defensive rebounder in the history of the NBA (National Basketball Association). In turn, this complex presentation of self encourages us to render problematic the essentialism of the impost to come out, not to mention its ethnocentrism. Black critics point to the way that the white gay movement's privileging of being out has ignored the importance in many "heteronormative" black families of putting unity against racism before the expression of minority sexuality.

As important a disincentive as financial cost to sportsmen and women coming out is their vulnerability to homosexual abuse from sports competitors and fans. For example, in 1995 the Australian rugby league player Ian Roberts, after many years of street gossip and media innuendo about his euphemistically named "lifestyle," came out in spectacular fashion on the cover of a popular magazine, *New Weekly*. Roberts, who it appears was about to be involuntarily "outed" in any case, was paid for his story not only because of the shock value of his sporting celebrity status, but also because, as a famously large, aggressive and tough player in the demanding position of "prop," he challenged the widely-held stereotype of how a gay man should look and act.

The defiantly non-camp Roberts, as is reported in his biography, was subjected to considerable abuse both before and after his official coming out. At one point he says:

> When I ran out on the field for Manly, I was starting to cop heaps, every game. Every game. From the crowd. The guys at Manly got used to it, so it didn't bother them. Sometimes, I copped it from other players. Once, when I got cut, a Norths player was yelling "Don't let that bastard fucking bleed on us."

Roberts goes on to observe that such behavior is endemic, commenting that:

> I know guys say things like that when they are geed up for a game or frustrated. When you see them off the field socially, they're fine. But for them to have said it means it must be a problem for them. I've been called "poof" and "faggot" that many times on the field. It's a part of the game, abuse.

Abuse has, indeed, long been part of the game for gay men and women in sport, and the stigma attached to sexual "otherness" still retains considerable force in contemporary sport. Such practices are explained away as relatively harmless "gamesmanship," but, as Roberts notes, for sexual vilification tactics to be used in the first place requires an already existing cultural structure of sexual oppression.

It is hardly surprising, in view of the personal and professional perils of "fessing up" about their sexuality, that few sportspeople have been able to find the courage to proclaim to the world of sport that they are, indeed, proud to be gay.

Of related interest

Cahn, Susan K. (1993) "From the 'Muscle Moll' to the 'Butch' Ballplayer: Mannishness, lesbianism, and homophobia in U.S. women's sport," *Feminist Studies* vol 19, no 2.
"Ian Roberts Tribute Page," http://www.dstc.edu.au.
Pronger, Brian (1990) *The Arena of Masculinity: Sports, Homosexuality and the Meaning of Sex*, St Martins Press.
Rogers, Susan Fox (ed.) (1995) *Sportsdykes: Stories from On and Off the Field*, St Martin's Press.

DAVID ROWE
TOBY MILLER

Gleneagles Agreement, the

In 1977, the heads of government of Commonwealth nations met at Gleneagles, Scotland, to formulate an agreement "vigorously to combat the evil of apartheid by withholding any form of support for, and by taking every practical step to discourage contact or competition by their nationals with sporting organizations, teams or sportsmen from South Africa." The agreement was made by governments rather than sports governing federations and, as subsequent events showed, the ability of governments to overrule individual organizations was often tested.

The origins of the Gleneagles agreement lie in 1968 when Basil D'Oliveira, a black cricket player from South Africa's Cape who had settled in England, reached peak form. Selected for the English national team, he scored a triumphant century against Australia and was, almost without question, the premier batsman in the country. Yet, when the team for the winter tour of South Africa was announced, D'Oliveira's name was missing.

David Sheppard, a former England player later to become Bishop of Liverpool, led a protest, accusing selectors of submitting to the requirements of apartheid, which included the strict separation of those deemed to belong to different "races." D'Oliveira, having relatively pale brown skin, was officially classed by South Africans as "colored" and so had no legal right to share facilities with whites.

Needless to say, the South African team included only white players. Several England team members threatened to resign as the protest gathered momentum, prompting the selectors to include D'Oliveira in the team as a replacement for an injured bowler. South Africa's Prime Minister John Vorster promptly denounced the squad as "not the team of the MCC but the team of the Anti-Apartheid

Movement, the team of SAN-ROC [the South African Non-Racial Olympic Committee]."

The MCC, England's governing organization, pulled out of the tour. But in 1970, the MCC was prepared to receive a South African team to tour England. The announcement of this was met with a "Stop the Seventy Tour" campaign and series of disruptions to the South African rugby team's tour of Britain. Progressively, more and more sports minimized or severed contacts with South Africa, effectively ostracizing that country's sports.

The D'Oliveira episode was not the first to surface: the political significance of South Africa in world sports had been realized for at least ten years. But 1968 was a year of great upheaval. John Carlos and Tommie Smith's black power salute at the Mexico Olympics, Muhammad ALI's emergence as a symbolic leader of black people and antiwar protesters and the student revolts in both Europe and the USA contributed to a culture of change.

In 1956, South Africa had made a formal declaration of its sports policy program, which, it insisted, should stay inside the boundaries of its general policy of apartheid (an Afrikaans word meaning "apart-ness"). The physical segregation embodied in apartheid was instituted in 1948 and encouraged by pass laws, police brutality and a repressive state that dealt harshly with challenges to its authority, as the slayings in Sharpeville in 1960 illustrated. Sports performers and teams visiting South Africa were expected "to respect South Africa's customs as she respected theirs," according to an official statement (quoted in M. Horrell, *South Africa and the Olympic Games*, Johannesburg Institute of Race Relations, 1968).

Blacks, who constituted over 70 per cent of South Africa's population at the time, were barred from a new rugby stadium in 1955, prompting Bishop Trevor Huddlestone, a leading member of the anti-apartheid movement, to point out that sport was South Africa's Achilles heel. To deny South Africa the opportunity to demonstrate its excellence would, as Huddlestone put it in his influential *Naught for Your Comfort* (Collins, 1956), "shake its self-assurance very severely." South Africa was a world power in rugby, and one of its rivals, New Zealand, had traditionally picked Maoris in its national team. But, it capitulated to South Africa and chose only white players for a 1960 tour. Against the background of the 1960 Sharpeville massacre (69 black people dead, 180 wounded at a black township after a show of black resistance), the New Zealand tour went ahead.

SAN-ROC, which was launched in 1962, asked for recognition from the IOC in preference to the whites-only Olympic and National Games Associations of South Africa. In 1964 the government banned SAN-ROC, which was made to shift its base to London. The IOC responded by banning South Africa from the Tokyo Olympics of 1964. Racial discrimination is forbidden in the IOC charter, and South Africa was also expelled from the Olympic movement. Virtually every attempt to continue sporting links with South Africa met with protest: tennis, rugby, cricket as well as track and field events were all subject to disruptions.

In 1971, Vorster announced what he called a "multinational" sports program in which "whites," "Africans," "coloreds" and "Asians" could compete against each other as "nations," but only in international competitions. This was a devious move, allowing black athletes to compete provided they were affiliated to one of the government's "national" federations. It divided blacks: some wished to compete and felt compelled to affiliate; others rejected the racist premise of the divisions and refused. With international links receding, the government permitted domestic contests between "nations" and, later club-level competitions between "nations."

Rugby union resisted the international trend and, in particular, New Zealand set itself against world opinion by willfully maintaining contacts. During a New Zealand tour of South Africa in 1976, the Soweto uprising (official figures: 575 dead, 2,389 wounded) prompted ever more searching questions. African nations argued that, as New Zealand seemed intent on prosecuting links regardless of the upheavals, it too should be ostracized. New Zealand's admission to the Montreal Olympic games of 1976 caused a mass boycott by African states and sympathizers.

In the following year, the Gleneagles Agreement was drafted. Commonwealth governments unanimously committed themselves to overcome the autonomy of sports federations by applying sanctions to organizations and individuals ignoring the agreement. In 1981, a United Nations special committee published its first "blacklist" (an embarrassing misnomer) of sports performers who had worked in South Africa.

Rugby robustly defended its autonomy and, in 1979, Britain entertained a "mixed" Barbarians (South African) team that included eight whites, eight "colored" and eight blacks. British cricket player Robin Jackman, who had played in South Africa, was deported from Guyana in 1981 just as a test match against the West Indies was about to begin. The game was abandoned. Other British cricketers, like Geoff Boycott and Graham Gooch, were banned from test cricket as punishment for playing in South Africa. In 1989 the International Cricket Conference (ICC) passed a resolution to formalize sanctions against players, coaches or administrators who worked in South Africa. Automatic suspension from test cricket was the penalty. It was the most unambiguous pronouncement on sport and apartheid since the Gleneagles Agreement. It was hailed by Sam RAMSAMY of SAN-ROC as "a victory for sport over racism."

The election of Nelson Mandela as president of South Africa in 1993 and the collapse of apartheid which preceded it effectively ended the isolation of South Africa in all senses and sporting relations were resumed. South Africa was readmitted into the Olympic movement, and its soccer team was welcomed by FIFA into the World Cup competition of 1998. Its rugby teams were allowed to tour and its cricket teams were allowed to play test series against the world's other cricket powers. The West Indies team was the first national team to tour South Africa after the announcement of the end of apartheid. Black representation in the country's national rugby team remained scant for several more years, prompting controversy and resignations. "Deracializing" sport, as the process was called, was a slower process than many anticipated.

Of related interest

Bose, Mihir (1994) *Sporting Colours: Sport and Politics in South Africa*, Robson.
Payne, A. (1991) *The International Politics of the Gleneagles Agreement*, Round Table.

—— (1993) "The Commonwealth and the politics of sporting contact with South Africa," in Binfield, C. and Stevenson, J. (eds), *Sport, Culture and Politics*, Sheffield Academic Press.

globalization

World cultures and world markets

Considering the near-unanimity on the existence of globalization, there is little agreement on its precise meaning and consequences. For example, Tony Spybey (1996) writes: "Globalization is the tendency for routine day-to-day social interaction to be imbued with patterns that are to an increasing extent shared across the planet." In his discussion of sports in globalization, Joseph Maguire refers to "the emergence of a global economy, a transnational cosmopolitan culture and a range of international social movements" ("Sport, identity politics and globalization," *Sociology of Sport Journal* vol 11, 1994). Roland Robertson, in his *Globalization: Social Theory and Global Culture* (1992), points out that there is a subjective element when he argues that "the expansion of the media of communications has made people all over the world more conscious of other places and the world as a whole." Anthony Giddens opts for a short, but encompassing definition: "the general term for the increasing interdependence of world society" (*Sociology*, 3rd edn, Polity Press, 1997).

All share the view that substantial transformations have occurred in which economic orders, cultural patterns and configurations of information the world over have developed common tendencies and characteristics. The prime movers behind such transformations are unclear. Some argue that it is a logical development of capitalism: private capital's tendency to exploit markets is seen as key to the process of globalization. Others point to the emergence of a genuine worldwide information system, made possible by satellite TECHNOLOGY and the megalomaniac propensities of certain media moguls. Still others point out that the time–space compression facilitated by air travel and telecommunications have led to a cultural convergence.

Whatever the causes, there is no doubt that phenomena resembling a global culture and global market appeared complete by the second half of the twentieth century. In a sense, this was the product of an initiative begun by colonial traders in the early days of IMPERIALISM, or perhaps even before. The interdependence written of by Giddens disguises what others believe to be an economic dependence of underdeveloped nations on the traditional imperial powers of western Europe and the USA. In fact, the inordinate influence of the United States on globalization has led some to believe that the term itself is a euphemism for "Americanization."

If globalization were confined to the homogeneity of culture that became apparent in the 1980s, then it would be possible to accept Todd Gitlin's contention that: "American popular culture is the closest approximation there is today to a global lingua franca." Gitlin's *New York Times* article was entitled

"World leaders: Mickey *et al.*," an allusion to the ascendant cultural hegemony of all things Disney (*New York Times*, May 3, Section A, 1992).

Certainly, sport and the culture it has propagated has its roots in the England of the nineteenth century, its trunk in the USA and branches all over the world. It is possible to see young people wearing NBA replica shirts in practically any part of the world, regardless of whether they actually ever see basketball games on TELEVISION. The fact that some may be able to see NBA games on television is testimony to the globalization of the communication systems. Their interest piqued, they may then seek to buy the replica shirts, themselves made available by a worldwide network of manufacturers and distributors controlled ultimately by an American or European corporation. NIKE is the exemplar in this instance.

Three levels of globalization

It is possible to discern three levels of sports globalization. First, there has been the creation of global tournaments that attract competition on a universal basis. The Olympic Games were launched with this ambition in mind. Second, there has been the development of satellite communications: the first satellite, Telstar, was sent into orbit in 1962, and today a large number of different transponders offer a daily diet of news, sports and entertainment to a planetary audience. Third, there was the emergence in the 1980s of sports goods manufacturers which were able both to mine new sources of manufacture in hitherto neglected economies, and to develop new markets all around the world. The fact that markets existed owed much to the interest generated by the media coverage, itself dependent on the existence of big sports tournaments. Today, large-scale sports events cannot exist without television coverage on a global scale, and the promoters/organizers of such events derive a large part of their income from sales of merchandise. The interdependence is clear.

The earliest globalized sports tournament was the modern Olympics, which owed much to the vision of de Coubertin and which began in obscure circumstances in 1896. By the 1956 Olympics at Melbourne, television had taken an active interest such that the IOC was able to start charging for broadcasting rights. In 1930, FIFA held its first ever World Cup championships in Uruguay. Television was instrumental in changing the competition from an international sports event to a genuine global spectacle. The 1966 World Cup staged in England was televised around the world and became a benchmark for successive tournaments.

Both tournaments were representative in the sense that nations sent teams. International club competitions have been rarer. FIFA inaugurated the world club championship in 2000, bringing together top clubs from all over the world to compete in Brazil. More adventurous was Rupert Murdoch's – to some – outrageous attempt to bring together the top rugby league clubs from Australia and Europe to compete in a play-off competition after the conclusion of regular domestic seasons. The initiative was made possible by Murdoch's ownership of the television companies that would cover both the regular season and playoff games. In this sense, the whole enterprise was media-driven.

While the supremacy of the United States in its three cardinal sports, baseball, basketball and football, has never been in doubt, the lack of competition from elsewhere in the world denies the nation a forum for demonstrating this. It has no peers in baseball: Japan has a professional league, but tends to recruit American professionals who have not made it in MAJOR LEAGUE BASEBALL. After realizing the interest in Europe during the 1980s, the NFL tried to promote football in Europe, at first through the World League of American Football and then, from 1998, through NFL Europe, which featured six teams all based in Western Europe. Basketball, an American invention, was adopted by several countries around the world, but never played at the level of the NFL, which, in the 1990s, followed football's path in promoting itself in Europe. Professional basketball's progress was helped by European satellite and cable television stations that broadcast games "live." The decision to send teams of professional players to Olympic games was a controversial one, but it placed elite players on a world platform and expanded the NFL's horizons far beyond Europe.

The reverse process was in evidence in 1994 when FIFA agreed to stage the World Cup competition in the United States. FIFA president João HAVELANGE was eager to penetrate the largest unconquered market in the world, and attached conditions when he vouchsafed the tournament to the United States: MAJOR LEAGUE SOCCER had to be up and running within two years. While the growth of soccer in the US was slow, its popularity among three key groups, ethnic minorities, women and young people, maintained market interest. FIFA's global expansion was abetted commercially by Coca-Cola, a company that has associated itself, either through ENDORSEMENTS and SPONSORSHIP, with most international sporting events since the 1980s.

Dominance and dependence

Sport in the way we conventionally understand it is a phenomenon of western industrial society. Its emphasis on competition, achievement and athletic excellence reflected features of cultures in transition. The export of such sports from colonial times to the present day represents the intrusion of western values, particularly ones related to the PROTESTANT ETHIC, into cultures that have been subordinated economically or politically. Even a cursory examination of the Asian Games, for instance, reveals the extent to which Western sports have supplanted traditional events.

In this sense, the globalization of sports is part of a more generic pattern in which Western powers have sought to conquer and control developing countries and maintain their dominance through the imposition of cultures; sport, no less than religion, television and movies, has played a vital part in this process. C.L.R. James's *Beyond a Boundary* is an almost classic study of how cricket in the British Caribbean was integral to the colonial culture, but eventually became instrumental in challenges to British dominance.

Similar observations have been made about the effect of baseball in South American countries, but here there has been an additional process that feeds into globalization. Having successfully inculcated local populations with the values and creed of organized baseball, Major League Baseball teams were able to attract outstanding players with salaries that could not possibly be matched anywhere but in North America. In a similar fashion, European soccer clubs reaped a rich harvest from African nations. This benefited the few individuals involved, but often left local teams bereft of their standout players. The transfer of KENYAN RUNNERS to US colleges is another example of the African sporting exodus.

Again, this process has to be set in the context of globalization and perhaps what some call world systems analysis. This approach sees the co-existence of MODERNITY/POSTMODERNITY as a structure of continuing exploitation. Traditional political and economic powers at the center or core of a system remain connected to nations that were historically oppressed and rendered dependent by trade and commerce rather than political dominion. Athletes in the dependent, or peripheral, states may be regarded in the same way as the natural resources that were exploited and shipped out during colonial times: they are developed locally, but quickly move out to central metropolitan nations once their labor becomes valuable.

Of related interest

Rees, C. Roger, Brettschneider, Wolf-Dietrich and Brandl-Bredenbeck, Hans P. (1998) "Globalization of sports activities and sports perceptions," *Sociology of Sport Journal* vol 15, no 3.
Robertson, Roland (1992) *Globalization: Social Theory and Global Culture*, Sage.
Spybey, Tony (1996) *Globalization and World Society*, Polity Press.

Goolagong (Cawley), Evonne

b. 1951, Australia

Born in Barellan, New South Wales, Goolagong was the first internationally recognized female athlete of aboriginal background. She remains one of the few aboriginal competitors to have succeeded at world level, despite the emergence of Cathy Freeman as a track star in the late 1990s.

Historically, minority groups that have been denied opportunities to progress through conventional career routes, have sought betterment through sports. When RACISM has worked to close off career paths, many minority groups members have opted for sports as a way out of their circumstances. The material circumstances of Aboriginals have been especially dire, and few have been granted even the most rudimentary facilities for sports. Even in the team sports in which Australia has excelled (cricket, rugby), Aboriginals have been absent. Those that have risen to fame have either emerged from mixed parentage, as in Goolagong's case, or have been fostered by white Australian families, as in the case of Lionel Rose, who in 1968 became the first Aboriginal to win a world title when he beat Fighting Harada in Japan for the world bantamweight title. (Rose eventually retired in 1976, aged 29, and declined into alcoholism.)

Goolagong was a blithe presence in tennis: she betrayed no nerves on court, remained even-tempered throughout games, never resorted to PSYCHING opponents and seemed joyous even in defeat. She came to attention in 1970 when she won the Australian Junior championship at the age of 19. The following year she won Wimbledon, and reached the finals in 1972, 1975 and 1976, losing on the latter three occasions. She won the Australian Open four times, the French championships once and the South African Open in 1971 and 1972. Goolagong also played under the name Evonne Cawley after her marriage to Bill Cawley.

Goolagong, unlike Freeman, refused to use her position to publicize the Aboriginal cause and remained apolitical throughout her career. This angered Aboriginal activists, who pointed out that housing conditions were atrocious, job opportunities were scarce and life expectancy was shorter for Aboriginals than for other Australians. In 1998, Aboriginal advisers to the Sydney Olympic games of 2000 urged an international boycott of the event in protest at the worsening RACISM that affected Aboriginals.

Of related interest

Jacobs, Linda (1975) *Evonne Goolagong: Smiles and Smashes*, EMC-Paradi.

Graf, Steffi

b. 1969, Germany

Graf's often puzzling relationship with her father Peter raised interesting questions about the issue of PARENTHOOD and the sporting prodigy. Playing competitive tennis from the age of six, Graf was vigorously encouraged by her mother and coached from the outset by her father, who also managed his daughter's financial affairs. Yet the relationship with Peter Graf was controversial, and the most serious of the scandals surrounding him resulting in his serving two and one-half years in prison for tax evasion. It is also possible that the disciplined training regimen that she followed as a child was responsible for the momentous injuries she endured in her late twenties.

Born in Bruehl, in the former West Germany, Graf was groomed for tennis, practicing daily as a child. In 1982, at the age of 13, she turned professional and was the second youngest player ever to be computer-ranked. Within three years she was ranked sixth in the world. Despite persistent injuries, she competed at the highest level: in 1986, she won eight out of fourteen singles finals, claiming significant wins over Chris Evert and Martina Navratilova.

Her best period began in 1987 when she won forty-five consecutive matches and eleven out of thirteen tournaments, including the French, Italian and German Opens and the Women's International Tennis Association's indoor and outdoor championships. In 1988, victories at Wimbledon and in the Australian, French and US Opens made her the fifth person to achieve the Grand Slam (winning all four titles in one year). Later, she went on to become first player of either sex to win all four Grand Slam titles at least four times.

Much of Graf's success was based on her formidable physical power. Eschewing the backcourt style traditionally associated with female players, Graf favored a more aggressive approach, forcefully rushing the net in a manner not dissimilar to the serve-and-volley type of tennis played by men. Presumably this style derived from her childhood coaching and strength conditioning. But there were costs: her punishing competitive style and exacting training led to a series of injuries that began seriously to affect her play.

Continual hand, knee and ankle ailments – she had surgery on her right hand in 1998 and her left knee was surgically repaired in 1997 – might have ended the career of a less motivated competitor, and her problems were compounded by the incarceration of her father. In 1998, at the age of 29 and seemingly past her best, Graf won straight tournaments to qualify for a season-ending tournament in Madison Square Garden. Her run ended when her right hamstring gave out when leading the number one-ranked Lindsay Davenport. Graf's astonishing competitive urge manifested itself when she refused to retire and hobbled out after a three-set defeat. Another defeat by Davenport in the 1999 Wimbledon singles final prompted Graf to announce her retirement.

She explained her persistence in the face of daunting injuries as of someone trying to cling onto to a doomed relationship: "If you love the game so much, it is very difficult to part from it" (*Sports Illustrated* November 30, 1998). Never a popular player, Graf's travails earned her fans in the autumn of her career. Like Monica Seles, who also overcame considerable adversity, though of a different kind, she became a crowd favorite only after showing signs of vulnerability.

Of related interest

Heady, Sue (1995) *Steffi: Public Power, Private Pain*, Virgin.

grass

Grass is the surface of choice for most outdoor sports. While synthetic alternatives have been found to yield superior performances in many sports, most obviously track and field, grass has generally been favored as providing the truest and most reliable surface for competition: a literal as well as proverbial "level playing field." Even tennis, which employs a variety of playing surfaces, tends to venerate the verdant planes of Wimbledon.

Level grass playing surfaces are made possible by many factors, the most fundamental being good drainage. Artificial land drainage was used by Romans in Britain, though it was not until the Middle Ages that irrigation work of any significance was carried out. During the seventeenth century, land enclosures and field ditch systems began to take shape. The Agricultural Revolution of the eighteenth century paved the way for further social changes. Industrialization fed a movement away from rural areas and to the urban centers that housed the factories. This created a demand for food and led to the Enclosure Acts, which were legal landmarks in the development of modern farming. The first effect of these acts was to show the need for more efficient drainage systems to provide environments conducive to the growth of grain and vegetables. Experiments with underdrainage proved profitable.

One of the products of industrialism was automated cutting tools. Precursors to the lawnmower were indispensable in maintaining even, short grass which would permit the true bounce of a ball.

Grass surfaces flourish where there is good light all year round, adequate ventilation and sufficient rainfall. Some parts of the world manage this throughout the year, though most parts can produce good playing surfaces only in particular seasons. In the first two decades of the twentieth century, when sports began to attract masses on a regular basis, the stands used to accommodate spectators were crude and, by and large, uncovered. As sports professionalized and attracted more affluent customers, more comfortable seating and standing arrangements were needed. This introduced problems as stadiums became bigger and more covered. The light and air needed to promote good growth were at a premium.

In the 1960s, US and European stadiums made use of sand to improve permeability by ameliorating topsoil, or confining sand to an integrated by-pass system of vertical slits linked to underdrains. In some parts of the world, natural surfaces were replaced by synthetic turf. Teams in places such as Minnesota and Detroit were able to accrue benefits, especially in winter months. In Britain, soccer teams at Luton and Queens Park Rangers in London switched to artificial turf in the 1980s, though only on an experimental basis. The Football Association instructed a return to natural grass after observing the unusually high bounce of the ball and the worrying amount of injuries (including burns) to players. And, as John Bale (1993) points out: "Plastic pitches also have the effect of increasing player discomfort by having, on average, summer temperatures 4°C (7°F) higher than those on grass. As solar radiation increases, the synthetic carpet, helped by the layer underneath which acts as an excellent thermal insulant, becomes significantly hotter than natural grass." While the American football teams that continue to play on synthetic surfaces enjoy advantages when playing at home, none has ever won a Super Bowl.

The grass used for playing fields is typically grown outside the stadium and imported in four-foot-square trays, each about four inches deep. Theoretically, they may be imported from anywhere in the world. Because soccer's world governing federation FIFA insisted that all the 1994 World Cup games be played on grass, the Kingdome in Detroit had to ship in specially-grown grass from California.

In Europe where the winters can be severe, many clubs utilize undersoil heating to prevent the surface freezing over. This necessitates two rudimentary pieces of technology. First, there is approximately twenty-five miles of piping that acts as a conduit for boiling water, which lies between six and ten inches beneath the playing surface. Second, there is an efficient drainage system to take away the excess water once the ice or snow has been thawed.

In the late 1990s, sports clubs of all kinds tried zealously to attract the most affluent spectators by building more capacious stadiums with bigger and more luxurious boxes for corporate clients. Aesthetically, modular roofs were preferred, but lack of air and light then became a serious problem. New strains of grass helped: a particularly durable Poa Supina grass, which needed only minimal light and could prosper even in the shadow of large overhanging stadium roofs, was developed at Purdue University, Indiana, and widely exported. An alternative, or augmentation, was the see-through roof: transparent materials were used for the roofs of many stadiums to allow natural sunlight to shine through.

Air was a different proposition. Apart from suffocating stadium designs, an additional problem arrived when clubs came under pressure from sponsors to adorn their fields with logos or messages. These were literally painted on the grass, preventing the grass from breathing. Solutions to this were not easy to come by, especially as teams were loathe to either upset sponsors or redesign their architecture. New types of dye helped; ninety gallons of green dye were applied to the Miami field for Super Bowl XXXIII after the grass developed a disease that discolored it. The surface was playable, but the color was not aesthetically pleasing and certainly was not TELEVISION-friendly.

Another solution, albeit an expensive one, originated in $46m ($74m) Arnhem Dome in Holland, where the playing field was literally slid in and out of the stadium whenever it was needed. The operation took about seven hours to complete. The grass was grown off-site in concrete trays and remained outside when not in use for sports events. Emptied of grass, the 26,000-seat stadium was used for rock concerts and a variety of other functions.

One of the world's most notorious grass surfaces is the playing field at Sabina Park, Kingston, Jamaica, which is used for cricket. Historically, the West Indies team has included several fast bowlers, who favor a hard, unyielding surface from which they can extract maximum lift – the height at which the ball pitches – and speed. Ground staff at the stadium traditionally prepared the grass in such a way as to keep it dry and firm. The grass at Sabina Park was dug up and relaid in 1967. The following year, the surface dried out completely and cracks appeared all over the twenty-two-yard wicket. The constant barrage of balls caused divots to fly up, leaving an uneven surface, meaning that the balls either skidded through at ankle height or veered upward toward the batsmen's heads. The cricket pitch broke up again in 1976 when a West Indian attack comprising Michael Holding, Wayne Daniel and Vanburn Holder wreaked havoc with an Indian team, leaving five men injured as a result of unpredictably bouncing balls.

England's Mike Gatting needed reconstructive surgery on his nose after a wickedly bouncing ball from the Sabina surface in 1986. And, in 1997, a whole test match was called off after less than an hour's play between the West Indies and England when the surface was declared sub-standard. In a move unprecedented in over 120 years of test cricket, umpires halted play after witnessing players suffer a series of injuries. The pitch had baked, leaving scarcely any grass at all and an uneven surface off which the ball caromed into batsmen's heads and bodies.

Of related interest

Bale, John (1993) *Sport, Space and the City*, Routledge.
Frederick, E.C. (ed.) (1984) *Sports Shoes and Playing Surfaces*, Human Kinetics.
Stewart, V.I. (1994) *Sports Turf: Science, Construction and Maintenance*, E.F. Spon.

Griffith Joyner, Florence

b. 1960, USA; d. 1998

Griffith Joyner's importance lies in three areas. First, she re-defined popular conceptions of femininity, both in and out of sport. Second, she was the subject of considerable speculation as to whether her dramatic improvement in track performance was attributable to drugs. Third, she was one of the first sports performers to bridge the spheres of sports and entertainment.

Her image was the opposite of the small, fragile female: she exuded strength and durability. She offered a very different, yet distinctly female conception of femininity and one which subsequently became integrated into mainstream fashion. In her prime, during the 1980s, Griffith Joyner was the epitome of radiant athletic sexuality: an unconquerable female who had re-defined the standards by which women sprinters should be assessed, and a fashion model. An exhibitionist on the track, often wearing extravagant costumes and copious jewelry, she seemed blessed with an uncanny ability to judge the cultural zeitgeist.

Her track appearances were occasions for hardened media hacks to turn into fashion correspondents, recording every detail of her outfits, often down to the color of her nail polish. Flo-Jo, as she was known, represented the coming of age of female athletics when women could be flamboyant and sexually attractive as well as dedicated athletes. Other female athletes who displayed their ample, muscular bodies without compromising their heterosexual appeal followed; they included Gabrielle Reece and Lisa Leslie.

Griffith Joyner emerged as a world class performer at the 1988 US Olympic trials, when her winning time of 10.47 seconds in the 100 meters obliterated Evelyn Ashford's world record of 10.84 seconds. Griffith Joyner's time was better than the men's national records of several countries. She also captured the 200 meters record with a time of 21.34 seconds. In terms of Griffith Joyner's own development, it was an exponential leap: her previous best of 10.99 seconds had been set four years before and she had hovered around 11 seconds prior to 1987 when she began a new weight training regime, which she later claimed was the key to her success.

The following year she reappeared on the track having undergone what looked to be a metamorphosis: her muscular separation was clean and distinct, her skin was thin and vasculated and her chest was flat. Her stunning, powerful torso may have been shocking at the time but, in the years ahead, the muscular, athletic body became a fashionable look for young women. Yet Griffith Joyner left no room for doubts over her sexuality: she had a long mane of lustrous black hair, wore figure-hugging Lycra outfits, many of them specially designed for her, and draped herself in glittery jewelry, as if emphasizing that, for all her musculature, she was very much a woman. Her trademark nails were several inches long and always immaculately manicured.

Yet, even after her Olympic triumphs in the 100 meters, 200 meters and 4 × 100 meters relay events at Seoul in 1988, the media would not accept her as a unique yet legitimate athlete. The beaten Ashford's question to the media, "Why don't you guys write the real story?" might have been regarded as sour grapes;

but Carl Lewis, who had been given the men's 100 meter gold only after the disqualification of Ben Johnson, added to the suspicion that Griffith Joyner's rapid improvement may have been enhanced. Later reports from other Olympic Games confirmed that many positive test results had been willfully concealed.

Griffith Joyner had been tested for drugs, but never positively. Her decision to retire after the Olympics was surprising to all except those who believed that a pact had been made between her and the International Olympic Committee. The rumor ran that the IOC, rather than risk further damage to its credibility after the Johnson dismissal, either did not test Griffith Joyner or ignored the results on the condition that she retired soon after the games. She was 29 when she retired from active athletics, her reputation intact; she then went on to co-chair the US President's Council on Physical Fitness and began modeling clothes.

In 1996 she suffered a seizure when flying from her native California to St. Louis and spent a day in hospital with her family; no further details were released. Two years later she suffered another heart seizure in Mission Viejo, California, and died. She was 38. Her death revived stories of her alleged yet unproved use of performance-enhancing drugs. The British newspaper the *Observer* ran a story that linked Griffith Joyner's death with a batch of human growth hormone (hGH) stolen from a London hospital. According to writer Duncan Mackay, Darrell Robinson, a former 400 meters runner, sold the German magazine *Stern* a story claiming that he had supplied Griffith Joyner with a 10cc vial of hGH. While Griffith Joyner repudiated the story, she did not take legal action against either the publication or Robinson. Mackay speculated that an infected batch of hGH may have been traded on the black market in California. It is a highly conjectural argument, but one which added to the spiral of rumors around Griffith Joyner.

At the time of her death, her world records remained unbroken. Marion Jones' 10.61 and 21.62 were the closest at that stage; no one had run under 10.60 or 21.60, underlining the dimensions of Griffith Joyner's accomplishments. Whether they were chemically assisted or not will never be known, although it seems reasonable to assume that, if she were using drugs, then it is likely that her contemporaries in the 1980s would also have had access to similar substances.

Of related interest

Aaseng, Nathan (1991) *Florence Griffith-Joyner: Dazzling Olympian*, Lerner.
Koral, April (1992) *Florence Griffith-Joyner: Track and Field Star*, Watts.
Mackay, Duncan (1998) "London drugs link to Flo-Jo's death," *Observer*, September 27.

haka

In 1888–9, the first Maori rugby union team to tour Britain introduced an unusual pre-game ritual. Immediately before kickoff, the whole team would form a semi-circle and issue a warlike chant, stamping feet and making aggressive gestures in unison. The ceremony ended with the players jumping in the air and screaming ferociously. It seemed an effective way of intimidating opponents. Over the years, every game played by the New Zealand team, the All Blacks, was preceded by the same ritual, known as the haka.

The term "haka" is a generic concept for Maori dances and the ceremony performed by the rugby players is but one of several. Like all Polynesian peoples, the Maori, who began to occupy the Pacific islands about 1,000 years ago, composed, memorized and performed laments, prayers and war chants. There is a complex mythology to explain the meanings of the "haka and the condition of the Maori".

According to Greg Ryan (1993), the 1888–9 tour was an eventful one. British fans were disappointed to find that the players, far from being savages – as they expected – were civilized and conventional in appearance. A writer in *The Times* suggested that the Maoris might play barefoot; of course, they did not. However, the haka added to the image of savagery that was current in the nineteenth century. Some commentators saw the haka as little more than a gimmick, while others believed there was a circus-like quality to the Maori's game, which helped draw crowds. Few appreciated the cultural significance of haka. "But all of these responses to the team were more a matter of ignorance and misunderstanding than any kind of deliberate racism," writes Ryan. There was, however, one racial slur before a game against Rochdale, when local players "positively asserted that they would not play against the 'darkies' for no one, for they are only half civilized" (quoted in Ryan).

Although the All Blacks' version of the haka predates psychological studies of mental preparation for competition, it reveals a similar type of conditioning: its purpose, like that of the war chant from which it derived was in heightening the team's arousal and instilling in the team a combative, even warlike, state of mind.

At the same time, the sheer sight of fearsome players beating their chests, stamping their feet and chanting aggressively left opponents in no doubt of their hostility and perhaps initiated some anxiety. In other words, it was an early indication of the value of PSYCHING and of the role of SUPERSTITION in developing an appropriate mindset.

In recent years, opponents have understood the importance of the haka and have evolved methods of neutralizing it, such as turning their backs or walking through the semi-circle. New Zealand's rugby union governing organization has objected to such maneuvers on the grounds that they disrespect a ritual of religious significance.

Of related interest

Cuddon, Charles (1996) "Haka," in *Microsoft Encarta Encyclopedia* (CD-ROM).
MacDonald, F. and Ryan, G. (1996) "The game of our lives: The story of rugby and New Zealand and how they've shaped each other," *New Zealand Journal of History* vol 30, no 2 (October).
Ryan, Greg (1993) *Forerunners of the All Blacks: The 1888–89 New Zealand Native Football Team in Britain, Australia and New Zealand*, Canterbury University Press.

Harding *vs* Kerrigan

As sporting rivalries go, Tonya Harding *vs* Nancy Kerrigan had no equal. It had resonance far beyond the sporting arena: disputes over sexual identity, gender politics and social class made Harding *vs* Kerrigan a *cause célèbre* in its own way every bit as involving as the O.J. SIMPSON case and the Lewinsky affair – as evidenced by the television viewer ratings it claimed.

Harding and Kerrigan were figure skaters vying for a place in the US team to compete at the 1994 Winter Olympics at Lillehammer, Norway. In the run-up to the games, both were scheduled to appear at the US National Figure Skating Championships in Detroit. The clash never materialized on ice: on January 6, Kerrigan withdrew from the competition after being attacked after practicing. She was assaulted by a man who struck her right knee with a telescopic metal baton in an unprovoked attack. Her assailant fled, only to be captured and ultimately revealed as an acquaintance of Harding's ex-husband, Jeff Gillooly.

Shawn Eckardt, Harding's bodyguard, was charged with plotting the attack on Kerrigan. Two other men thought to be a hired hitman and a getaway driver were also brought in, giving rise to speculation of a contract attack designed to disable Kerrigan and remove her from Olympic contention. On January 25, an Oregon newspaper alleged that Harding herself was involved in the incident. Within three days, Gillooly agreed to testify against Harding and, two days after that, a television station claimed that Harding would be charged.

The US Olympic Committee dropped Harding from the Olympic team, but reinstated her after she threatened it with a $20 million lawsuit. Her effort was supported by Phil Knight, of NIKE, who contributed $25,000 toward Harding's cause; Kerrigan endorsed Nike's main competitor Reebok. Television stations carried daily news updates of the case and were rewarded with spectacular ratings. Harding was herself the victim of attack when walking in a public park near her home in Beaverton, Oregon: her knees, elbows and wrists were injured. Faced with possible prosecution, Harding eventually plea-bargained, admitting to hindering the prosecution of the then alleged attackers of Kerrigan. Her fines totaled $160,000, and she was ordered to complete 500 hours of community service and make herself available for three years of psychological treatment.

Kerrigan meanwhile recovered and captured the silver medal at the Olympics; the Ukraine's Oksana Bayul finished first. Harding was allowed to compete, but skated disastrously and left empty-handed. Kerrigan was feted at DisneyWorld and assembled a portfolio of product endorsements valued at $10 million (including a contract with Mattel to act as a model for a children's doll). Harding was also offered lucrative contracts, the most notable coming from a Japanese company that wanted her to wrestle for $2 million. Her appearance on *Saturday Night Live* gave the comedy show its highest audience rating in six years.

The United States Figure Skating Association stripped Harding of her national title for "unsportsmanlike behavior" and banned her for life. Her former bodyguard and ex-husband were given prison sentences. Yet, far from being disgraced and discredited, the vanquished Harding became something of a feminist hero. Her vilification by the media, her belligerent will to win – at any price – and her working-class credentials positioned her as a model of femininity in sharp contrast with that of Kerrigan, whose media image had been carefully nurtured. Kerrigan was presented as the clean-scrubbed, wholesome, middle American girl; hence the contract with Disney. After her attack she also became a victim, which served to enhance her appeal to mainstream audiences.

Even before the attack, media characterizations of Harding and Kerrigan tended to polarize the two rivals, "Tonya as the artless athlete, Nancy as the personification of elegance whose athleticism was not worth mentioning," as Ellyn Kestnbaum puts it in her essay "What Tonya Harding means to me, or images of independent female power on ice" (in Baugham (1995)). These representations were augmented following the Detroit incident, as Jane Feuer reveals:

> Tonya was never "artistic." Her skating reputation was made on the basis of her triple jumps and power. Her image prior to the attack was one of an "athlete," so that when she became newsworthy, it was easy to add on "working class" and "slut." Then Tonya could be opposed to Nancy, who was artistry/ middle class/princess.
>
> (Baugham 1995)

Kestnbaum asks if "the mode of being a woman Nancy projected, on at least as much as off the ice, was more acceptable to collective American ideologies of femininity than Tonya's?" Harding was outspoken about her pursuit of money as opposed to pure glory, her failed marriage was well-publicized, and her wedding night activities were captured on videotape; all these signaled what Robyn Wiegman and Lynda Zwinger call "her refusal to be a nice, feminine girl" ("Tonya's bad boot," in Baugham (1995)).

If there was a quality possessed in abundance by Harding which cleaved the American population, it was her white trashiness. It endeared her to some, but was anathema to others. While the term "white trash" (as opposed to poor whites) has all manner of negative connotations – slatternly, lubricious, dishonest – it also registers, with some, several admirable traits, including stubbornness, prickly pride and a lurking suspicion that those who succeed, do so by foul means more than fair. In Harding's almost classic case of white trashiness, there was an additional, and for many an attractive, quality: a refusal to be beaten by a favorite, who herself epitomized the middle-class lady. This rendered Harding's misdemeanors comparatively venial sins.

Widening the scope of the rivalry, we should notice how the entire sport of figure skating, or ice dance, is feminized by its conventions. Kestnbaum believes that women have "been complicit in offering their glamorized, eroticized bodies for spectatorial consumption"; though the same could be said for many other sports. Male figure skaters also present themselves in flamboyant costumes and frequently perform with great ostentation; they too offer themselves for "spectatorial consumption." There has been an association between figure skating and gays and, as Judith Mayne argues in her "Fear of falling," "televised coverage of the men's competition often wavers uncomfortably between a submerged acknowledgment of that [gay] sensibility and an affirmation of heterosexual and/or 'masculine' identities" (in Baugham (1995)).

Of related interest

Baugham, Cynthia (1995) *Women on Ice: Feminist Essays on the Tonya Harding/ Nancy Kerrigan Spectacle*, Routledge.

Haight, Abby and Vader, J.E. (1994) *Fire on Ice: The Exclusive Inside Story of Tonya Harding*, Time Books.

Reisfield, Randi (1994) *The Kerrigan Courage: Nancy's Story*, Ballantine.

Havelange, João

b. 1916, Brazil

Between 1974 and 1998, Havelange presided over the Fédération Internationale de Football Associations (FIFA), the organization that governs world soccer. During his presidency, FIFA's membership grew from 122 national sports bodies to 198, drawing affiliates from Africa, Asia and the former Soviet states to complement its core of European and Central and South American countries. Havelange was responsible for brokering a variety of commercial deals that helped soccer toward its position as the most popular and richest sport in the world. According to John Sugden and Alan Tomlinson, the projected revenues for the 2002 and 2006 World Cup championships are $2.6bn (£1.6bn).

Havelange was born in Rio de Janeiro, the son of affluent Belgian migrants. After studying law, he went into his father's business. Never a good soccer player, he concentrated on swimming and water polo and twice represented

Brazil in Olympic Games. He left his family's business to work for the Brazilian Sports Federation. Between 1958 and 1962, the Brazilian national team dominated world soccer, winning two world championships and producing players such as Pelé and Garrincha who are acknowledged as among the greatest players of all time.

Havelange was able to use Brazil's supremacy on the field to negotiate a greater political role for his country. Historically, FIFA was an organization run by Europeans. In terms of voting power, Europe held 33 votes as against South America's 10. FIFA's president was Sir Stanley Rous of England, who campaigned for re-election in 1974. Havelange was able to marshal the support of Africa, Asia and North and Central America by promising the global expansion of the sport. Developing countries, said Havelange, would share in an unprecedented expansion of soccer. No sport had ever developed such ambitious plans. Buoyed by the additional votes, Havelange ousted Rous and ended the European hegemony.

FIFA itself was at this point approaching bankruptcy. Its primary purpose was as an organizer of the World Cup competition, which was staged every four years and alternated between European and South American venues. The championship was contested by sixteen nations, with the African and Asian states having to compete in an elimination tournament for a single place. Havelange set about changing the structure of the competition so as to accommodate nations from all quarters of the world.

Assisted by Horst Dassler, the one-time head of Adidas, and Coca-Cola, which, from the 1970s became progressively interested in sports sponsorship, Havelange began building a financial base for FIFA. Over a twenty-four-year period he added a series of competitions to FIFA's portmanteau, including the Women's World Cup, the World Football (indoor soccer) Championships and the Confederations Cup. All were handsomely sponsored, with Coca-Cola continuing its commercial interest.

During his reign, he had several contretemps, including a well-publicized row with Pelé, an argument over the 1994 world youth championship venue and a visit to Nigeria at the time of the execution of dissidents. Perhaps the most embarrassing dispute arose over Japan's hosting of the 2002 World Cup. South Korea objected and was eventually granted the status of co-host.

In 1998, Havelange, then aged 82, stepped down from his presidency. While many regarded his reign as autocratic and unhealthy for soccer, he left behind a commercially prosperous governing organization that had operations in all six continents and had 170 affiliated states.

Of related interest

Dauncy, Hugh and Hare, Geoff (eds) (1999) *France and the 1998 World Cup: The National Impact of a World Sporting Event*, Frank Cass.

Sugden, John and Tomlinson, Alan (1998) *Fifa and the Contest for World Football: Who Rules the People's Game?*, Polity Press.

Hillsborough

A total of ninety-four Liverpool fans died as the result of a tragedy at the Sheffield Wednesday soccer club's Hillsborough stadium on April 15, 1989. It was later found that more than six hundred too many spectators may have been allowed into a section of the Hillsborough stadium, and that the wrong size barriers had been fitted, resulting in fans being crushed. The disaster, which was witnessed on television by many relatives of the victims, took place prior to a game between Liverpool and Nottingham Forest in the semi-finals of the FA Cup. In an effort to relieve a crush outside the stadium, the police ordered a large gate to be opened, allowing hundreds of fans to pour into the overcrowded enclosures at the Leppings Lane end of the stadium.

A government inquiry into the incident, chaired by Lord Justice Taylor, laid the blame squarely on the South Yorkshire police who, he concluded, failed to plan for the arrival of large numbers of fans. But, to the fury of relatives of the deceased, senior police officers refused to admit any responsibility at the inquiry. Rumors that Liverpool fans caused the crush by arriving at the stadium late, drunk and without tickets compounded the grief of relatives. At the inquest held in 1991, the coroner refused to admit evidence relating to events later than a cut-off point of 3.15 p.m. on the day. The jury returned a verdict of accidental death.

Two years later, families of six of the victims applied for judicial review, asking the High Court to quash the verdict and order a new inquest that could lead to a verdict of unlawful killing. This was refused. However, in 1996 the TELEVISION docudrama *Hillsborough* uncovered new evidence suggesting that the police must have known the severity of the overcrowding when they opened the gate. A closed circuit camera was said to have been working, contrary to evidence at the inquest. The police video and new medical evidence disclosed in the television program precipitated a review in 1997 to establish whether a fresh inquiry was justified. This was ruled out in February 1997.

A disaster comparable in kind and scale to Hillsborough occurred in Guatemala City on October 16, 1996 when 82 people died beneath an avalanche of bodies at a World Cup qualifying game between Guatemala and Costa Rica. A crush in a tunnel and fans trapped against fences at the densely packed Mateo Flores stadium evoked parallels with the Sheffield tragedy. FIFA speculated that forged tickets may have triggered the crush: fans holding tickets were denied access and proceeded to kick down an entrance, causing fans inside to cascade down to lower levels.

In both stadiums, there were fences that effectively prevented the free movement of spectators and there was no monitoring of crowd density inside the stadiums. These were but two of a series of stadium disasters that occurred through the twentieth century. Ibrox Park, Glasgow, was the scene of tragedies in 1902, when a stand collapsed and 25 fans were killed, and in 1971 when 66 died after barriers gave way. In 1968, 74 were killed when fans headed toward a locked exit and were crushed against the doors. Forty-nine people were trampled to death in a Cairo stadium in 1974. In 1985, thirty-eight people died at the Heysel Stadium, Brussels, when HOOLIGANISM was blamed. A grandstand collapsed at Corsica in 1992, killing 17 spectators. However, the worst sports tragedy occurred in 1982 in Moscow where a reported 340 people were killed at a European Cup soccer game.

Of related interest

Frosdick, S. (1996) *Risk and Responsibility: The Disasters of the 1980s Highlighted the Importance of Stadium Safety*, Panstadia International Quarterly Report, vol 3, no 4.

Maguire, Joseph (1994) "Patriot Games? English identity, nostalgia and media coverage of sporting disasters," in Allison, Lincoln (ed.), *Working Papers in Sport and Society*, vol 3.

Scraton, Phil (1999) *Hillsborough: The Truth*, Mainstream.

Walvin, James (1986) *Football and the Decline of Britain*, Macmillan.

Hoch, Paul

b. 1942, USA; d. 1993

The context of *Rip Off the Big Game*

Hoch was arguably the most important of a small group of academic writers who, in the early 1970s, formulated a critical approach to the analysis of sport, in Hoch's case based on Marxist foundations. While much of the analysis offered in the 1970s is now familiar, and in some cases dated, Hoch's work was truly pioneering in its day and, even in retrospect, looks a powerful and challenging attack on sports.

Hoch himself was educated at New York's City College, from which he graduated with a degree in mathematics, and at Brown University, Rhode Island, where he completed his doctoral research in theoretical physics. He continued his work in theoretical physics at the University of Toronto between 1966–8, and then moved to the University of London where he conducted research in the philosophy of science. While in London he became involved in the anti-Vietnam War movement: he was arrested and imprisoned after a demonstration, and later deported. Between 1973 and 1979 he held a professorship of humanities at Dawson College, Montreal, and then returned to Britain where he worked on research projects at several English universities.

He published widely on subjects such as the history of solid state physics, the role of refugee migration on scientific development, the history of sexual and racial stereotyping and the British and American educational systems. However, it was his book *Rip Off the Big Game: The Exploitation of Sports by the Power Elite* that established his reputation as an international scholar; it outsold his other books by some way, and was (and is) cited by every quality sports science textbook.

The book was written during his first period in England, when Hoch's thought was at its most radical. In the second half of the 1960s, a number of sports biographies had begun to express criticisms of sport as an institution. Hoch was influenced by, for example, Dave Meggyesy's *Out of Their League* and Bernie

Parrish's *They Call it a Game*, both of which departed from the more orthodox sanitized biographies and reflected caustically on some of the practices encouraged in professional sports. Other critics, like Harry Edwards and Jack Scott, were also commenting on the darker aspects of sport, such as racism and drug taking. Hoch saw a critique of sports taking shape: his effort was to define that shape more clearly.

The Marxist influence in *Rip Off the Big Game* is made clear in Hoch's early acknowledgment of Antonio Gramsci. Gramsci's concept of hegemony, though not used by Hoch, describes a way in which exploitative capitalist systems are kept intact, not by force or coercion but by persuasion and consensus. The domination of the working class, for Gramsci, is part of a control apparatus that serves the interests of power-holding groups: the working class consent to their own control and, in some cases, even oppression. This is not a passive type of consent, less still a capitulation: culture prescribes certain types of values and beliefs, and growing up in such a culture inclines working-class people toward such values and beliefs. The right of the ruling class to rule, the inevitability of gross inequalities and the uselessness of trying to transform the system might be instances of such values and beliefs. All work in a persuasive way to convince working-class people of the rightness of the *status quo*. The way things are appears to be "common sense." Hoch takes up Gramsci's observation that there is an entire apparatus responsible for diffusing ideas that complement and encourage consensus. These include the Church, education, the media, political institutions and, most crucially for Hoch's purposes, sports.

Up until Hoch's book, the prevalent view of sport by social science was that sport should be analysed as a functional element of the social whole, contributing to the resolution of conflicts or tensions and assuring a continuity of beliefs and orientations through training and co-ordination. Other perspectives derived from ethology also saw sport functionally, analysing it as an outlet for aggression that might otherwise be channeled into areas that would be destructive for society. Hoch found both conclusions unsatisfactory: neither, he reckoned, even asked the right kinds of questions about sport. What groups in particular benefit from it? What are its effects on fans? What would Marx have said about sport were he alive in the second half of the twentieth century? For Hoch, these were the relevant questions.

Sport as a new opiate

"Five generations ago, Karl Marx called religion the opiate of the masses. Today that role has been taken over by sports," Hoch wrote. Marx had drawn an analogy between the effect of religion on followers with that of opium on its users. Temporarily gratified by the agreeably uplifting consequences of the drug, users become dependent and seek ever greater amounts to compensate for meaninglessness and routine nature of their everyday lives. The feeling of well-being provided by the drug takes their minds away from the practical problems of existence and makes it possible for them to face another day. Yet the relief they find in the drug is, in a sense, illusory: it leads them only into misery.

Similarly, religion captivates its adherents and affords them feelings of euphoria; the succor it brings balances the ill effects of their material circumstances. By promising a salvation, religion encourages believers to endure hardships in the here and now in anticipation of the afterlife. For Marx, religion was the perfect foil for capitalism: workers were prepared to tolerate exploitation in the expectation that salvation would be theirs.

Hoch wrote of the coming of mass production, the division of labor and the growth of an industrial working class, or proletariat (a term that Hoch, following Marx, preferred): "So in a situation in which workers were given less scope for creativity and decision making in production, it was only to be expected that they should seek (and be provided with) some sort of pseudo-escape and pseudo-satisfaction." Sports had an added benefit: "The sort of passive attitudes industrial workers learn in watching a baseball game serve as a useful socializer for the deadened passivity necessary to function in a capitalist society."

In sports, Hoch found a kind of reflection of capitalist power arrangements, a small elite group owning and controlling the means by which profits are produced and a mass of paid workers/players who performed in their service. Cross-ownership has meant that a virtual monopoly exists, with a relatively small number of power-holders owning major franchises. He also found echoes of industrial production in the way players are trained to perform almost as dehumanized factory workers. And the disciplined, regimented approach that had crept into team sports in the postwar period suggested a militarism that dovetailed neatly with notions of NATIONALISM and loyalty to one's country. The belligerence fostered in most sports and even the lexicon employed (blitz, attack, destruction) encourage a militarized conception of the world in which there is always an enemy to be conquered. Hoch believed this complemented the ideology behind US economic imperialism.

Hoch described contemporary sports as "ultra-macho," and found sexist values at almost every level of sports participation: competition is a testing ground for masculinity and women are, in a sense, the prizes for success. Writing as the first wave of feminism began to take effect, Hoch proposed that women's position in sports destined to mirror their position in society generally, "as a reserve army of labor ... or, in the case of non-working housewives, as a barrier against their husbands' ability to go on strike."

RACISM in sports also came under scrutiny. Building on Edwards's *The Revolt of the Black Athlete*, Hoch examined the racial issues of sports. Racist stereotypes were fed by blacks being allowed entry into certain sports and not others. Sports would, he felt, be used increasingly as a platform for publicizing discontent over the racial discrimination that continued unabated after the civil rights legislation of the mid-1960s. In this respect, Hoch anticipated many of the debates that would rage through the 1980s and to the present day.

Rip Off the Big Game shared a premise with many other Marxist analyses of the 1970s: that the class division created by capitalism is the root of all evil. Crime and deviance, educational imbalances and massive inequalities in income and wealth distribution were all attributable to the workings of the capitalist system. Like other Marxist studies of the period, it can be criticized for its occasionally overwrought attempt to reduce everything to byproducts of economic processes. Hoch, at times, showed a Procrustean zeal to force facts into his theoretical framework. However, Hoch's work should be evaluated as a prototype from which came several later versions. The perspective he offered was so fresh and surprising that it all but threw down a gauntlet for subsequent analysts of sport. Disagree as they may with his brand of MARXISM, they could hardly ignore such a damning critique which remains one of the most defiant studies of contemporary sports.

Of related interest

Brohm, Jean-Marie (1978) *Sport: A Prison of Measured Time*, Ink Links.
Hoch, Paul (1972) *Rip Off the big Game: The Exploitation of Sports by the Power Elite*, Anchor Doubleday.
Gruneau, Richard (1983) *Class, Sports and Social Development*, University of Massachusetts Press, 1983.

hooliganism

History and development

The term "hooliganism" became popularly associated with British soccer fan culture in the 1960s. The term itself had been around for much longer, possibly dating back to a nineteenth century family of Irish migrants named Houlihan, members of which were prone to VIOLENCE. The name underwent changes in pronunciation and became applied to any young person with delinquent tendencies. Its specific application to soccer fans came after a series of incidents at English and Scottish soccer stadiums in which rival sets of fans fought, at first on the fields of play immediately following games, then in the terraced areas surrounding the field, and later in the vicinity of the stadiums.

Violence runs like a ribbon through the history of soccer. Early violence normally took the form of trying to kill the referee. In 1921, fans of Arsenal and Tottenham Hotspur met in the streets of North London armed with knives and iron bars. Police baton charges on crowds were commonplace. One club took the view that a game should not be stopped unless the bottles being thrown were full rather than empty. In the 1930s, invading the field of play and attacks on players and police were the subject of public disapproval. Then came a relative calm in the 1945–60 period.

Many of the eruptions of violence were at meetings between local teams, such as Rangers *vs* Celtic in Glasgow and Everton *vs* Liverpool. The rivalry between fans in these cities was intensified by a Catholic *vs* Protestant edge, with the Celtic and Everton clubs having Catholic ancestry. At a time when sectarian violence in Northern Ireland was raging, soccer "wars" seemed a logical, if perverse, counterpart. Anti-semitism was thought to be behind the age-old conflict between fans of Tottenham and Arsenal, the former being traditionally a Jewish-owned club. However, the violence, or "aggro" (aggravation), became, in the words of the tabloid newspapers, mindless. Every Saturday, local stores boarded up their fronts, pubs were demolished and hospitals filled up with casualties.

The violence was impersonal and often ritualistic; weapons, or "tools," became commonplace and serious casualties were frequent. Far from being friendly rivalries, the hooligan encounters were fiercely factional and passionately fought. At first thought to be the work of a few irascible and feckless youths, hooliganism spread throughout the country, attracting more mature and calculating fans. By the end of the 1960s, all soccer teams had a corps of fans who delighted in media descriptions of them as "animals": one memorable chant that issued from the stadiums was used as the title of a book by David Robins, *We Hate Humans* (Penguin, 1984).

Localized at first, hooliganism took on a European complexion in the 1980s. It was exported initially by the traveling groups of fans following British teams in the competitions governed by FIFA's European affiliate UEFA (Union des Associans Européenes de Football). Exposed weekly to the extensive *television* coverage afforded hooliganism, fans in countries such as Germany, Holland and Italy became well-tutored in British hooliganism and were sometimes prepared to engage in pitched street battles.

Far from being marauding masses, hooligans acquired more organizational control during their European sojourns. Tactical planning and quasi-military structures became features of hooliganism in the 1980s. Some groups spawned cells, each of which had functions in the overall scheme of things. Hooligans gave themselves names, such as the Inter-City Firm, Zulu Warriors and Headhunters; some even had the audacity to leave business cards behind after vandalizing trains or pubs. The constant cries that the violence was the result of only a minority seemed a puny defense, as it seemed the entire character of soccer fandom was changing.

European hooliganism reached its grisly climax in 1985 when an explosive encounter between fans of Liverpool and Juventus, of Turin, took place at the Heysel Stadium in Brussels, Belgium. Thirty-eight fans were crushed to death and 200 others injured in the worst tragedy in soccer's history. After blame was apportioned, all English clubs were suspended from European-wide competition for five years and Liverpool for seven years. Juventus and its fans were exonerated.

While hooliganism was *not* a factor when four years later, 94 fans died at the HILLSBOROUGH stadium in Sheffield, England, this tragic event served to sharpen the focus on the physical structures of stadiums and the behavior of spectators within those structures. The report of the inquiry that followed Hillsborough recommended that standing-only areas of stadiums should be removed. The government, in response, adopted a number of measures which led to a decline in violence at games: in particular, alcohol was banned from all stadiums in 1985. The 1986 Public Order Act made provision for the exclusion from games of those convicted of offenses against the public order. The 1991 Football Offenses Act and the introduction of surveillance cameras also reduced the incidence of criminal behavior at games.

Thereafter, hooliganism slid from the news and, eventually, from the stadiums. Chastened by report after report that documented the mass media's role in amplifying – and thus promoting – soccer violence, newspapers and television began turning their gaze away from fans in an attempt to starve hooligans of the publicity they presumably sought, in a process described by Eric Dunning as a "deamplification." Soccer generally and British soccer in particular began a slow transformation from a predominantly working-class sport and one which offered disreputable pleasures to barbarous youths to an altogether more "respectable" pastime. The old-style terraces on which fans would traditionally stand and which were well suited to hooliganism were replaced by seats. Many fans stood on seats as if to signal their resistance to the changes, but they were practically immobilized: the terrace surges that used to start mass violence were stopped and hooliganism was curtailed.

Sporadically, there were reports of a return to more primitive times. Occasional outbreaks of violence, usually outside stadiums, were rarely given the chance to form a pattern; police control of hooligan activities had, by the 1990s, progressed far beyond baton charges. The Football Intelligence Unit, set up in 1990, was an anti-hooligan squad that operated as part of the British National Criminal Intelligence Service (roughly the equivalent of the FBI). The unit maintained a database of intelligence on individuals known or suspected of violence at stadiums, and offered this information to overseas police forces when English teams played abroad. The information was gathered from all sources, including a number of undercover operations, one of which is dramatized in the film *I.D.*

The reputations of British fans continued to earn them the special attentions of police forces around Europe. In one notable incident in 1997, traveling fans of the England team that played Italy in Rome were given an especially harsh time by Italian police. It seemed that the violent elements of soccer's FANDOM had receded, leaving a body of people that had shared more features with a market than with the motley assemblies of the 1960s. Fans became eminently exploitable, devouring expensive replica shirts, computer games, videos and all manner of other merchandise that added to the costs of being a fan in the 1990s. Admission prices rose out of proportion with inflation; clubs justified this as a way of offsetting the cost of stadium refurbishment. The once "rough" working class became respectable, although, according to some interpretations, violence was still lurking not too far beneath the surface.

Sociological explanations

Writing in 1971, the writer Ian Taylor identified the 1961–2 season as the beginning of hooliganism ("Soccer consciousness and soccer hooliganism," in Stanley Cohen (ed.), *Images of Deviance*, Penguin). Interpreting this and the series of similar occurrences that followed as a disguised form of political resistance against a sport that had detached itself from its working class origins, Taylor examined the emerging disorder among spectators against a background of changing class composition and a culture that was increasingly taking on bourgeois characteristics amid postwar affluence. In other words, when fans' loyalty to their clubs spilled over into AGGRESSION against fans of other clubs, it signaled a loss, that of the club itself. It no longer belonged to fans: its players were highly paid celebrities, its owners were wealthy capitalists and its boundaries were no longer local, but international.

Fans were mainly young lower-working-class males, who sensed they were no longer an organic part of the club and had no effective control over the destiny of what they regarded as *their* team. One of the ways they could assert themselves was to invade fields of play, disrupt the game and, perhaps most importantly, seize the attention of the popular media. In other words, Taylor explained the upsurge in violence in and around the soccer stadiums in the early 1960 in Marxist terms: it was a class revolt against powerlessness.

Though popular in the 1970s, the somewhat rigid Marxist approach gave way to more nuanced explanations. Eric Dunning and several of his colleagues at Leicester University, England, had been schooled in the work of Norbert ELIAS. Historically, Dunning and his colleagues discerned a continuity in the norms of aggressive masculinity that generally prevail in patriarchal societies. This is consistent with Elias's theory of a civilizing process in which violence has been brought under control, external and internal, giving way to planning and the emergence of the modern state. However, this has been an uneven process, and some sections of the working-class population of Britain were not incorporated into dominant patterns of values. Although one of the norms was control of violence, sections of the working class, which Dunning *et al.* describe as the "rough" working class, contravened such norms.

The Leicester school found that the crowd behavior that was zealously magnified by the media from the 1960s had actually been going on from the end of the nineteenth century through until the First World War. Then came a period of greater incorporation, and as this proceeded, crowd violence decreased. The "new hooliganism" was attributable to the attraction into the sport of "young males from the still relatively unincorporated sections of the working class, a process which led to the moral panic which had been generated earlier around the teddy boys and the mods and rockers to be transposed into a football context," as Dunning himself put it in his essay "The social roots of football hooliganism" (in Giulianotti *et al.*, 1994).

Historical research indicates that soccer, even as far back as the 1890s, has provided a context for the expression of local rivalries, and the violence associated with hooliganism is actually part of an older, recurring pattern. Males, regardless of social class, were expected to fight under certain circumstances or risk being called "unmanly." The rough or unincorporated segments of the working class would have been socialized on the streets and so been exposed to the aggression which often conferred prestige on the best fighter in the locality. "Forms of violent fan disorderliness are a virtually universal accompaniment of the Association game [soccer]," writes Dunning, concluding that the most recent manifestations are not new at all; the media have reported them *as if* they were new and this in itself is new. In the process, the media's amplification of the hooliganism created awareness of and fascination with the violence and set in motion a self-perpetuating spiral. Only when the media lost interest did hooliganism disappear.

Psychological and ethological accounts

The first set of arguments about the hooliganism of the 1960s came primarily from journalists, whose observations of games and crowd disorders led them to believe there was a connection between the two. As more money began to circulate in British soccer, so the competition between teams increased and cash incentives for winning games or trophies introduced a rawer, more ruthless and often brutal type of play. The violence among the crowd was a reflection of the violence on the field of play, with fans mimicking the aggression of players. Robert Arms and his colleagues replicated several earlier studies into this phenomenon and concluded that: "the observation of aggression on the field of play leads to an increase in hostility on the part of spectators" (R. Arms *et al.*, "Effects on the hostility of spectators of viewing aggressive sports," in A. Yiannakis *et al.* (eds), *Sport Sociology*, 3rd edn, Kendall/Hunt, 1987).

Dismissed at first as crude and mechanical, this theory returned in the early 1990s, albeit in a different form. Two murders in Britain were blamed on video *Child's Play 3*, which was watched by the culprits shortly before their crimes. The Rodney King riots of 1992 were thought by many to have been perpetuated by the mass media which, in transmitting images of rioters, virtually invited people to duplicate their behavior. In other words, once the media focused on an event, the copycat effect is triggered. By presenting an event as more important, more serious or more widespread than it really is, the media inadvertently creates conditions under which their images are likely to become a reality. None of the theories covered so far would dismiss the active role played by the media in the persistence of hooliganism, but the copycat account accords the media primacy in the cluster of causes.

Alternatives influenced by ethology (the study of animal behavior) dwelt on the ritualistic elements of the fan violence, viewing it as part of a huge dramatic performance in which youths acted out their parts without risking life and limb. Examining the sometimes quite elaborate hierarchies around which clubs' fans were organized, Peter Marsh, Elizabeth Prosser and Rom Harre of Oxford University concluded that, while the belligerent behavior witnessed at stadiums appeared to be chaotic and unplanned, there were, on closer inspection, what they called *The Rules of Disorder* (Routledge & Kegan Paul, 1978).

Absent from many of the theories of hooliganism is the perspective of the hooligan. John Kerr, in his *Understanding Soccer Hooliganism* (Open University Press, 1994), addressed this in what he calls "reversal theory." Basically, Kerr argues that young people who get involved in fan violence are satisfying their need for stimulation through forms of behavior that involve risk and novel or varied situations. One of the attempts behind this approach is to get away from theories that offer the impression that humans are consistent. "This means that a soccer hooligan who on one occasion smashes a shop window may on another occasion do something completely different," writes Kerr. This depends on a "metamotivational state": we can "reverse" between them as easily as a traffic light changes red to green; it all depends on the situation, or contingent circumstances.

"The soccer environment provides a rich source of varied pleasures for those who wish to pursue and enjoy the feelings of pleasant high arousal," Kerr concludes. Most regular fans reach a satisfactory level of arousal; others do not, and develop their own extreme variation in their quest for excitement. This results in destructive behavior which can, given the right motivational state and a conducive situation, be as gratifying as watching a good movie or poring over a work of art. Kerr detects that one way of achieving a high arousal is through "empathy with the team."

What becomes clear from such a brief survey of the strikingly different theories is that no single account is satisfactory in accounting for a cultural phenomenon that remained part of soccer's landscape for nearly thirty years. Interestingly, hooliganism seemed almost impervious to police control, stringent court sentences and panopticon-like surveillance. Even when it did seem to fade, it was at the onset of what Steve Redhead calls *Post-Fandom and the Millennial Blues* (Routledge, 1996) when soccer fans were brought to order not by social control measures but by the power of market forces. They were pacified by replica shirts, videos, logo-plastered bedsheets, face painting and a miscellany of commodities derived from a sport that realized that the only way to prosper was to re-invent itself.

Of related interest

Armstrong, Gerry (1997) *Football Hooligans – Knowing the score*, Berg.
Buford, Bill (1992) *Among the Thugs*, Mandarin.
Giulianotti, Richard, Bonney, Norman and Hepworth, Mike (eds) (1994) *Football, Violence and Social Identity*, Routledge.
Murphy, Patrick, Williams, John and Dunning, Eric (1990) *Football on Trial: Spectator Violence and Development in the Football World*, Routledge.

Hoop Dreams

A documentary film directed by Steve James, Fred Marx and Peter Gilbert, *Hoop Dreams* was released in 1994 to unanimous acclaim. Taking as its main narrative the efforts of two young African Americans to make it to basketball's professional ranks, the movie revealed the profligacy of sports in a way that was often out of the grasp of academic writers or journalists. It raised the question of how many young basketball hopefuls it takes to produce one Michael JORDAN. Its implicit answer is that the number is beyond calculation.

The lives it chronicled were those of Arthur Agee and William Gates, two black teenagers who live in Chicago and, more pertinently, live in the hope of becoming NBA players. The film trails them for seven years from the age of fourteen. Both aspire to play "downstate" for the interstate school championships and, after that, to play professionally. Both show promise and are accepted into St. Josephs, a private school which nurtured the talent of Isaiah Thomas.

When Thomas revisits his old school to give the boys a pep talk, the look of rapture on Agee's face makes it clear that he is gazing at an ICON of black redemption. Both youths' boredom in classes apart from sports is evident in their every movement. Their single-mindedness is never approximated by their peers. The magnetic pull of stars like Thomas is aided by the push given to the aspirants by family members, particularly Agee's ne'er-do-well father and Gates's brother, himself a failed basketball player. It becomes apparent that the youths are effectively beasts of burden, freighting much more than their own personal ambitions.

The odds of their making it into the ranks of the professionals are slim: each year, 500,000 boys play high school basketball, a coach tells them, and of the 14,000 who go on to play intercollegiate basketball, fewer than 25 ever play a single season in the NBA. Agee and Gates are not destined to be among those few.

The films contrives to make several points about the ruthless, unforgiving nature of professional sport and its links with the black experience. Agee's and Gates's forays into sport are microcosms: their reversals are those of hundreds of thousands of other would-be basketball stars. It is this resonance that gives *Hoop Dreams* a parable-like quality. The disappointments of the youths at the film's center are the prices paid for blacks' sporting excellence.

The St. Joseph's school took out a lawsuit after the film had, it claimed, "misrepresented the nature of their work as not-for-profit." According to the official transcript of the court proceedings, "the film was not an accurate reflection of St. Joseph's High School or its staff or students." The video version of the movie carried an apology from the film makers. Agee capitalized on the media attention afforded him by the film and became number one draft choice. He did not make the cut. Gates failed to make the grade at all and became a sports announcer for radio WMAQ-AM in Chicago.

Of related interest

Axthelm, Pete (1971) *The City Game*, Simon & Schuster.
Hoop Dreams, directed by Steve James, Fred Marx and Peter Gilbert, 1994.
Joravksy, B. (1995) *Hoop Dreams: The True Story of Hardship and Triumph*, Harper Perennial.
Malec, M.A. (1995) "Hoop shots and last dreams," *Journal of Sport and Social Issues*, vol 19, no 3.

horses

Totem animal

No animal has been more central to the sports experience than the horse. Horses were tamed and ridden for recreational purposes in the pre-Christian cultures of Egypt, Greece and Rome, although, of course, the barriers that now separate sports from other pursuits were indistinct; certainly the hunting and racing activities for which horses were trained have contemporary counterparts.

Through the entire civilizing process, horses have been raced, harnessed and used for both military and hunting purposes; they have been bred for speed, strength, endurance and the ability to perform expressively. They continue to fascinate gamblers, breeders, trainers and owners as well as fans throughout the world. Anthropologist Kate Fox, in her monograph *The Racing Tribe*, argues that the source of this fascination is in the horse's totemic status. "A 'totem' animal is said to be a symbolic representation of the tribe," writes Fox, suggesting that the aficionados constitute a tribe. "The control/disinhibition contradictions in racing culture are precisely mirrored in the tribe's treatment and expectations of the racecourse."

Fox argues that, in sports, horses are saddled, bridled, led and ridden, "controlled and constrained by leather, metal and rigorous training in acceptable behavior." Yet, in racing sports, the animal is encouraged to give free rein to its most basic instinct: to run with the herd. Horse racing in particular provides its followers with "precisely the balance of security and freedom that they need." So, horse racing fulfills a "fundamental human need for escape from the restrictions of mundane existence," concludes Fox. While not all horse sports accentuate the speed of the horse, all involve some degree of control – the rider's ability to subordinate the animal to his or her (most horse sports have permitted women riders) wishes – while allowing the horse behavioral expression of its own abilities.

Horse sports have two sources. Most racing derives from the attempt to recreate the excitement of hunting and the horse racing that sometimes accompanied the hunt. Other sports emphasizing the performance of the horse under testing conditions have military origins.

Industrialism and hunting

Many of the organized equestrian sports as we recognize them predate industrialism, though their popularity and formalization owe much to the coming of steam power and the new means of transport it introduced. When railways superseded horses as the main mode of transportation in the mid-nineteenth century, the functional importance of horses diminished sharply. Horses had pulled ploughs, stage coaches, wagons, barges and many other kinds of conveyances vital to preindustrial life; they were also the most effective means of travel, particularly in North America with its sheer size and relatively undeveloped terrain.

In Britain, the steam engine made long-distance transportation by horse all but redundant by the late nineteenth century, and motor cars had replaced horses on the roads by the beginning of the First World War. Yet the acceptance of and affection for horses – and a general interest in competitive sports – meant that sports involving them endured. As with many other folk games and recreational pursuits, equestrian sports reflected the design, organization, structure and other features of industrial society. Governing associations regularized meetings and formalized rules. The codification of the lengths of courses, heights of fences and permitted weights made sports involving horses as ordered as the other major sports. The British were responsible for diffusing interest in horse sports throughout the former Empire (see ANIMAL RACING).

Military origins

According to Jane Kidd (1996), dressage has foundations independent of horse racing. She traces its beginnings to ancient Greece, although "the start of modern dressage was during the Renaissance"; the first riding academy was created in Naples in 1532 and attracted members of European aristocracies. More an art than a competitive activity, dressage was fashionable in France in the seventeenth century. Over the next 200 years, it was practiced throughout Europe. Germany introduced standardization and testing into the art, rendering it a competitive activity, principally for members of the military. As with many sports, it was, at first, a way of preparing riders and horse for war, and, later, a competition in itself. The trials of dressage ensured that the horses were highly disciplined and responsive to the wishes of their riders; both vital attributes of military horses. After dressage was admitted to the Olympic games at Stockholm in 1912, the prescribed sequences of movement became more formalized and criteria for evaluating were stipulated. In 1921, the *Fédération Equestre International* was created as a governing organization for all horse sports at international level, including dressage.

The US Army Cavalry had an influence on another very different sport, that of endurance riding, in which horses competed in time trials, covering a specific distance within a predetermined maximum time. The US Cavalry began this type of event in the 1920s, in 1955 the Tevis Cup was established, which was contested over a hundred miles between Nevada and California. The sources of inspiration for this event are not difficult to find: during the westward advance of the nineteenth century, the horses of cavalry, frontiersmen, Pony Express employees and others would often need to travel great distances across difficult terrains. The Tevis Cup was designed to embody the same kind of challenge.

Although they share similar origins, endurance racing and dressage represent extremes, the former testing the horse and rider's stamina and conditioning, the latter their closeness and control. Eventing brings these two aspects together, integrating dressage, cross-country (a test of endurance and courage) and show-jumping, in which horses are expected to surmount artificial obstacles in an enclosure. Again, the military purpose of all three disciplines is apparent. Before the Second World War, all competing teams at major events were from the military.

The relationship between horse and rider is scrutinized during eventing: an understanding of sorts is said to develop between animal and human such that the horse reacts to the minutest of instructions. Similarly, mounted games (formerly known as gymkhana races) allow this understanding to manifest by making animal – usually a pony – and human complete a series of intricate tasks while in motion. As its name suggests, gymkhana has Indian roots: it was started by British Army units stationed in India in the nineteenth century.

Horses feature in a variety of other competitive pursuits that emphasize restraint, poise and mastery. Rodeo, started by American ranchers, is perhaps the most vivid example of this. Vaulting, which involves the performance of gymnastics while on horseback, originates in Europe. Both test skills that were once essential to survival but which are now surplus to requirements. Traditional proficiencies were preserved by translating them into competitions.

For many people, horses symbolize a golden age gone by, which they seek to recreate. In America, large numbers of horse riders take pride in the authenticity of their turnouts as cowboys or as riders of Morgan horses in the ante-bellum South. In Britain, the same impulse has led to a phenomenal revival in side-saddle riding and in harness classes, for which people take great care to recreate the carriages of gentry or the carts of tradesmen from the nineteenth century.

As with other commercial sports, the professional horse sports, specifically racing, were – and continue to be – affected by CORRUPTION. As with any sport in which stakes are high, the temptation to try to influence the outcome of competition has been great. Wray Vamplew's history (1996) suggests that corruption (NOBBLING) in horse racing is practically as old as the sport itself.

Of related interest

Fox, Kate (1998) *The Racing Tribe*, Social Issues Research Centre.
Kidd, Jane (1996) "Horseback riding, dressage," in Levinson, D. and Christensen, K. (eds), *Encyclopedia of World Sport: From Ancient Times to the Present*, ABC-Clio.
Vamplew, Wray (1976) *The Turf: A Social and Economic History of Horse Racing*, Allen Lane.

human growth hormone

Known as "the drug of champions," human growth hormone (hGH), or somatotropin, became popular among elite athletes in the late 1990s, largely as a result of ever-more rigorous testing procedures. Because it is a naturally occurring substance, no reliable test to detect it had been discovered. Human growth hormone shared many of the benefits of anabolic steroids, including increased body strength and lean muscle mass. But, its prohibitively expensive price – about $800, or £500 per 2.5 centimeter vial (late 1990s prices) – put it beyond the reach of all but top competitors.

Like erythropoietin (EPO), which facilitates the production of extra red blood cells but does not show up in urinalysis, and Insulin Growth Factor (IGF1), hGH mimicked nature, in this case by duplicating the functions of the pituitary gland, which secretes the growth hormone. This hormone controls the body's rate of growth by regulating the amount of nutrients taken into the body's cells and by stimulating protein synthesis. Overproduction of the hormone may cause a child to grow to giant proportions (a condition known as "gigantism"), whereas too little can lead to a retardation, sometimes referred to as "dwarfism." The hormone is administered by injection.

Human growth hormone also affects fat and carbohydrate metabolism in adults, promoting a mobilization of fat, which becomes available as fuel, and sparing the utlization of protein. It provides immense strength for short periods of time, allowing performers to train harder and recover more quickly. The potential of this mechanism for promoting growth has not been lost on field athletes, weightlifters, bodybuilders and others requiring muscle bulk. However, it is in the area of swimming that hGH gained notoriety.

Human growth hormone was produced from human corpses in the 1960s to treat children with serious growth problems. When the hormone's potential for sports performers was realized it was sourced from doctors, who would scrape the pituitary gland during autopsies. Although it was banned in 1986 (after children being treated with it died) markets in the growth hormone extracted from human foetuses were uncovered. A 1988 article, "Growth hormone: A review" (by S. Haynes in *New Studies in Athletics*, Supplement 1), spelled out its potential.

A synthetically manufactured version called somatonorm made the illicit trade redundant. Somatonorm was thought to be safer than the natural hormone, but its effects included the broadening of bones and elongation of the jaw. Females developed masculine facial hair and Adam's apples. As somatonorm was also undetectable, it became one of the DRUGS of choice for top sports performers, though the extent of its use remained unknown.

Then, in 1997, customs officers at Sydney, Australia found thirteen vials of Norditropin, the brand name of somatotropin, in a bag belonging to Yuan Yuan, a member of China's team in the World Swimming Championships. Yuan Yuan, at 21, was the youngest member of the team and ranked thirteen in the world for the breaststroke. It was speculated that, as a relatively lowly member of the team, she was a guinea pig intended to ascertain whether hGH could be detected through conventional equipment. In the event she did not have chance to use the drug, which was confiscated.

Between 1990 and the Sydney incident, Chinese swimmers returned twenty-three positive tests for banned substances. In 1994, China's female swimmers won twelve of sixteen events at the World Swimming Championships in Rome. Two months after their successes, in the 1994 Asian Games in Hiroshima, seven Chinese competitors tested positive for dehydrotesterone, an anabolic steroid. And, while China's women won only one swimming gold medal at the 1996 Atlanta summer Olympics, two set world records in Shanghai the following year; both swimmers, Chen Yan and Wu Yanyan, were ranked outside the world's top fifty. There were also suspicions surrounding the record-breaking feats of several female Chinese distance runners in the early 1990s. Known collectively as "Mao's army," the athletes' secret was said to be caterpillar droppings, though few believed that this was the only substance ingested by the runners.

Of related interest

Stone, M.H. (1995) "Human Growth Hormone: Physiological functions and ergogenic efficacy," *Strength and Conditioning* vol 17, no 4.

Wirth, V.J. and Gieck, J. (1996) "Growth hormone: Myths and misconceptions" *Journal of Sport Rehabilitation* vol 5, no 3.

Yarasheski, K.E. (1994) "Growth hormone effects on metabolism, body composition, muscle mass and strength," *Exercise and Sport Sciences Reviews*, vol 22.

Hustler, The/Color Of Money, The

A quarter of a century separated *The Hustler* (released in 1961) from its sequel *The Color of Money* (1986), during which time Fast Eddie Felson, the flighty, overconfident young pool player of the original, had matured into a somewhat jaded liquor salesman whose grip on the game was, at best, tenuous; he scouted promising young players. Paul Newman – who featured in memorable sports movies, such as *SOMEBODY UP THERE LIKES ME* and *Slap Shot* – played the fast-lane hero who finally slowed down, perhaps to find himself. *The Hustler* was based on Walter Tevis's 1959 novel of the same title.

Both films, of course, center on pool, which was also the subject of a close-up study by Ned Polsky in 1964, *Hustlers, Beats and Others*. Polsky spent time with the real-life hustlers, players who played badly at first in order to set up their opponents: convinced the hustler is truly mediocre, the victims are seduced into raising the stake money of a side bet. The hustler then plays at his best and wins.

Eddie Felson is fictional hustler of the first film, and he jokes and teases his dupes. The film's most memorable scenes are pool battles: there is genuine exhilaration in the edgy tension, particularly between Felson and his big prey Minnesota Fats, played by Jackie Gleason. Director Robert Rossen (working from Walter Tevis's source book) enclosed much of the film in smoky, grimy, almost claustrophobic pool halls. The pool milieu is a stage for the two main characters who charm and infuriate in roughly equal measures. Polsky's book, noted above, is also a study of the poolroom scene of the 1960s, depicted as "no-woman's land" that "caters to refugees from the world of female-imposed gentility, catering to men who wanted to be able to curse and spit tobacco, fight freely, dress sloppily, gamble heavily, get roaring drunk, whore around." Yet there are customs and conventions that must be obeyed.

Fast Eddie, however, flouts all the informal codes of the pool circuit in his effort to force a confrontation with Fats. The film suggests that the pool playing fraternity recognizes all manner of procedural rules, a key one of which is respecting senior players. Eddie makes a deliberate policy of ignoring this. His relationship with Fats, whom he irritates incessantly, is mirrored in *The Color of Money*, though by the 1980s, Fast Eddie himself had become the player who expects respect and Vince, played by Tom Cruise, is a clone of himself twenty-five years before. Recognizing in Vince his own youthful qualities, Eddie takes him under his wing and mentors him. It becomes clear that Eddie is trying to recreate himself, though Vince is less compliant than he had hoped and a brittleness develops in the relationship.

Martin Scorsese's *The Color of Money* shows how, by the 1980s, the pool circuit had acquired an organizational structure and a certain respectability. The efforts of Vince and Eddie are geared to winning a national tournament taking place at an Atlantic City hotel. This kind of glitzy showcase for pool co-exists with the greasy pool hall games that were a staple of the first movie.

The breakup of the mentor–acolyte relationship agitates Eddie back into competitive action, and much of the film is devoted to his sometimes painful road back. His decline is symbolized by a pair of eyeglasses he needs to wear in order to see the pool balls clearly. Inevitably, he brings his experience to bear and fights his way into the Atlantic City tournament, where he meets and beats Vince. His elation at having proved himself again evaporates when Vince reveals that he eased up to win a bet he has placed. Eddie's triumph turns to disaster as he learns that the old hustler has been hustled.

The Hustler and its sequel span a period in which the structure and shape of sports changed appreciably. Television had barely sensed the potential of sports as a means of hiking ratings and, so, increasing advertising revenue, and commercial sponsors were several years away from realizing the advantages of having their products associated with something as wholesome as sports – though pool could hardly be described as such, certainly not in the 1960s. By the 1980s, though, the kind of tournament depicted in *The Color of Money* would have been a clean, sponsor-friendly affair, far removed from the strictly men-only subculture seen in the first movie. By the 1990s, women's pool was an organized competitive activity that had acquired the kind of respectability that had eluded the men's game, which never totally severed itself from the disreputable pleasures of old.

Of related interest

Polsky, Ned (1964) *Hustlers, Beats and Others*, Aldine.
Tevis, Walter S. (1959) *The Hustler*, Harper.
The Hustler, directed by Robert Rossen, 1961.
The Color of Money, directed by Martin Scorsese, 1986.

I

icons

Creating icons

The word icon is from the Greek *eikon*, meaning image. Today, it typically refers to the image that is conferred, granted or attributed to an individual by a collection of others, usually fans. In a sense, the popular cultural icon exists almost independently of the individual, who is usually a sports or rock star: popular perceptions, expectations and beliefs define the icon much more powerfully than the person.

Historically, we can find occasional examples of this. Jack JOHNSON "was not merely a fighter but a symbol," according to Lawrence Levine in his *Black Culture and Black Consciousness* (Oxford University Press, 1977). In 1912, it was widely believed that the then heavyweight champion had been refused passage on the doomed *Titanic* because he was black. This enhanced his status even further: he had been divinely spared, thought his followers. This is not so unusual. In Christine Gledhill's collection of essays, *Stardom: Industry of Desire* (Routledge, 1991), Stacey writes of the "god-like" status of icons in the eyes of their fans: "Stars are fabulous creatures to be worshipped and adored." They are seen as more than "ordinary mortals."

As Johnson achieved iconic status among blacks in the first two decades of the century, so Muhammad ALI did in the 1960s and 1970s, his every feat seeming to elevate him above "ordinary mortals." Not only could he defy overwhelming odds and beat seemingly invincible opponents, like Sonny Liston and George Foreman, but he could also predict the round in which he would win fights. By converting to Islam and refusing the military draft, he surprised everyone while at the same time making himself an enigma. His extraordinary capacities were underlined when he regained the world title at an age when other sports stars were contemplating retirement (an event documented in the movie *WHEN WE WERE KINGS*).

Contemporary sports icons continually have beliefs built around them, about their affairs, their earnings, their sexual proclivities; indeed, there is a willingness to believe almost anything about some icons. In the 1990s, sport's iconography took an almost Manichaean character in which icons personified either good or evil. There was an asymmetry between, on the side of good, Michael JORDAN and George Foreman, and, on the other side, Dennis Rodman and Mike TYSON. All had iconic status: stories about all of them proliferated, they enjoyed wide fan bases and their every move was monitored by a voracious media.

Superlatives must accrue to the sports icon. He or she must express the highest or very high degree of a valued quality: as Jordan was the supreme basketball player, so Tyson was, for a while, "the baddest man on the planet," Rodman the nonpareil rebounder, Michael Johnson the fastest man alive. The people themselves are dissolved into the superlatives to the point where they become indistinguishable from them: they *become* superlatives. In some cases, they can seem to be part of a different order of being. What the actual person is becomes irrelevant: what matters is that a following, or FANDOM, believes this to be so.

The advent of cross-marketing and the general commodification process of which this is part has facilitated the creation of sports icons. Jordan is the supreme example: his affiliation with NIKE, in particular, worked as a component in what was a carefully coordinated process of icon construction. The deliberate confusion of Jordan the man with Jordan the athlete *extraordinare* encouraged a general belief in his super-humanity: someone who defied the laws of gravity with his ability to hang, whose unerring shooting defined new levels of perfection, whose unrivaled mastery of all facets of basketball elevated him above all others.

However, sporting performance is but one component of the icon creation process: Rodman, like other basketball players, ventured into movies, adopting personae that were only fractionally different from the one he portrayed on court (see *Double Team*). Foreman became a spokesperson for burgers and unsuccessfully piloted a television sitcom in which he virtually played himself. No sooner had French soccer star Eric CANTONA been suspended for fighting with a fan (in 1995) than Nike featured him in a series of ads that both highlighted his "bad boy" image and made a virtue of it.

The importance of fandom

The power of the icon lies in the relationship with the audience. Fans imitate icons by fashioning their hair, piercing their bodies and so on; they identify through wearing replica shirts or items of apparel that proclaim their allegiance; they sometimes project, which means that they actually wrap up their own lives with that of the icon. This enables fans to index their own experiences with that of the icon, as if they are "living through" another's experiences. Jenson (1992) suggests ways in which fans live vicariously through what they understand to be the lives of the famous. In this sense, the relationship to the icon might be a way of fulfilling dreams or fantasies by imagining oneself in the position of another. It is hardly surprising that some icons have attracted fans whose projections have bordered on the pathological.

Alberoni (1972) described stars as a "powerless elite," groups of people "whose institutional power is very limited or non-existent, but whose doings and way of life arouse considerable and sometimes even a maximum degree of interest." Alberoni argued that stars who commanded strong and widely diffused followings operated in their own spheres and posed no effective danger in a political sense. There are, however, instances when sports icons have capitalized on their obvious adulation to transfer into political spheres. Olympic track star Sebastian Coe, for long regarded as a gifted athlete, became a politician after retiring from competitive sports. The indications are that more sports icons will follow this path and convert the obvious influence they have over fans into political influence.

Rodman

The *fin de siècle* sports icon Dennis Rodman was perfectly suited to an age when mass media and multimedia were pre-eminent. Through his company, the Rodman Group, the Chicago Bulls and LA Lakers rebounder recycled himself into every possible television talk show, into movies and into books. Rodman, with his pierced nose, navel and scrotum, incessantly sought notoriety, swearing in front of millions of TELEVISION viewers, kicking a photographer and head-butting a REFEREE. During the 1997 NBA play-off finals, he found himself in Salt Lake City where the Bulls played (and beat) the Utah Jazz. "You've got a bunch of asshole Mormons out here," Rodman told reporters, in a state where more than two-thirds of the population are Mormon.

Rodman's wardrobe was what might be described as sexually confused, and his hair changed hue with virtually every appearance. His body was plastered with tattoos. His best-selling books, *Bad as I Wannabe* and *Walk on the Wild Side*, boasted of his sexual dalliances with, among others, that other postmodern icon *suprême*, Madonna. Rodman confided to the world's media that he wished to change his name to "Orgasm" and that, on his death, he wanted to be stripped naked, frozen and be placed in a see-through freezer.

Of related interest

Alberoni, F. (1972) "The powerless elite theory and sociological research on the phenomenon of the stars," in Dennis McQuail (ed.), *Sociology of Mass Communications*, 1972.

Dyer, R. (1979) *Stars*, British Film Institute.

Jenson, J. (1992) "Fandom as pathology: The consequences of characterization," in Lisa A. Lewis (ed.), *The Adoring Audience: Fan Culture and Popular Media*, Routledge.

i.d.

Director Philip Davis' first film, *i.d.* (1994), was made more relevant three years after its release when a Manchester police officer revealed that his experience as an undercover agent who had infiltrated a gang of soccer hooligans was as turbulent and stressful as that of the chief character in the movie. *i.d.* focuses on an ambitious twenty-something London detective who goes deeply undercover to build relationships with a group of highly organized hooligans, who have proved impervious to conventional police tactics.

Like other movies essaying undercover themes, such as William Friedkin's *Cruising* and Mike Newell's *Donnie Brasco*, *i.d.* details the officer's immersion into the subculture and his periodic attempts to disengage himself and recover objectivity. John, played by Reece Dinsdale, insinuates himself into a group of soccer fans at their "headquarters," a London pub. He and a fellow agent prove themselves with displays of machismo in front of rival gangs. But while John's colleague senses the dangerous appeal of FANDOM and draws back, John goes with the FLOW, taking on the manners, attitudes and, ultimately, the identity of a fully-fledged fan.

His objectivity lost, John begins to relish the habitual drinking and fighting, the racist attacks and the belligerent chauvinism typical of hooligans. Compared to the excitement and the respect he enjoys among the hooligans, his "real" life appears drab and featureless. Like the agents in *Cruising* and *Donnie Brasco*, he discovers facets of his own identity which are clearly incompatible with his official role as a police officer.

By concentrating on the officer's metamorphosis while undercover, the film manages to expose the attractions of HOOLIGANISM without becoming judgmental about the people who structure their lives around it. John scales the hierarchy of the hooligan structure, at one point celebrating his position in front of his fellow police officers. "I'm a top boy!" he boasts to his incredulous colleagues. The viewer is left to ponder: has he become a hooligan, or is it just part of his cover? By the end of the film, it is clear that there is no pat answer. At the same time, the film shows that there can be no pat solutions to soccer VIOLENCE: the seemingly irrational, though often ritualistic, AGGRESSION is rendered both comprehensible and as functional as churchgoing to the hooligan himself (women feature little in this depiction).

The film's additional relevance came to light only after Detective Constable David Burton, of the Greater Manchester Police, opened up about his own undercover work with the Omega squad, an elite team of detectives in Manchester set up to target hooligans. His early work was to infiltrate English hooligans at the World Cup and the European Championships in Sweden, where he pretended to be an armed robber. His next assignment was to act as a drug dealer. The operations lasted about six to eight months each, after which Burton would get a new identity. While working undercover, his wife and three children saw him only occasionally and he was shunned by parents at his children's school.

At the end of 1994, Burton was informed that he was "overexposed" and made to give up his double life to return to normal policing. But, he argued, he was given insufficient support from police colleagues in his attempts to reassimilate and became physically ill, taking eleven months sick leave. He separated from his wife and started taking Prozac. On his return to work in 1996, he was given an administrative position. Many of the hooligans he helped convict remained in circulation and he feared for his own safety. By contrast, the fictional character in *i.d.* finishes with the police and embraces the hooligan subculture completely.

Of related interest

Dunning, Eric, Murphy, Pat and Williams, John (1988) *The Roots of Football Hooliganism*, Routledge & Kegan Paul.
Guilianotti, R., Bonney, N. and Hepworth, M (eds) *Football, Violence and Social Identity*, Routledge.
i.d., directed by Philip Davis, 1994.

imperialism

Militarism and conquest

The relationship between sports and imperialism is an intimate and complex one, involving as it does imperialism not only in its military form, but also in its economic and cultural manifestations. In order to establish this point, it is first necessary to recognize that what we call "sport" is a specific cultural creation of nineteenth-century imperial Britain, one that is so deeply wedded to a particular sense of Englishness that, in 1936, the German writer Stiven observed that the English technical language of sport was becoming globally dominant in the same way as Italian terms in music had become universal (cited in Norbert Elias and Eric Dunning's *Quest for Excitement: Sport and Leisure in the Civilizing Process*, Basil Blackwell, 1986: 126).

This is not to suggest that physical play of various kinds has not existed in many societies for millennia, nor that the founders of official sports in Britain did not imitate and combine elements of many forms of play from around the globe (think, for example, of the influence of native American games on the development of tennis and on a closer relative, lacrosse). Indeed, to conceive of imperialism in sports as only the imposition of alien games on the peoples of conquered territories is to underestimate the degree to which it also involves the partial and selective appropriation of subordinate cultural forms. It is also to ignore the extent to which imperial sport may be used strategically by both social elites and subordinate groups in post-imperialist or post-colonialist societies.

The British origins of sport as a social and cultural institution lie in a formative combination of factors: the desire within ruling economic, political and religious groups to regulate the leisure activities of the industrial and rural working class and the more dissolute male scions of the aristocracy and bourgeoisie; the establishment of physical education and the healthy minds, healthy bodies ethic in school education; and, of particular significance here, the deployment of sport in the great public (independent) schools of England as a training aid for what was seen by Matthew Arnold, Thomas Hughes and others as a decline in the military preparedness of the nation and in the fitness for leadership of the hereditary officer class.

Sport figured, therefore, both as a metaphor for war and as representative of the life that British imperialism was trying to defend and extend. For example, in Herbert Havens's *Scouting for Buller* (first published in 1902 by Thomas Nelson), an adventure novel of the Boer War, the Cape Town-born protagonist finds himself, just prior to battle, introduced to the arcane language of association football (soccer) by his fellow soldiers. Sitting in the trenches, he found the talk drifted into some mysterious subject which he could not follow: "It had nothing to do with the coming battle, I knew, but the men were greatly excited." Bemused by all the "strange talk" about the Wolves, Throstles, Babes and Saints, it was not until much later that he learned that these were the popular names of various football clubs engaged in an annual tournament for the possession of a silver cup. In this instance (fictional, though no doubt based on reality), sports provided a distraction for the working-class soldiery in the imperial wars as they thought nostalgically of England.

From the same era but further up the class hierarchy, Frederick Courteney Selous's travelogue *Sport and Travel: East and West* (first published in 1900 by Wolfe Publishing, of Arizona) makes a more literal connection between sport, militarism and imperialism. Here sport means hunting, as the imperial sportsman roams exotic locations like Asia Minor and the Rocky Mountains, providing illustrations of a "Swarthy Type of Turkish Peasant", shooting and then mounting on walls as trophies the heads of various species of deer and big cat. It is hard not to see some of this impulse to conquer the wildlife of the world anthropomorphically, with an imaginary victory also achieved over the peoples who seem to merge, symbolically, with the animal world.

Similar connections are made in Sir Henry Newbolt's famous poem *Vitaï Lampada*: "The Gatling's jammed and Colonel dead, And the regiment blind with dust and smoke … But the voice of a schoolboy rallies the ranks: 'Play up! play up! and play the game!' " Later, in its twentieth-century deviant working-class variant, xenophobic British soccer fans, as Colin Ward recalls in his autobiographical *Steaming In: Journal of a Football Fan* (Simon & Schuster, 1989), set out to take the territory of rival fans during forays into Europe which self-consciously invoked previous wars against the French, Germans, Italians and so on.

Class and culture

The connection between sport and imperialism has also been made by those on the political left, but in this case sport is regarded as a means by which imperialist powers can control the underdeveloped nations of the earth. MARXISM has inspired several polemics on sports, one of the most notable being that of Jean-Marie Brohm. In *Sport: A Prison of Measured Time* (Pluto, 1978), he proclaimed that: "Britain exported her main forms of sporting practices along with her commodities and gun-boats, to India, southern Africa etc. *The birth of world sport parallels the consolidation of imperialism.*"

Brohm goes on: "The great international sports federations were set up at the turn of the century around the time of the First World War, at the same time as the other great supra-national organizations such as the League of Nations. Today the international authorities of world sport are completely integrated into the mechanisms of imperialism" (1978: 175–6). From this perspective, the spread of sports from the imperial centers was a device to retain influence by monopolizing the administration of international sporting competition. For such a strategy to be effective, it was necessary to persuade other countries that they should wish to emulate the success at sport which brought with it a sense of national progress. Hence, for Brohm, beaming images of the decadent Western life glimpsed through global media events like the Olympic Games and the soccer World Cup into the lives of the world's poor was part of a process of post-imperial psychological enslavement, so that:

> *The Olympics objectively form part of imperialism's development at the expense of the third world. The Games allow third world countries to witness, through the medium of television, the exhibitionist displays of the bourgeois world, gorged and wallowing in the prodigalities of the consumer spectacle.*
>
> (1978: 120) [emphasis in the original]

This somewhat conspiratorial view of sporting imperialism is, clearly, not always shared by the people of the Third World, who, while perhaps ambivalent about the origins of sport, may see success at the international level as an opportunity to strike back at the former imperialist aggressor. The Caribbean Marxist C.L.R. James, for example, while loving the game of cricket, also understood the manner in which it could achieve psychologically what could no longer be seized unquestioned by force of arms.

The presence of the English MCC (Marylebone Cricket Club) in the colonial enterprise is apparent in James's analysis. As he explains in *Beyond a Boundary* (first published in 1963), cricket formed part of a seductive cultural package including many magazines on W.G. Grace, Victor Trumper and Ranjitsinhji that meant that he was a British intellectual "long before I was ten, already an alien in my own environment among my own people, even my own family" (James, 1963: 18). The sovereign publication *WISDEN* would have been among those magazines.

This form of imperialism is principally cultural, leaving a deep legacy that binds both parties far into the future, most notably in the Commonwealth (formerly Empire) Games, which are held every four years in some corner of the former British Empire. Yet the success of the West Indies cricket team – itself a neo-colonialist construct of sovereign nations which exists only for the purpose of international cricket – is felt by many of its players and supporters to be supportive of anti-imperialism, just as President Nelson Mandela in post-apartheid South Africa was happy to celebrate its rugby union World Cup victory in 1995, despite the traditional lack of black South African involvement in the sport and its deep (though not absolute) affiliation with white RACISM. Sport has been used as a vehicle for resisting the world's most powerful nations in a variety of contexts; by Ethiopian and KENYAN RUNNERS, for example, or by Dominican baseball players.

Post-imperial ironies

The historical and geographical development of sport around the world has also produced some slightly curious circumstances, such as those which prevail in Australia. This former white-settler colony embraced sport so enthusiastically in the twentieth century that, for many commentators, sport became its defining cultural institution. Yet, as Colin Tatz points out in his 1995 book

Obstacle Race: Aborigines in Sport (University of New South Wales Press), the sporting aspirations and achievements of Aboriginal Australians have frequently been obstructed or neglected, thus denying them the kudos that, despite some elitist disparagement, attaches to sporting success in that country.

As in other spheres of Australian society, then, it has been necessary for Aboriginal sportspeople to fight for recognition in challenging the legacy of imperialist domination. The gesture by the indigenous runner Cathy Freeman at the 1994 Commonwealth Games – where she waved both Australian national and Aboriginal flags in a victory lap – entailed the use of sport as a means of affirming and celebrating Aboriginal identity at the very moment when post-imperial white nationhood was itself being affirmed and celebrated. (Compare Freeman's gesture with the apolitical approach of Evonne GOOLAGONG in the 1970s.) The politics of such a gesture cannot simply be reduced to the "prodigalities of consumer spectacle."

Yet it would be equally misguided to ignore the manifest economically and culturally imperialistic dimensions of contemporary sport. It is difficult, when observing the scarce resources that small nations plough into Olympic sport or the huge sums expended by developing nations like South Korea and China in bidding for the right to host global sports spectacles, not to judge international sport as a potent force for shaping the economic priorities of such countries in a manner likely to favor the sports superpowers who largely control the governance, production and communication of world sport.

Here Americanization comes to the fore alongside – or perhaps coterminously with – GLOBALIZATION. The extraordinary success of African American ICONS like Michael JORDAN (who is repeatedly named by children as their favorite sports person in countries like Australia where basketball is still a relatively minor sport) and of US-style sports attitude and marketing in general may be regarded as an aggressive new form of cultural imperialism in and through sport. Not only does US sport spread out across film, music, magazines and other forms of popular culture, but its associated endorsed and sponsored products – Coca Cola, Pepsi, McDonalds, NIKE, Philip Morris and many other brands – are sold alongside it, while US broadcasters and advertising agencies dominate the transmission of sports content across the globe.

New imperial ironies emerge at this point where positive images of (formerly enslaved) African American men are used, in stark contrast to their negative profile in other respects, to sell products and market messages of individualism through consumption. At the same time, there have been protests that this process also involves the systematic exploitation of workers in poor countries like Indonesia, often under contract from suppliers in other still developing countries like South Korea. Imperialism in and of sport, it seems, is putting on a different and more exotic mask.

Imperialism in its various forms, of course, stimulates objection and assertion of local difference, and, as noted above, there are few nations exercising their right to opt out of international sport. There is little evidence that forms of sport can be foisted on an (at first) unwilling population, as the history of the NFL and NBA in Britain and of MAJOR LEAGUE SOCCER in the USA have shown. The former or currently dominant imperial powers have also been challenged in various international sports associations like FIFA (Fédération Internationale de Football Associations) and the International Cricket Council (itself an outgrowth of the MCC). In sport, however, as in other social and cultural institutions, old Western imperial influence has displayed considerable resilience.

Of related interest

Birley, Derek (1995) *Land of Sport and Glory: Sport and British Society, 1887–1910*, Manchester University Press.
James, C.L.R. (1994) *Beyond a Boundary*, Serpents Tail.
Klein, Alan M. (1991) "Sport and culture as contested terrain: Americanization in the Caribbean," *Sociology of Sport Journal* vol 8.

DAVID ROWE

instant replay

In 1998, a spurious decision by REFEREE Phil Luckett in an American football game between the New York Jets and Seattle Seahawks sparked off a renewed clamor for the restoration of instant replay facilities in National Football League (NFL) games. It was suggested that they be used as early as the 1998–9 post-season. The request was denied, but the pressure to use cameras as aids to referees and umpires continued. The NFL had experimented with instant replay from 1986–91, but discontinued it because of the time it added to a typical game; the three-hour slot that had been so convenient for TELEVISION was extended indeterminately, making program scheduling difficult.

In other sports, instant replay had proved a successful adjunct to refereeing. Cricket, already a slow game (up to five days), was slowed down by a further sixty-nine seconds in 1993: this was the time it took to study three video replays and decide that Robin Smith would earn the distinction of being the first player given out after study of the "magic eye." This was a highly controversial technological innovation in a sport that clung dearly to age-old traditions, but its utility was recognized. As in football, the delays often seemed excessive, though the more ordered pace of cricket made an accommodation possible. Cricket also discovered that video evidence, while valuable in many close decisions, was inconclusive in certain areas; for example, catches behind the wicket and catches at bat-pad.

Rugby League introduced a video referee who had the authority to adjudicate on in-goal decisions by watching a range of replays. Crowds watched the same replays on a large screen that also displayed the verdict, "try" or "no try."

In the late 1990s, a series of questionable decisions by English soccer referees prompted calls for the instant replays in the Premiership. Every game in this league was covered by the television cameras of BSkyB, owned by Rupert MURDOCH, meaning that video evidence was already available. Referees resisted the move, pointing out that their authority would be undermined and that the abiding principle that "the referee's decision is final" would be violated.

The introduction of instant replay in several sports and the pressure to introduce it in many more is the product of what the sociologist Jay Coakley calls "VIDEATED sports," that is, those sports that are represented to viewing audiences through video technology and which use "dramatic, exciting and stylized images and messages for the purpose of entertaining viewers." From the 1960s, sport's FANDOM was accustomed to television and expected the kinds of visuals that only television could provide. Pieces of action could be shown from different angles, at different speeds and, in the 1990s, from the perspectives of the players (virtual technology made this possible). As television's incursions into all sports deepened, so video technologies were made available to sports governing organizations, many of which chose to exploit the possibilities they offered. While some believed the undermining of referees' authority to be a regrettable break with tradition, others reasoned that it was a logical extension of televised sport.

In some senses, the instant replay, or more specifically the appeals for its use, were also logical extensions of a culture which had accentuated the importance of surveillance. The metaphor of a panopticon was used to suggest how people's lives were systematically laid bare for public examination. Popular television shows specializing in "confessions" dramatized the *quid pro quo*: people demanded to know the innermost, often prurient details of others' lives, and were prepared to disclose details of their own in exchange. Concerns about civil liberties violations were raised in the late twentieth century when a bar code could contain a person's profile, from birthdate to credit rating. People were inured to being inspected. With so many technological procedures available for inspection, it seemed only rational to use a fairly rudimentary video TECHNOLOGY for determining ambiguous situations in sports. The concept of employing fallible human beings without the formidable array of technological surveillance available seemed somewhat primitive.

Of related interest

Coakley, Jay J. (1998) *Sport in Society: Issues and Controversies*, McGraw-Hill.
Garbner, Greg (1997) "Finally, replay might be reborn" *ESPN.com*
    (http://espn.go.com/gen/columns/garber/00973288.html).
Henderson, John, Buckley, Will, Marks, Vic and Wilson, Andy (1999) "The video verdict," *Observer*, February 7.

IOC

Origins

The International Olympic Committee was formed in 1896 to govern the organization and development of what were understood to be a modern version of the ancient Greek Olympic Games. Its first president was Dimitros Vikelas, himself Greek, and its secretary was Pierre de Coubertin, whose vision was in many respects the prime mover behind what became the Olympic movement.

Coubertin assumed the presidency following Vikelas's retirement after the first modern games, which took place, appropriately, in Athens in 1896. There were twelve founder members and, while Argentina was one of them, South American applications to host the games were consistently refused over the next century.

While the 1896 games are often accepted as the first of what have become the summer Olympics, Greece had staged two sports festivals designed to restore the Olympics, and while the first, held in 1859, was a modest success, the second, in 1870, was a chastening failure. Coubertin's effort was to introduce an organizational structure to the games. No doubt mindful of the various governing associations that had developed in England in the previous three decades, he understood the need to liaise with national sports federations rather than individuals.

Coubertin's prejudices during the early years of the IOC are well documented. His attitude toward women embodied Victorian sentiments. The sight of the "body of a woman being smashed" was for Coubertin "indecent." Women were prohibited from competing in the inaugural Olympics; indeed, they were encouraged only to participate in gentler sports, such as croquet, skating and tennis, the latter then being a much more playful activity than the power game it has become today. "No matter how toughened a sportswoman may be, her organism is not cut out to sustain certain shocks," said Coubertin (quoted by E. Snyder and E. Spreitzer in *Social Aspects of Sport*, 2nd edn, Prentice-Hall, 1983, pp. 155–6).

Despite these reservations, women were admitted to a restricted number of events at the next Olympics, held in Paris in 1900. It is difficult to think of a summer Olympics without the world's media and multinational sponsors having strong interests, but the 1900 games were all but dismissed as insignificant. In fact, it was not until 1914 that the IOC was able to claim genuine international interest. Various countries sent delegates from their national sports federations, and this served to validate the official status. The IOC introduced its recognizable five-ring symbol (now seen on Kodak color film packages and McDonald's boxes, of course).

The First World War introduced divisions in the IOC, with representatives of member states aligning themselves with their own nations. Coubertin relocated the organization's headquarters from France to Switzerland, which was neutral. The IOC limped through the postwar years and into the 1930s depression. The games were held at four-yearly intervals from 1920, with the Los Angeles Olympics of 1932 being of particular relevance in bringing world attention to what was then an insignificant arid region of Southern California. The next games held in Los Angeles were in 1984 and were hailed as the biggest, most overtly commercial games and, for many, crassest betrayal of the Olympic spirit in history. They were also the most spectacularly profitable, although, true to IOC non-profit stipulations, the $150 million (£91m) accrued was rendered as a "surplus."

Still patriarchal in outlook, the IOC allowed women entry to the games but only on a limited scale: the initiation of a Women's Olympic Games (*Jeux Olympiques*) in 1921 was a response to this. The IOC wanted its blue riband events to be men-only competitions, while the Fédération Sportive Féminine Internationale, the organization behind the Women's Olympics, pressed for inclusion. The pressure paid off in 1928, which was something of a watershed in IOC history: at Amsterdam, a limited program of women's track and field events was included, much to the horror of many who witnessed exhausted women sweating, straining and painfully dredging up their last drops of effort in exactly the same way as their male counterparts. Despite the mixed reactions to the sight of women in states of athletic distress, the games showcased women's sport, although the 800 meters event was excluded for the next thirty years as women were thought to be in danger over this distance (some women collapsed after the event, which was won by Germany's Linda Radke). Over the next several years, a worldwide proliferation of women's sports organizations ensured that the IOC would be unable to exclude female athletes from subsequent games.

The political uses of the Olympics

It is perhaps to the lasting embarrassment of the IOC that its most memorable games have been ones saturated in political controversy. The first of these came in 1936, when the tournament was used as an occasion for celebrating National Socialism. From this point, POLITICS and the Olympics became intertwined. Rarely has a sporting event been used so blatantly for propagandist purposes: Hitler's presence was felt everywhere and his Aryan ideals were promoted at every turn. Leni Riefenstahl's film chronicle *Olympia* is considered a classic of its kind.

The IOC's capacity for unity was again tested by world war between 1939–45, but the games resumed again in 1948, although the complement of nations was depleted by the absence of Germany, Italy and Japan. In the same year, winter Olympics resumed. These had been a very low-key series of games that had first come into existence in 1924 and continued, albeit in virtual anonymity. They were a far cry from the grand, much publicized and televised games in Lillehammer, Norway, in 1994, held two years apart from summer games to maximize exposure.

Up until the dissolution of the former USSR, the IOC was much concerned by the issue of amateurism. The difference in approach between Eastern bloc and Western states gave rise to anomalies, the main one of which was the state-sponsored athletes of the former, ostensibly amateur but effectively full-time sports performers. Soviet countries came to dominate track and field, with the only opposition provided by the USA. No resolution of this was found. Soviet power was exaggerated, particularly in women's events, by the experiments with performance-enhancing drugs. The IOC tested for some substances in 1968 and instituted systematic drug-testing at all Olympic games from 1972. Thereafter, Soviet dominance faded.

South Africa proved to be a thorn in the IOC's side for many decades. The republic had been an IOC member since 1908 and, while its racist policy of apartheid clearly offended IOC principles (countries were not denied participation in games "for reasons of race"), its all-white representative teams came under scrutiny in the 1960s. In this decade several African nations, previously under the colonial control of European states, gained independence and began to ask questions of the IOC president Avery Brundage. Supported by Soviet countries, the African states campaigned against South Africa's presence at Olympic games. The IOC withdrew invitations to South Africa in 1964 and 1968 before expelling it from the organization in 1972. Twenty years later, South Africa, its apartheid system dismantled, re-entered the games.

Racism was also the source of a controversy that exploded at the Mexico games of 1968. It is difficult to think of a more dramatic sporting image than that of black militant sprinters Tommie Smith and John Carlos, heads bowed, holding gloved fists in the air while standing on the victory rostrum. While newly independent African states began to assert themselves internationally, African Americans were eager to publicize their own plight. Civil rights were slow in arriving, and many major cities had been scenes of incendiary violence as frustrated blacks expressed their protest at America's institutional racism (as Stokely Carmichael and Charles Hamilton termed it in their book *Black Power* (Penguin, 1967)). The stunning gesture eclipsed all other news and made the IOC an unwitting partner in a worldwide political imbroglio. Brundage condemned the behavior of Smith and Carlos and made the US Olympic Committee send them both back to the States in disgrace. In fact, they were transformed into martyrs and, while they were never again allowed to run competitively, their history-making stance has conferred a kind of honor on them. The names of Smith and Carlos will forever be linked with Olympic history.

There is a barely detectable irony in the IOC's embarrassment over Smith and Carlos's black power protest. Were it not for the fact that TELEVISION and the world's media were on hand to record the moment, it is unlikely that it would have made such an impact internationally. Indeed, it is possible that the protesters and the organizations of which they were part would have considered the gesture futile without the attentions of a massive audience. Yet, it took place only eight years after the IOC first consented to a deal that allowed a commercial television network to broadcast the games.

Brundage opposed television on the grounds that the Olympics should not be cheapened as a form of entertainment. Under his leadership, the IOC became involved in an argument over the 1956 Melbourne games and this resulted in the formulation of a new rule, stating that any television broadcasting longer than three minutes or broadcast more than three times per day should be paid for by the television company rather than freely given by the IOC as news items. By this point, the immediate postwar austerity had given way to an era of affluence and consumption was spiraling. Domestic television was in the middle of its growth phase and advertisers were realizing the value of reaching the kinds of mass audiences that television was attracting. Almost 90 per cent of America's homes had television sets in 1960, compared to only 10 per cent at the start of the decade.

CBS and its rival NBC (ABC had not yet become a major player) had glimpsed the potential of sports in gaining high audience ratings. Boxing, professional football and baseball were proving successful instruments in cutting into what was a large market with more disposable income than ever. The Olympics seemed a logical extension, and CBS was prepared to pay the IOC a then staggering amount, \$394,000 (£240,000), to broadcast the Olympics of 1956. Buoyed by the effect, the IOC upped the price to \$2 million (£1.2m) for the combined winter and summer Olympics of 1964. By century's end, the asking price was \$750m, the amount paid by NBC for the Sydney games. NBC actually contracted to pay more than \$3.5bn for all summer and winter games between 2004 and 2008, with the IOC allowing host cities to keep 60 per cent in 2004, reduced to 49 per cent in 2008. IOC President Juan Antonio Samaranch, who took up office in 1980, made it clear that he would try to extricate his organization financially from governments and become economically independent. Hence his embrace of television and commercial sponsors.

For all the money brought to the IOC by television, its ill effects were formidable. In 1972, cameras were on hand to record the shootings that took place at the Olympic Village in Munich. A Palestinian terrorist group gained entry to the village and took a team of Israelis hostage before killing them. Five of the eight Palestinians were also killed. The IOC insisted that the games would continue, although the atrocity caused many to wonder whether the spectacle had grown so out of proportion with its original ideal that it had become a target for politically motivated organizations seeking global attention.

Repackaging the games

Internal problems continued to beset the IOC. The 1976 games at Montreal were financially ruinous, with labor disputes and allegations of corruption compounding a tournament weakened by the withdrawal of several African nations in protest at the presence of New Zealand. The country's rugby team had played games against South Africa in spite of the IOC's instruction to member nations not to compete against South African teams. The GLENEAGLES AGREEMENT of 1977 forbade sporting links with South Africa. Sixty-two nations, including the USA, withdrew from the next games, this time in Moscow, protesting the Soviet invasion of Afghanistan. In reply, the Soviets led a boycott of the next summer Olympics, held in Los Angeles..

The Los Angeles Olympics redefined the shape of the contemporary games. Mindful of the financial debacle of the previous games held in North America, a committee headed by Peter Ueberroth approached the IOC and asked it to consider a new type of games run on manifestly commercial lines. Commercial sponsors would provide the money to stage the games and, in return, they would be entitled to use the Olympic symbol as a logo with which to attract the consumers who would be either watching at home or at the games themselves.

In straight monetary terms the games were a colossal success, though any vestige of Coubertin's original concept was surely lost amid an orgy of burger and beer advertisements. The Olympic games ended up as little more than a gigantic marketing instrument, its departure from the type of festival depicted in *CHARIOTS OF FIRE* complete. As if to underline this, it was revealed years later that some positive DRUGS tests were ignored rather than risk a major embarrassment.

In fact, that embarrassment was only four years away: Ben Johnson's dismissal from the Seoul Olympics in 1988 became perhaps the best-known drugs-related sports story of all time. While it served the IOC's purpose in sounding out a warning to all prospective drug users, it also raised doubts over whether the public had been watching (and would continue to watch) human athletes or steroid-pumped missiles. It also raised doubts about whether they actually care: Johnson's 100 meters sprint in 9.73 seconds was one of the most electrifying sports performances in history. Regardless, the IOC continued its vigilance in doping control, working with the International Amateur Athletics Federation (IAAF) to introduce ever-more sophisticated testing techniques to successive games in an effort to keep pace with less detectable drugs.

If the Olympic spirit envisaged by Coubertin had been damaged by the IOC's decision to allow corporate sponsors into the Los Angeles games, this was dealt another swingeing blow in 1992 when the IOC permitted the USA to enter a basketball team comprising highly-paid professionals from the NBA (National Basketball Association). In the 1988 games, the US team, which had won 84 out of its previous 88 games in six decades of Olympic play, lost in an upset to the Soviet team. Entering the professional team was a form of retaliation. The International Basketball Federation had agreed to allow professional players to play at Olympic level; in this respect, it came into line with track and field and tennis. The move permitted the inclusion of the world's finest professionals from a league whose capital value exceeded the gross national product of many of the other nations in the competition. It cemented the status of the Olympics as an openly professional tournament.

Over the years, indeed the decades, the IOC has striven to become all-inclusive, embracing many, sometimes minority sports. Some, like synchronized swimming, have risen in popularity as a result of the exposure gained. Amateur boxing, whose inclusion in Olympic programs has been the subject of much debate, has arguably suffered as a result of IOC-influenced modifications. During the mid-1990s there was a strong lobby to integrate ballroom dancing into the Olympic movement. One effect of this has been to diffuse interest from track and field, the traditional centerpiece of any games. It has been suggested that, given the prime financial importance of television, that medium more than any other factors influences the content of Olympic competition.

It has also been suggested that the World Athletics Championships which are held either side of Olympic years have assumed a greater status than the Olympics: they typically feature eight days of concentrated track and field competition between the world's best athletes. It is possible that the mantle of World Champion may come to be prized over that of Olympic Champion.

But, in terms of *cachet*, the Olympics have been unbeatable. Cities compete ferociously for the right to host an Olympic games and always enjoy guarantees of taxpayer support. This is vital, as infrastructures can cost (at current prices) up to $7.1bn (Buenos Aires's estimate of the cost of rebuilding when submitting its bid for the 2004 games). The SALT LAKE CITY SCANDAL of 1999 suggested that the prizes accruing to the hosts of Olympic games may have been *too* tantalizing, leading to CORRUPTION: bidding cities were known to have bribed IOC officials in their attempts to gain favor.

Of related interest

Conrad, Derek and Smith, Marc (1984) *The Olympics: The First 90 Years* (videocassette), Conrad Film Associates.

Guttmann, Allen (1992) *The Olympics: A History of the Modern Games*, Human Kinetics.

Lucas, John A. (1992) *The Future of the Olympic Games*, Human Kinetics.

Simson, Vyv and Jennings, Andrew (1992) *The Lords of the Rings: Power, Money and Drugs in the Modern Olympics*, Simon & Schuster.

J

Johnson, Earvin "Magic"

b. 1959, USA

While Johnson was a notable basketball player, he will also be remembered as the first sports performer of international stature to declare openly that he had contracted the HIV virus. He retired immediately from basketball and, while he made two short comebacks, finally left the sport while still at the peak of his game.

Born in Lansing, Michigan, Johnson grew to 6 foot 9 inches and became an outstanding NCAA player for Michigan State. The nickname "Magic" was given to him during his high school years by an enthusiastic sports reporter. His rivalry with Indiana State's Larry Bird continued when they both turned professional, Johnson for the Los Angeles Lakers and Bird for the Boston Celtics. In fact, theirs was one of the great RIVALRIES that helped pump up interest in the NBA in the early 1980s.

During his period with the NBA, from 1979 till he retired in 1991, he was named the league's Most Valuable Player three times. His extraordinary ability necessitated a new statistical measure, the triple-double, which refers to a player who reaches double figures in points, rebounds and assists in a single game. He also became commercially attractive to advertisers during a period when African Americans were being used more frequently than ever to endorse products. Guarded in his comments on racial issues but unsparing in his charity work, Johnson became for a while one of the few sports performers to challenge Michael JORDAN's overwhelming popularity in the United States.

On announcing his retirement, Johnson stated that he contracted the virus from unprotected heterosexual sex. Tales of his sexual exploits with sports groupies circulated in the press and, somewhat paradoxically, Johnson became a talisman for safe sex, reminding anyone who wanted to listen that the unseen malefactor of AIDS did not respect any distinctions: black, white, men, women, heterosexual, homosexual. This was noted by Converse, the sports equipment manufacturer whose products were endorsed by Johnson: "Anyone can get the Aids virus" became a strapline in one of the Converse advertisements. Sympathy for Johnson prompted a bitter response from Martina Navratilova who reasoned that, had a high profile female athlete made a similar declaration, she would be damned as a "slut." Navratilova believed that a commercial company such as Converse would have dropped a woman from their ENDORSEMENTS in comparable circumstances.

Further debate centered on the women with whom Johnson had professedly had sex. Apart from his wife, who undertook an Aids test and was declared negative (as was their child), there were a number of women who had presumably been exposed to the virus by having unprotected sex with Johnson. Their plight was downplayed by the media, as it had been in situations where SEX CRIMES by athletes have been alleged.

In her article "The politics of the body and the body politic: Magic Johnson and the ideology of Aids," Samantha King (1993) analyses the media's reaction to Johnson. She argues that the accentuation of Johnson's "hypermasculinity and heterosexuality" in the aftermath of the announcement served to "distance him and his socially constructed healthy, heterosexual body, from the anxiety and loathing that usually accompany Aids because of its connection with gay men and drug use." Thus the normality of heterosexuality was reaffirmed. Images of Johnson with a supportive wife reinforced the values of family life. King also makes the point that Johnson, as an African American male, represented an "other," a member of a group that is irredeemably distinct from "white, Christian, heterosexual, middle- to ruling class, male" selves. She believes that white middle-class America looked on "with smug approval" as Johnson, at once a hero and victim, unwittingly justified people's fears and prejudices about black athletes.

Of related interest

Gutman, B. (1992) *Magic, More than a Legend: A Biography*, Harper Paperbacks.
King, Samantha (1993) "The politics of the body and the body politic: Magic Johnson and the ideology of Aids," *Sociology of Sport Journal* vol 10, no 3.
Pascarelli, P. (1992) *The Courage of Magic Johnson*, Bantam.
Sperling, Don and Bennett, John (1991) *Magic Johnson: Always Showtime* (videocassette), Fox Video.

Johnson, Jack

b. 1878, USA; d. 1946

In 1908, when Johnson challenged Tommy Burns for the heavyweight championship of the world, he carried to the ring far more than his gloves and gear: he carried the hopes of black America. "When Johnson battered a white man to his knees, he was a symbolic black man taking out his revenge on all whites for a lifetime of indignities," wrote Johnson biographer Al-Tony Gillmore (1975). Johnson did indeed batter Burns, so much so that police had to enter the ring in the fourteenth round of the prize fight to rescue the outclassed champion. In a memorable description of the fight, Jack London wrote: "Plucky, but absolutely helpless, the white man seemed to be a victim of a playful Ethiopian who did just as he would" (quoted in Gillmore).

In victory, Johnson became the first black boxer to hold what was – and arguably remains – sport's most prestigious and richly symbolic prize. But, the status and attention that came with the heavyweight title became an uncomfortable burden for Johnson, whose career was bedeviled by scandal and legal cases.

Born in Galveston, Texas, the son of a janitor, Johnson ran away from home at age 12 and worked on a milk wagon, in livery stables, in bakers' shops, at the docks and in various other occupations while establishing himself as a prize fighter. Sports, like other sectors of American society, were segregated, although boxing, because of its historical roots, permitted black and white pugilists to fight. Still, there were white prize fighters who refused to set foot in the same ring with African Americans. "Gentleman Jim" Jeffries was one of them; he retired, vacating the world championship rather than face Johnson. Burns, a lesser fighter, was more obliging, and received what was then the extraordinarily generous amount of $30,000.

The symbolic significance of having a black heavyweight boxing champion of the world was not lost on Jeffries, who was persuaded to return to the ring for the purpose of re-establishing white dominance and, as Jeffries himself put it, "remove that golden smile from Jack Johnson's face" (quoted in Weston and Farhood (1993)). In less than fifteen rounds, however, Johnson had dispatched Jeffries. Johnson reflected: "It was my honor, and in a degree the honor of my race." The aftermath of the fight was tumultuous with blacks, enraptured by the triumph, celebrating in the streets all over the country. Whites responded angrily, provoking a nationwide conflict which became known as the "Jack Johnson riots." Gillmore suggests that Johnson's win "had the effect of a second emancipation."

Within days, calls for the abolition of boxing were heard and films of Johnson's fights were suppressed for fear of further outbreaks of violence. Many blacks were also concerned, particularly after Johnson displayed a liking for escorting white women. Their apprehensions were summed up by the *New York Age*: "As a black champion, he has given the Negro more trouble than he did in twenty years a black tramp." Black leader Booker T. Washington charged Johnson with being "a man with muscle minus brains," but Marcus Garvey, who rivaled Washington as an influential African American, lauded Johnson and held him up as man who should be revered for his achievements. However one interpreted Johnson's impact, there is little argument about his status as a folk hero of black America. The myths that grew around Johnson were immeasurably bigger than the man himself. Lawrence Levine credits Johnson with being part of a tradition of "bad niggers," moral hard men who were "admired because they had the strength, courage and ability to flout the limitations imposed by white society." Mike TYSON might be seen as an extension of that tradition.

One folk tale about Johnson concerns the extraordinary power that protected his well-being. In 1912 he attempted to board the ill-fated liner *Titanic*. The racist rule that prevented Johnson traveling actually saved his life. Many black Americans regarded the *Titanic* disaster as a kind of divine retribution. Johnson's outrageous fortune seemed like evidence of his special status rather than of RACISM.

Martyrdom was forced on Johnson in 1913, when he was arrested under the Mann Act for taking a white woman, Belle Schreiber, from Pittsburgh to Chicago "for immoral purposes." Fleeing to Europe, Johnson defended his title three times in four years. He was still heavyweight champion, and efforts were made to bring him to book. The search for the Great White Hope began in earnest: it eventually produced Jess Willard, who in April 1916 challenged Johnson in Havana, Cuba. Sixteen thousand people watched an astonishing fight as Johnson was knocked to the canvas in the twenty-sixth round and made no attempt to regain his feet, seeming only to shield his eyes from the sun. Allegations of "fix" went unsupported, but rumors were rife. It was suggested that the promoter Jack Curley had negotiated a pardon for Johnson on the understanding that he lost the title. Willard redrew the color line and the heavyweight crown was thereby insulated from black threats; at least until 1937, when Joe Louis beat James J. Braddock to start a succession of black champions.

In 1946, when Louis was nearing the end of his far less controversial occupation of the world champion's berth, Johnson was killed in a road accident in North Carolina. His career had slipped into an ignominious decline following his deposition and he had spent time in prison in Kansas, fought bulls in Barcelona, performed stunts in circuses, played Othello across the country and even boxed all comers in exhibitions at the age of 68.

When Johnson began his professional career in 1897 (he last fought in 1928), he joined an assembly of black fighters who had seized one of the very few opportunities they had for fortune. This had been the case since the era of slavery. Prize fighting was the earliest introduction of black people to organized sports, and dates back to the contests of the eighteenth century. Slaves were taken from plantation work and made to fight other slaves, sometimes from other plantations. Slave owners would wager on their own slaves. Many of the notable pugilists who traveled Europe were ex-slaves who had gained their freedom as a result of their fighting prowess. Masters who amassed gambling winnings sometimes showed their appreciation in this way. Tom Molyneux was one such former slave who found fame. Farr (1964) writes that Molyneux "showed how prize fighting could be the means by which a man of his color might gain prominence and a certain undeniable importance akin to a theatrical star." A few others achieved comparable status. Molyneux's campaigns involved him in many fights with white pugilists; in fact, his classic fight with the English heavyweight champion Tom Cribb, in December 1810 – won by Cribb – was the most celebrated match of the age. Black achievement in this period, and indeed for many years after, was confined to prizefighting and other individual sporting events.

Of related interest

Farr, Finis (1964) *Black Champion: The Life and Times of Jack Johnson*, Macmillan.

Gillmore, Al-Tony (1975) *Bad Nigger! The National Impact of Jack Johnson*, National University Publications.

Johnson, Jack (1927) *Jack Johnson in the Ring and Out*, National Sports Publishing.

Weston, S. and Farhood, S. (1993) *The Ring: Chronicle of Boxing*, Hamlyn.

Jordan, Michael

b. 1963, USA

The two Michael Jordans

In a sense there have been two Michael Jordans: the human being, born in 1963 and, in the 1990s, regarded as the best basketball player in history; and the icon, endorser of dozens of products, movie actor, role model and an idol about whom it was possible for many to believe just about anything, including his ability to defy the laws of gravity.

Jordan the player was the youngest of three sons of a corporate executive. He attended North Carolina University from 1981–4. He was drafted third to the Chicago Bulls in 1984 after co-captaining the United States basketball team which won the gold medal in the Los Angeles Olympics of 1984. He was named rookie of the year in his first professional season. Represented by PROSERV and his agent, David Falk, Jordan quickly established himself as a marketable commodity through his own line of basketball shoes and apparel courtesy of NIKE. In his *Playing for Keeps: Michael Jordan and the World he Made* (1999), David Halberstam credits Falk with helping to "revolutionize the process of representing a basketball player, going into a team sport and creating the idea of the individual players as a commercial superstar, an iconographic act that was considered breathtaking at the time." It is probable that many others followed Falk's example in using the media to assist in creating sports ICONS.

In 1993, Jordan surprisingly announced his retirement from the NBA at the age of thirty. He signed as a free agent to play MAJOR LEAGUE BASEBALL with the Chicago White Sox and made his professional baseball debut for their affiliate team, the Birmingham Barons. The venture into baseball was ill-judged, and within a year Jordan made a comeback to basketball; interestingly, at a time when another African American icon, Mike TYSON, was also coming back (although, in Tyson's case, after a period in prison). In his "second coming" – as his return was coined – Jordan averaged 31.5 points in the NBA playoffs (second highest in the league). The media hyped mythology surrounding Jordan's return provided the subject in a *Sociology of Sport Journal* special feature entitled "Deconstructing Michael Jordan: Reconstructing postindustrial America," in 1996 (edited by David L. Andrews; *Sociology of Sport Journal* vol 13, no 4).

The commodification of Jordan

The rise of Jordan the icon is attributable in part to his mutually rewarding relationship with Nike and, in part, to the surge in popularity of the NBA. More generally, the commercial success of both Nike and the NBA was made possible by a more general transformative process in which major sports were exported around the world via TELEVISION and the opportunities of using sports as instruments for entering world markets was realized.

Jordan's 1985 endorsement contract with Nike was a watershed in athletic ENDORSEMENTS. The contract was also revolutionary in that signature sports products had up to then been primitive and largely untested. Jordan's original $2.5 million deal amounted to a signing bonus, annuities, a part in leading Nike advertisements and royalties on every pair of basketball shoes sold. "Air Jordan" became the best selling endorsed product range in history, and made well over $100 million for Nike in its first year on the market. Enthused by its success, Nike produced a new line every year. Jordan remained the most visible of the Nike endorsers until his second retirement in 1999.

The relationship was symbiotic. As Jordan's name and image enhanced Nike's products, so Nike's dramatically original advertising elevated Jordan to national, then international prominence. Of course, Jordan's on-court performances were so good that he, at times, carried an aura of invincibility; but the Nike commercials featured him as an almighty figure with boundless skills and literally fantastic gifts. Jordan acknowledged: "Nike has done such a good job of promoting me I've turned into a dream." And, while *USA Today* reported that "He himself [Jordan] is tired of being this godlike hero," Jordan seemed comfortable when addressed as "your royal airness" or just "the light."

Jordan was the highest paid endorser in sports history: his $33 million-plus salary of the 1990s was dwarfed by endorsement fees. McDonalds, Coca-Cola, Oakely, Gatorade, Hanes, Chevrolet, Bigsby and Carruthers suits were among the names linked with Jordan. Toward the end of his career, he launched lines of his own special sportswear and cologne. *The Chicago Tribune* labeled Jordan as the "world's most popular marketing commodity." Originally, Jordan's phenomenal market appeal stemmed from his peerless playing skills, his clean-cut image as an all-American and a devotion to children. In 1995 Jordan was adjudged the most popular sports person "on earth" in the *China Sports Daily.*

Perhaps the most outrageous example of Jordan's iconic appeal was his co-starring role in the movie *Space Jam.* His co-stars were the Warner Brother's Loony Tune cartoon characters Bugs Bunny, Daffy Duck and Elmer Fudd. The film was conceived out of the Nike commercial "Hare Jordan." The movie's plot involved Jordan's being kidnapped by Bugs Bunny and helping the Loony Tune characters defeat a team of aliens, who had come to earth to steal the other NBA players' skills, in a basketball match.

Jordan's ascent was largely free of controversy. As an African American, his status as the world's premier sports figure was always precarious: any hint of misconduct would have been severely punished. The examples of Muhammad ALI and Mike Tyson in sport, or Michael Jackson in entertainment, were reminders that the black person's acceptance by a predominantly white culture is always conditional. Jordan's only brush with authority came in 1992, when he declared that his image could not be used by the NBA for the licensing of leisure wear and memorabilia in the run-up to the summer Olympics of that year. Furthermore, at the Barcelona games, Jordan and several other Nike endorser athletes initially refused to wear the official sponsor Reebok's warm-up suits, stating that they would effectively be in breach of contract. The issue was resolved when Jordan and his team mates wore the US flag and extra long lapels to cover the offending Reebok logo.

Jordan's ability on the basketball court and the packaging and consumption of the worlds greatest sports icon has at times perpetuated a conflict behind Jordan the player and Jordan the icon. Sam Smith's book *The Jordan Rules* (1992) alludes to the special tactics developed by the Detroit Pistons to stop Jordan scoring. Smith writes of the extra attention afforded to Jordan, and Horace Grant, a Jordan team–mate, observed: "The media projects that it is Michael's show, but we know within ourselves that it is not. And he knows it". However there seems only one strategy to employ when the Bulls were losing: "Give it to Michael."

The black athlete as commodity

Jordan's Nike advertisements were the precursor to the effective commodification of black athletes. In *Taking to the Air*, Naughton (1992) writes that, in warming to Jordan, "the marketplace surmounted racial prejudice and created an icon." David Falk commented that: "The problem from a corporate point of view, was that he was black." It is widely acknowledged that Jordan has managed to transcend race and has a crossover appeal to consumers. Jerry Reinsdorf, owner of the Chicago Bulls asked the question "Is Michael Jordan black? . . . Michael has no color."

Jordan has largely eluded controversy, though he was once criticized for a gambling habit and his failure to intervene in areas of ethnic conflict and politics. In particular, he issued a statement in support of Nike when Jesse Jackson's PUSH movement organized a boycott of Nike products, and he was unwilling to help unseat a seemingly racist politician. The question remains as to whether black athletes such as Jordan helped to de-racialize the largely white America. Or does their success simply exacerbate the mythology surrounding blacks in sport and society by racial codes represented in popular media culture that continue to define RACISM and racial ideology in the United States?

Of related interest

Greene, B. (1992) *Hangtime: Days and Dreams with Michael Jordan*, Doubleday.
Halberstam, David (1999) *Playing for Keeps: Michael Jordan and the World He Made*, Random House.
Naughton, J. (1992) *Taking to the Air: The Rise of Michael Jordan*, Warner Books.
Smith, S. (1992) *The Jordan Rules*, Simon & Schuster.

ERWIN BENGRY

K

Kenyan runners

A single nation has rarely dominated a sport as completely as Kenya did men's middle-distance and long-distance running in the 1980s and 1990s. The extraordinary capabilities of Kenyans both on the track and cross-country was expressed time and again through two decades, never more so than in 1997 when an unprecedented seven world records fell in a one-month period, all but one to Kenyan athletes. The emergence of Kenya as a force, for a time *the* force, in world track athletics can be traced to the late 1960s when Kip Keino became the first Kenyan to win a gold medal (at Mexico in 1968 over 1500m). Prior to him, Kenya's premier runner was Nyandika Maiyoro.

Keino, born in 1940, first emerged as a star in 1965 when he became the first Kenyan to set a world record (7 minutes, 39.6 seconds for 3,000 meters). In the same year he ran the third fastest mile with a time of 3:54.2; in the process becoming another record holder of sorts, as the first black man to run a sub-four minute mile. Racist plaudits followed. For example, *The Times* described him as running with "primeval joy and strength, with full-blooded zest replacing tactics." At the 1968 Summer Olympics, Keino attempted an unprecedented triple. He failed to finish the 10,000 meters, but took the silver medal in the 5,000 meters and the gold at 1500 meters. His time of 3:44.91 was exceptional at altitude. Kenya won seven other medals, all in running events. Four years later at the Munich Olympics, Keino switched to the 3,000 meters steeplechase and emerged with the gold. It is worth noting that Kenyan athletes trained in Kenya and did not enjoy the kinds of advantages associated with US university athletic scholarships. The first Kenyan to take up such a scholarship was Steve Machooka, who went to Cornell University.

Keino's achievements might have been eclipsed by Henry Rono, who broke four world records in the 1980s but was denied an Olympic medal by Kenya's boycotting of two Summer Olympics. In 1976, the South African tour of the New Zealand rugby team caused African nations to pull out. Then, in concert with the USA, it boycotted the Moscow games of 1980 over Russia's invasion of Afghanistan. Rono never competed for the titles that his form suggested were well within his grasp. Together with Some Muge's success at the 1983 world cross-country championships, Rono's performances were evidence of deeper potential.

The key to the continuing success was a training camp set up in the foothills of Mount Kenya, where trails were at levels of 7,010 feet (2,300 meters). The Kenyan Athletics Federation financed the project in the mid-1980s. The inspirational head coach was Mike Kosgei, who supervised training regimes that were once described by the French sports publication *L'Equipe* as *démentiel*. The advantages of living and training at altitude had been accepted in athletic circles, but the long-term evidence had not been shown until Kenya's demonstration. (Interestingly, the Moroccans, who in the 1990s became the Kenyan's most serious challengers, also trained at altitude, specifically at Ifrane between Fez and Meknes.)

Basically, a rarified atmosphere encourages the natural production of haemoglobin in the blood; as highly oxygenated blood increases, so athletic performance improves. The athlete then descends to sea level for competition still retaining the oxygen-rich blood he or she has produced at high altitude, and their performance is often dramatically enhanced. While barred by athletics authorities, BLOOD DOPING essentially reproduces these effects by removing an athlete's blood after a period of training at altitude and transfusing it immediately prior to a race. Training regularly at altitude proved a winning formula. Kenya won the 1986 world cross-country team race and, from then on continued to win the men's senior team title every year. The apotheosis came in Auckland in 1988 when Kenyan men won the first four places and eight of the top nine in a field of 300.

In the same year at the Seoul Olympics, Paul Ereng won the 800 meters, Peter Rono won the 1,500 meters, John Nguge won the 5,000 meters and Julius Kariuki won the 3,000 meters steeplechase. Only Ereng was not a Kosgei protégé. Kosgei's partner in his endeavors was, oddly, Father Colm O'Connell, an Irishman who was teaching at St Patrick's High School in Iten, about thirty miles from Keino's home before he was recruited into the training camp. O'Connell was instrumental in the discovery and development of one of Kenya's most celebrated track stars of the early 1990s, Moses Kiptanui, one of several previously unheard of runners that came out of the foothills including William Tanui, Patrick Sang and Joseph Keter.

Together with Kosgei, O'Connell supervised the training of Daniel Komen who, at 20, broke his first world record in September 1996 when he broke Noureddine Morceli's 3,000 meters world record. He then broke world records at two miles and 5,000 meters (winning an Olympic gold medal at this distance in 1997). Wilson Kipketer left the Kenyan training camp to study electrical engineering in Copenhagen in 1990, and returned only occasionally. His move prevented him from competing for Kenya at the 1996 Olympics in Atlanta, though there was no doubt about his supremacy in his event, the 800 meters; he beat the Olympic champion, Vebjorn Rodal, five successive times either side of the games. In 1997 he equaled, then broke the world 800 meters record held by Sebastian Coe (1:41.73), which had previously stood for sixteen years (Kipketer's time was 1:41.11).

In contrast to home-grown track successes, US universities have fostered Kenyan athletics, though Bale and Sang (1994) believe "exploited" is a more appropriate verb. In their view, Kenyan talent migration to the USA can be interpreted as a form of cultural IMPERIALISM leading to the underdevelopment of local sporting resources. Bale and Sang argue that: "Athletes come to devalue their own country, its traditions and its culture." Indeed, in the 1980s, Kenya did consider not selecting US-based athletes for representative teams at major events.

Far from seeing Kenya's domination as the result of national systems or even the outcome of US interest, Bale and Sang conclude that it has come about because of an athletic GLOBALIZATION. "The global sports system shares several characteristics with the world political and economic system," they write. "There exists a three-tiered structure of inequality with a sports-core, a semi-periphery and a periphery." According to Bale and Sang, countries at the core have incorporated emerging nations (at the periphery and semi-periphery) into a global system of "Eurocentric sports competition, sports aid, and the importation of (sporting analogues of) natural resources." In this system, there is a trans-national migration of sporting talent and Kenyan athletics has become part of this.

Of related interest

Bale, John and Sang, Joe (1994) "Out of Africa: The 'development' of Kenyan athletics, talent migration and the global sports system," in Bale, John and Magure, Joseph (eds), *The Global Sports Arena: Athletic Talent Migration in an Interdependent World*, Frank Cass.

O'Connell, C. (1996) "Environmental conditions, training systems and performance development of Kenyan runners," *New Studies in Athletics* vol 11, no 4.

King, Billie Jean

b. 1943, USA

Feminist champion

"In 1981, when Billie Jean King acknowledged her lesbian relationship, the flurry of media attention included no statements of public support from the USTA [United States Tennis Association] or WTA [Women's Tennis Association] or any of the other women professional tennis players," writes Pat Griffin in her book *Strong Women, Deep Closets: Lesbians and Homophobia in Sport*. It was the first example of a female sports performer being outed, and it cost King dearly. A lucrative portfolio of endorsements shrank immediately as commercial companies panicked at the prospect of having their products associated with a lesbian, although in fact King initially denied that her relationship with her former secretary, Marilyn Barnett, was anything more than a one-off affair. King, having defended a palimony suit brought by Barnett, was forced to make a comeback to meet her legal costs. She performed quite respectably, advancing at the age of 40 to the 1983 Wimbledon semi-finals, where she lost to Andrea Jaeger. (Jaeger's career had an abrupt decline thereafter as she became a casualty of BURNOUT.)

There was irony in the icy reception she received from fellow women professionals after the outing. King was the single most important figure in the movement that secured for women prize money comparable with that available to men. At a time when the incipient women's movement was making demands for equal pay, reproductive rights and an end to sexist discrimination, King was a strident campaigner for women's rights in sports.

Born in Long Beach, California in 1943 as Billie Jean Moffatt, she began playing tennis at the relatively late age of 11. She learned the game on the municipal parks circuit, rather than through private clubs or academies. Playing at a time when tennis was strictly amateur, she entered her first Wimbledon tournament in 1961. Two years later she advanced to the final, losing to Margaret Court. By 1965, when ranked number four in the world, she married Larry King. It was in many senses a "modern marriage," with both partners avowing that domestic considerations were subordinated to career interests.

King won her first Wimbledon title in 1966, when aged 22. Her prize was a £45 ($60) gift voucher for Harrods. She went on to win thirty-nine Grand Slam titles. Professionalism was already under consideration in tennis, and, echoing the remonstrations of "women's liberation," King began demanding prize monies for women players.

Although ostensibly an amateur (she worked as a playground director), King was "professional" in her approach to the sport. Her preparations were careful and disciplined and her on-court behavior was often belligerent. It was she rather than John McEnroe who introduced the histrionic protests against umpires' decisions. She was admired for her ruthlessness in some quarters, but crowds turned against her.

King's major professional initiative was to organize an exclusively women's tennis tour, which began in 1968. Operating outside the auspices of "official" organizations, King's tour was openly professional in much the same way as men's tours such as the Kramer Pro Tour. King was able to recruit fellow player Rosie Casals, but few of the other top players. Interestingly, Wimbledon allowed professionals within three months of the start of the King/Casals tour, and the rest of the world's tournaments went open soon after.

Having taken charge of her own career, King aligned herself with the pro-abortion campaign that had grown in momentum and with the TITLE IX legislation of 1972. And, as if to cement her position as a feminist champion, she negotiated a deal with the Philip Morris TOBACCO company to set up the women-only Virginia Slims tour. Virginia Slims cigarettes were marketed in such a way as to appeal to newly independent women. King had no compunction about accepting SPONSORSHIP money from a tobacco company. The USTA set up a rival women's tournament, but it was clear that King's ascendancy during 1972–5, her most prodigious championship-winning period, and her sheer notoriety made the Virginia Slims tour the major attraction in women's tennis.

"The Battle of the Sexes" was a largely media-driven exhibition game between King and self-styled "male chauvinist pig" Bobby Riggs, who was defeated in the packed Houston Astrodome, watched by a huge ABC TELEVISION audience, in 1973. The 55-year-old Riggs had previously beaten Margaret Court, but was no match for King's serve-and-volley play. Hailed by many as a symbolic win, the event was in fact little more than a $100,000 payday for King and far less significant than her other struggles, the principal one of which was to follow in 1981.

Lesbianism

In reflecting on her conflict-strewn career, King has made it clear that: "My sexuality has been my most difficult struggle." It had been known in tennis circles that many of the world's top female players engaged in lesbian relationships, though few had come out voluntarily. In 1981, King's former hairdresser and secretary Marilyn Barnett took legal action against her to ascertain property rights, or "palimony." King at first denied that she had an intimate relationship with Barnett, then acknowledged it. The case was thrown out after the judge heard that Barnett had threatened to publish letters that King had written her.

Despite this and the fact that King was married (she divorced in 1987), King's sexual proclivities had become a matter of public record and the detrimental consequences forced her into resuscitating her playing career. There had been no other lesbian sports ICONS. In the 1930s and 1940s, Babe DIDRIKSON, the track and field star and golfer, worked hard at presenting a feminine and heterosexual front in spite of suspicions about her sexuality (suspicions that were not actually confirmed until years later with the publication of her biography, which contained details of her friendship with Betty Dodd).

Women who were rumored to have lesbian tendencies were mindful of the commercial implications of having their "secret" known. Even today, GAYS in sport remain under pressure to stay in the closet or lose commercial sponsorship deals. Martina Navratilova's relationship with writer and lesbian activist Rita Mae Brown was revealed in a 1981 *New York Post* article. Unlike King, Navratilova never concealed her lesbian relationship, though she probably missed out on the kind of commercial opportunities available to other, more conspicuously heterosexual players. By the time of Navratilova's era in the 1980s and 1990s, there had been a liberalizing of attitudes and a greater, though far from total, acceptance of homosexuality.

Given the historically male-oriented character of sport and its function in demarcating MASCULINITIES/FEMININITIES, it is hardly surprising that the presence of high quality female performers with attributes and achievements to rival those of men would be regarded as threatening. This is the gist of Griffin's thesis. She argues that: "One of the most effective means of controlling women in sports is to challenge the femininity and heterosexuality of women athletes." Calling a female sports performer a "dyke" limits what Griffin terms "her sport experience" and "makes her feel defensive about her athleticism." This effectively perpetuates the stigma attached to lesbianism and deters new recruits. Griffin gives several examples of young women college athletes either moving to different universities or being forcibly transferred by parents on the suspicion that there is a lesbian presence. She also notes the pressures of the Fellowship of Christian Athletes and other religious organizations which have condemned homosexuality. University and professional coaches have made public their disapproval of LESBIANISM, and this has had the effect of further demonizing lesbian performers.

Acceptance of women in sports has been a slow process. As early fears of virilism and TRANSSEXUALS subsided, many sports tentatively integrated women into their assemblies. Tennis, of course, was one such sport. There seemed to be a resolution that women would remain "feminine" and not betray any signs of "butchness." Griffin makes the point that: "Femininity, however, is a code word for heterosexuality." Lesbians threaten sports: because of the stigma they continue to bear, sports governing bodies are afraid they will scare away (a) new recruits and (b) commercial sponsors.

Although Griffin does not cite it, the hugely publicized and widely watched COMING OUT episode of the sitcom *Ellen* in 1997 constituted something of a symbolic event. As Billie Jean King was the first prominent sports performer to proclaim her sexuality, so Ellen Degeneres was the best-known television star to do likewise, in her case through a rather transparent television character. After King, women's tennis became one of the few areas where gay and straight athletes could co-exist peacefully, although Amélie Mauresmo was derided by her opponents at the 1999 Australian Open.

"Most major institutions in the United States are grappling with lesbian and gay issues in some way," writes Griffin, citing the military, the government, the legal system, health care, education, religion and the media. "How can we think that athletics will evade the call to address the broad gap between our professional ideals of fairness and justice and our treatment of lesbian, gay and bisexual athletes and coaches?"

Of related interest

Festle, Mary Jo (1996) *Playing Nice: Politics and Apologies in Women's Sport*, Columbia University Press.

Griffin, Pat (1998) *Strong Women, Deep Closets: Lesbians and Homophobia in Sport*, Human Kinetics.

King, Billie Jean and Deford, F. (1982) *Billie Jean*, Viking.

Mosbacher, Dee (1992) *Out for a Change: Addressing Homophobia in Women's Sport* (videocassette), University of California Extension Center for Media and Independent Learning.

King, Don

b. 1931, USA

Early career

Don King was the leading boxing promoter of the late twentieth century. He grew to prominence principally through his association with Muhammad ALI, but later secured his position through a network of operations, including management and TELEVISION. It would not be an exaggeration to describe him as the most powerful figure in professional boxing during the 1980s and 1990s, and a symbol of African American business success. He wholeheartedly endorsed the achievement ethic, rarely missing the opportunity to boast that his ascent was possible "only in America."

King courted fame and infamy in equal proportions. In 1990, he said of himself: "The Justice Department has charged me with every known crime and misdemeanor – kickbacks, racketeering, ticket scalping, skimming, fixing fights, preordaining them, vitiating officials and laundering money … But the missing link is the burden of factual proof" (quoted in Lidz 1990).

In 1967, King was imprisoned in Marion Correctional Institution, Ohio, for manslaughter after killing a man in a fight on a Cleveland Street. After serving four years, King, who had been involved in numbers rackets as a youth, befriended three people who were to prove crucial to his rise: Don Elbaum, a small-time boxing promoter who operated in Pennsylvania and Ohio; Lloyd Price, a rock'n'roll singer who recorded on Art Rupe's Specialty label (and sold one million copies of his own "Lawdy Miss Claudy" before it was covered by Elvis Presley); and Ali, the premier boxer of the period and the symbolic leader of countless blacks in the USA and perhaps the world over.

Price had known King for many years. He also knew Ali, who had been beaten by Joe Frazier some months before. King persuaded Price to ask Ali to box an exhibition at a Cleveland hospital which was in danger of closing. The hospital had a mostly black staff and patients. Ali agreed and King sought the expertise of Elbaum in running boxing shows. At this stage, King knew little about booking referees, doctors, renting a ring, applying for licensing and so on. Eight and a half thousand people watched Ali spar with four men. Price also used his influence to bring singers Wilson Pickett, Marvin Gaye and others to the show, and they performed a concert before the boxing began. The gross take was $81,000, an astonishing amount for an exhibition. Elbaum's recollection is: "Ali got ten thousand for expenses. I got paid one thousand instead of five thousand. The hospital got about fifteen hundred. And King pocketed the rest" (quoted in Newfield 1995).

Soon King had incorporated himself into a standing business partnership between Elbaum and Joseph Gennaro, who were cultivating a number of promising fighters including soon-to-be contender Earnie Shavers. By 1974, Elbaum was out of the picture and Gennaro was suing King for a share of the profits from boxing ventures. This was settled, with King paying $3,500. It was one of many boxing-related disputes to which King was a party, but it did not stop his progress. King was perfectly poised on the space-time curve. The new consciousness that had inspired riots in the streets had counterparts in sport. The memorable black power salute by Tommie Smith and John Carlos at the Mexico Summer Olympics in 1968 signaled a newly politicized black athlete.

Ali converted to the Nation of Islam, better known as the Black Muslims, and spoke acerbically about the "white devils" who controlled western society. As a black entrepreneur with an interest in boxing, King could present himself as the embodiment of what the Black Muslim strove for: black economic independence in the face of RACISM. Acting as an agent of a company called Video Techniques, King was able to convince Ali to let him promote one of his fights.

Fortuitously for King, it was one of Ali's most momentous fights, when he regained the world heavyweight title at the age of 32, knocking out George Foreman in Zaire in 1974. "The Rumble in the Jungle," as the fight became known, was as much a showcase for King as it was for the protagonists. He presided over press conferences, gave interviews and made his presence felt at every opportunity. He cut an unforgettable figure with his electric shock hairstyle. The film centering on the fight, *WHEN WE WERE KINGS*, shows King as a keen publicist, though not yet the flamboyant extrovert he later became.

King's next major venture was a $2 million boxing tournament televised by ABC television. Allegations of kickbacks, fixing and mob connections surrounded the show, but King became adept at neutralizing them, often by arguing that every successful black person is immediately suspected of misdeeds. Jack Newfield's book, *Only in America: The Life and Crimes of Don King*, charts King's contacts with the underworld and his phenomenal resourcefulness in avoiding conviction. King emerged unscathed from an FBI operation codenamed Crown Royal, which attempted to link him with organized crime. One of the investigators in this operation, Joseph Spinelli, recorded details of this for the magazine *Sports Illustrated* (November 4, 1991).

King kept an interest in the heavyweight championship, either by promoting fights or managing champions. The World Boxing Council (WBC) was extraordinarily careful in its treatment of King, giving rise to rumors that its president, Jose Sulaiman, was unduly generous. For example, when Ali lost his title to Leon Spinks in 1978, the fight was promoted by rival Bob Arum, who held a contract giving him options of Spinks's first three title defenses. It worked greatly to King's advantage when the WBC stripped Spinks of the title and declared it vacant, allowing King to promote a title fight between fighters he effectively controlled. The decision broke up the world heavyweight title into two different versions and King was later to capitalize on this, promoting a $16 million HBO subscription television tournament to unify the title again.

The Tyson years

Mike TYSON left his manager Bill Cayton to enter into a business relationship with King. Interestingly, Tyson refused to criticize King even after several other boxers, like Larry Holmes, Tim Witherspoon and Mike Dokes, had turned against him, claiming financial peculiarities. Coming from African American boxers, these were trenchant criticisms of King. Witherspoon complained robustly after defending his world heavyweight title against Frank Bruno in 1986. He agreed to fight for $550,000, but received only $90,094, while Bruno, the challenger, made $900,000 (challengers typically earn 40 per cent of the total purse). King received revenue from HBO, BBC, Miller Lite and the live gate, earning him at least $2 million. Witherspoon's deductions included $275,000 to King's stepson, Carl King, who acted as the boxer's manager.

Unlike many of the other boxers who complained, Witherspoon pressed his claims against King and, in 1992, received a one million dollar settlement. His verdict on King reads like a misanthropic epigram: "Don's speciality is black-on-black crime. I'm black and he robbed me" (quoted in Newfield 1995). Former heavyweight champion Larry Holmes once said of King: "He looks black, lives white and thinks green."

Despite his personal wealth, his extensive contacts and his obvious gift for promoting sports and entertainment, King either avoided or lacked the acumen for building a stable structure for his many enterprises. Don King Productions was ostensibly the master organization, but King harbored too many suspicions, sometimes bordering on paranoia, to delegate tasks on the scale needed for a large-scale corporation. Because of this, he remained a maverick. In one of his most reflective interviews, with Richard Regen ("Neither does King" *Interview*, vol 20, October 10, 1990), King suggested that he was the epitome of the American Dream: "But instead of getting plaudits and accolades, I get condemnation and vilifications."

Even allowing for King's questionable practices, one can understand his irritation with the media. Business deals are done in sport every day. When King approached Mike Tyson, he elicited the following description from James Dalrymple, a journalist writing for the respected British *Sunday Times:* "Like some dark, crooning nemesis, he came to Tyson, when he was down and beaten and bewildered, took him in his arms and whispered to him that it was time finally to leave the white man's domain for good and join the brothers" (*Sunday Times Magazine,* September 18, 1994, p. 21). One can barely imagine the same prose being applied to any other sports entrepreneur.

Tyson's return to the ring after his imprisonment for rape between 1992–5 augured well for King, especially after Tyson regained the World Boxing Council heavyweight title in 1996. But King's grip on heavyweight boxing loosened dramatically after Tyson lost the title to UNDERDOG Evander Holyfield, then had his license to box revoked for one year by the Nevada State Athletic Commission after he severed a piece of Holyfield's ear in the 1997 rematch. Holyfield's victory established him as the premier heavyweight of his day, and he insisted on remaining independent of promoters.

King's ten-year association with Tyson soured in 1997 when it was revealed (by the *New York Daily Post*) that the boxer had made $110m (£68m) in his six fights after his release from prison, yet still owed $7m in unpaid taxes. A meeting to resolve this situation ended in a scuffle. King's three-year partnership with British promoter Frank Warren ended acrimoniously in 1996 and the two became locked in a High Court case in London. The initial conclusion, reached in March 1998, was that Don King Productions Inc. was entitled to share the profits made by Warren's Sports Network from the World Boxing Organization featherweight champion Naseem Hamed. King was also embroiled in a criminal insurance and fraud case brought by the US government, and faced suits from Bill Clayton, a former manager of Tyson, and Murad Muhammad, one of his own former partners.

Of related interest

Hoffer, Richard (1998) *A Savage Business: The Comeback and Comedown of Mike Tyson*, Simon & Schuster.
Lidz, F. (1990) "From hair to eternity," *Sports Illustrated*, December 10.
Newfield, Jack (1995) *Only in America: The Life and Crimes of Don King*, William Morrow.

Korbut *vs* Comaneci

While there was only six and one-half years in age between gymnasts Olga Korbut and Nadia Comaneci, this was equivalent to a generation gap in gymnastics terms and the actual head-to-head competition was unimportant. Unlike most historic RIVALRIES, that between the two Eastern European gymnasts was played out not on the floor but in the imaginations of sports spectators, who were charmed by the pair. Perhaps unwittingly, Korbut and Comaneci vied for the affection of millions.

In the 1970s, Korbut and Comaneci effectively redefined gymnastics, enlarging its appeal from a minority pursuit to a mass spectator sport. They were assisted by an increased interest in sports from TELEVISION and technological advances that made it possible for vast proportions of the world's population to view Olympic competition either "live" or via delayed transmission.

Belarus-born Korbut first came to international prominence at the 1972 Olympic games at Munich. She was then 17. Selected only as an alternate, or reserve team member, she got her chance to perform after a team-mate was injured. Her routines were radical, taking her to the boundaries of athletic competition and art. The high-risk endeavor was rewarded with three individual gold medals and a rapturous audience that had been entranced by her impish audacity.

Korbut was a product of the Soviet sports machine, entering a government sports school at the age of eleven and being subject to often punishing training and conditioning regimens into her teens. Her nymph-like representations on the floor belied the grueling years of preparation and her own steely competitive determination. In the year of her Olympic triumph, she was voted Associated Press's Female Athlete of the Year and, in 1973, her presence in a touring Soviet gymnastics team guaranteed football-size attendances around the USA. Enrollments at gymnastics clubs multiplied as a result of her popularity.

But by the next Summer Olympics, at Montreal in 1976, Korbut was eclipsed by a new celestial body, that of Nadia Comaneci from Romania. The defeat of Korbut in the individual competition was expected: she was then a relatively mature 21. Her place in the public's affection was assured. But Comaneci, then 14, found a way of sharing that place: she became the first athlete to be awarded a perfect score of ten by all judges in all routines and, thereafter, became known as "Little Miss Perfect." The drama of her success was heightened when the electronic scoreboard indicated that she had earned the score of 1. In fact, the device had not been programmed to show the figure 10 and it was not until the announcer clarified the result that fears of an injustice were allayed. Comaneci's competitive decline was not as sharp as Korbut's: at the Moscow Olympics in 1980, she won the silver medal in the all-round competition and gold medals in the balance beam and floor exercises.

The fortunes of the two "rivals," albeit only rivals for the public's fondness, differed quite markedly. Korbut was inducted into the International Gymnastics Hall of Fame in 1988, by which time she was 33 and, according to reports from Belarus, suffering physically from years of hard training. Her health was poor and she had aged alarmingly. She was involved in the relief effort after the nuclear accident at Chernobyl in 1986 and, in 1991, moved to the USA where she began teaching gymnastics in public schools. Comaneci also moved to the USA, defecting in 1989 to marry fellow gymnast Bart Conner. Still only 28, Comaneci remained youthful and healthy enough to gain modeling assignments. She then built a career in professional gymnastics training.

Of related interest

Oglesby, Carole A. (1998) "Nadia Comaneci," in Oglesby, Carole A. (ed.), *Encyclopedia of Women and Sport* Oryx.

—— (1998) "Olga Korbut" in Oglesby, Carole A. (ed.), *Encyclopedia of Women and Sport* Oryx.

Pierce, Barbara E. and Burton, Dawn (1998) "Scoring a perfect 10: Investigating the impact of a goal-setting program for female gymnasts," *The Sport Psychologist* vol 12, no 2.

L

law

Professionalism, commercialism and regulation

The law has developed a more specific and visible role in regulating sports since the 1960s. This development has occurred at different points in different countries, but, everywhere that sports have become professionalized – and commercialized – law has inevitably played a significant part in the process. The countries where this has occurred most obviously are the USA, Australia and Western European states; in countries where there is little professional sports, the involvement of law is less common.

The law has had most impact in the most advanced industrialized societies. Because so much in professional sports involves commercial activity, it has become subject to much the same legal regulation as any other commercial operation. In the USA, law's increasing regulatory role became evident in the 1960s, and by the 1980s this was also true in Britain. Despite the number of high-profile legal interventions in recent years, law has provided guidance and remedies for commercial sports organizations for much longer, specifically in the areas of employment contracts and in providing legal frameworks for sports clubs that have developed into corporate enterprises.

The impact of law on the commercial dynamics of sports can be illustrated by the 1995 decision of the European Court of Justice in the BOSMAN CASE. The case concerned an attack on the legal legitimacy of soccer's transfer system and the freedom to move to a new employer without the requirement for the payment of a transfer fee, and the operation of quota systems on foreign players in European soccer. The likelihood of a successful challenge under European law was one that had been noted for quite a period of time, and it was perhaps only a question of when someone would pursue a discrimination case to court. The Bosman ruling states that professional sport is subject to Article 48 of the Treaty of Rome concerning freedom of movement provisions; and Articles 85 and 86 concerning the ability of sporting bodies such as Union des Associans Européenes de Football (UEFA) to operate monopolies supervising particular sports in ways that restrict competition.

It was speculated that this would usher in the end of the traditional transfer system and a move to other forms of economic structuring, such as SALARY CAPS and revenue-sharing mechanisms commonly used in North America. In terms of the greater freedom for individual players to move from club to club, the decision reflected the changes that were introduced in the United States with the concept of FREE AGENCY. The chain of events that led to this was started by the Flood decision of 1972. The rule resulting from the case – brought about by Curt Flood – stated that any player who had ten years of service, the last five with the same team (as had Flood), would have the right to veto any trade. Some players were given control over where they played for the first time since 1879. The case spelled the end of MAJOR LEAGUE BASEBALL's reserve clause.

Law and culture

It is too simplistic to see law's intervention as due purely to increasing commercialization. Another factor seems to be the propensity of individuals involved in sporting disputes to seek legal remedies. This may reflect an increasingly litigious culture. Historically, law has been used to implement state policy that prohibits sports activity. This has revolved around a number of issues. The control of land and the rights to hunting have been a perennial issue, dividing on class grounds the English aristocracy and landowners, on the one hand, and the masses, on the other. The needs of war also dictated the legitimacy of many sporting activities until the fifteenth century. The maintenance of order has been a major concern, both in nationalistic terms (with alarm at foreign influences in certain sports) and the disorder implicit in many team sports (the specter of the uncontrollable mob has been a constant fear, particularly in terms of sports spectating). The perceived dysfunctional effects of GAMBLING (for example, family breakdown, absenteeism from work and fecklessness) have also been of concern.

Sport today continues to be regulated by law in terms of the need to control activities that are seen as morally reprehensible, contrary to public policy and a threat to social order. This can result in the prohibition of certain sports, such as foxhunting and boxing, the regulation of the frameworks of sports (particularly in respect of safety standards) or the control of illegitimate activities, such as drug taking and excessive VIOLENCE.

In Britain, the Football Spectators Act (1989) and the Football Offences Act (1991) introduced an element of regulation that bore close resemblance to the legal instruments used to control other forms of popular culture. The legislation may be seen as responses to moral panics. With football, there has been the need to control the unruly football hooligan; the legislation was precipitated by the HILLSBOROUGH tragedy, which was not caused by HOOLIGANISM but primarily by inappropriate policing. Panic law is invariably bad law.

Legal issues that occur in several nations with large-scale professional sport include marketing, sponsorship agreements and intellectual property rights. The role of law in the control of DRUGS in sports is one common to a wider range of countries. Issues such as this also have an international component, with the legality of bans on players by international sporting bodies, such as the

International Amateur Athletics Federation (IAAF), needing to comply with national legal systems.

In other areas, the legal framework of sports has national specificity and operation of the law is very different. For example, in the USA, collective bargaining agreements are important in regulating contractual relations in professional sports, while in Britain, individual contracts are normal; remedies for sports field injuries in the United States are almost exclusively based on civil law compensation, while in Britain, prosecutions under criminal law became increasingly common in the 1990s.

One of the interesting issues with legal regulation in sports is the interaction of laws with sports' internal rules. Sport as a social practice is, of course, highly rule-bound. Individual sports are regulated by their own constitutional rulebook and adjudication machinery. The volume of rules varies between different sports. Some are particularly multifarious. Rules in sports exist for both its organization and playing. Explicit codes of ethics are also relatively new developments as largely informal but written normative statements. Sports are also surrounded by strategies and practices that are not explicitly stated and recorded, but partly amount to the "working culture" of particular sports, such as the tackle from behind in soccer or the collapse of the scrum in rugby. The law's increasing regulation of sports needs to be understood within the context of how it interacts with the quasi-legal and non-legal rules that operate in the sports world.

Sports law or "sport and the law"?

There are also many ethical issues to be determined in sport, and the law has a role to play in helping provide solutions. But the law's intervention itself provides ethical issues: does the law have a role to play or not? If intervention is seen as legitimate, then to what extent? There are many issues of policy where the law is used as an instrument to prohibit and regulate sports activity.

The regulation of sports field violence between players is an example where the legitimacy of the law's involvement is contended. There are precedents which suggest that the sports field is not a "private area" where the law cannot intervene, as reinforced by the statement that "the law does not stop at the touchline." Support for the intervention of law is often predicated on the belief that sport is more violent today than in the past. However, there is a counter that the most effective mechanism for controlling violence on the field of play and providing effective punishment and compensatory remedies is more likely to come from the national governing federations' internal mechanisms or quasi-legal alternative dispute resolution machinery: the view is that sports administrators rather than lawyers are the best arbiters for disputes that arise.

To conclude, a debate has developed concerning whether we can describe law's intervention in sports as "sports and the law" or sports law. Some commentators believe there is no identifiable area of sports law, but rather the proliferation of the application of legislation, litigation and arbitral decisions to sports disputes. Others believe that it is possible to see a recognizable sports law, and note the debate concerning whether an "identifiable legal subject" exists has occurred in other developing and burgeoning legal areas. The latter position is one that is increasingly persuasive: it is not a pure area of legal principle, but an area of "applied law." This has essentially been developed by legal practitioners dealing with disputes as they have arisen in sports, involving the applications of pure legal areas in the context of a human activity – sports – and moving from a loose association such as sports and the law to a more recognizable body of sports law. It is true to say that this field is largely an amalgam of interrelated legal disciplines involving such areas as contract, taxation, employment, competition and criminal law; but dedicated legislation and case law has developed and will continue to do so.

Of related interest

Barnes, John (1996) *Sport and the Law in Canada*, 3rd edn, Butterworth.
Gardiner, S., Felix, A., James, M., Welch, R. and O'Leary, J (1998) *Sports Law*, Cavendish.
Grayson, Edward (1994) *Sport and the Law*, 2nd edn, Butterworth.
Greenberg, Martin (1998) *Sports Law Practice*, 2nd edn, Lexis Publishing.

SIMON GARDINER

left-handedness

Reasons for left-handedness

Left-handed athletes, often known as "lefties," have a special place in sports culture. Babe Ruth, Rod Laver, Martina Navratilova, Marvin Hagler; every sport can boast a great left-handed player. Statistically a minority group, the left-handed have to overcome the multiple disadvantages of being left-handed in a world designed for right-handed people. Various studies have shown that left-handed people live shorter lives, are more prone to accidents and mature more slowly than right-handers. Yet in some sports, their achievements are legion. The explanation as to why this is so must begin with why people are left-handed at all.

About 10 per cent of men and 8 per cent of women are left-handed. These figures have remained stable for centuries. Left-handedness is a distinctly human trait: other animals show no bias or preference in claws, paws, hoofs, fins and so on. The precise reasons for human preferences are not clear. Most theories are based on the lateralization of the brain, that is, the degree to which the right and left cerebral hemispheres of the brain differ in specific functions. The human brain is divided into two hemispheres, the left side often being described as the dominant half because that is where the centers of language and speech and of spatial perception are located in most people. Nerves on the two sides of the body cross each other as they enter the brain, so that the left hemisphere is associated with the right-hand side of the body. In most right-handed people, the left hemisphere directs speech, reading and writing while the right half is responsible for emotions.

It was thought for years that left-handedness was the result of a kind of reversal of the more usual pattern, with the main functions of the brain being on the right. But in the 1970s, research by J. Levy and M. Reid (in *Science* vol 194, 1976) showed that in fact most left-handers are still left-brain dominant and have their centers of language, speech and spatial perception in the same place as right-handers. A minority of lefties are reversed, and there is a simple way of identifying such people, by watching a left-handed person writing and noting the placement of the hand. The study found that about two-thirds of left-handed people write with a hooked hand (with the left wrist curling over the paper and the fingers pointing down) and these are still left-brain dominant. Only the third of left-handers who write with a straight, or unhooked wrist are actually reversed. Of course, many cultures use scripts that move from right to left margins, in which case right-handers must write with hooked wrists.

The word *sinistral*, meaning a left-handed person, has an interesting etymology, deriving from the Latin for "left," *sinister*, which also means an evil omen (sinister-looking person) or something malignant (sinister motive). Historically, there was little difference: left-handed people were associated with malevolence. As that myth receded it was replaced by more enlightened empirical research, much of which still suggested some sort of undesirable characteristics or even pathology. Two lines of research led to the conclusion that there was a close connection between left-handedness and physical fitness. The most influential theory was that of Geschwind and Galaburda, who, in 1987, proposed that there was an association between a left-handedness and immune or immune-related disorders. This stemmed from birth-related problems. Left-handedness was also related to disabilities such as stammering and dyslexia. Later studies cast doubt on these conclusions.

A second line of research came to light in 1991 in a widely reported article by Coren and Halpern in *Psychological Bulletin* (vol 109). The authors claimed that left-handers die sooner than right-handers; the mean age of death for left-handed people was 66 compared with 75 for right-handed people. Coren and Halpern gave two explanations for this. First, there is environment: we live in a world that has been designed and built with right-handed people in mind. Door handles, telephones, cars and countless other technological features reflect right-handedness. So, when left-handed people perform even the simplest of functions, they find them slightly more awkward and so have a higher risk of accidents (and accident-related injuries). Several subsequent studies confirmed that left-handed people were more prone to accidents.

Second, there are birth problems. Referring back to the Geschwind and Galaburda studies, Coren and Halpern hypothesized that exposure to high fetal testosterone at birth may lead to developmental problems for left-handed people. This particular aspect, and indeed the whole early death theory, did not go unchallenged and other studies both refuted the findings and uncovered others. For instance, Warren Eaton and a research team from the University of Manitoba took one strand of Coren and Halpern's research and argued that: "Indirect evidence for an association between sinistrality [left-handedness] and matura-tional lag can be found from the fact that males, who are more likely to be left-handed, are less advanced in language and skeletal development than are females" (*Journal of Child Psychology and Psychiatry and Allied Disciplines* vol 37, no 5, 1996). On closer examination, however, direct evidence was not forthcoming.

Advantages and disadvantages of left-handers

The research supporting or refuting the relationship between left-handedness and early death, accident proneness, physical immaturity and other pathologies continues, although little light has been thrown on the exceptional sphere of sports. If, as most of the evidence suggests, left-handed people are disadvantaged in some way, why do so many of them rise to the top in sports? One interesting theory came from a French biologist, Michel Raymond of the University of Montpellier, who published his views in the *Proceedings of the Royal Society* (December, 1996). Marshaling data about athletes, including both amateurs and world class professionals, Raymond concluded that, compared to their total size in the population, left-handed people are over-represented in sports.

The reason for this is that left-handers have an advantage in confrontation sports, those sports in which an opponent is directly confronted, including boxing, fencing and tennis, as well as team sports such as baseball, cricket and basketball. There is no over-representation of "southpaws" in non-confrontation sports such as track or swimming in which opponents compete alongside each other. Not only are left-handed people over-represented in confrontational sports, they are also especially good at them; and, the closer the interaction between opponents, the greater the prevalence of left-handers. So, we would expect more southpaw boxers than lefty baseball hitters or pitchers, and even fewer left-handed rugby players.

Yet even in sports like baseball and cricket where competitors face each other at several yards distance, there are more than the expected number of left-handers. The researchers found that, over a six year period, about 16 per cent of top tennis players were left-handed, as were between 15–27 per cent of bowlers in international cricket and pitchers in MAJOR LEAGUE BASEBALL. For close-quarter sports, the difference is more pronounced: 33 per cent of competitors in the men's world foils championships, increasing to 50 per cent by the quarter-final stage of the competition, were left-handed. It needs to be remembered that this is a group that represents about 10 per cent of the total male population. The pattern was less marked for women, though there was still over-representation at the fencing championships.

One tempting thought is that, if left-handed people are disadvantaged in several areas of development and functionality, they may be overcompensated when it comes to sports skills like hand-to-eye coordination, quick reflexes, astute judgment, tactical awareness or just raw strength. Or, it could simply mean that the sheer fact of favoring one's left arm in a context geared to right-hand biases lends the left-hander a strategic advantage? Because of the frequency of right-handers in any given population, sports performers are habituated in training and in competition to facing other right-handers. Thus left-handers, because of their relative scarcity, have an edge of sorts: they hit, run and move in unexpected ways.

Certainly sports are full of stories of orthodox (left leg forward) boxers who detest fighting southpaws because of the special problems they pose. These include having to jab along the same path as the opponent's jab and constantly having one's front foot trodden on. Baseball hitters swing at the ball in such a way that their momentum carries their bodies in the direction they want to move to get to first base; saving fractions of a second in this way can be vital in a game where fielding is crisp and accurate. Pitchers, like cricket bowlers, can deliver at unfamiliar angles. Returning serve in tennis against left-handers is known to be difficult for a right-hander, especially defending the advantage court; left-handers are known for their ability to cut the ball diagonally across the body of the receiver. In basketball, a left-handed player typically tries to pass opponents on the side they least expect; there is barely time to determine whether the opponent is left-handed or not.

The strategic advantage of playing against opponents who are used to a different pattern of play seems to be the answer to the preponderance of them in some sports. In others, where being left-handed counts for little, their prevalence is about the same as in the general population. According to Raymond *et al.*, 9.6 per cent of goalkeepers in soccer are left-handed, and left-handed field eventers account for 10.7 per cent of all competitors. At the top levels of darts, snooker, bowling and gymnastics, lefties are actually under-represented. Somehow, they gravitate toward the sports in which they possess a natural advantage.

An anonymous journalist with *The Economist* (in "Left-handedness: Sinister origins," February 15, 1997) adds an evolutionary level to this argument: over the years, the strategic advantage enjoyed by left-handers has outweighed the other possible disadvantage uncovered by the afore-mentioned psychological research. Natural selection, of course, favors the best physically equipped (strongest) species, which survived and were able to pass on their genes to their children. This would account, albeit in a crude way, for the persistence of left-handed people in an environment built largely by and for right-handers and in which social pressures (such as associating sinistrality with wrongdoing) might reasonably have expected to pressure lefties to change their biases.

Of related interest

Coren, Stanley (1992) *Left Hander: Everything You Need to Know About Left-Handedness*, John Murray.

Harris, Lauren J. (1993) "Do left-handers die sooner than right-handers? Commentary on Coren and Halpern's (1991) 'Left-handedness: A marker for decreased survival fitness'," *Psychological Bulletin* vol 114, no 2.

Muris, P., Kop, W.J., Merckelbach, H. (1994) "Handedness, symptom resorting and accident susceptibility," *Journal of Clinical Psychology* vol 50, no 3.

Pass, K., Freeman, H., Bautista, J., and Johnson, C. (1993) "Handedness and accidents with injury," *Perceptual and Motor Skills* vol 77, no 3.

Raymond, M., Pontier, D., Dufour, A. and Moller, A.P. (1996) "Frequency-dependent maintenance of left-handedness in humans," *Proceedings of the Royal Society of London*, Series B, 263, 1627–33.

lesbianism

True womanhood

Until relatively recently, any female athlete able to reach levels of adequacy in sports would expect to have her sexuality questioned and be eyed suspiciously as a "mannish" woman, or freak of nature. "Sport," as understood in the early twentieth century, writes Kathleen McCrone, was "perceived as a basically masculine phenomenon in which female participation, apart from providing applause and respectability as spectators, was an anomaly" (in "Play up! Play up! And Play the Game!" in Mangan and Park 1987). Even after the conclusion of the First World War, when notions of ACCEPTABILITY/NONACCEPTABILITY were revised as certain competitions were seen as appropriate for women, advocates of women's sport "denounced the few sports-crazy girls, who eschewed conformity and went to extremes by exhibiting the roughness and offhand masses of young men as 'hoydens' "[a term that means wild, boisterous girls and derives from "heathens"].

It was decent for women to compete in sports that accentuated aesthetic and graceful qualities, but not in those that required speed and strength. McCrone's essay is one of a number collected by J.A. Mangan and Roberta Park in *From 'Fair Sex' to Feminism: Sport and the Socialization of Women in the Industrial and Post-Industrial Eras* (1987), all of which emphasize that there was a total conflict between sport and womanhood. The women who persisted in sports, especially those sports that demanded physical exertions, refused to comply with traditional dichotomies of MASCULINITIES/FEMININITIES; every effort they made to excel in sport was a violation of what was seen as their sex's true nature. They were not regarded as "true women."

The dominant MEDICAL DISCOURSE of the day determined that these women were either a perversion of nature themselves or that their participation in sports would pervert their nature. They challenged not only conceptions of natural womanhood, but the sexual division of labor as well: women were "properly" wives, housekeepers and childbearers. Unladylike behavior was strictly discouraged and even subject to stigmatization.

The dangers of competing in sports were often hidden. Jennifer Hargreaves, in her essay "Victorian familialism and the formative years of female sport," writes: "Cycling for women was described as an indolent and indecent practice which would even transport girls to prostitution" (in Mangan and Park 1987). Those women who favored sporting activities were burdened with the task of demonstrating that their femininity and athleticism were not incompatible, although many suspected they were and were supported by medical evidence about the effects of sports. Among the popular beliefs was the theory of virilism: women who competed regularly in sports would eventually acquire secondary masculine features, such as facial hair and broad shoulders. Their ability to bear children would be impaired, perhaps irredeemably, and their menstruation patterns would be disrupted. The eugenicist doctor Arabella Kenealy, in 1899, warned of sexual transformations brought about by physical sports and, according to Sheila Fletcher, likened the process to "that of male antlers in female deer" (in "The making and breaking of a female tradition," in Mangan and Park 1987).

While they were members of the "weaker sex" – even if only notionally – sportswomen were not helpless. In fact they posed moral problems, first, because they were regarded as *morally* rather than physically weak, and second because, as Donald Mrozek indicates: "the emergence of women to athletic excellence could be seen as a threat to social order and as a violation of the tradition of 'true womanhood' " ("The 'Amazon' and the American 'Lady': Sexual fears of women as athletes," in Mangan and Park 1987). They were "mannish."

There is no doubt that one of the most significant features of sports was, indeed is, that they provide validation of masculinity. Throughout the nineteenth and for the early decades of the twentieth centuries there was an earnest search for distinguishing features between men and women: as well as skeletal, hormonal and other physical characteristics, cultural differences were also essayed. Women were not just different being, they inhabited different cultures. Sportswomen usurped this and so affronted the male's sense of selfhood, specifically his sense of self-efficacy. If sports were physical endeavors designed to affirm man's prowess in a period when the value of labor was being eroded by the onset of mechanization, then a woman capable of equaling men's tasks was a menacing aberration. It needed to be kept an aberration, rather than becoming a more regular phenomenon.

Women were prohibited from entering sports both by medical opinion and social stigma: sport was simply "unladylike." This was dramatically publicized at the 1928 Olympic Games, in which women were allowed to run an 800 meters event. The finish saw straining athletes drained and wearied, as they might well be after a fast race; but this was thought to not be fitting for a lady, and the event was excluded until 1960.

The cultural prohibitions on women's sports ensured that women who were prepared to compete knew that they risked undesirable physical effects and possibly cultural disgrace. The slurs about Mildred "Babe" DIDRIKSON and Eleanora Randolph Sears reminded other aspiring sportswomen of the 1920s and 1930s of what to expect. Both Didrikson and Sears were subject to rumors about their sexuality at a time when lesbianism was far more scandalous than today. It is at least possible that women who were unafraid to enter sports were prepared to have their sexuality questioned or even pathologized.

In 1943, with the American and National Baseball leagues weakened by the war effort, Philip Wrigley, head of the famous chewing gum company, sponsored an all-women's league. Women who played baseball were popularly regarded as tomboys, who habitually mimicked men with their unladylike behavior, such as chewing tobacco and using expletives. Wrigley believed that he would have more commercial success with the league if the players were more conspicuously heterosexual. To this end, he made makeup compulsory, provided uniforms that accentuated "femininity" and penalized violations of a code of conduct appropriate to young ladies. The "boyish" behavior of the women is spoofed in the movie *A League of Their Own*.

The significance of Wrigley's All-American Girls Baseball League was that it made the association between overtly heterosexual female sports and commercial success. Although the league lost popularity after the war when the male players resumed, the female league had attracted enough interest to suggest a financial future for women's sport. The decorative functions of women approved of by Coubertin at the start of the modern Olympics was still in evidence with the cheerleaders (who still perform, of course). But a more competitive role for women became fully realized in the postwar period. Ridding women's sports of its associations with lesbianism was a precondition for its commercial success.

The power of the label

In 1986, Helen Lenskyj pointed out that: "Many female athletes still feel compelled to flaunt their heterosexual attractiveness; labels like 'masculine' and 'lesbian' retain their power to divide women." One of the obvious reasons they do this is to enhance their marketability. Martina Navratilova for long complained that her associations with lesbianism prevented her from capitalizing on endorsement and other market possibilities. In contrast, her tennis contemporary Chris Evert and golfer Nancy Lopez were never short of endorsement opportunities; both were prepared, as Lenskyj notes, "to have intimate details of their married lives revealed in magazines." (We might add baseball player Sheryl Swoopes and volleyball player Gabrielle Reece to a growing list of women who are prepared to publicize their heterosexual credentials.)

Perhaps they were mindful of the fate of Billie Jean KING, who, in 1981, acknowledged her lesbian relationship with her former secretary, Marilyn Barnett. Almost immediately, her portfolio of endorsement contracts shrank as companies panicked at the idea of having their product associated with a lesbian. King's income fell and she was made to fight a costly court battle; all of which left her so short of money that she was forced to make a comeback.

King's experience was a cautionary one for many athletes who might have considered COMING OUT about their lesbianism: she was the first prominent sportswoman to disclose her lesbianism and she suffered financially as a result. Few homosexual sports performers, male or female, have openly discussed their sexuality, perhaps for fear of losing public favor and commercial endorsements. Pragmatic considerations seemed to supersede all others. Yet, women's tennis as a sport has not suffered financially, despite widespread, unspoken assumptions that there are a great many lesbians on the circuit.

The golfer Muffin Spencer–Devlin disclosed her lesbianism in 1996. She did so voluntarily through the pages of *Sports Illustrated*. Interestingly, there was little fanfare. Whether this reflects a "softening" of public opinion about lesbians, an indifference or perhaps a resignation is not clear. But one suspects that the "demonizing" of lesbians in sport, as Pat Griffin (in *Strong Women, Deep Closets*) calls it, is not over.

For the first half of the twentieth century, women who excelled in sports were regarded as anomalies, if not freaks. But now, as Martin Polley writes, "approval has come through increasingly sympathetic media coverage, as well as through private and public sponsorship of women's sport initiatives" (in *Moving the Goalposts: A History of Sport and Society since 1945*, Routledge, 1998). Yet the approval of women in mainstream sports is, in some senses, conditional. It was as if women needed to convince the sports world that it was possible to succeed in sports and be heterosexual. The sometimes overt display of female heterosexuality among women athletes is a reminder of the pact: approval is granted on the condition that most female athletes are unambiguously heterosexual. An occasional coming out, such as that of Spencer-Devlin, failed to stir much public sentiment because it was but one. Sportswomen are continually involved in providing reassurances that it is possible to be an athlete and still feminine. Female athletes still go to some lengths to distance themselves from lesbianism. As Griffin spells out: "Femininity, however, is a code word for heterosexuality."

Of related interest

Griffin, Pat (1998) *Strong Women, Deep Closets: Lesbians and Homophobia in Sport*, Human Kinetics.
Lenskyj, Helen (1986) *Out of Bounds: Women, Sport and Sexuality*, The Women's Press.
Mangan, J.A. and Park, Roberta J. (eds) (1987) *From 'Fair Sex' to Feminism: Sport and the Socialization of Women in the Industrial and Post-Industrial Eras*, Frank Cass.

Lombardi, Vince

b. 1913, USA; d. 1970

The American football coach Vince Lombardi, more than any other sports figure, epitomized the "winner takes all" philosophy that began to permeate professional sports as TELEVISION money flowed in during the 1960s. With more at stake than mere pride or honor, a more ruthless creed developed and Lombardi's famous – some might say infamous – dictum "Winning isn't everything, its the only thing" seemed to affirm a new attitude. There is some irony in this, as Lombardi's actual pronouncement had a quite different import, one which allied it to the *CHARIOTS OF FIRE* spirit he was thought to oppose: winning, Lombardi insisted, "is not everything, but *trying* to win is." But, the myth surrounding Lombardi grew to be appreciably bigger than the man himself, and he remains one of the great sporting ICONS of the postwar period.

Lombardi's parents had planned for him to enter the Roman Catholic priesthood, but he became involved in football coaching at a New Jersey high school. His outstanding record secured him an offer from the US Military Academy, where he worked as an assistant coach. After a spell with the New York Giants, he moved to Green Bay in 1959. The Packers were then an ailing team with abysmally poor losing records. Over the next nine years, Lombardi guided them to six National Football Conference titles and, in 1967 and 1968, two Super Bowls. After he left, it was another thirty years before the Packers recaptured the dominance they had enjoyed under Lombardi.

Lombardi's martinet style was described by one his players: "Lombardi is very fair – he treats us all like dogs." A disciplinarian throughout his career, Lombardi stood down from the Green Bay head coach's position after the second Super Bowl triumph, but was tempted into a return with the Washington Redskins in 1969, when aged 56. While he never approached the kind of glories he brought to Wisconsin, Lombardi brought respectability to a club, which was then on a streak of fourteen losing seasons.

The NFL named the trophy awarded to Super Bowl winners after Lombardi in commemoration of his achievements. While his actual win–loss record has been surpassed, no other coach has quite captured the success ethic so integral to North American society as well as Lombardi.

Of related interest

Lombardi, Vince (1997) *Strive to Excell: The Will and Wisdom of Vince Lombardi*, Rutledge Itill Press.
Wells, Robert (1997) *Lombardi: His Life and Times*, Prairie Oak Press.
Wiebusch, John (ed.) (1997) *Lombardi*, Triumph Books.

Loneliness of the Long Distance Runner, The

Tony Richardson's film *The Loneliness of the Long Distance Runner* was released in 1962, at a time when the British working class were being encouraged to undergo what sociologists of the time were calling *embourgeoisement*: "You've never had it so good," Britons were reminded by Prime Minister Harold Macmillan: all the trappings of the affluent society, including televisions, cars and that consumer icon the washing machine, were available to the entire population.

The film features Tom Courtney as Colin Smith, a young unemployed youth in the Midlands city Nottingham. After being convicted of theft, he is incarcerated in a Borstal (a juvenile correctional facility) where he discovers he has a raw talent for long-distance running. Identified by the Borstal's governor as someone who can bring glory to the institution, Smith is given special dispensations to train and wallows in the limited freedoms he is granted, such as being released temporarily to go on long, unsupervised runs.

The film intercuts periods in Smith's life before his sentence. He is shown witnessing his father's death in the family home: his father refuses to go to a hospital for treatment and spurns medicine. On his death, he accompanies his mother to his father's former place of work where they receive £500 widow's allowance. He regards it as a derisory sum for a lifetime's work. As he later reflects:

> My dad was a laborer, sweated his guts out for £9 a week and he "never had it so good" … Mom and dad were at it like cat and dog. My dad used to smash mom's face 'cause she was doing it on him with other blokes, mom cursing dad for not bring enough money into the house. That's how most people live and I'm beginning to see it should all be altered.

His rebelliousness manifests not in political activism, but in small acts of class hatred: he robs a fruit machine, breaks into a bakery and steals a petty cash box, steals a car and masquerades as a rich son who has just received it as a birthday present. When in the Borstal, he resists authority at every turn, satirizing a psychologist who insists he wants to "help" him, sneering at guards who object to his obvious contempt and mocking the governor whom he refuses to address as "sir." "Say 'sir' when you talk to the governor!" he is ordered by a guard after answering the request for his name as just "Smith." He snaps back "*Sir* Smith," only to be told that his attitude will not get him far.

Asked by fellow inmates what he would do if granted a wish, he has no hesitation in saying that he would assemble all police, guards, governors and politicians, line them up against a wall and "let 'em have it." Yet, his rage against authority dissipates after his selection for the institution's cross-country team to face a local public (fee-paying) school at a sports day event. His peers notice his belligerence disappear as he concentrates on his running and finds comfort in his training. The anger that was once vented at any symbol of authority is recycled in his sporting pursuit. Watching him train, the governor remarks to a colleague that the secret of rehabilitation is to "rechannel their [inmates'] natural aggression into a new direction." He coaxes Smith into training by whispering dreams of Olympic glory. Before long, Smith is known by fellow prisoners as "the governor's blue-eyed boy."

"Who's side you on?" asks a friend who knew him on the outside and cannot believe the transformation. It makes Smith reflect on his changing posture. On the day of the race, he meets his main rival, a well-heeled youth from a rich family to whom Smith is about as recognizable as an alien. Before his imprisonment, Smith would have spat at the youth; on race day, he shakes his hand and wishes him well. Yet, during the five-mile race and while surging ahead of the field, thoughts flood into Smith's head; of the TELEVISION bought by his mother (with the £500) that affronts his senses with commercials; of the advice he once gave to someone who asked why he would not work ("I don't like the idea of slogging my guts out so the bosses can take all the profits"); and of the way he has been groomed as if a "thoroughbred racehorse" (as he puts it).

A few yards from the finish line, he has something of an epiphany and realizes that his success in sports has been exactly as the governor designed it. The rebel has become a champion. At least, a *potential* champion. A sly grin breaks across his face as he spots the governor in the crowd. The moment brings a triumph of sorts as Smith sees the fury in the governor's face: his plans of bettering a school from the other extreme of the class spectrum are ruined by the mischief of a feckless youth. But, there is a political message concealed within the action: Smith celebrates his own minor key victory as he watches his public school rival romp past him, glancing incredulously at the stationary Smith.

Like other Alan Sillitoe stories, *The Loneliness of the Long Distance Runner* is a parable of class antagonisms. Smith is the product of a generation of young people who grew up in the 1950s with no memory of war. Like the "rebel without a cause," Smith assails everything and everyone. Yet in many ways, the objects of his wrath are quite precise. He despises his mother for buying into the affluence dangled like a carrot in front of the working class. He hates capitalism for exploiting the likes of his father. He opposes the police for no better reason than the fact that they represent authority. And yet, he is almost seduced into the mainstream by the very first taste of success: a win on the sports field. The assuring words of an authority figure and a few favors are all he needs to suspend his ill will toward all. The anticipation of "bettering himself" brings new perspectives. It is when success on the sports field becomes palpable that he realizes that there is greater satisfaction in challenging than in achieving for others.

Of related interest

Richardson, Tony (1962) *The Loneliness of the Long Distance Runner*.
Segrave, J. and Hastad, D. (1982) "Delinquent behavior and interscholastic athletic participation," *Journal of Sport Behavior* vol 5, no 2.
Sillitoe, Alan (1959) *The Loneliness of the Long Distance Runner*, W.H. Allen.

Lopez, Nancy

b. 1957, USA

The golfer Nancy Lopez was a genuine child prodigy who developed into an indomitable competitor. In the process, she redefined women's golf. A sport that was once seen as a poor and not entirely serious version of a "man's game" was turned into an earnestly competitive pursuit of excellence – and money. Lopez was, for a while, the highest earning female in sports.

Born in Torrance, California and educated at Tulsa University, Lopez started playing golf at the age of eight and won the New Mexico Women's Amateur title at the age of only 12. She went on to finish in a tie for third in the 1975 in the US Women's Open as an amateur. In 1977 Lopez turned professional and began what was to become an epic career. In her first year as a professional she won nine tournaments, including a record five consecutively. Her commercial impact was tangible: attendance at LPGA tournaments tripled and Lopez's earnings soared. As Olga Korbut inadvertently converted a generation of young girls to gymnastics, Lopez introduced a generation of women to golf. She proved something of a catalyst in promoting the media's recognition of the demographic significance of female spectatorship, and the market women collectively defined.

Lopez's achievements are legion: she was Player of the Year five times, set stroke average records and qualified for the LPGA Hall of Fame after her 35th win. But her importance was not only in her tournament wins. After marrying baseball player Ray Knight and having two children she resumed her playing career and, while she never recaptured her peak form, she laid to rest outmoded theories about the relationship between sports and fertility and the impact of pregnancy on sporting performance.

We should also note the fact that Latinas have been consistently under-represented in sports, making Lopez a member of minority within a minority. Popular explanations of this under-representation rest on the strong family bonds, male dominance and traditional female expectations that work as obstacles to Latina's participation in sports. However, Katherine Jamieson and Maxine Baca

Zinn, in their essay "Latina in sports" (in *Encyclopedia of Women and Sport in America* edited by Carole A. Oglesby, Oryx Press, 1998), attribute this to three factors: (1) low levels of school enrollment at the secondary level and in higher education; (2) neighborhood and social segregation; and (3) lower-than-average levels of family income.

Of related interest

Cahn, Susan K. (1995) *Coming on Strong: Gender and Sexuality in Twentieth Century Women's Sport*, Harvard University Press.
Daddario, Gina (1998) *Women's Sport and Spectacle: Gendered Television Coverage and the Olympic Games*, Praeger.
Oglesby, Carole A. (1998) "Nancy Lopez," in Oglesby, Carole A. (ed.), *Encyclopedia of Women and Sport in America*, Oryx Press.

luck

Creating unpredictability

"Competence alone is not enough to secure success in a chancy world," writes Nicholas Rescher (1995) in his treatise *Luck: The Brilliant Randomness of Everyday Life*, "there is always the prospect that even the best possible effort may not meet with the success it deserves." In sports, as in other realms of human affairs, luck plays a prominent role. No matter how well prepared an athlete or team may be, the "best-laid plans" are often at the mercy of fortuitous chance, those ineffable circumstances beyond our control. Luck is a formidable and ubiquitous factor in sports, and it is this that preserves sports from the domesticating influences of rational management, at the same time maintaining our fascination with the unpredictability that competition always creates.

The word "luck" can be traced back to fifteenth-century England. It derives from the Middle High German *gelücke*, modernized to *Glück*, which translates as both happiness and good fortune. Rescher notes that, "Virtually from its origin, the term has been applied particularly to good or ill fortune in gambling, in games of skill, or in chancy ventures generally."

There is, of course, a big difference between luck and fortune. If something nice happens to a person in the normal course of events, then they are fortunate; luck intervenes when something nice happens despite there being odds against its happening. A highly rated team that comes through a hard game with no injuries is fortunate, but not lucky in the strict sense. But, a team that is an UNDERDOG that benefits from injuries to several of the opposition's key players and wins the game is lucky. Catching a cold is just unfortunate, whereas catching one on the day before you are due to appear in the Super Bowl is terribly unlucky. Sam Huff, the linebacker for the New York Giants and Washington Redskins, was fortunate to possess the talent and skills to be a powerful defensive player; he was also lucky to start a thirteen-year career at exactly the same moment that

TELEVISION was growing out of its infancy and so became one of the NFL's first media superstars.

For Rescher, luck involves three elements: (1) a beneficiary or maleficiary; (2) a development that is benign (positive) or malign (negative) from the standpoint of the interests of the affected individual; and (3) unforseeability, that is, it must be unexpected. The first two elements have clear relevance in sports. A soccer team that is leading 3–0 when the floodlights fail and then loses the replay is clearly the maleficiary of luck, while the opponents get lucky. The third element is absolutely crucial to the enduring appeal of sports competition, even in times when every effort is made to leave nothing to chance.

Much of sport is founded on the concept of merit. Coaches liberally dispense *bon mots* such as "you only get out of this game what you put in" and "nobody ever got anywhere without hard work." Losers will sometimes cite bad luck as the cause of their defeat; winners rarely invoke good luck, and when they do, it is often with the qualification, "you create your own luck." There is sense in this: honest human effort can contribute greatly to a set of circumstances conducive to one competitor's victory. Winners may well be fitter, better prepared tactically, aware of specific weather demands (like wearing appropriate footwear) and so on.

Yet, the fascination of sports lies in the very fact that, if talent+work=merit, merit is not always rewarded. Otherwise, much if not all of sports competition would be calculable. As long ago as 1929, A.A. Brill constructed a timeless argument about the attraction of sports. His article, "The why of a fan," offered an insight into the drabness and formality of much in the world and the security it holds for most of us. "The restrictions of modern life," as Brill called them, meant that our lives were governed by predictable patterns. "Life organized too well becomes monotonous; too much peace and security breed boredom."

Incalculability

Luck involves departures from the calculable by ensuring that life is never too organized. The possibility of erratic interventions in sports is never completely absent: if we could run the competitors' recent form through a computer and come up with an unerringly accurate result, our interest would soon wane. We watch, read about and gamble on sports events because things do not always run their usual course.

It is always possible that there is an order to what we variously describe as chaos, randomness or haphazardness: but, if there is such a pattern, it is beyond our comprehension. Professional gamblers at racetracks make livings from forecasting the outcome of races; the successful ones are privy to information not usually available to outsiders. A mysterious and – to most – unpredictable result in which an outsider wins may have been accurately conjectured by someone with insider's knowledge. So, we cannot assume that results that appear to be beyond the scope of rational prognosis are, in fact, freak results. Technically, we could predict much more with the benefit of greater knowledge of contingencies. For example, a detailed knowledge of weather conditions and the electrical arrangements that affected the power supply to the floodlights might have enabled a forecast that the above game of soccer would be abandoned. In practical terms, of course, such perfect knowledge is not attainable.

Professional tipsters occasionally appear to defy form, logic and even common sense, but they are usually armed with the knowledge that enables them to do exactly the opposite. Like the good tipster, sports performers are aware of the dangers of relying on luck. Yet, they are just as aware that luck is an ineliminable part of any contest. For this reason, they tend to try anything in their efforts to reap good luck. SUPERSTITION is rife in sports: rabbits' feet, lucky numbers, charms and old shirts are primitive when compared with some of the complex rituals undertaken by competitors. They typically stumble across a particular piece of behavior that precedes an exceptionally good performance, and then repeat the behavior before every game. The procedures are often basic, like always putting on the right shoe before the left or laying out one's clothes in a predetermined pattern before changing into them. Another common attempt to encourage good fortune is by carrying a photograph of a loved one or writing the latter's name on a strip of tape or on the skin. Among the more elaborate rituals was that of NFL linebacker Kevin Greene, who would leave the locker room exactly thirty minutes before a home game's kickoff and venture onto the field to search for his wife, who would always be seated in the front row of the lower levels. They would then begin an almost liturgical pregame performance that involved recitations and punching.

No matter how elaborate the ritual or how fastidiously it is followed, its benefit was always subjective: performing these rituals made the competitors feel good. However, these rituals could not achieve their stated aims of bringing good luck. Luck can of course never be invoked; if it could be, it would not be luck.

Of related interest

Brill, A.A. (1929) "The why of a fan," *North American Review* part 228.
Plaschke, Bill (1996) "Rite angles," *Sporting News* vol 220, no 38, September 16.
Rescher, Nicholas (1995) *Luck: The Brilliant Randomness of Everyday Life*, Farrar Straus Giroux.

M

Major League Baseball

Baseball's governing body has its origins in the year 1858, when the National Association of Base Ball Players (NABP) was formed as an organization that prohibited remuneration for the players. As the Civil War drew to a close and baseball's popularity spread, many began to sense opportunities for exploiting the sport's financial potential. Some teams enclosed their parks and charged between 10 and 25 cents admission to games. Some players flouted the rules and accepted a share of gate receipts, while others procured phantom jobs such as winding up a stadium clock every day, leaving them most of the day to practice.

"Base ball," as it was then called, was already a popular participation sport, although there were two sets of rules; these were amalgamated with by the NABP. While the convention has it that baseball was and is "America's game" and sprang fully formed from the American imagination, its origins can be traced to English bat and ball games that were popular in the eighteenth century. The children's game of "rounders" has similarities with baseball, and Jane Austen's *Northanger Abbey*, published in 1818, contains a reference to a game of "base ball." In its original conception, it was to be a gentleman amateurs' game, reflecting concerns similar to those of cricket's MCC (formed in 1787): to promote upper-class and upper-middle-class participation in a sport which was to be played only by those who could afford it.

However, as Peter Levine points out (in his *A. G Spalding and the Rise of Baseball* (1985)), "almost from the outset, however, this amateur gentlemen's game was transformed," and baseball became one of the first professional spectator sports. In 1858, fans were charged 50 cents admission to watch a three-game championship series between teams from New York and Brooklyn. In 1862, enclosures were built especially to accommodate paying fans and exclude those who wanted to watch games for free. As gate fees went up, so players began to reap some benefits, although their salaries were to prove a source of dispute for many years to come.

The NABP was never more than a loose structure, and was not adequate as an institutional framework once baseball began pursuing commercial opportunities. There is a section in Dean Sullivan's collection *Early Innings* (1995) which records William Hulbert's critique of the NABP; this is followed by Hulbert's own self-interested proposals. In 1876, Hulbert, the owner of the Chicago White Stockings, mapped out a new baseball league based on territorial monopolies and a restricted number of financially solid franchises. Hulbert's idea was to keep the number of teams to a minimum so as not to swamp the market with too many clubs; franchises in cities with less than a 75,000 population were excluded. His National League of Professional Baseball Clubs (NL) started in 1876 with just eight franchises paying $100 annual dues. It is probable that only the strong Chicago club made any profit, and several franchises dropped out of the NL within two years.

The introduction of what became known as the "reserve clause," which affected the contracts of players and depressed salaries, gave rise to alternative leagues that offered players free contracting. Of these, the American Association (AA), founded in 1882, succeeded in presenting the NL with a challenge; so much so that Hulbert was forced to make a pact with the fledgling organization. One of the effects of this was to restrict players' contracts. In response, players started the Brotherhood of Professional Base Ball Players (in 1885) as a way of protecting their material interests. However, club owners were intransigent and the Brotherhood announced plans to establish its own competitive organization, to be known as the Players' League (starting 1890) and which would be run on a co-operative basis (for example, gate receipts were to be divided evenly among all clubs regardless of their size).

The League survived only one season and was soon absorbed by the NL, whose head, A.G. Spalding, worked tenaciously at staving off competitors. The most formidable of these was the Western League, later the American League (AL), which drew many NL players with better offers. The AL's salary cap of $2,400 was still in place at the turn of the century. In 1902, the AL attracted 2.2 million fans to its games, compared to the 1.7 million who attended NL games. A truce was signed in January 1903, and this agreement established the framework of what became Major League Baseball. The agreement effectively finished league rivalries and consolidated the reserve clause, which had proved a persistent cause of problems for the NL: each league would recognize each others' reserved players and establish a three-man commission to oversee all professional baseball. The agreement provided for the drafting of players from minor league teams at the conclusion of each season. In 1905, the leagues formulated a plan for a post-season World Series, which has of course remained ever since.

The agreement also introduced a new phase in organized baseball known as "the golden age." New stadiums were built, high schools adopted the sport, books and plays were written, newspapers carried reports and radio stations carried play-by-play commentaries. New ICONS emerged, including pitchers Cy Young and Christy Mathewson and, most revered of all, the record-breaking batter Babe Ruth, who helped establish the New York Yankees dominance in the early century.

Spalding presided over and in no small way encouraged an era in which baseball transformed itself from a pastime to a commercial entertainment. He was puzzled by the fact that traces of the old amateur mentality still affected the sport: "I was not able to understand how it could be right to pay an actor, or a singer, or an instrumentalist for entertaining the public, and wrong to pay a ball player for doing the same thing in his way" (quoted by Levine 1985). Spalding had little respect for the "gentlemen's game": he approached baseball as if it were an industry and he a captain of that industry. For him, baseball was pure business and his influence shaped the sport. New organizational structures were built to provide stability, specialization in roles and procedures was introduced and disciplinary mechanisms for maintaining control of players were brought into play. The Fordist emphases on divisions of labor, regulation and efficiency were all features of Spalding's vision of baseball. He saw the USA changing to a complex modern state in which there were "experts" in all aspects of society, including religion, commerce and culture. Sport was no exception; it too needed efficient management.

The American population was growing and shifting rapidly, and the values of self-reliance, the work ethic and aggressive individualism were accentuated as the USA became an urbanized industrial power. All these values were reflected in baseball, and no doubt contributed to its appeal. By 1910 – five years before Spalding's death – attendances had soared to 7.25 million, though players' salaries were still kept artificially low, averaging under $2,500. Eventually, player resentment manifested itself in a strike in 1912, after the Detroit Tigers' Ty Cobb was suspended following a fight with a fan. The Cobb incident was a catalyst for wider discontents over pay and conditions.

In 1913, Major League Baseball's hegemony was challenged by the Federal League (FL) which was able to offer double the salaries of Major League players in some circumstances. Hal Chase moved from the Major Leagues to the Buffalo-based FL club, and became the center of a New York State Supreme Court case. The court's key ruling was that Major League Baseball was not subject to antitrust laws (laws that prevented monopolies); baseball was not a commodity or article or merchandise but "an amusement, a sport, a game." Some FL clubs were incorporated into Major League Baseball as a result of the judgment, while the rest folded. The import of the decision was that Major League Baseball had a legitimate monopoly and was exempt from many of the rules that affected other businesses. Players were still bound to accept restricted wages.

The sense of grievance resulting from this added to the increasing amount of professional gambling on baseball led to the infamous 1919 World Series featuring the Chicago White Sox, which paid the league's lowest salaries. Seven Chicago players were suspended for life after allegations of fixing. The case led to a re-evaluation of the position of baseball's leading executive. Judge Kenesaw Mountain Landes, the then commissioner of baseball, ruled in the White Sox case. His power to suspend, fine or disqualify players was consolidated in 1921, and in 1922 a Supreme Court further strengthened Major League Baseball's antitrust exemption in *Federal Base Ball Club of Baltimore, Inc. v. National League of Professional B.B. Clubs and American League of Professional B.B. Clubs.* The bribery scandal sent reverberations through professional sports in the USA, alerting the public to the fact that sport was far from being immune to the kind of corruption that seemed to be everywhere else. The film *EIGHT MEN OUT* centers on the episode, and the book *Baseball Babylon: From Black Sox to Pete*

Rose (by D. Gutman, Penguin, 1992) charts the various scandals that followed in its wake.

During the 1920s, Major League Baseball as a whole prospered and the salaries of some players rose disproportionately. For example, in 1927 Babe Ruth earned $70,000 when the median salary of the league's highest paid players was a mere $7,000. (Ruth's memorable line, "I had a better year than him," came in 1928 when he was told how his $80,000 meant that he earned $5,000 more than President Hoover.) Despite falling attendances in the 1930s and 1940s, Major League Baseball stayed profitable, offsetting lower receipts with lower salaries.

In the 1940s, Mexico, which had supported a Mexican Professional League since 1925, began a new initiative. The Mexican League developed under the leadership of Jorge Pasquel, who lured many players south of the border in search of higher pay. One such player was Danny Gardella, who played in Mexico but later tried to return to Major League Baseball only to find himself blacklisted. He went to court and won damages of $300,000. But, more embarrassing for Major League Baseball was the court's references to "involuntary servitude" and "peonage of the baseball player."

This opened the way for a spate of antitrust cases against Major League Baseball. The reserve clause that bound players to particular clubs remained a contentious point, even though in a sense it was the cornerstone of Major League Baseball's continuing operational success. Major League Baseball's argument was that this method of player retention was the only way of preserving a competitive balance in the league. Baseball's immunity from antitrust laws gave it a unique self-regulating status, and this continued to be debated until 1976 when free agency was introduced, thus allowing out-of-contract players voluntarily to move from club to club.

FREE AGENCY had been discussed for at least a decade before it finally came to pass. Marvin J. Miller's appointment as executive director of the Major League Players' Association (formed in 1956) in 1966 signaled the start of a much tougher approach to negotiations. Miller's first significant victory came in 1972 when he won the right to independent salary arbitration. Free agency had the effect of unlocking Aladdin's cave: average yearly salaries shot from $29,000 in 1970 to just over $1 million in 1992. Alarmed owners tried to interrupt the trend in 1981, but were met with a seven-week industrial dispute.

Players went on strike again towards the end of the 1994 season, and the World Series was aborted for the first time in ninety years. It was the longest and most expensive strike in the history of professional sports, lasting 234 days and costing an estimated $800 million (£490m). The strike ended when the owners accepted an offer by the players' union to go back to work without a collective bargaining agreement, leaving open the possibility of another strike should the owners try to impose a salary cap as they had before.

Historically, Major League Baseball's exemption from antitrust laws dated from a 1922 Supreme Court ruling known as the Holmes decision, which afforded baseball a blanket antitrust exemption on the basis that it was not involved in interstate commerce. The Gardella ruling of 1949 seemed to have removed the protection provided by Holmes, but in 1953 in a case involving player George Toolson against the New York Yankees, the Supreme Court affirmed the 1922 ruling. The introduction of free agency in 1976 allowed players to move freely between clubs. Contrary to earlier defenses of the reserve clause, free agency brought an evening out of competition, with twelve different teams winning the World Series over fifteen years. The days of the baseball dynasties were ended (the Yankees, for example, won nine of twelve World Series from 1949–64).

It is possible that there is no sports governing body comparable in legitimate authority over its players and teams. Major League Baseball has enjoyed the kind of monopoly not countenanced in any other sphere of American commercial life, its protected position being based on the premise that it is unlike other businesses: it is the organization that runs America's national game. As such, it has held a unique position in sports culture. Its panoply of heroic figures have, in many ways, signified America itself, all of them being tough-minded individualists from humble backgrounds who have risen to positions of wealth and respect.

Baseball is perhaps the most studiously chronicled sport of all time, more so than even cricket. Baseball is intricately quantified, with virtually every move of the game being convertible into statistics that baseball fans can pore over. It is possible for games that took place a half-century ago to be analysed in great detail, allowing fans imaginatively to reconstruct every play. It is this potency to recall bygone days that gives baseball a special place in American culture and permits myths, even legends to be built around it.

The All-American Girls Baseball League

The All-American Girls Baseball League was started in 1943. The brainchild of Philip K. Wrigley, of the chewing gum company and owner of the Chicago Cubs, the league was made up of women's teams. Major League Baseball's ranks were depleted by the number of male players who were drafted into the armed services in the war effort, and it was feared that a sub-standard competition would drive away fans. Women had been playing baseball and softball at a competitive level at colleges from at least the turn of the century, and possibly before. The war demanded that many women leave their traditionally defined domestic duties and work in factories or other parts of industry; it seemed perfectly consistent for women sports performers to occupy positions previously held by men too. The league's popularity waned when men returned home from war, though attendances took a long while to recover in the postwar period. The women's league is the subject of the Penny Marshall film *A League of Their Own* (1992).

Of related interest

Chadwin, Dean (1999) *Those Damn Yankees: The Secret Life of America's Greatest Franchise*, Verso.

Levine, Peter (1985) *A.G. Spalding and the Rise of Baseball: The promise of American Sport*, Oxford University Press.

Rader, Benjamin (1992) *Baseball: A History of America's Game*, University of Illinois Press.

Sullivan, Dean (ed.) (1995) *Early Innings: A Documentary History of Baseball, 1825–1908*, University of Nebraska Press.

Major League Soccer

When the USA presented its bid to stage the 1994 World Cup soccer tournament, FIFA responded by laying down a condition: the USA would need to make arrangements for starting a national soccer league that would guarantee at least a short-term future for the sport in North America. Two years after the World Cup, the first Major League Soccer season began, its eventual champions being Washington DC United.

The structure of Major League Soccer was designed to avoid the failings of the North American Soccer League, which was launched in 1968 with the backing of Warner Communications. This had collapsed in 1984 when many of the clubs were financially ruined, mainly as a result of the free-spending New York Cosmos, which counted Pelé and Franz Beckenbauer among its players. Other teams strove to match the Cosmos' star-filled roster and ran up extravagant salary bills. In contrast, the new Major League Soccer structure controlled all league revenues centrally, distributing monies evenly so that all franchises had the same amount to spend on players' wages.

Major League Soccer offered investor-owners 49 per cent of each club and paid for its running costs, while retaining a 51 per cent controlling interest. It attracted high-profile investors such as George Soros, who owned part of Washington DC United, and John Kluge, the Manhattan-based owner of the New York/New Jersey MetroStars. Original investors paid $5 million (£3m) for an original stake in a franchise in 1995. By 1997, a stake in two expansion teams at Chicago and Miami cost investors $20m (£12m). Only three (of twelve) clubs were actually owned by the league: Tampa Bay Mutiny, Dallas Burn and San Jose Clash.

The first season's attendances averaged 17,400, the highest gate being 92,000 at a Los Angeles Galaxy game. Games shown on the TELEVISION sports channel ESPN earned a 0.55 rating, meaning that over half a million homes watched. This declined slightly to 0.54 in the 1997 season; attendances also slipped to less than 15,000. The decline was most marked in the annual All-Star games, which attracted 78,000 fans to the Giants Stadium in 1996 for a double-header which included a Brazil vs FIFA XI game; a year later, a similar event (minus Brazil) drew only 25,000.

Over $100m (£60m)was spent in establishing the league, which lost $18m on turnover of $60m. The second season's revenues were buoyed by the interest of the ATV network which telecast Saturday afternoon games. ATV's logic was – presumably – that the league's nucleus of support came from white, upper-middle-class suburban families, many of them young and well-educated. Compared to others sports' fandoms, soccer had a disproportionate number of women who both watched and played: of approximately twenty million Americans who played soccer regularly in the late 1990s, 40 per cent were female. Another component was the Hispanic following: in 1996, there were twenty-five million Latinos in the United States (10.2 per cent of the total population). Projections suggested that by 2020 they would be the largest ethnic minority group, with forty-nine million. Demographically, this was well-suited to a network looking for advertising dollars. In soccer's third season, NIKE invested $120m (£75m) into a youth development scheme. Soccer was, at the time, the most popular sport among under-15s.

Of related interest

Giulianotti, R. Bonney, N. and Hepworth, M. (eds) (1994) *Football, Violence and Social Identity*, Routledge.

Rosentraub, Mark S. (1997) *Major League Losers: The Real Cost of Sports and Who's Paying For It*, HarperCollins.

Shropshire, K.L. (1995) *The Sports Franchise Game: Cities in Pursuit of Sports Franchises, Events, Stadiums and Arenas*, University of Pennsylvania Press.

marathon

No sport integrates competitive sports and playful culture as effectively as marathon running. Over the last thirty years of the twentieth century, marathons have been held in virtually every national capital and several other major cities throughout the world, attracting both serious competitors and whimsical participants, all seeking to complete the 26.2 mile (42.195 kilometers) distance. City marathons, as opposed to marathons that were part of wider athletic events, became occasions for casual runners and keep-fit enthusiasts to line up with some of the world's elite distance runners. In this sense, the marathon was a unique event.

Origins

The competitive marathon was introduced as part of the modern Olympic Games in 1896, the idea being that the event would echo the Greek Olympics, even though the Greek games did not feature such a contest. The word "marathon" is taken from the town of Marathon in Greece. According to legend, in 490 BC a Greek soldier ran from Marathon to Athens to take news of a Greek military victory over the Persians. The runner collapsed with exhaustion and died shortly after arrival. An alternative tale was told by Herodotus who related that a trained athlete named Pheidippides was sent from Athens to Sparta before the battle to request assistance from the Spartans. He was said to have run about 150 miles over two days. Appropriately, the first winner of the Olympic marathon (held over 25 miles, the approximate distance between Athens and Marathon; the event was changed to its present distance in 1924) was a Greek runner, Spiridon Louys.

Most major track and field meets eventually integrated marathons into their schedules. The event provided vivid athletic images, one of the most arresting coming at the 1954 Empire Games held in Vancouver. Of sixteen starters, only six finished. One of those who did not was Jim Peters, who had set a world's best time earlier in the year and led what remained of the field into the stadium. (The fastest marathon runs are not "records," as no two courses are exactly alike.) His intrepid attempt to reach the end saw him stagger, then crawl as the effects of dehydration and exhaustion took their toll. He was rescued on all fours and taken to an oxygen tent where he spent the next seven hours. The sight of Peters prostrated on the track drew the admiration of many; but it repelled others, who saw the ordeal as debasing and dangerous.

Improvements in training and conditioning made it possible for an athlete like Emil Zatopek to win the 1952 Olympic marathon after having already won gold medals in the 5,000 meters and 10,000 meters races. Other memorable accomplishments were witnessed in the 1960 and 1964 Olympic marathons, both won by the slight-framed Ethiopian Abebe Bikila who seemed effortless in his victories, the first of which he achieved running barefoot. Bikila began a tradition of middle-distance and marathon running among Ethiopians.

Women's impact

One of the most significant marathons took place in 1967 when Kathy SWITZER made her historic run at Boston. A year after the first modern Olympics, the City of Boston Athletic Association inaugurated what was to become the most famous marathon in the world. It became an annual event, held on Patriots Day (April 19). Although women had been running marathons for decades before (Violet Percy's 3:40.22 run in 1926 was the first recorded for a woman), the dominant MEDICAL DISCOURSE of the first half of the century suggested that it was unsafe for women to run such distances. The International Olympic Committee (IOC) did not introduce an Olympic marathon for women until 1984.

Switzer entered the Boston marathon as "K.V. Switzer" and began her run, only to be spotted by a zealous official at about the four-mile stage. The image of the official running onto the course to yank at Switzer's shirt only to be shoved away by Switzer supporters took on symbolic dimensions as the years passed: the thwarting of a male guardian of official rules as he tried to interrupt the progress of a woman who was determined to shatter a patriarchal myth.

Switzer's win had the effect of stimulating marathon running for women and the Amateur Athletic Union of the United States came under pressure to legitimize the event. By 1972, when the organization did so, city marathons, in which "keep fit" enthusiasts as well as competitive athletes participated, were beginning to grow in popularity. Greta Waitz of Norway forced re-evaluations of women athletes, principally through her accomplishments in the city marathons that proliferated in the 1970s and 1980s. In 1972 and 1976 she ran the longest available distance for women, which was then 1500 meters, and in 1978 she won the World Cross-Country Championship. But it was in the city marathons that Waitz came into her own. In the mid-1970s, NARCISSISM began to penetrate Western culture: people began to take an earnest interest in themselves, trying to avoid sickness and aging by exercise and any number of therapeutic means. The "health craze," as it was known, cut across class, gender and ethnic divisions: the search for personal well-being (or "wellness") took place on a mass scale.

The New York marathon of 1976 became a touchstone after its organizers, the New York Road Runners' Club, opened its annual event to all comers as part of the USA's bicentennial celebrations. Two thousand people of various abilities participated in the race, which attracted wide publicity. The following year the number of entrants more than doubled and, by 1978, there were 10,000 starters in a race that snaked through the streets of New York City. Soon applications began arriving from all over the world, so that by 1986 the entrants list had grown to over 20,000.

In the 1979 New York marathon, Waitz became the first woman to break the 2:30 barrier. Waitz won a total of nine New York marathons, eventually lowering the world's best time to 2:24.41. In a remarkable career, she also won Olympic and several other city marathons, but it was at New York that Waitz established herself. Her final win there came in 1988, by which time the American Joan Benoit had risen to join the women's marathon elite. Waitz's natural successor was fellow Norwegian Ingrid Kristiansen, who, more than any other runner, brought athletic legitimacy to the city marathons. An underachiever on the track, Kristiansen won thirteen city marathons at places like Chicago, New York and Stockholm in the 1980s. In the 1985 London marathon, Kristiansen set a women's world's best time of 2:21.45, which stood until Tega Loroupe's run of 2:20.47 in 1998. Loroupe's time was also set in a city marathon, in her case in Rotterdam. From the 1980s onward, both women's and men's world's best times were set outside major track and field tournaments.

Opening up the marathon

While the New York race grew, other cities that had for long hosted marathons (Boston being the obvious example) widened their admission criteria, allowing less competitive runners to take part. New marathons sprang up in places like London and Rotterdam. As with the New York event, they measured their entrants at first in thousands and later in dozens of thousands. Also, as with New York, most city marathons needed an active entrepreneurial promoter. Fred Lebow is credited with being the man who turned the New York marathon into an international festival. In London, former track star Chris Brasher performed a similar function, not only organizing the race but attracting sponsorship money. Increasingly, as entrants grew, arranging emergency medical services became a priority. Injuries and even fatalities began to multiply as the marathons broadened the scope of their entrants.

The purposes of the competitors were mixed. A minority were competitive, often world-class runners, many of whom had run in World and Olympic games. Others were well-conditioned enthusiasts whose aims were personal; typically, to complete the course in a personal best time. Still others – perhaps the majority – were involved in the less serious, though no less worthy, pursuit of raising money for charity. This was evidenced by the rise in entrants dressed in all manner of garb: many dressed as if attending a masked ball, in clown's outfits or as animals. A runner dressed as an English butler completed the whole course carrying a silver tray of drinks. Two runners ran the 26.2 miles inside a pantomime "horse." Such entrants would be sponsored by companies or groups of people, who would make donations to a charity. The idea of twinning sport with charity was novel, and marathons were well-suited to the purpose: they were occasions not only for serious sports, but also for circus-style entertainment. Spectators would line the courses, encouraging even the most inept runners to complete the course. What was once a competitive event was transformed into spectacle.

One of the significant features of marathons was the steady increase in the number of competitors with a DISABILITY of some kind. As with the general mixture of entrants, some disabled participants approached the race with a seriousness of competitive purpose, while others were bent on achieving personal goals or raising money for charities. While wheelchair users were the most conspicuously disabled competitors, marathons were run by persons with several other kinds of disabilities.

Of related interest

Cooper, Pamela (1996) "Marathon and distance running," in Levinson, D. and Christensen, K. (eds), *Encyclopedia of World Sport: From Ancient Times to the Present*. ABC-Clio.
Oglesby, Carole (1998) "Joan Benoit," "Kathrine Switzer" and "Greta Waitz," in *Encyclopedia of Women and Sport in America*, Oryx.

Marxism

Marx

As the writer of the most influential and exhaustive analysis and critique of modern capitalism, Karl Marx has commanded the attentions of scholars and activists for years. His theories have inspired political revolutions as well as scholarly debates. The fact that his name has been appended with an "-ism" suggests not only the depth of his analysis, but the faith-like devotion of those who accept it and, indeed, use it as a practical program. Marx's favorite motto was *de omnibus dubitandum* (We ought to question everything). Every single aspect of social life was open to criticism. Because sports were not as important in Marx's time as they are today, it was left to later writers to subject them to critical scrutiny.

At the time of Marx's writing (in the middle of the nineteenth century), sport was undergoing a transformation to the organized form we now recognize, but it was still some way short of the commercial activity so central to twentieth century capitalism. Marx himself did not include organized sport in his examination of capitalism. However, more contemporary theorists believe that he left appropriate analytical tools to dissect sports.

Because Marx's own thought was subjected to so many different interpretations, it was inevitable that no single analysis would emerge that could claim to be "what Marx would have written about sport had he been alive today." When theories of sports bearing Marx's imprimatur began to surface in the early 1970s, they were far from uniform, their linking characteristics being that sports were geared to the interests of the bourgeoisie, or middle class, had the effect of neutralizing any political potential in the working class, and contributed in some way to the preservation of the status quo. Sports were, in other words, to be criticized, not just analysed.

The principal scholars claiming to work with a Marxist approach were Paul HOCH, the French writer Jean-Marie Brohm and the German theorist, Bero Rigauer. Other commentators, such as Rob Beamish, John Hargreaves, Richard Gruneau and William Morgan, later contributed toward what has now become a respectable corpus of Marxist literature on sports. There have been three tendencies in the literature. The first, as represented by Brohm and Rigauer, is informed by the spirit of the Frankfurt School, and can be described as critical theory. The second takes as its starting point the theories of the Italian Marxist Antonio Gramsci, whose central concept of hegemony has provided a focus for studies of sport. The third is an ambitious attempt by Morgan to amalgamate various schools of Marxist thought and fuse them with his own particular interpretation.

Critical theory

Critical theorists draw their inspiration from the work of Marx published before 1845, when his work had a more pronounced humanism than his later theorizing. Underlying this humanist approach is a stress on the prime importance of human labor. Through labor, the human being expresses his or her unique creative ability to imagine and build. The engagement of the human and material worlds is the crucial nexus, which allows free expression or, under restrictive capitalist conditions, alienation. Both Brohm and Rigauer see sporting activity as a form of labor and, in the "prison of measured time" (as Brohm calls it), a highly alienated form. Its patterns, forms and functions derive from work: its techniques and movements could easily be applied to the process of industrial production; the discipline and practice it requires are similar to that of factory work. Sport does not just reflect labor: it actually is a form of industrial labor and is no more than a "subsystem" of the larger capitalist system.

Brohm writes in terms of the "performance principle" which applies equally to industrial labor and sport and entails competition, quantification, a division of labor, normative standards of individual conduct and the methodical manner and rationalized style of bourgeois life. The inescapable conclusion is that sport is just another repressive force utilized by capitalists to perpetuate the system that has served them – but not workers – so well.

Rob Beamish is prepared to allow that some related cultural expressions, such as TELEVISION, writing and other art forms, have a potential that can enable participants to form critical ideas about society. Sports, however, have no subversive potential and can serve only the established order of things. Beamish has engaged with the debate in several articles (for example, "Understanding labor as a concept for the study of sport," *Sociology of Sport* vol 2, 1985). While disagreeing on finer points, he concludes with Brohm and Rigauer that sport as an institution is homologous to work; that is, it is similar in position and structure if not in function.

Sport, in this conception, is not merely a convenience for capitalism: it serves a vital purpose in inculcating bourgeois beliefs and actions, such as respect for authority, the achievement ethic, obedience to superiors, a sense of duty, self-sacrifice, all of which are integral to both sports success and the continuation of capitalism. The beauty of all this is that sports *appear* to be quite disconnected from the productive sphere, so no one suspects they are guided by the same logic. So, critical theorists go further than the conventional sociologists' argument that sports reflect society. Yes, sports mirror labor relations: but they are also central processes that contribute to keeping the capitalist system intact. Sport is a profoundly conservative force.

Hegemony theory

Writers such as Gruneau and Hargreaves were persuaded of sport's centrality in the capitalist system, but found the critical theorists' interpretation too mechanical. Surely, they argued, sport does not exist in such a fixed relationship to the productive base of society, its character and purpose deriving from the imperatives of the capitalist economy. If this was the case, sports would be epiphenomena – byproducts of the economy – rather than lived experiences that actually *mean* something to participants and have potential to *change* them and their surroundings. Hegemony theorists wanted to restore the role of the human being to that of an agent, someone who was active and could intervene in practical matters rather than just respond to the logic of capitalism.

Although critical theorists were inspired by the humanism in Marx and the effectiveness of human beings in changing history, their actual theories on sport offered little hope for change. According to hegemony theory, there is nothing intrinsic to sports that makes them conservative or subversive: they have no essential qualities. Under capitalism, sports have been supportive of the existing order of things; but there is no necessary reason why, given different circumstances, they could not have a liberating effect. However, for Gruneau in particular, as sports become more structured in their institutional forms, they constrain and regulate much more than liberate their participants. The kind of liberating features of sport he has in mind are spontaneity, freedom of expression and aesthetic beauty. Politically, sports can yield the kind of solidarity that contributes toward the women's movement, civil rights campaigns and other types of protests against injustice and inequality. In sports, there are opportunities to mobilize against the status quo, not just comply with it.

Historically this has not been the case and the enthusiasm for sports, particularly among the working class, has bolstered the social order. Flocking to sports as amusement, the working class assimilates sports' values and principles, most of which dovetail perfectly with those of the wider society. Fair play and the opportunity to go as far as one's ability allows are sacrosanct in sports: meritocratic ideals are important in society as well. One legitimates the other. Forgotten is the fact that, in any capitalist system, there are gross, structured inequalities in the distribution of income, wealth and prestige, and that these are replicated one generation after the next through an inheritance system that favors rich over poor. For hegemony theorists, it is important that those at the poorer end of the class structure regard this as common sense; they are not constantly questioning the legitimacy of a system that consigns them to the status of "also-rans." Sports encourage this by promoting the good of meritocracy and the equality of life chances that seem to be available to everyone, but, in reality, are not.

Hargreaves adds to this the view that sports can have a depoliticizing impact, feeding the enthusiasm of the working class for fun and fantasy while rendering them more vulnerable to the commercial exploitation that today accompanies commodity sports (*Sport, Power and Culture*, Routledge & Kegan Paul, 1986) . Yet Hargreaves is also keen to emphasize the fragility of the hegemonic domination of the ruling class. Sport is not "universally evil," writes Hargreaves. It can be useful as a builder of solidarity, bringing together working-class groups in a common purpose. "It is precisely this type of solidarity that historically has formed the basis for trenchant opposition to employers," Hargreaves concludes. Public gatherings have always generated a potential for disorder and have attracted the state's agents of control. Involvement in sports can facilitate challenge as well as accommodation.

Hargreaves and Gruneau both argue against a firmly negative view of sports and proffer a more flexible Marxist interpretation. Sports can fragment, divide and atomize the working class by splintering into regions, localities and so on. But they can also provide a basis for unity, and resistance to dominant interest groups.

Reconstructed critical theory

The philosopher Alisdair MacIntyre's distinction between practices and institutions is crucial to Morgan's (1994) analysis of sports. Sports are practices in that they are skillful, complex, cooperative and virtuous in their conduct and strive through sophisticated means to achieve excellence. The "goods" produced by sports are internal: they are achieved and judged only by those who are fit to do so. "Sporting practices," as Morgan calls them, are all contrived pursuits that seek to overcome unnecessary obstacles. The ends they are geared to, such as crossing the finish line, putting the golf ball in the hole and so on, are not important in themselves: "they are considered worth pursuing only if they include a quite definite specification of the way such ends may be attained." The logic of inventing obstacles is unintelligible outside the logic of sporting practices; but the "gratuitous logic" is a "contingent universal condition of its practice."

From the turn of the century, the practice of sports have been corrupted – not just changed – by institutions. In the 1940s and 1950s, economic and political forces have rendered sports an article of mass consumption. "The same entrepreneurial initiatives that had organized our factories and shaped the character of our work were now well on their way to doing the same to our leisure and sporting pursuits," writes Morgan. Investors flocked to build new franchises, and sports performers "milked their newly-won FREE AGENCY." Morgan argues that this "mass commodification" amounted to "the capitulation of the practice side of sport to its business side."

On this account, the two Marxist versions of sports covered earlier both missed an ideological shift in the way powerful classes ensured their dominant position: they became less dependent on repression and increasingly dependent on the market. A new managerial class emerged to direct and administer the apparatus of mass production and consumption. Accompanying this shift was an open admission that the pursuit of profit was a perfectly reasonable goal in itself without the need for any superior-sounding rationale, like making the world a better or safer place. This point is important to Morgan because he feels that sports as a practice were once thought to be pure and autonomous. More recently, sports, like all other components of culture, have been rendered a business affair, offering careers to those who have requisite abilities. The fact that sport is a commodity is not new; what *is* new is the open acknowledgment of this. While Morgan describes his theory as reconstructed critical theory, it bears little resemblance to the earlier Marxist version: it is driven by a similar critical spirit, but modifies the central relationship between sport and the economy – which is vital to all Marxist accounts – by suggesting that sport is corrupted by the market forces of capitalism rather than being an extension of its activities.

Of related interest

Brohm, Jean-Marie (1978) *Sport: A Prison of Measured Time*, London: Ink Links.
Gruneau, Richard (1983) *Class, Sports and Social Development*, University of Massachusetts Press.
Morgan, William J. (1994) *Leftist Theories of Sport: A Critique and Reconstruction*, University of Illinois Press.
Rigauer, Bero (1981) *Sport and Work*, Columbia University Press.

masculinities/femininities

Sport as the "natural domain of men"

Historically, sport has been so closely identified with men and masculinity that the two have become synonymous in many Western societies. In Victorian Britain, sport became institutionalized in the public (independent) schools. In this setting, team games such as rugby, football and cricket provided the dominant image of masculine identity in sports. It was believed that these "cults of male physicality," as Robert Connell calls them, would turn boys to men. Organized sport became a symbol of bourgeois masculinity: the athletic field was a place to encourage the development of muscular and moral strength (the ethic of MUSCULAR CHRISTIANITY), AGGRESSION and physical power, the essential elements of manhood both on and off the field.

Sport became important in the construction of male solidarity, encouraging men to identify with other men. In contrast, femininity developed around women's roles as wives and mothers in the home. Victorian ideas about women's reproductive functions and the essential biological differences between men and women provided the main justification for excluding women from sport. As Jennifer Hargreaves (1994) explains: "The belief in innate and biological differences between the sexes constituted a powerful and pervasive form of sexism – experienced as 'unproblematic common sense behavior' – which systematically subordinated women in sport for years to come." Sport was an arena in which the bodily differences between men and women were celebrated; it was undoubtedly, as Hargreaves outlined, the "natural domain of men."

Organized sport thus developed as one of the most masculine of social institutions created "by and for men," as Messner and Sabo (1990) put it. Even in the 1990s, sports clubs and organizations ranging from England's MCC to the Formula One racing circuit remain male preserves. Robert Connell argues that in the late twentieth century, "Sport has come to be the leading definer of masculinity in mass culture" (*Gender and Masculinities*, Polity Press, 1995).

As a gendering institution, organized sport has played – indeed, continues to play – an important role in the reproduction of male power. Numerous studies examining sports institutions, discourses and subcultures (from rugby to surfing) have demonstrated sport's role in the ideological and structural domination of women by men. However, power relations between men and women in sport are not fixed. "Sport does not simply and unambiguously reproduce men's existing power and privilege," states Michael Messner in his *Power at Play* (1992). To understand the complexities, unevenness and discrepancies in men's exercise of social, economic and physical power, it is useful to adopt a more fluid model of gender oppression that, as Connell outlines, "focuses on the processes and relationships through which men and women conduct gendered lives." The "gender order" may be seen as a *relational* process through which power relations between men and women are constructed, negotiated and contested. As Messner and Sabo write: "A relational conception of gender necessarily includes a critical examination of both femininity and masculinity as they develop in relation to each other within a system of structured social inequality."

Furthermore, masculinity is not some innate characteristic or behavior type. As cross-cultural research demonstrates, stereotypes of "male" behavior, such as being competitive and adventurous, are historically, socially and culturally constructed. With an increased awareness of the interplay between such factors as gender, race and class, it has become recognized that there are many masculinit*ies* and femininit*ies* .

An overriding concern among feminists in recent years has been a recognition of the diversity of women's experiences and the multiplicity of feminine identities. Feminists recognize that social oppression varies among women according to class, "race," ethnicity, religion, age, sexuality and DISABILITY. These factors will have an effect on women's ability to participate in sports and will color their experience of it. Likewise, to understand the ways people understand masculinity in sport, it is important to consider the range or diversity of masculinities that are produced in a particular cultural setting. However, as Connell argues, we need also to recognize that there is a "gender politics within masculinity." By focusing on gender relations among men, we need to distinguish the hierarchical relations between the different types of masculinity; relations of alliance, dominance and subordination. In their article "Towards a new sociology of masculinity," (in *Theory and Society* vol 14, no 5, 1987), Carrigan *et al.* developed the concept of "hegemonic masculinity" to understand "how particular men inhabit positions of power and wealth and how they legitimate and reproduce social relationships that generate dominance."

Hegemonic masculinity is thus a particular variety of masculinity within a gender-based hierarchy among men under which women and "other" men (for example, GAYS and non-whites) are subordinated. It is supported and maintained by a multitude of patriarchal institutions, but particularly by sport. As Garry Whannel suggests, in his *Blowing the Whistle* (Pluto, 1983), to be good in sport is central to being a real man, which is to be "strong, virile and macho." This hegemonic masculinity reinforces the *naturalness* of heterosexuality.

Sexualities

Sport thus reinforces a construction of male sexuality based on conquest and the objectification of women. Demonstrating sporting and heterosexual prowess are tests of masculinity even for those boys who detest sport. However, as Connell explains, hegemonic masculinity is not a fixed character type but a contestable position. As Messner (1992) argues, sport is an institution within which "power is constantly at play," for example, in the contestation between black and white masculinities, or between hetero-social and homo-social aspects of male sporting masculinities. Nevertheless, many of these "masculine" characteristics such as being physically strong and skillful are reproduced through sport.

Sports imagery in particular reflects dominant conceptions or stereotypes of both masculinity and femininity. For example, "emphasized femininity," as Connell terms it, the form of heterosexual femininity that is organized around the theme of sexual receptivity, still dominates magazine and newspaper photographs of celebrity sportswomen. The runner Florence GRIFFITH JOYNER, figure skater Katerina Witt and Russian tennis star Anna Kournikova have all been photographed in glamor style poses focusing on their sexuality, not their sporting performance. However, these co-exist with images of femininity emphasizing sportswomen as active, strong and muscular, images that challenge the stereotypes of female frailty.

In consumer culture, physical activity for women has become desirable. The body NARCISSISM that began in the 1960s contributed to physical exercise becoming more widely available, popular and significant in the lives of many (albeit predominantly young, able-bodied, professional and white) women. Women penetrated many of the traditional as well as more recent bastions of masculinity, like bodybuilding, boxing, soccer and ice hockey. So, what has been the effect of women's increased involvement on the existing gender order of sport? If sport is still such a proving ground for masculinity, then surely it can only be preserved by the continued exclusion of women from the activity.

Challenge or incorporation?

Some feminist scholars have argued that women's increased participation in physical activity is a form of resistance that challenges the naturalization of gender difference and inequality, and thus the male hegemony of sport. Messner outlines that some consider women's movement into sport "represents a genuine quest by women for equality, control of their bodies and self-definition." If this is to be accepted, then we must consider women's presence in sports as a "challenge to the ideological basis of male domination."

Yet, mere presence in sport does not guarantee empowerment for women. Sport in the main is defined and organized around the potential of the male body, particularly its potential for physical strength and endurance. As women can never be expected to measure up to male standards, the belief that inequality is part of the natural order is enhanced, according to Messner. As Hargreaves argues, women's influx into traditionally male activities is contradictory; it is not clear to what extent these "potentially radical forms of sporting femininity" are supporting or challenging broader power relations. "Women are being incorporated into models of male sport which are characterized by fierce competition and aggression," Hargreaves contends. "Instead of a redefinition of masculinity occurring, this trend highlights the complex ways male hegemony works in sport and ways in which women actively collude in its reproduction."

Feminist analyses inspired by the work of Michel Foucault have focused on the body as a key site in women's struggle around the subordination of their physicality. However, for many of these theorists, the significance of the fitness and health craze has been in controlling and disciplining the body and in surrendering to regimes of BODY REGULATION. The body has been made into a commodity. As Judith Butler wrote in her "Revising femininity," "you only have permission to be this strong if you can also look beautiful" (in R. Betterton (ed.) *Looking On*, Pandora, 1987). Sports women still need to "prove" their femininity by displaying traditional constructions of womanhood, looking sporting, but still sexy. For sportswomen, compulsory heterosexuality is a powerful form of control.

Nevertheless, studies of masculinities/femininities in sport have demonstrated strains in the association between sport and masculinity. In the media, for example, increasing objectification and sexualization of the (especially black) male body is apparent. Sporting masculinities have and are diversifying. The rejection of overt competition and of the emphasis on winning in many new "lifestyle" sports such as skateboarding, in-line skating, windsurfing and snowboarding broaden the range of sporting masculinities. Such developments will expose some of the contradictions within both the reproduction of traditional sporting femininities and masculinities and, using Messner's phrase, the status quo of hegemonic masculinity.

Of related interest

Hargreaves, Jennifer (1994) *Sporting Females: Critical Issues in the History and Sociology of Women's Sports*, Routledge.

Messner, Michael A. (1992) *Power at Play: Sports and the Problem of Masculinity*, Beacon Press.

Messner, M. and Sabo, D. (1990) *Sport, Men and the Gender Order*, Human Kinetics.

BELINDA WHEATON

MCC

The origins of cricket

Once described by Lord Hawke as "the Parliament House of Cricket, not only in Great Britain but of Overseas Dominions," the Marylebone Cricket Club (MCC), was formed in 1787. The club grew out of the White Conduit Club, which itself was formed out of the *Je ne sais quoi* or Star and Garter Club, the perpetual chairman of which was the then Prince of Wales, subsequently George IV. Established by men of high status, the club has throughout the years been dominated by titled, upper-class men educated at public schools and Oxford or Cambridge universities.

The origins of cricket itself can be traced to a number of sixteenth- and seventeenth-century bat and ball games such as "stoolball," "trap-ball," "tip cat" and "cat and dog." Rules were relatively few and simple, often transmitted orally rather than in written form. Variations were such that identical games could have a variety of different, locally specific names, or such that an identical name could be given to a number of games played under a variety of localized rules. The common thread, however, is that all these games consisted of a stationary batter, who struck a ball or piece of wood away from his/her body and who could subsequently score (points, notches, runs) by running between two or more fixed points. Cricket, in a manner similar to other sports such as football and golf – though in contrast to basketball – was not therefore invented but, rather, emerged from a cluster of folk antecedents.

After the English Civil War, the activities of the aristocracy became increasingly focused around the twin focal points of government and social life, around Parliament in London and the country estate. By 1700 adverts for cricket matches appeared regularly in the local press and indicate that cricket was being played by aristocrats for whom gambling was both significant and common. Although incipient levels of organized cricket existed in rural areas (most notable in this regard was the Hambledon Club in Hampshire), it was not until the aristocracy adopted the game and began to organize its playing that cricket took on its specifically modern form.

The MCC's emergence out of a number of similar, overlapping clubs (such as the White Conduit Club) indicates what the MCC was originally designed to be: a loosely structured association of high-status gentlemen whose main purpose was to facilitate cricket playing. The founding of the MCC and the establishment of Lord's as the club's home (though not at this stage its property) marked a significant turning point for cricket. The White Conduit Club, named after the White Conduit Fields where games were normally played, staged matches on common land. As it proved impossible to save games from outside interference, Thomas Lord, acting on the advice of the Earl of Winchilsea, leased a piece of land in Dorset Fields in London in 1786. The establishment of a private playing area, which was subsequently enclosed, marks the beginning of one of the major characteristics of both English cricket and the MCC, namely, status exclusivity. In 1808, Lord's, as it was to become known, moved to North Bank in Regents Park, and finally in 1812 it moved to its current location in St John's Wood.

As the MCC was to become the "Parliament House of Cricket," so Lord's was to become cricket's "spiritual home."

Gentlemen and players

It would be a mistake however to conclude that the MCC assumed the role of the supreme authority of cricket at this early stage. During the early 1800s, members of the MCC were happy just to turn up and play cricket. Members held influence over the game simply because they were part of the elite of society, but until the 1830s the MCC had no formal or coherent administrative structure. Despite regular law revisions (for example, in 1811, 1817, 1821, 1823 and 1825), 1828 was the first time that proposals were put to a general MCC meeting. Even though the three great matches – Eton *vs* Harrow, Oxford *vs* Cambridge and Gentlemen *vs* Players – became annual events in this period, the MCC might well have disappeared entirely had it not been for the efforts of James Darke. He purchased the leasehold for Lord's in 1835 and, driven mainly by profit, transformed the stadium facilities and upgraded the MCC fixture list. MCC minutes record that, in 1850, Lord's was drained at Darke's "sole expense" and in 1853 that "Mr Darke receives all subscriptions and Entrances and undertakes the expenses of all matches made by the Committee." At this point Darke *was* the MCC's day-to-day administration.

What the MCC did manage to organize in these early days was the employment of its first professionals. In 1825 the club employed four groundsmen to act as bowlers and two boys to act as fielders. In 1835, this was increased to five bowlers and five boys. This move helped to establish the two-tier amateur–professional status of players, which remained until the distinction was abolished in 1962. With one exception, before the Second World War, all captains of county sides were amateurs. Playing roles were informally divided into professional bowlers (mostly working class) and amateur batsmen (gentlemen-players from the upper classes). Various status-emphasizing practices were employed to symbolize the division, including the use of separate gates for entering and exiting the field of play, separate and usually inferior travel and changing facilities for professionals, and the use of professionals to help prepare the playing area, doubling up as gatemen and bowling to the amateur batsmen in the "nets" to provide them with practice. Professionals addressed amateurs as either "Mr" or "sir," and on scorecards the professionals' initials were listed after their surname while the amateurs' initials were listed before.

However, the continuing weak structure of the MCC at this time is evident from its role in the major cricketing controversies of the nineteenth century; the introduction of first round-arm (1835) and then over-arm (1864) bowling. Both introductions were the initiatives of professional players, partly seeking to improve their employability and partly seeking to advantage the bowler in the face of increasingly smooth, and therefore batsman-friendly, pitches. Such was the weakness of the MCC that they failed in their attempts to stop either innovation. So disillusioned was the influential journal *The Sporting Life* with the MCC's role that it fostered a campaign, albeit unsuccessful, to establish a new administration to oversee the running of the game.

The golden age

By the end of the century, however, the MCC had become, in Lord Harris's words "the most venerated institution in the British Empire" in what is generally considered the "Golden Age" of cricket. Two factors were important: the fractured nature of the county clubs and the changing composition of the MCC. The County Championship, which remains the premier first-class cricket competition in Britain, was first competed for in 1873 by nine counties (there are now eighteen). However, there was no administrative body for the competition and the scoring system was so complex that the press were normally left to decide the winner. The major obstacle was one of definition: which counties could be deemed "first class"? It took twenty-one years for the MCC eventually to succumb to pressure and make a ruling. The 1894 "Classification of Counties" marks the beginning of the MCC's reign as the central administrative body for cricket in Britain. The establishment of a coherent County Championship was closely followed by establishment of the Minor Counties Cricket Association (1895), the Board of Control to administer test matches in England (1898) and the Imperial Cricket Conference or ICC (1909).

The changing composition of MCC membership facilitated this process. Between 1860 and 1914 the dominance of Eton–Harrow and Oxford–Cambridge old boys among the membership waned (although the proportion of titled and aristocratic members remained static at around 45–50 per cent). The new MCC leaders were more businesslike than their predecessors, and more committed to the idea of empire. Many, like Lord Harris (Under-Secretary for India) and Hon. F.S. Jackson (Governor of Bengal), took up administrative posts in foreign countries. Many felt that Britain's world dominance was attributable to team games and influential MCC members such as Lord Harris and Lord Hawke explicitly argued that cricket could "civilize" the Empire and strengthen its bonds. As the premier cricket body, as the MCC had by this time become, it was natural that its President should assume the chair of the ICC; this protocol existed until 1989. Despite changing its name to the *International* Cricket Conference in 1965 (and International Cricket Council in 1989), cricket remains a game dominated by nations of the former Empire, or Commonwealth. Indeed, 35 of its 74 current member nations have been part of the British Empire or Commonwealth at some time.

The role of the MCC has somewhat reduced in recent years. Indeed, from 1993, the ICC was no longer administered by the MCC and became an independent body. As other nations have become more powerful in the ICC, so the County Clubs, the Test and County Cricket Board and the National Cricket Association have increasingly taken responsibility for the running of the game in Britain. The establishment of the England and Wales Cricket Board in 1997 has centralized cricket's administration further, and what power the MCC retains is largely symbolic and resides mainly in tradition and emotional attachment.

International cricket

In the late 1990s, nine nations were afforded "test match" (that is, full international) status. These were (in chronological order of their being granted this status) England, Australia, South Africa, West Indies, New Zealand, India, Pakistan, Sri Lanka and Zimbabwe. At first sight, North America appears to be a striking omission from this list. In fact, the first international cricket match was between the United States and Canada in 1845, and the first tour by an England XI, in 1859, encompassed both countries. The failure of the sport to sustain interest in North America is generally attributed to the Civil War (1861–65) and the subsequent growth of MAJOR LEAGUE BASEBALL. Baseball is thought to have more closely equated to American culture and to have satisfied desires for developing an American national identity. A small amount of cricket is still played in the USA, in the Philadelphia area, and in California, where there remains a small cricket league started in the 1920s and featuring a Hollywood XI. It is also played in Canada, mainly by migrants and their offspring. In recent years India and Pakistan have attempted to popularize the game in North America by playing a number of international one-day matches under floodlights in Canada.

Of related interest

Bradley, J. (1990) "The MCC, society and empire: a portrait of cricket's ruling body, 1860–1914," *International Journal of the History of Sport* vol 7, no 1.
Brookes, C.(1978) *English Cricket: The Game and its Players through the Ages*, Weidenfeld & Nicolson.
Sandiford, K. (1994) *Cricket and the Victorians*, Scolar Press.
Williams, J. (1989) "Cricket," in T. Mason (ed.), *Sport in Britain: A Social History*, Cambridge University Press.

DOMINIC MALCOLM

McCormack, Mark

b. 1931, USA

The founder and managing director of International Management Group, or IMG, McCormack was described by *Sports Illustrated* in 1990 as "The most powerful man in sports" (May 21). At that stage he presided over a web-like organization that covered all aspects of sports management. IMG's clients included tennis players Martina Hingis and Aranxta Sanchez Vicario, Grand Prix drivers Jacques Villeneuve and David Coulthard, golfers Bernhard Langer and Ian Woosnam and sports associations and events such as the Japanese J-League (soccer), Wimbledon and the Water Ski World Cup. In addition, IMG had interests in classical music (clients included Kiri Te Kanawa and Itzhak Perlman), literature (Pat Conroy), modeling (Niki Taylor), British royalty (Captain Mark Phillips), education (Oxford University), world affairs (the Nobel Foundation and the World Economic forum) and religion (Pope John Paul). On every day of every year since 1980, somewhere in the world, there has been at least one sporting event taking place in which McCormack has had an active interest.

The son of a farm journal publisher, McCormack grew up in Chicago where he began playing golf as therapy after suffering a fractured skull in a car accident. He met his first client, Arnold Palmer, while playing at William and Mary College. After graduating from Yale Law School, McCormack joined a Cleveland law firm and, in his spare time, arranged exhibitions for professional golfers. Palmer was one of several golfers who approached McCormack to review his endorsement contracts. McCormack sensed a business opportunity and, in 1960, set up on his own as a golf agent, representing at first Palmer and then, soon after, Gary Player and Jack Nicklaus. These three players all but dominated world golf, and McCormack's fortunes followed theirs.

Within six years McCormack had opened a London office, his clear objective from the outset being to have as many international branches as possible and sign the best – that is, best-known – sports performer in each country. Having an association with the top performer afforded McCormack a way of insinuating himself into big events organized by sports federations. Within a year of starting the London operation, McCormack had signed Britain's top golfer, Tony Jacklin, who in turn introduced McCormack to the Royal and Ancient Golf Club of St Andrews, Scotland. The St Andrews golf club eventually became an IMG client.

In 1968, McCormack sought the signature of Jean-Claude Killy, then the world's top skier, who had taken three gold medals at the Grenoble Winter Olympics. Killy was instrumental in persuading the Albertville Olympic Committee to let IMG handle the marketing of the 1992 Winter Olympics. In the same year, tennis went open and paved the way for a fully professional sport; McCormack was in position at the outset and took advantage of the growing number of professionals who needed financial representation.

By 1990, IMG had established offices in ten European cities and had eyes on Asia. McCormack became known for his secrecy about IMG structure. Its company brochure listed an office in Neuchâtel, Switzerland, but the official register of Swiss companies revealed another IMG office in Geneva. This Geneva branch had the same address as Molard, a Swiss firm of accountants. Also registered at the address was Marksmen Investment, which had one director, Julian Jakobi, manager of the late racing driver Ayrton Senna. Marksmen was described as a *conseil fiscal*, or tax adviser. McCormack was famously reluctant to discuss the web-like nature of his organization.

IMG was organized into three divisions, each controlling a sector. Golf was the principal activity, but tennis came to the fore after McCormack successfully negotiated to handle the Wimbledon marketing. TELEVISION occupied the third sector. McCormack moved from representing performers to representing the events in which the performers participated and then to the production of television coverage for those events. Some of the effect of IMG's efforts can be gauged by the successful golf tours that have developed in, among other areas, Europe, Japan, Australia and South Africa, all of which attract television interest.

Given his position as the chief negotiator for so many top sports performers, it was perhaps inevitable that McCormack acquired the reputation as one of the least liked men in sports. Promoters wishing to attract golfers or tennis players would need to deal with hard-bitten business types before they could secure the services of the performers, and IMG players were known not to come cheap.

And, after one case in the 1980s, they were also known to work hard. Bill Rogers was the 1981 PGA Player of the Year, Ryder Cup player and winner of three PGA tournaments (seven in total). Secure financially and seemingly burned out by the demanding schedule set for him by IMG, Rogers descended abruptly from the limelight and won only one more tournament. Ten years after his triumph, he slipped out of competitive golf at the comparatively young age of 38.

But, for every "casualty" there are many other successes. Jennifer Capriati, for example, had not even won a major tournament when IMG negotiated her a $5 million (£3m) endorsement contract at the age of 14. At any one time, IMG has interests in about one-third of the top thirty tennis players in the world. One of the ways McCormack achieved this was by buying one of the world's top tennis academies (Nick Bollettieri's in Florida) in 1987. Andre Agassi, Monica Seles and Jim Courier were all graduates of the academy who signed with IMG.

But, while McCormack is known as a players' agent, his focus in the 1990s moved to event management. Of all the tennis Grand Slam events, only the French Open remained untouched by IMG. And, as exclusive agent for the ATP's sponsorship rights and television sales, IMG virtually controlled the tour (comprising more than 70 events).

McCormack's shift was precipitated by two changes in sports. First, the rise of team players as public figures prompted more cut-throat and cut-price competition. For example, IMG's typical commission would range between 20 and 25 per cent; as team players came to the fore, agents were known to pare down commissions to as little at three per cent in order to gain the cachet of a well-known NFL, MAJOR LEAGUE BASEBALL or, later, NBA player. In the early 1980s, when McCormack was in his ascendancy, it would not have been viable for him to pursue players in a league that had made little impact in terms of visibility. During the late 1980s, the likes of Michael JORDAN, Magic JOHNSON and Larry Bird opened up a new market.

This led to the second change, a proliferation of sports agents, not just rival organizations but independent individuals who operated outside any formal structure and could give clients the personal attention lacking in the larger, more anonymous IMG. The movie *Jerry Maguire* charts the progress of an independent who breaks away from an IMG-style agency with just one client.

In 1997, IMG's once unassailable position as the number one sports marketing and events management organization was tested by the creation of two serious rivals. Interpublic, a large US advertising group, acquired two sports agencies – Advantage, of the USA, and AAPI in Britain – to produce what it claimed was the second largest organization behind IMG. Then Marquee, a relatively new company, acquired PROSERV, a well-known sports agency founded in the 1960s by former tennis player Donald Dell. The merger, which valued ProServ at $15 million, created a group with estimated annual billings of about $400m, compared with IMG's of $800m–1 billion, and Advantage–ATP's of about $500m. Intensifying the competition even more was NIKE's decision to create Nike Sports Entertainment to stage sports events.

McCormack also made serious errors. For example, IMG attempted to build its interests in European golf in the 1990s, and to this end it joined forces with the Professional Golf Association (PGA) to form the European Tour Courses (ETC).

The golf course market in Britain was near saturation, but elsewhere in Europe courses were coming onto the market cheaply. The strategy was to buy real estate and develop twenty quality courses capable of staging major championships. These events would be awarded by one of the stockholders – the PGA – and managed by the company with the assistance of IMG. The exposure of television would virtually guarantee increased interest in the courses and inflate their values. But the acquisitions proved disastrous, and both media and professionals criticized the condition of the courses. The initiative made losses from the outset, and the project was heavily scaled-down. With losses estimated at over a million dollars, PGA–ETC announced that it would concentrate only on "flagship venues."

IMG owned the French soccer club Strasbourg and, in the late 1990s, began targeting other European clubs in Italy, Germany and Hungary. This was an innovation in strategy for IMG and prompted the FIFA-affiliated Union des Associans Européenes de Football (UEFA) to stipulate that commonly-owned clubs could not compete in the same competition.

When McCormack started IMG, he was the pioneer of a different type of approach to sports, one which was perfect for what was, in the 1960s, a professionalizing culture. By the 1990s, the entire sports landscape had changed. Professionalism had pervaded all sports. Even as recently as 1990 there were perhaps less than 15–20 organizations in sports marketing; by 1998, there were at least 500. IMG was unique in its positioning, but it was unlikely to enjoy the kind of complete domination it had during the thirty years from its founding in 1960.

Of related interest

McCormack, Mark (1984) *What They Don't Teach You at Harvard Business School*, Collins.
—— *McCormack on Managing*, Century.
Swift, E.M. (1990) "The most powerful man in sports," *Sports Illustrated* vol 72, no 21, May 21.

medical discourse

Man: the measure of all things

Medical discourses in the nineteenth and a large part of the twentieth centuries contained explicit warnings about the dangers of female participation in sports. Scientific opinion held that women's bodies were not designed to withstand the rigors of physical exercise required of athletes: they were too frail, too vulnerable and too prone to the injuries that were commonplace in athletic competition. There were additional, less apparent dangers: reproductive dysfunctions and profound, irreversible hormonal changes could result from many forms of sporting endeavor. Medical science discouraged women's entry into sport and supplied a rationalization for the kind of mandatory exclusion that was typified by the first modern Olympic games in 1896. The Olympics, declared their founder, Pierre de Coubertin, in a memorable phrase, were dedicated to the "solemn and periodic exultation of male athleticism ... with female applause as a reward."

Nelly Oudshoorn's book *Beyond the Natural Body: An Archeology of Sex Hormones* (1994) analyses how this conception of the female had dominated medical discourse through the eighteenth and nineteenth centuries. In this period, intellectual curiosity centered on the dissimilarities between men and women. The fact that the reason men and women differed was not perfectly evident illustrates how dramatically understanding of the human body can change. Oudshoorn's work underlines that new knowledge does not just make the body more transparent: it actually alters its nature.

Oudshoorn acknowledges that her account was influenced by the work of two scholars, Thomas Laqueur and Londa Schiebinger. Laqueur's studies of medical texts indicate that the concept of a sharp division between male and female is a product of the past 300 years and, for two thousand years before that, bodies were not visualized in terms of differences. In other words, there were people, some of whom could have children and others of whom could not; sexual difference was not a concept, so it was impossible to conceive of a distinct bifurcation of types based on sexual identity. Even physical differences we now regard as obvious were not so obvious without a conceptual understanding of sexual differences. In some periods, a woman's clitoris was thought to be a minuscule protuberance, an underdeveloped version of the equivalent structure in men (the penis).

For most of human history the stress was on similarities, with the female body being just a "gradation," or nuance of one basic male type. This vision complemented and bolstered a male-centered worldview in which, as Laqueur puts it in his *Making Sex: Body and Gender from the Greeks to Freud* (Harvard University Press, 1990), "man is the measure of all things, and woman does not exist as an ontologically distinct category."

The tradition of bodily similarities came under attack, particularly from anatomists who argued that sex was not restricted only to reproductive organs but affected every part of the body. Anatomists' interest in this was fired by the idea that even the skeleton had sexual characteristics. Schiebinger's medical history *The Mind Has No Sex: Women in the Origins of Modern Science* (Harvard University Press, 1989) shows that anatomists in the nineteenth century searched for the sources of women's difference and apparent inferiority. Depictions of the female skull were used to "prove" that women were naturally inferior to men in intellectual capacities. In the process, the concept of sexual differences was integrated into the discourse, so that by the end of the nineteenth century, female and male bodies were understood in terms of opposites, each having different organs, functions and even feelings.

Oudshoorn's work extends the analysis by identifying how the female body became conceptualized in terms of its unique sexual essence in the 1920s and 1930s. In these decades, sex endocrinology created a completely new understanding of sexual differences based on hormones. Eventually, hormonal differences became accepted natural facts. Knowledge, on this account, was not discovered but produced: research on hormones created a different model of the sexes which was adopted universally and served to reshape our most fundamental conceptions of human nature. Women were different to men in the most profound, categorical and immovable way, and the impact this had on their relationship to sport was immense.

The weaknesses of womanhood

Females were not only discouraged from participating in sports and exercise, but were warned against it. "Medical advice concerning exercise and physical activity came to reflect and perpetuate understandings about women's 'abiding sense of physical weakness' and the unchangeable nature of her physical inferiority," writes Patricia Vertinsky. Her article, "Exercise, physical capability, and the eternally wounded woman in late nineteenth century North America," explores how physicians' interpretation of biological theories of menstruation led them to discourage taxing physical exertion (*Journal of Sport History* vol. 14, no. 1, 1987).

Menstruation – the eternal wound – was seen as a form of invalidity, and its beginning meant that young women would need to be careful in conserving energy. Growing up had quite different meanings for young males and females, as Vertinsky observes: "Puberty for boys marked the onset of strength and enhanced vigor; for girls it marked the onset of the prolonged and periodic weaknesses of womanhood." This was the popular view at a time (1880s) when the full ramifications of sexuality were the subject of great debate.

Disabled by menstruation, women were less than perfect when compared to men. Their physical inferiority prohibited them from competing against each other, let alone men. As in so many other instances of exclusion, the justification was based on patronage: it was for women's own sake. If they tried to emulate their physically superior male counterparts, they would be risking damage to themselves. Scientific studies of how menstruation defined and delimited a woman's capacity for physical activity shaped popular thought, their credibility enhanced by their apparent symmetry with folk beliefs and taboos concerning impurity and contamination. Vertinsky notes that scientific and medical theories were "strongly colored by these traditional beliefs."

Women were thought to be so handicapped during monthly periods that they were prone to accidents and hysteria, making sport and exercise unsuitable areas of activity. Another scientific view was that women possessed a finite amount of energy and, unlike men, were "taxed" biologically with special energy demands necessitated by menstruation and reproduction. Women could never aspire to the kind of intellectual and social development pursued by men because they were simply not built for that purpose: they were naturally mothers.

There were some schools of thought that held that the enfeebling effects of menstruation could be offset by cold baths, deep breathing and mild exercising, such as beanbag-throwing, hoops or golf. Especially appropriate, according to Alice Tweedy, writing in *Popular Science Monthly* in 1892, were "homely gymnastics" (i.e. housework). Other physicians prescribed rest and energy conservation. While these may sound like (if the reader will pardon the phrase) old wives' tales, they had the status of scientific fact in the period when organized sports were coming into being. Sports were intended for men only.

Vertinsky quotes a passage from influential physician Henry Maudsley who, in 1874, wrote that:

> women are marked out by Nature for very different offices in life from those of men ... special functions render it improbable she will succeed, and unwise for her to persevere in running over the same course at the same pace with him ... women cannot rebel successfully against the tyranny of their organization.

The same natural tyranny that dictated women's exclusion from sports and exercise restricted women's activities in all other areas of social life.

"Scientific definitions of human 'nature' were thus used to justify the channeling of men and women ... into vastly different social roles," writes Schiebinger in her article "Skeletons in the closet: The first illustrations of the female skeleton in eighteenth-century anatomy." "It was thought 'natural' that men, by virtue of their 'natural reason,' should dominate public spheres of government and commerce, science and scholarship, while women, as creatures of feeling, fulfilled their natural destiny as mother, conservators of custom in the confined sphere of the home" (in Gallagher and Laqueur 1987). Even the most tremulous suggestions about activities for women was likely to incense those whose interests were best served by passive women. For example, toward the end of the nineteenth century, cycling was a popular pastime in North America and Europe. Both men and women cycled, though to mixed reactions from the medical community. While the advantages to men's health were acknowledged, there was suspicion about whether women's bodies were up to the rigors of cycling. Many doctors believed that the pedaling motion when operating a sewing machine gave women sufficient exercise, according to Helen Lenskyj.

This did not stop women who wanted to get involved in sports, and in her *Out of Bounds: Women, Sport and Sexuality*, Lenskyj provides examples of competitors in several sports and women's organizations that would cater for them. She also points out that sportswomen were generally seen as odd. Labeled as tomboys or hoydens, they were thought to lack "femininity" and even represent a moral degeneracy that was thought to be creeping into society. "Although some doctors advocated exercise therapy in the early 1900s, a time when rest, not exercise, was the accepted medical treatment for virtually all diseases and injuries, they rarely made the connection between exercise therapy and women's full sporting participation," writes Lenskyj.

Despite these fears, women were cautiously admitted to the more taxing track events of the Olympics, although the sight of exhausted females fighting for their breath as they crossed the line of the 800 meters in 1928 was so repugnant to Olympic organizers that they removed the event from women's schedules. Not until 1960 was the distance reinstated for women. Yet, women continued to steal their ways into competition, giving rise to different fears. Contemporary biologists Lynda Birke and Gail Vines use a cautionary quotation from a 1939 book on women and sport: "Too much activity in sports of a masculine character causes the female body to become more like that of a man" (in "A sporting chance: The anatomy of destiny" *Women's Studies International Forum* vol. 10, no. 4, 1987) "Virilism" is the term for the development of secondary male sexual characteristics in women, and there is evidence that continued use of synthesized testosterone-based products is responsible for facial hair, deep voice, broad shoulders, muscle mass and other typically male features. In the 1930s, this evidence was not available. The assumption was that exercise and competition in themselves would cause female genital organs to decay and so pervert woman's true nature.

Not only was a woman's body regarded as too weak and liable to serious hormonal dysfunction if she went into sports, "but the competitive mentality was antithetical to her true nature," reported the respected *Scientific American* journal as late as 1936, adding that women had an "innate tendency to shun competition." By this time, women were already showing competence in a variety of Olympic sports, including track and field, swimming and many team sports. Yet, fears about the long-term effects persisted and physical prohibitions were reinforced by social ones.

The repression of women's bodies

Lenskyj's study reveals how sneering comments about tomboys added to alarm over the masculinizing effects of sport grew into fully-fledged condemnations of sporting females' alleged sexual proclivities. Women aiming to succeed in sports were burdened with scientific and popular beliefs and images about the rightful place of women. Any achievement of note was a subversion of established wisdom. Lenskyj's thesis is that, in all other social contexts, women's femininity served to validate male identity and male power at both individual and social levels. A woman who defied scientific orthodoxy and excelled in areas defined by and for men was a threat.

Women who managed to negotiate a successful passage into sports, or any other traditionally male domain for that matter, were in a paradox. Lenskyj argues that male heterosexual standards were applied to sports and women who succeeded were immediately suspected of being lesbians. If they were not lesbians before they went into sports, they would be before long. Their achievements were undermined by the presumption that they were not natural women at all; or, as Lenskyj puts it, by "the equating of any sign of athletic or intellectual competence with masculinity, and by extension, with LESBIANISM."

No culture that promotes masculinity could surrender one of its bastions of masculine pride to women. But, preaching conformity to male standards requires a transgressive influence as an example of otherness. It appeared that women athletes might fill that position; their transgressions being punished with the stigma of homosexuality, or the stain of virilism. All this would be grossly offensive today; but, as the mid-twentieth century approached, it was nothing of the sort. In fact, it was seen as common sense, and rested on a scientific discourse that had been in progress for a couple of centuries.

The thought of female sports performers functioning within these kinds of restrictions was not a promising one. Yet, women showed that their talents were more supple than it may have seemed. Struggling through the fears and prejudices, women showed that their bodies were sturdier than they appeared and their minds as competitive as any man's. Besmirching sportswomen remained commonplace through the 1940s and 1950s. At the 1952 summer Olympics, the achievements of brawny Soviet field athletes and tenaciously competitive Japanese volleyball players were regarded with skepticism. Appeals for sex tests followed. Calls for some form of standardized sex-testing had in fact been growing since 1946, when three female medal winners at the European athletics championships declared themselves to be men. They had "male-like genitals" and facial hair as well as chromosomal indicators of maleness. In 1952, two French female medalists were later exposed as males. The cries for testing reached full pitch in 1955 when it was revealed that the German winner of the women's high jump at the 1936 Berlin Olympics was in fact a man who had been pressured into competing for the glory of the Third Reich.

Other individual competitors, like Stella Walsh, the Polish–American track and field athlete, were the subject of widespread discussion in the 1930s and 1940s. It was not until her death in 1981 that it was discovered that she had irregular sex organs. The innuendo about Walsh was mild compared to that about Irina and Tamara Press, of the former Soviet Union. Both disappeared suddenly from active competition soon after the introduction of mandatory sex testing in 1966. Prior to this, certificates from the country of origin were sufficient proof, but visual examinations from gynecologists replaced this at the European athletics championships in Budapest. Chromosomal testing was introduced in 1967, when Polish sprinter Eva Klobkowska was disqualified from competition after failing such a test. To her apparent surprise, she was found to have internal testicles (a condition that is not as uncommon as it sounds).

At the time, knowledge of the extensive performance-enhancing programs being pursued in Soviet bloc countries, especially the Soviet Union and East Germany, was obscure. The connection between taking anabolic steroids and the acquisition of male features was not widely known. In retrospect, it is probable that many of the female athletes who were suspected of being men had been inducted into steroid use, probably at an early age.

Lenskyj's comment that "it has served male interests to stress biological differences, and to ignore the more numerous and obvious biological similarities between the sexes," returns us to where we were before the emergent scientific discourse of the eighteenth century started taking effect. The implication of Lenskyj's statement is that women's experience in sport would have been radically different if they had not been the subject of an intense yet tortuous debate on the precise nature of the woman's body.

Women were never intended to be in sports. Historically, sports, particularly those that involve strenuous competition, have certified masculinity: by providing the kind of unmediated athletic challenge rarely encountered in working days, sports made possible a strong and assertive proclamation of men's strength, valor and, above all, physical superiority over women. Industrial society brought with it, among other things, a less physical life, one in which manual labor, while still essential in many spheres of work, was less dangerous and taxing than in pre-industrial times. The proliferation of organized sports toward the end of the nineteenth century is due in large part to the desire for an expression of canalized AGGRESSION to counteract what was becoming an increasingly sedentary lifestyle. Sports had the added benefit of providing a sense of traditional masculinity which was in the process of erosion as the seas of industrial and urban change swept against it.

The developing medical discourse over the female body elevated two themes that fitted perfectly the masculine purposes of sports. Lenskyj summarizes them as: "Women's unique anatomy and physiology and their special moral obligations." Both derived from nature and were immutable; both effectively disqualified women from sport. As we have seen, the perils of competing in sports lay not in the effects of exercise on women's bodies, but in the reaction of society to their achievements. Jennifer Hargreaves summarizes the wider relevance of this when she writes: "The struggle over the physical body was important for women because control over its use was the issue central to their subordination: the repression of women's bodies symbolized powerfully their repression in society" (in *Sporting Females: Critical Issues in the History and Sociology of Women's Sports*, Routledge, 1994).

Of related interest

Gallagher, Catherine and Laqueur, Thomas (eds) (1987) *The Making of the Modern Body: Sexuality and Society in the Nineteenth Century*, University of California Press.

Lenskyj, Helen (1986) *Out of Bounds: Women, Sport and Sexuality*, The Women's Press.

Oudshoorn, Nelly (1994) *Beyond the Natural Body: An Archeology of Sex Hormones*, Routledge.

medicalization

The influence of medicine

Medicine has played an increasingly central role in sports since the 1950s. It has been important in the treatment of sports-related injuries and in establishing procedures for maintaining levels of safety. Medicine also has extended into areas of sports where its presence is not so obvious. Health care corporations often employ sports performers to endorse their products. Performers themselves take pharmaceuticals either to alleviate pain, accelerate recovery from injury or fatigue or improve performance.

The manner in which medicine has established itself in sports reflects a more general process in which many aspects of personal and social life have become redefined by medical practitioners. This process has been called medicalization. Medicine's influence is pervasive, according to Ivan Illich, whose 1982 book *Medical Nemesis* (Random House) was both an analysis and critique of the power of medicine. The formal power to define illness and prescribe treatments rests with physicians. That much is clear. However, medicine and the medical model have come to play a role in many areas of life not typically associated with health and illness.

The sheer growth of health care, particularly in Europe and the United States, indicates the value we place on wellness. While there have been attempts to challenge medicine as the paramount model, most alternatives have been designated exactly that; alternatives, rather than the accepted template for analysis and method. But, medicalization includes medicine's encroachment on territories that ostensibly have no relevance to issues of health and illness. For example, giving birth once involved no medical practitioners or expertise; it did not even take place in a medical environment. Today, it is a highly controlled procedure involving highly trained medical specialists and complex technologies.

Other areas which have been integrated into medicine's portfolio include alcoholism, depression, DISABILITY, EATING DISORDERS, hyperactivity, obesity, stress and mental disorders. It is conceivable that, under different conditions, such issues may be handled in non-medical ways: all, it could be argued, have origins in social or psychological provinces and could be treated with this in mind. Medicine's dominance allows its practitioners to define, for instance, alcoholism or eating disorders as akin to diseases, or if not actual diseases then perhaps inherited conditions. By approaching them as illnesses, medicine asserts its authority to "medicalize" and manage with treatments that the medical profession recognizes.

While Illich's tirade against medicalization was founded on the premise that the process was dangerously controlling in its implications, Eliot Freidson's more calculating examination revealed the skillful political maneuvers through which the medical profession was able to achieve and perpetuate its position of absolute supremacy. Freidson's *The Profession of Medicine* (Dodd Mead, 1970) analysed the profession's internal control, noting how medicine's central claim is to be privy to a corpus of esoteric knowledge which is simply not available to those without long, complex and ritualistic training. The profession has successfully insulated itself against the criticisms of outsiders through often cryptic processes, demanding the right to police itself and to make pronouncements on an ever-widening range of topics in a variety of domains. Sport is one such domain.

In the late nineteenth and early twentieth centuries when competitive activities were taking the shape we now recognize as organized sports, medical practitioners took only a passing interest in performers. John Hoberman, in his *Mortal Engines* (1992), believed sports competitors as curiosities or "freaks of nature" deserving of scientific investigation, but perhaps in the way a practitioner might look at someone with an extraordinary condition. Medical practitioners of the late Victorian era were attracted to unusual organisms. One can imagine a physician's being fascinated by an outstanding athlete as he (they were all males) would be fascinated by Joseph Merrick, *The Elephant Man* as featured in David Lynch's 1980 film. There was no effort to apply medicine to the improvement of performance.

Medical concern over the consequences of overexertion in training and competition brought some practitioners into conflict with Pierre de Coubertin, who founded the IOC (International Olympic Committee) in 1896 and who himself believed women unsuitable for physical competition. Women were allowed into the Olympics in 1928, the first games after Coubertin's retirement from the presidency of the IOC. There were five events for women including an 800 meters race, won by Linda Radke of Germany in 2:16.8. After this race, some woman collapsed with exhaustion. Male officials were appalled by this and took the race out of program; it was not reintroduced until thirty years later, this time with no distress among competitors. After this, women's events were progressively expanded. But, in the early decades of the century, female frailties were thought to be so self-evident that medical investigation of the phenomenon was considered almost irrelevant.

The application of pharmaceuticals

The medicalization of sports began in earnest only in the postwar period. Medical science and the technology it generated led to all manner of developments from open inoculation against disease to heart surgery, all of which greatly increased longevity in industrial societies. Industrialization itself precipitated advances in medicine: the increasing incidence of factory-related injuries meant that new treatments needed to be developed. So, the relationship between industrialization and the growth of medicine is a close one.

Sports did not command attention in the same way as industry, as injuries incurred during training or competition were after all self-inflicted. The steadily growing emphasis on winning and breaking records was frowned on by a medical profession with no interest in applying its knowledge to the improvement of athletic performance. As the emphasis grew, sports began to take note of the advances made in the areas of health maintenance and treatment of sickness. The possibility that techniques and products appropriate to the general population may have specific applications in sports was raised. This was first recognized by sports practitioners in the former Soviet Union.

In the early 1950s, Soviet-bloc athletes were given a synthesized version of testosterone as part of an experiment designed to test the effectiveness of various pharmaceutical products on performance. Clinical trials were already underway when the physician accompanying a US weightlifting team in Vienna obtained some testosterone and tried the steroid on himself and on a team coach. The medical profession had for long known some of the anabolic properties of testosterone and, indeed, the commercial potential of a synthesized version of the male hormone was not lost on the large pharmaceutical corporations, which were already engaged in research on the product. The CIBA company first produced the branded product Dianabol, an anabolic steroid intended for use by patients suffering from burns and certain other conditions.

A book, *The Male Hormone* by Paul de Kruiff, published in 1945, recorded research into the impact of testosterone on the endurance of men involved in muscular work, and this alerted some coaches to the potential of what was supposed to be a medically prescribed treatment. Dianabol was given to weightlifters, whose gains in weight and strength were impressive enough to convince coaches and competitors as well as administrators of the value of medical science in sports. During the 1950s and 1960s there were no rules forbidding the use of pharmaceuticals: the death of cyclist Tommy Simpson in 1967 alerted the sports world to the dangers and effectively started the movement that led to outright bans across the majority of sports.

The first attempts to create organizations dedicated to exploring the application of medicine to sport were less about treating injuries and more about boosting performance through the administration of DRUGS. Waddington gives the examples of the German College of Physical Culture, the Research Institute for Physical Culture and Sport, the Central Institute for Microbiology and Experimental Therapy and several other organizations which handled the controlled administration of drugs to competitors. Sports federations and medical institutions worked closely together, not just in the development and application of pharmaceuticals but in the application of other branches of medical science to sports. Exercise physiology, biomechanics and nutrition were integrated into sports.

In the United States, the American College of Sports Medicine was founded in 1954. One of its founders was Joseph B. Wolffe, a renowned cardiologist who was already a member of the Federation Internationale Medico-Sportive et Scientifique. This organization had its roots in physical education. By this time, the concept of "sports medicine" was beginning to be used, although, according to Waddington (1996), in Eastern Europe at least, "it is not possible to separate out the development and use of performance-enhancing drugs from the development of sports medicine."

The irony of this is that the medicalization of sport was given fresh impetus by the efforts of sports federations to eliminate the use of the very products that medicine gave to sports. Simpson's death set in train a series of attempts to rid sports of substances which could prove lethal if taken inappropriately. While the initial effort of sports federations was paternalistic, later efforts were aimed at the expulsion of cheats: taking drugs was redefined as cheating. Medical knowledge was invoked to find ways of discovering who took proscribed substances. Elaborate, sophisticated and expensive (the testing center for the 1988 Olympics cost £3m) testing institutions were set up to identify competitors who had taken performance-enhancing substances.

Ostensibly, medicine's role in the effort to stamp out drugs remains paternalistic – to protect competitors' health and welfare – rather than investigatory, although increasingly the profession has opted for a more moralistic position, making pronouncements of the unethical aspects of taking drugs to improve performance. During the 1990s when sport added more substances to its banned list on a yearly basis, medicine's power increased: the profession affected substantially the patterns of testing, the appropriate standards of practice and the costs associated with testing procedures.

Of related interest

Berryman, Jack W. (1995) *Out of Many, One: A History of the American College of Sports Medicine*, Human Kinetics.

Hoberman, John (1992) *Mortal Engines*, Free Press.

Waddington, Ivan (1996) "The development of sports medicine," *Sociology of Sport Journal* vol 19.

Modahl case, the

In 1994, British runner Diane Modahl was banned from competition for four years after failing a drugs test at a meeting in Lisbon, Portugal. The test was administered under the auspices of the Portuguese Athletics Federation. From the sample taken at the meet, Modahl's urine showed a testosterone to epitestosterone ratio (T–E ratio) reading of 42:1. Any ratio above 6:1 provides evidence of the presence of an excessive amount of testosterone and thus grounds for suspension. A reading of six times the permitted ratio suggested that Modahl had taken gross amounts of a prohibited substance; much more, in fact, than Ben Johnson had when he was banned after the Seoul Olympics in 1988.

After being banned, Modahl appealed to an independent panel constituted by the British Athletics Federation and an investigation opened up questions about the testing procedures followed. Several of the questions considered by the panel revolved around the reliability of the sample. The laboratory at which the original sample was analyzed was questioned, as were the procedures followed. Most importantly, the environmental conditions under which the samples were kept was brought into doubt, giving rise to the possibility that the samples may have degraded. If this were the case, then a misleading reading may have been given. The sample had been stored for two days following the race, but not in a refrigerator; the first sample, A, was then refrigerated at 39°F (4°C) while sample B was kept in a locked freezer until thawed for analysis on June 30, 1994.

While the panel was satisfied that protocol had been observed and that both samples showed a reading in excess of a 6:1 T–E ratio, it entertained the possibility that the cause of the T–E ratio many not have been ingested testosterone but degradation resulting from unrefrigerated storing of the sample and action of bacteria present in the urine. This may have caused a rise in the amount of testosterone detected. Lacking conclusive evidence, the panel determined that there was reasonable doubt over whether or not Modahl had taken proscribed substances. The British Athletics Federation (BAF) agreed, the International Amateur Athletics Federation decided not to refer the case to an arbitration panel and Modahl resumed her running career. Her ban lifted on appeal, Modahl sought up to £500,000 in damages from the BAF, which became bankrupt in 1997.

In July 1999, the British House of Lords dismissed Modahl's right to sue the BAF for adopting the drug test results of the Portuguese laboratory in its decision to ban her. Her lawyers argued that the Lisbon laboratory moved to different premises without notifying the IAAF or the IOC, and so lost its accredited status. The BAF denied that the move had any such effect. Modahl continued to pursue a £1 million damages claim against the BAF on other grounds, claiming that there was bias in the disciplinary proceeding brought against her which resulted in her being banned from international sports for nearly a year before she was cleared.

In a comparable case, British runner Dougie Walker, who was suspended in March 1999 after his test results showed the presence of nandrolone in his sample, was cleared four months later. The explanation provided by UK athletics was that "the substance found in Doug Walker's sample could have come from substances which were not prohibited." Walker had been taking protein supplements.

Modahl was one of a number of female athletes who were found to have a T–E ratio beyond acceptable parameters. German marathon runner Uta Pippig challenged the finding of her test by pointing out that she had recently stopped using oral birth control and this had affected her hormonal system; she also pointed out that each of her drug tests following her wins in the Boston MARATHON from 1994–1996 came up clean.

In the SLANEY CASE, the decorated US middle-distance veteran Mary Slaney (once Mary Decker and Mary Decker Slaney) appealed against an excessive T–E reading, citing several ways in which the T–E could be changed. Slaney tested positive in 1996 when she was 37. A woman's testosterone levels can be affected naturally by aging.

Of related interest

Downes, S. and Mackay, D. (1996) *Running Scared: How Athletics lost its Innocence*, Mainstream.

Powell, David (1997) "Athlete wins right to sue official over drugs claim," *The Times*, July 29.

Thompson, Laura (1997) "Diane Modahl: Beaten off the track," *Guardian*, August 2.

modernity/postmodernity

Uncertain origins

In its most general sense, postmodernity refers to the decomposition of the complex of economic, political and social systems brought into being somewhere around the eighteenth century and known collectively as modernity. While its origins are uncertain, incipient postmodernity advanced from the 1970s, being dramatically embraced in academic and artistic circles from the late 1980s. As the end of the twentieth century approached, postmodernity became something of a debate: were we living in the postmodern condition, or was it simply a buzzword used to capture the changes in specific areas of contemporary culture?

The former view held that the whole of western capitalism had changed so radically that it was appropriate to describe the modern age as over and acknowledge its replacement. Postmodernity on this account was everywhere. One of many other alternatives favored a more limited conception of postmodernity: it was a perspective or impulse that informed areas of mass culture, including rock music, film, magazines, the Internet and, of course, sport.

All of these areas have been elevated by postmodernity's re-evaluation of all things cultural. Reversing the previous scale of priorities that privileged economic or material domains over areas of culture, postmodernity prompted a recognition of the importance of culture in social life. Sport may have been considered as peripheral to the core areas of work and production for much of its history, but the postmodern approach to culture forced a reappraisal: it became a constituent power of postmodern society in its own right, endowed with much the same status of many other aspects of culture and granted the respect of serious scholars and writers. To understand how this came about, we need to examine the tradition from which postmodernity broke.

The grand project of modernity at work and play

The particular set of cultural or aesthetic styles visible in, for example, architecture, poetry, literature and the visual arts have taken the epithet "modern" to distinguish them from classical, traditional or older forms. Modern forms emphasized newness, experimentation and alternative modes of viewing, understanding or appreciating. The project of modernity, having its origins in the eighteenth-century Enlightenment, was predicated on the belief that a deeper knowledge of something – anything – could be revealed if we could strip away surface appearances. In contrast, postmodernity is characterized by an abandonment of any definitive search for "deeper" realities.

In the seventeenth century, the "new" mode of knowledge called science promised to unravel the hitherto unfathomable mysteries of the world and beyond. The scientific tradition had sources in sixteenth-century Protestantism. The application of science to TECHNOLOGY set in motion not only an exponential growth in human knowledge, but a startling ability to rearrange and change the world in accordance with human priorities. Far from being role-players in a divine plan with no control over their own destiny, humans discovered an ability to change both the world and their own future. In the scientific worldview, the human being was a prime mover. This recognition had implications for every conceivable aspect of social life.

Playful activities and games that were popular all over Europe in the nineteenth century were converted into structured sports, each with its own rules or codes that regulated conduct and encouraged orderly competition. Industrial society was never random: it ran according to patterns, times and measurable output. The newly emerging sports reflected changes in what John Hargreaves terms "tempo and quality of industrial work." In his *Sport, Power and Culture* (Routledge, 1992), Hargreaves notes the symmetry between modernized industry and sports, pointing to "a high degree of specialization and standardization, bureaucratized and hierarchical administration, long-term planning, increased reliance on science and technology, a drive for maximum productivity, a quantification of performance and, above all, the alienation of both producer and consumer." Organized sports embodied many facets of industrial work. They also shared the emphasis on individuality, the PROTESTANT ETHIC of hard work and acquisitiveness and the commitment to achievement, all features that were integral to modernity.

Buoyed by the success of the natural sciences, social sciences tried to emulate them, constructing comprehensive explanatory frameworks within which all social life could be interpreted. Newton, Einstein, Darwin and others had made heroic attempts to build holistic, unifying theories that linked together all material phenomena in the natural world. The grand theories of Freud, Marx,

Durkheim and, later, Parsons are examples of narratives that purport to explain everything in the social world by reference to a single encapsulating theory. Freud in particular seemed to suggest that even something as enigmatic as the unconscious could be explained in terms of secular rationality.

The urge to wrap things together, to integrate and to unify had its counterparts in sports. The creations and amalgamations which gave rise to centralized governing bodies were in themselves grand narratives, compositions that facilitated continuity and uniformity to otherwise incoherent miscellanies of activities. Federations such as America's National League (precursor of MAJOR LEAGUE BASEBALL) and England's Football Association were two of several other modern organizations to emerge in the late nineteenth century. We can also interpret the creation of large-scale worldwide tournaments, such as the modern Olympics and soccer's World Cup, organized under the auspices of the IOC and FIFA respectively, as part of the same trend toward grand and exalted global competitions.

One of the features of the many theories that poured out of modernity was that history had a definite direction. Another was that reason could, indeed, should be the basis for all human activities. Together, these formed a credo: modernity ushered in a search for reliable and generalizable knowledge. Progress was unstoppable. This belief had resonance in athletics, where advance was once thought to be prohibited by physical limitations. The traditional *ne plus ultra* beyond which it was thought impossible to progress was revised. In much the same way, conceptions of the finite relationship between humanity and the natural world were radically changed by science.

While it may have been once thought that the human body could only run so fast, jump so far and throw missiles only a set distance, a new understanding of progress removed such limiting thoughts. Careful preparation of the body, much of it informed by science, cleared the way for radical reassessments of progress. Fostering this was the use of sophisticated timepieces. Athletic progress could be recorded and documented precisely without reference to subjective evaluations. Records did not stand still: year-by-year improvements in performance were chronicled as proof of a seemingly never-ending advance.

By the twentieth century, the demonstrable potency of industrial society and the prestige of modern science and technology seemed to confirm the confidence of the intellectual tradition. The Holocaust of the Second World War was a horrific reminder that such confidence was misplaced and that technologically advanced societies do not guarantee goodness. It became apparent that the grand theories that were intended to enrich humanity were never more than a short step away from being turned into dogma. Stalinism had laid this bare.

Not even the modern Olympics, conceived in a spirit of universal camaraderie, were immune to NATIONALISM and POLITICS: the "Nazi Olympics" of 1935, staged in Berlin, were testimony to this. A blatantly ideological platform for Hitler, the Games attempted to introduce the principles of fascism to the world through the medium of sport. Sport was clearly not off-limits to politicians.

Faith in the prospects of modernity was dealt a further blow by the act that concluded the war. Hiroshima forced the recognition that the locks to which science had keys were sometimes better left unopened. Modernity may have produced irresistible intellectual and cultural currents, but its moral insufficiency created tensions.

Culture, consumers and sports in postmodernity

In his article "Reaching beyond enlightenment," Peter Scott employs a metaphor to describe the contrast between the modern age and the one that many believe replaced it. " Modernists see culture, science and perhaps society too as a Grand Hotel, linked enterprises organized according to a commanding theme," writes Scott. "Postmodernists see them as a shopping mall, an infrastructure that supports disparate enterprises without any common authoritative thread" (*Times Higher Education Supplement*, August 8, 1990).

The aftermath of the war witnessed a sharp recoil from the grand ideologies that had led ultimately to totalitarianism and mass destruction. Suspicion replaced the faith once placed in the grand narratives of modernity. Some theorists speculated on a kind of political and economic "convergence" in which all societies would resemble each other structurally and that ideological differences would make little difference.

Added to this skepticism about ideology was a new enthusiasm for what the writer Daniel Bell called *The Coming of Post-Industrial Society* (Basic Books, 1973). Bell had earlier written of *The End of Ideology* (Free Press, 1960), and popularized the idea that the period after the war had brought about a pluralistic consensus politics to the West, removing ideological conflict to the international arena and developing countries. The latter book was in hindsight a naively pragmatic essay that was to be undermined by what became known as the *evénéments* of 1968 and the student revolt in the USA. But the concept of post-industrial society was a powerful one. It referred to the fact that, as manufacturing was being superseded by service industries as a mass employer of labor, knowledge-based industries in science and technology were replacing primary production. The role of the consumer, as opposed to that of the producer, was becoming more pronounced. In other words, the staples on which modern society had been nourished were disappearing.

The resistance to ideologies and the grand theories that had in many ways complemented them was expressed in scholarly circles by a number of highly influential French philosophers, the most prominent of whom were Michel Foucault and Jacques Derrida; although it was Jean-François Lyotard who first described what he called "the postmodern condition" (*La Condition Postmoderne*, Minuit, 1974). Lyotard's target in this work was scientific knowledge, which he wanted to expose as self-legitimated in its reference to a universal truth. There are varieties of knowledge, argued Lyotard, indeterminate and particular truths, but no single, absolute truth about which there is consensus. Consensus, for Lyotard, spells the end of freedom.

Foucault too rejected all notions of invariant truth that hold good in all contexts. He denied that knowledge and language and all that derive from them could be anything but provisional, indeterminate, subjective and relative. Derrida's deconstructionist method of analysis invited the reading of knowledge not as a description of an objective reality, but as a linguistic discourse in which the meanings of words derive from their relationship to each other rather than anything else. The thrust of all three (and many others) was against the privileging of any type of knowledge: there could be no legitimate canon, no authoritative source of knowledge. The intellectual movement deriving from theoretical positions such as these became known as *postmodernism* and it is fair to say that it influenced practically every academic sphere of activity and beyond.

Complementing this intellectual movement was an aesthetic shift away from modern styles of architecture, which were typically stark, sleek, streamlined, angular, pure and minimalist. Postmodern styles echoed the intellectual calling for the abandonment for a single type and the embrace of a plurality of different, possibly incompatible styles. As scholars had encouraged heterogeneity in thought and knowledge, so postmodern architects essayed with collage, eclecticism and incongruous juxtaposition.

A reappraisal of sports

Drawing together the elements that have become hallmarks of postmodernity, we can establish that: (1) all-encompassing theories, grand narratives, or ideologies are rejected; (2) knowledge is always indeterminate and truth is contingent on the particular circumstances of time and space; (3) variety and plurality are preferred over uniformity and singularity; (4) work (or production) which was once regarded as the nexus of social life and has been supplanted by consumption, which includes how we spend our time, our money and our energy. This final hallmark points to a new evaluation of the role of culture in the human experience.

Sport was very much a phenomenon of modernity: its structure and operations reflect the wider context of its origin and development. It could be argued that some of the sports emerging in the 1990s represent a postmodern turn: the RISK-filled extreme sports that owe more to the thrills they engender than the pursuit of athletic excellence might serve as an example. The contrived TELEVISION-driven AMERICAN GLADIATORS (known in Britain simply as "Gladiators") that developed in the early 1990s made no pretense to be anything but what Jean Baudrillard would call "a mutation of the real into the hyperreal." It was a sport without origin or reality separate from its existence in the media – a *post*-sport.

Baudrillard's work, particularly on the force of electronic media in consumer society, invites analyses of postmodern sports as owned, controlled, organized and run by mass and multimedia corporations. The trend in the 1980s and 1990s was for magnates such as Ted TURNER and Rupert MURDOCH to extend and then consolidate their interests in sports. Baudrillard's image of postmodern society is one in which the media dominate: excesses of information available to us has led to what he calls a "loss of the real." The distinction between a "real" world out there and the one represented by the media has disappeared. The images we receive are no longer depictions of reality, but simulacra, bearing "no relation to any reality whatsoever."

For Baudrillard, the conversion of populations into consumers is the equivalent of the indoctrination of rural populations into industrial labor in the nineteenth century. Consumption is the central mode of postmodern existence; we are all skillful, willing and voracious consumers. And, while Baudrillard has nothing to say specifically about sports, his observations of Disneyland – which confirms the hyperreal as the real and conceals the fact that there is a "real country" – have relevance. Disneyland's authenticity derives from the fact that it makes no attempt to represent anything but its own artificial self, its ICONS, images, signs and illusions. Sports too play the Disney game: they are sites of leisure and recreation with no links to any reality other than their own. Sports is a reality, or to use Baudrillard's word, hyperreality that is sustained, dramatized and presented by the electronic media and consumed by a FANDOM which implicitly confirms its reality.

Postmodernity is inspired by Foucault's argument that representation *is* power: the way reality is expressed, imagined or signified does not reflect an outside reality, but is constitutive of that reality. It follows that the cultural realms that were forced to the wings while matters of the economy dictated were moved to center stage. By the 1990s, sport had become an integral part of culture. As such, sport came to command serious attention not only from the electronic media, but from journalists, academic writers and teachers. Perhaps this is the most significant impact postmodernity has had on sport. The postmodern elevation of culture's significance led logically to a fresh evaluation of the role of sport in all areas of society, especially politics. The political potential of mass televised sports events was evident in the 1960s, especially after the Smith–Carlos Black Power gesture at the Mexico Olympics in 1968. At the time, this was seen as having symbolic value; in postmodern times, it would be a cultural sign, an active agent in itself, evoking substantial changes rather than purely expressive ones.

Sport has no single meaning, nor purpose, nor utility. As postmodernists favor approaching everything that is intelligible as text, we can view sport as text, one that is amenable to endlessly different readings. A political reading is but one of these. To repeat a previous point, sport may have been considered as peripheral to the core areas of work and production for much of its history, but the postmodern approach to culture has forced a reappraisal. The postmodern emphasis on social context and construction of knowledge and culture has meant that sport is now subject to the kinds of critical appraisal associated with key areas of social life.

Of related interest

Berger, Arthur Asa (1997) *Postmortem for a Postmodernist*, Sage.
Bertens, Hans (1995) *The Idea of the Postmodern: A History*, Routledge.
Smart, Barry (1993) *Postmodernity*, Routledge.

motherhood

Evidence of the effects of motherhood on athletes is contradictory. In 1948, mother of two Fanny Blankers-Koen, of Holland, undermined the MEDICAL DISCOURSE of the time by winning four gold medals at the London Olympic games. Norway's Ingrid Kirstiansen set world records at 5,000 meters, 10,000 meters and in the MARATHON within two years of her son's birth in 1983. In both cases, pregnancy resulted in improvements in athletic performance.

Evelyn Ashford of the USA matched her track achievements either side of her pregnancy. A world champion in 1979 and double gold medalist at the 1984 Olympics, Ashford took time off to start a family in 1985, returning in 1988 to take gold and silver medals at the Seoul Olympics and, later, a gold at the 1992 Barcelona Olympics when aged 35. Scottish distance runner Liz McColgan returned to training only twelve days after the birth of her daughter in 1990 and, a year later, became the world 10,000 meters champion in Tokyo. Russian Svetlana Masterkova gave birth in 1995 and won Olympic gold medals at 800 meters and 1500 meters in 1996 at Atlanta.

On the other hand, neither Mary Slaney (also known as Mary Decker Slaney) or Joan Samuelson recaptured their previous world class form after motherhood, and triple Commonwealth Games track winner Kirsty Wade, of Wales, never approached her best times after the birth of her first child.

Women are advised to exercise throughout their pregnancies, though athletes often maintain demanding regimes. For example, Irish middle and long-distance runner Sonia O'Sullivan was running ninety miles a week four months into her pregnancy; she was aged 29 at the time. The potential benefits of the hormones produced in early pregnancy have long been recognized by sports science. During the first three months, the mother's body generates a natural surplus of red corpuscles rich in haemoglobin. These assist cardiac and lung performance and improve muscle capacity by up to 30 per cent. A pregnant woman also secretes increased amounts of progesterone to make muscles more supple and joints more flexible. Olga Karasseva (or Kovalenko, as she became), a gymnastics gold medal winner at the 1968 Summer Olympics, in 1994, revealed to the British newspaper the *Sunday Times* (section S1: 23, November 23) that she had deliberately become pregnant and had an abortion shortly before the games to prepare her body. Karasseva, who was a product of the Soviet system, also alleged that during the 1970s, females as young as 14 were ordered to have sex with their men friends or coaches in an effort to become pregnant.

However, if the physiological consequences of pregnancy are accepted as beneficial to athletic performance, the effects on mentality are more ambiguous. Reflecting on her loss of form, Kirsty Wade reasoned: "You stop being self-oriented. You have a baby who becomes very much a pull on your energies. For me that took away some of the hunger for athletics. But for some people it can ... put their athletics in perspective in a way that helps them" (quoted in the *Independent on Sunday*, February 21, 1999). Rather than sinking into a depression or engaging in critical self-evaluation after a poor performance, a mother may prioritize her family over her athletic career and be gratified by her efforts rather than her results. In some athletes, this may lead to complacency or resignation; but, in others, it may release them from the pressure of winning, perhaps even enhancing the possibility of FOCUSED performances.

Of related interest

Lutter, J. and Jaffee, L. (1996) *The Bodywise Woman*, 2nd edn, Human Kinetics.

Penttinen, J. and Erkkola, R. (1997) "Pregnancy in endurance athletes," *Scandinavian Journal of Medicine and Science in Sports* vol 7, no 4.

Wiggins, D.L. and Wiggins, M.E. (1997) "The female athlete," *Clinics in Sports Medicine* vol 6, no 4.

motivation

Types of reward

Motivation conventionally refers to the forces either within or external to a person that arouse enthusiasm and persistence to pursue a course of action. In sports, it is part of the manager's, coach's and trainer's job to channel motivation toward the accomplishment of goals.

In sports, as in other areas, there are two types of rewards: intrinsic and extrinsic. The former are the satisfactions a competitor derives from performing a piece of action, the latter are the more tangible dividends made available by persons or organizations. Money is the most apparent of extrinsic rewards and, as sports have become increasingly professional, so hard currency has become more important as a motivating force.

The word amateur has its origins in the Italian *amatore*, itself derived from the Latin root *amare*, for love. The amateur sports performer was motivated strictly by intrinsic rewards: he or she practiced and competed for the pleasure, the joy, the rapture of the activity itself. The love of participating counted most. The coming of the professional sportsman (and early professionals were all male) in the late nineteenth century introduced extrinsic motivations. The historical study of rugby by Dunning and Sheard, *Barbarians, Gentlemen and Players* (Martin Robertson, 1979), demonstrates how early sports in England cleaved into two spheres and how the motivations of working-class players were quite different from those of the comfortably well-off gentlemen, who regarded making money from sport as vulgar and base.

Through the twentieth century, more and more sports professionalized, introducing coexistence between amateurs and professionals and a corresponding mixture of motivations. In sports that have both amateur and professional divisions (basketball, boxing, football and so on), there was the possibility of transferring from one to another, and so the motivational forces were very close, if not the same: extrinsic rewards were available in the medium, if not in the short term. The fictional but credible film *BLUE CHIPS* suggests they were in fact available in the short term to those who sought them. Added to this was a relentless emphasis on winning that emerged in the mid-1920s and which gradually seeped into the ethos of all sports. As early as 1925, Ty Cobb dispelled any romantic notions about baseball professionals when he said: "Most of the players are in the game for the money that's in it – not for the love of the game" (quoted in Coakley, *Sport in Society: Issues and Controversies*, 6th edn, McGraw-Hill, 1998).

(As an aside, we might note the limitations of money as a motivating factor. In his book *Mike Tyson: Money, Myth and Betrayal* (Grafton, 1992), Montieth

Illingworth outlines the terms of Tony Tubbs's fight with Mike Tyson in 1988: "For this fight Tubbs would earn around $500,000, plus a $50,000 bonus if he came in under 235. He unrobed at 238.")

The CHARIOTS OF FIRE spirit was dampened in the 1940s, and all but extinguished in the 1960s when television took an active interest in sport. The ethos was personified by Vince LOMBARDI, whose epigram about winning drew more approval than condemnation.

Theories of motivation

While professional sports performers and aspirant professionals are unquestionably motivated by money, this is not the only component that accounts for energizing, directing and stopping behavior. Several theories have offered formulae to account for what makes people "tick." Perhaps the most widely quoted account is that of Abraham Maslow, who argued that humans have a hierarchy of strong needs; those needs that go unsatisfied will act as motivators. Once one tier of basic, or lower level needs (for food, water, air, shelter) are satisfied, we strive to satisfy higher needs (for security and affiliation/friendship) before moving on to the pursuit of others (for esteem and self-actualization). We are all motivated by the desire to fulfill the needs, though, as studies have shown, age, class, ethnic origin and other cultural variables affect the definition of needs at the higher levels. According to this model, a highly paid baseball player, having satisfied a need for security with a multimillion dollar contract and for affiliation with a loving wife and family, will no longer be motivated at these levels. Instead his motivation will be for the esteem that comes through winning trophies and the self-actualization that accrues through perfecting his own game. An up and coming player, having not reached such levels, will be motivated by needs lower in the hierarchy.

In sports, it is possible to find sports performers moving both up and down. Boxers are famous for their profligacy and often, having squandered a fortune, fight not for adulation and self-actualization but for more basic needs. Other sports performers who never earn the fortunes sometimes wind up performing for nothing more than a paycheck. Maslow, and other scholars who modified his approach, accounted for this type of situation by stating that, if a person is continually frustrated in attempts to satisfy "growth" needs, "relatedness" needs will re-emerge as motivating forces.

In his book *The Achieving Society* (Van Nostrand-Reinhold, 1961), David McClelland stayed with Maslow's original concept of human needs, but argued that we are not born with these needs but rather acquire them through cultural experiences. Early life experiences determine whether people acquire some needs rather than others. McClelland believed the three most common needs are for achievement, affiliation and power. So, if children are encouraged to do things for themselves and receive reinforcement from parents to do so, the chances are that they will have the need to achieve. If they are reinforced in forming warm human relationships, they will develop the need for affiliation. If they are encouraged to control others, they will manifest the need for power. In this scheme, successful sports performers would be driven by the need to achieve. As part of an experiment, McClelland assigned tasks to children in the presence of their parents, some of whom were tense and demanding. Other parents were more relaxed, joked and made suggestions without interfering with their children's performance. The latter group of children performed better.

Few people dispute the fact that parents play a role in the development of motivation in future sports performers. Precisely what that role is remains unclear. Also, its consequences are nowhere near as clear-cut as McClelland seemed to think. Joan Ryan's exposé of forceful parents abetted by almost tyrannical coaches, *Little Girls in Pretty Boxes* (Virago, 1997), shows how achievement-oriented parents in the USA displace their own motivations onto their children. The consequences are dire: teenage gymnasts and skaters are pushed beyond their physical limits. They are made to train when injured, encouraged to diet to the point where they develop EATING DISORDERS and abused for failing to live up to coaches' often unreasonable expectations. Far from being edifying instructors in how to succeed, win-oriented parents propel their children toward the premature end known as BURNOUT.

By contrast, research in the 1980s by Cashmore (*Black Sportsmen*, Routledge, 1982) revealed that high-achieving African Caribbean sports performers in Britain had little or no support and, in some cases, discouragement from parents, who were interested only in professional or business careers for their offspring. As they matured, the children acquired a potent motivation to succeed, a motivation often mistaken for "natural ability" linked to race.

Many writers have acknowledged the crucial role of parents in motivation, but have rejected the idea that needs are in us waiting to energized. Rather, the motivations we manifest are put there by parents and all sorts of other influential figures. This school of thought is based on the principles of B.F. Skinner and the behaviorist psychology he pioneered. In this model, we are born *tabula rasa* – blank tablets. We learn from experiences in our material and human environments. The mechanism through which we learn is stimulus–response. We perform a piece of behavior which is rewarded and we repeat it again and keep repeating it while the rewards are forthcoming. We perform another piece of behavior which results in a punishment, or negative reinforcement (there is a difference in Skinner's theory) and we do not repeat it.

Skinner's operant conditioning built on the classical Pavlovian theory: as long as the behavior keeps eliciting rewards, we will keep repeating it. Any mystery about the deep origins of motivation disappears in Skinner's theory: all behavior can be accounted for in terms of learning outcomes. We are not so much driven, as responding to reward. Coaches probably use behaviorist techniques, possibly without knowing it: good performances are met with congratulations, compliments and even flattery, while poor performances are berated, castigated and denounced. It was often said that Vince Lombardi's players were too terrified of him to produce anything less than a 100 per cent performance.

Less domineering coaches, such as basketball's Phil Jackson or soccer's Fabio Capello, emphasize the reward side: they coax and cajole players into performing optimally. Skinner himself would approve of the carrot as a more effective instrument than the stick. Jackson, Capello and other top-flight coaches operate in an environment in which the extrinsic reward of money is so bountiful it has lost much of its power to motivate. All the players in major professional sports are paid relatively well, in some cases spectacularly so. Money may continue to provide a stimulus for aspiring athletes, but the professional coach must devise other kinds of reward structures.

Jackson was known to initiate his players into the techniques of meditation, yoga, visualization and other forms of RELAXATION. In 1989 when he became coach of the Chicago Bulls, he took over a squad of skilled individuals eclipsed by Michael JORDAN, who once referred to his team mates as "my supporting cast." Jackson summarized his task: "I had to convince Michael that the route to greatness was in making *others* better." It proved to be one of the most brilliant motivational strategies ever, and Chicago went on to become the NBA team of the 1990s.

Theories of motivation are at their strongest when attempting to account for why individuals perform optimally at times and below par at other times. They are less useful in explaining why, for example, so many young blacks are highly motivated in sports, or why class background seems to have an impact on the kinds of sport people pursue. Answering these questions necessitates a wider examination of the context of sport.

Contexts of motivation

An old English aphorism was: "Shout down any coal pit and half-dozen fast bowlers are sure to appear." The idea behind this was that, in days when the working class in the coal-mining districts had little option but to follow their father's occupation and work in the coal industry, any opportunity to earn a living in a less miserable fashion would be greeted enthusiastically. Both types of work involved physical exertion. Even a raw, completely untutored young miner would soon pick up the rudiments of cricket if their only alternative was a return to the mines. Bowling was infinitely preferable, and that was motivation enough to guarantee a decent bowler.

The saying is a variation on the "hungry fighter" theme: the best boxers tend to be the ones who come from socially deprived backgrounds and have no other options open to them. Boxing has for decades functioned as a ticket out of the ghetto for many Jewish, Latino and, of course, black people. The motivation needs little elaboration: the extrinsic reward of money is usually sufficient. Sometimes, in a manner that invites interpretation from Maslow, boxers who have reached the top lose their hunger and, with it, their motivation. The process has been dramatized in the *ROCKY I–V* movie series. Some believe the fall of Mike TYSON can be explained in similar terms.

Track coach Brooks Johnson described the mental state of his athletes; they "wake up with the desire and the need and the compulsion and the obsession to win and they go to sleep with it." He believed that to become an Olympic champion, a competitor has to be clinically sick, so great is the pressure at the highest level. Sport is replete with stories of great athletes motivated by seemingly inhuman desires to succeed. Their motivations often become transparent when more is known about the poverty from which they emerged. KENYAN RUNNERS dominated world middle-distance events for over thirty years: many of them came from rural areas afflicted with poverty, starvation and other misfortunes. Motivation derives from the daunting prospect of the alternative to sporting success.

Writing of such motivational disincentives, the sports journalist Ken Jones referred to Livia, the wife of Augustus in Robert Graves's *I Claudius*. Disgusted at the lack of effort of some of the gladiators, she decides to motivate them, not by offering inducements, but by threats. "These Games are being degraded by more and more professional tricks to stay alive," she tells gathered gladiators before a contest. "I won't have it. So put on a good show, and there'll be plenty of money for the living, and a decent burial for the dead. If you let me down, I'll break this guild, and I'll send the lot of you to the mines."

The persuasion coaches use sometimes borders on coercion. In concert with other specialist personnel, such as coordinators, conditioners and scouts, they will decide on training techniques and, in team sports, team selection as well as day to day matters. Ultimately they stand or fall on the results. Its axiomatic that managers and coaches occupy invidious positions: their reputation and, indeed, destiny is never in their own hands, but always in those of others; their competitors.

At the other end of the motivational spectrum, we find intrinsic rewards which are likely to be paramount in sports that typically attract the affluent. Some of these have retained amateur or semi-professional status and the prizes for success could be described in terms of self-actualization, personal accomplishment or affiliation (gaining the approval of others or just being with friends). Polo remains a sport of the aristocracy and the rich. The equipment needs are prohibitive enough to exclude all but the moneyed.

Another sports that attracts well-off groups yet is utterly professional is motor racing. The rewards that accrue to successful drivers compare with those of the elite of other lucrative sports, including baseball, basketball, boxing, football and golf. While the monetary rewards are high, aspiring drivers are almost certainly motivated by them. Already having money is a precondition of going into the sport in the first instance. There is certainly a school of thought that holds that we are drawn to pursuits such as motor racing, mountain climbing, and extreme sports because of the danger they hold. A diverse range of writers from John Adams (*Risk*, UCL Press, 1995) to Frank Furedi (*Culture of Fear*, Cassell, 1997) have speculated on our RISK-taking (or risk-avoiding) propensities, some believing that the reward that some sports offer is the chance to cheat death or serious injury. Many sports performers have recounted the ADRENALINE RUSH associated with a close call. Maybe Maslow would have regarded this as a form of self-actualization, achieved in this instance through a transaction with danger. In a culture that has raised our awareness of the limitless perils that lie in the world, we have become increasingly security-minded.

According to Ulrich Beck, in his *Risk Society* (Sage, 1992), we have reached the stage of modernization where TECHNOLOGY has introduced new and unmanage-able threats to our security, indeed our existence. Our response has been to become much "safer" in our attention to, for instance the water we drink, our financial affairs, the security of our homes and, of course, the way we have sex. In such a safety-conscious environment, it may be that the possibility of commerce with danger, or even DEATH, offers a powerful motivator.

Finally, we might consider the deterrent factors of work at a time when market pressures flatten, downsize and destabilize workplaces all over the world. The often mortifying dead ends that loom in many occupational sectors all but encourage people to dream or plan for exit strategies. Success in sports is, for most, an idle fantasy about six-figure salaries and even bigger endorsement contracts. Some are willing to take whatever chance they have, not because the fantasies loom large, but because the prospect of what the writer Douglas Coupland once called McJobs is so dispiriting. As the deskilling of work has yielded corrosive, low-grade jobs, the single chance some young people occasionally get becomes an attractive and potent source of motivation.

Of related interest

Daft, Richard L. (1997) *Management*, 4th edn, Harcourt Brace.
McClelland, David C. (1985) *Human Motivation*, Scott, Foresman.
Roberts, Glyn (ed.) (1992) *Motivation in Sport and Exercise*, Human Kinetics.

Munich disaster

On February 6 1958, twenty-three people died as the plane carrying the English soccer team Manchester United home from a European Cup game in Belgrade crashed on takeoff after refueling in Germany. Eight of the dead were players. Many remember the news of the disaster in the same way that they recall hearing of the car crash that killed the Princess of Wales or the assassination of President John F. Kennedy. The tragedy consecrated Manchester United: the team became legendary, and the widespread sympathy for the club's loss translated over the following decades into worldwide support. The club has probably the largest sports FANDOM in the world.

Manchester United was not the first club to lose players in an air crash, nor was it the last. Torino, of Italy, flew into the Superga Basilica, near Turin, while returning from a game in Lisbon in 1949. In 1961 the team of Green Cross, of Chile, was killed. A Bolivian team, The Strongest, perished in the Andes after a 1969 crash. The Pacific ocean claimed the lives of the Alianza team of Lima, Peru, in 1989. In the same year, four Surinamese members of Netherlands clubs died when their aircraft attempted to land in fog at Paramaribo. And eighteen Zambian players were killed when their plane dived into the Atlantic in 1993.

What made the Manchester club's loss more poignant was that the average age of the players who died was under 24; they were part of a team known as the "Busby babes" after its manager, Matt Busby, who had cultivated a celebrated youth policy. Duncan Edwards, 21, was the most promising of Busby's prodigies. A midfield player from Dudley in the English West Midlands, Edwards seemed destined for a glittering career.

A maximum wage was in effect at the time; this meant that clubs could afford to have squads, or rosters, of about 40 full-time players. The most players could earn was £14 per week during the season, or £10 during the close season.

International games between British clubs and continental opponents were unusual in the 1950s. The Union des Associans Européenes de Football (UEFA) was formed in 1956 to oversee a European-wide club competition and became affiliated to FIFA. Manchester actually went against its own league's policy when it accepted an invitation to compete in the European Champions' Cup, which was then sponsored by the French newspaper *L'Equipe*. The period was one of change in soccer: its boundaries were being extended and many of its governing organizations had decided that the future of the sport lay in international competition. This became a central feature of a sport.

Busby was an advocate of European soccer, at the time dominated by the peerless Real Madrid, which boasted Alfredo DI STEFANO, by common consent the most brilliant player in the world and the first international soccer superstar. Stung by having been beaten previously by the Real team, Busby was probably hoping for a rematch. His team had beaten the Red Star club, of Belgrade, shortly before the disaster.

The club chartered a British European Airways (BEA) 47-seater plane for the Belgrade game. Having stopped to refuel in Munich, the plane twice failed to take off because of snow and ice. On the third attempt the plane experienced a sudden loss of speed; its undercarriage lifted but the plane careered through a fence and across a street, ripping off a wing and part of its tail. The plane's fuel ignited, causing an explosion. Four subsequent inquiries established that slush on the runway, rather than ice on the wings, was the cause of the crash. The captain, James Thain, was dismissed by BEA in 1960; he never flew again.

Of the survivors, some, like Bobby Charlton and Harry Gregg, went onto to celebrated careers, while others, such as Ken Morgan and Johnny Berry, never fully recovered their previous form and Jackie Blanchflower – who had the last rites administered to him at the crash scene – never played again. Busby was badly injured, but resumed his managerial role after several months on crutches.

Of related interest

Maguire, Joseph (1994) "Patriot Games? English identity, nostalgia and media coverage of sporting disasters," in Allison, Lincoln (ed.) *Working Papers in Sport and Society*, vol 3.
Roberts, John (1998) *The Team That Wouldn't Die: The Story of the Busby Babes*, Vista.

Murdoch, Rupert

b. 1931, Australia

The growth of Murdoch's empire

During the 1990s, Australian-born US citizen Murdoch was the owner of arguably the world's most powerful multimedia complex. This included several newspapers, publishing houses and, most importantly, three TELEVISION networks, the combined "footprint" of which covered the globe. He held influence undreamed of by previous media tycoons, such as Randolph Hearst or Robert Maxwell.

In 1952, Murdoch inherited an Australian publishing group from his father, Sir Keith Murdoch. Sir Keith had worked as the editor and later managing director of the *Melbourne Herald*, but he also owned a small Adelaide newspaper, the *News*, which he vouchsafed to his son. Still in his twenties, Rupert Murdoch bought another small newspaper in Perth and tried to move into television. The latter venture was opposed by the Australian Prime Minister Sir Robert Menzies, whom Murdoch's publications had criticized.

Over the next forty years Murdoch built up his global business, progressing from Australia to Britain and the USA, and then to Asia. In 1968, Murdoch defeated Robert Maxwell's bid to take over the British Sunday newspaper *News of the World* and, the following year, he bought the ailing daily the *Sun*. Within nine years, the *Sun* was the best-selling newspaper in Britain and was making £250,000 per week profit; the total price Murdoch had paid for the publication. Murdoch's strategy was to include a daily topless model on page three, bingo games and, perhaps most importantly, a comprehensive television guide. Other newspapers had shrunk from television coverage, believing that television was a rival medium.

Murdoch believed that printed and visual media actually complemented each other in the lives of consumers: people wanted to read about as well as watch television. In 1981, Murdoch strengthened his grip on the British newspaper market by purchasing two "quality" papers, *The Times* and the *Sunday Times*. All his titles were housed in a high-tech plant at Wapping, London, which disallowed labor unions. A self-proclaimed socialist during his student days at Oxford, he later turned into a champion of the free market, a supporter of Margaret Thatcher and an anti-unionist.

Having unsuccessfully tried to take control of London Weekend Television, he decided that his best chance of breaking into television was through cable. He witnessed the success of the US cable industry in the 1980s, particularly the sports-dedicated ESPN and HBO, which specialized in movies and prestigious sports events. In 1983, he bought a struggling satellite operator, Inter-American, which he turned into Skyband. The purchase proved a disaster and Murdoch lost $20m within six months. In the same year he tried unsuccessfully to buy Warner, the Hollywood studio (later to merge with Time). The film studio Fox was then struggling and, in 1985, Murdoch bought at first a 50 per cent stake and, later, full control from its then owner, Marvin Davis. At the time, US network television was divided among ABC, CBS and NBC. Fox was insignificant in the television market, but Murdoch grew it into the fourth major network.

In 1993, Murdoch-owned News Corp's most powerful operation, Fox Broadcasting, then the fourth biggest broadcasting network in the USA behind ABC, NBC and CBS, obtained the rights to televise National Football League (NFL) games for four years. The cost was thought by many to be absurdly high, $1.6b, and Fox lost an estimated $100m in broadcasts in the 1994/95 season alone. Undeterred, Fox also signed contracts with MAJOR LEAGUE BASEBALL and the

National Hockey League. Murdoch's motives were longer term: by wresting the popular Sunday afternoon games from CBS, he had established Fox as a major player. Many local television stations changed their affiliations as a direct result of the coup and, of course, advertising revenue soared. Solid audience ratings helped Fox advertise its other shows in the commercial spots, thus increasing viewer awareness of the station's menu.

The somewhat surprising decision to show Mike Tyson's second fight after his release from prison in 1995 was the result of a temporary alliance with Don KING. The original plan was to schedule the Tyson–Buster Mathis, Jr fight on the same night as a Time Warner pay-per-view show headlined by Evander Holyfield against Riddick Bowe. Explaining his sudden contact with Murdoch, King is quoted by Richard Hoffer as saying: "In searching to do things, you are led spiritually by God, and I found Rupert" (in *A Savage Business: The Comeback and Comedown of Mike Tyson*, Simon & Schuster, 1998).

Extending his interest in football, Murdoch, through Fox Television, took a 49 per cent stake (i.e. co-ownership rather than just broadcasting rights) in the NFL initiative known first as the World League of American Football and, later, NFL Europe. He was then able to show "live" games from places like Amsterdam, Barcelona and London in the USA and, through his subscription cable/satellite network BSkyB, in Britain. He could also beam the games to Asia via his company, Star.

In 1998, Murdoch bought the Los Angeles Dodgers. The club was the last major baseball team in family hands; its sale by Peter O'Malley signified the passing of the national pastime into corporate hands. As part of a $350m deal, Murdoch secured not only the team but the 56,000 seat Dodgers stadium in LA and the surrounding land, as well as team facilities in Florida and the Dominican Republic. Baseball's response was quite accommodating, compared to that of the FIFA-affiliated Union des Associans Européenes de Football (UEFA) when Mark McCORMACK's IMG began acquiring European clubs.

Owning the Dodgers also assured Murdoch long-term access to Dodgers games for broadcast on Fox, which in the 1990s tightened its grip on sports rights in much the same way as Murdoch's BSkyB acquired sports events from traditional broadcasters in Britain. In 1998, Murdoch announced his intention to buy Manchester United, the best-known sports club in the world. The price, $1 billion, seemed exorbitant, though it paled beside the $4.4 billion Murdoch had paid to keep the NFC football games on the Fox network. This represented a price hike of about 30 per cent annually, though CBS had paid over twice (again, on an annual average) what NBC had paid for the previous contract to screen the AFC divisional games. Disney had paid three times greater annual payments for their ESPN and ABC channels to screen Sunday and Monday night games than its 1993 agreements. In other words, Murdoch's seeming extravagance was, in fact, just a case of staying abreast of the opposition.

In the same year, Murdoch signed a 50–50 partnership with Liberty Media and bought a 40 per cent stake in the Staples Center, Los Angeles, which was to be a home stadium for the NBA teams the Lakers and the Clippers, and the NHL ice hockey team, the Kings. The deal included a 40 per cent option on the Kings franchise. A similar deal between Murdoch's Fox Entertainment Group and

Rainbow Media Holdings, a subsidiary of Cablevision, gave Murdoch access to the New York franchises of the Knicks, of the NBA, and the Rangers, of the NHL, as well as an interest in Madison Square Garden. The strategy seemed to be aimed at gaining an interest in the major franchises of both Los Angeles and New York. Less publicized though still important acquisitions included a one-third stake in the Outdoor Life and Speedvision channels and the launch of Fox Sports Cafés. Murdoch also extended his interest in horse racing by forging an agreement with the National Thoroughbred Racing Association.

Murdoch's "glue"

In the early 1980s, cable/satellite television was not available in Britain and Murdoch had little chance of breaking into a market conveniently shared by BBC, Independent Television and Channel 4. But, by acquiring the pan-European advertising-driven Sky Television, which had been launched in 1978 and had served mainly continental Europe, Murdoch gained leverage in the British market. When Sky television was launched in 1989, market response was unpromising and there was no operating profit until 1992. A rival company, BSB, merged with Sky to form BSkyB.

A critical moment in BSkyB's history was the signing of a £304m deal with English soccer's Premier League (later renamed Premiership) in May 1992. The contract to show "live" games exclusively on BSkyB's subscription network was renewed in 1996 for £670m. It included a clause that made provision for the broadcast of games on a pay-per-view basis. The soccer deal initiated a U-turn in BSkyB's fortunes, and sharp increases in subscriptions and advertising revenue made BSkyB one of the most profitable companies in the country. In 1990, the company's losses were estimated at £10m a week; by 1995, it was making profits of £5m a week. While the original plan was to draw most revenue from advertising, this yielded only 12 per cent of BSkyB's income, with the majority coming from subscriptions.

Also in 1996, Sky Sports 2 was added to the existing dedicated sports channel, Sky Sports, and later a third sports channel was launched. In the interim, BSkyB had also added more soccer to its schedules and later negotiated with the Rugby Football Union the rights to screen rugby from Twickenham. In 1996, BSkyB broadcast Britain's first pay-per-view event, the heavyweight title fight between Mike TYSON and Frank Bruno. Later in the year, the company announced profits of £257m.

During his rise, Murdoch made no secret of the fact that he viewed sports as his "battering ram": with this instrument, he could find his way into millions of homes around the world. Murdoch's predatory acquisition of some of the world's most popular sports for his television companies gained him leverage in markets that had remained beyond the grasp of other media tycoons, China being a notable example.

Through his Star Television which covered Asia, BSkyB operating from England and the US-run News Corporation, Murdoch, during the 1980s and 1990s, assembled a complex of assets that allowed him to reach over two-thirds of the world's television-owning households and affect many more people through print media and movies. "More than any other company, News Corp. is the intertwining of the two trends of megamedia and globalization," writes Kevin Maney in his book *Media Shakeout* (Wiley, 1995). By megamedia, he refers to clusters of information highways, multichannel television companies and digital communications networks. By the mid-1990s, the $12 billion (£7.5 billion) company's reach far exceeded that of any other media corporation in the world.

In contrast to Murdoch's own preferred metaphor, Maney calls sport Murdoch's "glue" with which he sticks together his worldwide assortment of companies. Beside football and soccer, he has created a professional golf tour to rival the PGA and the world's first genuinely globalized club-based competition in rugby's Super League. He also secured the rights to National Hockey League games and cricket's World Cup. And, in 1998, the purchase of the Dodgers mirrored the actions of fellow media proprietors Ted TURNER, and Silvio Berlusconi and sports entrepreneur Mark McCORMACK.

Demonized by many, hailed as a visionary by others, Murdoch arouses many passions. No sport was thought be have adequate protection against MURDOCHI-ZATION, the process by which the tycoon has integrated clubs or even entire leagues into his media empire and was able to assert unprecedented media control over the shape of sport. According to Horsman (1997), Murdoch's guiding philosophy was that: "There were really only three kinds of programming that people were willing to pay extras for: movies, sport and pornography."

In 1999, Murdoch's influence on world sports could be gauged by an itinerary of his sports-related interests, which included clubs such as the Los Angeles Dodgers, Manchester United, New York Knicks, New York Rangers, Los Angeles Lakers and Los Angeles Kings. Media outlets included BSkyB, Fox Broadcasting, Fox Sports Net, FX and Star TV, plus regional US sports networks. Sports stadiums included Dodger Stadium, Madison Square Garden and Staples Center. Print media included the *New York Post*, *News of the World*, the *Sun*, the *Sunday Times*, *The Times*, *TV Guide* and HarperCollins. Miscellaneous companies included SkyLatin America Studios, Century Fox, Fox Filmed Entertainment and Fox TV.

Of related interest

Horsman, Mathew (1997) *Sky High: The Inside story of BSkyB*, Orion Business.
Munster, Georg (1985) *Rupert Murdoch: A Paper Prince*, Penguin.
Shawcross, William (1992) *Rupert Murdoch*, Chatto & Windus.

Murdochization

Integrating assets

Murdochization refers to a process by which corporations primarily involved in mass media of communications appropriate and integrate into their organizations sports clubs. In doing so, the media groups gain access to and control of the competitive activities of the clubs, which they can distribute through their networks. The exemplar is Rupert Murdoch's organizations, which operated as News Corp. in the USA, BSkyB in Europe and Star TV in Asia. There are however many others, and in the late 1990s, media companies owned at least twenty top clubs in baseball, football, basketball and ice hockey.

Time Warner acquired MAJOR LEAGUE BASEBALL's Atlanta Braves and the Atlanta Hawks basketball club after its takeover of Ted TURNER's holdings, which included his several cable TELEVISION channels; it also became owners of the Atlanta Thrashers ice hockey team. Disney owned the Mighty Ducks of the National Hockey League and the Anaheim Angels baseball club; it also owned ESPN. Wayne Huizinga, former owner of Blockbuster Video, owned baseball's Florida Marlins and the Florida Panthers hockey club. The *Chicago Tribune* owned the Chicago Cubs; Cablevision owned the New York Nicks; Ascent Entertainments owned the Denver Nuggets and Comcast owned the Philadelphia 76ers. Italian media magnate Silvio Berlusconi owned the AC Milan soccer club of Serie A. The French cable television company Canal Plus owned the Paris St. Germain club. These are but a few illustrations of media–sports cross-ownership patterns in North America and Europe. But, on a global scale, Murdoch's operations had no counterpart.

Murdoch's zeal in acquiring sporting assets and creating sports-dedicated television stations in the late twentieth century led many to believe that his commercial activities were driven by a sense of mission. His ownership of three media corporations gave him access to an estimated two-thirds of the world's population and a afforded him a formidable sphere of influence.

Murdoch's interest in sport was not confined to merely broadcasting sports competitions. He bought parts of, and in some cases entire sports clubs in order to affect a vertical integration of his assets. this meant that he was able to control not only the channels of communication, but the content of those channels. For example, his abortive bid for the purchase of the Manchester United football club in 1998 was designed to give him access to the games of one of the world's richest, most famous and most popular sports clubs in the world. His intention was to distribute the club's games throughout the world. In a similar way, his acquisition of the National Football League's prized NFC broadcast rights brought him the opportunity to establish his Fox Network, a terrestrial service, as a serious rival to the USA's other main networks, ABC, CBS and NBC. Murdoch's News Corp. owned the Los Angeles Dodgers baseball club and options on the LA Lakers of the NBA. Some of these acquisitions were costly. For example, Fox lost an estimated $350m (£215m) on its first four-year contract to screen the NFL's National Conference games; yet this did not prevent it contributing a further $4.4 billion to the next $17.6 billion package. This compares with other deals: Disney paid $600m for exclusive rights to NHL games, while Cablevision paid the New York Nicks $486m over twelve years. Expensive as the mega-deals of the 1990s were, they were guided by sound business logic, as Murdoch's actions demonstrated.

Sports were Murdoch's most effective instrument in creating new markets for his media outlets. While his methods for doing this were, from a business viewpoint, straightforward, the recognition that sport could be used effectively for this purpose was not. It is perfectly possible that, had Murdoch attempted this method in the mid-1980s or before, he would have failed. To understand why Murdochization was able to materialize, we need to take stock of the changing historical, cultural and technological conditions under which the process took place.

The new cultural equation

Commenting scathingly on the "circle of corporate domination" that surrounds social life today, Thomas Frank writes: "TV is no longer merely 'entertainment,' it is on the verge of becoming the ineluctable center of human consciousness, the site of every sort of exchange" (in his essay "The new gilded age," in Frank and Weiland, 1998). Frank argues that much of what we understand as reality is mediated by television. The news we receive, significant parts of our education, even portions of our work are conducted through television. Television has become so pervasive that it is now inescapable, and the relentless multiplication of channels means that we are served an almost endless supply of VIDEATED content around which to structure our lives.

This has two implications for Murdochization. First, most of us possess and organize some part of our day around television; which means that we are primed as consumers. Second, advertisers can deliver their messages efficiently from creator to consumer in the safe knowledge that the content of television programs has divided the viewing populations cleanly. Markets can be broken down into specific demographic groups on the basis of their viewing proclivities. This is a boon for the supplier of sports programs: the media corporation can deliver with dependable accuracy the precise target group that advertisers want to reach.

In the early 1980s, Murdoch was impressed by the ways in which dedicated cable channels such as ESPN and MTV were able to isolate specific portions of the population. This was an agreeable development for advertisers, and the enduring commercial success of both of these channels confirms this. While he had no intrinsic interest in sports, Murdoch realized how effective these were in attracting a particular group of consumers, which he could in turn deliver to potential advertisers. At Fox and at BSkyB, Murdoch was prepared to bear punishing initial losses in anticipation that sports would ultimately woo demographically-desirable viewers; the kind that drink alcohol, drive cars and have pension plans, for example.

The concept of using sports to sell products, possibly products only tangentially connected to sports (cars, beer, pension plans and so on) seems blindingly obvious today, but in the 1960s it was a daring innovation. Even in the 1970s, the possibilities were never totally explored. Only in the late 1980s and through the 1990s was sport's potential fully realized. On reflection, the linking of consumerism with sports may be the single most influential development since the advent of organized sport itself.

The link was strengthened by the emergence of a new cultural equation in which sports' stock soared. In the early 1990s, "Sports had arguably surpassed popular music as the captivating medium most essential to being perceived as 'young and alive'," writes Donald Katz in his *Just Do It: The Nike Spirit in the Corporate World* (1994: 25–6). "Sports, as never before, had so completely permeated the logic of the marketplace in consumer goods that by 1992 the psychological content of selling was often more sports-oriented than it was sexual." Companies such as NIKE, Coca-Cola and McDonald's in some measure hitched their wagons to sport's star; and profited enormously as a result. Nike's pursuit of sports stars who had the reputation of being "rebellious" was a brilliant marketing strategy: the likes of Agassi, CANTONA and McEnroe had images that were perfectly suited to Nike's target market. This trio and other members of Nike's pantheon enjoyed status comparable with rock stars and movie stars. Their credibility derived as much from their public personae as their sporting prowess. While Nike was not the only company to have exploited the new status of sports performers, it did more than any other to enhance the status. Nike's television commercials were famed for their resemblance to MTV videos. The company positioned its endorsers as ICONS.

The new cultural equation encouraged the interest of all manner of companies in sports, especially televised sports. Car firms, clothes makers, food manufacturers and other organizations with no particular interest in sports save for the ability to sell their products began to express interest. This took the form of both signing athletes to endorse products and advertising in the commercial spots that punctuated sports competitions.

The zest with which Murdoch bought television rights, often for sums that other major networks believed to be suicidal, attests to his confidence in the cultural power of sports to deliver its followers to his programs and, by implication, his customers – the advertisers. Murdoch, like Berlusconi and Time Warner, also controlled several print media outlets, including newspapers, which he used to promote interest in the sports themselves and the television companies that screened them. The symmetry did not please all, of course: in particular, fans of the Los Angeles Dodgers and Manchester United tried to resist his takeovers.

A world without frontiers

The main reason Murdoch was able to engineer a multimedia, multisports conglomerate on an unprecedented scale was that he had meticulously built up a worldwide network of television channels and other media, sometimes in areas that were not considered worthy or even impenetrable. In their *Swoosh: The Unauthorized Story of Nike and the Men who Played There* (HarperBusiness, 1993), J.B. Strasser and Laurie Becklund write of Murdoch's Star TV: "Asian MTV and other stations and television commercials sent skywards by Star TV landed not only in Hong Kong and China. The same signal was received by Australia, Thailand, Japan, Sri Lanka, Kuwait and the seventeen other nations now served as a result of Hong Kong-based Star TV's quadrupling of viewership between the summer of 1992 and the summer of 1993."

GLOBALIZATION of production meant that companies were able to disperse the creation and assembly of products throughout the world. A microwave oven might comprise components made of materials from four or more different countries, assembled in several more then shipped all over the world. Globalization of consumption involved selling identical or near-identical products to multiple markets. For it to work effectively, those markets need to be refined, voided of resistant tendencies and primed for the same products. In other words, local market preferences needed to be subordinated to global uniformity. As head of media organizations that could reach intimidatingly tough but potentially lucrative markets, like China, Murdoch could lay legitimate claim to be responsible for cultivating (some might say creating) world markets.

During the 1990s, sports became a cultural Esperanto. NBA stars enjoyed adulation in places they had never been near, thanks solely to their regular appearances on television screens. The English soccer club Crystal Palace signed two Chinese players and immediately found a demand for their games to be beamed to China. It became a perfectly acceptable option to watch a televised game of baseball between two American teams rather than travel across town to witness firsthand a game between locals. It would be hard to imagine any other sphere of entertainment – including film – where the cultural pleasure was shared so amply by a global population. As an illustration, soccer's World Cup competition of 1998 was watched by a total of 37 billion television viewers, including 1.7 billion – a quarter of the world's total population – for the final 90 minutes alone. While Murdoch's companies did not hold rights to televise this tournament, the lessons he would have drawn from it are clear.

In the 1980s, Neil Postman wrote a book that warned of the damaging effects of television. Its title, *Amusing Ourselves to Death* (Viking Penguin, 1985), conveys its message: consumers were allowing themselves to be lulled into a state in which all they sought was the shallow entertainment offered by television. Postman was convinced that the dire impact of too much television watching would be felt in politics, in the public sphere and in our mental states. He would have been appalled by the Murdochization process that followed his caution. Not only was the content and much of the format of television channels standardized, but the saturation of sometimes whole networks with sports would have caused Postman to supplement his argument. Postman lamented what he considered the waste of brain cells on television; he would have deplored the inordinate waste on sports events alone.

Scholars and sports fans alike express revulsion at the global trend. For many, Murdochization typifies the fearful consequences of the information age. A small number of corporations have extended their influence not by the use of political rule nor military power, but by controlling the media of information. Media corporations in general and Murdoch's group in particular have identified commonalities in the human experience; their acumen has been in catering to these commonalities without excessively damaging local cultures. Sports have become a serviceable way of enticing people to their television sets and commanding a significant share of their attention spans, while leaving most local proprieties and customs intact. Murdochization in itself does not homogenize different cultures: it gratifies a human longing for thrills, transcendence and fantasy. Sports, especially televised sports, have what may be a unique capability for accommodating all of these.

Of related interest

Barker, Chris (1997) *Global Television: An Introduction*, Blackwell.
Frank, Thomas and Weiland, Matt (1998) *Commodify Your Dissent: The Business of Culture in the New Gilded Age*, Norton.
Franklin, Bob (1997) *Newszak and News Media*, Arnold.

muscle dysmorphia

"Body dysmorphia", or "muscle dysmorphia," describes the syndrome of men who are fixated with their own bodies. According to researchers in the 1990s, a growing number of males, who were perfectly healthy in most respects and regularly attended gyms, became obsessed with their physical appearance. Their preoccupation went beyond the point where they simply trained: they actually suffered as a result of their quest for the perfect body.

Typically, the sufferer would have a low muscle-to-fat ratio, a flat abdomen and well-vasculated limbs. They would weigh themselves several times daily, check their appearance in mirrors constantly and wear baggy tee-shirts even in the summer to hide their bodies. A.M. Wroblewska has studied the relationship between taking performance enhancing drugs and the state of body dysmorphia ("Androgenic-anabolic steroids in young men," *Journal of Psychosomatic Research* vol 42, no 3, 1997). A study led by Harrison G. Pope, of McLean Hospital, Massachusetts, and Precilla Choi, of Keele University in England, concluded that men became so acutely distressed that they needed counseling to help them break their obsession. In their unpublished article, " 'Muscle dysmorphia': an underrecognized form of body dysmorphic disorder" (Keele University), the psychologists argued that the disorder was comparable to anorexia nervosa: the muscular males who thought they looked feeble suffered from a similar delusion as the adolescent females trying to mimic models who thought they looked fat. Both had a distorted perception of their own bodies. In an anorexia case, a woman diets until she is severely underweight, yet she perceives herself as fat; many women have died by literally starving themselves. In the same way, a muscular but dysmorphic weight trainer would see himself as out of shape, even though the perception was inaccurate.

Dysmorphic men often sacrifice career, family and social life to spend hours at the gym. They are too ashamed of their bodies to go to the beach or swimming pool; many take anabolic steroids in an effort to build more muscle. Missing a day of training causes enormous distress. Some men seek pectoral and calf implants similar to the silicone breast implants favored by some women in the 1990s.

The specific reasons for muscular dysmorphia are not clear. It has been variously suggested that high-intensity training leads to the release of endorphins, a group of neurotransmitters with morphine-like effects. These neurotransmitters – natural chemicals secreted in the brain – inhibit the production of nerve impulses by neurons associated with the perception of pain (it has been speculated that the effectiveness of needle acupuncture is due to the release of endorphins). If this is to be accepted, then training may induce a type of dependency among some people, who become habituated to the agreeable effects of endorphin release. Other accounts stress the ADRENALINE RUSH that accompanies some types of training. The expansion of blood vessels in the heart, brain and limbs, the contraction of vessels in the abdomen, the release of glycogen from the liver and the diminishing of fatigue contribute to the sensation commonly experienced by intense trainers.

Sociological explanations identify cultural changes. Legislative changes that have led to equal pay for women and men and the outlawing of sexual discrimination have combined with the greater availability of oral contraceptives and abortion to enable women to become more independent, economically, legally and domestically. One consequence of this may be that women grew more choosy about their partners. Men have responded by paying closer attention to their physical appearance.

A more general change that began in the 1970s was the switch toward a culture of NARCISSISM in which people became increasingly self-centered in their pursuit of happiness through their own bodies. The cultural change involved a fear of aging, or of sickness, an intense regard for one's own esteem and recognition of one's own mortality. The development of late twentieth-century consumer culture was a willing ally in the generation of a market which caters for every conceivable need of the individual; and the emphasis has been very much on the individual. In the 1990s, a surfeit of magazines, such as *Mens' Health* and *FHM*, contributed to images of masculinity that were clearly derived from Schwarzenegger-like exemplars.

The researchers who coined the term believed that the muscular dysmorphia they detected in men was an inevitable feature of a culture that judged people in terms of their physical appearance rather than other facets of their makeup. While the historian Christopher Lasch wrote in the late 1970s of developing narcissism, he did not anticipate the extent to which appearance would create pathologies related not to actual bodily disorders, but *perceptions* of bodily disorders which ultimately created physical problems.

In his article "Muscle murders," William Nack (1998) reported that dissatisfaction with one's own body can have violent consequences. Nothing satisfies the craving to look big and well-cut, so bodybuilders experience a sense of powerlessness. They begin using or increase dosages if already using, steroids or other bulk-related DRUGS. This, according to Nack, produces a combustible combination: he relates the number of violent episodes, including homicidal ones, involving bodybuilders.

Of related interest

Lasch, Christopher (1979) *The Culture of Narcissism*, Norton.
Nack, William (1998) "Muscle murders," *Sports Illustrated* vol 88, no 20, May 18.
Pope, Harrison G., McIlroy, Susan, Keck, P.E. and Hudson, James (1995) *Disorders of Impulse Control: Impulsivity and Aggression*, Wiley.

muscular Christianity

Religion, education and athleticism

Muscular Christianity was the creed that approved of the moral values of sports and games. First used in 1857 by a reviewer of Thomas Hughes's novel *Tom Brown's School Days*, the term came to describe a Christian life in which young gentlemen would develop a hearty character and strong-mindedness to complement healthy bodies. It opposed the traditional Protestant church condemnation of the pursuit of "devilish pastimes" on Sundays, the only days when the mass of people had the opportunity for physical recreation.

Muscular Christianity chimed with British elite beliefs and attitudes in an era of predatory IMPERIALISM, militarism, NATIONALISM, industrial capitalism and Darwinism. From the middle of the nineteenth century, the Christian missionary ethos associated with conquest and imperialism was exported to colonies such as Australia, Canada and New Zealand. In Australia and New Zealand, rifle shooting and gymnastics were justified as invaluable to military fitness and the training of army recruits.

Darwin's evolutionary ideas, aided by Herbert Spencer's endorsement of muscular Christianity in his *Education: Intellectual, Moral and Physical* (first published 1861), supported the concept of the gradual progression of the "race," in this case the British race. This was popularized as the "survival of the fittest" and its contiguous aphorism, "a sound mind in a sound body"; intellectual superiority and physical robustness were highly complementary and contributed to the fitness of the race.

Charles Kingsley, a theologically liberal English cleric and author of *The Water Babies*, idealized human movement and spiritual embodiment through sports and games. He believed that this, along with love of family in serving God, would combat the social malaise of Victorian society. While the import of his message was the same as that of muscular Christianity's, Kingsley preferred the term "manly Christianity." Kingsley's many influential essays and Hughes' semi-autobiographical novel inspired the growth of muscular Christianity in the second half of the century. Sports became central features of the British public schools. The Christian socialist aspects of the creed united both Hughes and Kingsley with its links to medieval notions of chivalric service transmuted into social conscience and public service, especially among the poor urban working class. Many former public (independent) schoolboys and graduates of Oxford and Cambridge, particularly clergymen, took their love of competitive sports with them into urban factories and parishes. This led to the formation of rugby and association football clubs and cricket teams from the 1860s. Many of these clubs endure to the present day.

In 1864, the Clarendon Report on the reform of public schools accelerated the muscular Christianity movement in its recommendations that sports and games provided a healthy, competitive impetus to the character training deemed essential to Britain's future leaders. Yet, from the early 1880s it became apparent that, with religion increasingly becoming a matter of habit rather than commitment, muscular Christianity was falling out of favor and being replaced in schools and universities by more secular notions of athleticism and amateurism. The new ideal of *espirit de corps* was based on affiliation to the group, as exemplified by football.

The export of the creed

Muscular Christianity, and indeed "Britishness," were exported to colonies where educational institutions were modeled on the British matrix. From the 1860s, muscular Christianity and its attendant range of organized sports were rapidly integrated into Australian life. Rugby was embraced heartily by New Zealand's high schools, a fact that helps explain the extraordinarily strong tradition and success of the nation's rugby union teams. Following an education at the Rugby public school, Australian Thomas W. Wills returned to his homeland and was instrumental in devising a new variant of the game, which became known as Australian Rules.

From the mid-nineteenth century, members of the American elite also extolled muscular Christianity and wholesome leisure pursuits. This was in response to the need for social reform in urban areas which were centers for mass migration. English weavers had taken cricket to the northeast, Germans introduced gymnastics and the Irish took boxing to various states. Reformers such as the Reverend A.A. Livermore, the Boston Unitarian preacher, Thomas Wentworth Higginson, the Harvard football player, and Oliver Wendell Holmes, himself a noted oarsman, crusaded for participation in organized sports as a way of creating a healthy urban environment and physically fit citizenry.

The muscular Christianity movement did not reach its peak in the USA until after the Civil War. Recreational facilities, such as parks, were situated far from the cities and therefore out of reach of the working class. The first Harvard–Yale boat race took place in 1852. America's first sports icon was in fact a literary character, Frank Merriwell, who appeared in 208 books published between 1896 and 1916. The author was Burt L. Standish (real name Gilbert Patton). Not to be outdone, social reformer Catherine Esther Beecher propounded a concept of acceptable but differentiated female physical exercise and sport (such as calisthenics, croquet and gymnastics) to encourage robust women as both cultural progenitors and reproducers of a Christian society.

The essentially masculine character of muscular Christianity was confirmed in the late nineteenth century by major figures such as Luther H. Gulick and James Naismith. The former became chair of physical training at the Young Men's Christian Association (YMCA) at Springfield College (established in 1895). The YMCA was the birthplace of both volleyball and basketball; Naismith invented basketball during a cold winter in 1891. Many Springfield alumni carried the muscular Christian gospel of basketball to other colleges and high schools and started a sport that would later be organized as the NBA.

The YMCA's marriage of morality and competitive team sports was inspired by muscular Christianity with its character-building emphasis, and this, combined with the gymnasium and playground movements either side of the turn of the twentieth century, led to the first major inter-scholastic sports league. In 1903, Gulick was appointed as director of physical training for public schools in greater New York. American football was an expression of late nineteenth-century civil religion, and reflected a growing national self-interest as well as aggressively competitive qualities normally associated with industrial capitalism. Such qualities were expressed in the annual Thanksgiving games between Ivy League colleges, which attracted national interest.

As America industrialized, the PROTESTANT ETHIC so vital to the development of capitalism took root. The stress on hard work, goal-directedness, achieved status, competitiveness, moral asceticism and individualism had ready partners in the emerging sports creed. However, while sports and recreation programs became part of the reform gospel espoused by Protestant churches in most American cities outside of the southern states, in Chicago they were associated with the Roman Catholic church. By 1910, it boasted the largest church-sponsored baseball league in the country. By the beginning of the twentieth century the Catholic Youth Organization, which was sponsored by the churches, had established leagues for bowling and softball. During the 1920s, the then small Catholic college of Notre Dame achieved national fame as a football-playing power. In 1947, Holy Cross became the first Catholic college to win the NCAA basketball championship.

After the Second World War, muscular Christianity yielded to what some called "Christian muscularity," meaning that sports seemed to generate near-religious emotion, fervor and zealotry. It is significant that the evangelist Billy Graham selected sports venues such as the Yankee and Wembley stadiums and the Los Angeles Coliseum for his early crusades. Athletes in Action was founded in 1966 as a division of Graham's Campus Crusades for Christ: star athletes were invited to "share" their conversions publicly. This strategy was also employed by the Pro Athletes Outreach organization which sent professional sports performers around the country on what were called "speaking blitzes."

Canadian novelist W. P. Kinsella challenged organized religion with his notion of "sports religion." His *Shoeless Joe Jackson Comes to Iowa*, the source novel for the film *FIELD OF DREAMS*, discloses the profundity of sports as a way of experiencing personal religiosity. But, despite articles in the popular press with headlines like "Super Bowl as Religious Festival," there is only a superficial resemblance between contemporary pro sport and religion. In his article "Muscular Christianity, holy play and spiritual exercises: confusion about Christ in sports and religion," Robert Higgs observes: "There is no doubt that play is closer to the idea of the holy than is sports competition" (*Arete* vol 1, 1983). Any understanding of the connection between religion and what we now recognize as organized sports must take account of the historical significance and cultural meanings of muscular Christianity.

Of related interest

Bloomfield, Anne (1994) "Muscular Christianity or mystic? Charles Kingsley reappraised," *International Journal of the History of Sport* vol 11.
Brown, David W. (1986) "Muscular Christianity in the Antipodes: some observations on the diffusion and emergence of a Victorian ideal in Australian

social theory," *Sporting Traditions: The Journal of the Australian Society for Sports History* vol 3.

Money, Tony (1997) *Manly and Muscular Diversions: Public Schools and the Nineteenth-Century Sporting Revival*, Duckworth.

GEORGE PATON

N

narcissism

The so-called "health craze" that started in the 1970s and led to a preponderance of health clubs, nutrition stores and domestic athletic apparatuses had its sources in a particular kind of culture, one that promoted individualism and "wellness." This culture was analysed by the historian Christopher Lasch who, in 1979, published his book *The Culture of Narcissism*, in which he reflected on the changes of the previous decade.

Lasch observed a society in the throes of its own mutation, its citizens spurning community or any other kind of collectivity in preference for an unyielding self-regard. People, argued Lasch, became preoccupied with themselves: they admired themselves, pampered themselves, attended to themselves. Like Narcissus who fell in love with his own reflection, people became emotionally and intellectually fixated with their own images. This almost obsessive self-centeredness translated into a demand for physical perfection, an avoidance of substances that were potentially harmful, and a fascination for any new product that promised youth. This final point was important, for the devotees were the products of mid-war and postwar years and were on the cusp of middle age as the 1980s approached.

"The therapeutic outlook" is how Lasch described the mentality that transformed every collective grievance into a soluble personal problem. As the promise of the 1960s radicalism waned, people looked for a therapeutic intervention in their own lives, rather than theirs *and* others. Jerry Rubin, a one-time member of the radical left-wing group the Yippies, confessed that after the passing of the 1960s, he moved to the West Coast, confronted his private anxieties and, between 1971–5, experienced e.s.t., gestalt therapy, bioenergetics, rolfing, massage, jogging, health foods, tai chi, Esalan, hypnotism, modern dance, meditation, Silva Mind Control, Arica, acupuncture, sex therapy and Reichian therapy: a smorgasbord course in New Consciousness.

Rubin's "journey into self" (as he called it) was part of a new movement in the 1970s that was driven by a quest for self-understanding or self-perfection; in other words, personal growth. This "inner revolution" had as one of its central components what became known in populist terms as the "health craze." This involved a fear of aging, or of sickness, an intense regard for one's own esteem and recognition of one's own mortality. The development of late twentieth-century consumer culture was a willing ally in the generation of a market which catered for every conceivable need of the individual; and the emphasis was very much on the individual. Lasch had been critical of the rise of industries geared to the requirements of overprivileged first-world citizens, living in a material cornucopia and apparently bored to the point where they took interest only in their own narrow lives.

The latter day narcissist, unlike the legendary Narcissus who was consumed with fantasies of omnipotence and eternal youth, was not selfish, self-assured or egotistical. He or she was a "minimal self" whose preoccupation with self-preservation and psychic survival was an adaptation to a culture that was disintegrating before their eyes. Other writers, like Richard Sennett, wrote about the end of public life as meaningful social relations, family life and a loss of faith in social institutions all waned. The narcissists' reaction was to turn inwards, spurning social contacts and commitments while gratifying themselves with consumer goods and self-improvement of one kind or another.

In the 1970s, it was felt by many that this self-absorption was limited to middle-class Americans and Europeans, whose inner search served to insulate them from the poverty, racism and injustice that raged about them. This proved to be an oversimplification: the mentality affected all segments of society. The endless avoidance of signs of aging and ill health pervaded Western culture.

The response was an industry comprising health clubs, nutritionist shops and a sports apparel industry, all organized around creating both new forms of insecurity and new forms of conquering that insecurity. A new hypochondria emerged, with hitherto undetected pathologies feeding inventive remedies. Without doubt, the most potent and pervasive ailment of the health-crazed *fin de siècle* was stress, a malady so ill-defined, with so many manifestations and so resolutely immune to conventional therapies that it was near-pathological to be without it.

Of related interest

Falk, Pasi and Campbell, Colin (eds) (1997) *The Shopping Experience*, Sage.
Lasch, Christopher (1979) *The Culture of Narcissism*, Norton.
Wolf, Naomi (1991) *The Beauty Myth: How Images of Beauty are Used Against Women*, Morrow.

nationalism

National identities

At times, modern international sporting events seem to be on the point of being overwhelmed by the trappings of nationalism. Political leaders routinely attend such events, national anthems are played, national flags are flown and newspapers report the outcome in terms of national joy or despair. Less frequently but no less significantly, ethnic communities such as the nationalists in Northern Ireland, will promote sports that emphasize their own distinctiveness within the nation state while others, in Canada and Spain for example, will seek to subvert the dominant sporting culture by their fiercely partisan support for local or regional teams.

Despite the routine association of sport with nationalism and sub-nationalism, the link between sports culture and identity is far from clear. Indeed, nationalism itself is a highly disputed concept. While there is agreement that the nation is distinct from other forms of collective identity such as class, tribe or race, there is considerable confusion and disagreement about the mix of features that constitute a nation. Objective features such as territory, religion and language need to be balanced against a series of subjective features such as a shared sense of history and mythology. To add to the conceptual complexity, one needs to distinguish between "bottom up" identity, which is the product of ethnicity, and "top down" identity that is facilitated, stimulated or even imposed on the population within a territory by the state. The state's concerns with defending the integrity of the national territory and maintaining its own legitimacy impose considerable pressures upon it to attempt to manage national identity.

Finally, while some believe that "national identity" is fixed and that members of a nation simply require periodic reminders of "who they are," an alternative – and a more persuasive – view is that, as an ideological construction, national identity needs to be constantly nurtured, reinvented and maintained. It is the combination of the fugitive nature of national identity, the quest for continuing state legitimacy, and the potential challenge to state defined identity from ethnic identities that lead to the involvement of sport in the politics of nationalism.

During the twentieth century over sixty new states have been established, many as a result of the process of decolonialization, the ending of the Cold War or of the redrawing of the world map in the wake of two world wars. Many of these new states were, and some continue to be, faced with the acute problem of establishing and then maintaining a sense of national identity. For former colonies, the unity brought about by the anti-colonial struggle often evaporated once the colonial power had withdrawn, and this often resulted in previously subsumed divisions of race, tribe or wealth commonly resurfacing. These divisions had either to be allowed an expression that did not challenge the state's fragile stability, or subsumed under a stronger loyalty to the new state. Sport has regularly been seen as a potential contributor to both strategies.

Perhaps the most systematic use of sport as a contribution to the development of a sense of national identity was in the communist states of central and eastern Europe. For the German Democratic Republic (GDR), the objective was not only to foster a sense of national identity distinct from West Germany, but also to eradicate any lingering association between sport and Nazism. For Walter Ulbricht, the State Council Chairman, sport played an important role in the development of the "socialist personality" and demonstrating the superiority of socialist democracy over its bourgeois rival. The sports system of the GDR was closely modeled on that of the Soviet Union, which also used sport to support the state's attempt to stimulate feelings of Soviet nationalism to help preserve national unity in a polyglot society which has over 100 nationalities, and in which the ruling Russians were in a minority. The collapse of the Soviet empire and the reunification of Germany has undermined the claims of those who argued that sport had a capacity to build an identity in the face of historic and deeply entrenched ethnic identities. The eagerness of the East Germans for reunification, and the development of nationalist movements in the Baltic states, Russia and Georgia as well as in Yugoslavia are indications of the superficiality of the sense of East German, Soviet and Yugoslav nationhood.

Despite the lack of firm evidence of the effectiveness of sport as a foundation for national identity most states seek to influence, if not control, the development of sport within their boundaries. However, for many states the sports culture they are attempting to manipulate in order to enhance national identity is rarely one that has an association with any of the ethnic communities within the state. Indeed, for many the sports they have available not only have no lengthy cultural association with the country but are frequently part of the cultural baggage of an IMPERIALISM.

Colonialism and cultural division

Many colonies were exposed to the sporting traditions of the imperial power, often with the intention of undermining traditional sports or with the aim of "civilizing" the colony. While some ex-colonies (such as Ireland through the promotion of Gaelic sports) rejected the imperial sporting culture, most sought an accommodation with it. However, the accommodation can be uncomfortable. In studies of the cultural significance of cricket for West Indian regional identity, there is a conflict between on the one hand, those who see cricketing success as a process of self-denigration of black culture and simply being good at the white man's game, and on the other hand, those who argue that cricket has been a positive focus for West Indian identity and has been reshaped in sympathy with the culture of the West Indies has been used as a means of fostering nationalist sentiment and racial pride.

A somewhat different situation existed in the British ex-colonies of Australia and Canada, where the indigenous population was both small and systematically marginalized by the late nineteenth century. The problem for these states was similar to many other ex-colonies insofar as, by the middle of the twentieth century, they wished to build a separate identity from the imperial power; but it was different in the sense that they clearly shared a common sporting and cultural heritage with Britain. Sport played a substantial role in the process of cultural differentiation. Cricket, especially cricket matches against England, in particular was of such symbolic importance that it was frequently promoted as the only true test of a country's worth. Beating England was an important means of asserting Australian equality and demonstrating its vitality. Indeed, so important is sport to Australian identity that the poor performance of its athletes in the 1976 Montreal Olympics prompted a government inquiry. Similar claims may be made for the importance of sport in Canada, where the government of Pierre Trudeau invested heavily in elite Olympic sport as a partial means of overcoming the problems arising from Canada's strong provinces, small dispersed population and cultural divisions between English and French speakers.

It is not just British ex-colonies that have to come to terms with the sporting traditions of hegemonic cultures; the experience of a number of states within the cultural sphere of the USA have led to analyses similar to those relating to the experience of British ex-colonies. For example, in his *Sugarball: The American Game, the Dominican Dream* (Yale University Press, 1991), A. Klein discusses the significance of baseball in the relationship between the Dominican Republic and the United States. He argues that baseball mirrors the political economy of other commercial businesses in poor countries, which leads to systematic under-development. He demonstrates how Dominican baseball talent is fostered, traded and discarded by the large US clubs, which are simultaneously undermining the development of a strong baseball league in the Republic. However, he also argues that baseball has also provided the basis for cultural resistance, becoming less a measure of American cultural superiority than a demonstration of Dominican excellence.

Former imperial powers have also experienced threats to their cultural identities. Britain is an example of a country which has sought to respond to a perceived threat to its national identity arising, in part, from membership of the European Union by investing heavily in the production of sports heroes and heroines. The funding of an elite sports development center and the emphasis on traditional team sports in the school curriculum were both products of nascent cultural insecurity.

In conclusion, sport, because of its apparent malleability, will remain subject to state attempts to manipulate its symbolism for purposes of nation-building. However, two caveats are necessary: the first is the reminder of the shallow roots of fifty years of state-sponsored sporting excellence in the former GDR, and the second is to draw attention to the difficulty of controlling sports culture. In many countries, sports symbolism is contested terrain with state attempts to control symbolism often subverted by dissenting ethnic communities. Northern Irish nationalists have very effectively used Gaelic sports as a basis for challenging English and unionist cultural dominance, and in Spain the Catalans and Basques have used support for local soccer teams, particularly when playing against the Real Madrid (the symbol of Spanish unity), as an opportunity to demonstrate their distinctive cultural identity. The link between nationalism and sport is well established and close, but it is far from straightforward.

Of related interest

Beckles, H. and Stoddart, B. (1995) *Liberation Cricket: West Indies Cricket Culture*, Manchester University Press.

Cashman, R. (1995) *Paradise of Sport: The Rise of Organised Sport in Australia*, Oxford University Press.

Houlihan, B. (1994) *Sport and International Politics*, Harvester-Wheatsheaf.

Smith, Anthony D. (1995) *Nations and Nationalism in a Global Era*, Polity Press.

BARRIE HOULIHAN

NBA

Origins

In 1976, the National Basketball Association (NBA) was an ailing professional basketball league. Within fifteen years it had risen to challenge the traditional powers of the National Football League and Major League Baseball as the leading sports association in the United States and, by extension, in the world.

The NBA was formed in 1949, the result of a merger of two struggling leagues, but its deep roots lie in a YMCA training college in Springfield, Massachusetts. In the midst of a bitterly cold December in 1891, a training instructor gave his students an assignment: to devise an activity that could be practiced indoors and would have enough competitive interest to hold the attentions of healthy young men through the long New England winters. James Naismith's project involved a soccer-style football and two peach baskets. The game of basketball was born.

Within five years, modifications were made and the game became a regular part of YMCA activities. The YMCA allowed the Amateur Athletic Union to govern the sport according to strict amateur standards and, as the game grew steadily in popularity among colleges, the National Collegiate Athletic Association (NCAA) took an interest. In 1915, the three organization drew up a single set of rules and an organizational structure to rule the sport.

At around the same time, professional teams were beginning to emerge. These were originally itinerant clubs which competed in challenge games around the country, as their names suggest (The Wanderers, The Globe Trotters and so on). The main difference between the professional game and its amateur equivalent was in the former's emphasis on entertainment. The Harlem Globetrotters, who still tour to this day, are an exemplar: starting life in 1927, the Harlem team, comprising extrovert African American players, evolved from a playful yet competitive outfit to a virtual circus, complete with clownish antics, accompanying music and all sorts of gimmicks.

The professional teams came and went but the college game thrived, especially in the interwar years. The first NCAA playoffs were held in 1939 as a response to another challenge series known as the National Invitational Tournament. At this stage, basketball was regarded principally as an amateur sport played by college students. Then in 1946, an organization known as the Basketball Association of America was founded by a group of industrialists who had experience in sports and entertainment marketing. Their plan was to introduce some organization to the loose collection of professional teams that played around the country.

In 1949 the group pooled its resources with another league, known as the National Basketball League, which operated in the Midwest. Together they created a slimmed-down, profit-driven organization, the National Basketball Association. The attractiveness of the NBA-style game was enhanced by the distinctive contributions of black players, many of whom specialized in explosive slam-dunks, electric speed and staccato play rhythms. These were the kind of extravagant techniques that brought kudos on the hard inner-city parking lots where the game was learned, rather than in the colleges.

However, it was an African American ex-college player, Bill Russell, who became pivotal in the fortunes of one of the NBA's most successful dynasties of the 1960s. Under their coach Red Auerbach, the Boston Celtics utterly dominated the NBA, winning eleven straight championships in the years leading up to 1969. Another black player, Lew Alcindor, later to become Kareem Abdul-Jabbar, was a key player in a comparably dominant NCAA team, UCLA, which won nine national titles between 1964 and 1975.

Thwarting challenges

The NBA's position as the sole professional league was challenged in 1967 when the American Basketball Association (ABA) sprang to life. The ABA's search for talent took it beyond college undergraduates all the way to city high schools. One of its major finds was the center Moses Malone, who eventually went on to an NBA career and a place in the Hall of Fame. The ABA lasted nine years before it did a deal with the NBA, which saw four of its franchises become part of the NBA structure. At this stage, the NBA had acquired characteristics of other major employing organizations, and a Players' Association had been formed to negotiate for better salaries and conditions of work. The problem was that basketball was still not a major sport and its TELEVISION ratings were not impressive enough for it to contemplate challenging the big two, the NFL and MAJOR LEAGUE BASEBALL.

Three developments helped change this. The introduction of the three-point shot, scored from outside 23 feet 9 inches (7.23 meters), clearly added to the aesthetics of the action: the long arcing eye-pleasing shots that sometimes won games were a boon, and particular players became adept at scoring from this range. Great RIVALRIES became focal points: the one which pitched the Celtics' player, Larry Bird against the Lakers' Magic JOHNSON had carried over from their days as NCAA players. Third, there was a new intensity in sports marketing. The health craze that began in the late 1970s alerted many sports goods manufacturers to the value of associating their goods with sports generally and individual sports stars in particular. The lessons were not lost on the likes of NIKE and its arch-rival Reebok, both of which aggressively pursued NBA players and featured them in their often dazzling advertising campaigns. So successful was the NBA's commercial approach through the 1980s and 1990s that, by 1997, the New York Knicks' franchise was valued at $250 million (£153 million), second only to football's Dallas Cowboys in terms of overall worth (measured by gate receipts, broadcasting revenues and operating expenses). Chicago Bulls were worth $214 million. The average value of an NBA club was $134m.

Nike's cardinal player was Michael JORDAN, and CEO Phil Knight gambled on building a whole line of sports apparel around him. The "Air Jordan" line of products ensured that the name of the Chicago Bull's player was imprinted on the mind of virtually everyone. Jordan became synonymous with the NBA, and his international fame was instrumental in establishing the league's cachet even in countries where basketball is not habitually played.

In 1992, in a move deplored by many, the NBA sent an all-star team to the Barcelona summer Olympics. While this was a perfectly legitimate move and professional players were eligible to play under the Federation of International Basketball Associations rules, it was regarded as a snub to NCAA players who had previously represented the USA. The so-called "dream team" which brought together the NBA's multi-millionaire players found itself playing penniless amateurs from underdeveloped African nations and war-racked East European countries. Predictably, the NBA team won the gold medal in one of the most obvious Olympic foregone conclusions ever.

The league's 1998–9 season was disrupted by one of the most significant STRIKES in NBA history, which resulted in about half the regular season games being canceled as players pressed for contractual changes and club owners remained obdurate. Much of the negotiating was conducted by David Falk, one of the principal figures in the PROSERV agency which handled several of the leading players' business affairs, and David Stern, the league's commissioner.

Women's leagues

Women's basketball has a slightly longer history than the men's game: the first college game was held at Smith College in 1893, and the first official women's game, between Berkeley and Stanford, in 1895, predated the first official men's game by two years. Originally, the sports differed in that women used six-player teams. Women eventually changed to five per side in the late 1960s. The first flowering of public interest came in the 1970s when there was an overall interest in women's sport. Players such as Nancy Lieberman were the first nationally-known representatives of the sport and, in 1976, women's basketball was recognized as an Olympic sport.

In 1978, the Women's Professional Basketball League attempted to launch professional basketball for women, extending its affiliates to nine within two years. Lacking the backing of TELEVISION or any parent organization, the league folded in 1982. An attempt to revive women's professional basketball came in 1995 with the American Basketball League (ABL), but it soon had a potent rival in the form of the Women's National Basketball Association (WNBA), which was affiliated to the NBA and enjoyed the considerable advantage of the NBA's marketing power behind it.

As with most major sports, the key to the WNBA's relatively successful opening season in 1997 was television. A three-way deal with the all-sports cable network ESPN, the female-oriented cable channel Lifestyle and the NBC network enabled the WNBA to establish itself nationally. ESPN reported 1.2m viewers, Lifestyle 900,000 and NBC averaged over 3m viewers in the traditionally slow summer months. Playing in the NBA's close season also helped ticket sales with an average of 9,669 per game.

Although the ABL signed most of the USA's best women players, including 29 of the 51 invited to the US national team trials, its eight teams tended to be near women's college hotbeds, while the WNBA clubs were all in NBA cities. After only one year, the WNBA expanded from eight to twelve franchises.

Of related interest

Fox, Stephen (1994) *Big Leagues: Professional Baseball, Football and Basketball in National Memory*, Morrow.

Halberstam, David (1990) *Playing for Keeps: Michael Jordan and the World He Made*, Random House.

Stern, David J. (1994) *The Official NBA Basketball Encyclopedia*, 2nd edn, Villard.

NCAA

The NCAA (National Collegiate Athletic Association) was an outgrowth of the Intercollegiate Athletic Association (IAA), which was formed in 1906 in response to a crisis in college football. In 1897, southeastern universities canceled the final month of the season after a player was fatally injured during a game. Although it was vetoed, the state of Georgia's subsequent attempt to make playing football a felony indicated the strength of the anti-football lobby. In the 1906 season alone, there were eighteen deaths. Stanford and the University of California switched to rugby, and many other colleges were similarly minded. The IAA was formed to avert an impending crisis.

The organization comprised a broad base of universities. Its remit was to first rescue and then to popularize football. Several departures from rugby had already made American football a unique game, but the use of lateral passes as in rugby encouraged compressions of play and enhanced the chances of collisions. The forward pass – illegal in rugby – was a major innovation and one which cut down the injury rate. It proved to be a significant factor in reshaping the game: open play, lightning-fast receivers and long passes thrown by powerful quarterbacks became the staples of the sport.

But the NCAA had wider purposes. Like its ancestor rugby, which had developed the Rugby Football Union (RFU) to organize its affairs in 1871, the American game needed the stability of an organizational structure to ensure its future as a competitive sport. Rugby divided into two distinct organizations in the period 1893–5, each controlling a different version of the game, or "code": the RFU remained amateur, while the Northern Rugby Union, later to become the Rugby Football League, permitted payments. In 1907, when American football brought in the forward pass, rugby league implemented a series of rule changes designed to make it faster, more open and so more attractive to spectators.

Even in this role, the significance of organizations in standardizing rules and making competition more attractive is clear. But, the NCAA, like all similar sports associations, came into its own in the 1920s when mass spectatorship became a feature of sport. An ability to negotiate with other industries, particularly communications industries, was crucial to the development of any sport, and the NCAA was equipped to make its game the most marketable team sport in the country. It was also able to perform the same functions for basketball, a sport that was dominated by YMCA teams up to the 1930s. Modifications of rules quickened the pace of the game and, in the 1950s, with the sport embroiled in several money-related scandals, the NCAA stepped in to regulate forcefully. In a decisive move, it restricted the number of "live" basketball games on television and distributed TELEVISION revenues to its affiliates. Competition from the aggressively marketed NBA in the 1980s meant that college basketball lost some of its shine and, like amateur football, had to content itself with a shrinking share of the – admittedly huge – market.

The concept of US universities functioning as free training schools for the NFL and NBA and, to a lesser extent, MAJOR LEAGUE BASEBALL and the National Hockey League was brought under scrutiny by Tracy McGrady, who, in 1997, signed a $12m (£7.3m) six-year deal to promote Adidas sportswear. He was then picked ninth in the NBA annual draft, which guaranteed him a minimum income of $3.5m over the next three years. He also did not graduate from university, only from high school. Kobe Bryant also short-circuited the NCAA, signing to the Los Angeles Lakers straight from high school.

McGrady's and Bryant's eschewing of college was not welcomed by the NCAA. The Corinthian ideal of producing "scholar athletes" who would compete at the highest levels of amateur sport and graduate as well-rounded academicians was integral to NCAA philosophy. The conventional understanding between the NFL and the NBA on the one hand and the NCAA on the other was that amateur players should be left to pursue academic study without the lure of professional contracts. Universities were prepared to arrange timetables and adjust standards to keep students for the full four years. Only occasionally would a player drop out. Wilt Chamberlain, for example, was enrolled at the University of Kansas but resented the rules that prevented his individual domination of basketball games. He left to play professionally with the (independent) Harlem Globetrotters until his four years had expired; after this he went on to a long and distinguished career in the NBA.

When colleague stars Kareem Abdul-Jabbar and Elvin Hayes boycotted the US Olympic team in 1968, Spencer Haywood, a then obscure center from Trinidad (Colorado) Junior College led the USA to a gold medal. After only a year at college, Haywood signed with the American Basketball Association, which started in 1967 as a challenger to the NBA (it lasted nine years, then merged with the latter). The fledgling league's most notable recruit was Moses Malone, who was eventually inducted into the Hall of Fame. Less distinguished high school graduates who signed directly to the NBA in the same period included Darryl Hawkins and Bill Willoughby.

Professional basketball was not nearly as lucrative in the 1960s and 1970s as it became in the 1990s, and there was little attraction in abandoning academic studies. But, as the NBA expanded and became a marketing force, competition for quality players intensified and promising high school players were scouted more vigorously. McGrady was the fourth high school graduate to be drafted in three years. Kevin Garnett, drafted directly by the Minnesota Timberwolves in 1995, signed a contract worth $5.5m over three years. Two years into the contract, he turned down a proposed six-year extension worth $103m, preferring an arrangement that earned him $20m per year.

Staggeringly successful experiences such as Garnett's were potentially damaging to the ideal of amateur sports, but the NCAA's conception of amateurism was itself open to question. While players were not allowed to receive any monies apart from their scholarships, coaches typically earned more than the top-salaried professors and sometimes more than university presidents. The universities were able to justify this by appeal to the revenue brought in by amateur sports. For example, the University of Michigan consistently attracted crowds of 100,000 for football games and, with the advent of commercially sponsored "bowls" in the 1990s, could expect in the region of $6m for an appearance in such a bowl. The NCAA-sanctioned amateurism was amateur only for the competitors: all other aspects were highly professionalized. After Garnett and McGrady, college scouts were ever more vigilant in their search for high school talent, but their efforts were undermined by professional agents who patrolled the inner cities with a view to signing outstanding players straight to professional clubs.

Of related interest

Feinstein, John (1989) *A Season on the Brink: A Year with Bob Knight and the Indiana Hoosiers*, Fireside.

Wiggins, David (ed.) (1995) *Sport in America: From Wicked Amusement to National Obsession*, Human Kinetics.

Yaeger, Don (1996) *Indue Process: The NCAA's Injustice for All*, Sagamore.

NFL

Roots

The NFL (National Football League) is one of – if not the – wealthiest and most powerful sports governing organizations in the world. Its richest franchise, Dallas Cowboys, alone is worth an estimated $320 million (£195m), and it claims seven of the top ten richest US sports clubs with an average value of $205 million. Considering it only came into existence in 1970, its commercial growth has been extraordinary and reflects the power and influence of TELEVISION. Although American football is its *raison d'être*, the NFL is a media-driven organization.

The ethic in which American football is grounded is MUSCULAR CHRISTIAN-ITY, and the sport on which the NFL is founded has its roots in English rugby, which was played in Eastern colleges from the 1870s. Harvard refused to play soccer. Yale responded and introduced changes in rugby that seemed more in keeping with American cultural norms. The need for precision in measurement, for certainty, for clear demarcation of possession of territory; all these features reflected an America that was pressing west in the epic effort to extend its frontiers and using the products of an industrial society (guns, railroads, construction equipment) to do so.

The rules of the American game were devised by Walter Camp, who played for Yale. He began reformulating rugby in the 1870s. In 1880, he completely broke one of rugby's central rules by introducing downs: this contrasted with the to-and-fro of rugby where the ball stays live while play continues, even after tackles. Instead of rugby's scrummage with possession remaining unclear until the ball breaks free of a sheltering group, Camp changed to a scrimmage in which players lined up and the spectators were able to see a clear snap of the ball backwards. This provided for the kind of episodic play that was to prove so vital to the sport's compatibility with television in the next century. Equally as drastic was the change in 1906 to the forward pass, which was proscribed in rugby but which permitted the possibility of long, spectacular throws which could turn a game in an instant. The "Hail Mary" remains one of the most dramatic moves in any sport today.

The sport was played in the main by students and stayed very much the preserve of an elite group of north-easterners. Professionalism came long after the college game had been established, though some players did receive payment as early as the 1880s. Athletic clubs, as they were mostly called, traveled about the country playing each other. Some college players would play under assumed names to safeguard their amateur status. Midwest teams were the best professional outfits in the early 1900s. Ex-college players hired themselves virtually by the game.

Professionalization

In the same way as many soccer clubs developed in England, many professional football franchises started as factory teams. The Indian Packing Company of Green Bay, Wisconsin had its own team in the first decade of the twentieth century, as did the Staley Starch Company of Decatur , Illinois. Players were paid about $50 per week and given time off to train. In 1920, both companies affiliated their teams to a new organization that also include teams from New York and Washington. The teams evolved into the Packers, Bears, Giants and Redskins respectively. Quite soon it was possible for the teams to divorce themselves from their industrial backgrounds and become independent employers: players who had learned their skills at colleges could earn a decent living once their years of study were over. This seamless transition from university to professional club has been a feature of American football ever since, with the draft being brought into play in 1936 as a mechanism for equalizing the league and avoiding an imbalance of power.

While the transfer of quality university players to professional teams has obviously provided a rich source of talent, there has been an element of tension in the relationship between amateurs and professionals, the former always mindful of the popularity of the latter and of the possibility of an eclipse. The tension was tightened by the climactic playoffs brought in by the professionals in 1957, compared with the somewhat indeterminate rankings and multiple "bowls" of the college game. The college game had been more popular until the 1960s, but it could do little to interrupt the rise of the professionals thereafter.

The 1950s was the decade of television. In 1949, only two per cent of American homes had television sets, then priced by Sears, Roebuck at a hefty $149.95. A year later, 10 per cent had sets, and a year after the number had risen to 13 per cent. By 1955 the number had risen to 65 per cent, and the growth continued to 90 per cent in 1963 and 95 per cent in 1968. Like many other sports, football, especially college football, was wary of inviting television cameras to the games. Sport was a cheap option for the networks: production and personnel costs were relatively inexpensive and the rights were not prohibitive. From 1951 the NCAA tried to control the telecast of college games, but eventually in 1984 a Supreme Court decision allowed colleges to negotiate their own agreements with television companies.

The National Football League (not yet the NFL as we know it) prospered from the coverage it received from television. Its solution to the problem of hurting live attendances was a blackout within a seventy-five-mile radius. Its other innovation was to pool the revenue and divide between its franchises. This was another example of its strategy of avoiding the formation of elites. It allowed clubs in smaller and less lucrative markets (Green Bay and Pittsburgh, for example) to coexist and compete with the teams in the bigger urban areas (like New York and Chicago). NFL Commissioner Bert Bell made a clever concession to television in 1958 when he allowed "television time-outs," stoppages specially to permit networks to screen commercials. CBS was delighted with the result: as more homes acquired television sets, so the popularity of professional football grew all over the nation.

The football–television liaison

So successful was the liaison between the then National Football League and television that, when the fledgling television network ABC came on the scene, seeking to challenge the big two (CBS and NBC), it chose football as its weapon. ABC virtually sponsored the formation of a rival to the NFL, the American Football League. This was in truth a second-rate affair, full of players who could not make the grade with the rival league; but it was competitive enough to make progress in the slipstream of the NFL.

ABC had no reservations about featuring a strictly fabricated league created for the sole purpose of giving it more leverage with advertisers. In fact, the AFL had a contract with the network even prior to a ball being kicked. It existed only for television. During its first five years its credibility solidified, so that in 1965 the AFL was able to loose ABC's apron strings and negotiate independently. A deal with NBC television brought the league $42 million (£25m) for five year's coverage. The extra revenue enabled the AFL to sign better players, like Joe Namath, and become a legitimate equal of the NFL. In fact, it was too equal for comfort, and in 1966 the NFL agreed to a merger which resulted in the National Football League as we now know it. A playoff finale to the season between the NFL and the AFL was, of course, the precursor to the Super Bowl, itself a television phenomenon which commands record-breaking audiences both domestically and internationally.

Monday Night Football was another brilliant innovation designed to heighten the impact of football on television. The brainchild of ABC's Roone ARLEDGE, the Monday night game was geared to a family audience, rather than the more male-dominated Sunday games. It began life in 1970 and continued to command impressive ratings for the next three decades.

NFL Commissioner Pete Rozelle is credited with negotiating the landmark five-year, \$2.1 billion contract with television's three major networks in 1982. Rozelle then expanded to cable, establishing a Sunday night series with the ESPN network in 1986. Rozelle steered the NFL through periods of often severe industrial unrest with player STRIKES over salaries and conditions in 1974, 1982 and 1987 which disrupted league schedules.

One of the features of the NFL's success is its robust defense of its relationship with television. It has been protective in the extreme. In 1983, for example, a rival league, the United States Football League (USFL), began a spring schedule which did not clash with the August–January season of the NFL. While its television ratings were not nearly as impressive as the NFL's and it appeared to be no challenge, the NFL made concerted efforts to ensure its modest success was short-lived; the USFL folded within three years. The lucrative liaison enjoyed by the NFL with network television continued unabated into the 1990s, with each contract surpassing its predecessors by some margin. For example, the broadcasting rights package sold to the ABC, CBS and Fox networks in 1998 was worth \$2.2 billion (£1.38 billion) a year, twice as much as the previous package. The price was too heavy for NBC, which had broadcast the NFL since 1965 (before the merger).

Of related interest

Neft, David, Johnson, Roland and Cohen, Richard (1974) *The Sports Encyclopaedia: Pro Football*, Gross & Dunlap.
Roberts, Randy and Olsen, James (1989) *Winning Is the Only Thing: Sports in America Since 1945*, Johns Hopkins University Press.
Schwartz, Donna (1997) *Contesting the Super Bowl*, Routledge.

Nike

The ubiquitous brand

By the mid-1990s, Nike had become one of the world's most recognized brands alongside Coca-Cola, Disney and McDonald's. Starting in 1964 as a sports shoes outlet, the company grew to the market leader in footwear and apparel before diversifying into a range of activities, including sports event promotion. Owned by Phil Knight, who headed operations at the purpose-built headquarters at Beaverton, Oregon, Nike became virtually synonymous with worldclass sport; so much so that it became automatically associated with every major event. As if to emphasize this, a survey to test public awareness of the sponsors of the Atlanta summer Olympics revealed a high awareness of Nike – despite the fact that Nike was not among the sponsors. The name *Nike* comes from the winged Greek goddess of victory who sat beside Zeus at the pantheon in Olympus and was the inspirational figure behind Greek military victories.

So confident was Nike of its own recognizability that it ran TELEVISION commercials without even mentioning its own name, using just the checkmark logo known as the Swoosh. This was originally the name used for the fiber in the first nylon athletic shoe designed by Carolyn Davidson in 1971, and was said to be a graphic representation of one of Nike's wings.

Nike's ubiquitous status in the athletic shoe and sportswear market was based on what marketers call *referent power*: the effective marketing of particular sports ICONS and linking the identity and characteristics of the icon to the product. Richard Donohue, President of Nike, once said: "We really start with authentic athletes, with prestige icon athletes, and we drive down from that pinnacle of the pyramid."

As part of its strategy, Nike has often positioned itself as an iconoclast of the governing bodies of world sport. Donald Katz (1994) writes of Nike's "anti-bureaucratic and anti-authorisational streaks," which clearly manifest themselves in Nike's relationship with governing bodies. Most noticeably, Nike avoid paying to become official sponsors of such events as the Olympics. Nike was known to be an ambush marketer and ran highly visible advertising campaigns *around* world sporting events intended to create a tie with the consumer. As Knight put it: "we actually like the kind of publicity that pits us against the establishment."

Knight's project

Knight was a competent middle distance runner at the University of Oregon who was coached by Bill Bowerman, who later became head coach to the US Olympic team in Munich 1972. Knight graduated in 1959 and decided to go to Harvard Business School, where Nike was originally conceived out of a paper and seminar he delivered in a business and entrepreneurship class.

Bowerman often designed and produced innovative footwear with the provision that "shoes should be light and go the distance". He believed that light, well-made athletic shoes could improve athletic performance. His shoes were on average 2oz lighter than the then market leader Adidas's shoes, since he used nylon mesh instead of the traditional leather. However, Bowerman was never able to attract a manufacturer to mass produce designs to his specifications.

Knight had a fascination with Japanese culture, and believed an opportunity existed to import Japanese manufactured shoes made with cheap labor into the United States and undercut the German companies Adidas and Puma, which then dominated the athletic shoe market. He had noticed how Japanese technology particularly in camera manufacture was increasingly becoming evident in the United States. On a visit to Japan in late 1962, Knight observed counterfeit Adidas shoes being manufactured and sold. Adidas had failed to protect its three stripe logo internationally, and copies were being made by the Onitsuka Co. Ltd. (Asics Tiger), under the brand name Tiger. Ever the opportunist, Knight visited the company in the seaport of Kobe and presented himself as an athletic shoe importer and distributor whose fictitious company's name, made up in haste, was known as Blue Ribbon Sports, or just BRS.

Knight was shown a number of new samples about to be manufactured and he noticed their superior quality over traditional athletic footwear. These shoes were made of leather as opposed to the usual canvas material. Onitsuka was enthusiastic at the opportunity to sell athletic shoes through distributors who had a particular interest in specific sports. Knight chose Onitsuka over the more established Mizuno brand.

In early 1964, both Knight and Bowerman each contributed $500 (£300) and with a handshake, Blue Ribbon Sports became a reality. Bowerman offered his assistance in endorsing the shoes with the athletes he coached and the extensive network of coaches he knew. Knight would handle the financial side of the business. In February, Knight placed his first order, which amounted to $1,107 supported by a letter of credit from the First National Bank. Onitsuka gave Blue Ribbon Sports the rights to sell Tigers in thirteen Western States, with the rights due to expire in November 1965.

Selling athletic shoes out of his father's basement, which was used as an office and a storeroom, and his car boot at track meets was the precursor to the Nike idea that their shoes were made *by* athletes *for* athletes. Adidas was the market leader, and the trademark Adidas trefoil was conspicuous at practically every major sporting event. Knight wrote to Onitsuka: "Adidas will not relinquish its number one position without a stiff fight."

By 1965, Blue Ribbon Sports had taken on it's first employee. Jeff Johnson a graduate student in anthropology, became the catalyst of ideas that catapulted the emerging company into imaginative advertising in running magazines, gaining the sole distribution rights for Tiger track shoes in the United States and Tiger logo T-shirts, which were originally distributed for free to race winners as a marketing strategy. In November 1966, BRS established its first retail outlet which made the company a mail order, retailer and wholesale specialist. When the original contract expired, turnover was $20,000 and profits were $3,240. Johnson was taken on full time in 1966. Knight himself began to work full time at BRS in 1969, when he signed a new contract with Onitsuka to distribute Tiger shoes until the end of 1972. By this time sales were in excess of $10 million. BRS was well-placed to cash in on the health craze born of the 1970s NARCISSISM.

Faced with Onitsuka's continued production problems, lack of product development and believing that BRS were about to lose its distribution rights or have their rights divided up when the current contract expired in 1972, Knight began in 1970 to look for alternative manufacturers. Onitsuka was seemingly communicating with other potential distributors of Tiger shoes. Such a move would have ended the ambitions of BRS. Onitsuka, aware that Knight had a $400,000 loan note to repay, used its position in an attempt to force Knight into accepting a merger. Knight had two options: either to accept Onitsuka's terms and give up control, or to find an alternative manufacturer and create a new brand and a trademark that was not subject to a contract. After considering "Bengal" and "Dimension Six" as potential names, Nike and the Swoosh logo and trademark was born.

Knight flew to Japan in 1971 to meet representatives of Nippon rubber (the most advanced shoe manufacturer in Japan) and ordered ten thousand pairs of Tiger Cortez, tennis, wrestling, basketball and casual shoes. On the boxes Knight had printed the now familiar: "Nike sport shoes are manufactured to the exact specifications of champion athletes throughout the world. Nike and the Swoosh name and stripe are your guarantee of quality." In January 1972, Onitsuka announced to the Japanese financial press that they were to merge with BRS.

Knight refuted this statement to his bankers, Nissho Iwai, and confirmed that Nike was going to be at the forefront of BRS's future plans while at the same time placating Onitsuka; shipments were still required to keep the company afloat whilst it was in transition.

The star endorsers

To endorse new tennis shoes, BRS paid tennis star Ilie Nastase $3,000. A temperamental player, he would become Nike's first venture into the use of sports stars to sell shoes. ENDORSEMENTS were to become a central marketing strategy of Nike. The Nike Cortez shoes were priced to undercut the near-identical Tiger shoes. Initially, the quality of the shoes was unpredictable and a high percentage of returns ensued. Shipments were sporadic, so much so that a delivery had to be airlifted to meet the growing demand. With inventories very small, Onitsuka cut BRS's supply of original Tiger shoes, an action which was to lead to court proceedings.

As the supply of shoes dwindled, the opportunity to market Nike shoes fortuitously arrived. The US Olympic trials were held in Eugene, Oregon. Bowerman was named head coach to the Olympic team and Nike representatives, many of them former athletes, worked to put Swooshes on the athletes' feet and to give away Nike logo T-shirts.

In 1969, Steve Prefontaine, an athlete described by *Sports Illustrated* as "America's distance prodigy" went to the University of Oregon and fell under the auspices of Bill Bowerman. Though he narrowly missed a medal at the Munich summer Olympics in 1972, he embodied the type of rock 'n' roll attitude and spirit the Nike brand required. When Prefontaine graduated and his scholarship expired, it was left to Nike to subsidize his training to the tune of $5,000. His death in a road accident in 1975 led to his immortalization as a "Nike guy," a term that Knight was to invoke many times over the following decades.

Bowerman experimented with a sole modeled on the grid of his wife's waffle iron. He felt that the square rubber spikes molded from the iron would make an excellent traction device for cross-country runners and football players especially on artificial surfaces. The development led to the Nike "Moon Shoe" and "Waffle" sole.

In 1977, Athletics West was established to nurture the talents of post-collegiate athletes. Athletics West allowed the financial support and recourse to sports science which was available to Eastern Bloc athletes. Although technically an infringement of The Athletic Congress's (TAC) amateur conventions, the club continued to support athletes and no athlete was ever suspended from competition because of their membership. In 1978, BRS changed its corporate name to Nike.

Frank Rudy is credited with developing the patented Air sole, which was originally evident in the Tailwind shoe. Design problems led to the return of half the manufactured stock. The idea was later rekindled in the Air Max, which included a visible air compartment, in 1987. In 1985 Nike, in a period of transition and difficulty stemming from a slowdown in the running market, signed the NBA player Michael JORDAN to a groundbreaking $2.5 million deal which included the Air Jordan line of basketball shoes and apparel and his own "Jump Man" logo. The Air Jordan proved to be the best-selling athletic endorsement in history and made over $130 million in its first year (to date, there has been a new line of Air Jordan shoes each year). The shoes were originally banned from the NBA. Nike countered with the advert "On October fifteenth, the NBA created a revolutionary basketball shoe. On October eighteenth, the NBA threw them out of the game. Fortunately the NBA can't keep you from wearing them."

Although Jordan was the most visible icon of the Nike endorsers, Nike has signed among others John McEnroe, Michael Johnson, Bo Jackson, Andre Agassi and Tiger WOODS. Each athlete was given an effective screen personality by Nike's advertising agents Wieden & Kennedy, which was intended to enhance the possibility of image transfer from the stars to the products they endorsed.

Response to criticisms

In the early 1990s, Nike, by then the market leader, attracted criticism from a number of sources. Jesse Jackson tackled Knight over his poor record of equal opportunity. Despite using African Americans to endorse Nike products and selling to African American youths, the Beaverton headquarters did not have many black senior level managers. Knight rode out a threatened boycott and promised to review his equal opportunity program.

Further criticism was leveled at Nike's labor practices of its subcontractors in East Asia. Investigators exposed the menial wages Nike paid to workers in developing countries, and compared these to the retail prices of its products in the West. To counter this, Nike and other sporting goods companies drew up a Memorandum of Understanding as a code of practice. Nike formed NEAT (Nike Environmental Action Team) in 1993: this was a tactic to appease environmentalist critics by encouraging the recycling of worn shoes and creating inner city playgrounds and sports areas. PLAY (Participate in the Lives of American Youth) was launched in 1994 with Michael Jordan and Jackie Joyner-Kersee as figureheads: this was aimed at reclaiming public spaces for youth.

Nike advanced its relationship with athletes further than just endorsements. Charlotte Hornets basketball player Alonzo Mourning signed an arrangement for Nike to handle his entire career development. And, in perhaps his most outrageous deal, Knight in 1996 signed a $200m (£121m) deal with the Brazilian National Soccer Federation to exploit "exceptional commercial opportunities." The deal formed the core of Nike Sports Entertainment (NSE), the company's event management arm. NSE promoted and produced five Brazil exhibition games per year around the world as well as several other events featuring the company's roster of sports stars. It also promoted the first World Championship of Beach Volleyball. NSE seemed to herald the development of the worlds first sports and media conglomerate: the inclusion of the word "entertainment" revealed something of Knight's ambitions.

In sporting terms, the 1990s belonged to Nike: it demonstrated how to use commodities to penetrate popular culture. The irreverent brand persona was in tune with image-oriented youth who wore clothing in an effort to define status and identity. The notion that logos denote status and create identity and the late twentieth century's fascination with consumption is said to offer the individual a sense of empowerment. Faced with a diverse and dispersed population around the world, Nike delivered a product loaded with the kinds of values that would be recognizable to young people, whether in Hong Kong, Croatia or Colorado.

GLOBALIZATION, for Nike, would have meant a single homogeneous world consumption culture based on sports rather than ephemeral fashion. As Phil Knight observed (quoted in Katz 1994), sport "is the culture of the United States ... before long, it will define the culture of the whole world."

Of related interest

Halberstam, David (1999) *Playing for Keeps: Michael Jordan and the World He Made*, Random House.
Katz, D. (1994) *Just Do It: The Nike Spirit in the Corporate World*, Random House.
Strasser, J.B. and Becklund, L. *Swoosh: The Unauthorised Story of Nike and the Men Who Played There*, HarperBusiness.

ERWIN BENGRY

nobbling

To "nobble" means to tamper with a racehorse to prevent its winning. The word probably derives from the old English slang "nob" or "knob," which is to hit or knock over the head, usually with a stick (or even the Afrikaner term *knopkierie*, a short stick with a knobbed head used as a weapon). In sports, it refers to dishonestly attempting to obtain money by slowing down a horse. Horse-racing has attracted many forms of CORRUPTION, but nobbling has historically been the most popular.

The horse must be a favorite or at least strongly fancied to win: by implication, other horses would have longer odds. When a favored horse is nobbled, it is certain to lose and the potential for profit becomes significant, with two possibilities available to those with inside knowledge. The first is obvious: back all the remaining runners with any chance of winning. The second is to approach a bookmaker who can offer the nobbled horse at better odds than rival bookies to attract as much backing for it as possible. When the horse is beaten, the knowing bookie keeps the money.

British racecourse history is full of stories, many of them apocryphal, of nobbling. In 1811, for example, Daniel Dawson, a stable lad at Newmarket, was found to have poured arsenic into the water trough used by three of his own horses. Bookmakers who had laid big bets against all three had paid Dawson simply to incapacitate them, but he measured the amounts of arsenic incorrectly and the horses died. To attempt to defile the Sport of Kings was a heinous offense in early nineteenth-century England, and Dawson was hanged on Newmarket Heath in front of a massed gathering of 15,000 people.

While nobbling does not exclude cruder and more obvious ways of slowing down the horse, by far the most popular and effective method involves some sort of dope. At the end of the nineteenth century, a group of American owners and gamblers used cocaine to great effect by purchasing poor horses and administering a dose of the drug before placing wagers on them. While, strictly speaking, this was not nobbling because it was intended to enhance the horses' performances, it paved the way for the use of other substances whose effects would not be so conspicuous. The Jockey Club of the day had no rules to forbid the use of such substances. This prompted George Lambton, a leading trainer, to give cocaine to five of his horses; four won and the fifth finished second. Convinced by the demonstration, the Jockey Club imposed bans on doping, although a betting syndicate whose members were aware of cocaine's potency won an estimated $2 million before the ban became operational.

In 1961, the ante-post favorite for the DERBY race was Pinturischio. The horse's trainer believed the colt to be his finest ever and a certainty to win the big race. But the horse was nobbled and could hardly stand, far less race. Another hot favorite, Gorytus, finished last in a 1983 race, prompting suspicions that it had been nobbled. The horse seemed to have been irreparably damaged by particularly powerful dope, and never raced again. In 1990, the unbeaten Bravefoot was nobbled and lost.

Perhaps the biggest nobbling case in recent times came in 1998 when four men, three of them professional jockeys, were arrested in the south of England following a police investigation into two races in March 1997 in which horses were found to be nobbled and a number of other races were thought to have been manipulated. In two of the races, strongly favored horses were doped with Acetylpromazine (ACP), a mild but fast-acting tranquilizer, and performed way below expectations. One of the horses, Lively Knight, started at 1–7 for a two-horse steeplechase and finished second.

During the 1990s, ACP became the drug of choice for nobblers. Veterinarians used the tranquilizer to sedate horses on occasions such as when it was being examined or having its coat clipped. It was an available and freely used drug administered easily by nasal spray or tablet. It was also convenient to conceal. Its effects are variable: some horses remain alert while others become drowsy almost immediately. For some horses, the consequences of the drug can be ruinous, as in the case of Lively Knight and Avanti Express, another horse believed to have been nobbled in 1990.

ACP is at its most effective about an hour after its administration, so the nobbler must obtain access to the horse at the track. While security tightened considerably after the 1990 cases, it is probable that attempts to prevent nobbling will always prove futile. The practice is as old as the sport itself.

Of related interest

Crist, S. (1982) "Was justice served?" *Thoroughbred Record* vol 216, no 25.
Nack, W. and Munson, L. (1992) "Blood money," *Sports Illustrated* vol 77, no 21.

Vamplew, Wray (1988) "Odds against: The punter's lot is not a happy one," *Sporting Traditions* vol 5, no 1.

North Dallas Forty

In the 1970s, books such as Jack Scott's *The Athletic Revolution* (Free Press, 1971) disclosed aspects of professional sports that sat very uncomfortably with the media-generated images. While the public was being served a picture of sports as populated by young, healthy, often high-minded people with their sights set on achievement, Scott's book in particular conveyed a much seedier version: drugs, unbridled machismo and player exploitation were, he argued, the hallmarks of professional sport.

Consistent with this view was Ted Kotcheff's film *North Dallas Forty*, based on former Dallas Cowboys wide receiver Pete Gents's detailed account of pressure and partying. In the movie, Nick Nolte plays a hard-bitten, pragmatic American football player whose youthful aspirations have been replaced by a purely instrumental attitude. He wakes every morning aching from head to toe from injuries that have never had time to heal. The only way he can make it to the training field is by swallowing a cocktail of painkilling DRUGS. When he arrives, he welcomes a battery of analgesic shots that all but anaesthetize his body.

Nolte is a "seen it all, done it all" pro: he knows the rather narrow limits of his ability, but equally knows that he can perform a useful job for the club. For him, playing football is as meaningless as a day at the factory. Indeed, Kotcheff leaves the viewer with the impression that his fictional football club operates very much *as* a factory. The management is openly exploitative in its relationship with all but the star players. Nolte has an almost self-destructive disregard for his own body: he smokes dope seemingly in every waking moment away from the playing field, drinks alcohol and seems hell-bent on dissipation. His only concessions to fitness are made because he has no other way of earning a living.

Many of the movie's most interesting scenes involve a young, idealistic player who refuses to take painkillers because he feels he may exacerbate an injury. He dismisses the advice of more experienced colleagues, all of whom carry some sort of injury. Gradually, his grander aims recede: he realizes that a prolonged spell on the disabled list will do his career no good, especially as he is under pressure from management to take the shots and play. Toward the end of the film, he relents and troops out with the rest of the walking wounded.

Today, much of the film's impact is dissipated by the frequent revelations of competitors' drug use, SEX CRIMES and other forms of deviant behavior. *North Dallas Forty* would tell most sports fans only what they already know. But in the late 1970s, idealistic conceptions of sport were just about holding their credibility, and the values sport was thought to embody were not yet totally undermined by the infusions of cash; although, of course, TELEVISION money was paving the way for the era of the multimillionaire athlete. It is interesting to compare *North Dallas Forty* with *CHARIOTS OF FIRE*, which depicts a different sport in a different context in a period when ruthless competition was creeping in but before professionalism had completely taken over.

Of related interest

Ardolino, F. (1987) "Sex violence and castrated cowboys in *North Dallas Forty*," *Arete* 2.

North Dallas Forty, directed by Ted Kotcheff, 1979.

Umphlett, Wiley Lee "*North Dallas Forty* and the tradition of the American sporting hero," in Umphlett, Wiley Lee (ed.), *American Sport Culture: The Humanistic Dimensions*, Bucknell University Press.

P

parenthood

The sports parent

"In the organization of every sport to which young people are initiated there is a special breed of person," writes Dorcas Susan Butt in her early text *Psychology of Sport* (1976). "This is the sports parent, more commonly known as the 'baseball father,' or 'the tennis mother,' who pushes the child onward in the sport." Butt questions the value of parents who go to great lengths to encourage their children. Many parents are prepared to sacrifice their own interests in order to further those of their children; but, according to Butt, the sports parent's concern to maximize the performance of his or her child does the child a "disservice."

There are countless children who have suffered because of the competitive urgings of parents, many of whom have displaced their own sporting ambitions onto their offspring. Perhaps frustrated at lack of opportunity or an untimely injury that ruined a promising career, a parent may transpose his or her ambitions onto children. Or, they may just push the child towards goals that their ability does not equip them to achieve.

Great advantages are conferred on the child: coaching, equipment and other facilities are provided by enthusiastic parents. Yet, Butt argues that the child "cannot psychologically accept the advantages extended to him because of favoritism." She marshals the support of David McClelland (*The Achieving Society*, Van Nostrand, 1961) and Robert Sears *et al.*, who in the 1960s studied children who were asked to perform tasks in front of tense and demanding parents. The children performed less well than those who had tried to complete the same tasks in the presence of relaxed and jokey parents. The studies also indicated that, in the longer term, children of less demanding parents grew more confident, honest and mature (Sears, R., Rau, L. and Alpert, R. *Identification and Child Training*, Stanford University Press, 1965).

High-achieving parents

There is, of course, abundant evidence of children who have profited handsomely from the coaxing of parents, especially fathers, who have had successful sports careers. English soccer star Jamie Redknapp's father Harry was himself a decent class player (and, later, club manager). Ken Norton, Jr.'s father Ken was of course a heavyweight champion, best known for his three fights with Muhammad ALI.

Having a parent, or two parents, with sporting accomplishments provides the child with evidence, however insubstantial, that someone like him or her is capable of achieving in sports. The parent may then function, unwittingly perhaps, as a role model. The psychologist Albert Bandura, best known for his *Social Learning Theory* (Prentice-Hall 1977), argued that we copy, or model, the behavior of significant others. These are figures who are important to us for a variety of reasons, including their status, authority and the care they take over us. Parents fall into this category, and a child will learn from sheer observation of them. We all acquire characteristics from our parents, ranging from mannerisms to moral qualities, and also including career paths.

The implications for children of professional athletes are manifold. Observing that a parent earns his or her living from sports inclines the child toward a sports career, even if only for a period during adolescence. Showing an aptitude, the child may seek the counsel of a supportive parent who will encourage them in their ambitions. A successful career can ensue if the parent retains enough distance to allow the prodigy to bale out at any stage.

On the other hand, there are sons who have suffered seemingly because of their parent's inflated ambitions. Joe Frazier was another heavyweight champion of Norton's era who groomed his son Marvis for a boxing career, even to the point of coaching his son to fight in a style closely resembling his own. Possessed of none of his father's renowned power or durability, Marvis had a disappointing and unfulfilling sports career which ended in punishing defeats.

Fathers who have been successful boxers often discourage their children from active boxing career (for fear of injury), yet many sons of boxers pursue their father's sport. One of the reasons they rarely repeat their father's success is that they are driven by a different set of motivations. The father may have pursued his sport because of lack of viable alternatives; in other words, he became a "hungry fighter." Motivationally, no amount of parental coaching or encouragement can make up for a lack of raw desire for success.

This is especially damaging for young athletes desperately trying to duplicate their parent's success and aware of the high expectations on them. Defeat is less easily assimilable for them than their peers who are under less pressure to excel. In a sense, the latter are unfettered by the anticipation of success that as often constricts as releases aspirant sports stars.

While there are several examples of sons following in fathers' footsteps, examples of daughters are not always so apparent. A study in the early 1990s found that parental sports involvement was associated with sports participation for young women. The study also found that women who participated in sports often had "masculine behavioral attributes" ("Sport participation in middle childhood – association with styles of play and parental participation," by A. Colley, E. Eglinton and E. Elliott, *International Journal of Sport Psychology* vol 23, no 3, 1992).

Constructive or destructive?

Robert Griffin's book *Sports in the Lives of Children and Adolescents: Success on the Field and in Life* (1998) was written in response to a letter from a father who asked Griffin, a professor at the University of Vermont, to advise as to whether he should go against the wishes of his wife and encourage their daughter to participate in sports. Griffin's reply is part academic analysis, part "how to" manual.

Among his many conclusions is that the adage about sports building character has no empirical foundation (no matter how one defines "character") and that, in some circumstances, involvement can lead to an unhealthy compulsion that actually inhibits the growth of maturity often associated with "character." Griffin also observes how much contemporary sport is suffused with a "self-centeredness." He writes: "Parents will have to watch how much sports encourages a philosophy that rationalizes winning at any cost, cheating, and aggression to get what you want as long as you can get away with it." Sports culture today is distinguished by "excessive commercialization, violence, autocracy, the use of DRUGS" and a variety of other features that should at least make parents think twice about encouraging their children.

While there are examples of young black athletes who have been inspired by parents and who have had sports careers, the weight of evidence suggests that ethnic minorities are discouraged by parents. There is evidence that African American youths do not receive parental support in their athletic efforts, but respond positively to the encouragement of friends, coaches and especially teachers ("Race, Sport and social support," O. Harris, *Sociology of Sport Journal* vol 11, no 1, 1994). My own British study in the 1980s (*Black Sportsmen*, Routledge & Kegan Paul, 1982), and that of Gajendra Verma and Douglas Darby in the 1990s (*Winner and Losers*, Falmer, 1994) record a pattern that cuts across different ethnic minority groups: parents do not typically regard sports as a legitimate career. They either discourage children from pursuing sports for a living, or remain neutral about their prospects. Yet, the success of African Americans and African Caribbeans in sports is disproportionate to their size in the total populations of the USA and Britain, and attests to either the insignificance of having pushy parents, or the positive benefit of not having them.

Exceptions are often dramatic. The movie *HOOP DREAMS* conveys a sort of achievement by proxy in which the promising basketball player becomes the unwitting recipient of his family members' dashed aspirations. This can be a pernicious displacement of ambition in which the young competitor is freighted with unreasonably high expectations of success. As we have seen, Butt was critical about any parent, of whatever ethnic origin, who burdened their children in this way. Of course, when a black player from a pushy family achieves spectacularly, thoughts of the many others who fail recede; witness the rapturous acclaim for Tiger WOODS.

Typically, ethnic minority sports performers come from lower classes. Griffin notes that fewer parents from higher socioeconomic brackets saddle their children with high ambitions than parents from lower brackets. Given the indifference of many ethnic minority group parents to sport, we can presume Griffin refers to white families. He encourages them to familiarize themselves with their children's chances of success: the odds of a high school athlete making it to the NFL are 6,318 to 1; to the NBA, 10,345 to 1; and to MAJOR LEAGUE BASEBALL, 7,325 to 1. Despite this, Griffin approves of parents who encourage young children to participate in sports, though with a great many qualifications, the main one of which is that "the choice must be the child's." In fact, Griffin believes that parents who fail to nurture their children's interest in sport are errant in their parenting duties.

Of related interest

Butt, Dorcas Susan (1976) *Psychology of Sport: The Behavior, Motivation, Personality and Performance of Athletes*, Van Nostrand Reinhold.

Griffin, Robert S. (1998) *Sports in the Lives of Children and Adolescents: Success on the Field and in Life*, Praeger.

Wolff, Rick (1997) *Good Sports: A Concerned Parent's Guide to Competitive Youth Sports*, 2nd edn, Sagamore.

paternity

In May 1998, *Sports Illustrated* carried a cover story that argued that a disproportionate number of professional athletes were the subjects of paternity suits and several others, who had never been involved in civil litigation, were fathers of illegitimate children. It listed an NBA "All-Paternity" team of basketball players who had fathered children out of wedlock; it included Latrell Sprewell, who had three children by three women before he turned 21.

The efflorescence of fatherhood was not restricted to basketball players. The article, "Paternity ward," by Grant Wahl and L. Jon Wertheim (1998), went on to name baseball players, boxers, football players, hockey players and other professional sportsmen who paid support for children. Nine out of ten paternity cases involving high-profile athletes are settled quietly before they become a matter of public record, the article suggested.

In the absence of evidence, we must speculate on the reasons for the high number of paternity suits involving pro sports stars. A number of them are baseless and fail to stand up in court. Former NBA All-Star Jeff Malone, for example, was the subject of a paternity suit filed by a one-time college lover. He submitted to genetic tests to prove that he was not the father of the woman's child, and eventually needed to recruit NBA security to prevent the woman from harassing him. Today, professional sports performers are highly paid and, in some ways, are targets for such actions.

The substance of the report was that a large number of athletes either succumb to the charms of sports groupies or involve themselves in sexual relationships that result in children and then absolve themselves of responsibility – or, at least, try to. The result is what Wahl and Wertheim describe as a "staggering" number of illegitimate children fathered by sports stars who find themselves subjected to paternity suits.

The incidence of illegitimate births and subsequent legal actions involving sportsmen is full of possibilities for the student of sports culture. Interestingly, there has been no academic research on the subject. Yet it still presents us with an example of several aspects of sports culture. The phenomenon is not intrinsic to any game: its consequences are felt far beyond the basketball court or football field, and it exists outside the public purview.

Some might discount the idea that this is a sports issue at all; or at least only in the sense, that there are a disproportionately high number of black athletes in some sports, particularly basketball and football. Black males in the USA and, for that matter, in Britain account for a inordinate number of illegitimate children relative to their numbers in the total populations of both societies. The statistics (were they available) in sport would simply reflect the pattern in culture at large, according to this view. So, it is a simple statistical phenomenon, with sport replicating the rest of society. However, other perspectives would suggest that there is something singular about the culture of sports that promotes behavior that in turn results in pregnancies and civil cases. For example, received wisdom has it that sportsmen are more sexually active than most males, the exception being rock stars whose affections are pursued by promiscuous groupies. The various biographical and anecdotal accounts of athletes support this. From Wilt Chamberlain's seemingly superhuman conquests to Magic JOHNSON's boasts, sports stars have enjoyed the reputation of sexual as well as sporting athletes. The stories may or may not be true: there is no secret about the fact that sex sells and respectable publishers as well as tabloids no doubt encourage some hyperbole in the biographies of sports performers. But, even accepting an element of exaggeration, it is certainly possible that well-known sports performers have become sought-after people and that they attract a ready supply of available women.

Sports stars have not suddenly become desirable to some young women, of course. Babe Ruth used to brag about his sexual adventures in the 1920s. He was a genuine celebrity in an age when baseball players were notoriously exploited. In 1927, Ruth's salary was $70,000, when the median salary on the highest-paid Yankees team was barely a tenth of that amount. In the 1960s, the exploits of American football player Joe Namath earned him the nickname "Broadway Joe." An acclaimed libertine, Namath had an adoring FANDOM that afforded him a status comparable with musicians and movie stars. The British equivalent was the Manchester United soccer player George Best, a boulevardier of considerable repute.

Today, virtually every male sports professional (and many college athletes) enjoys celebrity standing. Cultural changes have ensured that athletes are frequently rich, often famous and have lifestyles to match. The changes involve the mass media, especially TELEVISION, the marketing strategies used to promote sports, the general process by which sports have been transformed into high-priced commodities and the increasing importance of agents in handling the affairs of their clients. The newfound glamour, visibility and money possessed by athletes has no doubt increased their value as trophies for the sports equivalent of groupies, and it is at least possible that some have approached the athletes in anticipation that a quick out of court settlement will ensue. The *Sports Illustrated* article estimates that 90 per cent of athlete-related paternity cases are settled and hushed up. Image is integral to sportsmen's market appeal. So, changes in the culture surrounding sports has fostered an environment in which conspicuously successful male sports performers have become valued sex partners, albeit short-term partners. Their earnings and public profile has made it probable that women whom they may or may not have made pregnant can pursue their cases with a reasonable chance of having a cash settlement or support payments.

Also feeding into the equation are cultural factors inside sports. Sports are traditionally male pursuits: historically, they have been used as proving grounds for young men, ways of establishing sexual identity and the dominance it typically entails. Competitive sports have had the effect of demarcating MASCULINITIES/FEMININITIES. Women have, of course, made a deep impact on contemporary sports, and this has made it more imperative that men emphasize their physical masculinity. Women play basketball at a decent level, likewise soccer, tennis, track and field, and even boxing. Perhaps the self-evident superiority of men in sports has come under such threat that men have sought proving grounds elsewhere, like in the bedroom. Here, the physical prowess they demonstrate in competitive play can be translated into sexual prowess. In fact, the latter may compensate crudely for the former.

No one doubts that there is something immature about taking advantage of every sexual opportunity to reinforce one's own sense of masculinity or to prove to others one's virility. But, being a competitive sports performer frequently involves being infantilized. Most successful professional athletes have transferred seamlessly from high school to college to professional club. Their frames of reference are tightly defined by the organization in which they operate. Team players are taught the value, indeed, the necessity of discipline, of subordinating one's own interests and preferences to those of the team. Coaches, managers and other authority figures must wield an unquestioned authority. All this is facilitated by ensuring that players do not grow up, by locking them into a subculture where the norms of obedience and respect for authority prevail. The preponderance of alcoholism, recreational drug use and VIOLENCE on women may all be explained in part by the attempt to forestall the maturational process.

Sports-related paternity is not just about individual athletes getting single women pregnant. It incorporates a compound of cultural issues, including questions of race and ethnicity, masculinity, commodification and money.

Of related interest

Lapchick, Richard (ed.) (1996) *Sport in Society: Equal Opportunity or Business as Usual?*, Sage.

Messner, Michael and Sabo, Donald (eds) (1990) *Sports, Men and the Gender Order*, Human Kinetics.

Wahl, Grant and Wertheim, John (1998) "Paternity ward," *Sports Illustrated* vol 88, no 18.

politics

Political groups have found major international sports events an attractive means of expressing interests. The series of government led boycotts over the issues of apartheid and Cold War rivalry that affected the Olympic Games from the mid-1960s to the mid-1980s illustrate sport's political utility. However, not all sports politics depend on government action. The 1968 Olympic Games, for example, provided an opportunity for two black American athletes to protest against the continuation of discrimination in their home country. In 1994, six Catholics were killed by Unionist terrorists while they watched Ireland play Italy in a soccer World Cup match at a local bar in Loughinisland, Northern Ireland. The campaign by Sydney to host the 2000 Olympic Games provided an opportunity for aboriginal groups to draw attention to their marginalization in Australian society. In the 1990s, a campaign was launched to achieve greater gender equality at international track and field competitions. The association between politics and sport is now firmly established and, as can be seen, is highly varied.

One difficulty in understanding the relationship between politics and sport is the ambiguity of the concept of politics. For many, politics is best defined narrowly as essentially the activities of governments, while others prefer a broader definition which suggests that politics is present wherever and whenever there is conflict about goals and the means of achieving them, and is consequently to be found in a much wider range of organizations and settings including sports bodies.

There is little to be gained by attempting to engineer a consensus from these competing conceptualizations of politics. Rather, it is important to acknowledge the variety of definitions and the tensions that exist between them. For present purposes, a distinction will be made between politics *and* sport, and politics *in* sport. The study of politics *and* sport directs our attention to the use made by governments of sport. The study of politics *and* sport is therefore concerned largely with an examination of the relationship of politics to sport in the public domain defined by recognized institutions of the state. A focus on the politics *in* sport leads to a consideration of issues concerned with the way in which organizations use power to pursue their own sectional interests at the expense of other social groups. Issues of gender equity, racial discrimination and class advantage would all be legitimate focuses for examination.

Politics and sport

One of the earliest examples of government intervention in sport was the prohibition of particular sports such as some mainly urban and working-class BLOOD SPORTS; for example, bull-baiting and bear-baiting. Both Britain and the

United States have legislated to outlaw certain blood sports, and in Sweden boxing has also been made illegal. A second common motive for governmental intervention is to improve military preparedness. Canada, Britain and France all used legislation in the 1930s or early 1940s to create opportunities for physical training and fitness, while more recently in the former Soviet Union, the GTO (Ready for Labor and Defense) scheme provided a framework for sports development for most of the Soviet period and contained shooting as one of the set range of sports.

A third motive for state involvement in sport is the belief that participation in sport facilitates social integration/control. In Britain, successive governments invested in sports facilities and programs as a solution to urban unrest, and in Northern Ireland there was an extensive program of investment in public sport and recreational facilities aimed at bridging the gap between the nationalist and unionist communities. In France, sport was seen as making a contribution to social discipline and controlling the behavior of French youth, while in post-Maoist China sport was seen as a force for developing the virtues of unity and mutual effort. Sport has also been used routinely by governments to aid the development of a sense of national identity (see NATIONALISM).

Closely related to the use of sport for nation-building was the use of international sport to project a positive image of the nation abroad. Success in sports events, and particularly the hosting of sports events, provide a benign and uncritical backdrop for the parade of national achievement. The intensive investment in recent years by Britain, France, Hong Kong and Australia in elite programs and specialist academies confirms the continuing attractiveness of international sporting success.

A more recent motive for government involvement is to support economic development whether in the form of hosting major events such as the World Cup or in developing sports that help to promote tourism. In Ireland, for example, the government has invested heavily in the provision of opportunities for golf, fishing and long-distance walking routes, following tourist board surveys which found that one-third of all tourists participated in sport when on holiday and that the availability of sports opportunities influenced their holiday choice.

Finally, governments have found sport to be a highly versatile tool of diplomacy. The Americans used a boycott of the 1980 Olympic Games in Moscow as a way of showing displeasure at the Soviet invasion of Afghanistan. Just as sport can be used as a vehicle for registering disapproval, it can also be an effective vehicle for signaling the re-admission of a state to the "international community." The hosting of the 1964 Olympic Games by Tokyo marked Japan's return to diplomatic respectability and the visit by the South African cricket team to India in November 1991 and the attendance of a South African team at the Barcelona Olympic Games in 1992 confirmed the establishment of a non-racial South Africa. International sport has also been used as a means of improving relations with previously hostile states, most notably when an American table tennis team visited China in the early 1970s and helped to pave the way for Nixon's meeting with Mao Zedong in 1972.

A further use of sports diplomacy has been to maintain good relations with one's allies and with neighboring states. The Commonwealth Games and the quadrennial Francophone Games are both examples of the former, while the extensive program of bilateral sporting contacts between the Soviet Union and its Warsaw Pact neighbors was an example of the latter. The willingness of governments to utilize sports diplomacy should not be interpreted as clear evidence of its effectiveness; it may simply be a reflection of the high visibility and low cost of the resource and the lack of viable alternative diplomatic responses. Although it is not impossible for governments to intervene in sport because of a concern to support an intrinsically worthwhile activity most governmental involvement has been motivated by an instrumental attitude towards sport where sport is a convenient means to an end whether that end is diplomatic, social welfare, economic or military.

Politics in sport

By contrast to the politics of sport, where the focus is on governmental action, politics *in* sport is concerned with the significance of sports organizations in affecting access to, and the nature of, sports opportunities for individual sportsmen and women or of groups which may be defined, for example, geographically, or by sport or gender. Among the issues which currently dominate the character of politics *in* sport are commercialization, gender, and RACISM and ethnicity. None of these issues is discrete, each overlaps and intertwines with the other, and each has both a domestic and a global political aspect.

Commercialization involves examining sport as both a source of profit and also as a vehicle for the transmission of capitalist values. In addition to sports goods manufacturers, such as NIKE and Adidas, that have a clear interest in the growth in interest in the particular sports they manufacture for there is a growing number of multinational-national corporations for whom sport sponsorship is part of a global marketing strategy for non-sports goods and services. Major TELEVISION companies have a close interest in sports programs as products and also see sport as a means of selling advertising. In addition, all capitalist enterprises have an interest in the capacity of sport to contribute to the assimilation of capitalist values in general and consumerist values in particular and finally, there are the sports organizations, ranging from individual clubs and leagues to the IOC who operate in an increasingly competitive environment and are concerned to secure market growth for their particular club, sport or competitions.

A second major political issue in sport is the question of equality of access and especially the relationship between gender and race, and sporting opportunity. Both these aspects of sport are covered elsewhere in this book, and it is sufficient here to emphasize the extent to which both these dimensions of inequality are intensely political insofar as they can have a profound impact on individual choice and career opportunity. For both ethnic minorities and women there has been a general, if slow, improvement in opportunities for competition both in domestic leagues and at the highest international level. However, significant progress remains to be made in terms of access to coaching, administration and management in sport. The most significant gap, though, is the level of representation in those organizations that exercise increasing influence over the future shape and direction of sport, namely the television companies, corporate marketing units and sports goods manufacturing companies.

Of related interest

Allison, Lincoln (ed.) (1993) *The Changing Politics of Sport*, Manchester University Press.

Guttman, Allan (1992) *The Olympics: A History of the Modern Games*, University of Illinois Press.

Hargreaves, Jennifer A. (1994) *Sporting Females: Critical Issues in the History and Sociology of Women's Sport*, Routledge.

Wilson, J. (1994) *Playing by the Rules: Sport, Society and the State*, Wayne State University Press.

BARRIE HOULIHAN

Program 1425

Between 1960 and 1989, the former East Germany (then a communist state) pursued a policy in which about 10,000 young people were inducted in sports academies where they were trained, conditioned and supplied with copious amounts of performance-enhancing DRUGS. This operation enabled East Germany, or the German Democratic Republic (GDR) as it was known, to dominate women's swimming and field events and excel in several men's sports. State Program 1425, as it was called, was administered by Mandred Ewald. It has been described by sports journalist Paul Howard as "sport's answer to the Holocaust."

It was for long suspected that the remarkable athletic achievements of East German competitors were due, at least in part, to performance-enhancing drugs. After the end of the Cold War, a special team of prosecutors began sifting through the files of the Stasi secret police. The names implicated included those of administrators, coaches, doctors and physiotherapists. By the time of the trial in March 1998, it was concluded that at least 2,000 competitors had at some time taken performance-enhancing substances. Four swimming coaches and two doctors stood trial, accused of inflicting grievous bodily harm on athletes. The trial took place in a fortress-like courthouse in Moabit, Berlin, and was intended as only the start of a process that would eventually involve nearly 700 people who were in some way connected with the program.

The first group of accused had all worked for the swimming section of the prominent Sporting Club Dynamo, the Stasi's own club. One of the most important members of the club was Dieter Lindemann, who coached Franziska van Almswick. Rolf Gläser, another one of the accused, was working in Austria at the time he was charged. Indeed, only one of the four trainers accused of encouraging the use of drugs had failed to find a job in sports by the time trial started in March 1998.

The charge sheet named seventeen athletes whose health was adversely affected by the anabolic steroids they had been forced to take. The "vitamins," as they were sometimes called, had side effects that included liver damage, hormonal imbalances and mood changes. The investigators produced evidence of a total 350 athletes whose health was affected, including four fatalities.

Jerg Sievers was a swimmer who was found dead in a training pool. The official cause of death was given as influenza, though it was known that he had been given "vitamins" – which may have been Oral Thurinabol, an anabolic steroid – for several years before. At the age of 16, he was diagnosed as having an abnormally large heart and advised to give up sports. After taking the advice he was ostracized by his coach and former team-mates, so he continued to train.

Rica Reinisch, a three-times Olympic swimming gold medalist, denounced her former coaches, in particular Uwe Neumann who later secured employment at Leipzig. Some of the accused were actively coaching. For example, Bernd Henneberg was the coach of the Olympic champion Dagmar Hase, who had also coached swimming star Kristin Otto. The former doctor of 1997 TOUR DE FRANCE winner Jan Ullrich was also accused.

The trial was conducted against a background of sport's continuing policy against drug use. The 1998 World Swimming Championships at Perth had been preceded by the seizure of quantities of HUMAN GROWTH HORMONE from the luggage of a member of the Chinese team. The East German former star shotputter Heidi Krieger had undergone a sex change operation as a result of the dramatic hormonal consequences of steroid use; her disclosures led to suspicions that there were other TRANSSEXUALS in sport who were too embarrassed to admit that they had taken drugs to enhance their athletic performances.

As the investigations proceeded, reports emerged that a similar state-sponsored program had taken place in the former Czechoslovakia (later divided into the Czech Republic and Slovakia). It was also thought that Program 1425 was East Germany's response to what the nation considered to be the USA's use of academic environments as training facilities (through sports scholarships) and its less systematic but no less prevalent use of performance-enhancing drugs.

Of related interest

Howard, Paul (1998) "Time to swallow the bitterest pill," *Sunday Tribune* (Ireland), July 26.

ProServ

The sports agency ProServ was started in 1969 as a marketing division of a law firm in Washington, DC. Thirty years later it was still vying with Mark McCORMACK's International Management Group (IMG) for position as the world's leading sports agency.

Donald Dell was the captain of the US Davis Cup-winning teams of 1968 and 1969. His fellow team members included Arthur Ashe, Stan Smith (both Wimbledon champions) and Bob Lutz. A partner of the law firm Dell, Craighill, Fentress and Benton, Dell worked with Jack Kramer to establish the Association of Tennis Professionals (ATP) in 1972. Dell's company represented the ATP. Kramer, a Wimbledon winner in 1947, was an active entrepreneur in professional tennis: he founded the Kramer Pro Tour which featured players such as Pancho Gonzales, Ken Rosewall and Lew Hoad.

Shortly after the formation of the ATP, ninety affiliated players boycotted the Wimbledon tournament of 1973. The decision was not Kramer's but that of a committee, including Ashe and Smith, though Kramer was known for pressing for higher payments for tennis pros. Kramer's bullish approach may have had some effect on Dell. Certainly, the example of McCormack was not lost on him: McCormack had launched his IMG in the late 1950s, when the concept of a sports agency was unheard of. McCormack's role was to exploit the market potential of golf players, like Arnold Palmer, Jack Nicklaus and Gary Player, then premier players on the professional circuit but without the showbusiness connections that are essential to today's sports top sports figures.

Dell sought to duplicate McCormack's strategy, but with tennis players. He introduced them to sponsors, set up television deals and, generally, advanced their financial interests. Ashe and Smith were highly ranked players and gave Dell the purchase he needed to negotiate with corporations.

As one of the significant agencies of the day, ProServ was able both to represent the players and the financial backers of tournaments, a situation that today might be regarded as involving a conflict of interests. ProServ's staff grew from five people at its inception to fifty executives by 1983. The addition of David Falk in 1975 was an important step, as Falk diversified into college football, selecting promising players whom he would interest when they were drafted into the professionals.

In 1983, two of ProServ's original partners, Frank Craighill and Lee Fentress, broke away to form their own agency known as Advantage International, leaving Dell in control. Advantage's focus was narrower than that of ProServ: it chose exclusively to represent sports performers and eschew the promotion of competitions (thus removing the potential for conflicts of interest). As well as its ATP interests, Advantage's specialty became basketball players. Its rise was proportionate to that of the NBA, which went from strength to strength in the 1980s.

ProServ also spotted the growth potential of basketball and scouted Michael JORDAN when he was at North Carolina. Jordan wished to turn professional before graduating, and Dell was prepared to handle his career. ProServ's NBA portfolio came to include some of the best-known names in the sport, including Patrick Ewing and John Stockton, both among the league's highest earners; but it was Jordan whose ascent guaranteed that the agency rivaled McCormack's.

Falk was something of an architect, designing a complex structure of corporate links for Jordan: endorsements for the likes of McDonalds, Gatorade, Wheaties and so on positioned Jordan at the fore of every TELEVISION viewer's mind. And, while there had been media-friendly African American sports stars before, none had quite escaped the more traditional and, by implication, racist roles reserved for blacks. Jordan was anything but brutish or self-mocking: there was a certain dignity in his presentation (if indeed there can be dignity in endorsing a breakfast cereal). His unalloyed brilliance on court and avoidance of scandals off secured him a unique place among the late twentieth century's popular ICONS.

Falk masterminded what might be called the commodification of Jordan, the crucial phase of the process being Jordan's association with Phil Knight's NIKE. This was to prove a match made in heaven, and the company and the player assisted each other's advance to the forefront, Nike becoming the world leader in sports clothes and equipment and Jordan becoming the best-known sports performer in the world.

The precise conditions of Jordan's contract with ProServ were not clear, but typically the agency would be entitled to 4 per cent of a player's annual salary for his or her club and between 15 and 25 per cent of other commercial deals, including the lucrative endorsements. In the 1990s, Jordan's yearly earnings would ordinarily exceed $30 million (£18m). ProServ's annual billings would top $150m.

In 1997, ProServ, then valued at $15m, merged with another sports agency, Marquee, creating an organization with annual billings of about $400m. This was still less than half of IMG's estimated billings. The move was part of a more general realignment of agency powers (Advantage had previously been acquired by Interpublic, a large US advertising group). The market in sports agencies had changed dramatically since Dell's initiative in 1969, when there just two main rivals: by the year 2000, there were over 500 significant sports agencies. Some measure of the worth of this market can be gained by the $80 million that Falk received when he sold his own agency to Robert Sillerman's SFX Entertainment in 1998. The market value of US sports reached $152 billion (£94 billion) in 1995, making it the country's eleventh largest industry with two per cent of the GDP. In Europe, a similar ratio would have valued the sports market at $185 billion in 1997. Sports marketing as an industry in its own right was worth about $16 billion worldwide by the end of the millennium, with about 38 per cent of this in the USA.

Of related interest

Halberstam, David (1999) *Playing for Keeps: Michael Jordan and the World He Made*, Random House.

Naughton, Jim (1992) *Taking it to the Air: The Rise of Michael Jordan*, Time Warner.

Sheehan, Richard G. (1996) *Keeping Score: The Economics of Big-Time Sports*, Diamond Communications.

Protestant ethic, the

Evolution of the ethic

The design, form and spirit of contemporary sports has been significantly influenced by the Protestant ethic, which embodies a constellation of values, attitudes and behaviors including rational asceticism, goal orientation, constancy, thrift, individual achievement, work as a "calling" and time consciousness. The ethic evolved during the sixteenth-century Protestant Reformation within the social context of Calvinism. Central to its formation was the Calvinist doctrine of predestination, which created intense anxiety among individuals regarding their state of grace. In response, Calvinists began to interpret worldly success as a sign of salvation. The systematic application of the above virtues promoted the attainment of success in the world and thus served as means for reducing salvational anxiety.

Martin Luther's idea of a "calling" was amplified by the Calvinists to promote a strong commitment to vocation. This commitment and the mandate to reinvest the fruits of labor were important factors in the development of entrepreneurial capitalism. Adherence to this ethic promoted success among Protestant groups in the newly emerging capitalist economies of Europe and in the New World. The ethic also became an important factor in the secularization and rationalization of Western society, as elucidated in Max Weber's *The Protestant Ethic and the Spirit of Capitalism* (translated by Talcott Parsons, Scribners's, 1958).

The institutionalization of the work ethic

The secular Protestant ethic influenced both individual and institutional behaviors, shaping not only economic enterprises but a wide range of social and political institutions including government, education, the family, social welfare agencies, and the organization of work and leisure. The work ethic promoted human labor to a central position in the moral life of the individual, while it elevated the business entrepreneur to an exalted status. Laboring in one's chosen vocation was extolled in sermons and in popular literature (for example, the writings of Cotton Mather, Benjamin Franklin and Thomas Carlyle) as both a duty and vehicle for personal fulfillment.

The uses of leisure and the role of ludic activity remained problematic within the constraints of Protestantism. The English-speaking Calvinists, the Puritans, expressed discomfort with sensual pleasures and harbored a distrust of free time, while condemning idleness as an occasion for sin. Recreation, when it was not banned outright, was tolerated only to the extent that it offered refreshment prior to a return to work. Laudable recreation was to "be used for sauce but not for the meat," in Mather's words. The pragmatic view of Protestants toward the uses of leisure is reflected in Franklin's maxim, "leisure is time for doing something useful." The sporting impulse had to be tied to worthy ends in order to be justified. Recreation could improve health or physical stamina, but could not be used as an escape from the duties which await.

Embedded in these severe doctrines were the seeds of their failure. N. Struna, in "Puritans and sport: the irretrievable tide of change," shows how common people could not live up to the strict standards of the Puritan Saints (in *Journal of Sport History*, vol 4, 1977). The futility of eradicating idle play from their communities prompted the Puritans to forge a synthesis between compromised virtue and persistent vice. Sport was reconceptualized as *moral* activity instilled with the values of the Protestant ethic. Spontaneous games gave way to supervised recreation; physical training supplanted hedonistic play. Sport assumed work-like forms and values. Achievement of worthwhile goals through physical recreation eclipsed experiential qualities of play. Once transformed, the successful pursuit of recreational avocations gained parity with traditional vocations. The revised moral calculus allows for a career in baseball or soccer to assume the mantle of a "calling" such as teaching.

Sport, once legitimized by the Protestant ethic, was institutionalized. What had been marginal activity in Western society became central through support by religious institutions, the political structure, the business community and the educational system. Sport would come to both reflect and shape societal values. Public and private enterprises were organized to promote sport and recreation, turning them into cornerstones of Protestant capitalism. While employers provide recreation programs for employees, children are steered into sports as a component of liberal education. To justify the sponsorship of sports, schools and colleges invented the extra curriculum, as cities and states established recreation departments to steer their citizens into worthwhile leisure activities.

The Protestant sport ethos

In the United States and Protestant Europe, a sport ethos emerged which reflected the values of the Protestant ethic. This ethos not only determines the forms and meanings of sport in Protestant nations, but has spread to other cultures through international competition so that it now constitutes the dominant spirit of contemporary sport. The core elements of the Protestant sport ethos are rationalization, the work ethic, goal-directedness, achieved status, competitiveness, moral asceticism and individualism.

The rationalization of sport and recreation emulated the rationalization of work during the course of the industrial revolution. The application of scientific principles to human movement in the workplace carried over into competitive sport, where it led to efficient and intense training programs, sophisticated game strategies, and intrusive coaching. The industrial artifacts of specialization and division of labor became evident in team sports.

Sports governing bodies instituted standardization of rules, procedures, equipment and facilities. The proliferation of rules and regulations brought about an increasingly litigious climate within and peripheral to sport. Rationalization promoted the quantification of human performance, resulting in a preoccupation with measurement, records and statistics. In the twentieth century, the applied sciences of exercise physiology, biomechanics and sport psychology have exploited knowledge and technology to enhance competitive performance.

When the work ethic spilled over into sport, forms of play increasingly came to resemble patterns of labor. The more regulated and intense pace of work displaced what was once the leisurely pace of play. The non-serious ambiance of play took on a work-like sobriety, and the freedom of play gave way to the inherent constraints of structured competition. Athletes have become producers of performances and records under the supervision of trainers and coaches, whose objective is to increase productivity. Sports champions are heroes of efficiency. The restructuring of sport along the lines of the work ethic brought about a decline in the spirit of amateurism while bolstering professionalism. Allen Guttmann's *From Ritual to Record* (Columbia University Press, 1977) elaborates on this point.

The Protestant sport ethos succeeded in transforming sport into a regimen of goal-directed behaviors which are the antithesis of pure play. Through a series of goal displacements, the intrinsic goals of games and contests were subjugated to extrinsic and more pragmatic goals. The nature of activity on the playing field was increasingly limited to the singular focus on winning. Concurrently, sport became the vehicle for achieving larger ends: personal, political, commercial, educational and moral. This focus on goals which reoriented the institution of sport also is coopting the contemporary athlete, who often competes for money or status rather than the love of the game.

The focus within the Protestant ethic is to assign worth to individuals based on their achievements. The medium in which achievement occurs is less important than the accomplishment itself. Thus, social status can be acquired by demonstrating achievement in sport as well as in business or politics. Sport in its public venues provides a highly visible form of status, incorporating status rituals, symbols and labels. Sport competition is uniquely adapted to promoting status through achievement, for in this medium the ascribed status provided by birth, social class or ethnicity counts for little. The sports arena, in theory, provides a "level playing field" which reaffirms the credo that success comes not through privilege but through the Protestant virtues of hard work, self-control and perseverance. While the sport ethos supports equality of opportunity, at the same time it condones elitism among an athletic "elect."

The Protestant ethic promotes an agonistic view of life as a moral contest in which few rise to an elite status. Competitive sport, by its very nature, establishes differences among its participants, dividing the players into winners and losers at the end of the contest. As in life, the status which accompanies winning in sport is not a "given" but a contested prize which must be earned. The ethic implies that winners achieve something more than victory; they acquire a sense of moral worth. The stigma attached to losing is equally compelling, as forms of competition proliferate and the level of competition escalates. The Protestant sport ethos has led to an unbridled competitiveness encapsulated in the American coach Vincent LOMBARDI's dictum, "Winning isn't everything. It's the only thing."

The Puritan legacy of moral asceticism leads to an ironic posture in which personal affirmation is realized through denial. This form of asceticism works to stifle the experiential and sensory qualities of life in general, and of ludic activity in particular. "Moral athleticism" eclipses a sense of "disporting" as the athlete, in a test of will, subjects the body to discipline, denial and discomfort. The joyless quest for record performances and uninterrupted victories becomes little more than a duty performed to fulfill the expectations of self and significant others. The athlete and the coach are obsessed with control: control of the body, control of the will and control of circumstances. Sport is championed not for its celebratory or aesthetic features but for its contributions to morality, character development and social cohesion.

The Protestant ethic holds that personal salvation comes through individual initiative. This ethic propels the athlete toward personal achievement even where team sports predominate in the broader culture, which reciprocates by focusing on individual athletic performances. The scrutiny of print and electronic media highlight individual styles and statistics. A team's victory or defeat is often attributed to the actions of a single player. Typical honors, such as "most valuable player," are bestowed upon one member of a team. The credo of individualism impels athletes toward a preoccupation with the egocentric goals of careerism, while bargaining as free agents with management and routinely changing team affiliation for personal advantage. (The advent of FREE AGENCY in the 1970s hastened this process.)

Sport and the spirit of capitalism

Max Weber wrote convincingly of the long standing affinity between the Protestant ethic and the spirit of capitalism. The affinity between modern capitalism in its various guises – entrepreneurial, investment, consumer – and the Protestant sport ethos has facilitated the transformation of organized sport into a business and a profession. As global capitalism asserts its dominance, spectator sports increasingly are marketed as commercial entertainment.

Participant sport is recast as a form of consumer activity which one has to "buy into" by purchasing equipment and/or access to facilities. Business entrepreneurs routinely purchase sports teams or franchises as financial investments. Professional athletes and teams are judged by how much money they make as often as by their performances in the sports arena. Amateur sport, where it continues to exist, mimics the business model. While this development is most apparent among athletic programs in American colleges, it even filters down into youth sport programs.

Of related interest

Geldbach, E. (1975) *Sport und Protestantismus: Geschichte einer Begegnung*, Theologischer Verlag R. Brockhaus.

Guttmann, A. (1978) *From Ritual to Record: The Nature of Modern Sports*, Columbia University Press.

Nixon, H.L. (1974) "The Commercialization and Organizational Development of Modern Sport," *International Review of Sport Sociology* vol 9.

Overman, S. (1997) *The Influence of the Protestant Ethic on Sport and Recreation*, Avebury Press.

STEVEN J. OVERMAN

psyching

The term "psyching" came into popular use during the 1970s, a period when the applications of psychology to sports were being discussed in both scholarly and practical circles. Psyching emphasized the importance of mental rather than physical preparation for competition; its utility was in gaining an advantage, however slight, over opponents either through heightening one's own arousal (psyching *up*) or initiating anxiety in one's opponent (psyching *out*).

Psychologists offered suggestions on how these might be achieved, though coaches and performers often created their own. It is probable that they had been doing so for decades before psychology started to formalize psyching strategies. The publication of *Problem Athletes and How to Handle Them* (Palham, 1966) by academic writers Bruce Ogilvie and Thomas Tutko marked a significant break in sport psychology. While the discipline had an ancestry stretching back to the 1920s and research had been carried out on motor learning, it was not until the late 1960s that an attempt was made to demonstrate the utility of academic work to sports practitioners.

At its most basic level, psychology's message was that sporting performance required mental as well as physical preparation; and, while practitioners knew much about the latter, their knowledge of the former was speculative rather than empirically based. Psychologists argued that scientific experimentation was needed to discover how best to facilitate optimal performance from an athlete. As the results of their efforts were disseminated, so more and more sports practitioners came to accept the value of mental preparation. Terms like "mental toughness," "psychological advantage" and "positive thinking" became part of the sports lexicon and indicated an approval for psychological conditioning to complement physical training.

Some performers and coaches had intuitively used psyching techniques with no assistance from academic researchers. In the 1960s, heavyweight champion boxer Sonny Liston pioneered a method of psyching out opponents by staring them down during pre-fight preliminaries. Liston glared into opponents' eyes, as if challenging them to make eye to eye contact or divert their gaze. Opponents would often blink, or just look away, intimidated by Liston's scrutiny. Muhammad ALI, who took the title from Liston in 1964, gave the impression of being brash before their fight, but later admitted: "Just before the fight, when the referee was giving us instructions, Liston was giving me that stare. And I won't lie; I was scared."

Vince LOMBARDI ruled his formidable Green Bay Packers team of the 1960s with a rod of iron: his strict disciplinarian approach completely subordinated players to his command. While his domineering style may not have met success in later years when FREE AGENCY made it possible for players to become superstars and even ICONS, Lombardi's quasi-military system was perfect for his time.

Today, a Lombardi-style approach would be considered somewhat crude. Psychologists have found that coaches run the risk of overactivating some anxiety-prone athletes by arousing them, that is pumping (or hyping) them up. Psyching an athlete for an event frequently involves allaying anxiety by downplaying the seriousness of an occasion or the importance of the winning rather than the opposite. In other words, RELAXATION is as much a part of psyching up as arousal.

Perhaps the finest example of a psyching strategy that backfired grotesquely was that of Butch Lewis, manager of boxer Michael Spinks, who in 1988 prepared to fight Mike TYSON. As is customary in world title matches, a representative of the opponent is permitted to watch as a fighter bandages his hands. In his book *Tyson* (Pan Books, 1990), Peter Heller recounts how Lewis noticed a lump in Tyson's bandage and insisted the whole hand be unwrapped and re-bandaged. It was a tactic Lewis believed would irritate Tyson and gain an advantage for Spinks. Instead, Tyson grew furious. After Lewis left the changing room, Tyson promised "I'm gonna hurt this guy." He did: with barely controlled fury, Tyson dismantled his opponent in only ninety-one seconds.

Of related interest

Nideffer, Robert M. (1992) *Psyched to Win*, Human Kinetics.
Orlick, Terry (1997) *In Pursuit of Excellence* (audiocassette), Human Kinetics.
Tutko, T.A. and Richards, J.W. (1971) *Psychology of Coaching*, Allyn & Bacon.

R

racism

The sources of black excellence in sports

The dominance of sports performers of African descent or origin in several spheres of activity has given rise to several theoretical attempts to disclose the sources of black excellence in sports. The theories fall into two basic categories: those that locate the source in natural ability, and those that examine social conditions underlying the overachievement.

The most famous example of the former is found in Martin Kane's influential article "An assessment of black is best," first published in *Sports Illustrated* (vol 34, no 3) in 1971. In this, Kane argued that there were three main reasons for blacks' seemingly perennial success in sports. These reasons were physical, psychological and historical.

In terms of physiological structure, Kane compared blacks with their white peers and concluded that the former had several advantages in terms of muscle density, skeletal strength, reaction time and a catalog of other physical features. He marshaled evidence from Robert Malina, whose research was published in the volume *Physical Activity* (ed. G.L Rarick, Academic Press, 1973) and which examined the ways in which black youths in elementary schools seemed to possess different basic motor skills to whites. They could, among other things, run quicker, jump longer and grip stronger than their white counterparts.

Malina's study was entitled "Ethnic and cultural factors in the development of motor abilities and strengths in American children," and he was aware of the roles of poverty, housing conditions, poor diet and other cultural factors in affecting physical performance. However, the upshot of his investigation was that differences in motor skills do exist. Kane used this work somewhat selectively, neglecting cultural factors and emphasizing physical differences to support his contention that differences were linked to "race." Kane argued that black populations have: proportionately longer leg lengths, narrower hips, wider calf bones and greater arm circumference; they also had a greater ratio of tendon to muscle, giving rise to a condition often termed double-jointedness, a relatively dense bone structure and a basically elongated body structure which made them more efficient heat dissipaters compared to whites. The relative absence of top black swimmers was explained by Kane as the result of such factors as bone and muscle density, distribution of fat and small lung capacity. Weak ankles and an adversity to cold climates (because of body fat deficiencies) would account for the lack of black hockey players.

In addition to the physical advantages they enjoy in certain sports, Kane claimed that blacks have psychological advantages, specifically an ability to remain relaxed under pressure. To bolster this claim, Kane cited Lloyd C. Winter, an established US coach, whom he quotes as saying: "As a class, the Black athletes who have trained under me are far ahead of whites in that one factor – relaxation under pressure." There were no systematic findings to complement this.

As for historical reasons, Kane invoked his own version of Darwin's theory of natural selection to argue that weaker members had perished in harsh plantation conditions, leaving a fitter, well-equipped black population whose genes were passed through successive generations. "Only the strongest survived," concluded Kane. Lee Evans, the black Olympian renowned for his gesture at the Mexico games, was quoted by Kane: " ... on the plantations, a strong Blackman was mated with a strong Blackwoman. We were simply bred for physical qualities."

Kane's work has proved enduringly popular, though many scholars have pointed out the racist implications of both his premises and conclusions. America's original slaves were forcibly taken from West Africa and Kane speculated revealingly on the typical West African: "He had not ... reached that fine state of civilization in which he was able to make gunpowder ... he never invented the wheel and the plow."

The sports dream

Social scientists typically reject the concept of "race" as having value save as a nebulous justification for theories purporting to explain natural inequalities. Instead, research into the sports prowess of black people has been directed toward the particular social conditions under which so many young blacks enter sport. In his *Sociology of Sport*, former basketball player turned sociologist Harry Edwards argued that racialist practices in society generally work to limit the number of career avenues available to blacks and, as a consequence, they turn to sports as an alternative. On this account, the enthusiasm for sports is less the product of untrammelled ambition, more a result of blocked opportunities. It is hardly surprising so many get to the top when one considers the countless thousands of young blacks striving to make progress along one of the few career paths open to them.

The impression one might get from reading sports pages – that black sports performers dominate baseball, boxing, football, track and so on – is actually misleading. It disguises the huge numbers of blacks who do not even approach the stage where they can make a professional career out of sports. The sports journalist Jack Olsen wrote memorably of this: "At most, sport has led a few thousand Negroes out of the ghetto. But for hundreds of thousands of other Negroes it has substituted a meaningless dream." The reverie is brought to life in the movie *HOOP DREAMS* which plots the progress of two young NBA hopefuls whose dreams are eventually vanquished.

Early research by Sandra Castine and Glyn Roberts proposed that: "For Black youth the most obviously successful role models are Black professional athletes. The role attractiveness of the Black athlete coupled with the relative lack of Black high level achievers in other fields of endeavor, may lead to imitation of these roles by aspiring Black youths" ("Modeling in the socialization process of the Black athlete," *International Review of Sport Sociology* 3–4, 1974). Subsequent work supported this.

Empirical work in Britain has complemented these findings by noting the manner in which black youths are "sidetracked" into sports, often at the behest of schoolteachers who harbor stereotyped views on the suitability of blacks for sport, yet not for more scholarly pursuits. My own study (*Black Sportsmen*, Routledge, 1981) and that of Bruce Carrington indicate how the myth of the naturally gifted black athlete has become an almost permanent fixture of contemporary culture. Harry Edwards hinted at the self-fulfilling consequence of this in his *Sociology of Sport* (Dorsey Press, 1973), where he wrote that "many white athletes, some of whom may themselves be of exceptional athletic potential *believe* blacks to be innately superior as athletes. ... The 'white race' thus becomes the chief victim of its own myth."

John Hoberman argued that the myth has been a destructive force in American culture: the belief that the high numbers of successful blacks in sports indicates that sports have become a deracialized utopia where blacks are equal to their white team-mates, thus making American culture itself more egalitarian. Hoberman contends that this image actually contributes to the deepening racial divisions and the further degradation of the black experience. Hoberman's argument went beyond the kind of view offered in the 1980s by former tennis star Arthur Ashe, who implored young blacks to spend less energy on sports and more on academic study. In his *A Hard Road to Glory* (Amistad/Warner, 1988). Ashe asserted that black sports stars inadvertently gave weight to a "black pathology business." When high-profile blacks are involved in controversy, they simply add to existing stereotypes about blacks being rich in athletic gifts but poor in intellectual ones.

Of related interest

Carrington, Bruce (1986) "Social mobility, ethnicity and sport," *British Journal of Sociology of Education* vol 7, no 1.
Hoberman, John (1997) *Darwin's Athletes: How Sport has Damaged Black America and Preserved the Myth of Race*, HM Publishing.
Wiggins, David (1997) *Glory Bound: Black Athletes in a White America*, Syracuse University Press.

Raging Bull

However much he hated boxing, however much it disappointed him, Jake La Motta seemed to want more of it. *Raging Bull*, Martin Scorsese's celebrated film biography of the former middleweight champion, is a tragedy that dwells, often agonizingly, on the least likable aspects of the fighter. The film has a similar kind of mesmerizing power to a car wreck: we know it is repulsive, yet we cannot take our eyes away.

Raging Bull makes no attempt at hagiography. La Motta is depicted as a brutish, amoral misogynist; the "bull" of the title refers as much to his animalistic manner outside the ring as his style inside. The film focuses on the relationship between the boxer and his wife, a woman constrained by traditional role expectations of women in the 1940s and 1950s.

From the outset, La Motta, played by Robert De Niro, is introduced as monstrously unlikable. His brother and manager, played by Joe Pesci, feels the brunt of his early anger at not being big enough to challenge for the heavyweight title. He grows even angrier when he cannot clinch a shot at the middleweight title.

In fact, La Motta had been a ranked contender for several years after the second world war and had, on paper, earned his shot. He had beaten Sugar Ray Robinson (who then went another ninety-eight fights without defeat) and Fritzie Zivic, the former welterweight champion. La Motta's account of events is that organized crime syndicates which controlled boxing in the 1940s made him take a dive in a 1947 fight against Billy Fox before he could get a title chance. He obliged and was rewarded with a challenge against Marcel Cerdan in 1949. Even then, it cost him $20,000 to secure the fight.

The film follows La Motta's progress as champion. Even the acquisition of material comforts that might soothe lesser rages does little to sedate La Motta. He picks fights with his brother on the merest pretext, and accuses his wife of cheating on him. His bile manifests in the ring: we see him not just beating opponents but seemingly trying to obliterate them.

During La Motta's reign as champion, Robinson moved up from welterweight and pursued a second title. Although La Motta had taken a decision from him, he had reversed the defeat within three weeks and it was the only loss in Robinson's extraordinary 123 fight sequence (which also included two draws). La Motta went into his defense against Robinson with a record of 78 wins, 12 defeats and 4 draws.

Scorsese's portrayal of the fight spurns action realism in preference for a realism of feeling and even thinking. Slow motion, freeze frames and unexpected cutaway shots make the viewer privy to a different kind of action from those typically associated with sports movies. Cinematographer Michael Chapman takes his camera into the ring to convey the impressions of La Motta as he is faced by an incoming Robinson. De Niro is seen dumped against the ropes, arms draped helplessly, beckoning Robinson to hit him, defying him to make him take a count. "I'm still standing, Ray," he utters, as Robinson, played by Johnny Barnes, batters him to defeat in the thirteenth round. La Motta and Robinson had one of the great ring RIVALRIES, meeting a total of five times.

Robinson, at 29, was at his peak and continued to dominate the middleweight division as comprehensively as any champion in history. La Motta, as the film shows, slid away from the public gaze, to reappear several years later as a nightclub artist. La Motta gained over thirty-five pounds in his retirement and

De Niro replicated the experience (he actually had to maintain a strict regimen of eating ice cream and other sugary foods). La Motta is seen bathotically rehearsing the "I coulda been a contender" passage from *On the Waterfront* and clumsily knocking over a nightclub patron's drinks.

Many of the conventions and customs that governed women's lives in the postwar period are expressed through La Motta's story. Vicky, played by Cathy Moriarty, is at first attracted to La Motta's ostentation and vulgar exhibitionism; he parades her around the Bronx as if she were a badge of his worldly success. La Motta stays embedded in his natural habitat, enjoying the good life, part of which is patriarchal control of a beautiful woman who is the object of other men's desires. A passing reference by Vicky to Billy Fox as "a good looking guy" meets with terrible retribution: Vicky is immediately chastised and Fox, in his fight with La Motta, is battered into a hideous, bloody mess. "You don't look so pretty now," snarls La Motta before he leaves his victim.

Vicky is given little capacity for fulfillment of her own: she is strictly a ringside ornament for La Motta and a domestic factotum, in some degree a caricature of what later feminists were to call a house slave. Vicky joins La Motta in his life of consumer choice and material comforts, having surrendered real control of her fate. She accepts unflinchingly the relationship between the sexes, either too content or too afraid to rebel. Her subordination, like that of women in the 1950s, is seen as part of the "common life," the natural relationships among families, friends and neighbors. All her friends are equally as subjugated; by comparison she is well off, as she at least has money (albeit her husband's money).

Selflessly, Vicky supports and encourages her husband, never complaining, yet somehow adrift: any realization she achieves is always through Jake's fame. But, the viewer is always reminded that her interests stand in stark opposition to her husband's. The weightlessness of her character is counterpointed by La Motta's massive presence.

In some senses, the film's progenitor is Robert Wise's 1948 *The Set-Up* in which Robert Ryan's 35-year-old fighter, Stoker Thompson, is urged by Audrey Totter to quit fighting; she cannot bear to watch a fight he unexpectedly wins, yet waits stoically for him to return to their hotel after the fight. As in *Raging Bull*, fight fixing is a theme: in this instance, Thompson is such a rank UNDERDOG that his manager and trainer, who have taken bribes to ensure he takes a dive, do not consider it worth telling the fighter. They reason he will be well beaten anyway. In the event, Thompson's win lands him in trouble with the fixers, who assume (incorrectly) that he has reneged on the "set up" and crush his right hand as punishment.

Raging Bull actually revived interest in La Motta and he became a public personality all over again at the time of the film's release. De Niro's performance earned him the Best Actor Oscar at the 1980 Academy Awards.

Of related interest

La Motta, Jake, Carter, Joseph and Savage, Peter (1971) *Raging Bull*, Prentice-Hall.

O'Brien, R. (1991) "The Bull's daughter puts up a good fight," *Sports Illustrated* vol. 74, no. 1, January 14.

Raging Bull, directed by Martin Scorsese, 1980.

The Set-Up, directed by Robert Wise, 1948.

Ramsamy, Samba (Sam)

b. 1938, South Africa

Ramsamy is arguably the single most influential administrator in the history of South African sports. He came to prominence through his role as chair of the South African Non-Racial Olympic Committee (SAN-ROC), an anti-apartheid pressure group that was forced to base itself in London after being banned from South Africa in 1964.

South Africa's constitutionally enshrined RACISM ensured that the majority (consistently over 70 per cent) of its population were denied civil rights, excluded from the political process, lived in prescribed territories, had to carry passbooks to identify themselves, held only poorly paid jobs and were subject to habitual brutality at the hands of a predominantly white police force. Ramsamy, as a member of the country's majority and having grown up in the crowded ghetto of Magazine Barracks in Durban, was familiar with the experiences of South Africa's subordinated black population.

Under Ramsamy's leadership, SAN-ROC created a mandate to force the IOC (International Olympic Committee) to recognize that the white South African National Olympic Committee reflected the country's apartheid system and was unrepresentative of the whole South African population. As such, it contravened the first rule of the Olympic Charter, which states that there must be no discrimination of any form in a member country. South Africa was expelled from the Olympic movement in 1970, but continued international sporting relations with traditional allies, particularly in rugby.

Ramsamy symbolized international sports protest against South Africa and, as a consequence, was vilified in his home country for denying South Africa – a country where sport for the white population was something akin to religion – international sports contact.

Ramsamy was a competent athlete, excelling at boxing, soccer and swimming. He trained and qualified as a physical education teacher. It seems a crucial event in his development came in 1970, when he was 32. Internationally, the period at the end of the 1960s had been one of great change. In particular, the tumultuous events of 1968 had involved African American athletes in dramatic protests against racism. Muhammad ALI was still in exile after his refusal to serve in the US armed forces. There was a growing recognition that sport, for long regarded as a separate sphere of activity, was actually a powerful political instrument that could serve the interests of many masters.

No doubt mindful of this, Ramsamy, when invited to organize a sports event at the teacher training college where he was a junior lecturer, turned the event into an anti-apartheid demonstration. Aided by his students, Ramsamy engineered a spectacular mockery: outraged white dignitaries watched on as the long jump became the short jump, runners ran backwards and the thrower of the shortest javelin distance was declared the winner. Ramsamy also became involved in the organization of "non-racial" sports: he was national trainer for the South African Amateur Swimming Federation, a member of the South African Amateur Athletics Association and president of the Natal Senior Schools Sports Association.

In 1972, Ramsamy fled to Britain after discovering that he was being investigated by the South African Special Branch for his anti-apartheid activities. In London, Ramsamy initially worked as a physical education teacher and received a scholarship to study swimming coaching in Leipzig, Germany. He joined SAN-ROC and, in 1974, was appointed executive chairperson. Working with limited resources, Ramsamy was responsible for the intensification of international sports protest against South Africa's policies. In 1977, the South African Council on Sport (SACOS) appointed Ramsamy to speak on its behalf at any international meeting he attended. SACOS was the umbrella body that represented non-racial sport in South Africa. Its members were unable to travel abroad, as the South African government withheld their passports.

In 1980 Ramsamy addressed the United Nations, where he highlighted the fact that there was still significant international sporting contact with South Africa. In response, the UN established its Register of Sporting Contacts with South Africa, which, combined with the Gleneagles Agreement, served as perhaps the two most important international statements against South African sport. SAN-ROC was primarily responsible for maintaining the profile of both in the international media.

Ramsamy's global profile peaked between 1987–92. Acknowledged as the figurehead of international sports protest, he initiated an intensive public relations campaign at the third International Committee Against Apartheid in Sport Conference in 1987. After being appointed as one of the two special advisors to the IOC Commission on Apartheid, he used his position to galvanize the Association of National Olympic Committees of Africa (ANOCA) and the IOC to more forthright action against South Africa. This introduced strains between him and SACOS: the latter felt that Ramsamy's willingness to negotiate with the African National Congress (ANC) and its allies compromised its policy of non-collaboration with political parties. In response, Ramsamy made it clear that international sport would pursue the abolition of apartheid in sport through the eradication of apartheid generally.

By the time of Nelson Mandela's release from prison in 1990, the ANC had developed an explicit proactive role in sports, fueled by the belief that readmission to international sports could be used as an incentive to white South Africans to continue to negotiate a democratic constitution. In the same year that Mandela was set free, Ramsamy met with the National Sports Council, an organization dedicated to a single non-racial body for each sport in South Africa. Also in 1990, Ramsamy returned to South Africa as a representative of ANOCA with the remit of studying progress toward the dismantling of apartheid in sport.

In the following year, apparently encouraged by the preceding events and the prospect of democratic elections, Ramsamy ended his exile and settled in South

Africa where he was elected chair of an IOC-recognized organization, the National Olympic Committee of South Africa. In this capacity, Ramsamy negotiated the re-entry of South Africa into the Olympic movement. South Africa participated in the 1992 summer Olympics in Barcelona.

Ramsamy is frequently credited with being the person most responsible for South Africa's readmission to international sports, yet, even by the late 1990s, a number of sports had not unified into a single governing federation and had no structures in place to develop sports among black and what South Africans call "colored" people. Critics claimed that South Africa had returned to the international arena too quickly. Despite this, it is clear that Ramsamy played a significant role in the international anti-apartheid movement. His contacts with the IOC resulted in his being invited to become a member of the IOC in 1995.

Of related interest

Archer, R. and Bouillon, A. (1982) *The South African Game*, Zed Press.
Bose, M. (1994) *Sporting Colours: Sport and Politics in South Africa*, Robson.
Ramsamy, Sam (1981) *Apartheid: The Real Hurdle*, IDAF.

MARC KEECH

referee

Fair play, "sportsmanship" and competition

As the name suggests, the sports referee was once a person to whom disputes arising in a contest were referred for a decision. Changes in the condition, purpose and ethos of sports ensured that the referee was required to apply rules impartially and consistently as well as remain responsive to disputes. In some sports, the official figure was called the umpire, another resonant name which derives from the French *noumpere*, meaning "not equal." Authority was said to reside with the umpire and, in every contentious circumstance, the referee or umpire's decision was final and beyond question. This principle came under severe pressure as sports were professionalized and financial incentives became a feature of contemporary competition.

It is possible that the functional equivalent of neutral arbiter would have acted in competitive games and organized sports since antiquity, though the paid official that we now recognize as a referee or umpire emerged in the period when sports themselves were becoming formalized. Tony Mason, in his *Sport in Britain* (Faber & Faber, 1988) notes how by the 1880s, newspapers specializing in sports provided referees and judges as well as trophies. As the competitions were subject to codes of rules devised and administered by governing associations, referees and umpires were delegated the responsibility for implementing them during actual contests.

The professionalization of sports increased the need for neutral referees. No sports competitions at any level has not contained a situation that has been contested in some way. It became important for individuals or teams to enter in a contractual relationship prior to the competition in which they agreed to abide by the neutral official's verdict. This was intended to be accepted unreservedly and without question, a principle that had its basis in a conception of "sportsmanship."

In 1880, at the inception of the modern Olympics, its founder Pierre de Coubertin declared: "The important thing in the Olympic games is not winning, but taking part." In a similar spirit, the American Sportsmanship Brotherhood, which was assembled in 1926 to spread the gospel of sportsmanship adopted a slogan that summed up the Corinthian ideal of sporting competition: "Not that you won or lost – but how you played the game." The Brotherhood is quoted by James W. Keating in his essay "Sportsmanship as a moral category," which examines the central precept of early sports. "The primary purpose of sport is not to win the match," reasons Keating, "but to derive pleasure from the attempt to do so and to afford pleasure to one's fellow participants in the process" (in Morgan and Meier 1988).

However, Keating maintains that sport has been displaced by athletics which, for him, places much more emphasis on winning and is more demanding on its participants. Victory is, of course, essential to financial success in professional sports and sportsmanship, in its original conception, became vitiated. Contests that may once have played out without recourse to neutral judgments became more rigorously competitive. "Taking part" was still an honorable endeavor, but "playing to win" became equally as honorable and more rewarding. As victory superseded participation as the principal objective, so the role of an objective adjudicator became more central.

Fair play was – and, for many, still is – the pivotal virtue in contemporary sports. This was perfectly compatible with the ruthless pursuit of athletic excellence and superiority. If victory was to signify athletic supremacy, then an unbiased application of the rules of play was essential. Ostensibly, referees and umpires were supposed to ensure the abiding presence of "gentlemanly conduct," but increasingly their purpose was to penalize infractions of the rules.

Signs of gentlemanly play were still in evidence with the likes of golfers Bobby Jones and Arnold Palmer, both of whom were known to have called penalty strokes on themselves, but for the most part, referees were burdened with the task of making judgments. Competitors motivated by the incentives of victory were unlikely to own up to infractions, although there have been exceptions. For example, in 1997 Liverpool soccer player Robbie Fowler was awarded a penalty after the opposing goalkeeper, David Seaman of Arsenal, had, according to the referee, fouled him. Fowler risked censure by insisting to the referee that Seaman had not in fact fouled him. The referee was adamant that the penalty stood and Fowler duly took it. While Fowler's spotkick was saved and driven into the goal on the rebound, one wonders what might have happened had the player remained true to his original confession and deliberately sliced the ball wide of the goal. The probability is that he would have been fined by his club and disciplined by the Football Association for his "ungentlemanly conduct," that is, for effectively ridiculing the referee. In an earlier era, his initial honesty may have been rewarded.

More typical of the contemporary approach to referees and their decisions is the response to the faulty call of NFL referee Phil Luckett, who awarded New York Jets a touchdown against Seattle Seahawks in 1998. The ball was clearly short of the endzone, and several Jets players (as well as millions of TELEVISION viewers) knew this. Yet, with a playoff spot at stake, none of the New York team tried to correct Luckett. In common with most competitors, they prioritized victory over all other considerations, including fair play.

While the principle of the finality of the referee's decision has been widely observed by most sports governing organizations, there have been occasional examples when the referee has been overruled. In boxing, for example, it has been known for a commissioner or medical officer to intercede in a contest independently of the referee. In soccer, games have occasionally been replayed when a referee's decision at a crucial moment was shown to be flawed. In 1999, a referee's failure to observe a customary protocol based in sportsmanship resulted in a game between Arsenal and Sheffield United being played again. Technically, the referee was correct in observing the rules of soccer, but the Football Association considered the breach of etiquette that led to Arsenal's second (and decisive) goal should not have gone unpunished.

Violence and competitors

This indicates how the nature of the relationship between referees and competitors has changed over the decades. Once seen as partners in a pursuit that was both cooperative and competitive, the two parties became more adversarial, particularly in major professional sports. Baseball umpires were often subject to verbal and, occasionally physical assaults from players and managers. In 1996 alone there were four incidents in the USA. Roberto Alomar, of the Baltimore Orioles, was suspended after spitting in the face of umpire John Hirschbeck. Basketball player Dennis Rodman was also suspended and fined for head-butting a referee, and in the same sport, LA Lakers' Nick Van Exel shoved a referee and Magic JOHNSON was fined for a similar offense.

In 1998, Italian soccer player Paulo di Canio, then playing for the English club Sheffield Wednesday, pushed a referee to the ground during a dispute over a decision. Even cricket, for long the exemplar of gentlemanly conduct, found its umpires being questioned: Sri Lanka's Arjuna Ranatunga was censured after vigorously arguing with a referee and poking him in the chest, a serious breach of conduct.

Controlling violent conduct was prioritized by the National Hockey League, which, in 1999, announced that it would use two referees during play-off games. An experimental period using two referees resulted in a decrease in penalty minutes, an increase in flowing play and a shortening of games.

Changes in the cultural meanings of sports have transformed the sports referee from a guardian of rules and conduct whose role was to support and assist players in a spirit of moderation and generosity into an agent of restraint, discipline and surveillance. Buffalo Sabre's general manager David Poile's choice of words after the NHL's introduction of two referees was revealing: "Two policemen in a community are better than one." The referee's purpose in today's sports is regulatory: to maintain order in a competitive struggle in which extrinsic rewards have supplanted the intrinsic joys once thought to derive from sporting activity.

Of related interest

Brailsford, Dennis (1997) *British Sport: A Social History*, Lutterworth Press.
McIntosh, Peter (1980) *Fair Play: Ethics in Sport and Education*, Heinemann Educational.
Morgan, William J. and Meier, Klaus V. (eds) (1988) *Philosophic Inquiry in Sport*, Human Kinetics.

relaxation

Relaxation is an integral part of many athletes' mental preparation for a competitive event. While PSYCHING up has conventionally been regarded as a matter of activating the organs and mechanisms under the control of the central nervous system, it also involves decreasing levels of anxiety and tension. As the incentives for success have promoted a win-at-all-costs mentality in many professional sports and NATIONALISM has increased the amount of pride to be gained from sporting success, so the costs of failure have been magnified. Apprehension, strain and trepidation over the prospect of failing have necessitated the introduction of techniques designed to allay concerns and enhance the performer's chances of optimizing performance.

It is doubtful that any training regime today does not incorporate some element devoted to proper relaxation. From the 1960s and the increased recognition of the mind's role in sporting achievement, more attention has been concentrated on mental preparation in itself rather than as an adjunct to physical preparation. In the 1980s and 1990s, the all-purpose malaise of postmodernity, stress, paid scant respect to occupational groupings. If the volumes of literature on the subject are to be believed, it afflicted virtually everyone, from chief executives to office cleaners, from cosmonauts to truckers. City dwellers, suburbanites and the homeless were all, to some degree, stressed. Men, women and children of all ethnic backgrounds and all religious persuasions could be prone to stress. For a time, it seemed, no one lived a stress-free life: everyone was entreated to chill out, unwind or loosen up at some point.

There is some irony in the fact that taking up a sport or joining a gym were – and are – often prescribed remedies for relieving stress. The remedy becomes less useful as the levels of competition are raised and the pressure to succeed become more intense. At such levels, the kind of stress or anxiety that is apparently diffused throughout society affects the performance of an athlete. It would have been odd if sports had not been impressed by the trend toward stress management as manifested in innumerable self-help manuals, tapes and instructional videos, all designed to promote relaxation in the user. Over the past few decades, sports performers have used a variety of methods of relaxing before and, in some cases, during competition. Perhaps the most commonly used technique was popularized by rock stars and others who had little if any connection to sports.

The NARCISSISM of the 1960s and beyond brought with it a plethora of techniques for self-discovery or self-improvement, many based on Eastern beliefs and practices. Yoga was extremely influential, whether as a route to self-fulfillment or as a practical remedy for relieving the tensions of everyday life. One of the techniques that was popularized during the period was transcendental meditation (TM), and this had clear applications in sports. Essentially, the concept behind TM was that the meditator should think of a single image or sound and exclude all others from his or her consciousness. As an aid to this, a simple word may be repeated over and over again as an incantation or mantra (this being a Sanskrit word for "instrument of thought"). Tennis players Jimmy Connors and Boris Becker were both known to employ yoga-style techniques in the breaks between games. Connors was often seen repeating words over and over to himself; Becker would drape a towel over his head, breathing deeply as he prepared for the next game. Arthur Ashe also favored mid-game meditation. Tennis is one of the few sports where breaks in play allow meditation during the contest. Competitors in other sports compose themselves prior to competition or unwind after training by using yoga.

Toni Schumacher, the goalkeeper of the German national soccer team for many years, was an advocate of autogenics as a means of relaxing and improving his playing performance. The technique is German in origin: it pioneer was Johannes Shultz, who experimented with methods of self-hypnosis. Inducing a trance-like state in oneself is the aim of autogenics; this is achieved through months, if not years, of assiduous attention to specific practices. Alternatively, audio and video tapes based on autogenic methods have been produced and sold commercially. Practiced users of autogenics have astonishing powers of rapid relaxation and can induce deep states of inner calmness within minutes. They report sensations of relaxation so intense that their limbs feel lifeless and their whole bodies consumed by warmth.

Without doubt, the most controversial of relaxation techniques has been hypnotism induced by others. Some sports performers have admitted using hypnotists as part of their training schedule, while there are doubtless many others who have concealed the fact – for obvious reasons. While using hypnotism has not been debated in the same way as using DRUGS, it is a matter of conjecture whether it confers an unfair advantage on the acceptor of the hypnosis. British boxer Nigel Benn acknowledged the contribution of his hypnotist to his athletic performance. Irish boxer Steve Collins was less clear. Prior to his fight against Chris Eubank, he made it well-known that he was seeking the counsel of a hypnotist. He entered the ring first and sat stoically in his corner, his head covered, while the razzle-dazzle Eubank showboated through the introductions. Immediately prior to the first bell, Collins emerged and fought the fight of his life. The defeated Eubank complained that Collins' hypnotism had made him impervious to punishment and that this had given him an advantage. Collins replied that, in fact, the hypnotism was merely a ruse and that he had successfully psyched Eubank out of the fight.

While Eubank's remarks might be disregarded as the belly-aching of a beaten athlete, there was actually a serious point being made. While hypnotism has been used in sport principally as an aid to relaxation, post-hypnotic suggestions would technically facilitate something similar to what Eubank had in mind. The psychologist Richard Cox, in his book *Sport Psychology* (1998), states that "Ken Norton was given posthypnotic suggestions for his fight with Muhammad Ali." Post-hypnotic suggestions are recommendations for action given by a hypnotist while the subject is in a hypnotic state. In contrast to the state of waking hypnosis in which subjects are asked to carry out actions while in a trance, post-hypnotic suggestions are carried out at a later stage.

The concept of post-hypnotic suggestions takes the application of hypnosis in sport some way from a method of enhancing performance via relaxation: one can easily see how it might be used, generally, to get competitors FOCUSED and to improve particular facets of play. But, there are limits; as Cox points out, "hypnosis may be able to help a successful athlete, but it cannot make a good performer out of a poor one."

Of related interest

Cox, Richard (1998) *Sport Psychology: Concepts and Applications*, 4th edn, McGraw-Hill.

Levleva, Lydia (1997) *Inner Sports: Mental Skills for Peak Performance* (two audiocassettes), Human Kinetics.

Morgan, W.P. and Brown, D.R. (1983) "Hypnosis," in Williams, M.H. (ed.) *Ergogenic Aids in Sport*, Human Kinetics.

Reynolds case, The

In 1992, a US federal judge in Ohio awarded Harry "Butch" Reynolds, then world 400 meters record holder, $26 million (£16m) after determining that the International Amateur Athletics Federation (IAAF) had acted in error to ban him from competition for two years for testing positive for drugs. Reynolds had tested positive following a race in Monte Carlo in August, 1990, but challenged the IAAF's decision to ban him. The IAAF had no assets in the jurisdiction covered by the Ohio court and opted not to defend the case, on the assumption that no order could be enforced.

The case was an unprecedented reversal and the scale of the award prompted the International Amateur Athletics Association (IAAF) to establish legal defenses against recurrences. Prior to the Atlanta Summer Olympic games of 1996, all competitors were made to sign a declaration that, in the event of a dispute over drug testing, they would not seek legal redress outside the Court of Arbitration for Sport.

Reynold's lawyers pursued their award, obtaining orders in several US states in which the IAAF held assets. The IAAF was forced to respond and appealed the original decision. Eventually the case reached the Supreme Court. In 1993, a US Court of Appeal overturned the Reynolds award, ruling that the Ohio judge had no jurisdiction over the IAAF, which was then based in London.

Reynolds, having served his ban, had since resumed his athletic career. International sports bodies hailed the appeal verdict as an important milestone, but were braced for the legal conflicts that followed as more athletes who had been banned for alleged drug use sought atonement and restitution through the courts. Germany's Katrin Krabbe fought for damages from German and international athletics federations, and the MODAHL CASE in Britain indicated how litigious athletes were prepared to become in attempting to clear their names and claim damages.

The Reynolds case bears some resemblance to the SLANEY CASE, in which veteran middle-distance runner Mary Slaney contested a positive test for testosterone, which was conducted in 1996 when she was aged 37. Slaney was cleared by USA Track and Field, but remained under suspicion by the IAAF which suspended her and called for an arbitration meeting.

Of related interest

Downes, S. and Mackay, D. (1996) *Running Scared: How Athletics lost its Innocence*, Mainstream.

Ferstle, J (1922) "I want to clear my name," *Runner's World* vol 27, no 7.

Nelson, V.A. (1993) "Butch Reynolds and the American Judicial System v. the International Amateur Athletic Federation: a comment on the need for judicial restraint," *Seton Hall Journal of Sport Law* vol 3, no 1.

risk

The appeal of fear

While the trend in sports over the past century has been to remove or minimize potentially harmful elements, many sports entail some exposure to risk and peril. Without the prospect of danger, some sports would lose their character and probably their fascination. Paradoxically, the effort to render mainstream sports safer has been accompanied by attempts to invent competitive activities in which the risk factor is paramount.

It is at least possible that the apparent lust for danger is a product of a "safety first" culture in which personal security, public protection and environmental management have become priorities. Panics spread easily among populations sensitized to the hazards of pollutants, foodstuffs, sex and a seemingly endless list of other potential dangers that lurk both within and without. In the 1980s, as the search for safety gained momentum, the ways to escape it become more ingenious. Established practices like mountain climbing, stunt cycling and potholing continued as newer adaptations flourished. Zorbing, bungee jumping and whitewater rafting contained ersatz dangers: they offered thrills, though under controlled conditions. Other responses, such as hang gliding, kayaking off waterfalls or extreme sports, were less amenable to control and so had genuine risks attached.

The sociologist Frank Furedi argues that by the 1990s, societies all over the world had become preoccupied, if not obsessed, by safety. Risk avoidance became an organizing principle for much behavior. Safety was not something that people could just have: they needed to work toward getting it. So, human control was extended into virtually every aspect of cultural life: nothing that was potentially controllable was left to chance.

The title of Furedi's book, *Culture of Fear* (1997), describes an environment in which risks are not so much there, as they are created. We started to fear things that would have been taken for granted in previous times: drinking water, the nuclear family, technology all came to be viewed as secreting previously unknown perils. Furedi despairs at this "worship of safety," as he calls it. The most significant discoveries and innovations have arisen out of a spirit of adventure and a disregard for perils.

While we avoid risks that lie outside our control, we are quite prepared to take voluntary risks. The so-called "lifestyle risks" such as smoking, drinking and driving are examples of this. But sports present us with something quite different: they are manufactured risks that are actually designed in such a way as to preserve natural dangers or build in new ones. Horse racing always contains some risk for both jockey and horse, particularly in steeplechases. Lowering fences would reduce the hazard, but the governing associations have resisted doing so.

On the other hand, boxing, especially amateur boxing, has done its utmost to reduce the dangers that are inherent in combat sports. Yet both sports are fraught with risk, and both continue to prosper. According to Furedi's thesis, it is probable that they would continue to prosper with or without safety measures. He cites the example of rock climbing, which had some of its risks reduced by the introduction of improved ropes, boots, helmets and other equipment. Furedi writes: "The fact that young people who choose to climb mountains might not want to be denied the *frisson* of risk does not enter into the calculations of the safety-conscious professional, concerned to protect us from ourselves."

Furedi is one of a number of writers who have speculated on the rise of what Ulrich Beck calls the *Risk Society* (Sage, 1992). Beck believes that advances in science and technology have expanded our knowledge not only of how the world works, but of the perils it holds. Many of the perils have actually been fostered by our desire to know more. In other words, many of the anxieties have been produced by knowledge, not ignorance.

Social fragmentation

Furedi believes the preoccupation with safety has come about through a "tendency for society to fragment," itself the result of economic dislocation and a weakening of social institutions. We have become "individuated": survival has become a personal concern, not a social one. Matters of health, work, crime and the provision of services have become individual issues. In the midst of this transformation of the relationship between the individual and society, tradition and cohesion have been lost. We are all concerned with ourselves. In many ways, Furedi's argument extends that of Christopher Lasch, whose observations of the 1970s led him to believe NARCISSISM had taken grip of Western culture.

The problem, as Furedi and others see it, is that risk is still an important element in human life: we can become too secure and lose what has been a vital and heroic trait. As Michael Bane (1997) suggests: "In our personal lives, we accept the government's (and the legal system's) position that life should be free of risks. . . . Our businesses have been hampered – even crippled." Yet, the more we find ways of controlling or even wiping out risk, the more we find ways of flirting with danger. John Adams, in his book *Risk* (UCL Press, 1995), believes that we have inside us a "risk thermostat" which we can set to our own tastes, according to our own particular culture. "Some like it hot – a Hell's Angel or a Grand Prix racing driver, for example; others like it cool," writes Adams. "But no one wants absolute zero." We all want to retain some danger in our lives, and sport is one of the preferred ways of doing this. Most people would not go to a restaurant declared unsafe by state sanitary inspectors, but some of those same people might ski off piste, go scuba diving or go on survivalist expeditions. A game of chess may offer no hint of danger: skiing, surfing and all air, combat and motor sports certainly do. Sitting in a crowd watching such sports can carry a vicarious sense of danger.

Even safe sports carry concealed risks. Witness, for example, the case of Gunther Parche, an obsessively devoted fan of Steffi GRAF, who in 1993 attacked Monica Seles with a knife because he feared she rivaled his idol as the world's premier female tennis player. Seles was seriously injured, but survived and eventually returned to competition, though without fully recapturing her best form.

Risks are not confined to active competitors. Managers and coaches do not typically enjoy rude health. Football coach Mike Ditka and boxing manager Lou Duva both underwent major heart surgery. British soccer manager Brian Clough developed a well-publicized drinking habit during and after his successful professional career.

Often the risks involved in sports do not become apparent until years after the sports performer has finished competing. The symptoms of brain damage incurred during competition often do not manifest until years later. Stories of retired boxers experiencing medical problems are legion. Much more unusual is the case of Billy McPhail, a Scottish soccer player in the 1950s, who suffered pre-senile dementia at the age of 70 and claimed in court that his condition was the result of persistently heading the ball. There is some research that suggests a neurological link between playing soccer and brain damage.

It is against this background that we must understand the enduring presence of DEATH in sports. For risk to be a factor in the calculus that makes sports attractive, there has to be a genuine possibility of harm. Otherwise, people would be content to go to any number of theme parks that feature "death defying" white knuckle rides. They typically promise all the benefits of an ADRENALINE RUSH with no attendant dangers. Sports can be dangerous and, as such, fatalities often occur.

Of related interest

Bane, Michael (1997) *Over the Edge: A Regular Guy's Odyssey in Extreme Sports*, Gollancz.
Füredi, Frank (1997) *Culture of Fear*, Cassell.

Groves, D. (1987) "Why do some athletes choose high-risk sports?" *Physician and Sportsmedicine* vol 15, no 2.

rivalries

Head to head

Rivalries are an integral part of sports. They feature two individuals or teams that are so evenly matched in terms of capability, technique, determination and other values associated with sports success that every contest between them ensures the kind of intense competition that provides outstanding audience entertainment. One of the conditions of rivalries is that one rival's supremacy is transient and always open to challenge.

Track events have yielded some keen rivalries, none keener than that between British middle-distance runners Sebastian Coe and Steve Ovett, who in 1981 traded the world mile record three times in nine days. In any other era, either man would have probably dominated distances between 800 and 3,000 meters, but the fact that they both peaked in the early 1980s meant that neither established dominance over the other. In fact, they never met in a one-mile race.

TELEVISION woke up to the audience appeal of rivalries too late to bring Coe and Ovett together in a special event, but, in 1985, British commercial television brokered a race featuring Mary Decker Slaney and South African Zola Budd. Budd had accidentally tripped Slaney, or Decker as she then was, at the Los Angeles Summer Olympics the year before, leaving Slaney crying at trackside. The 3,000 meters "needle match" was held at London's Crystal Palace, but was in no sense a genuine confrontation: Slaney romped home, while Budd trailed twelve seconds behind her in fourth place. Ironically Budd, who was billed as the villain of the piece, earned $125,000 compared to Slaney's $75,000. The victor later became embroiled in a DRUGS-related issue that became known as the SLANEY CASE.

Carl Lewis was locked into two lucrative rivalries in the 1990s. After being beaten into second place and then reinstated as the winner of the 100 meters in the Seoul Olympics, his rematch with Ben Johnson in Lille in 1991 (after Johnson had served out his drugs suspension) turned out to be an anticlimax. Johnson, who was found to have traces of an anabolic steroid in his system after his Olympic "win," managed only seventh place, while Lewis was beaten into second place by fellow American Jon Drummond. Briton Linford Christie and Lewis shared $320,000 for a one-off race in 1993, but again Drummond produced a surprise by running a close second to Christie, leaving Lewis a distant third.

Such an embarrassment was avoided in June 1997 when "The Challenge of Champions" featured just two protagonists, Canada's Donovan Bailey and the USA's Michael Johnson, who held the world 100 meters and 200 meters records respectively. Both were also 1996 Olympic champions, Bailey at 100 meters, Johnson at 200 and 400 meters. They met head to head (with no other competitors) at the Toronto Skydome over the neutral distance of 150 meters. A supplementary coincident rivalry was dubbed "Swoosh vs the Stripes," an allusion to the shoes worn by the runners: Johnson wore NIKE, Bailey wore Adidas (neither pair weighed more than 3.5 ounces).

One of the most bitter rivalries involved figure skaters Tonya Harding and Nancy Kerrigan, who clashed at the 1994 Winter Olympic games; Kerrigan took the silver medal, with Harding finishing eighth. Rarely has there been such a dramatic rivalry as HARDING VS KERRIGAN. Harding's near-obsession with her media-friendly rival drove her to extraordinary lengths to eliminate her from competition. She became involved with friends who physically attacked Kerrigan prior to the games, hoping that she would be injured too badly to appear. The attack backfired: Harding was taken to court, plea bargained a single felony count of hindering a Federal prosecution, and was punished with three year's probation, 500 hours of community service and a $160,000 (£98,000) fine, which was apparently paid for out of appearance fees at various functions. Harding was stripped of her 1994 US Figure Skating title and her membership of the Figure Skating Association was canceled.

Kerrigan, while only a silver medalist, was feted; her wholesome image brought her several lucrative contracts, including one from Disney. Harding, who years earlier had established her credentials as a world-class skater (she was ranked number two in 1991), never recovered from her poor performance in 1994 and disappeared from competition in the same year at the relatively early age of 24.

Rivalries beyond competition

Unlike any other sports rivalry, the one between Olga Korbut and Nadia Comaneci was never played out in an arena: the two gymnasts never met head to head in a competition. Their rivalry was for the affections of television viewers all over the world. Korbut, who was born in the Soviet Union in 1955, was six years older than Comaneci and, for four years from 1972, was the most popular and inspirational gymnast ever known. The Munich Summer Olympics were televised internationally, and viewers became infatuated by the fresh-faced, cherubic Korbut, who leapt euphorically at every triumph and dissolved into tears when setbacks threatened. Korbut's gentle play at the aesthetic borders between art and competitive sports produced a visual extravaganza that captured television viewers' imaginations. The games were known as the "Korbut Olympics." Gymnastics as a sport received its biggest boost ever as young children followed Korbut's inspiration. Korbut could lay claim to being the best-known female athlete in the world.

But Korbut was replaced within four years. Still only 21, Korbut admitted to being burned out by the rigors of training through her pre-pubescent years. Nadia Comenici of Romania was only 14 when she appeared at the Montreal Olympics of 1976. She was awarded an unprecedented perfect score of 10 for her performance on the asymmetric bars; she then repeated the score six times to earn the nickname "Little Miss Perfect." Even smaller than the diminutive Korbut (5 foot; 84 lbs), Comaneci, like her predecessor, charmed the world's television audiences with impish floor displays and outrageously acrobatic work on the bars.

In one Olympic cycle, the rivalry was over. They had contrasting fortunes in later life. Korbut married Leonid Bartevich, a pop singer, and retired to become a full–time homeworker. By her mid–twenties she was showing the effects of her early training regimes; haggard beyond her years, she became prone to bouts of depression and slipped into premature obscurity. Comaneci avoided BURNOUT and defected to the USA in 1989; there she married former Olympic gymnast, Bart Connor, and remained healthy. KORBUT VS COMANECI is an example of a sporting rivalry that was played out in the imaginations of fans.

Tennis has witnessed some unusual rivalries, often played out against a backdrop of sexual politics. The 1981 "Battle of the Sexes" was a televised showcase event between 55–year–old ex–professional Bobby Riggs and a peak–form Billie Jean KING, who dispatched him with relative ease. Riggs had earlier beaten Margaret Court, and claimed even an aging male player of reasonable proficiency could beat a top–class woman player. It was an embarrassingly foolish contention.

In her book, *Strong Women and Deep Closets: Lesbians and Homophobia in Sport* (Human Kinetics, 1998), Pat Griffin argues that "the longtime rivalry between Chris Evert and Martina Navratilova had an unspoken subtext of Beauty (Queen) versus Butch (Lesbian)." Navratilova was one of a number of GAYS known to be on the professional tennis circuit, but her well–publicized outing in 1982, coming so soon after the unsuccessful "palimony" suit brought by King's female secretary, reinforced the view that there were predatory lesbians lurking in the locker rooms. Griffin believes that this posed a threat to the established gender order of sports and threw up new sorts of rivalries, specifically about the male provenance of sport itself.

Team sports have also yielded often intense rivalries that owe more to factors lying outside sports. In soccer, for example, the bile secreted in any game between Barcelona and Real Madrid is due to ethnic bitterness: Barcelona is the capital of the region of Catalonia, whose residents regard themselves as independent of Spain and have their own language, customs and beliefs to maintain this. Madrid symbolizes the homogenizing presence of a nation that denies Catalans a separate existence. The two Glasgow clubs, Celtic and Rangers, for long represented sectarian halves of a city divided by religion, with Celtic recruiting only Catholic players and Rangers Protestants. In the 1990s both clubs relaxed their policies. At an international level, games between France and Germany are still affected by the vestigial asperity of the Second World War, when France was occupied by Nazi Germany.

Of related interest

Aaseng, N. (1985) *Pro Sports' Greatest Rivalries*, Lerner Publishing.

Baugham, Cynthia (1995) *Women on Ice: Feminist Essays on the Tonya Harding/ Nancy Kerrigan Spectacle*, Routledge.

Reeves, R.A. and Tesser, A. (1985) "Self–evaluation in sports teams rivalries," *Bulletin of the Psychonomic Society* vol 23, no 4.

Wynne, E.A. (1987) "Competitive sports: inevitably controversial." *Journal of Physical Education, Recreation & Dance* vol 58, no 3.

Robinson, Jackie

b. 1919, USA; d. 1972

Baseball's great experiment

On April 15, 1947, Robinson became the first African American to play Major League Baseball when he started for the Brooklyn Dodgers against Boston Braves. In doing so, Robinson broke what was then known as sport's "color line."

There had been black baseball players for many years, and some had played with whites until the milestone Plessy vs. Ferguson case of 1896, which enforced the legal segregation of blacks and whites. Moses Fleetwood ("Fleet") Walker, for example, played for the American Association's Toledo club in the 1880s. Walker featured in what is probably the first drawing of the color line in baseball: in 1884, his club was instructed by the visiting Chicago White Stockings, under the ownership of A.G. SPALDING, to keep its "colored man" off the field when Chicago came to town. Demands such as this were widespread and ultimately resulted in a segregation of sports. By the 1890s, players like Walker were excluded from the Major Leagues and the only blacks used by baseball clubs were the club mascots. Black players were forced to organize their own loosely-structured Negro Leagues.

Robinson, the son of sharecropper and grandson of a slave, excelled in several sports before serving in the US Army, where he was court-martialled on a trumped-up charge. This incident became the subject of an interesting TELEVISION movie, *The Court-Martial of Jackie Robinson*, directed by Larry Peerce (1990). As a baseball player in the Kansas City Monarchs in the Negro Leagues, Robinson was evidently talented. Although strict segregation had held firm for years, Robert Peterson (1970) observed that: "By the early [nineteen] thirties, gentle waves were washing against the hull of organized baseball." The Brooklyn Dodgers' general manager, Branch Rickey, was a known pragmatist and it is unlikely that his bold attempt to integrate Robinson into the Major League was an idealistic gesture. More probable is his guess that Brooklyn's increasing black population would flock to fill the empty bleachers at Ebbets Field. There were other outstanding players in the Negro Leagues, including Cool Papa Bell, Josh Gibson and Satchel Paige.

In 1946, Robinson went to Florida to try out for the Montreal Royals, the Dodgers' farm team. The South was known for its hostility to blacks: in the same year that Robinson was trying out, nine African Americans were lynched and over twenty others had to be rescued from a mob of whites. Also in 1946, a black war veteran in military uniform was dragged from a bus, beaten and blinded by a police chief in Batesburg, South Carolina.

In Florida, there were segregation laws that prohibited whites and blacks from sharing the same restaurants, hotels, schools, theaters and a variety of other public places, included the baseball field. At Daytona Beach, Robinson was made to find a "coloreds-only" hotel. Unable to get a flight, he had to sit at the back of a Greyhound bus during a sixteen-hour journey. This suggested to Robinson that he would not get a fair try-out in Florida and, according to Chris Lamb, he considered returning to the Negro Leagues. Robinson threatened several times to quit during the spring training, but each time he was persuaded to try again. He could not stay in the same hotels as his team-mates, nor eat in the same restaurants. But, Robinson impressed enough on the field of play to ensure him a start with the Montreal team.

It was thought that a gradual integration in the more liberal environment of Canada would help prepare him for the inevitable abuse he would get when he moved up to the majors. He led the International League in hitting and showed enough potential to play in Major League Baseball. Relatively old at 28, Robinson made his debut amid opposition from his own team-mates, several of whom signed a petition asking Rickey not to bring Robinson to Brooklyn. The St Louis Cardinals threatened not to play against the Dodgers if Robinson was in their lineup. The National League's president, Ford Frick, warned that anyone who refused to take the field against Robinson would face a lifetime ban. "The National League will go down the line with Robinson, no matter the consequences," Frick told the Cardinals. "If you go through with your intentions, you will find you have been guilty of complete madness." The threat subsided and "baseball's great experiment," as the Robinson's integration was known, continued, though not smoothly.

In the first two months of the season, Robinson was hit by pitches six times, spiked by base runners and taunted by both fans and players. He did not retaliate and ended the season being voted Rookie of the Year. Later, he was to become the league's Most Valuable Player. During his ten years with the Dodgers they won six National League pennants and, in 1955, their first World Series. His effect off the field was arguably greater: by the end of the 1947 season, four more black players were playing for Major Jeague clubs and, by 1959, every Major League team had at least one black player. (Basketball's equivalent of Robinson was Chuck Cooper, who in 1951 signed for Boston Celtics and precipitated a rush of black players to the major clubs.) In 1997, the fiftieth anniversary of his debut, the three highest-paid baseball players – Barry Bonds, Ken Griffey Jr and Albert Belle – were African Americans and four managers were black or Latino. In the interim period, great black players like Willie Mays and Hank AARON had made their mark and both the National and American Leagues had black presidents.

In his book *The Negro Revolt* (Hamish Hamilton, 1963), Lewis Lomax described Robinson as a "moderate" and his sympathies with the National Association for the Advancement of Colored People (NAACP) underlined his initial reluctance to get involved with mass direct action. The NAACP favored social change through legal processes. Robinson became much more confident and outspoken in the 1950s, and eventually criticized the NAACP for its gradualist policies. Presumably, his testing years as the first black player affected his perceptions. Edwin Henderson (*The Negro in Sports*, Associated Publishers, 1949) noted that, at one point, Robinson came near to a nervous breakdown. At the same time, Robinson was "wrapped in all the dreams and aspirations not only of negro people but of all Americans of whatever color who knew that segregation was wrong."

Interestingly, Robinson's impact was largely confined to the diamond. Fifty years after his path-breaking entrance, baseball remained a white spectator sport, even in the American inner cities. Black players comprised about sixteen per cent of Major League rosters in 1997, reflecting the competing attractions of basketball (80 per cent of NBA team players were black) and football (the NFL had 65 per cent black players). In management, African Americans have been under-represented. Of the 234 managerial appointments following the hiring of Frank Robinson, who became the first black manager in 1972, only ten were from minorities.

Robinson, a diabetic, died in 1972, aged 53 and was buried in Cypress Hills Cemetery, Brooklyn. His headstone bears an epitaph provided by himself: "A life is not important except in the impact it has on other lives."

Plessy *vs* Ferguson

In the Plessy *vs* Ferguson decision of 1896, the Supreme Court upheld the state of Louisiana's requirement that seating on trains be segregated. The doctrine emerging from this decision was that blacks and whites were "separate but equal." Mr. Plessy was, he claimed, seven-eighths "white," yet he was, for all intent and purposes, a "negro" and therefore not allowed to travel in "whites only" railroad cars. The doctrine of "separate but equal" spread throughout the South and, by 1910, there was a virtual caste system in practice. This served to maintain blacks in positions of perpetual subordination, if not servitude. While some individual sports performers, most notably Jack JOHNSON and, later, Jesse Owens, were permitted to rise to the top of their sports, black players were not allowed to compete in major team sports. The "separate but equal" doctrine was eventually declared unconstitutional by the Brown vs Board of Education decision of 1954.

Of related interest

Lamb, Chris (1997) " 'I never want to take another trip like this one': Jackie Robinson's journey to integrate baseball," *Journal of Sport History* vol 24, no 2.
Peterson, Robert (1970) *Only the Ball Was White*, Prentice-Hall.
Rowan, Carl and Robinson, Jackie (1960) *Wait Till Next Year*, Random House.
Tygeil, Jules (1983) *Baseball's Great Experiment*, Oxford University Press.

Rocky I–V

The *Rocky* film series comprised five movies, released between 1976–90, all revolving around the fortunes of the eponymous professional heavyweight boxer, all featuring Sylvester Stallone and all heavily-endowed with lurid, blood-drenched boxing action that owed much more to choreography than to real boxing.

The original, low-budget production *Rocky* (1976), adapted from Stallone's own script, was directed by John G. Avildsen and became a surprise artistic and box office success, winning the Best Picture Oscar and launching Stallone as one of the most bankable action movie stars ever. The story contrasts the innocence of club fighter Rocky Balboa with the manipulative cynicism of promoters and managers eager to exploit his whiteness, his Italian background and his rank UNDERDOG status in any way they can. The business backers of world heavyweight champion, Apollo Creed, an African American, pick Balboa's name from the lower orders of the rankings and publicize their champion's magnanimity in giving even no-hopers a shot at the world title. The fact that Balboa is white and can be billed as "The Italian Stallion" adds ethnic spice.

The Balboa character was thought to have been inspired by Chuck Wepner, who, in 1975, was plucked from obscurity and thrust into a challenge for the world heavyweight title against Muhammad ALI, who was making the first defense of the title he had famously regained by beating George Foreman in Zaire. Like Wepner, who sustained cuts but gutsily lasted until the fifteenth round before the referee stopped the fight, Balboa puts up unexpectedly durable resistance before dropping a decision. The Ali-like Creed rules out a rematch in the immediate aftermath of the fight.

His valiant challenge vanquished, Balboa returns to his hometown Philadelphia a new man. No longer an illiterate working man who works out on cow carcasses instead of heavy bags, he is now a legitimate contender with newfound aspirations. The plot of *Rocky II* (1979) surprised no one: directed by Stallone himself, this sequel saw a second death or glory effort from Balboa. If anything, there were more fluid ounces of blood spilt in the rematch than in the original. Rocky leaves the ring looking like an abattoir, but with the title belt around his waist.

Rocky III (1982) effectively completes the hungry fighter cycle. Balboa, now champion, begins to luxuriate in the fame and adulation. Far from a starving nonentity striving to make good, he relaxes into a world of easy living, hardly noticing how all the elements that made him such a formidable warrior have been dissipated. The fighter once driven by the will to survive falls prey to the hubris that has visited many a great champion. The Italian Stallion finds himself struggling after Clubber Lang defeats him. Having lost both his title and his manager, Rocky relies on his wife's support to help him make it back to the top, enlisting former adversary Apollo Creed as his trainer.

Stallone directed *Rocky III*, but, not content to let the trilogy rest, he was tempted to add another, perhaps superfluous chapter. *Rocky IV* (1985), again directed by Stallone, opens with Rocky's one-time opponent, Apollo Creed, getting battered literally to death by a new Russian sensation named Drago, played by Dolph Lundgren. (In the fight sequences, Lundgren dwarfs Creed, played in the series by Carl Weathers: one story has it that former pro heavyweight-cum-actor Ken Norton was lined up for the part, only to be turned down after he made Stallone look too small in the fight scenes.) Most of the film contrasts Drago's high-tech training techniques with Balboa's more primitive methods; and this alone makes the movie quite interesting, especially as most of Drago's supposedly futuristic training apparatuses and techniques are now in common use.

Stallone did with the film series what most aging fighters do with their careers: prolong them. *Rocky V*, released five years after its predecessor and totally lacking any semblance of freshness or originality, was no more than an appendix. John Avildsen returned to direct this tale of Balboa – ruined by a crooked accountant and brain damaged – trying to resume his fighting career, albeit vicariously. His charge, Tommy "Machine" Gunn, is played by boxer Tommy Morrison, in 1990 a useful heavyweight prospect who would go on to become a heavyweight champion (he later declared himself to be HIV-positive). The film sees Rocky re-evaluate himself, returning to his old haunts in an effort to redeem himself. Gunn is lured away from his mentor by a promoter who owes much of his style to Don King. Having won the heavyweight title, Gunn is derided at a press conference for beating a "paper champion." The true champion is Rocky, say the press: he never lost the title in the ring. Gunn hunts down Balboa, but comes a poor second after a hammer and tongs street fight

After fifteen years, the series seemed to have exhausted itself. The emergence of Mike TYSON as heavyweight champion and the melodramas that followed made the fictional Rocky stories seem almost quaint by comparison. But, it is interesting that the series made its impact at a time when boxing's heavyweight division was less than thrilling. Dominated by Larry Holmes, the heavyweight class featured several decent though dull fighters, such as Tim Witherspoon, Greg Page, Trevor Berbick and James "Bonecrusher" Smith. Compared with the Ali–Frazier–Foreman era it followed, the Holmes era was unexciting, with the highlight of Holmes's career probably coming with his defense against Gerry Cooney; and only the unfortunate racial ingredient gave this match added interest (Cooney was white). Set against this backdrop, the fantastic adventures of Rocky Balboa seemed a better, if preposterous, choice.

Of related interest

Rocky, directed by John G. Avildsen, 1976.
Rocky II, directed by Sylvester Stallone, 1979.
Rocky III, directed by Sylvester Stallone, 1982.
Rocky IV, directed by Sylvester Stallone, 1985.
Rocky V, directed by John G. Avildsen, 1990.

S

salary caps

The salary cap is a maximum amount a club can spend on its *total* wage bill, rather than on individual players. Its aim is to maintain a balance in a league: because all clubs are restricted in the money they may offer players, wealthier clubs are prevented from continually attracting the best players. They can pay the same total wage bill as less rich clubs. In this way, leagues are kept competitive and the chances of domination by one team or by an elite few are minimized (although not eliminated).

The NBA (National Basketball Association) introduced the concept of a salary cap in 1984, a year that coincided with the beginning of its ascent to become a major American sport. As genuine stars such as Larry Bird and Magic JOHNSON began to gain national exposure, the league tried to ensure that the entire NBA benefited. The league's commissioner, David Stern, is credited with the salary cap initiative. While the maximum salaries were meager in early years, by 1998 the NBA cap was set at 51.8 per cent of the league's "defined gross revenues." This was determined as $26.9m (£16.5m) per twelve-man team, or an average of over $2m per player per year.

The system was probably a contributory factor in the NBA's commercial success: rather than let franchises operate independently (as, for example, MAJOR LEAGUE BASEBALL and, to a lesser extent, the NFL did), the NBA subordinated its members to the central organization and demanded compliance. A balance established, the NBA maintained interest in its competition by creating the chance that an UNDERDOG always stood a fighting chance against its more favored rivals, which were never allowed to exercise fully their financial might. However, the salary cap became less effective in the 1990s when a Chicago Bulls team, boosted by the exceptional Michael JORDAN, was able to assume an historically unprecedented supremacy.

The NFL's salary cap was placed under stress by the advent of FREE AGENCY, which meant that out-of-contract players were able to negotiate their own terms with whichever club they chose. Jerry Jones, owner of Dallas Cowboys, is known to have bypassed the NFL's salary cap on team salaries by paying only moderate wages, but offering huge signing-on bonuses that ensured that he could attract the best players around. This loophole was closed in 1997 by fixing bonus payments at no more than 15 per cent over the maximum of $41.4m per 53-man squad. Only 63 per cent of all revenues were to be allocated to salaries. The cap needed to be revised with each successive TELEVISION contract, of course.

Historically, Major League Baseball has granted its clubs a high degree of autonomy in their dealings, but it levied a "luxury tax" on the five teams with the highest payrolls in the form of a charge of 35 per cent on any amount over $55.6 spent on annual salaries per club. While this seemed punitive, it did not prevent all five teams progressing to the 1997 playoffs, though the fifth-ranked club in terms of salary expenditure – Florida Marlins – actually won the World Series in that year.

The salary cap option was rarely discussed in Europe where wealthy soccer clubs, like Juventus of Italy, Manchester United of England and Barcelona of Spain, were typically the biggest spenders. While the BOSMAN CASE of 1995 was thought to presage a glut of NFL-style salaries, the transfer system held firm and much of the monies continued to be exchanged between clubs in the form of transfer fees rather than between clubs and players.

In 1998, rugby league introduced a two-tier salary cap. In Australasia, twenty clubs that competed in television-driven merger between the European Super League and the Australian Rugby League were each made to work under a salary cap of A$3m (£1.2m). British clubs had their cap defined as 50 per cent of "relevant income," including television rights fees, season ticket sales and sponsorship. The move was inspired by the competition between clubs from the two hemispheres brokered by Sky television, owned by Rupert MURDOCH. After its first season, it became apparent that the Australian clubs were embarrassingly dominant.

Of related interest

Rosentraub, Mark S. (1997) *Major League Losers: The Real Cost of Sports and Who's Paying For It*, HarperCollins.

Scully, Gerald W. (1995) *The Market Structure of Sports*, University of Chicago Press.

Sheehan, Richard G. (1996) *Keeping Score: The Economics of Big-Time Sports*, Diamond Communications.

Salt Lake City scandal

The Salt Lake City scandal arose out of allegations that International Olympic Committee (IOC) officials had received gifts tantamount to bribes when reviewing the various bids to host the 2002 Winter Olympic games. The IOC's decision to award the games to Salt Lake City was announced in 1995 in Budapest. Four years later, six of the organization's officials were suspended with a recommendation that they resign following disclosures of bribery in the bidding process. It was reported that they and perhaps others had received "gifts" and "donations" from Salt Lake City's Olympic bid committee. The investigation into the reports revealed a more extensive pattern of CORRUPTION in the Olympic movement, particularly in the way it had allocated sites of Olympic games.

The calumny was started in 1997 when Marc Hodler, a senior IOC vice-president, announced to the media that there were four "agents" who, for a commission of between $500,000 and $1m, would deliver blocks of votes to cities bidding for the rights to host the games. Losing cities had informed Hodler of a numbers of IOC officials whose votes could be "bought." The allegations quickly multiplied and stories of past Olympic games came to light, each suggesting that far from being a neutral assessment process, the way in which cities were awarded games was racked with venality. In effect, the city prepared to offer the most generous bribes to officials won the bidding.

The bribes were said to include tuition expenses to an IOC member to send his son to a US university, thousands of dollars worth of medical services, prostitutes and hard cash. Sergio Santander Fantini, the president of the Chilean Olympic Committee and an IOC member since 1992, denied taking a $10,000 donation from Salt Lake City to help finance his re-election campaign in Santiago, although he was one of the officials asked to resign.

The scandal prompted investigations into other Olympic venues, including the Japanese city of Nagano which held the Winter Olympics of 1998. The bribes to secure the games were described by IOC officials as "astronomical," and documents related to the bid were said to have been incinerated. Manchester, which lost out to Australia in its bid to host the Summer Olympics in 2000, revealed that IOC members solicited gifts and cash. Limits of $150 for gifts per member in the later stages of bidding ($50 in earlier stages) were imposed in 1986, after the Los Angeles games. Yet, even IOC chairman Juan Antonio Samaranch accepted a gift of guns worth $2,000 from Salt Lake City, and defended this by pointing out that the limit applied only to those responsible for voting. He also insisted that the guns would be displayed in an Olympic museum.

Samaranch had chaired the IOC from 1980 and, in many eyes, saved the Olympic movement from ruin. The 1980 Summer games in Moscow had been boycotted by the United States, and the previous games in Montreal had been a financial débâcle. Only two cities competed to stage the 1984 games, which was eventually awarded to Los Angeles. In 1981, Samaranch met with Horst Dassler, of Adidas, to develop a marketing strategy for the Olympics. Central to this strategy was the branding of the image of the five interlocking rings that form the Olympic symbol.

Prior to the Seoul Olympics of 1988, the IOC had no power to license its five interlocking rings symbol on a worldwide basis; under rule 53 of the Olympic charter, exclusive rights to use all Olympic names and symbols was held by individual member countries. Basically, the problem was solved by buying the rights from the 150 member countries. Companies were then invited to become official Olympic sponsors and, for a price, permitted to use the world famous symbol on their products and in their advertising. The biggest sponsor paid $14m (£9m).

The IOC was able to sell the games in this way because of television's interest. Without global exposure, the sponsorship would have been less attractive.

However, television continued to buy the rights to broadcast the games. ABC television paid 45 per cent toward the cost of staging the Los Angeles Games. NBC contributed only marginally less than the South Korean government to Seoul for the 1988 games. At the time of the Salt Lake City scandal, NBC held the exclusive American rights to five winter and summer Games, for which it paid $3.55bn.

While the IOC continued to present itself as embodying the spirit originally revived by de Coubertin, its ideals became progressively diluted. Samaranch had made clear his intention to extricate the Olympic movement financially from governments and become economically independent. In doing so, he made pacts with companies and the mass media; and these, in a sense, surrendered the Olympics' independence to other more overtly commercial organizations and, more generally, to market forces.

After the announcement that the 1984 games had made a surplus (Olympics do not make "profits") of $220m (£133m), other countries were encouraged to bid for future Olympics. As well as sharing in the largesse provided by TELEVISION and sponsors, countries profited from the extra business Olympic Games typically attract. The bidding became intense. Even before the Salt Lake City disclosure, rumors about the bidding process and other irregularities were rife. Two books by British writer Andrew Jennings did much to discredit the IOC's reputation as an honorable and wholesome organization. The Salt Lake City investigation led to suspicions about previous bids, the belief being that the money potentially available to host cities made bribes a small, albeit illegal, investment.

Of related interest

Jennings, Andrew (1996) *The New Lords of the Rings: Olympics, Corruption and How to Buy Gold Medals*, Pocket Books.

Simson, Vyv and Jennings, Andrew (1992) *The Lords of the Rings: Power, Money and Drugs in the Modern Olympics*, Simon & Schuster.

Swift, E.M. (1999) "Breaking point," *Sports Illustrated* vol 90, no 4, February 1.

Season On The Brink, A

John Feinstein's *A Season on the Brink: A Year with Bob Knight and the Indiana Hoosiers*, is hailed by its publishers as the "best-selling sports book of all time." Feinstein was given a year's leave of absence by his employer the *Washington Post* to shadow volatile head coach Bob Knight for the 1985/86 season; and while the season ended disappointingly for Indiana University – a first round exit from the NCAA tournament – the insights into Knight's restless quest for success distinguish the text from many other "insider" accounts. Knight himself, having granted the author access to what were hitherto no-go areas, such as the post-game locker room, was dissatisfied with the book, though Feinstein invokes one of the coach's precepts – the ends justify the means – to defend the unflattering frankness with which he depicts a man he describes as "brilliant, driven, compassionate – but not patient."

Feinstein's sprawling fresco, centered around the Hoosier's fluctuating fortunes, portrays Knight's tropes and peculiarities. The team's indifferent start to the season makes Knight explode with anger. His mean-spirited scapegoating of individual players on whom he often blames a defeat is almost inhumanly severe. He refuses to allow players on the plane back from road games, making them take a separate flight. "The reason we lost this game was *you*," he blares at Steve Risley, one of his players on another occasion. "It was *your* fault." Coaches are famously reluctant to single out individuals, doing so rarely for success and almost never for failure.

Knight's savage criticism continues, and players are subjected to unsubtle barrages of insults. Knight never misses a chance to compound their indignities. Yet, when the wins start to come with more regularity, Knight is almost as fierce in his condemnation. A close, hard-fought victory against Wisconsin meets not with warm approval but with: "You almost let them take this game away from you."

Knight is yoked with Vince LOMBARDI and Red Auerbach with Feinstein. And his track record bears the comparison. His consistently overachieving Indiana University teams earned him the job as coach of the US national team that won gold at the 1984 Olympics. "Some wondered why players like Charles Barkley and Antoine Carr weren't selected [for the Olympic team]," writes Feinstein. "The answer was simple: Knight wanted players who would take his orders without question." In the book, Knight is revealed as a total disciplinarian: he demands not just loyalty but absolute, unquestioning obedience. Individual talent is subordinated to Knight's method. When he sees evidence of spontaneity on court, he reminds players: "Playing my game is what got you here, boys, not playing your game." One ex-player is quoted as saying of Knight: "He's not a man, he's a set of rules."

By infantilizing his players, Knight maintains his role of paterfamilias; his players are "boys," who must surrender themselves to his wishes or be banished. Feinstein relates how a "rebellious" player, Ted Kitchel, made a point of reciprocating a Knight "glare." Despite a secret admiration for the player's stubbornness, Knight made his life miserable. Only when Kitchel's career was at an end did Knight express his appreciation. It was a Knight trademark: active players were rarely congratulated even after stellar performances. Once they had left the ranks, Knight was unsparing in his loyalty.

It has been suggested that one of the reasons for Knight's popularity is that his autocratic rule had the effect of reinforcing the cultural preference that young people should submit to parental control. In his *Sport in Society* (McGraw Hill, 1998), Jay Coakley makes a more general point about obsessional coaches such as Knight: "Sport reproduces a form of age relations in which adult power and privilege is defined not only as good but as a 'natural' and necessary aspect of social life."

Knight's world is a masculine one: "The women in his life have very defined roles: Nancy Knight has been a wife in the most traditional sense – mother, cook housekeeper, fan of the husband's basketball team. Knight has two secretaries."

The people he respects, scolds, manipulates, provokes, embitters and endears are all men. There seems barely room for women in Knight's life. There is certainly no room for them in Feinstein's book, which is in a sense a study of maleness: of male bonding, male conflicts, male ambitions and, above all, male monomania.

For Knight, basketball holds everything life has to offer. Bill Shankley, who managed the Liverpool soccer team in the 1960s and 1970s, was once queried over his attitude toward his sport which always seemed "a matter of life or death." Shankley replied: "It's more important than that." It was a sentiment that Knight would surely endorse. Every win for Knight is just a board over an abyss. The euphoria of success is always short-lived, and the possibility of defeat never disappears for long. Feinstein creates a vision of a man forever balancing, never stable long enough to establish the solidity that many find in middle age (Knight is in his mid forties as the book is being written).

Perhaps this is the key to his success: the indomitable, fractious spirit that guides him forbids contentment, less still calmness. Feinstein shows that Knight's rants and outbursts are not mere posturings, tricks in his repertoire of MOTIVATION techniques. Toward the start of the book, Feinstein relates Knight's now infamous eruption when he picked up his chair and threw it across the court, earning himself an immediate ejection from the game in front of 17,000 spectators and several million TELEVISION viewers. "Always and forever more, Knight and that chair would be linked," writes Feinstein. It continues to haunt him.

Surprisingly, there are few moments of humor: Knight's cussed passage through the season permits only the occasional, supercilious remark that might pass for humor. "Do you really think that God is going to help a team that *I'm* coaching?" he asks Steve Alford, his star player whose constant appeals to God run counter to Knight's self-help philosophy. God enters Knight's humor again when he comments sarcastically on Andre Harris' reach for a pass with one hand: "If God had wanted you to play this game with one hand you would have an arm growing out of your ass." But for the most part, Knight is consumed by the need to succeed in his own world. Years after the book, Frank Deford (1994) wrote: "Knight's mind is too good to be wasted on a mere game – and he probably recognizes that – but he's personally not comfortable away from the precisely circumscribed environment in which college basketball is played. Therein lies the great conflict in him."

None of the players on the Hoosiers' roster at the time of the book went on to emulate Isiah Thomas, Knight's most celebrated ward. Steve Alford, who was a member of the 1984 Olympic team, was voted the 1987 Big Ten Most Valuable Player and went on to become head basketball coach at Southwest Missouri State.

Of related interest

Deford, Frank (1994) "The rabbit hunter," *Sports Illustrated* vol 80, no 1.
Feinstein, John (1989) *A Season on the Brink: A Year with Bob Knight and the Indiana Hoosiers*, Fireside.
Yaeger, Don (1996) *Indue Process: The NCAA's Injustice for All*, Sagamore.

sex crimes

On September 19, 1991, Mike TYSON was indicted by a Marion County grand jury on a charge of raping Desiree Washington, a contestant at a Miss Black America pageant, who claimed Tyson had forcibly had sex with her in an Indianapolis hotel room. On February 10, 1992, Tyson was convicted of rape and sentenced to six years in prison. Washington later alleged that Tyson had given her a venereal disease. Tyson was released from prison in March 1995, and resumed his professional boxing career five months later under the guidance of Don KING. During his imprisonment, the boxer converted to Islam and claimed to be a reformed person. The blaze of publicity that accompanied Tyson's case turned it into a *cause célèbre*. There had been no comparable lawsuit since the arrest of another notorious heavyweight, Jack JOHNSON, under the Mann Act when he tried to cross state borders with a white female companion in 1913 (Johnson was forced into exile for seven years).

Less than two years after Tyson's release, the world's media were feasting on another celebrated sports star, when football player Michael Irvin of the Dallas Cowboys and his team-mate Eric Williams were accused of rape. Wide receiver Irvin was caught in an hotel with two "self-employed models" (as they described themselves), three ounces of marijuana, two ounces of cocaine and a vibrator. Although the charges did not stick, there had been enough football players convicted of similar charges to give the complainant's claim superficial credibility. Only months before, police reported that they were investigating a woman's complaint that she had been sexually assaulted by a member of the Philadelphia Eagles. A University of Southern California player was charged with rape; four players on the Grambling State University football team in Georgia were accused of raping a 15-year-old girl in a campus dormitory; and two players at Virginia Tech were each charged on one count of rape and one of attempted sodomy.

In 1998, former heavyweight champion boxer Bruce Seldon pleaded guilty to supplying a 15-year-old woman with marijuana and having unspecified sexual activity with her at his house. In 1999, the British soccer coach and former player Graham Rix was charged with having unlawful sex with a 15-year-old woman. There had been lesser known cases involving sports performers, enough of them to encourage the suspicion that many sportsmen were unable to restrain the testosterone rage required in the ring or on the field from spilling over into their off-game activities.

Academic enquiry on the subject of sexual AGGRESSION among male athletes has brought other perspectives to bear. The main question informing this research has been, as Jeffrey Benedict and Alan Klein (1997) put it: "Whether being a celebrity athlete provides a male athlete charged with sexual assault certain built-in advantages in the legal system." While the answer would seem to be "no" in the case of Tyson, this is not necessarily so: a high-profile athlete may actually have escaped conviction on previous occasions, or received lenient treatment, as a result of his status. Benedict and Klein set out to find the real answer.

Research on rape outside sports has demonstrated that acquaintance rape – as opposed to stranger rape – is most prevalent and that as many as 80 per cent of all sexual victims are known to their assailants. Benedict and Klein found that this pattern also holds good for sex crimes committed by sports performers; but the legal implications are different.

Susan Estrich's *Real Rape* (Harvard University Press, 1987) detailed the difficulties facing anyone trying to bring a prosecution on a rapist. The burden of responsibility falls very much with the victim, whose credibility is questioned at virtually every stage of the legal process. In 1995, research by Crosset *et al.* (1995) uncovered a correlation between participation in high-visibility college sports and reported incidents of sexual assault. The debate over whether male sports performers are more likely to be involved in sexual assaults than non-athletes was opened in 1993 by Gaines and Koss. Lawyer Alan Dershowitz, famed for his defense of Claus von Bulow, came to the defense of athletes, and academic Richard Lapchick pointed out several flaws in the research that purportedly linked sports performers with rape. The link would seem to be, at best, tenuous.

Benedict and Klein examined a more tangible aspect of the debate: whether sports performers accused of rape received preferential treatment once in the criminal justice system. As with any research on rape, the results need to be tempered with the recognition that a large number of sexual offenses are not reported. Benedict and Klein collected information on cases that were actually dealt with officially and not on those that were dealt with through nonjudicial means, such as civil courts or university judicial hearings.

From the 217 official police complaints lodged against sports performers, 45 (21 per cent) resulted in no formal action being taken. In other words, the police together with the district attorney's office determined that there was no sufficient cause to warrant an arrest. In some cases, the victim herself may have stopped the process because of the prohibitive prospect of publicity. Of those who were arrested, 32 per cent had charges against them dismissed; typically, cases that are unlikely to result in a conviction are screened out.

Of the remaining 117 sports performers, eight (7 per cent) had charges against them dismissed prior to trial, 43 (37 per cent) plea-bargained and 66 (56 per cent) stood trial. Of those who went to trial, 50 (76 per cent) were acquitted by a jury. Ten (15 per cent) were found guilty by a jury and six (9 per cent) ended in a hung jury. Adding the plea bargains with the jury convictions results in 53 convictions out of an original total of 172 arrests (31 per cent). Seen as a percentage of the number of athletes who were formally reported to the police for the commission of a sex crime, only 24 per cent were successfully prosecuted.

Always remembering the undisclosed amount of rapes, the researchers compared their findings with those nationally and found a significantly higher percentage (79 per cent) of complaints involving athletes that resulted in arrests. This may be accounted for by zeal with which police officers pursue high profile personalities. Because the media are likely to cover cases that involve such personalities, the police stay mindful of the possible attention and respond accordingly. One of the accusations they try to avoid is that of treating celebrities lightly. Yet discrepancies still occur at a national level: 54 per cent of arrests for rape result in convictions generally, while only 31 per cent of athletes arrested for rape are convicted. "A 23-percentage point difference indicates that something in the sport-law nexus is working to the advantage of athletes over their accusers," conclude Benedict and Klein. Factored into the higher arrest rate for sports performers, this yields an even greater discrepancy. In other words, more athletes get arrested, but fewer get convicted.

The question then becomes: what happens after the arrest? One thing that militates against a conviction is that the victim's credibility is called into doubt. Virtually every study of rape has turned up similar evidence. This takes on a peculiar importance in the sphere of sports, which is, on the accounts of many biographers, populated by young, available women whose intention is to procure the sexual favors of well-known athletes. Even if the extravagant claims of NBA stars like Magic JOHNSON and Dennis Rodman are to be considered exaggerations, there may still be enough truth concealed within them to accept that sports has its equivalent of groupies (Wilt Chamberlain famously claimed to have sampled the sexual favors of 20,000 different women). Accusers may not be groupies, but the fact that groupies are known to follow male sports performers will always damage the accusers' case.

Sports performers, especially celebrities, usually have sufficient resources to employ expensive legal defenses. Sometimes this backfires, as it did in the case of Tyson. At other times, it can work. Former football star O.J. SIMPSON, while tried for murder rather than rape, showed the benefits of a high-powered legal team, costing between $4–5 million (about £3m).

Perhaps the most tragic aftermath of a sexual assault charge came after soccer player Justin FASHANU fled from Maryland to his native England and committed suicide following accusations from a teenage boy. Fashanu was one of a number of GAYS in sport who had voluntarily outed themselves.

When allegations of rape are made, they are nearly always contested; when the alleged perpetrator is a known sports performer, that contestation is even greater. Good legal defenses apart, the stigma that attaches to anyone having casual sex, consensual or otherwise, with a sports performer makes it likely that the accuser will be as much on trial as the defendant.

Of related interest

Benedict, Jeffrey and Klein, Alan (1997) "Arrest and conviction rates for athletes accused of sexual assault," *Sociology of Sport Journal* vol 14, no 1.

Crosset, T.W., Benedict, J.R. and Mcdonald, M.A. (1995) "Male student-athletes reported for sexual assault: Survey of campus police departments and judicial affairs offices," *Journal of Sport and Social Issues* vol 19, no 2.

Miracle, A.W. and Rees, C.R. (1994) *Lessons of the Locker Room: The Myth of School Sports*, Prometheus Books.

Simpson, O.J.

b. 1947, USA

It has been argued that the trial of Orenthal James Simpson for murder was Americas' defining cultural experience of the 1990s. It claimed the front page news of every newspaper in the USA, Britain and probably everywhere else in the world. TELEVISION companies afforded it gavel-to-gavel coverage and were rewarded with record-breaking viewer ratings.

Simpson, until then relatively unknown outside the United States, became perhaps the most talked about person in the world. A rich and decorated former football player, Simpson had made the transition to comedy actor, featuring in the *Naked Gun* series, before he was charged in June 1994 with the murder of his estranged wife Nicole Simpson and her friend Ronald Goodman. His defense, led at great cost (estimated $4–5 million) by celebrity lawyer Johnnie Cochrane, Jr., revolved around the claim that the Los Angeles Police Department (LAPD) had planted evidence. In the wake of the Rodney King case, it was not unreasonable to suppose that RACISM was a motive in some LAPD actions, and Cochrane skillfully played the "race card." Simpson was acquitted.

Born in San Francisco to a poor family, Simpson developed rickets soon after birth, a condition that left him bowlegged and pigeon-toed. His father, Jimmy Lee, abandoned the family. His mother Eunice encouraged O.J. to pursue sport, mainly to ameliorate his physical problems; he soon showed enough promise to win an athletics scholarship at a parochial school, where he played baseball. After moving to a different school, Simpson became an outstanding football player. Despite his physical handicap, he was big for his age. Also on the team was Al Cowlings, who became his close friend and confidante in years to come.

Simpson enrolled in the City College of San Francisco and continued to impress on the football field. Teresa Carpenter (1994) tells of a SUPERSTITION Simpson held for many years: his head was so large that the City College needed to order a new helmet. There was no time to paint the college's logo and Simpson played so well that he insisted on wearing a plain helmet from that stage on. This aided his instant recognition by the local media.

With offers from fifty universities, Simpson opted for University of Southern California (USC) where he distinguished himself as the 1968 Heisman Trophy winner. USC was a predominantly white school and Simpson was not, it seems, eager to become involved in the racial politics of the late 1960s. He did not support the attempt to boycott the Mexico Olympic games in 1968, and was not conspicuously supportive of the Black Power revolt of the era. The Nation of Islam's best-known athlete member, Muhammad ALI, was embroiled in all manner of controversy and his acts of defiance inspired many black sports performers to pledge their allegiance. But Simpson was noncommittal. "A lot of my brothers in sports have joined the Black Muslims," he once said. "But ... they're not allowed to eat pork – and I love bacon too much" (quoted in Carpenter 1994).

A semester before he was due to graduate in public administration, Simpson dropped out and signed a three-year deal with Chevrolet worth $250,000, the first of several highly lucrative ENDORSEMENTS that would make Simpson one of the wealthiest athletes of his time. By 1985, it was estimated that he had earned $10m from sponsors such as Schick, Foster Grant and Tree Sweet orange juice. The money pales beside that earned by Michael JORDAN in the 1990s, but in the 1980s companies involved in SPONSORSHIP were only just learning the value of having products endorsed by sports performers. All the same, Simpson was an African American and commercial companies were known to favor white product endorsers.

Drafted by the then unfashionable Buffalo Bills in 1969, Simpson failed to deliver for three years. But in 1972 a new head coach, Lou Saban, played him with protective blockers, who released him to exploit his speed (he was a useful track athlete in his early career). The records went tumbling: he topped 1,000 yards rushing five consecutive times, had six 200-yard games and broke Jim Brown's season record for rushing yards with 2,003 in 1973. He was traded to San Franciso 49ers in 1978, but injuries dogged him and he was forced to retire the following year, age 32. He was inducted into the Professional Football Players' Hall of Fame in 1985.

The expected glut of film offers did not materialize, but he picked up some minor parts and became well known for his role in David Zucker's 1984 comedy *The Naked Gun*, which spawned a series. He had a brief but ill-starred spot as commentator on ABC's Monday Night Football. Hertz Rental Cars featured Simpson in its advertising and, interestingly, did not void the contract during Simpson's trial.

Stories of Simpson's alleged abuse of his first wife, Marguerite Whitley Simpson, had circulated during their twelve-year marriage in which they had three children. Simpson left her and sued for divorce in 1978. But Marguerite Whitley refused to be drawn and filed no official complaint. In fact, the first recorded account of O.J.'s violence was not until New Year's Eve, 1989, when Nicole Simpson called the police. When the police arrived, Nicole was hiding. O.J. received a $200 fine and two year's probation. Simpson had met Nicole in 1977, when she was waiting tables. They had an affair and married shortly after she became pregnant in 1985. Over the next four years, it is understood that Nicole made up to thirty emergency calls to the police without pressing formal charges or filling out incident reports.

His dramatic arrest, flight, trial and subsequent civil suit have been exhaustively documented. Coming so soon after the *causes célèbres* involving Marion Barry, the black former mayor of Washington, DC, and Mike TYSON, the Simpson trial became yet another prism through which to view America's racial condition. As well as the racist dimensions inhering in the case (including taped racist remarks of LAPD officers), there were other factors that went beyond the courtroom. Research conducted while the trial was in progress revealed that a majority of African Americans believed Simpson to be innocent, while a majority of whites thought him to be guilty.

Simpson was acquitted of the charges in 1995. The acquittal did not bring immediate rehabilitation as far as commercial America was concerned; there was not a glut of movie or endorsement offers. Simpson had been demonized. A successful athlete turned movie actor with millions in the bank, Simpson was widely regarded as fortunate: had he been just another African American without the kind of resources to hire formidable defense teams, it is at least statistically probable that the verdict would have been different.

Of related interest

Carpenter, Teresa (1994) "The man behind the mask," *Esquire* vol 122, no 5.
Dershowitz, Alan (1996) *Reasonable Doubts: The O.J. Simpson Case and the Criminal Justice System*, Simon & Schuster.
Mixon, L., Foley, A. and Orme, K. (1995) "The influence of racial similarity on the Simpson, O.J. trial," *Journal of Social Behavior and Personality* vol 10, no 3.

Slaney case, the

Background

Mary Slaney burst to world prominence in 1983 when she won the 1500 meters and 3000 meters at the first world athletics championships. An outstanding middle-distance runner, Slaney, or Decker as she was before her marriage to Richard Slaney, represented the USA at four summer Olympics and was ranked in the world top ten for every distance from 800 to 10,000 meters. Slaney broke world records at the mile, 5,000 meters and 10,000 meters. She competed at world class into her thirties, capturing the US Indoor Championship for 1500 meters at the age of 38.

Paradoxically, she was perhaps best known for being tripped by Zola Budd during the 3,000 meters final at the Los Angeles Olympics of 1984. The image of Slaney dissolving into tears at trackside, her chance of a medal gone, is one of the most expressive in Olympic history. She rebuffed Budd's apology, setting up a British TELEVISION-sponsored rematch in London. As sports RIVALRIES go, Decker Slaney *vs* Budd was hardly a "natural": Budd, a native South African granted citizenship in Britain, was outclassed by the more experienced American.

The irregular T–E ratio

In June 1996, Slaney qualified for the Olympic games for the fourth time at the US trials. A mandatory DRUGS test followed and Slaney's sample showed positive. The testosterone-to-epistestosterone, or T–E, ratio is normally 1:1; if an athlete's sample shows a ratio of 6:1 or higher, then further tests are necessary. It was reported that Slaney's urine contained ten times the normal ratio of testosterone.

The USA Track and Field (USATF) organization, the sport's governing association, was informed of Slaney's test results but allowed her to compete at the summer Olympics of 1996 at Atlanta, Georgia. Seven months later, in February 1997, the International Amateur Athletics Federation (IAAF) changed its rules to give itself the authority to suspend athletes even when national organizations had decided not to. Meanwhile, the USATF had taken no action against Slaney. The IAAF banned Slaney from competition pending a hearing held by the USATF. The hearing, in October 1997, exonerated Slaney.

The role of NIKE in the defense of the athlete was crucial. In a web article, "Nike's muscle helped clear Slaney," Don Allison wrote: "Nike, which sponsors both Slaney and USA Track and Field, put its resources behind the runner in her fight to clear her name. Nike would not say exactly what that support was but [Jim] Coleman [Slaney's lawyer] said it was invaluable in compiling the overwhelming evidence that resulted in the three-member board reaching its quick decision" (*News from Running Around the World*, September 19, 1998). In the same article, Nike chair Phil Knight was quoted as saying: "Both Mary and track and field have been stained by the accusations raised in this case, which were false." Nike had previously paid for the legal defense of German sprinter Katrin Krabbe when she tested positive in 1992. On the other hand, Nike dropped Harry Reynolds, who hired a lawyer and spent two years protesting the legality of his suspension. Contracts with Nike, as with most sponsorship deals, contain clauses that allow for their negation in the event of drugs violations.

The basis of Slaney's defense was similar to that in the MODAHL CASE, in which British runner Diane Modahl appealed a suspension and won her fight to race again. Unusually high levels of testosterone in women may be attributable to several factors other than administered drugs. Another runner, Uta Pippig, of Germany, when suspended after a drugs test, argued that she had stopped taking birth control pills after fifteen years and this had led to hormonal changes, which in turn affected the T–E ratio. Drinking alcohol and menstruating may all contribute to an abnormal T–E ratio. The aging process also affects how a female hormonal system operates. Slaney was 37 at the time of the positive test. Modahl and the Irish swimmer Michelle De Bruin, who also challenged the reliability of the samples, suggested that samples can degrade when not kept under suitable conditions. Because testosterone is a naturally occurring hormone, the onus is on drug testers to prove that it has been administered by an athlete or accomplice. Modahl won her case and was reinstated.

Slaney insisted that she had not taken testosterone, though Professor Christiane Ayotte, of the IAAF's doping commission, remained unsatisfied by the USATF's conclusion. "I am convinced there has been a significant doping violation," he said in the aftermath of the hearing (quoted in the *Sunday Times* November 29, 1998). The IAAF continued to examine evidence and called for an arbitration hearing. In April 1999, the IAAF's arbitration panel handed Slaney a retrospective two-year ban without right of appeal, having concluded that there had been a "failure to establish by clear evidence that an abnormal T-E ratio was attributable to pathological or physiological conditions."

Issues raised

The Slaney case raised important issues, not least of which concerned the extent of commercial intrusion in a process that had little to do with financial considerations. Nike's precise influence remained unclear, though the corporation had been thought to have intervened in other major decisions affecting sports, such as the inclusion of Nike-sponsored soccer star Ronaldo in the Brazil team that lost the World Cup Final to France in 1998, even though the player was known to have been injured.

Friction between the world's governing federation and national organizations were not unknown before the Slaney case, although the relationship between the IAAF and USATF was especially abrasive. With the Slaney arbitration hearing pending, the IAAF opened up another case after reports that US sprinter Dennis Mitchell, who failed a drugs test in April 1998 and was suspended by the IAAF, was cleared by the US board in the following December. No reason was given, though a report in the British newspaper the *Daily Telegraph* maintained that Mitchell escaped a ban by claiming the night before giving his urine sample he had sex four times and drank five bottle of beer. The IAAF drugs commission decided to open its own investigation into the Mitchell case.

Another issue related to finance was that of compensation. In 1992, another US athlete who appealed against an alleged doping violation, Butch Reynolds, was awarded $26 million by the US courts, although he never actually received it. The REYNOLDS CASE reminded sports governing organizations how expensive it could be when a suspended athlete successfully challenged its test findings.

A third issue concerns confidentiality. Slaney and her coach Alberto Salazar, the former MARATHON runner who was also a Nike executive, believed the major injustice was that the positive test result should not have been made public under the USATF confidentiality rule. It became public knowledge after an apparent leak from someone in the organization. Sports performers who test positive for drugs have a tendency to stay associated in public awareness with a positive dope test, even though they may have been cleared of the offense.

Of related interest

Downes, S. and Mackay, D. (1996) *Running Scared: How Athletics lost its Innocence*, Mainstream.

Goodbody, John (1997) " Slaney denies drugs claims," *The Times*, May 16.

Kardong, D. (1997) "Bright Speed: in nearly 25 years of world-class racing, Mary Slaney has elevated women's running to new heights," *Runner's World* vol 32, no 7.

Somebody Up There Likes Me

Robert Wise's 1956 film *Somebody Up There Likes Me* of the life of Rocky Graziano – based on the boxer's autobiography of the same name – was one of several dedicated to exposing the underside of a sport that was coming under increasing police scrutiny in the 1950s. Police investigations into organized crime's involvement in professional boxing, allegations of fixing and "manu-facturing" fighters were all ingredients of what became a virtual sub-genre with films such as *The Harder They Fall, Requiem for a Heavyweight* and *Night and the City*.

Somebody Up There Likes Me was the least sensational and least cynical of these films. In fact, it was a straightforward narrative biography of Rocky Graziano, who held the world middleweight title between 1946–7. Graziano is played by Paul Newman. As a "hungry fighter" fable, the film is an archetype: Graziano, born in poverty in New York's East Side, scrambles his way out of the slums and becomes, in his own words, "homeowner, a good citizen on a good street in the good city of Brooklyn." On his own account, he earned a million dollars in his ring career.

Graziano was born Rocco Barbella in 1922 and spent his early childhood running wild, spending time in reformatories and remand homes. His misdemeanors also earned him a sentence in an army prison and he was dishonorably discharged from the military. In 1947, he had his boxing license revoked in New York for failing to report an attempted bribe.

Much of Graziano's reputation was founded on his three fights with Tony Zale, their first two meriting inclusion in all-time great middleweight battles. There were 40,000 fans at Yankee Stadium on the first occasion, September 27, 1946, and gate receipts totaled $350,000. Zale won in the sixth round, despite cuts to mouth and eye. The rematch was in July 1947 and is often cited as one of the most brutal in sports history. Graziano himself described it as a war and, years later, confessed: "I get nightmares that I am back in the ring on that hot July night and I am looking out through a red film of blood."

Graziano was cut and floored inside the first three rounds, but his cornermen pleaded with the referee not to stop the fight. In *Somebody Up There Likes Me*, Graziano expatiates: "I was an animal in a cage of ropes, a bleeding, cornered, half-blind, aching, sweating, snarling animal who had to kill or be killed. ... I yelled that I was going to kill that stinking rat bastard and I tore into him and never stopped" (1956). Graziano imposed himself so utterly that the referee stopped the fight in the sixth round. A third meeting confirmed Graziano–Zale as one of the great RIVALRIES of boxing. Zale, then 35, saved the *pièce de résistance* of his career for this fight and finished Graziano in three stunning rounds. Graziano described it as the lowest point in his life and admitted that his active career was effectively over at that point. He was 31.

Graziano then parodied himself in a moderately successful stand-up comic act. One of his oft-told gags was about when he and his trainer entered the ring. On one occasion, the trainer asked him: "Have you got your cup?" Graziano replied: "Nah, I'll just drink outta the bottle like the other guys." A.J. Liebling's observations on the fight scene of the early 1950s in *The SWEET SCIENCE* provide an interesting backdrop against which to view the Graziano movie.

Of related interest

Graziano, Rocky (with Rowland Barber) (1956) *Somebody Up There Likes Me*, Hammond, Hammond & Co..
Liebling, A.J. (1956) *The Sweet Science*, Gollancz.
Somebody Up There Likes Me, directed by Robert Wise, 1956.

Spalding, A.G.

b. 1850, USA; d. 1913, USA

Industrialism and professionalism

A.G. Spalding's plaque in the Baseball Hall of Fame describes him as the organizational genius of baseball's pioneer days. He was star pitcher of the Forest City club in the late 1860s, a four-year champion with Boston, 1871–5, and manager-pitcher of the champion Chicago team in the National League's first year. He was the Chicago president for ten years and, in 1888, organized baseball's first world tour. Spalding became known as the "father of American baseball," and is usually referred to by his initials, A.G. He developed the precursor to MAJOR LEAGUE BASEBALL and established a highly profitable sports equipment business.

Spalding opened his first sports store with his brothers in Chicago in 1876, making an initial investment of $800. Thanks to his business acumen, baseball became America's first truly professional team sport. His involvement in baseball coincided with a period that provided America with the opportunity to dominate economically the twentieth century. The cultural transformation of turn-of-the-century America reflected the rugged individualism and embodied the PROTES-TANT ETHIC that helped define the inexorable industrialization process.

There was widespread migration to and industrial unrest across America. Baseball represented the dominant male ideology and became something of a rite of passage for young men. Baseball's organization incorporated wider social processes of modernization and rationalization. Peter Levine, in his *A.G. Spalding and the Rise of Baseball*, states that "AG was caught up in the mood of an industrializing America."

Spalding managed to create a stable business structure for baseball: he was ruthless in controlling the economic practices of his competitors and employees. Players' interests were often secondary to the expansion of the game. He famously declared that "everything is possible to he who dares." His brand of MUSCULAR CHRISTIANITY integrated the idea that sports was a great builder of character and should be part of American culture with a hard-headed approach to sports as a business.

In 1867, Spalding decided to seek a living from playing baseball. Clubs were still officially amateur. In his autobiography, he lamented: "I was not able to understand how it could be right to pay an actor, or a singer, or an instrumentalist for entertaining the public, and wrong to pay a ball player for doing exactly the same thing." The amateur rule was later removed. In 1871, Spalding was signed to the Boston Red Stockings on a salary of $1,500. By 1875, he and three other players were powerful enough to split from the Boston club and create, with entrepreneur William Hulbert, the Chicago White Stockings. Spalding was pitcher, captain and manager while Hulbert was president, making $2,500 per year and 25 per cent of the gate receipts.

Hulbert and Spalding created the National League of Professional Baseball Clubs (NL) in 1875. The league's management structure consisted of club owners who codified and enforced rules. The bureaucratic organization of baseball provided the impetus for maximizing profit through paying fans. The American Association rivaled the National League. A competition between the respective leagues' champions was played between the St Louis Browns and the White Stockings.

Professional baseball exacted widespread criticism, and the trade in players drew especially stinging comment. "When Spalding wants a man, money is no object," wrote one reporter of the day. In 1882, the NL passed the infamous reserve clause that tied a player to the club that originally gave him the contract. The clause kept player salaries artificially low and strengthened the position of team owners, lasting until the advent of FREE AGENCY in the 1970s.

One board member of the White Stockings was also the owner of the *Chicago Herald*, and Spalding took advantage of this. He instructed the ball club's press secretary to release news, good and bad, on the premise that "good, liberal roasts in newspapers of wide circulation are much more effective than fulsome praise."

The early sports industry

In 1876, Chicago newspapers announced the opening of Spalding's Baseball and Sporting-goods Emporium. The business published *Spalding's Official Guide* that also advertised his merchandise. The company also supplied baseballs and uniforms for league use. The uniforms were standard issue, and the only way of differentiating the teams was by their socks. The firm manufactured baseball bats, croquet equipment, ice skates and fishing tackle. By 1887, a million baseball bats had been sold. Spalding was acquisitive and bought out potential competitors, so that the *Sporting News* was able to declare that "A.G. Spalding and Brothers are without a rival." However, America's unease about monopolies, or trusts, forced Spalding to trade under the names of the companies he acquired, always being careful to conceal his monopolistic tendencies. Levine writes: "A.G. outstripped all his rivals, overwhelming several of them, in pursuit of the American dream."

Spalding promoted his products as "the standard of comparison the world over," and stamped his logo – a baseball with "Spalding" between the seams – on his goods. Counterfeiters were zealously traced by Spalding. For the St. Louis Olympics of 1904 Spalding's company designed the stadium, provided the equipment and organized the competition. Spalding himself declared that the Olympics "selected Spalding Athletic implements for exclusive use because of their acknowledged superiority, reliability, and official standing." In this sense, he anticipated many of the strategies of later sports goods companies.

Spalding published an *Official Cycling Guide*, featuring pictures of bicycles, sweaters and shoes. The guide stressed "to our lady friends ... all our pages are addressed to them, equally with husbands and brothers." He anticipated later trends to sign players to ENDORSEMENT, and signed three professional cyclists to a contract that required them to use his cycles. The association ended shamefully when the endorsers were accused of CORRUPTION.

Levine writes that Spalding "consciously sought to capitalize on his reputation as a famous ballplayer and baseball magnate, both to capture and to extend an expanding market for athletic equipment among middle class Americans." Spalding's enterprise was as particular to Fordism as Phil Knight and NIKE are to post-Fordism. Considered together, Spalding and Knight can be seen to represent the MODERNITY/POSTMODERNITY transition. Spalding's organization was a blueprint for what became the sports industry – an industry which, in the 1990s, Knight dominated. But, while Spalding used his influence in sports organizations, often to the detriment of players, to market his equipment, Knight used players to market his products.

Spalding's later years were confined to writing and politics. His autobiography, *America's National Game*, traced baseball's historical roots and its emergence into popular culture. Spalding himself represented the first in a line of sports entrepreneurs, such as Tex Rickard, Don KING, Phil Knight, Ted TURNER and Rupert MURDOCH, all of whom in some way exploited the commercial value of sports.

Of related interest

Hardy, S. (1990) " 'Adopted by all the leading clubs': Sporting goods and the shaping of leisure, 1800–1900," in Butsch (ed.), *For Fun and Profit: The Transformation of Leisure into Consumption*, Temple University Press.

Levine, Peter (1985) *A.G. Spalding and the Rise of Baseball: The Promotion of American Sport*, Oxford University Press.

Zimbalist, Andrew (1992) *Baseball and Billions: A Probing Look Inside the Big Business of Our National Pastime*, Basic Books.

ERWIN BENGRY

sponsorship

Sponsorship is defined by Frank Jefkins in his book *Advertising* (Pitman, 1994) as:

> the giving of monetary or other support to a beneficiary in order to make it financially viable, sometimes for altruistic reasons, but usually to gain some advertising, public relations or marketing advantage. The support could consist of money as in the cash of prizes, but may comprise trophies or other gifts in kind. ... While some sponsors may simply wish to be philanthropic, this is seldom so today when the object is more often deliberately commercial.

In 1983, England's Football League and its governing organization, the Football Association, failed to reach agreement over a £5.3 million ($8 million) contract for TELEVISION rights to soccer over a two-year period. The television companies insisted that the rules of international broadcasting would not allow a new form of advertising introduced by the soccer organization, displaying the brand name or logo of a commercial sponsor on the uniforms of the players. The Football League felt the sponsorship was more valuable than the revenue promised by the television companies, which was a sizable amount in the early 1980s.

By 1997, the Football Association had created an elite division called the Carling Premiership, its name taken from the beer brand owned by its sponsors,

Bass, which paid £36 million ($50 million) over four years to sponsor the division. Every club in the league had at least one sponsor. There were also sponsors – for example, Ford – for programs featuring soccer. Today, it is inconceivable for major sports events not to have at least one, and more probably several sponsors which seek to have their products identified with sports. Many competitions would not be viable without the revenue derived from sponsorship deals. For commercial companies, sports have become an extension of the overall marketing strategy: a way of familiarizing as many people as possible with their brands. Major sports have such vast audiences, both "live" and, more importantly, through television, that they have become an almost logical site for advertising. Sponsors effectively buy advertising space on the apparel of competitors, on the hoardings surrounding the contest, on scoreboards, on car panels, on the drink bottles; literally everywhere it is possible to find open space, even on the players themselves. Sponsors also buy advertising time: announcers frequently cite the name of sponsors when referring to, for example, "the Nike Golf Tour," "the Virginia Slims Tournament" or cricket's "Benson and Hedges' Cup."

In the late 1990s, there were indications that at least some of the large sponsors of sport were prepared to enlarge their role. NIKE, while ostensibly the sponsors of the Brazilian Football Federation, were allowed under the terms of their 1996 contract to arrange games and tournaments for which the company retained television rights. Nike was the effective promoter of Brazil's games. Budweiser, which sponsored many sports competitions and popular music concerts, also moved to a more central position in initiating and organizing events rather than just sponsoring pre-existing events. Nike's rival Adidas promoted the Adidas Two-Mile Race in Hengelo, Holland, in June, 1997: this event pitted two Olympic gold medalists, Noureddine Morceli and Haile Gebrselassie, against each other but controversially excluded the then world's fastest two-mile runner, Daniel Komen, because he had signed a deal with Nike.

TOBACCO companies were the largest sponsors of sports events through the 1970s and 1980s but, in 1997, their enterprise was curtailed in Britain when the newly-elected Labour government introduced legislation that outlawed tobacco advertising at sports. In Britain alone, there were 120,000 tobacco-related deaths each year. The outlawing of tobacco sponsorship came at a time when the USA's largest tobacco companies were embroiled in legal cases. Part of the legal dispute involved the tobacco companies' style of advertising, some of which, it was argued, was aimed at young people. Also in dispute was the question of whether habitual tobacco use was to be regarded as a physical dependency or a matter of choice.

The exact amount of money spent by tobacco companies on sports was estimated to be over £300 million ($500 million). Motor sport's Formula One teams received about £200 million from tobacco sponsorship, the biggest being: the Williams team (£20 million from Rothmans), the McLaren team (£12 million from West Brand) and the Jordan team (£10 million from Benson & Hedges). Snooker received £54 million from Embassy and £4 million from Benson & Hedges. Rugby received £2.1m from Silk Cut. In total, thirty-four British sports events were sponsored by tobacco companies at the time of the legislation (in May 1997). Benson & Hedges' links with sports were the strongest and one of the oldest. The B & H International golf tournament began in 1970; the B & H Cup in cricket started in 1972; the B & H Masters in snooker began in 1975. In 1992, the company provided the B & H Cup in ice hockey and, through Silk Cut, another branch of the parent company Gallaher, there was sponsorship of the Rugby League Challenge Cup from 1985.

There had been a voluntary agreement between the tobacco companies and the British government since 1972, which prevented the industry sponsoring sports that attract a young following, such as soccer, or what is known in the tobacco industry as "puff" sports, including track and field, swimming or cycling. The agreement also limited the use of cigarette names and logos on Formula One cars.

In a typical sponsorship deal, Demon Internet, one of Europe's largest Internet providers, paid Fulham Football Club, of London, £1.5m ($2.4m). The club had been bought for £30m in 1997 by Mohammed Al Fayed. The owner appointed high-profile manager Kevin Keegan in a successful attempt to attract the kind of sponsorship money Demon was prepared to pay. In return for the money, Demon had its name emblazoned on Fulham players' shirts and merchandise, free use of a ten-seat executive box and free tickets for home games.

Of related interest

Scully, Gerald W. (1995) *The Market Structure of Sports*, University of Chicago Press.
Sheehan, Richard S. (1996) *Keeping Score: The Economics of Big-Time Sports*, Diamond Communications.

spousal abuse

The connection between spousal abuse and sports culture is by no means clear, although research reveals that both male fans and sportsmen are prone to outbursts of AGGRESSION against their wives or female companions.

Fans

Some studies have discovered that, during the annual Super Bowl, there is a 50 per cent increase in calls to the police and battered women shelters. Others have identified a cultural mélange in which sports is an ingredient but not the main one: economic adversity when mixed with the passion and the frequent hard drinking that accompanies sports events often results in domestic VIOLENCE. Still others believe that the general masculine ethos that permeates sports culture promotes an approach to women that permits, if not commissions, hostility and outright violence against them. The Super Bowl findings prompted the inclusion of advertising in the commercial breaks during the broadcast of the 1996 and 1997 games offering women advice and providing a helpline number for the National Domestic Violence service. The organization found in a 1995 study that only 14 per cent of women who are beaten by their spouses or male companions ever reported the incident(s).

There is nothing new in suggesting that sports encourage the thrill and sense of drama often missing from everyday life. The title of the book by Norbert Elias and Eric Dunning, *Quest for Excitement* (Blackwell, 1986), conveys the whole purpose of sports, whether for participants or spectators. Aggression and violence remain integral to a great many popular sports, including one of the earliest sports, soccer. It is possible that, long before the advent of research on the subject, women were habitually traumatized by males returning from events. Part of British soccer lore was that wives would often quail at the defeat of their menfolk's local team for fear that they would have to feel the brunt of their frustration. There is perhaps too much truth concealed inside this anecdotal narrative for it to be dismissed.

Sportsmen

Yet, it is not only fans who instigate violence against women. Several violent cases involving high-profile British soccer and American football players seem to indicate disdain for women among top sportsmen. There are several explanations of this. The first – and weakest – is self-selection: only men who have violent proclivities excel at competitive sports, and the same streak that enables them to get to the top also animates their aggression toward other humans, including their female partners.

More plausible is the "win at any price" mentality that pervades much professional sports and which means that only the most ruthlessly competitive athletes survive at the upper echelons of sports. Even athletes who were not merciless at the beginning of their careers acquire virulence as they progress. This becomes part of their character and spills over into all aspects of their lives, including domestic spheres.

Sports culture is by definition competitive, and sportsmen embody that culture: they are shaped by the conditions in which they mature and develop. Infantilized by coaches and managers, enclosed in structured environments, pampered by the mass media, they are in many ways cocooned in a world in which they enjoy an exalted status, yet where they lack meaningful control. Aggression against women might be seen as a perverse attempt to assert the control denied them in virtually every other sphere. The status enjoyed by sportsmen publicly does not apply in the home, and violence against spouses may be interpreted as an angry reaction against this. It is at least possible that this leads to a denigration of the female's role in the partnership and helps support a code of conduct in which casual violence against women is commissioned.

There is a certain symmetry between this type of explanation and the neo-Freudian account offered by Germaine Greer in her feminist classic *The Female Eunuch*. She argued that male violence is a condition of the degradation of women, and that men's response to women varies between fear and contempt; these stem from a deeper anxiety about their own sexuality. In this scenario, the penis becomes a weapon. Extending this argument to sports, we might say that women are feared, despised and sometimes damaged by sportsmen because women remind them of the precarious control – or lack of control – they have over their own sexuality. This contrasts with the high degree of control they habitually exercise over all other aspects of their body. Being excellent in sports necessitates control over the body during competition.

Sports constitute an area of society in which male strength, muscular power and aggression are well rewarded. These attributes were also highly valued in a world in which the economy depended on steel industries and shipbuilding and in which freedom sometimes depended on armed conflict. But in the information society, these attributes count for little: there is hardly anything a man can do that a woman cannot.

Anticipating this trend in 1978, a *Newsweek* article that bore a question as its title – "Are men *really* changing?" – concluded that: "The crunch will come ... as women gain something closer to equality in the office and men find their protected status eroding both at work and at home." Today, many men have passed through the resistant stage and have accommodated the appreciable changes in sex roles since the 1970s. Sportsmen may be different: they are ensconced from their early teens in a culture that privileges masculinity, champions virility and rewards combativeness. Sports culture provides an effective insulation from many of the changes in the sexual milieu, changes that have ruined what the *Newsweek* article called the "masculine mystique." In this view, sportsmen's violence against their female partners is a belligerent defense of what they regard as their manhood. The culture in which they spend most of their lives has not recognized that this conception of manhood is a vestige of a bygone age.

Of related interest

"Are men *really* changing?" *Newsweek*, January 16, 1978.
Greer, Germaine (1971) *The Female Eunuch*, Ballantine.
Jeffries, Daniel (1997) "Last night men scored and women hurt," *The Independent Tabloid*, October 27.
Putnam, Douglas T. (1999) "Beating the spread," in Douglas T. Putnam, *Controversies of the Sports World*, Greenwood Press.

spread

The "spread" refers to a range of possible results set by a bookmaker. The gambler wagers either side of the range; in this way, the gambler bets on a number of possible results rather than the more conventional single stake on a predetermined choice.

Bookmakers choose the most probable result, taking into consideration form and other factors; they then set a small range, or spread, either side of it and the gambler chooses. For example, a bookmaker may set a spread of only three points in an evenly balanced match between two American football teams. If the gambler believes the UNDERDOG team will win or that the favorite will win, but by less than the three points, he or she takes the bet. If the underdog does win or keeps the score within three points, the gambler wins. If the favorite wins by three points or more, the bookie wins.

A bookmaker can set spreads on potentially anything. In a game of soccer, a spread may be offered on the time of the first goal. A typical spread might be between the 36th and 40th minute. The gambler may believe the first goal will come earlier and bet at, say, £10 per minute. If the first goal is scored in the 10th minute, the bettor wins £260 i.e. 36–10=26 (× £10). If there is no score by the 36th minute, the bookie wins at a rate of £10 per minute, i.e. 38th minute goal gains £20. No score at all at the completion of 90 minutes play means the bettor has to pay £540. Conversely, the gambler may buy the spread, meaning that he or she wins if no goals are scored after the spread; in which case a 0–0 scoreline would win the bettor £500 (90–40=50 × £10). A goal in the first minute would mean the bookie wins £390.

While spread betting has been popular with Las Vegas gamblers, it was actually introduced in Britain in the 1960s, although not on sports. The bookmakers Joe Coral used spreads to encourage gambling on movement in the stock exchange index. Britain's Gaming Act permitted gambling on sports, and this opened up the way for bookmakers to take bets on horse racing off course. Betting on soccer was largely confined to pools, which meant predicting the games that would end in draws. Spread betting gained popularity in the late 1980s.

Potentially, a spread can be set on any event, like the number of home runs, the shirt number of the first player to score, the total number of minutes a player spends in the sin bin, the number of games in a tennis match, and so on. Typically, the bettor will have an account with a bookie and make the bet over the telephone. In Britain spread bets, unlike conventional bets, are legally enforceable and bookies have the right to take defaulters to court to recover debts.

Of related interest

Black, Jacques (1998) *Spread Betting to Win*, Oldcastle.
Rendall, Jonathan (1999) *Twelve Grand: The Gambler as Hero*, Yellow Jersey Press.

strikes

A strike, as conventionally defined, refers to a situation in which employees collectively withhold their labor until some grievance is remedied. In many sports, professional athletes are employed by clubs, teams or other types of employers. Occasionally, the athletes exercise their prerogative to refuse to engage in the activity expected of them; the most usual grievance is related to pay. When players strike, the whole competition in which their team or organization operates is either disrupted or immobilized.

Baseball has been brought to a standstill on many occasions, its owners sometimes initiating a "lockout" (a term derived from the days when company owners would literally lock factory doors either to close down plants or to lock in strikebreakers who would work in defiance of labor union instructions). MAJOR LEAGUE BASEBALL has experienced more industrial unrest than any other sport. For years, it enjoyed freedom from antitrust laws on the grounds that it was a "sport" rather than an "industry," and this has been a key feature of its history of salary exploitation and labour disputes. Baseball's first serious dispute was in 1889, and this proved to be a harbinger of over a hundred years of vexatious relations between players and club owners. Being a relatively old organized sport, baseball had a less systematic and accountable management style than other more recently developed professional sports and, at times, virtually invited disputes.

Major strikes in 1972 and 1984 led to costly delays, but even these paled in comparison to the dispute that began on August 12, 1994 and ended March 31, 1995. This resulted in the abandonment of the World Series for the first time in history. The strike was made all the more galling for the league by the fact that the preceding regular season had attracted a record 71 million spectators and revenues of $1.8 billion (£1.12 billion). Neither the players nor the owners triumphed: the strike ended after the US district judge Sonia Sotomayor upheld an injunction that ordered Bud Selig, the acting Major League Baseball commissioner, and the club owners to restore the collective bargaining agreement that had expired the previous season. The ruling provided the players with a reason to call off their action. But, the issue of cost-cutting through the enforcement of salary caps – which Major League Baseball strongly favored – was to return in other sports.

The particular way most professional league sports have been organized licenses disputes between players' organizations and ruling bodies. The National Football League (NFL) established something of a blueprint in the 1960s under the leadership of the then Commissioner Pete Rozelle. The NFL was set up as an agency that would award franchises to clubs, collect revenues from television, marketing and other sources and redistribute the monies among the member clubs. This plus the draft system prevented the formation of elite clubs in fertile market areas and ensured a competitive balance. The model was adopted by both the National Hockey League (NHL) and the National Basketball Association (NBA). In all cases, the negotiating power resides with the central governing organization.

In American football, there were serious player strikes in 1974 and 1987, though the longest (fifty-seven days) came in 1982 when each team had to have seven games deducted from its regular schedule. Rozelle was criticized for leaving negotiations to the NFL Management Council rather than personally interven-ing. Ice hockey lost 105 days during a 1994–5 lockout. The NBA's longest strike started on July 1, 1998, and much of the dispute centered on what was called the "Larry Bird exception": this allowed clubs to re-sign their own players once the players were out of contract. The league's FREE AGENCY arrangements made it possible for clubs to elude salary cap restrictions when negotiating with their players. The NBA wanted an end to this exemption, but the players wanted it retained. Both sides agreed to several new conditions, such as marijuana testing, more money for veteran players and two years added to the rookie cap. But the league insisted on the elimination of the Bird exception, which actually worked to the advantage of only a small minority of the 348 striking players, whose average salary in the preceding year was $2.6 million. The lockout finished in January 1999, just in time to salvage the remainder of the season.

"Player power" was the term sometimes used to describe the often outlandish sounding demands of players. Highly paid athletes, it was reasoned, were emboldened by the celebrity status they had acquired in the 1990s and were prepared to fight for an even greater share of the revenue that professional sports were attracting, particularly from TELEVISION and pay-per-view channels. In one notable case in 1998, the cricketers Brian Lara and Carl Hooper refused to tour South Africa with the West Indian cricket team. The tour was the first official visit of the West Indies to South Africa since apartheid ended and, as such, was regarded as an historic event. Lara, the foremost batsman in the world, and Hooper demanded better pay and their absence threatened the whole three-month tour. South African broadcaster SABC television insisted that the broadcasting contract rested on their inclusion as sponsors, and advertisers wanted a full strength team. The deadlock was broken, but only after a leading firm of London lawyers had been called in. Cricket has sporadic disputes involving players, dating back to 1912 when six Australian players refused to participate in a tournament with England and South Africa.

Tennis has hardly been affected by strikes, although in 1973, seventy-nine male competitors withdrew from Wimbledon in protest against the International Tennis Federation's suspension of Niki Pilic.

In an unusual case involving a single sports performer, soccer player Pierre van Hooijdonk, contracted to the Nottingham Forest club in England, staged a solo strike after his club had traded another player. Angered at what appeared to him to be a signal of his club's lack of ambition, he walked out and returned to his native Holland. Three months into the 1998–9 season the player was reinstated and returned to play for his club, though in the face of criticism from his fellow players. The only other comparable case in soccer lasted for just two days in 1996, when Italian footballers withdrew their labor over one weekend.

Of related interest

Scully, Gerald W. (1995) *The Market Structure of Sports*, University of Chicago Press.

Sheehan, Richard (1996) *Keeping Score: The Economics of Big-Time Sports*, Diamond Communications.

Sherman, Len (1998) *Big League, Big Time: The Birth of Arizona Diamondbacks, the Billion-Dollar Business of Sports and the Power of the Media in America*, Pocket Books.

superstition

The function of rituals

Superstitions, rituals and seemingly meaningless practices are rife in sports. Sports performers are notoriously superstitious, and habitually engage in often complex rituals in the belief that such behavior will enhance their performance and bring good fortune to them and their team-mates. While this may suggest that sports performers are more prone to believe in magic, chance and false conceptions of causation, their behavior is not unusual: there is abundant evidence that ritual acts are cross-cultural and have existed throughout the ages.

In his *Elementary Forms of Religious Life* (first published in 1912), Emile Durkheim discovered that ritual has several ways of influencing individual and group consciousness. First, ritual is a distinct form of public behavior routinized by the group. Second, the routine focuses the participants' attention upon a single definition of reality. Third, a concrete focus for thoughts and feelings is provided through words or other symbols. Such symbolic representations facilitate the recollection and endurance of the attitudes and beliefs developed during the ritual. Fourth, the ritual is performed as often as necessary to remind participants of the emotions and ideas which its symbols represent. Durkheim writes: "In the end, the point is not to exert a kind of physical constraint upon blind and, more than that, imaginary forces but to reach, fortify, and discipline consciousness."

One of the more extreme forms of ritual is rooted in the supernatural beliefs of the Ghost Dance religion (a blend of orthodox indigenous belief and Christian missionary teachings) practiced by the Sioux in the latter part of the nineteenth century. A ritualized article of clothing known as the "ghost shirt" was believed to protect the Indians from the white soldier's bullets. However, as soldiers and Sioux stabbed, clubbed and shot one another at Wounded Knee (1890), the ghost shirts proved ineffective as at least 150 Sioux died and 50 lay wounded. This illustration supports Durkheim's analysis of ritual, as the ghost dance effectively disciplined the consciousness of the Sioux to brave battle against the white soldiers.

Rituals and superstition in sport

There is no reason to believe that rituals or superstitions in sport are significantly different from other superstitious beliefs and practices. Over recent years, sociologists and psychologists have documented how the motivation of many athletes is partly rooted in superstitious beliefs. To date, most research studies have focused on the rituals, fetishes and taboos of athletes. Examples abound regarding athletes who must wear a particular piece of clothing or who must eat the same pre-game meal so many minutes prior to the game. However, only a few studies have examined the meaning of these behaviors to the athletes themselves, as superstitions are often private and disclosing such behaviors are frequently a source of embarrassment.

Thus, from an empirical standpoint, little is known regarding how sport superstitions develop and why. Yet, anecdotal evidence has provided consistent findings in the form of retrospective reports of athletes competing in a variety of sports. While athletes report that a large measure of control over performance in competition derives from training and practice, athletic competition is not certain but subject to chance. Uncertainty regarding the chance element contributes to lessened confidence and increased anxiety.

Superstitions provide specific patterns of behavior that allow athletes to feel some sense of certainty while engaging in high-stress, high-risk competitive events. Thus, superstitious behavior may act as a psychological placebo, building confidence, reducing anxiety and helping athletes to withstand the inherent uncertainties in sport. Superstition in sport may also act as performance rituals, allowing athletes to relax, focus and perform the task via an automatic motor-behavioral response such as stretching, visualizing and other behaviors associated with getting FOCUSED.

While pre-game rituals may ultimately promote ideal personal performance and team cohesion, the use of superstition and rituals in sport may also be dysfunctional. Hence, performance may be negatively affected if the athlete has become obsessed with the ritual and it has not been performed correctly. Overdependence on superstition may also deter athletes from concentrating on improving mental skills, physical skills and utilizing advances in equipment that can heighten performance.

Superstition and the athlete

Social scientists studying superstition in sport believe superstitious behavior begins when an athlete tries to duplicate the conditions present during a previous good performance. A laboratory experiment by Van Raalte *et al.* (1991) illustrates this finding. The researchers hypothesized that superstitions are more apt to develop among people who believe they can exert some control over chance outcomes through their own actions. Thirty-seven subjects completed a Chance Orientation Scale, which measures one's belief in maintaining control over chance events. In addition, the subjects attempted fifty putts on an artificial putting green. As the subjects had no prior golf experience, researchers were able to control for pre-existing golf-related superstitions.

Before each putt, the subjects selected one of four differently-colored golf balls. The researchers defined superstitious behavior as the selection of the same color ball after having made a successful putt with that ball. Van Raalte found that subjects who believed their actions could control chance events were more likely to select a "lucky ball" after making a successful putt. In addition, the researchers argued that the level of anxiety increases the more ego-involved an athlete is in sport. Ego-involvement is measured by the level of importance one attaches to task performance. Thus, greater ego-involvement would make the athlete more apt to develop superstitions to cope with anxiety in sport.

An analysis of ego-involvement indicated that subjects did attribute importance to their performance on the putting task. There were no significant gender differences in level of ego-involvement, Chance Orientation or number of made putts. As hypothesized, the more subjects believed their actions allowed an element of control over chance events, the more likely they were to choose the same ball or "lucky ball" following a successful putt.

One sport often associated with superstition or ritual is ice hockey. Judith Keating designed a study to identify professional hockey players' patterns of behavior as they prepared for a competitive game. Fifteen professional hockey players were observed and interviewed during the 1991–2 pre-season and National Hockey League (NHL) regular playing season. Keating observed that the team ritual which takes place two minutes before the start of the game is quite physical as each player moves in a deliberate pattern towards the net. Her conclusions. which were published as "Precompetitive preparations in professional hockey" (in *Journal of Sport Behavior* vol 18, no 4, 1995), were that the majority of players skate to the goaltender, tapping him on his arm or leg pads once or several times. At this point, words of encouragement are also exchanged between the goaltender and players. As the final act before players leave for the bench or blue line, the ritual promotes team cohesion, motivation, and focus.

Ritual may also take the form of abstention. One of the more prevalent examples of abstention in sport concerns abstention from sex. A study by Gloria J. Fischer focused on whether college varsity athletes believe abstention from sex prior to a game helps athletic performance. An anonymous survey was given to eighty-three varsity football players and seventy-three baseball players from three universities. Results showed that football players usually abstained from sex twenty-four hours before a game, while baseball players sometimes did. Moreover, football players were more likely than baseball players to believe their athletic performance was helped by abstaining from sex. Although research does not substantiate a causal relationship between coitus and impaired muscular strength, the main reason all players believed abstention helped their performance was by conserving strength and increasing energy. Fischer writes that abstention is presumably encouraged by football coaches, as they generally isolate athletes in motels/hotels prior to a game, while baseball players did not face similar isolation. Thus, coaching philosophies may also contribute to the acceptance of a "sexual abstinence myth."

Superstition and fans

The significance of personal rituals to sports fans is particularly evident when some fans appear to blame themselves when their favorite team loses, even when the event was only watched on TELEVISION. Others constructed their roles as fans of athletes or teams by insisting on certain foods, clothing and particular repetitive behaviors despite the distancing effect of television. The ritualized behaviors of fans viewing televised games is intriguing, as evidence does not support that such behaviors affect the outcome of games.

One explanation for such behaviors may be that fans are copying the ritualized behaviors of athletes. It is also possible that fans watching sports on television have adopted such stadium fan rituals as wearing team colors, displaying the team logo or waving pennants in support of their team. When cheered by fans present at the sporting event, players are thought to expend greater effort. However, as the behavior of fans viewing the games on television cannot be observed by the players, and thus would not directly affect game outcome, the question still remains regarding the ritualized viewing of fans watching televised sports.

A study conducted by Susan Tyler Eastman and Karen E. Riggs (1994) utilized interviews of adult sports viewers and the observations of sports viewers within their natural home environments. Findings were based on forty-six observations and interviews primarily of college students (24 per cent female, 76 per cent male) and were supplemented by 112 interviews reflecting all adult age groups and both sexes of self-identified sports fans. While most observations of fan viewing were based on nationally televised sports such as college and professional football and basketball, some fans chose televised tennis, hockey, golf, car racing, ice skating and exhibition baseball.

Fan behaviors were categorized into five components consisting of membership, participation, connection, reassurance and influence. These categories are not mutually exclusive. Being part of a FANDOM may be viewed as an activity which creates a sense of group membership which may be reinforced through wearing one's team colors in T-shirts, caps and sweatshirts while watching televised games. Participation may add an element of empowerment for televised sports viewers by creating a dynamic in which the fan interacts with the people/ sports event on the other end of the television screen. The third category is defined as the connection of the fan to other fans and to sports teams, which is evident in having a minimum of one favored team. Reassurance is characterized by rituals providing security and relief from the anxiety of awaiting game outcome. Finally, influence also reassures the fan by maintaining a ritual that the fan feels will directly influence the outcome of the game. However, whether or not the subjects truly believed their behaviors affected game outcomes, the researchers concluded that sport rituals provided a sense of participation, connectiveness and relief from the tension inherent in sport.

Nick Hornby's chronicle of an obsessional British soccer fan, *FEVER PITCH*, records a catalog of practices all intended to assist his team, Arsenal. These include smoking cigarettes at specific intervals, eating cheese and onion flavor crisps (potato chips) at an appointed time in the game, deliberately not setting the VCR to tape games, wearing lucky socks, shirts and hats, accompanying some friends and avoiding others, and biting the heads off mice-shaped candy then throwing the remains under oncoming cars. "We invest hours each day, months each year, years each lifetime in something over which we have no control," writes Hornby. He echoes Durkheim when he asks: "Is it any wonder, then that we are reduced to creating ingenious but bizarre liturgies designed to give us the illusion that we are powerful after all, just as every other primitive community has done when faced with a deep an apparently impenetrable mystery?"

The practice of rituals, wearing of special clothing and the possession of amulets, talismanic charms, pictures and other articles that have idiosyncratic value is clearly pervasive in all sports and at all levels. This is not to suggest that it is the exclusive preserve of sports performers. Far from it: such ritualistic and apparently irrational behavior is prevalent in all cultures and, in all probability, extends beyond the reach of recorded history. The fact that it remains and indeed flourishes in an area increasingly dominated by science and reason reminds us of the persistence and power of beliefs in forces that lie beyond our conscious control.

Of related interest

Eastman, Susan Tyler and Riggs, Karen E. (1994) "Televised sports and ritual: fan experiences," *Sociology of Sport Journal* vol 11.

Fischer, Gloria J. (1997) "Abstention from sex and other pre-game rituals used by college male varsity athletes," *Journal of Sport Behavior* vol 20, no 2.

Van Raalte, Judy, Brewer, Britton, Nemeroff, Carol and Linder, Darwyn (1991) "Chance orientation and superstitious behavior on the putting green," *Journal of Sport Behavior* vol 14, no 41.

AMY I. SHEPPER

Sweet Science, The

First published in 1956, A.J. Liebling's *The Sweet Science* is the best-selling sports book of all time, outselling the arguably better known *A Season on the Brink* by John Feinstein and Nick Hornby's *Fever Pitch*. Liebling's narrative on boxing is a collection of essays on fights and the cultures surrounding them in the early 1950s.

Liebling was a writer for the *New Yorker* magazine, and his essays were first published in that magazine. He saw his chronicles connected as if by molecular chain to the work of the boxing historian Pierce Egan, author of *Boxiana; or Sketches of Ancient and Modern Pugilism; From the Days of Broughton and Slack to the Heroes of the Present Milling Aera*, itself an assembly of essays first published in 1813 (Liebling detects a publisher's error in giving the date as 1812). Liebling's title is actually taken from this book, the full phrase being a description of pugilism "The sweet science of bruising."

Liebling's debt to *Boxiana* is acknowledged in his introduction. He notes Egan's influence on Dickens and how his prose is a literary version of Rowlandson. "Egan's round-by-round stories, with ringside highlights and betting fluctuations, are masterpieces of technical reportage, but he also saw the ring as a juicy chunk of English life, in no way separable from the rest." In this sense, *Boxiana* is the first genuine analysis of sports culture. Liebling's work follows in the same tradition.

The tableau-like chapters betray Liebling's belief that boxing is something of a lifeform in itself, a living organism crowded with fighters, managers, promoters, press reporters and audiences "whose ignorance of the ring is exceeded only by their unwillingness to face facts." Liebling's world is a male domain: women appear in only the most minor of roles. They are "broads" who can wait for their men, or interfering wives who undermine trainers by wanting to be near their husbands prior to a big fight.

Liebling's feel for boxing derives from his early interest. He recounts that the first fight he saw was on May 12, 1923, in Yankee Stadium. He would have been 19 then (he was 52 when *The Sweet Science* was published). The Stadium's show featured Jess Willard, the former heavyweight champion of the world, conqueror of Jack JOHNSON and one-time "Great White Hope," who had been persuaded to make a comeback despite having lost the title six years before. The writer's affection for the period and the years that followed is evident in his condemnation of the changes wrought in the early 1950s by TELEVISION, which he likens to the potato. "It is like the potato, which is only a succedaneum [substitute] for something decent to eat but which, once introduced into Ireland, proved so cheap that the peasants gave up their grain-and-meat diet in favor of it." The disapproving theme continues throughout: Liebling fears that younger fighters are rushed into big money fights without first having acquired requisite skills, largely because of the demands of television. Smaller club shows which functioned as apprenticeships were being squeezed out.

The crassness introduced by television has, according to Liebling, cheapened boxing. Television, in the 1950s, introduced "an era when the Sweet Science has become a free handout to encourage beer sales." Liebling's worries proved well grounded: at the height of its power in 1955, televised boxing was watched by 8.5 million homes, then about one-third of the available audience in the USA. But while people stayed at home to watch the fights, 250 of the nation's 300 small fight clubs shut down (in the 1952–9 period alone). By 1959 a decline had set in and, in 1960 NBC cut boxing from its schedules. The other channels followed suit so that, by 1964, hardly any boxing was seen on television.

But Liebling's book is much more than a tirade on televised boxing. Every *aperçu* is a revealing conspectus. He is able to conjure a sense of personal cataclysm meshed with public crisis as Archie Moore is dealt "a crushing defeat for the higher faculties and a lesson in intellectual humility" at the hands of the less technically gifted and far less cerebral Rocky Marciano, whom Liebling likens to Moby Dick. "Ahab couldn't even stagger him," he writes of the aging Moore. Marciano appears again in his destruction of Jersey Joe Walcott, another master fighter who succumbed to Marciano's relentless pressure and undeniable strength. Describing Walcott's demise, Liebling writes that he "flowed down like flour out of a chute. He didn't seem to have a bone in his body." Another Marciano victim, Ezzard Charles, seems to "resent the primitiveness of it all" as blood gushes from his opponent's nose. Marciano's corner treat his cut with "a quick-setting plastic called Thromboplastin, topped it off with a generous handful of Vaseline, which made the champion look as though he were wearing a Halloween false nose."

What might in some contexts seem descriptions of casual cruelty are handled with a bleak hilarity and inventiveness. Liebling records Moore's beating of Harold Johnson, noting particularly that Moore "hit Mr. Johnson at least one left hook in the chops that it is a pleasure to remember not having received." At times, Liebling seems to share one of humanity's worst secrets: that violence can be funny. Yet, Liebling is no respecter of raw violence; only the human facility that has been refined and perfected over centuries. He considers the implications of a contest between the Cuban Nino Valdes and the much cruder Hurricane Jackson, whose own handlers had described as "an animal." If the animal won, Liebling surmises, "the Sweet Science was mere guesswork, requiring not even a specialized intelligence ... it meant that two hundred and fifty years of painfully acquired experience had been lost to the human race; science was a washout and art a vanity." Valdes prevailed.

Between the fights, Liebling recounts bar room arguments, spectator riots and weathered reporters carrying typewriters around the world. He shares planes with former contenders, swaps stories with coaches, sneers at the grand overweening trends that he believes threaten his beloved science and celebrates the elegant dignity he finds in what is, for many, the most uncivil of sports. It is probable that, in the hands of a less loving writer, the material in Liebling's book might have become mere pastiche. Instead, it was turned into a widely-lauded epic that continues to sell over forty years after its first publication.

Of related interest

Liebling, A.J. (1956) *The Sweet Science*, Gollancz.
—— (1996) *A Neutral Corner*, West Point Press.

Switzer, Kathy

b. 1947, USA

On April 19, 1967, a 20-year-old Syracuse University student entered the Boston Marathon as "K.V. Switzer" and was given the number 261. About four miles into the race, a race official noticed that K.V. Switzer was a woman; as women were not allowed in the race, the official, Jock Semple, tried to remove her from the field. He was stymied, and Switzer went on to complete a historic MARATHON. Her well-publicized run demonstrated to the world that women were capable of competing in an endurance event that had, up to that point, been officially for men only. Women, it was thought, were not physically able to withstand the rigors of over twenty-six miles of road running.

The Olympics did not even include a 1,500 meters event for women until the Munich games of 1972, the same year as the passing of TITLE IX. It was 1984, seventeen years after Switzer's historic run, before there was a women's Olympic marathon. The world's best time for a woman was recorded in 1926, when Britain's Violet Percy ran 3 hours 40 minutes 22 seconds. After that, records were not kept until 1964 when another Briton, Dale Greig, ran 3 hours 27 minutes 45 seconds. Between then and 1998, the record improved by 1 hour 6 minutes 58 seconds. In the same period, the men's record was reduced by only 5 minutes 2 seconds. The difference between the two bests was 13 minutes 57 seconds. Incrementally, women's times improved more rapidly. The import of this would seem to be that, had women been allowed to compete with men earlier, then the disparity between best times would be smaller than it is.

Switzer maintained that she was unaware that women were not legally admitted to the event in the 1960s. She filled out her application form and signed her usual signature, enclosing this with a medical certificate. "I wasn't trying to get away with anything wrong," Switzer later insisted. "I wasn't trying to do it for women's rights." Her ingenuous use of initials, she claimed, was due to the fact that: "I dreamed of becoming a great writer and it seemed all the great writers signed their names with initials: T.S. Eliot, J.D. Salinger, e.e.cummings, W.B. Yeats."

Switzer was born and grew up in Fall Church, Virginia and attended Lynchburg College before transferring to Syracuse as a junior. Here she ran for the track team, competing over the mile distance. She began dating a distance runner who finished the 1966 Boston marathon in 3 hours 45 minutes, and through him heard of another woman, Roberta "Bobbi" Gibb, who had finished the course – though without an official number or fanfare. This inspired Switzer, who began training in earnest with a group of male track athletes, including her coach Arnie Briggs and hammer thrower Tom Miller, who would later become her husband.

The marathon became a sort of epiphany for Switzer: she became world famous for her run, which grew in symbolic terms over the next several years. The picture of Semple attempting to abort her run took on an almost iconic status: the picture was that of a male vainly trying to thwart a determined woman trying to break into male territory. Switzer ran eight Boston Marathons in total, and used her success as evidence in her campaign to have a women's marathon established as an Olympic event. She also approached the cosmetics company Avon, which sponsored a series of high-profile marathons for women 1978–85.

There is often special providence in an event. Seven months after Switzer's run, the United States National Organization for Women (NOW) under the presidency of Betty Friedan held a conference which drew publicity from all quarters in its attempt to create an agenda for women's issues. Although it was actually the second annual conference of NOW, the inaugural meeting had nowhere near the same impact. News of the conference reached Britain at a time when legislators were debating reforms. Among the eight-point "Bill of Rights for Women," there were demands for the endorsement of laws banning sex discrimination in employment, more daycare centers, equal educational and training opportunities and the right of women to control their reproductive lives. This final demand effectively called for greater contraceptive facilities and for the repeal of laws that limited abortion, demands that were already satisfied, at least partially, in Britain.

The conference functioned as a clarion call for the feminist movement which was to have resonances in every sphere of cultural life, including sports. Switzer may not have been self-consciously feminist, but in practical terms, her contribution to the feminist cause was extremely valuable. As well as attracting media attention, she effectively undermined sexist myths about the fragility of women and their inability to complete marathons without incurring physical damage. Because of the circumstances in which she made her run, she was virtually forced into becoming a spokesperson for feminism, a position she filled with growing assurance. Switzer may have started her historic run a complete unknown, but by the end of it she was on her way to becoming a cultural ICON.

Of related interest

Cohen, G.L. (ed.) (1993) *Women in Sport*, Sage.

Oglesby, Carole A. (1998) "Kathrine Switzer," in Oglesby, Carole A. (ed.), *Encyclopedia of Women and Sport in America*, Oryx.

Negron, C. (1991) "Camera ready," *Runner's World* vol 26, no 7.

T

technology

Technological and social determinism

While the Olympian ideal of *citius, altius, fortius* (higher, faster, stronger) was based on the concept of an athlete in naturalistic competition with the forces of nature, all sports – even classical events, such as running and jumping – have been shaped by technology. For example, synthetic running tracks are designed and "tuned" to levels of sophistication which make cinder tracks, such as the one on which Roger Bannister ran the first four-minute mile, seem medieval. The combination of digital and video technologies provides sports performers and their coaches/trainers with the means of monitoring the biomechanical aspects of sporting activity. The battle between administrators wishing to eliminate drugs and maintain "fair" competition and those wanting to employ biotechnologies to improve performance is fought with competing technologies.

There is agreement over the interdependent nature of social and technical systems, but disagreement over the relative importance of the two. Technological determinists, for instance, argue that technological development has its own driving force (inertia) which is self-propelling and self-sustaining. So, individual people or entire social systems must adapt to the demands of core technologies. Fordist assembly lines could be seen historically as one such development: Ford employees had no choice but to follow the dictates of the new, rationalized technology introduced in the first two decades of the twentieth century.

By contrast, social determinists argue that human beings have volition in the matter of technology and that they alone are responsible for change. New technologies are molded to the demands of social systems as the result of "strategic choices" by members of a dominant coalition. From this perspective, the synthetic material of which most tracks are made did not become all-pervasive because of its own developmental "logic," but because of the strategic decisions of influential members of track and field federations, the most significant of which was the International Olympic Committee (IOC).

Despite a wealth of empirical material, this dispute has not been satisfactorily resolved. While some insist that technology has its own driving force which compels humans, groups and indeed whole cultures continually to adjust, others refute the idea that technology is independent of human volition and believe this view "fetishizes" technology. Technological determinism is seen by D.F. Noble (1984) as "an impoverished version of the Enlightenment concept of progress" and, consequently, legitimizes capitalism (i.e., by making conscious choices that have exploitative effects that seem inevitable outcomes of rational progression). Noble also believes some social determinists are naive in failing to acknowledge the overtly political nature of decisions about technology. He suggests that we must identify the human choices, intentions and compulsions that underpin technological development. As he puts it: "For when technological development is seen as politics, as it should be, then the notion of progress becomes ambiguous: What kind of progress? Progress for whom? Progress for what?"

With this injunction, we might see the introduction of a newly developed football with extra layers of synthetic material (that made the ball move faster through the air) at soccer's World Cup Finals in the USA in 1994 less as an instance of technological progress, and more as part of FIFA's strategic attempt to advantage attackers over goalkeepers. This would mean more goals, which would make the games more viewer-friendly and attract the interests of TELEVISION companies which would be prepared to pay more money for screen rights in the future.

Noble describes the case of numerically controlled (NC) machines which were developed by the postwar US aircraft industry. There were three political influences on the development of NC technologies: (1) Massachusetts Institute of Technology (MIT) scientists/engineers, who were convinced of the desirability of eliminating unreliable human interference; (2) the view that the USA was under internal threat from communists in the labor movement and that it was necessary to eliminate labor from the defense industry; (3) the industrial–military establishment, which was convinced that the USA was under military threat from the USSR and that the Cold War served their purpose in building up a massive defense industry.

Technological innovation and sports

The majority of researchers focusing on technological innovation have concentrated on its impact on workers and their work. It appears that the relationship between technology and sport is an area that has been largely ignored. However, technological innovation has played crucial roles in all sports. Motor and air sports have obviously been made possible by new technologies, but innovations have transformed other sports such as skiing, pole vaulting, tennis and golf. In regard to the latter, the South African golfer Nick Price expressed "grave concern" about the prevalence of "outsize-headed drivers" and was quoted (in the British newspaper the *Guardian*) as saying: "These drivers with huge heads and made of space-age metals are turning mediocre players into good ones. They just stand there and whale away with the driver off the tee, knowing that it will go straight and far because of the technology" (February 11, 1998).

Traditionalists would endorse Price's comments, although changes in the rules of golf could lead to litigation from the manufacturers of golf equipment. One can imagine the response from the likes of NIKE if track and field athletics decided to change the rules about spikes. Interestingly, tennis attempted to solve a comparable problem. Faced with a preponderance of big hitting serve-and-volley players who were able to gain overwhelming velocity from aerodynamically designed rackets with large heads, made of synthetic materials, tennis authorities needed to slow the game down. Too many games won on service, too many points won on aces and not enough rallies produced boring games. The trend had begun in the mid-1980s, when steel and aluminum innovations signaled the end of wooden rackets. Manufacturers experimented with a range of materials, including fiberglass, boron, magnesium, ceramics and, most influentially, graphite. These lighter materials permitted the introduction of rackets with larger heads which gave players greater power and control. The success of Martina Hingis in winning Grand Slam titles at 16 could be attributed partly to the long-bodied 29 inch (73.66 cm) rackets she was using (wooden rackets were 27 inches long).

Tennis authorities deflated championship tennis balls in an effort to allow finesse players back into a game increasingly dominated by power. Andrew Coe, the International Tennis Federation's technical director, acknowledged that, as technology had changed the game, so technology must restore it: "The ITF must differentiate between innovations which aid the game and those which change the nature of the game ... we must devise ways of measuring the power of rackets so that we can set limits which retain the nature of the sport" (quoted in John Barrett's "Sport: Longer rackets serve up an advantage," *Financial Times*, May 30, 1997).

While new technologies have certainly changed – and continue to change – the nature of professional sports, the impact on those participating in leisure activities is not usually contentious. Conventional waterproof socks for hikers and skiers tend rapidly to lose their shape and become unwearable. Povair, a British-based company, spent over £1 million developing a waterproof, breathable sock which included a wide range of materials in three layers. The middle layer combined waterproof polyurethane with a membrane that absorbed water and then allowed it to evaporate. The inner and outer layers were a mixture of cotton, nylon and polyester.

While wet feet are uncomfortable, the condition is not likely to be life-threatening; whereas scuba diving in shark-infested waters is. A South African company spent three years developing the "Shark Pod," a device based on the knowledge that sharks are extremely sensitive to very small electrical impulses. The pod utilized a low-voltage electrical transmitter which was powered by a rechargeable six-volt battery. Although the device was harmless to other divers and to fish, it was effective in ensuring that sharks did not venture near the diver. Technical sports such as scuba diving also adopted technologies that were originally developed for the US space program. "Dive computers" which could be worn on the wrist provided a range of "intelligent" features to control gas mix and monitor ascent rates. Sports have benefited from the technological by-products of other initiatives.

Analyzing performance

Apart from their applications in sporting activities, new technologies have been used to analyze performance. For example, a rubber suit called "Datawear" has a range of sensors which span each joint on the human body, plotting their positions on computer-based graphics. Such a suit has obvious utility in monitoring the bodily movements of high jumpers, gymnasts and competitors in other technical events.

Even a sport as traditional as cricket has been revolutionized by the use of digital technologies. Castle Sport, a company based in Newcastle, England, developed a computer program linked to video that allowed the coach to carry out detailed analyses of players, including opponents. In soccer, the victory of German team Schalke 04 over Internazionale Milan in the 1997 European Cup was partly attributable to the imaginative adoption of existing technology. The Schalke coach, Huub Stevens, prepared for the penalty shootout (which decided the game) by analyzing the approach of his opponents' penalty takers on a laptop computer.

Sky Sport, one of Rupert MURDOCH's collection of media corporations, adapted a piece of technology originally developed for use in the Gulf War by ORAD Hi-Tec Systems of Israel to track Saddam Hussein's Scud missiles. The technology digitally transformed sporting action to a video game-like visual format, which allowed television analysts to reconstruct key events virtually from any angles. The uses for coaches and administrators in many sports is clear. REFEREES were less enthusiastic about the introduction of INSTANT REPLAY to assist or even supersede their decision making. This is another example of a by-product finding new applications in sports.

When examining the influence of innovation in sports, it is tempting to favor the technological determinist model. Technology does indeed seem to determine changes in both the structure and dynamics of sports and, in many cases, appears to have transformed the ways in which sports are played, coached, administered and refereed. However, the opposing argument is that those participating in sports have always sought to improve their performance by making use of technologies which have been developed elsewhere. The timepiece, for example, was not developed simply to time foot races; but it was seized on, refined and became indispensable for quantifying performances, not only in running but in a variety of other sports.

It could be argued that "demand pull" from sports leads to the application of technological expertise to improve athletic performance. Technologies that facilitated the growing of GRASS under adverse conditions were sought by US stadiums in preparation for the 1994 World Cup Finals. Cyclists, among others, searched for a way of optimizing training and found it in the heart rate monitor, a device comprising a chestband transmitter and a wristband receiver that indicated how fast the heart was beating. In other words, the impetus in this theoretical approach is the human competitor's thirst for excellence rather than the technological impulse. Also, there is often a strong political element attached to sporting prestige, as revelations about state-sponsored PROGRAM 1425 in East Germany and among Chinese swimmers and track competitors seem to indicate.

Political initiatives may have abetted a MEDICALIZATION of sports in which pharmaceutical companies have been encouraged to develop performance-enhancing technologies.

The emergence of new communication technologies (such as satellite transponders) in the 1980s and 1990s instigated a process that re-shaped sports at a global level. As discussed earlier, media magnate Rupert Murdoch used communication technologies to fashion what amounted to a personal GLOBALI-ZATION of broadcasting. Like his rival Ted TURNER, Murdoch seemed intent on utilizing market dominance to "shape" sports in a way that arguably benefited neither participants nor audience, but only advertisers and sponsors.

Of related interest

Dyreson, Mark (1996) "Technology," in Levinson, D. and Christensen, K. (eds), *Encyclopedia of World Sports* vol 3, ABC-Clio.
Noble, D.F. (1984) *Forces of Production: A Social History of Industrial Automation*, Knopf.
Roe Smith, Merrit and Marx, Leo (1994) *Does Technology Drive History? The Dilemma of Technological Determinism*, MIT Press.

OSWALD JONES

television

A brief history

About 140 million American viewers watch the television broadcast of the yearly Super Bowl in American football, and even this figure pales beside that of the number of viewers worldwide who watch soccer's World Cup Final every four years. Television has transformed sports into genuinely global events: it has heightened awareness of games, turned individuals into ICONS and rendered what were once leisure activities into a form of showbusiness. Television's close interest in sport has yielded many benefits, but there have also been a corresponding number of costs. Television's supporters claim it has universalized sport's popularity by making it accessible. Detractors argue that, in reshaping sport, television has extinguished the joy of competition that once gave sports their vitality.

The history of the relationship between sports and television dates from the postwar period. Although RCA in the USA and the BBC in Britain had been broadcasting to a few thousand receiving sets with five-inch screens since the late 1930s, television did not become the basis for a mass medium until after the Second World War. The war effort had stimulated research, development and the production of an effective communication system, and the vast electronics industry that made this possible was left with spare capacity during peacetime. The large radio corporations capitalized on this, producing relatively affordable television sets for domestic use. In 1949, 2 per cent of US homes had television sets, which were sold by Sears, Roebuck for $149.95. By 1950, nearly 10 per cent of homes had sets, by 1955 the figure had leaped to 67 per cent, and by 1963, 90 per cent of the nation's homes owned sets. In Britain, the rate of growth was almost the same.

Sports were almost natural events for television to transmit. The BBC had televised Wimbledon in 1937, and in 1939, RCA showed a college baseball game between Columbia and Princeton, though sets were then priced around $600 and were mainly sold to prosperous New Yorkers. Early television broadcasts were primitive. The *New York Times* reviewed the first televised game thus: "The players were best described by observers as appearing like white flies running across the screen. When the ball flashed across the grass it appeared as a comet-like white pinpoint."

Commercial interests detected the potential of linking their products with sports and having both reach into the homes of thousands. In 1947, Ford and Gillette paid $65,000 for the rights to sponsor baseball's World Series. While only 12 per cent of US homes were able to receive the television broadcast of the games, it represented an affluent area of the potential market. Sponsors of sports events have been guided by a similar logic ever since.

As prices dropped, television became more available to the middle and working classes. Sports were an obvious target for television companies. Broadcasting them required only a fraction of the production costs of drama or news, and the popularity of major sports guaranteed healthy viewing audiences; which, in the United States, at least, attracted advertising revenue. In Britain, the BBC held a state-sanctioned monopoly until the mid-1950s and was able to select its events without commercial considerations affecting its decisions.

After initial enthusiasm for television, in the 1950s sports governing bodies became more circumspect. Attendances dropped in almost direct proportion to the number of televised events. The armchair fan was asserting his (the typical fan would have been male) right to stay at home. The debate over which profited most from the relationship – sports or television – raged on until the 1980s. Gates diminished as a result of the televising of an event. (For example, boxing for a time in the 1950s became a virtual studio sport, such was the saturation coverage afforded it.) In response, governing bodies either increased charges or barred cameras completely. Local blackouts, especially for baseball and football, were useful ways of bolstering "live" gates without deterring television's interest.

The benefit to television on both sides of the Atlantic was beyond doubt. Even steep increases in fees could not curb the seemingly boundless enthusiasm television companies had for sport. ABC supplies a fitting case study. When a distantly poor cousin to CBS and NBC, ABC could ill afford to compete for major sports. In the early 1960s, convinced of the value of televising sports, it created its own competitions and fashioned them into events that resembled but were not quite sports. This policy was the brainchild of Roone ARLEDGE, who recognized few traditions or conventions in sports as he sought to elevate ABC in the viewer ratings.

Arledge's most audacious move was in supporting the fledgling AFL, a rival league to American football's established NFL which already had television deals. Criticized initially for being a totally fabricated phenomenon, the AFL soon gained a following of ABC viewers sufficient for the NFL to accept a merger in

1966. By this point ABC had become a major player, and its concept of Monday Night Football had shown the way forward for sports by packaging sports as family entertainment. Monday Night Football consistently featured in the country's top three rated programs for over three decades. By 1998, the broadcasting rights for the NFL were worth $2.2 billion (£1.38 billion).

In Britain, ITV pursued a similar tactic when faced with the near monopoly of the BBC, especially on Saturday afternoons when the latter's sport magazine program "Grandstand" led the ratings by a long way. ITV introduced its own form of professional wrestling, which was theatrical, often amusing, but always entertaining (much like today's WWF). Whether or not it was legitimate sport is a matter of perspective, but it achieved its goal in wooing viewers away from their customary Saturday afternoon's viewing. ITV captured five million viewers, as compared to BBC's four million.

Subscription television

The advent of subscription cable and satellite television, especially pay-per-view, has added a new dimension to television's relationship with sports. Home Box Office (HBO) began broadcasting in 1972, screening an ice hockey game from Madison Square Garden to 365 paying customers. By skillfully selecting not only sports events but general entertainment that people are prepared to pay for, HBO has risen to a position of prominence, commanding 16 million subscribers across fifty states and screening twenty-four hours a day. ESPN, of course, filled its schedules with sports only. Both indicated that the terrestrial networks had far from exhausted the public's appetite for televised sports.

Rupert Murdoch's BSkyB in Britain made the same point, starting operations in 1989 and venturing into hallowed BBC territory by securing the exclusive "live" rights to Premiership soccer and charging viewers monthly subscriptions. The initial cost of £304 million ($500m) seemed colossal in the context of the early 1990s when the deal was struck, but it enabled BSkyB to increase its market appreciably (to three million subscribers by 1995, when the contract was renewed) and, in the process, become one of Britain's leading blue chip companies.

Pay-per-view began life in 1980 when the Ray Leonard–Roberto Duran fight drew 170,000 customers, each paying $15 (£10) each. Rock concerts and operas followed until the establishment of TVKO, an agency owned by Time Warner, which also owned HBO. TVKO struggled to establish itself as an alternative way of viewing boxing until 1991, when it sold Evander Holyfield–George Foreman to 1.45 million homes at $34.93 (£22). By the late 1990s pay-per-view was the main medium for major boxing promotions. Britain's first pay-per-view show came in 1996 with the Mike TYSON–Frank Bruno fight being shown by BSkyB's pay-per-view arm, Sky Boxoffice. Within a year it had begun discussing regular pay-per-view transmission of Premiership soccer games. Making viewers pay for specific events effectively limited the market and had the effect of minimizing television's negative impact on gates: casual viewers who might have stayed at home to watch an event for free might, when forced to part with money to watch the event, have preferred to spend slightly more and see the event from a stadium seat. The

GLOBALIZATION of dedicated television services specializing in sports throughout the world suggests that the viewer's appetite for sports has not been slaked.

Discussions about the relationship between sport and television have moved beyond the effects of televising "live" events on attendance toward other concerns. One of these is the economics of televised sport. Andrew Zimbalist, for example, in his analysis *Baseball and Billions* (Basic Books, 1992) has shown how sports are no longer the inexpensive commodity they once were and, in fact, cost the "free" television networks dearly. The major players include them in their schedules to attract audiences so that they can include commercials for their other programs in the breaks. There is also the question of saturation: can that point ever be reached? In his book *Fields in Vision* (Routledge, 1992), Garry Whannel suggests not: he believes that simply including events in television schedules almost guarantees a wide enough audience for advertisers to take note.

Cross-ownership of media and sports organizations became a minor trend in the 1990s. Italian magnate Silvio Berlusconi owned multiple television stations as well as the AC Milan soccer club. Ted TURNER owned several Atlanta franchises, including the baseball team the Braves, to complement his many media interests. Rupert MURDOCH, whose media groups enabled him to reach two-thirds of the world's population, had interests in several sports franchises as well as media organizations. The integration of these into a single organization gave him unique power in sports. The Disney organization's byzantine interests extended as far as NHL and MAJOR LEAGUE BASEBALL clubs in Anaheim, California, as well as ESPN.

Clearly, there is little chance of a let up in the incessant barrage of televised sport. This has troubled some analysts. Anxiety about the – for some – inordinate amount of television time spent showing sports has centered on the abuse of women during or shortly after big events. The number of reported incidents of SPOUSAL ABUSE and related VIOLENCE rises disproportionately on each Super Bowl Sunday, for example. While the contribution of male-dominated sports to female oppression has been noted in many contexts, the specific contribution of televised sports, which have immediate impact in the home, has come under scrutiny, particularly with the introduction of digitalization and the plethora of sports it offers.

Of related interest

Barnett, S. (1990) *Games and Sets: The Changing Face of Sport on Television*, British Film Institute.

Chandler, J. (1988) *Television and National Sport: The United States and Britain*, University of Illinois Press.

Wenner, Lawrence (ed.) (1998) *MediaSport*, Routledge.

This Sporting Life

Set in a grim city in Northern England at the start of the 1960s, the film *This Sporting Life* (based on the 1960 novel by David Storey) follows the early professional career of Frank Machin (played by Richard Harris), whose only ticket out of his squalid dystopia is a career is rugby league football. Machin is a bruised loner whose "no prisoners" style of play reflects his approach to life: he likes no one and asks no one to like him. All around him he sees working class no-hopers, who live only to survive. "You've got to see what you want and go and get it," he tells anyone who will listen. The only way to get on is to fight. Machin never sees himself as anything but a born fighter: at night, he gazes at pictures of boxers, he spars in his mirror, he threatens his team-mates. Everything is organized around AGGRESSION, often fueled by alcohol.

The same quality benefits him greatly on the rugby field, and he signs a professional contract with his local club, insisting first on a £1,000 ($1,600) signing-on bonus – then, a considerable sum for a rugby league player. His lifestyle changes immediately: cars, suits, the adulation of fans and the advances of women enable him to live as he senses others want to. "I'm a hero to them," he says of his fans, noting that none of them has enough fight in them ever to emulate him. Yet, material possessions fail to satisfy his torment. Oddly, he falls in love with his steely, depressive landlady (Rachel Roberts), a widow who still polishes her dead husband's boots every night. At first repulsed by Machin's interest, she softens as he lavishes her with undreamed of gifts and takes her to the kind of restaurants where a meal costs more than her former husband's weekly wage. A raging argument precedes her collapse and death with a brain haemorrhage

Machin's caricatured ruthlessness and working class belligerence personifies rugby league in the postwar period. Divorced from its gentleman-amateur partner, rugby union, in 1895, rugby league was created out of twenty-one northern clubs that wanted to pursue a professional game. Dunning and Sheard's (1979) analysis of rugby suggests that the split was precipitated by players' demands to have their efforts rewarded: "Players began to ask for more than the small payments officially permitted under Northern union rules." Club officials in the northern counties of Lancashire and Yorkshire "saw little wrong in offering financial inducements."

Professionalization brought with it a new ethos. Winning became more important than just competing; the character-building qualities so beloved of union were replaced by a desire only to earn a living wage; and the class composition changed dramatically so that rugby league became the preserve of the working class, while union stayed with the upper class public schools and their old boys. The rules, or codes (as they are known) of rugby league permitted a faster game than rugby union and one in which the possibilities of VIOLENCE were great. In his "Rugby in Northern England, 1871–1895," the historian James W. Martens quotes a nineteenth-century sports journalist: "In Yorkshire rugby is played almost entirely by artisans. … Artisans differ from public school men in that winning is everything … artisans' desire to win results in dodges and trickery which public school men consider dishonourable" (in Nauright and Chandler, 1996).

Although rugby league players were paid, they often took other jobs and clubs considered they had no right to interfere with how their players conducted their lives away from the rugby field. This principle was established in the late nineteenth century, and remained in place at least until the 1980s. The film shows Machin drinking with club officials and his team-mates, frequently collapsing drunk in their presence. He draws no admonishment; in fact, much of the rugby league subculture was based on drinking exploits. But, as full-time profession-alism arrived, the hard-drinking customs of rugby league receded.

The club on which the film was based was Wakefield Trinity, one of the giants of the 1960s, although it was Wigan which, in the 1980s, paved the way for a fully professional game. For the most part, rugby league players, though paid, would need to supplement their income, sometimes with jobs provided by their clubs. Even in Yorkshire and Lancashire, rugby league never approached soccer in terms of popularity. When referred to as a star, Machin replies: "There are no stars in rugby; that's soccer."

A player such as Machin would actually have been something like a star had he played in the late 1990s, when rugby league underwent its most revolutionary change since splitting with rugby union. Tempted by an offer from media entrepreneur Rupert MURDOCH, the sport switched from a winter to a summer schedule and reorganized its club structure so as to engage in an international play-off tournament, which pitched the best Australian teams against the best English and French sides. The Super League and the World Club Championship were shown on Murdoch's subscription cable/satellite channels. Some clubs, like London Broncos (consciously modeled on the NFL's Denver Broncos), struggled to draw decent crowds in areas where rugby league was not a traditional sport. Others prospered, like the Bradford Bulls in northern England, which tripled its average gate to 15,000 in the first two seasons after the switch to summer play in 1995. The club's success built on a century-old tradition of rugby league in the city of Bradford.

Of related interest

Dunning, Eric and Sheard, Kenneth (1979) *Barbarians, Gentlemen and Players: A Sociological Study of the Development of Rugby Football*, Martin Robertson.
Nauright, John and Chandler, Timothy (1996) *Making Men: Rugby and Masculine Identity*, Frank Cass.
This Sporting Life, directed by Lindsay Anderson, 1963.

Title IX

The context

In 1972, the United States Congress passed Title IX of the Educational Amendments and so instituted a law that would seriously affect all educational institutions offering sports programs. The law specified that: "No person in the United States shall, on the basis of sex, be excluded from participation in, be denied the benefits of, or be subjected to discrimination under any educational program or activity receiving federal financial assistance."

The law was passed in a context of heady social change. A strong feminist movement on both sides of the Atlantic was calling for "women's liberation" from centuries of male dominance. Patriarchy had both ensured and justified a seemingly perpetual pattern of control in which most, if not all, the incumbents of society's key positions were men. Culturally, this reflected in the ways in which people ordered their everyday lives, thought about their own experiences and generally made sense of the world. Women, it was argued, had been subordinated historically and had yet to find an effective escape from their subordination. Modifications to the relationships between women and men in the period following the Second World War had left women in more comfort, but with no more economic independence or political influence.

Through the late 1960s and early 1970s, a series of medical and legislative breakthroughs ensured that women's overall status would be radically changed. The availability of the oral contraceptive pill made it possible for women to control their own reproductive functions in a way that had been unimaginable before the war. Abortion, for long the province of illicit practitioners, was legalized. In the United States, the *Roe vs Wade* decision was hailed as both a landmark case and a symbolic turning point for the women's movement.

Comparable in importance were the various pieces of legislation that outlawed discrimination on the grounds of sex. Employers were no longer allowed to pay women less than men if they performed the same work, nor were they allowed to specify that a man was required for an advertised vacancy. While the laws were no guarantee of immediate equality for women – and, indeed, were the subject of some reactionary backlash in the late 1980s and 1990s (especially the Abortion Law) – a certain momentum was established and it became clear that the days of legitimate sexual discrimination were over. Title IX was perfectly consistent with the surrounding legal, social and cultural changes. It provided for equal treatment and equal opportunity for women. Initially, its reception was mixed: many of those who organized and controlled the athletic programs of schools and colleges receiving federal money believed the new instruction to be unworkable. Sports programs that had been historically structured to meet the needs of males would need drastic and costly revisions if the law was to be obeyed.

Arguments that women were not seriously interested in sports looked pathetic, especially when set against the culture of NARCISSISM that had developed through the 1960s and led to women's deepening involvement in health and exercise. Evidence of this could be found at the educational level, where women's team sports were growing in popularity. The NCAA had initially ignored demands from women's groups who pushed for equal rights in the 1960s. In response, the National Association for Girls and Women in Athletics formed the Association of Intercollegiate Athletics for Women (AIAW) to organize and govern women's national tournament competition. The AIAW's ethos was very much in opposition to that of the NCAA, in that it rejected the value of competition and stressed the power of sport as a way of "knowing oneself," of "creating female leadership" and attacking "racial exploitation." After the enactment of Title IX, the presence of female athletes became more evident and women's sports were recognized as legitimate partners of their male equivalents. The AIAW was eventually absorbed by the NCAA, and the concept of developing a genuinely alternative women's sports with different values, priorities and ambitions disappeared.

The effects

Any thoughts that women would dutifully accept that Title IX was unworkable were exposed in 1979 when three women athletes from the University of Alaska sued their state for failing to comply with the Title IX in providing better funding, equipment and publicity for the women's basketball team compared to the men's. This set in train more actions, and by the end of 1979 sixty-two colleges and universities were under investigation by the Office for Civil Rights.

The fact remained that many educational sports programs were geared to activities that women either did not play or which were considered unsuitable for women. Football is the obvious example. This was, and is, a lucrative sport for colleges and universities, particularly after the advent of SPONSORSHIP. A disproportionate amount of sports budgets was devoted to the development of football. Women, it was argued, were not robust or physically powerful enough for the sport. Questions of fairness were also dragged in. For example, men's sports drew more crowds than women's; so gender equality would lead to men's sports subsidizing women. It was a powerful argument and it was never satisfactorily settled. Educational institutions insisted that changes to the structure of their most lucrative sport in the name of gender equality would have disastrous financial consequences.

Such arguments marred the progress of Title IX. A study by Ann Uhlir, "Athletics and the university: the post-woman's era," in 1987 revealed a whole catalog of gender imbalances in sports. For example, only 15 per cent of women's intercollegiate programs were under the supervision of a female director; four of the top ten salaried coaches of women's basketball teams were male; and 31 per cent of the NCAA participants were female, although college enrollments were 53 per cent female (*Academe*, vol 73, July/August). Even fifteen years after the enactment of the law, male athletes with scholarships outnumbered their female counterparts by about two to one in US universities and colleges, and men's recruitment budgets were generally three times larger than those of women. To address this imbalance, all NCAA member institutions were required by law to disclose resource allocation details. Complaints persisted every time an athletic program was shaved to accommodate the mandates of Title IX: if 50 per cent of the students were female, it was argued, then 50 per cent of the resources for sports programs should go to women's activities.

Arguments against Title IX gained credibility in 1984 when the US Supreme Court declared that the beneficiaries of federal funds in educational institutions were the students rather than the athletic programs. One immediate effect of this was that 800 cases of alleged discrimination under investigation were dropped or scaled down. The rejoinder to this came in 1988 with the Civil Rights Restoration Act, which affirmed that all programs in any organization that received federal money should implement policies that ensured equality of opportunity.

In 1992, another US Supreme Court ruling guaranteed the right of any person injured by an intentional violation of Title IX to sue for damages. In other words, a female athlete who believed she had been discriminated against by her educational institution could actually sue that institution. This had the effect of making all organizations that received federal funds accountable. It was a massive disincentive against not complying with Title IX. The reaction to this was understandably great as educational institutions warned that they would face the closure of entire programs if forced to comply with the ruling.

Perhaps the best way to evaluate Title IX is to ask not so much what it has achieved, but what would have happened without it. It is quite probable that considerable changes in the organization and administration of educational athletic programs would have been made regardless, although the scope of the changes would have been narrower. Certainly, changes in the public interest in female sports would have brought changes at the college level: gender inequality in education would have been aberrant. There are also commercial pressures to consider. As popular interest in female sports grew in the 1980s and 1990s, both from participants and spectators, so the opportunities for professional women's sports opened. A restriction in opportunities at the amateur college level would not have been logical. In other words, Title IX in all probability accelerated changes that would have happened anyway. This is not to diminish its importance, but merely to highlight how its development was part of a much wider swirl of cultural changes that swept through Western society in the final three decades of the twentieth century.

Of related interest

Birrell, Susan and Cole, Cheryl (eds) (1994) *Women, Sport and Culture*, Human Kinetics.
Coakley, Jay J. (1998) *Sport and Society: Issues and Controversies*, McGraw-Hill.
Nelson, Mariah (1994) *The Stronger Women Get, the More Men Love Football: Sexism and the American culture of sports*, Harcourt Brace.

tobacco

Sponsorship

Considering that overwhelming evidence linking tobacco with, among other things, cancer, heart disease and respiratory problems, its association with activities that are typically identified with health, wholesomeness and well-being might seem perverse. In fact, tobacco companies have deliberately sought affiliations with sports, especially after the enervating effects of tobacco became widely accepted in the 1960s.

Official recognition of the health risks relating to tobacco consumption, especially cigarette smoking, led to governments in the USA, Britain and elsewhere banning advertising and printing warnings on cigarette packaging. Tobacco companies diverted much of their advertising budgets to the SPONSOR-SHIP of sports events, the Virginia Slims women's tennis tour in the USA and the

Benson & Hedges cricket trophy in Britain being two examples of competitions that achieved high visibility. Tobacco's presence in sport is global: the CHINA FOOTBALL ASSOCIATION, for example, was supported substantially by Marlboro money when it started in 1993. All these sports benefited financially from sponsorship money, though Formula One racing was perhaps the main beneficiary of the tobacco corporations' wish to maintain their brand awareness among demographically desirable populations (i.e. young people with disposable income).

Tobacco companies started what became a considerable interest in motor racing in 1968 when Imperial Tobacco created the Gold Leaf team. Marlboro quickly followed, signaling a strong trend for cigarettes to maintain their presence on TELEVISION through racing cars flashing their logos across screens, or drivers wearing coveralls with the appropriate appliqué or even the words of a commentator announcing the "Marlboro team." The tobacco sponsorship of Formula One racing caused a political scandal in Britain in 1997 when the newly elected Labour government announced plans to ban tobacco advertising from sports. This affected darts, rugby, snooker, tennis and clay pigeon shooting (to which Imperial Tobacco had pledged £100,000 over five years) as well as motor racing. The government made it clear that the ban would apply equally to sponsorship of all sporting events. But, soon after the announcement, came news that sponsorship of Formula One would be exempted from the provisions of the draft bill. Britain encouraged the rest of the European Union to act similarly. At the time, tobacco companies had £100m ($164m) invested in Formula One sponsorship. The seventeen Formula One races each year attracted global television audiences of 350m viewers per race, exceeded only by those for World Cup soccer and the summer Olympic games. Amid accusations of a U-turn, it was revealed that Bernie Ecclestone, owner of Formula One Holdings, the television company that held the rights to the sport, had made a £1m contribution to the Labour Party prior to its election to government. The money was returned to Ecclestone.

A staple argument of sports-sponsoring tobacco companies has been – and continues to be – that its advertising is not designed to induce young people to start smoking, but to persuade existing smokers to swap brands. This argument was weakened by research commissioned by the Cancer Research Campaign and published in the influential medical journal Lancet in November 1997. After sampling 1,000 boys aged 12–13, a Manchester University research team found, that over 27 per cent who watched motor racing could recognize the names Marlboro and Camel, compared to less than 17 per cent of those who did not like the sport. Similarly, 10 per cent of those who followed motor racing were more than twice as likely as the other boys to become regular smokers. Members of the sample were asked which sports they liked to watch on television and whether they smoked. The same questions were then posed again a year later. The researchers found that, of those non-smoking boys who named motor racing as their favorite sport, 12.8 per cent had taken up cigarette smoking by the following year, compared to seven per cent of the boys who did not like motor racing.

Pete Harnisch

In 1997, New York Mets pitcher Pete Harnisch was placed on the disabled list while he tried to overcome his addiction to tobacco. Having ceased his habit of chewing tobacco, Harnisch became restless and unable to sleep. After three weeks, he became so ill that he was classified along with players with more traditional physical injuries, such as torn ligaments or sprained thumbs. While many other sports performers had been suspended or immobilized after using illicit drugs and many more had suffered from the effects of alcohol use, Harnisch was the first player to be incapacitated by withdrawal symptoms resulting from his attempts to quit tobacco.

Harnisch's case was important in that it occurred at the same time the Liggett Group, the smallest of five US tobacco companies, was settling with attorneys general suing the industry, agreeing to release documents that showed that the company was aware of the addictive properties of nicotine and that its marketing targeted young people. The Liggett settlement opened the way to understand tobacco addiction not as a matter of choice – as had been maintained by other tobacco companies, which had likened tobacco use to drinking coffee habitually – but as a matter of physical and chemical dependence. Other tobacco companies argued in lawsuits that smokers knew the risks of cigarettes, in particular, but continued to smoke voluntarily. The companies contended that tobacco products could not be powerful enough to take away a person's willpower and that individuals should still have personal responsibility for their own behavior. In 1988, a US Surgeon General's report declared that nicotine was addictive and that the "pharmacologic and behavioral processes that determine tobacco addiction are similar to those that determine addiction to drugs such as heroin and cocaine." After that, research began to focus on precisely how nicotine functions on the brain.

In August 1997, Florida became the second state to reach a settlement with the USA's big tobacco companies over liability for smoking related illnesses, winning a total payment of $11.3 billion (£7.1 billion), payable over twenty-five years. Florida had sued the tobacco companies for $12.3 billion to defray the costs of treating state-assisted patients for lung cancer and respiratory diseases associated with smoking. The settlement was several times larger than the £3.4 billion agreement reached between the companies and the state of Mississippi in July 1997. The two states were thus excluded from the "tobacco pact," as it became known, an overarching national settlement reached in June 1997 between the same group of tobacco companies and the attorneys general of twenty-two states. The separate arrangements with Mississippi and Florida meant that the two states would start receiving payments earlier and could avoid competing with other states over a share of the payout.

During pre-trial questioning in Florida, Geoffrey Bible, the chief executive officer of Philip Morris, the biggest US tobacco company, allowed that tobacco could cause fatal illness. "Maybe," he answered when asked if he accepted that 100,000 people might have died as a result of smoking. Under the "tobacco pact" between the twenty-two states and the companies, which include Philip Morris, RJR Nabisco and US Tobacco, a total payment of £368.5 billion would be distributed among the states over twenty-five years, a stronger warning would be placed on cigarette packages and stricter regulations on advertising would be introduced. In return, the companies would receive immunity from future class-action lawsuits.

The political background to the tobacco case was complicated by the fact that the USA was a major tobacco producer as well as consumer. Several states, especially in the South, depended on the tobacco industry for jobs and revenue, and the companies had historically been impressive contributors to the political campaigns of both major parties.

Of related interest

Cassissi, N.J. (1996) "Tobacco and sports don't go together," *NCAA Sports Sciences Newsletter*, Spring, 1996.

Coker, R., Brown, S., Chitwood, L. and Keith, W. (1996) "Nicotine use and athletic performance: a brief review," *Journal of Strength and Conditioning Research* vol 10, no 4.

Crompton, J.L. (1993) "Sponsorship of sport by tobacco and alcohol companies: a review of the issues," *Journal of Sport and Social Issues* vol 17, no 3.

Tour de France

Industrialism, technology and cultural change

The cultural conditions under which the Tour de France emerged were the interest in developing efficient pieces of technology capable of transporting people quickly and relatively cheaply, the availability of an expanding network of roads across France and beyond in continental Europe, and the presence of sponsors willing to invest money in an untested sport in anticipation of publicity and increased sales. Their willingness was predicated on the view that there was a population ready and eager to consume organized competition. Facilities for mass production, factories capable of metal extrusions and innovations in the use of pneumatic wheels, gears, levers and ball bearings all contributed to the growth of cycling sports. Thus the Tour de France was a product of both industrialism itself and the technology that industrialism diffused.

The TECHNOLOGY in question was, of course, the bicycle, itself an offspring of the *célèrifère*, a wooden frame with wheels first demonstrated in 1791. Improvements on this machine were made in both France and Britain, with the next significant innovation being a treadle-propelled machine built in Scotland. But the machine that brought on a new set of sports and pastimes was built in 1861 by Pierre Micheaux and his son Ernest, who called their invention a *vélocipède*.

The mass production of the *vélocipèdes* in France in the 1860s was quickly followed by organized races using the new technology. The races rapidly spread beyond Europe; for example, Chicago was hosting championships as early as 1893. In the first two decades of the twentieth century, New York's Madison

Square Garden was regularly used as a venue for fatiguing races, the winners determined by the distance covered over the six days. Enthusiasm for *vélocipèdes* was untrammeled: as well as racing them, people used them for recreational purposes. Despite the MEDICAL DISCOURSE of the day, cycling, as it came to be called, was considered safe for women and many of the early races were often "open."

The Tour de France was a different matter: longer and conducted under conditions far more arduous than any previous race, it developed out of a rivalry between two popular sports publications whose proprietors were striving to outdo each other by promoting the longest race across the roughest tracks. The concept of racing around France was credited to Henri Desgranges, whose paper sponsored what was more a carnival than a road race, each stage having its own festival to celebrate the riders' arrival. Cycling was already an accepted Olympic sport (it was included in the program of the first modern Olympic games) and had two governing bodies, the more powerful of which, the Union Cycliste International (UCI), was founded in 1900. But even in its infancy, the Tour had a more overtly commercial purpose.

Le Tour was intended as more a technological than a human challenge. Teams were selected by bicycle manufacturers whom they represented. While this practice ended in 1930, the Tour remained (and remains) an opportunity for cycle makers to try to demonstrate the superiority of their technology. The materials used became progressively lighter, from wood to tubular steel to aluminum and eventually to the more contemporary titanium and carbon fibers. After a brief period in which riders represented national teams, competitors were reconfigured into teams organized by sponsors, many of which had little affinity with the sport. After the Second World War, the Tour was shortened to around 4,500 meters (2,800 miles) and some of the rougher patches of terrain were smoothed over with concrete. The event took on an increasingly commercial character with team sponsors approaching the event as an exercise in product branding. Riders increasingly became ambulant advertisements for all manner of products and services. The caravan that traveled ahead of the leading group of riders was decorated with advertisements. With the growth of domestic TELEVISION in the 1950s, the value of the Tour to sponsors increased and the exposure it offered was matched only by the Olympic Games and soccer's World Cup.

In this crucial period, the Normandy-born rider Jacques ANQUETIL towered above other competitors, winning five Tours between 1957 and 1964. He was one of a small number of riders who dominated Tours, with others including the Belgian Eddy Merckx, who won four consecutive Tours from 1969–72; Bernard Hinault, who was pre-eminent in the 1980s; and Miguel Indurain, who won successive titles between 1991 and 1995.

Deaths and dope

In their ways, all these riders were sports ICONS, though it was an unsuccessful rider who made arguably the most lasting cultural impression on sports. In 1967, British rider Tommy Simpson collapsed and died at Mont Ventoux. Pills were found in his pocket and the autopsy revealed the cause of his death to be "fatigue, heat, alcohol and amphetamines." Simpson's DEATH alerted sports fans and governing federations alike to the dangers of DRUGS when used to boost athletic performance. It was a symbolic event that presaged the start of what eventually became an anti-doping policy accepted by almost every sport.

The idea of taking supplements to assist the performance of Tour riders was not new. In 1924 a Parisian reporter, Albert Londres, wrote an article "Les forcats de la route" (The chain gang), based on interviews with cyclists. It presented evidence of the widespread use of cocaine, chloroform and pills that were described as "dynamite." The article did not provoke instant condemnation. The race itself was thought to make almost inhuman demands on its competitors, so when they took stimulants, it was to enable their bodies to take the strain rather than to gain a competitive edge over opponents. Whatever the response, drug taking on the Tour – indeed, in cycling in general – continued and was conveniently ignored.

However, the death of Danish cyclist Knut Jensen at the 1960 Olympics in Rome prompted French authorities to ban certain drugs thought to be favored by cyclists. In a well-known case in 1966, a team of officials visited the hotel room of Raymond Poulidor – who, with Anquetil, was half of one of the sport's great RIVALRIES – and took a urine sample. The following day, the entire leading group (le péloton) stopped to protest against such invasions of "individual liberty." But Simpson's death, in front of television cameras, convinced Tour doctors that individual considerations had to be subordinated and that regular drug testing should be introduced.

Anquetil, an outspoken critic of this practice, admitted to using dope and argued that it was necessary if the Tour was to insist on making riders race through mountainous regions for three solid weeks. In other words, riders took drugs to keep going, not to gain an unfair advantage: cyclists raced for about six hours a day for twenty-three consecutive days. Anquetil attributed Simpson's death to the fact that he had resorted to relatively unproven products, rather than use the banned substance solucamphre to ease his breathing. Following Simpson's death, the Tour was re-routed so that riders would not encounter mountains until stage twelve. There were then complaints that the Tour had become dull and unchallenging.

No official announcement was made, but it was thought that the Tour did not adopt the vigilant approach to drugs testing of the International Olympic Committee (IOC) and some of the other sports governing organizations. Tensions between the IOC and the International Cycling Union rose, especially after research by the Italian Olympic Committee concluded that as many as 80 per cent of the worlds top riders were involved in doping.

The occasional memoir, such as Paul Kimmage's *Rough Ride*, and the low number of positive tests during the Tour was further inferential evidence of cycling's laxity. In 1988, Indurain, then wearing the *maillot jaune* of race leader, tested positive for probenecid, a drug that appeared on the IOC's banned list, but not on cycling's. There had also been sudden deaths that were rumored to have been related to dope: Bert Oosterbosch died of a heart attack in 1989 when aged only 32; Johannes Draaijer died in his sleep a few months earlier, aged 26; Joachim Halupczok, a world amateur champion in 1989, died unexpectedly.

These were unusual cases, but suspicions grew that drug taking on the Tour was being unofficially condoned. This changed dramatically in 1998, after a masseur with the Festina team was found to be carrying a supply of amphetamines, anabolic steroids, HUMAN GROWTH HORMONE (hGH) and erythropoietin (EPO). The team was ejected from the competition and several of its officials arrested. Its sponsors, the Spanish watch company, Festina, stood by the team. The team's sporting director, Bruno Roussel, acknowledged that his team had succumbed to what he called the "imperatives of success, the obligation to achieve results." The International Cycling Union responded by introducing regular drug tests on riders throughout the year, rather than after each race.

Despite the 1998 scandal, the Tour remained the distance cycling event *par excellence* and continued to enjoy more world attention than other prestigious events, such as Giro d'Italia and Vuelta de España. Despite growing interest in other cycling sports, such as BMX and mountain bike racing (both originating in America) and the steady appeal of track cycling in many parts of the world, no cycling event – indeed, few sports events generally – attracted universal interest on the scale of the Tour de France. Because of this, the Tour prevailed: the commercial gains in having a stage of the race routed through a particular area were huge. The Irish Republic estimated that it was worth between $16m and $32m (£10–20m) in tourism revenue to host a portion of the race. Other areas profited similarly. Sponsors who might have withdrawn their patronage or investment from any other sports event tainted as the Tour was in 1998 resisted pulling out of the Tour, presumably mindful of its seemingly boundless popularity. Far from being outraged by the infamy, sponsors continued to plow in their money, creating the impression that the Tour may have been the most shockproof sport of the twentieth century.

Of related interest

Abt, Samuel and Startt, James (1998) *In Purusit of the Yellow Jersey: Bicycle Racing in the Year of the Tortured Tour*, Van Der Plas.

Fife, Graeme (1999) *Tour de France: The History, the Legend, the Riders*, Mainstream.

Kimmage, Paul (1998) *Rough Ride: Behind the Wheel with a Pro Cyclist*, Trafalgar Square.

Voet, Willy (2000) *Breaking the Chain: How Drugs Destroyed a Sport*, Yellow Jersey.

transsexuals

Virilism

A transsexual is a person who believes that he or she has a body that is inappropriately sexed, with anatomical features, particularly genitalia, that do not align with the person's sense of self as a gendered individual. In other words, they feel they are men trapped inside women's bodies or vice versa and, to escape, they seek a reconstitution of sex status. The reassignment of sex status typically involves long periods of counseling followed by reconstructive surgery.

The issue of sex in sport had, since Victorian days, been dominated by the view summarized by Tony Mason in his *Sport in Britain* (Faber & Faber, 1988): "Many women shared the idea that their role was primarily domestic, their natures inherently unsuitable for 'manly' physical exertion." It was suspected that women had less available energy than men, and that engaging in intensive training and competition might lead to an atrophy of reproductive organs. The theory that physical exercise could have a detrimental effect on a woman's fecundity had no basis in empirical evidence, but it served to inhibit women's involvement in many kinds of sport.

Even more intimidating was the folk belief that involvement in sports not only interfered with fertility but actually affected a woman's endocrinal system, possibly leading to virilism (the development of secondary male characteristics). The idea was based on the fact that testosterone, the hormone responsible for facial hair, deep voice and broad shoulders, muscle mass and other typically male features and which is produced primarily in testes, is found in both sexes, though significantly less in females' adrenal glands. Prolonged exercise, it was speculated, induced an imbalance in women's hormones, causing an overproduction of testosterone and a resultant "de-feminization."

Scattered cases seemed to support this speculation. For example, a mysterious gold medal winner at the 1936 Summer Olympics confessed several years later that "she" was actually a man who had been pressured into competing for the glory of the Third Reich. In 1952, two French female medalists were later exposed as males. Speculation over the invincible Press sisters, Irene and Tamara, circulated in track and field athletics. Were they actually "sisters" at all? They retired rather suddenly when sex testing was introduced in athletics in the 1966 European athletic championships, thus fueling even more speculation about their sexuality. (In all, six female competitors missed the European championships in Budapest after it was announced that there would be sex tests; in the 243 tests, no one failed.) The questions persisted: had the Press sisters somehow trained themselves into men, or were they men in athletic drag all along? Had they experimented with synthetic testosterone so much that they had induced permanent sex changes, or did they simply have a typically masculine appearance (they were densely muscular, had squarish jaws and a masculine gait). Sex tests, it was thought, would establish beyond doubt the sexuality of competitors.

The Barr bodies sex test was designed to establish unambiguously whether contestants were male or female. This test required that a sample of cells be scraped from the inside of a competitor's cheek, or hair follicle, and subjected to a laboratory examination to determine whether a minimum number contain what are called "Barr bodies" (collections of chromatins). Although the exact number of these chromatins varies from woman to woman and may change over time for any given woman, usually about 20 out of 100 cells contain this characteristic. If the count dropped below a minimum percentage, the athlete would be disqualified from competition. In 1967, the Polish sprinter Eva Klobkowska failed a sex test because she showed an excess of male hormones. To her apparent surprise, she was found to have internal testicles. This condition is not as uncommon as it may at first sound.

Heidi Krieger

After the dissolution of the Soviet Union, it was revealed that extensive programs involving performance-enhancing DRUGS were carried out in, among other countries, the German Democratic Republic. The GDR's sports system was based on the Soviet model and was in no way separable from the country's POLITICS: excellence in sports was part of a highly organized attempt to foster NATIONALISM, and no effort was spared in pursuing track and field glory. One of the athletes concerned was Heidi Krieger, who won the 1986 European shot title and later admitted that she had been prescribed large doses of anabolic steroids from the age of 17.

In 1987, after competing in the world indoor championships in Indianapolis, Krieger returned home to Berlin, disappointed at having finished only fourth. Her coaches responded by stepping up the amounts of steroids, but her form continued to slump. At the time of the fall of the Berlin Wall in 1989, Krieger began suffering from acute back pain and quit athletics. In her retirement, she revealed that since the age of 19 (that is, two years after the programme of steroids had begun), she had felt a steadily growing urge to be a man. The feelings continued until, in 1997, Krieger voluntarily underwent surgery to have her female sex organs, including breasts, ovaries and womb, removed. Krieger legally changed her name from Heidi to Andreas and became officially a man, though s/ he did not pursue further operations which would have involved reconstructing male organs. Police mounted an investigation to establish whether Krieger's sex change was linked to the consumption of illegal substances when she was Sporting Club Dynamo's star shot-putter.

Renee Richards

The *cause célèbre* involving Renee Richards brought the issue of transsexualism in sports to world attention in the mid-1970s. Richard Raskind was a tennis pro, ranked by the United States Tennis Association (USTA) in the 35-plus age category. He had been active on the circuit, though without achieving much of note. Then, in July 1976, Rasking reappeared in a small-scale *women's* tournament in La Jolla, California, under the name Renee Clarke. A media reporter became suspicious about the 6 foot 2 inch, 147 lb player and researched her background. The reporter found that Clarke's real name was Renee Richards, and that Richards was in fact Richard Raskind. Raskind had undergone surgery to remove his penis and decided to resume his/her tennis-playing career as a woman.

After a convincing victory at La Jolla, Clarke/Richards accepted an invitation at a national tournament at South Orange, New Jersey. The USTA responded by withdrawing its sanction of the competition and the Women's Tennis Association (WTA) followed suit. Of thirty-two original competitors, twenty-five withdrew in protest. Richards, her "secret" now the subject of widespread controversy, was beaten in the competition, but signaled her intention of entering the US Open at

Forest Hills. Hastily, the USTA and the WTA introduced a Barr bodies sex test, which Richards refused to take. She was excluded from the competition. A year later, the New York Supreme Court ruled that requiring Richards to take the Barr test was "grossly unfair, discriminatory and inequitable, and violative of her rights." During the *Richards vs USTA* case of 1977, the USTA, the WTA and the US Open Committee opposed Richard's right to compete as a woman because "there is a competitive advantage for a male who has undergone 'sex-change' surgery as a result of physical training and development as a male." In other words, this argument revolved not around whether or not Richards was or was not a woman, but on the concept of fairness.

The USTA's apprehensions proved unfounded: Richards entered the 1977 US Open, but was defeated in straight sets by Britain's Virginia Wade in the first round. Thereafter the controversy died down and Richards pursued a middling professional career, retiring at the age of forty-seven to become Martina Navratilova's coach for a year before returning to opthalmology – the occupation of the former Richard Raskind. Her autobiography *Second Serve* (with J. Ames) was not published until 1983 when the fuss had died down; a made-for-television movie of the same title featured Vanessa Redgrave as Richards.

The transsexual presence in sports has not been restricted to competitors. In 1990, Sam Hashimi, a married Iraqi father of two, tried to buy the English soccer club Sheffield United; the plan collapsed when he failed to get the necessary financing. Eight years later Hashimi tried again, though this time as Samantha Kane, a woman. In the interim, Hashimi had undergone a sex-change operation.

The MASCULINITIES/FEMININITIES dichotomy in sports is also challenged by the presence of transvestites, especially in areas that have been claimed as male domains. Basketball player Dennis Rodman was prone to occasional cross-dressing. Parinya Kiatbusaba, known as Tum, was a transvestite Thai boxer who dressed in women's clothing outside the ring and wore makeup when fighting. During the late 1990s he attracted a strong following of GAYS to his fights, most of which took place in Bangkok.

Of related interest

Birrell, Susan and Cole, Cheryl (1990) "Double fault: Renee Richards and the construction and naturalization of difference," *Sociology of Sport Journal* vol 7.
Raymond, Janice G. (1979) *The Transsexual Empire*, Beacon Press.
Richards, Renee and Ames, J. (1983) *Second Serve*, Stein & Day.

Turner, Ted

b. 1938, USA

Owner of the Turner Broadcasting System (TBS), Robert E. Turner, better known as "Ted" Turner, pioneered a system of cross-ownership that was perfectly suited to a time when the interests of professional sports and those of the mass media became intertwined. The process was later perfected and consolidated by Turner's rival Rupert MURDOCH, whose own particular strategy became known as MURDOCHIZATION.

In the 1970s, Turner was prescient enough to anticipate that the future of sports lay in the hands of TELEVISION and that, in a rather different way, the future of television lay in the hands of sports. Rather than attempt to play one off against the other, Turner, already the head of a media corporation, formulated a strategy in which he acquired powerful interests in sports clubs, whose games he could then televise. It was an ambitious and unprecedented move, and one which established Turner as one of the most influential figures in sports.

At the age of 24, Turner inherited his father's billboard business and, with it, $6 million worth of debt. His father had committed suicide. After turning the business around, Turner bought two radio stations in Chattanooga, Tennessee and retitled the business the Turner Communications Corporation. He floated the company on the local stock exchange in 1970 to finance the acquisition of Channel 17, an Atlanta television station. At first, he filled its schedules with old movies and television show reruns, but in 1972, he agreed to pay the Atlanta Braves baseball team $2.5m for the rights to games for five years. In 1976, eager to deepen his relationship with the Braves, Turner offered to buy out the owners, the Chicago-based Atlanta LaSalle Corporation, for $9.65m payable over twelve years. The new owner was called the Atlanta National League Baseball Club, which was a subsidiary of Turner Communications. The same company acquired a 75 per cent interest in the Atlanta Hawks NBA franchise, in 1977, and in the following year it bought a partnership in the Atlanta Chiefs soccer club.

An obvious advantage of owning the Braves was that their games had high ratings and gave Turner's television station a strong presence in the local market. Perhaps more significantly, Turner was able to avoid the hard-fought negotiations that typically accompany a television–baseball club deal. The complementarity was enhanced by the boost given by television exposure to home game attendances. Eventually, this gave the Braves more money to attract better players and so contributed to the playing performance. Improving performances brought more viewers to their television screens and enabled Turner to crank up his advertising rates. Andy Messersmith, one of the key characters in the creation of FREE AGENCY in baseball, was the Braves' most expensive signing and, as if to underscore the importance of cross-ownership, he played with a "Channel 17" logo splashed across the back of his shirt.

Turner's flamboyant conduct was despised by the MAJOR LEAGUE BASEBALL authorities, and in 1976 he was suspended from all baseball activities for a year. But Turner was undaunted, and he continued to spend more money in the ultimately successful attempt to bring the World Series to Atlanta. As the team's win–loss record improved, so fees from television and radio broadcast rights rose, becoming the single biggest source of revenue; in the 1990s, these regularly exceeded $22m per annum.

The Hawks were also a poor team when Turner took over. Its owners were prepared to move the franchise out of Atlanta. As in baseball, clubs received a pro rata distribution of television revenues from telecasts by the national networks, but unlike baseball clubs they received none of the gate receipts from away games. It took only until 1979–80 before the Hawks began averaging crowds of 10,000 or more for home games and, although this subsequently slipped, attendance picked up again after 1988–9. This was the period when the NBA generally gained widespread popularity. Encouraged by this, NBC paid the NBA $600m for four years' broadcast rights (1990–4). The Hawks' share of this was $22m. Turner retained broadcast rights for the fifty-game regular season and, if appropriate, thirty playoff games; for this it paid the NBA £275m, of which the Hawks saw about $10m.

Turner's flagship television network CNN started life in 1979. This was a highly innovative twenty-four-hour all-news cable station and, as such, carried no guarantees of success. It would be six years before the network showed a profit, but as soon as it did, Turner boldly – some said outlandishly – announced plans to purchase CBS, a corporation then valued at $7.6 billion (or seventeen times the size of the renamed Turner Broadcasting System, Inc.). The bid failed but, still in predatory mode, Turner bought the MGM/United Artists Entertainment Company for $1.5 billion. With it, he gained a formidable film library and was able to launch a movie television cable, TNT, or Turner Network Television. In 1991, TBS entered into a joint venture with three other companies to form SportSouth Network, a regional sports network serving southeastern states. It carried Hawks and Braves games and was available to 2.5 million homes. In the following year, the Turner Broadcasting System was split into five divisions, one of which concentrated on sports activities. In 1996, CNN/SI was launched: this was an all-sports news cable in competition with ESPN's second channel.

Turner's mega-deal with media giant Time Warner was one of a number of mergers and transactions in the late 1990s, all of which saw sports franchises fall into media hands. Disney owned the Anaheim Angels and Mighty Ducks; the Tribune Group owned the Chicago Clubs, and the Texas Rangers were sold for $250m (£153m) to a consortium led by Thomas Hicks, owner of the Dallas Stars NHL franchise, whose group also owned radio and television stations in the Dallas area. Inspired by Turner, the media owners secured the lucrative broadcasting rights to the games of their teams. Turner's media mogul rival Rupert Murdoch, owner of multiple television and radio networks including Fox in the USA and BSkyB in Britain, followed the trend in 1996 by bidding $311m for the Los Angeles Dodgers. Turner bitterly opposed Murdoch's ultimately successful attempt to buy the Dodgers, though he was outvoted when the sixteen National League franchises took the decision in 1998. Turner's enmity was apparent when he promised: "I'll squish Murdoch like a bug." In fact, Turner's influence in sport waned as Murdoch's waxed. In 1998, TNT lost its NFL coverage to ESPN and the prolonged NBA lockout, which proved to be one of the costliest sports STRIKES in history, hit Turner hard. He continued to handle Time Warner's cable networks, including HBO, and ran the Braves, Hawks and Thrashers.

Husband of actress Jane Fonda, Turner was a regular on *Forbes'* list of the world's 400 richest people and was usually ranked as one of the most powerful persons in sport, along with the likes of Phil Knight of NIKE, Mark McCORMACK of IMG and Michael JORDAN.

Of related interest

Thompson, Arthur A. (1993) "Turner Broadcasting System in 1992," in Thompson, A.. and Stricklan, A.J. (eds), *Strategic Management: Concepts and Cases*, 7th edn, Irwin Inc.

twins

Twins who have performed in sports are statistically rare. The British heavyweight Henry Cooper, who had two memorable fights against Muhammad ALI, had a lesser known twin, Jim, who underachieved by comparison. Tim and Tom Gullickson were professional tennis players who were both regulars on the ATP circuit; interestingly, their greatest achievements were as partners in a doubles team. In the late 1990s, Holland's Frank and Ronald De Boer were both high-class soccer players and the Waugh twins were Test-class Australian cricketers. The Barber twins both played the NFL and Americans Troy and Terry Steiner were college wrestlers.

In 1993, *Sports Illustrated* reported an "outbreak of identical twins in women's basketball" ("Double trouble," vol 78, no 4). However, no sport is likely to duplicate the National Hockey League, which had four sets of identical twins from 1982–2000, including Rich and Ron Sutter, Patrik and Peter Sundstrom, Chris and Peter Ferraro, and Daniel and Henrik Sedin.

This phenomenon has given rise to a research tradition dedicated to discovering whether the basis of athletic ability is genetic. (The American College of Sports Medicine cooperated with the Chicago Athletic Institute to investigate this as early as 1961 and published the results as "Sports and genetics: A study on twins (351 pairs)".) By studying twins in sports, the research gave a different slant on the nature *vs* nurture debate. The evidence has so far been inconclusive. For example, the multiauthored study of Maes *et al* focused on 105 10-year-old twin pairs and administered fitness-related tests. "The hypothesis that performance-related fitness characteristics are more determined by genetic factors than health-related fitness was not supported." The balance of the research seems to favor the influence of cultural factors (though a significant exception is the Polish work of M. Sklad, J. Piotrowski and B. Krawczyk, "Development of general strength in mono- and dizygotic twins", *Biology of Sport* vol 9, no 2, 1992).

Those favoring the view that nature exerts the most influence on who we are and how we behave point to advances made in genetic science: genes have been identified that are, they insist, responsible for such complex behaviors as alcoholism, homosexuality and criminality. On the other side, social scientists prefer to accentuate the role of place, family, class, education, peer group and other factors that impinge on the individual.

Yet studies have found that twin brothers or sisters who have been separated at birth, or shortly after, and brought up by different families, sometimes miles away, or even in different countries, demonstrate remarkable similarities. Similarities in lifestyles, occupations, partners and criminal tendencies seem to indicate that nurturing differences do not play such a significant part and that genes exert the more decisive influence. The response to such findings is that the twin's social backgrounds, though not exactly the same, often share many common features that are excluded from the geneticist's analysis.

Twins can be dizygotic (resulting from the fertilization of two ova by two sperm cells, and can be either same-sex or different sex) or monozygotic (resulting from the fertilization of one ovum by one sperm cell), the latter being identical genetic copies of each other. They have exactly the same skeletal structure, body fat distribution and other bodily characteristics. Often, they have very similar political attitudes, tastes and other traits. Such commonalities are to be expected of twins reared in the same family. But, twins sometimes claim a special form of empathy that borders on telepathy. Some have claimed feeling pain when their twin has been involved in accidents, or to know when their twin is in distress. Even more mysteriously, some twins have declared knowledge of their twin's death even though they may have been a great distance away at the crucial moment.

The often disarming similarity between twins has been explained by the propensity of parents to treat them as one. Dressing them in the same way, sending them to the same school and treating them alike has the effect of denying them uniqueness of identity. Their filial relationship takes primacy over friendships with peers in and out of school and the twins cultivate mutual dependency. As they grow, they become more intensely involved with each other to the point where they become mirror images.

While it is convenient to assume twins who both achieve in sports do so because of their shared natural ability, the fact that they are reared in the same household, with similar influences on their behavior as well as their ambitions, is significant. PARENTHOOD is especially crucial: having a father, mother or both parents who are enthusiastic about sports and likely to encourage their children may, in some circumstances, assist twins to sports success. The twins' eventual accomplishments may then owe more to MOTIVATION and the provision of facilities than natural gifts.

Of related interest

Maes, H. *et al.* (1996) "Inheritance of physical fitness in 10-year-old twins and their parents," *Medicine and Science in Sports and Exercise* vol 28, no 12.
Sundet, J., Magnus, P. and Tambs, K. (1994) "The heritability of maximal aerobic power: a study of Norwegian twins," *Scandinavian Journal of Medicine and Science in Sports* vol 4, no 3.
Woodward, Joan (1998) *The Lone Twin*, Free Association Books.

Tyson, Mike

b. 1966, USA

Rise and fall

In 1989, a headline in the magazine *Boxing Illustrated* asked: "Is Mike Tyson becoming the most unpopular heavyweight in history?" Tyson's own behavior over the following decade could have been designed to answer this. In 1992, he was convicted of rape and spent three years in prison. The conviction coincided with several civil suits, most filed by women who alleged some form of sexual misconduct. In 1997, in a world title fight with Evander Holyfield, he bit a chunk out of his opponent's ear, an offense for which he was disqualified and suspended from boxing. Those who were prepared either to forgive him or give him the benefit of the doubt for his sexual malfeasance turned sharply against him for violating the macho code of boxing. Tyson had conclusively lived up to the epithet of "the most unpopular heavyweight in history."

Born in Brooklyn, Tyson was the product of a dysfunctional family. His father deserted his mother, leaving her to struggle in the Brownsville district, one of the poorest areas of the United States. By the time he was incarcerated at the Tryon School, a correctional facility in upstate New York, Tyson had accumulated an extensive criminal record; he was 13, and had been arrested some forty times. In 1980, he was introduced to veteran trainer Cus D'Amato, who had guided Floyd Patterson to the world heavyweight title. Impressed by the untutored power of Tyson, D'Amato offered to train Tyson at his Catskill Boxing Club, a sort of live-in training camp. D'Amato was later to become Tyson's surrogate father.

Tyson's ascent to world heavyweight champion was sudden. In November 1986, in his 28th professional fight, Tyson, at 20, became the youngest ever heavyweight champion, beating Trevor Berbick in two rounds. D'Amato had died a year before, removing what many believed to be a stabilizing influence in Tyson's life. His management was handled by Jimmy Jacobs, a former handball champion and boxing enthusiast, and Bill Cayton, an entrepreneur, both of whom were white. Of the two, Tyson enjoyed a closer relationship with Jacobs, and the latter's death in 1988 left Tyson's business affairs in the charge of Cayton.

As the first undisputed heavyweight champion since Muhammad ALI – and, in many people's eyes, the best – he was able to command higher purses than any boxer in history. In 1987, Cayton negotiated a $26.5 million (£15m), multi-fight deal with HBO. According to Montieth Williams, Cayton objected to having Don King as promoter. King had an existing contract with the cable TELEVISION company. The bitterness between Cayton and King was set to continue.

Discord marked Tyson's reign as champion. Don KING was able to persuade Tyson that his interests would be better served if he dispensed with Cayton, and an acrimonious legal dispute ensued. His marriage to actress Robin Givens overflowed with domestic and commercial conflicts, with Givens at one stage appearing on national television to announce – in Tyson's presence – that life with Tyson had "been torture ... pure hell," and that "he [Tyson] gets out of control, throwing, screaming." Givens continued to make allegations of physical abuse, though without producing proof.

Under the guidance of King, Tyson, having fired Cayton, turned against his long-time trainer Kevin Rooney, with whom he had lived and worked at D'Amato's camp. The decision to release Rooney seemed poorly judged: his style changed as a result and his boxing was never as effective. This became manifestly clear in February 1990 when he lost his world title to James "Buster" Douglas, perhaps the rankest UNDERDOG in heavyweight title history.

Invited to judge a Miss Black America Pageant in Indianapolis in 1991, Tyson took a special interest in Desiree Washington, one of the contestants. She alleged that he took her to his hotel room, where he raped her. Tyson was found guilty and sentenced to ten years imprisonment, four years to be suspended. At the time, he was preparing for a fight against Evander Holyfield that would have earned him $15 million. Even while in prison, Tyson continued to spark controversy. Various African American organizations campaigned on his behalf, while women's groups damned him. Like Malcolm X, Tyson underwent a conversion to Islam during his incarceration and promised to emerge a reformed character.

Resuming his boxing career after his release in 1995, Tyson failed to discover his peak form and foundered in a fight against Holyfield. The 1997 rematch revealed Tyson at his worst: trailing on points and subject to Holyfield's unpenalized headbutts, he spit out his mouthguard and bit a chunk from his opponent's ear. Serving his suspension, Tyson took part in a well-rehearsed wrestling match, in which he served ostensibly as referee. He also had a public argument with King in which he was said to have struck the promoter. In 1999, shortly after a win over François Botha (for which he received $10m), Tyson was sentenced to a year in prison for assaulting two drivers in a Maryland traffic accident in August 1998. Described in court as a "ticking timebomb," Tyson was given the opportunity to appeal, but only on the understanding that he could face a twenty-year sentence if found guilty.

Attraction and repulsion

Tyson's first professional fight was on March 6, 1985. Within twenty-one months, he was the world heavyweight champion. By the time of his 1997 suspension, he had become one of the highest earning athletes in history, challenged only by fellow ICON Michael JORDAN. Unlike Jordan's income, Tyson's derived mainly from sports rather than ENDORSEMENTS: sponsors tended to shy away from linking their products with disreputable figures. No sports performer is able to command purses of as much as $15 million per fight unless there is a public prepared to pay to see him or her. Tyson may have been a repulsive character, but he was also a potent attraction. His big fights were screened pay-per-view; ringside seats at his fights were rarely available, even at $1,500 each.

The simple explanation of the enduring fascination with Tyson is that he was a good boxer amid a dearth of decent heavyweights. However, following the Douglas defeat in 1990, Tyson never mustered another performance to match his early form, and his two fights with Holyfield confirmed that he was in terminal decline. Yet, still the interest in him would not abate.

In his book *Tyson* (Pan Books, 1990), Peter Heller quotes Robin Givens:

"There's something about Michael that's dangerous. As we all know, that's part of the attraction. It's like enjoying scary movies or roller coaster rides." Tyson assuredly did scare people: all the evidence pointed to the fact that he could not be contained, less still controlled. In the ring and out, he seemed in constant struggle. This has some relevance to understanding Tyson's extraordinary cultural power. Witnessing a Tyson fight or even just following his exploits may have had the effect of insinuating fans into a world which was at once strange but entertaining, perilous but beckoning. Daniel Lieberfeld uses a resonant phrase when explaining why blues music became popular, particularly with white fans, in the 1990s: they were made to feel "party to something primal and uninhibited," he writes in his article "Million dollar juke joint" (*African American Review* vol 29, no 2, 1995). "The allure of the exotic is fundamental to the appeal black culture holds for the mainstream."

Throughout Tyson's career, his feral side was emphasized. He was described as a caged animal, someone who fought on instinct, a fighter who traded on raw aggression. Such descriptions occluded the carefully perfected technique that was born of D'Amato and Rooney's coaching. But, they served to project a convenient marketing image: the inhumanly aggressive and invulnerable "Iron" Mike Tyson. Tyson himself was a willing, if occasionally unwitting, accomplice in this projection. For example, in 1986, following a win over Jesse Ferguson, Tyson told gathered journalists: "I tried to punch him and drive the bone of his nose back into his brain." The quote circulated for long after, a terrifying reminder of Tyson's principal objective when he was in the ring. The writer Joyce Carol Oates famously referred to Tyson's "impassive death-head's face" when trying to fathom out his seeming self-destructive urges.

It is at least possible that depictions of Tyson as driven by primitive drives on all levels, not just boxing, helped foster an image that was both frightening and marketable. "That was a stereotype, of course," writes Illingworth (1992), one quite common to blacks. Nor was it a new one. In their book *Unthinking Eurocentrism* (Routledge, 1994), Ellas Shohat and Robert Stam write of a process they call "animalization" that was used in racist discourses of imperial days, but which continues to inform present day debates. It involves "the reduction of the cultural to the biological, the tendency to associate the colonized with the vegetative and the instinctual rather than with the learned and the cultural."

Tyson was attributed the quality of "otherness": a presence somehow in but not *of* mainstream culture, a reminder of what lay outside civilized society on the fringes of barbarity. Here was a man with boundless wealth, who bought luxuries on an impulse and discarded them without a thought (he once gave away a Bentley to two police officers who were investigating a collision with a parked car). Yet for all his fame and fortune, Tyson was, in the eyes of the world, resistant to the most basic civilizing influences. Illingworth suggests that the popular depiction was: "Tyson as some kind of savage on whom the culture bestows all that is noble, only for him to reject the gifts, and the givers, and revert to life on the instinctual level." The adage that "you can take the man from the gutter, but never the gutter from the man" never seemed truer than when applied to Tyson.

In other words, Tyson was a living fulfillment of age-old racist images of black people, images that had sources in the "brute nigger" stereotypes of yore. Blessed with an abundance of brawn, Tyson was a fearful figure; his apparent lack of intellect made him more frightening. Yet, as Givens acknowledged, that was "part of the attraction." Following the misadventures of Tyson made the follower "party to something primal and uninhibited." It also provided evidence of sorts that, given the opportunity, even the most spectacularly successful blacks are prone to self-destruction. As such, Tyson was the perfect cipher for a culture eager to rid itself of the legacy of pre-civil rights segregation, yet uncomfortable with the prospect of accepting African Americans as fully-fledged equals.

Of related interest

Hoffer, Richard (1998) *A Savage Business: The Comeback and Comedown of Mike Tyson*, Simon & Schuster.
Illingworth, Montieth (1992) *Mike Tyson: Money, Myth and Betrayal*, Grafton.
Tyson, directed by Uli Edel, 1995.

U

underdog

Competitive balance

Literature and mythology are replete with satisfying tales of underdogs who either won through against daunting odds (David W Goliath KO1), or made sensational comebacks against much-fancied competition (1. Tortoise, 2. Hare) or were able to overcome lack of adequate equipment and training facilities and still emerge victorious (Cinderella 1 ... Ugly Sisters 0). Impartial observers typically support the less favored of two competitors, possibly in an inverse relationship: the less fancied, less heralded and less recognized the underdog, the more support he, she or it accrues.

The idea of an underdog is central to sports competition. While some contests are equally balanced, others have favorites – the person or team expected to win – and underdogs, who are expected to lose. But, the element of incalculability is essential for a competition to maintain fascination. Even in contests featuring strong favorites, the possibility of an upset win is present. Contests that feature overwhelmingly strong favorites always contain the slightest sliver of a chance that the underdog may prevail in the face of the odds. Without this possibility, sport ceases to be *sport* and becomes theater, entertainment or some other form of dramatic spectacle. Competition involves uncertainty. Fans never know the outcome with absolute certainty; and this is what creates the tension and excitement that are germane to all sports.

Early sports used to use handicapping as a way of maintaining the competitive balance of an event and eliminate the possibility of the underdog's elimination. Foot races would use staggered starts, the fastest runners starting behind the slowest. Shorter distances are related to par in golf. In a sense the NFL uses a similar approach when devising its schedules: teams with the poorest record in one season are granted the easiest schedule in the next. Conversely, teams which have reached the play-offs are given a hard program (based on the previous season's results). In this way a competitive balance is preserved and poorer teams are encouraged by not having to face the toughest teams, at least not unless they progress beyond the regular season. American football fans fondly remember the

Super Bowl success of rank underdogs New York Jets over Baltimore in the 1968 season. The Jets team, which included Joe Namath, was the first AFL team to win the premier trophy.

The opposite approach is employed by tennis and some soccer competitions: top competitors are selected and seeded, that is, separated in such a way that they cannot face each other until later stages of the overall competition. Underdogs, or unseeded competitors, are virtually assured that they will need to conquer an opponent with a superior record in order to make progress. This places underdogs under extreme pressure from the first round, although, as unseeded Boris Becker showed when he became both the only unseeded male to win Wimbledon and the youngest ever winner, ultimate victory is not impossible.

It might be argued that underdogs are doubly disadvantaged by the fact that they will meet the superior opposition early in a tournament, when public interest is lower. On the other hand, this disadvantage is tempered by the thought that competitors who have better recent form often fall prey to inferior opposition when their victory is popularly regarded as a formality and when public interest is low. Top competitors are typically those who are able to get FOCUSED for the big matches. Because of this, the NFL structure will inevitably favor better "big occasion" competitors. Once play-offs begin, the regular season's activities become irrelevant and teams that excel in one-off knockout contests succeed. This is why in NFL history, only one wild card team, which started the play-offs a rank underdog – Oakland Raiders in 1980 – has ever won the Super Bowl.

Facing underdogs introduces problems unique to a much-fancied favorite: the individual or team sometimes has difficulty in getting "up" for the job. This means that a certain complacency creeps into preparations, training is not quite as intense as usual, motivation declines and overconfidence brings with it contentment. The conditions for an upset are perfect. These were the conditions on which Buster Douglas was able to capitalize when he stopped the hitherto unbeaten (and, for many, unbeatable) Mike TYSON in what most regard as the biggest upset in boxing history. The "underdog comes good" story is re-cycled in the *ROCKY I–V* movie series in which the hero takes advantage of *and* falls prey to smugness.

Rooting for the underdog

Jimmy Frazier and Eldon Snyder (1991) have written interestingly on the concept of the underdog. They discovered the origins of the term in a nineteenth-century verse, "The under-dog in the fight": this describes a dog fight, one of many BLOOD SPORTS popular in the period. In the verse, the observer of the fight notes that most of the crowd cheer for "the dog on top," although he or she roots for "the under dog." Frazier and Snyder argue that this sentiment has been widely assumed to be shared by all sports spectators: we all wish and cheer for the unfancied outsider to emerge victorious. Frazier and Snyder try to incorporate this into a general theory of spectating and MOTIVATION.

The theorists' first suggestion to explain what they call the "underdog effect" is to assume spectators are hedonists: they seek the most rewarding experiences they can obtain. Some spectators have vested interests in wanting one competitor rather than another to win. For example, they might have placed a bet, or they might be loyal fans. The former loses money (and perhaps some reputation for sound judgment) if he or she has gambled on the favorite; the latter loses some local pride, or face, if they are fans of the unseated underdog. For neutrals, supporting or rooting for a favorite is not a sound emotional investment: they stand to win less than the other two groups if the favorite wins, and lose almost as much in the event of a shock defeat.

Watching and participating in sports has been described by, among others, Elias and Dunning, as a "quest for excitement": the pursuit of that *frisson* that accompanies organized competition. Watching a favorite comply with expectations and win in a predictable fashion brings very little excitement to the neutral spectator. On the other hand, as Frazier and Snyder point out: "If the underdog should win, the emotional investment is repaid with a good deal of excitement and emotional reward." Surprise, the thrill of the unexpected, the delight of witnessing hubris visit pride: these are all satisfying dividends accruing to a witness to an upset.

Frazier and Snyder believe that rooting for the underdog squares with the Western ideal of equality, and that there is a certain satisfaction in watching an underdog who comes close to winning without actually upsetting the odds. The favorite does not get his, her or its comeuppance, but at least things were evened up somewhat by a close call. This is by no means unique to sports, of course. "Many American movement ideologies – from abolitionism and populism to contemporary feminism and gay liberation – confront oppression and exploitation with calls for equity," write Frazier and Snyder, concluding that equity is the one value from an spectrum of choices available that spectators "use to legitimize their utilitarian based preferences for underdogs."

Frazier and Snyder put this proposition to the test by constructing a hypothetical scenario in which a highly favored team faced an underdog. Respondents were asked to record their preferred winner and their reasons for choosing one team rather than another. The common response was that an upset win for the underdog gave more pleasurable excitement to the neutral observer. The researchers conclude that rooting for an underdog is comparable to gambling. Presumably referring to thrill-seeking gamblers rather than professionals, Frazier and Snyder suggest that placing one's sentiments on the team (or individual) with the longest odds of winning enhances the level of excitement in the outcome of a contest while leaving the spectator "with everything to gain and nothing to lose."

The underdog's role is full of ambivalence. He, she or it is relieved of the burden of high expectations, but may be awed by the scale of the task ahead. The underdog may not have the benefit of the self-confidence that goes with the favorite's status, but equally they will not fall foul of overconfidence. They are susceptible to intimidation (as were Mike Tyson's early opponents) and this can often inspire a cautious performance; in some circumstances, caution can repay handsomely.

Perhaps the underdog's most significant advantage is the absence of pressure. Periods of adversity, or even mixed success, can help develop the kind of resilience that may not be a feature of the favorite's makeup. Strong recent form and a good overall record can add to a favorite's momentum; but it may not equip them well should they fall behind or experience poor form early in a competition. The underdog may habitually face grief and could be well used to dealing with it.

Managers and coaches, as well as sports performers, usually welcome the underdog status: they usually believe it augurs well for the contest. A manager/coach will remind his or her team that the opposition will feel the pressure that comes with favorite's territory. As underdogs they can disregard spectators' expectations and concentrate on job. It is known that the ability to get FOCUSED is often contingent on the ability to ignore surrounding circumstances – such as the odds – which may well distract and interfere with effective performance.

Despite these attractive features of the underdog role and the fact that facing obstacles can work as a potent motivator, it should be remembered that competitors are installed as favorites by calculating odds-makers who are guided by such unemotional factors as recent form, conditions and the relative merits of each contestant. Underdog upsets are exactly that: upsets. They do not occur often.

Of related interest

Elias, Norbert and Dunning, Eric (1986) *Quest for Excitement*, Basil Blackwell.
Frazier, Jimmy A. and Snyder, Eldon E. (1991) "The underdog concept in sport," *Sociology of Sport Journal* vol 8.

videated

The term "videated sports" is used by the sociologist Jay Coakley (1998) to define sports that are represented to viewing audiences through video technology "used to create dramatic, exciting and stylized images and messages for the purpose of entertaining viewers and maintaining sponsors." In other words, every major sport and several minor sports.

Before the advent of radio in the 1920s, sporting events would have been experienced directly by spectators. The advent of wireless technology, and later TELEVISION, introduced ever-widening audiences to sports. Since the 1960s, sport and television have existed in what Coakley, along with several other writers, regard as a symbiotic relationship, each depending on the other to create revenues. The interest of sponsors, advertisers and manufacturers seeking ENDORSEMENTS from sports performers is strongly linked to the "videation" – that is, the recording and broadcasting – of sports.

Coakley argues that the way people use messages and images in the construction of ideas about sports, about the world, and about their relationship to one another perpetuate ideologies related to "success, gender, race, nationalism, competition, individualism, teamwork, violence and consumerism." He encourages research on how people create their own video images on the internet and through video technology. An implication of Coakley's comments is that, from the 1980s, people have become habituated to watching sports in a videated way, whether through television screens or, more recently, computer screens. The GLOBALIZATION of sports has been commissioned by the availability of television networks throughout the world. Coakley uses impressionistic evidence to argue that younger people actually prefer creatively playing computer-generated sports than attending an actual event. Young computer-literate adults enjoy the interactive facilities of sports on the Internet.

While he does not spell out the argument, we can infer from Coakley's statement that he would endorse the view that sport in the raw, so to speak, is insufficient for viewers who are part of a generation weaned on videated sports: they would want it packaged and presented much like any other commodity.

After all, when viewers are asked to pay for a product, as has increasingly been the case since the start of the 1990s, they want more than roving-eye-style presentation. In sports, the action does not speak for itself: it needs the direction and narration that produce drama. (Readers who disagree may wish to push the mute button on their remote controls when next watching sports on television.)

The videated generation of sports followers are typically those who opt to wait and rent the video rather than going to the movies, who play computer games at home instead of playing ball in the park. Attendance at sports events may be experienced as one-dimensional. Deprived of INSTANT REPLAY, slo-mos, reverse angles, virtual replays, captioned statistics and knowledgeable comment, the videated FANDOM is disappointed.

Expectations and perceptions of sports have changed, as have patterns of viewing. Television, video and their progeny have gently encouraged spectators to read sports differently. Today, young people may watch the same piece of action as their forebears, but they do not necessarily interpret it in the same way. Videation allows them to relax: missing a touchdown, a knockdown, a homer or a hole in one is not a disaster when it will be reviewed again and again and from different vantage points. This, plus the comment, summaries and statistics that accompany the action, encourages a certain detachment and predilection for analysis. Today's sports fan watches sport argus-eyed, assimilating all manner of information audial as well as visual. Pre- and post-event features have all but supplanted the actual event. Analysing has become an integral part of videated sports, and the better-informed viewer can cast a clinical eye on proceedings. The content of sports may not have changed too drastically, but, as Coakley points out, "the experiences associated with them are rapidly changing."

Of related interest

Barnett, Steven (1990) *Games and Sets: The Changing Face of Sport on Television*, British Film Institute.
Cashmore, Ellis (2000) *Making Sense of Sports*, 3rd edn, Routledge.
Coakley, Jay J. (1998) *Sport in Society: Issues and Controversies*, McGraw-Hill.

violence

Internal control

Violence is defined by Michael Smith (1983) as "physically assaultive behavior that is designed to, and does, injure another person or persons physically." But, as Smith argues in his book *Violence and Sport*, the term "sports violence" is more difficult to pin down. This is because definitions change over time and space. Behavior that we might consider unacceptably violent might, in a different era, be viewed as relatively mild. The surrounding cultural context to a large extent determines how we see violence. Smith cites Elias's work on *The Civilizing Process*, noting how wanton acts of brutality that we would regard as repugnant were considered modestly entertaining when set against an historical background of day-to-day barbarity. In an uncivil society, uncivil sports would be the norm.

Despite the occasional de-civilizing spurts that seem to work as a reverse gear on the more general process, culture has raised the threshold of what is acceptable violence. It is no longer acceptable to smack children, less still to strike employees or settle disputes with duels. Violence has become regulated synchronously with our BODY REGULATION: we control our own behavior. Outright violence has not disappeared, of course, but it has diminished, and this has been reflected in sports activities which were once " unregulated, chaotic, and barely distinguishable from 'real' fighting." When there are instances of such "real" fighting, we are alarmed, concerned and usually moved to clamp down on it.

From the late nineteenth century, when sports governing federations began to impose organizational structure and control on what were once loose assemblies of competitive activity, restrictions on the use of outright violence were introduced. The violent content of many sports decreased systematically as governing organizations moved with the times: as the threshold of acceptable violence in society changed, so did sport's. Late football hits, overly savage beatings in the boxing ring, unlimited head-high balls bowled in cricket: these were instances of once-acceptable behavior that were reviewed and modified during the twentieth century. Even sports that were not ostensibly violent were assessed: whip abuse in horse racing was banned, as was racket abuse in tennis. Mindful of changing attitudes, sports authorities adjusted their thresholds, penalizing violators with fines and suspensions in a quasi-legal manner. Sports defended their rights to police themselves and to safeguard their own standards; their administration of justice served to insulate them from the attentions of the wider judicial system. Until the 1970s, this proved generally effective.

Legal interventions

Special rules apply to sports. Behavior that we would admonish in most contexts is condoned on the field of play, in the ring, on the ice or in a variety of other competitive situations. Yet, from the 1970s, courts of LAW have demonstrated a willingness to adjudicate on matters that had previously been regarded for the most part as sport's internal affairs. This has given rise to many notable cases and a sometimes perplexing and contradictory set of rulings. Yet, beyond the uncertainties, there is one constant: the increasing readiness of law to become involved in events that were once seen as the sole domain of sports' own governing bodies.

Ice hockey's popularity has increased as its level of AGGRESSION has been raised. A study by DeNeui and Sachau concluded that spectators' enjoyment of a game was related to the amount of aggression they observed. In their book *Hockey Night in Canada* (Garamond, 1993), Richard Gruneau and Dave Whitson write: "Hockey actually seems to celebrate fighting outside the rules as normal part of the game." Sticks are sometimes wielded like axes, fists fly furiously and players are bundled about the ice. "The belief that violence sells and that eliminating fighting would undercut the game's appeal as spectacle has been the official thinking among the NHL's most influential governors and officers," reason

Gruneau and Whitson. Yet, this has not prevented certain cases escaping into the legal domain.

In 1969, Ted Green of the Boston Bruins almost died as a result of a stick blow to the head that fractured his skull. In the following year, both Green and Wayne Maki, of St Louis, who had struck the damaging blow, appeared in separate trials in Ottawa, charged with assault causing bodily harm. It was alleged that Green provoked Maki. Both were acquitted on the grounds of self-defense. Within months of the case, a Canada-wide poll conducted by *Maclean's* magazine indicated almost 40 per cent of respondents, male and female, liked to see physical violence in hockey. They were not disappointed: over the next several years, the amount and intensity of violence in hockey increased, leading to a spiral of assault charges related to hockey. In 1976, the Attorney-General of Ontario ordered a crackdown on violence in sports. In the same year, a particularly wild brawl occurred during a World Hockey Association playoff game between Quebec Nordiques and Calgary Cowboys, whose player Rick Jodzio was eventually fined C\$3,000 (\$2,200; £1,360) after pleading guilty to a lesser charge than the original causing bodily harm with intent to wound. There were also convictions arising from a Philadelphia–Toronto game in 1976. The interesting aspect of this case was that, in legal terms, a hockey stick was designated a dangerous weapon.

While hockey cases were the most vivid, there were also relevant occurrences in other sports. Indeed, the first case in recent history happened in a 1965 Giants–Dodgers MAJOR LEAGUE BASEBALL game, when San Francisco hitter Juan Marichal hit Los Angeles catcher John Roseborough with his bat. Marichal was fined by the league and suspended, but Roseborough sought retribution through a civil suit that was eventually settled out of court.

In basketball, a case in 1979 involved not only the fining and suspension of the Lakers' Kermit Washington, but an accusation leveled at his club for failing to train and supervise the player adequately. He was ordered to pay damages. The player whom he struck, Rudy Tomjanovich, was effectively forced into premature retirement as a result of his injuries.

In football, in an NFL game during the 1975 season, Dale Hackbart of the Denver Broncos suffered a career-ending fracture of the spine following a big hit from Charles Clark of the Cincinnati Bengals. Taking his case to the District Court, Hackbart was told that, by the very fact of playing in an NFL game, he was taking an implied risk and that anything happening to him between the sidelines was part of that risk. An appeals court disagreed and ruled that, while Clark may not have specifically *intended* to injure his opponent, he had engaged in "reckless misconduct." This paved the way for his employer, the Bengals, to be held accountable.

This case had echoes almost two decades later in England, when a Chelsea soccer player, Paul Elliott, pursued a case against Dean Saunders, then playing for Liverpool. Following a tackle from Saunders, Elliott sustained injuries that prevented him from playing again. The court found that the context of sport mitigated the offense and that Saunders was not guilty of reckless or dangerous play. Elliott's case was weakened by the fact that play was penalized by the referee during the game and so the judge was effectively asked to use a video and other evidence to overturn the referee's decision.

The violence in all these cases was not integral to the sport itself and, though it could be argued that to strip away all violence from sports like hockey and football would leave them wan and colorless, the game could theoretically still be played. This is not so in boxing, of course, which makes the case of Italian middleweight Angelo Jacopucci more interesting. In 1978, British middleweight Alan Minter knocked out Jacopucci, who died some hours later. In 1983, after a protracted and complicated series of legal actions, a court in Bologna, Italy, acquitted the referee and Jacopucci's manager of second-degree manslaughter on the basis that they should have stopped the fight before the twelfth and last round. The ringside doctor, however, was convicted and ordered to pay Jacopucci's widow the equivalent of $15,000 (£10,000) damages and given a suspended eight-month prison sentence. Minter, whose punches actually did the damage, was not prosecuted.

Soccer player Duncan Ferguson was sentenced to three months imprisonment after head-butting a rival player in a 1994 game between his club Rangers and Raith Rovers, in Glasgow. Unlike the actions of Saunders, Clark and Minter, Ferguson's were not in the flow of the game: head-butting may be charitably regarded as accidental in boxing, but in soccer it is invariably predetermined. Also in soccer, the case of Manchester United's Eric CANTONA illustrated the preparedness of courts to intervene in on-field activities. Cantona was leaving the field of play having been ejected from the 1995 game, when he detoured into the crowd to attack a jeering fan. Cantona's actions elicit comparisons with those of Vernon Maxwell of the Houston Rockets, who set off in pursuit of a fan who had been verbally abusing him by striding twelve rows into the crowd and punching his tormentor.

Both players were dealt with sternly by their clubs and leagues; Cantona was actually charged by a court of law with common assault and sentenced to two week's imprisonment, which was later changed to community service. The case had a precedent of sort some two decades before. Henry Boucha, who played for the Minnesota North Stars of the NHL, became involved in a fight with Dave Forbes during a game against Forbes's club, the Boston Bruins. The two were sent to the penalty box. On their way back into the game, Forbes lashed out with his stick, dropping Boucha to the ice. Concussed and bleeding, Boucha was helpless as Forbes leapt on him and, grabbing his hair, slammed his head onto the ice repeatedly. Forbes escaped with a relatively light suspension of ten games from the NHL, but a Minnesota grand jury charged him with the crime of aggravated assault by use of a dangerous weapon. Forbes pleaded not guilty, and the jury was unable to reach a unanimous verdict after eighteen hours of deliberations. The court declared a mistrial and the case was dismissed. Boucha meanwhile needed surgery and never played again. *State vs Forbes* was a criminal case, and its lack of a definite verdict left several pertinent questions unresolved. Michael Smith believes the main ones revolve around whether Forbes was culpable, or whether the club for which he played and the league in which he performed were in some way responsible for establishing a context for his action.

It is also relevant that the actual violent event took place as the players were re-entering the playing area rather in the context of the contest itself, which is why it bears resemblance to the Cantona affair. Cantona had first committed a foul, for which he was dismissed from the game. The attack on the fan occurred in a contiguous area to the field. Had the fan run onto the playing area and provoked Cantona, it would have been more difficult, though certainly possible, for courts to intercede.

Sports governing federations have, in their attempts to regulate their own sports, imposed increasingly severe penalties on rule-violators. An example is the Latrell Sprewell case. Sprewell, a basketball player for the Golden State Warriors and an NBA All-Star, assaulted and threatened to kill his coach P.J. Carlesimo during a 1997 practice. Even in the light of the coach's reputation as a hard man, Sprewell's attack was thought inexcusable (though not entirely unexpected, as there had been tension between the two for many months). It boiled over on December 1, when Sprewell grabbed Carlesimo by the throat, dragged him to the ground and choked him for 15–20 seconds before other players pulled him off.

Golden State responded by first suspending Sprewell for ten games, and then, two days later, terminating his four-year $32 million (£20m) contract, which had nearly three years and $25m remaining, citing a conduct clause in the basic players' agreement (i.e. stipulating that players must conform to standards of good citizenship). Sprewell also lost an endorsement deal with Converse valued at $300,000–600,000 a year. The NBA then banned Sprewell from playing for any NBA club for one year. It was a harsh punishment for an offense that may have probably carried a far lesser penalty had it occurred in a parking lot or a bar. Other incidents that have taken place on the field of play or in practice would have been dealt with more severely had they happened in other social settings.

Of related interest

DeNeui, O.L. and Sachau, O.A. (1996) "Spectator enjoyment of aggression in intercollegiate college games," *Journal of Sport and Social Issues* vol 20, no 1.

Smith, Michael (1983) *Violence and Sport*, Butterworths.

Whitson, Dave and Gruneau, Richard (1993) *Hockey Night in Canada*, Garamond.

Werbeniuk, Bill

b. 1947, Canada

Snooker player Werbeniuk's professional career ended in 1993 when the World Professional Billiards and Snooker Association (WPBSA) banned one-half of the cocktail that allowed him to play. Vancouver-born Werbeniuk was known for his consumption of large quantities of lager; he was also a habitual user of Inderol, a beta blocker, the combination of which helped counteract the effects of an hereditary nervous disorder known as Familial Benign Essential Tremor which caused him to shake uncontrollably. The drink-and-drugs combination was actually prescribed by his doctors; it enabled him to steady his nerves and play without trembling. In fact, it was such an essential part of his diet that he was able to claim a tax deduction on the cocktail's constituents. A typical day's consumption would be 10 pints (1.5 US gallons; 5.68 liters) before morning practice, a similar amount during a morning session, same again before an evening session and again while he was playing the evening session. His phenomenal intake blew up his weight to 280lbs and this was only kept down by Werbeniuk's hypoglycaemia, which meant that his body burned off sugar at a high rate.

Werbeniuk's drinking habit made him something of a celebrity when snooker rose in popularity in the 1970s, due mainly to British television's embrace of the sport. Snooker was a game that could have been designed for color TELEVISION: it is meaningless on black and white television, of course. BBC2 became a full color channel in 1967; a full color schedule had been introduced in the USA three years earlier. Sales of color sets were sluggish to begin with, but picked up during the 1970s.

Werbeniuk's reputation endeared him to British audiences and he based himself in London, where he used to drive a Ford Lincoln. He earned handsomely from exhibitions as well as tournaments and was even paid to visit pubs and just drink – without even playing snooker.

Snooker was heavily sponsored by TOBACCO companies, and tournaments would regularly feature the name of cigarettes, such as Embassy and Benson &

Hedges. There was an obvious affinity: the origins of snooker, like those of pool, are rooted in BARS AND PUBS: the smoke-filled public house, complete with clinking glasses, was a natural environment. During the 1980s, however, disapproving eyes were cast on the sport and snooker, like pool, began a quest to find mass market appeal. The WPBSA reviewed its drugs policy and adopted the IOC's list of banned substances. While the policy was designed primarily to weed out illicit DRUGS, such as cocaine (which was known to be favored by some players on the professional circuit), Inderol was included.

Success in sports such as archery, darts, shooting, show jumping and so on is based on fineness of judgment, acuity of sight, sensitivity of touch and steadiness of hand: success comes to those who remain calm and impervious to "pressure." Werbeniuk's customary pre-game ten pints would have helped him relax, dulling his central nervous system and easing tensions. But, alcohol has serious drawbacks which include nausea and impaired judgment in the short-term and liver damage and dependency-related problems over a longer term.

Beta blockers, such as Inderol, are alternatives. Originally used by patients with irregular heartbeats, they relieve anxiety by controlling the release of adrenaline and by lowering heart rate; they are used by edgy showbusiness performers, and by horses. In 1994, a racehorse, Mobile Messenger, tested for Propranolol, a beta blocker, after winning a race at Southwell, England. The effect of the drug would have been similar to that on a human, to slow down the heart rate and thereby alleviate stress. In this case, some form of NOBBLING had taken place.

In 1989 Werbeniuk, then aged 41, protested against the WPBSA's judgment, claiming that he could not play without his prescribed beta blocker, which he had been using for the previous ten years, during which time he had slipped from eighth to forty-seventh in the world rankings – suggesting that the drug was not enhancing his performance. His protests were to no avail. The lager alone did not prevent him from experiencing dizziness and he was made to retire from the sport, returning to his native Vancouver. Within five years of his enforced retirement, he was existing on welfare.

Of related interest

Johnson, Martin (1998) "Big Bill is still lifting his elbow long after enjoying final pot," *Daily Telegraph*, February 14.

Wharton, Arthur

b. 1865, Ghana; d. 1930

Arthur Wharton was Britain's first black professional soccer player and the country's first Amateur Athletics Association (AAA) champion. However, he remains largely unacknowledged as a trailblazer and his biography was only written sixty-nine years after his death.

Wharton was born in 1865 in Accra, Ghana (then known as the Gold Coast). His father was a Wesleyan missionary, and his mother was the daughter of a

Scottish trader. His parents wished him to become a Methodist teacher and, in 1884, took him to Cleveland College in the north-eastern English town of Darlington, where he was meant to study. Here Wharton discovered his sprinting prowess: running a handicap event at a Darlington cricket club's annual sports meeting, he ducked under the finishing tape rather than breaking it and would have been disqualified had the second-placed runner not refused the first prize.

Wharton, who became known as "Darkie," was an oddity in Victorian England, though he was by no means the first black sports performer to have distinguished himself. From the late eighteenth century, slaves and ex-slaves were taken from their plantations and made to tour England as prize fighters. Some, like Tom Molyneux, became famous for his contest with Tom Cribb in 1810. In the second half of the 1800s, Britain received high quality pugilists such as Bob Smith and Bob Traver, who was noted for his fights with Jem Mace and Patsy Reardon. They were followed by Peter Jackson, who was born in St Croix, in 1861 (four years before emancipation) and traveled as a seaman to Sydney, Australia and San Francisco before moving to London, where he became a sporting celebrity and rubbed shoulders with the aristocracy. The other lauded black fighter of the day was George Dixon, who was sometimes known as "Little Chocolate." Born in Nova Scotia, Canada, Dixon moved to Boston before transferring to England, where he won the world bantamweight title. He later moved back to the United States. But, it is reasonable to assume that, with limited transportation facilities and no mass media as such, knowledge of black sports performers was limited, especially in the northeast.

Wharton came to national attention in 1886, when he won the AAA's 100 yards title in even time (ten seconds dead) at London's Stamford Bridge. He repeated the act a year later, when he won his second AAA title. As a measure of how significant his time was, we should note that it was bettered in a AAA championship only once over the next thirty-seven years; we should also note that they were achieved on a cinder track, wearing flats and from a standing start. At the time of his first AAA victory, Wharton signed to play professionally (as goalkeeper) for the Preston North End Football Club. He was the first black player in the English Football League. He later transferred to Sheffield United, a first division club.

Wharton continued not only to run, but to play cricket and to cycle. He ran in the Scottish professional Powder Hall races and seems to have made a decent living from sports, moving to Sheffield in 1888 and then to Rotherham Town Football Club in 1889. Five years later he moved back to Sheffield and played for Sheffield United, though without becoming the club's first-choice goalkeeper. He finished his soccer career with Stockport County, retiring in 1902 at the age of 37. (In the same year, a boxer, Andrew Jeptha traveled to London, working his passage from South Africa on a freighter; five years later, he became the first black boxer to win a British title when he beat Curly Watson for the welterweight championship.) As Wharton's athletic powers waned, so did his earning power and he slid into poverty in South Yorkshire, pushing coal trucks as a haulage hand at Yorkshire Main Colliery. He died in 1930 at Springwell Sanatorium, near Doncaster, suffering from syphilis and a facial tumor, and was buried in an unmarked grave (later, an appeal was launched which raised enough money to buy a headstone).

After Wharton's retirement, a steady stream of black sprinters, mostly from the Caribbean, continued to win major honors. These included Harry Edward, winner of seven AAA titles from 1920–22; Jack London, who represented Britain in the 1928 Olympics and was the first sprinter to use starting blocks in Britain; McDonald Bailey, who won a bronze medal for Britain in the 1952 Olympics and took sixteen AAA titles from 1946–53; and Arthur Wint, who was domiciled in England but won the 400 yards Olympic title for Jamaica in 1948. It took until after the Second World War before another black professional soccer player emerged; he was Jamaican-born Lloyd "Lindy" Delaphena, who played for Middlesbrough and then Portsmouth before drifting from the public eye in 1958.

Of related interest

Cashmore, E. (1982) *Black Sportsmen*, Routledge, 1982.
Jenkins, Ray (1990) "Salvation for the fittest? A West African sportsman in Britain in the age of the new imperialism," *International Journal of the History of Sport* vol 7, no 1.
Vasili, Phil (1999) *An Absence of Memory*, Frank Cass.

When We Were Kings

Winner of the 1997 Academy Award for best feature-length documentary, Leon Gast's film *When We Were Kings* centered on the extraordinary heavyweight title fight between George Foreman and Muhammad ALI which took place in Zaïre (now called the Congo Republic) in October 1974. The fight is frequently cited as one of the sports events of the twentieth century. Foreman, a prohibitively heavy favorite, was upset by the 32-year-old Ali.

When We Were Kings took two months to shoot, but almost twenty-three years to complete. By the time of its general release in 1997, the movie had become a social document as well as report of what was known as the "Rumble in the Jungle," or simply "The Fight." Originally the director conceived of the project as an "African Woodstock," his intention being to film the three-day music festival which was scheduled to precede the boxing. The concert included James Brown, B.B. King and the Spinners. But Gast's attention was caught by events related to the fight itself.

The newly acquired independence of many of Africa's states had brought world attention on the continent. In the USA, black people had been energized by political and cultural movements that emphasized the importance of acknowledging African roots. Ali had, years before, converted to Islam and joined the black Nation of Islam organization, which identified whites as "blue-eyed devils" and preached separatism. As part of his personal mission, he had refused to fight in a "white man's war" and justified his decision memorably: "I ain't got no quarrel with the Vietcong." He had lost three years of his career as a result.

On arrival in Zaïre, Ali won over the local population, encouraging them in their chant *Ali, bom a ye* ("Kill him, Ali") and constantly depicting himself as the real black man opposing someone who had tamely held the US flag at the Olympic Games, where Foreman won a gold medal. Foreman is shown in the movie doing himself few favors as he exits his aircraft with his dog, a German Shepherd, the breed used by the Belgian police (Belgium was Zaïre's former colonial overlord). Foreman was either shy or inept when dealing with journalists, qualities amplified by Ali's expert commandeering of the media.

The crux of the fight and, indeed, the film was the six week postponement occasioned by a cut eye picked up by Foreman in sparring. The fighters were not allowed to leave the country, and while Ali continued to build his support, Foreman languished in isolation. He was clearly upset at what was, for him, a virtual imprisonment. It is at least possible that the unwelcome interlude in his preparation marred his concentration in the fight itself: the fearsome, seemingly unbeatable champion looked ponderous by comparison with the older but more agile challenger.

As the fight progressed, Ali introduced his "rope-a-dope" technique. Gast's cameras catch Ali, his back arched over the top rope, Foreman bent forward at almost 90 degrees, burying his head into Ali's midsection but doing no damage. "Hit harder," Ali can be heard saying. "Is that the best you can do?"

As Gast captures the visual drama, a Greek chorus of writers, George Plimpton and Norman Mailer (both of whom covered the actual fight), Ali biographer Thomas Hauser and film-maker Spike Lee, provide narrative. Plimpton recalls how he had heard locally that Foreman had been visited in his sleep by a succubus and that, in the eighth round, when Ali unleashed his stunning, fight-winning barrage of punches, he was momentarily convinced that a succubus had indeed possessed Foreman.

Ali's astonishing, unexpected victory left no doubts about his claim to genuine sporting greatness, but Foreman's image was shattered. Although Ali started the fight as a betting UNDERDOG, he left the universally acclaimed champion of the heavyweight division and arguably the finest pound-for-pound boxer in history. Interestingly, the two men's lives were reshaped very differently by subsequent events. Foreman did not immediately recover his formidable fighting prowess: after another loss he retired and became a preacher, only to return to the ring and recapture the world title in 1994, when aged 45. Ali fought on until his career was in steep decline, and later suffered from the debilitating Parkinson's syndrome. At the Oscar ceremony, Ali looked feeble and was assisted to the stage, followed by the fresh and ebullient Foreman.

The reason for the delay between filming and release was money. Zaïre's President Mobuto contributed US$10 million of his government's money to bring the events to his nation. Gast was promised that post-production costs would be met by gate receipts from the concert. But, Mobutu declared it a free concert. Further misfortune came when the Liberian government, which was backing the film, was overthrown and Gast spent fifteen years trying to re-finance what became a labor of love. The original footage was augmented by reflective interviews filmed by Hollywood director Taylor Hackford, though the principal protagonists are featured only in the 1970s.

Gast's film has a supple structure that allows the audience to be privy to the tightest personal moments (like Ali deliberately avoiding the sight of Foreman's heavy punch bag, which had been dented by the power of his shots) while providing an appreciation of the context of the 1970s. It is a fitting record of a key sports event, and a historical document in its own right. "One cannot fail to see the reflection of America in Africa and of Africa in America; one cannot fail to see the aesthetics of music and the grace and the violence of boxing," wrote Marc Singer in his review for the *Journal of Sport History* (vol 24, no 2, Summer 1997). "In the figure of Muhammad Ali, these all come together. As he preaches in the film about the unity of African-Americans and Africans, one realizes that Ali himself was helping create the unity."

Of related interest

Early, Gerald (ed.) (1998) *I'm a Little Special: A Muhammad Ali Reader*, Jersey Press.
Hauser, Thomas (1991) *Muhammad Ali: His Life and Times*, Simon & Schuster.
Mailer, Norman (1975) *The Fight*, Little, Brown.
When We Were Kings, directed by Leon Gast, 1996.

Wisden

Origins

Wisden Cricketers' Almanack has been published annually since 1864. During the intervening years, it has evolved from being just one of many informal magazines and publications to a weighty and authoritative tome, the "bible of cricket." It is perhaps the most venerated sports publication in the world.

The second half of the Victorian era saw the emergence of a large number of ephemeral cricket publications in Britain. *Wisden* was early in the field and it alone survived, having transformed itself in a way that others did not. John Wisden (1826–84), the *Almanack*'s founder (but never editor) was a highly successful professional cricketer at a time when the game was beginning to expand from its predominantly amateur base and when its appeal was widening.

Unusually for his kind, Wisden was a considerable entrepreneur and a man aware of his market value. In 1852, he co-founded the United All England XI which toured the country, playing local teams. Together with Frederick Lillywhite (who published more than one almanac himself), Wisden set up a cricket outfitting business which he went on to manage. He was the first in a long line of cricketing – and, later, general sports – retailers. Wisden was in addition the Secretary of the Cricketers' Fund Friendly Society from 1857 until his death; he helped to pioneer tours abroad, with George Parr's team to North America in 1859. Then, in 1864, came the first edition of his *The Cricketers' Almanack*.

Wisden's *Almanack* differed little from its contemporary counterparts, which were responding to the growing popularity of cricket, appealing to the fast-expanding literate lower middle and working class of the 1860s and 1870s. The early editions contained the scores of matches and items such as players' biographies, gossip, a lot of advertising and miscellanea. "When John Wisden published his first annual edition in 1864, he was so bemused by the beauty of his own invention that he had not the remotest idea what to put into it," wrote Benny Green (1986) of early editions. Green went on to describe how Wisden "[filled] the pages with irrelevancies ... tables showing the length of British canals, the dates of the principal battles of the Wars of the Roses ... and a brief disquisition on the constitutional implications of the trial of Charles I." The early *Almanacks* bore only passing resemblance to those of today. At a shilling (about a dime) each, they were perhaps a little beyond the pocket of the ordinary worker and cricket follower, but could be afforded by the growing urban lower-middle class.

1864 not only saw the first *Wisden*, but also the debut of the 16-year-old W.G. Grace, whose phenomenal feats did much to publicize and popularize cricket. It was a year when seven of the present first-class counties began their existence or formed clubs. The early 1860s were boom years for cricket. The 1830s and 1840s had seen the beginnings of organized matches between county and regional teams and the laws of cricket had been revised and scoring methods standardized. Although the sport's governing body, the MCC (Marylebone Cricket Club) had been formed in 1787 and contests between county teams increased in number throughout the 1860s and 1870s, it was not until the 1890s that an organized "County Championship" was set up.

The reportage of organized cricket

The burgeoning of cricket from the 1860s was an urban phenomenon, meeting the summer recreational needs of the growing town populations whose leisure time was expanding rapidly. Cricket was also taken up with considerable enthusiasm by the fast-developing public (independent fee-paying) schools. Between the 1820s and 1870s, cricket changed from being a gentleman's sport, mostly country-based, to a mass spectator sport of urban centers. In 1864, the year of the first *Wisden*, there were only thirty-seven games played which were (later) regarded as first class. In 1878, there were eighty-six first class matches, and by 1895 there were 150 (as a result of the MCC-organized championship competition). It was not only domestic cricket that was flourishing: by the 1890s there were all manner of organized games for *Wisden* to cover. Overseas tours – to and from England – proliferated from the 1870s (there were no fewer than twelve England/Australia tours between 1876–88).

From its beginnings, *Wisden Cricketers' Almanack* shared the field with a number of rivals. That it outlasted them can be attributed to the ability of its editors from the 1890s onwards. They skillfully capitalized on the huge growth in the popularity of cricket. The sport attracted formidable crowds; in 1892, 30,000 spectators (mostly standing) attended the first day of the Surrey–Nottingham-shire match at Kennington Oval. The sport was by then well-organized, increasingly professionalized and fully integrated into the fabric of everyday life. Its transition from a play-like recreation to an organized and regulated professional activity reflected the PROTESTANT ETHIC which had appreciably influenced the organization, meaning and moral value of work in industrial

Europe and which had effectively legitimized competition in all spheres of social activity.

Between 1895 and 1914, the year of the outbreak of the First World War, cricket experienced a "golden age." The appointment of Sydney Pardon to the editorship of *Wisden* roughly coincided with this (his tenure began in 1891). He can be regarded as the father of the modern *Wisden*. Sydney Pardon succeeded his father and remained editor for thirty-four years. In 1895, Hubert Preston joined the staff and enjoyed fifty-six years service (occupying the editor's position from 1944–51). He in turn was succeeded by his son Norman Preston, who edited *Wisden* from 1952 until 1980. It is on this continuity that *Wisden* has based its strength.

From the Pardon era of the 1890s, *Wisden* began to develop many of the features which were to last to the present. "Cricketers of the Year" were introduced in 1889, obituaries in 1892. The "chatty," anecdotal tenor of the early days was replaced by a more authoritative reportage style. Continuity does not mean that *Wisden* did not change. "*Wisden* is … surrounded by an era of myth. One myth is that the Almanack somehow never changes," wrote a new editor on taking up his position in 1993. "*Wisden* has changed enormously over the years, just as the game has. For the most part – and rightly – it has done so slowly, organically, almost stealthily, mutating a good deal more carefully than cricket itself."

The contemporary *Wisden*

The contents of today's *Wisden* range across many aspects of the game, including reportage, analysis, cricket politics and, of course, cricket history and records. A definitive section contains the "Laws of Cricket." The appeal of *Wisden*, as that of the sport itself, lies in this complex blend. The "heart" of *Wisden* , for many readers, is in its reportage of English domestic cricket. *Wisden* is published each April, immediately before the start of the English season, and the full scores for each first class match of the previous English season are reported in detail.

Wisden was – and is – ambivalent about newer variations of cricket's standard three-day and four-day "first class" game, such as the one-day format. Reports of such competitions have lacked the kind of detail associated with the publication. It regards itself as a bearer of traditional standards, be these with regard to the format of the game, players' behavior or the increasing commercialization of cricket.

The "organic change" of the *Almanack* reflects changing social mores. In the 1950s, a typical *Wisden* would devote as much as 7 per cent of its space to reportage of public schools cricket, including full details of, for example, Stonyhurst vs Denstone, or Repton vs Malvern. Averages and performances of 16-year-old schoolboys would be solemnly listed. By the late 1990s, the section on "Public Schools Cricket" had been retitled simply "Schools Cricket." Although much the same schools were reported, the proportion of space diminished to 3 per cent, reflecting the relative insignificance of public schools cricket compared to the professional game and the diffusion of popularity across the class spectrum.

Matches involving the MCC and elite clubs received less coverage in the 1990s than in the past, and there was a decrease in articles by and about senior administrators and other establishment figures who still largely control the sport. *Wisden*'s increasing coverage of cricket in other parts of the world beside England is testament to the GLOBALIZATION of cricket.

Wisden is unique in that it is perhaps the only sports publication that has no rivals: its comprehensiveness of analysis and factual reporting, and its mixture of past and present ensure that the most cerebral and subtle of sports is served effectively. John Wisden's 1864 one-shilling paperback of 112 pages now sells throughout the world at £26 ($43) hardback, containing nearly 1,500 pages. (Old editions are eminently collectable: in July 1996, a run of fifty-two *Wisdens* 1864–1915, which were once owned by W.G. Grace, were auctioned for £94,100, or $154,300.)

Of related interest

Dunning, Eric and Sheard, K. (1979) *Gentlemen, Barbarians and Players*, Martin Robertson.
Green, Benny (1986) "Introduction," *The Wisden Book of Cricketers' Lives: Obituaries from Wisden Cricketers' Almanack*, Queen Anne Press/Macdonald & Co.
Sandiford, K. (1994) *Cricket and the Victorians*, Aldershot: Scolar Press.
Williams, J. "Cricket" in T. Mason (ed.) *Sport in Britain: A Social History*, Cambridge University Press, 1989.

DAVID PODMORE

Woods, Eldrick "Tiger"

b. 1975, USA

Woods' impact

On April 13, 1997, Tiger Woods became the first black golfer to win a major golf title when he won the Masters in Augusta, Georgia. At 21, he was also the youngest winner of the title and, in winning, set a Masters scoring record of 270 over 72 holes, finishing a record by the greatest number of shots ever, twelve strokes ahead of second-placed Tom Kite. He had announced that he was turning professional only a year earlier.

Much play was made of the fact that Woods' Masters win came two days before the fiftieth anniversary of the day Jackie ROBINSON broke the color line in professional baseball. There was more irony in Wood's first major trophy: it came at a club where African American professional Lee Elder had not been allowed to enter the Masters until 1975. Previously, black golfers such as Elder, Charlie Sifford, Rafe Botts, Pete Brown, Jim Dent and Chuck Thorpe were denied entry onto the Professional Golf Association tour until 1961 when the PGA removed its "Caucasians only rule," although many courses still prohibited blacks.

Florida-born Woods was US amateur champion 1994–96, NCAA champion in 1996 and US Junior Amateur champion 1991–93. He interrupted his studies at

Stanford to pursue golf on a full-time basis. In his first year on the professional golf circuit, Woods attracted $653.5 million (£408m) in "new money"; this included revenue from TELEVISION contracts and ticket and merchandise sales. Television ratings for golf soared as a result of interest in Woods. In 1996, 57.6 million homes watched the final round of the four major championships. In 1997, the figure was 91.5m, an increase of almost 59 per cent. This enabled the PGA to secure a CBS television contract worth $650m, about $325m more than the deal that expired at the end of the 1998 season.

Wood's own ENDORSEMENT had established himself as a multi-millionaire even before he had played his first professional tournament. Under the guidance of Mark McCORMACK's International Management Group, he secured key deals. His contract with NIKE was worth $7.5 million as a signing bonus, plus $6.5 million for five years, totaling $40 million. Sales of Nike golf apparel doubled to $120m in the fiscal year ending May 1997, though the company's profits slumped in the year following Woods' Masters win.

Woods' contract with Titleist was worth $3.5 million per annum to play with Titleist golf equipment and help design a range of apparel. He also negotiated $7m (£4.2m) worth of stock in the All Star Cafe chain, a subsidiary of Planet Hollywood. Later, he gained endorsement contracts from American Express, Rolex and Wheaties, which also used Michael JORDAN. The Rolex deal provided for the introduction of a line of Tiger Woods watches, retailing at $2,000. CBS television made a special show called "Tiger Woods and friends" in which Woods entertained Jordan, Ken Griffey Jnr and Kevin Costner. Woods's personal earnings in 1997–8 were $26.1m (£15.5m), according to *Forbes*.

Heralded by some as the first black champion in a sport from which blacks had been traditionally excluded, he was also received with caution by others who felt that the last thing the African American population needed was yet another sports superstar. At the time, only a minute fraction of the African American population held full-time positions in professional sports, though various pieces of research estimated that as many as 80 per cent of young blacks aspired to making a living from sports. Forty-five per cent of African American children lived below the poverty line.

Woods himself admitted that he received death threats and hate mail. His response was that this was inevitable: "When you play a sport in which you are not a majority, of course, there is going to be animosity. Until we understand and respect everyone for the kind of person they are, not just by looking at their pigmentation, of course that's going to happen." In his book *Training a Tiger*, Earl Woods, Tiger's father, wrote: "The Almighty entrusted this precocious child to me. He is orchestrating this entire scenario and has a plan to utilise Tiger to make an impact on the world. I don't know what it is, but I sincerely believe it will be spiritual and humanitarian and will transcend the game of golf."

Fellow golfer Fuzzy Zoeller made a racial gaffe when referring to Woods as a "little boy" and, joking, said he hoped that he would not order "fried chicken and collard green or whatever they eat" at an official celebratory dinner in Wood's honor. Zoeller apologized, but was stripped of his advertising contract. Yet Woods himself also made gaffes. In a *GQ* magazine interview, Woods went on record as saying: "What I can't figure out is why so many good-looking women hang around baseball and basketball." He went on speculate that it was because of a widespread perception that "black guys have big dicks." One wonders what would have happened if Justin Leonard, David Duval or any one of Wood's white peers had uttered such remarks.

While he was widely acclaimed (and, indeed, marketed) as the first African American to make a major breakthrough in golf, Woods in fact described himself as "of Asian descent," since his mother was Thai and his father claimed Chinese as well as North American Indian ancestry.

Black golfers in history

While Tiger Woods's win in the 1997 Masters was hailed as a breakthrough for African American golfers, there had been an "invisible presence" of African Americans in professional golf since the 1940s. In fact, as far back as 1895, John Shippen, the son of a Native American Indian mother and African American father, played and finished fourth in the second US Open, the oldest major tournament in the United States. Shippen and his brother were teaching professionals at some of the most elite clubs in the USA. John Shippen narrowly missed out on the US Open in 1896; his Scottish and English contemporaries refused to compete with Shippen and the American Indian, Oscar Bunn, but relented under pressure from the PGA. The segregationist Jim Crow legislation eventually forced Shippen out of professional tournaments.

The whole game of golf in America was based on exclusivity. During the 1880s it was associated with country clubs and prosperity. Blacks, like their white working-class counterparts were afforded little or no opportunity to compete. Interestingly, the first golf tee patent was taken out in 1899 by Dr. George Grant, a black dentist based in Boston, Massachusetts. In 1916, the PGA published its constitution: it stipulated that its members should be white. This forced African American players to organize their own tournaments, or rely on invitations. In 1926, a group of black physicians from Washington, DC established the United Golf Association (UGA) as a response to their exclusion from all other golf clubs. Clubs were affiliated and tournaments organized. During the 1930s, about 50,000 golf-playing African Americans were members, growing to 90,000 by the 1960s.

Although black college golfers were mostly at black institutions, some played at white Division I schools: A.D.V. Crosby, for example, played at the University of Michigan in 1930, and George Roddy played for the University of Iowa. In the 1950s, Forest Jones, Jr. was the leading player on the Indiana University golf team. Tuskegee Institute was the first HBCU (Historically Black Colleges and Universities) to have a golf course.

During the 1940s, many black players took the PGA to court in an effort to gain admission to its tournaments and to play at public courses. The first success came in 1948 when a Baltimore court ruled that the local course for blacks was not of equal standard to the three public courses that were reserved exclusively for whites; the order was that the whites-only courses be opened to black players. The landmark *Brown vs Board of Education* decision that ushered in the desegregation of schools, adding impetus to what became a legal movement, with blacks fighting for the right to use municipal golf courses. The PGA was sued by several black players, including Ted Rhodes and Bill Spiller, who was also a boxer associated with the Joe Louis camp.

The PGA promised to drop its discriminatory policy in an out-of-court settlement. But, in 1953, the boxer Joe Louis was invited to play in a San Diego tournament. Rhodes and Spiller were also in the tournament. Shortly before the competition began, all three had their invitations withdrawn, prompting more threats of writs. As civil rights gained momentum, so demands on the PGA grew more fierce. In one memorable gesture, Spiller threatened to picket the privately owned Brentwood Country Club, which hosted the 1962 PGA Championship, if black players were refused entry.

Not until 1961 did the PGA drop its racist policy, although it had in 1959 allowed Charlie Sifford an "approved player" card, which was a classification ordinarily reserved for overseas players; he received his Class A card in 1964. Sifford won the UGA National Professional Title six times between 1952 and 1960. He had earned a living as a part-time golf pro, tutoring singer Billy Ekstein, and as a chauffeur. Pete Brown won the 1968 San Diego Open and followed Sifford as the top black player. That position was later occupied by Lee Elder, who won four PGA events in the 1970s and represented the US in the Ryder Cup in 1975. Elder qualified for the 1975 Masters at the Augusta National Golf Course, in Georgia, run by the Augusta National Golf Club, which operated an openly racist policy. The only blacks allowed onto to its course were caddies. Elder joined the Senior Tour in 1984, and won seven tournaments and more money in seven years than he won on the regular tour in sixteen years. Calvin Peete and Jim Thorpe were successful professionals during the 1980s. Peete earned $2 million from golf by 1987, and Thorpe would probably have bettered this had a wrist injury not cut short his career.

While Woods's arrival on the world stage made the small but growing black presence in golf visible, the involvement of black females was largely ignored. In fact, there have been several notable women, amateur and professional, who have excelled in golf. Ella Abel and Lucy Williams played in the 1930s and 1940s, as did Thelma Cowan and Anne Gregory in the 1940s and 1950s. They were regular participants in (and winners of) the UGA National titles.

The Ladies Professional Golfers Association (LPGA) was created in 1950 and, like its male counterpart, excluded black players. When, in 1967, Renee Powell became the first black woman on the LPGA tour, she was subject to the same kinds of insults and threats that typically greet any black sports performer encroaching on white male territory (witness Jackie ROBINSON, Jack JOHNSON, Hank AARON and so on). Tennis star Althea Gibson was also an adept golfer and joined the tour briefly in the twilight of her tennis career.

Of related interest

Reed, Wornie L. (1991) "Blacks in golf," *Trotter Institute Review*, Winter/Spring.

Warren, S. (1983) "Blacks in the world of golf: Indianapolis style," *Black History News and Notes* 15.

Woods, Earl and McDaniel, Pete (1997) *Training a Tiger: A Father's Guide to Raising a Winner in Both Golf and Life*, HarperCollins.

Index

Page numbers in **bold** indicate references to the main entry.

Aaron, Hank **1–2**, 364
ABC television 29–31, 36, 116, 315–16, 406
Abdul-Jabbar, Kareem 309, 312
Abel, Ella 452
Aboriginals 161–2, 197
abortion 281, 411
Above the Rim (Pollack) 137
Abrahams, Harold 64–5
AC Milan 293
acceptability/nonacceptability **2–4**, 88, 231–2
accidents *see* death; injuries; risk
acetylpromazine (ACP) 95, 322
achievement 340
acupuncture 97
Adams, John 286, 359
adidas x, 312, 317, 318, 333, 386
adrenaline rush **5–6**, 9, 286, 298, 359
Advantage International 336
advertising x, 68, 109–11, 294–5, 414
    and ideal body 47–8
    and Tour de France 417
    see also endorsements; sponsorship
African National Congress (ANC) 350
Against All Odds (Hackford) 134
Agassi, Andre 111, 140, 263, 295, 320
age **6–8**, 58–60, 222
Agee, Arthur 182–3
agents *see* McCormack; ProServ
aggression 3, **8–11**, 35, 41, 62–3
    attraction of 428–30, 437–8
    as catharsis 9–10, 269
    and frustration 10–11

and masculinity 254
    see also hooliganism; *i.d.*; spousal abuse; violence
Aids/HIV **12–14**, 31–2, 47, 48, 74, 81–2
    and endorsements 111, 153, 206
Aikman, Troy 153
air crashes 82, 287–8
Air Up There, The (Glazer) 137
Akureyrar, Iceland 57
Alberoni, F. 191–2
Albertville Winter Olympics (1992), and IMG 78, 262
Alcindor, Lew 309
Alford, Steve 373
Ali, Muhammad 5, **14–18**, 156, 190, 366
    and Don King 218–20
    and George Foreman 139, 444–6
    and Henry Cooper 66–7
    and Islam 377
    and Joe Frazier 16–17, 116
    and Ken Norton 356
    martyrdom 15–16, 349, 444
    Parkinson's syndrome 445
    return from exile 16–18
    and Sonny Liston 342
All American Girls' Baseball League 137, 232–3, 245
All the Right Moves (Chapman) 134
Allison, Don 380
Alomar, Robert 353
alpha brain waves 141
altitude training 97, 214
    see also blood doping, EPO

Amateur Athletic Association (AAA)
442, 443
amateurism 201, 312–13
amenorrhoea 102
American Amateur Athletics Union (AAU)
89, 248, 308
American Basketball Association (ABA)
309, 312
American Basketball League (ABL)
114, 310
American College of Sports Medicine 273
Americans with Disabilities Act (ADA) 91
American Express 450
American Flyers (Badham) 135
American football 8, 86, 131, 134
and drugs 28
in Europe 160
films 137
rules 311, 313–14
strikes 391
and television 198
violence 438
see also NCAA; NFL; *North Dallas Forty*
American Football League (AFL) 315, 406
American Gladiators **19–20**, 136, 279
American Jockey Club 26
American League (AL) 242
Americanization 158, 197
see also globalization
Amies-Winter, Joanne 81
amphetamines 91–2, 97, 419
anabolic steroids 38, 81, 92–3, 96, 97, 99
and Aids/HIV 13
and blood doping 37
and cycling 419
and horses 95
and muscle dysmorphia 297, 298
Program 1425 334–5
and sex change 421
USSR 272
and virilism 269
Anaheim Angels 293, 424
analgesics 94
Andrews, John vii
'angel dust' 6
Angels with Dirty Faces effect **20–5**
animal racing **25–8**, 150

animal rights movement 43
animals 25, 39–40
anomie 22
anorexia nervosa 101–2, 297
Anquetil, Jacques **28–9**, 92, 417, 418
anti-semitism 177
anxiety 70
apartheid xi, 155–8, 202, 349–51
see also Gleneagles Agreement;
Ramsamy, Sam
Arledge, Roone **29–31**, 110, 315, 406
Arlott, John 75
arm-wrestling 34
Armer, J. Michael 22
Arms, Robert 181
Arnold, Matthew 194
Arum, Bob 220
Ascent Entertainments 293
Ashe, Arthur **31–2**, 335–6, 346
Aids/HIV 13, 31, 32, 81–2
meditation 141, 355
Ashford, Evelyn 166, 281
Asics Tiger 317–19
Asinof, Elliot 77–8, 104
Asprilla, Faustino 52
Association for Computing (ACM) 83
Association of Intercollegiate Athletics for
Women (AIAW) 411
Association of National Olympic Commit-
tees of Africa (ANOCA) 350
Association of Tennis Professionals (ATP)
335–6
Astaphan, Dr Jamie 99
Athletics West 319
Atlanta Braves 293, 423, 424
Atlanta Hawks 293, 423–4
Atlanta Olympics (1996) 78, 90
Atlanta Thrashers 293, 424
Atlas, Charles (Angelo Siciliano)114–15
Attell, Abe 104
Auerbach, Red 309, 372
Austin, Tracy 58
Australia 196–7, 300, 306
autogenics 355
Ayotte, Christiane 380
AZT 12–13

Babe, The (Hiller) 133
Baca Zinn, Maxine 237–8
badgers 40
badminton 69
Bailey, Donovan 360
Bailey, McDonald 444
baiting 39–40
Bale, John 164, 215
ballroom dancing 204
Bandura, Albert 326
Bane, Michael 358–9
Bang the Drum Slowly (Hancock) 134
Bannister, Roger 401
Barber twins 425
Barcelona 362
Barkley, Charles 372
Barnett, Marilyn 215, 217, 233
Barr bodies sex test 420, 422
Barrett, Tom 74
bars and pubs **33–4**, 442
Bartevich, Leonid 362
baseball
    black players 363–5
    films 137
    and left-handedness 229, 230
    and Rupert Murdoch 290
    salaries 146
    see also Major League Baseball; Spalding, A.G.
basketball 45, 160, 312
    and films 137, 139
    and left-handedness 230
    and Olympic Games 309–10
    violence 438, 440
    women's 310
    see also Hoop Dreams; Johnson, Earvin; Jordan, Michael; NBA
Basques 307
Baudrillard, Jean 279–80
Bayless, Skip 153
Bayul, Oksana 170
BBC 36, 407
Beamish, Rob 251
Beamon, Bob 139–40, 142
bears 40, 43
Beck, Ulrich 286, 358
Beckenbauer, Franz 246

Becker, Boris 355, 432
Becklund, Laurie 295
Beecher, Catherine Esther 300
Belgium 54–6
Bell, Bert 315
Bell, Cool Papa 363
Bell, Daniel 278
Bellah, Robert ix
Belle 83
Belle, Albert 364
Ben-Hur (Wyler) 25
Bend, Emile 22
Benedict, Jeffrey 24, 374–6
Benitez, Wilfred 7, 60
Benn, Nigel 355
Benoit, Joan 249
Benson & Hedges 34, 386–7, 414, 441–2
Benson, Rose 102
Berbrick, Trevor 18, 367, 427
Bergelin, Lennart 53
Berlin Olympics (1935) 138, 277
Berlusconi, Silvio 292, 293, 295, 408
Berry, Johnny 288
Best, George 110, 329
Best of Time, The (Spottiswoode) 137
beta blockers 93, 441, 442
Bible, Geoffrey 415
bicycle 415–16
    see also cycling; Tour de France
Big Boss, The (Lo Wei) 136
Big Daddy 19, **35–7**
Bikila, Abebe 248
billiards 34
Bird, Larry 206, 309, 368, 391
Birke, Linda 267
Birkett, Mr Justice 76
biting 39, 427, 428
black athletes 442–4, 449–52
    African Caribbeans 284, 327
    as commodity 212
    dominance of 344
    and endorsements 111
    as role models 346
    and social conditions 345
    see also racism
black managers 365
Black Muslims *see* Nation of Islam

black power 16, 156, 202, 219, 280, 377
'Black Sox Scandal' 77, 104–5
Blanchflower, Jackie 288
Blankers-Koen, Fanny 280
Blatter, Sepp 132
blood doping 37–9, 94, 112, 214
    see also altitude training; EPO (Erythro-
    poietin)
blood sports **39–43**, 107, 149, 331–2, 432
Blue Chips (Friedkin) **43–6**, 282
Blue Ribbon Sports 317–19
BMX 419
body
    dissatisfaction with 102–3
    see also anorexia nervosa; muscle dys-
    morphia
body regulation **46–50**, 96, 108, 112–13
    and gender 49–50, 108, 257
    'technologies of the self' 47–8
    and violence 437
bodybuilding 114–15, 138
    and human growth hormone (hGH) 186
    and steroids 81, 93
    and women 49, 115, 138–9
Bogotà Affair **50–2**, 87
Bonds, Barry 364
Borg, Björn 6, 10, **52–4**
Bosman case 52, **54–6**, 58, 63, 146–7,
    224, 369
Boston Celtics 309
Boston marathon 248, 275
Botha, François 428
Botts, Rafe 449
Botvinnik, Mikhail 84
Boucha, Henry 439
Bowe, Riddick 290
Bowerman, Bill 317, 318, 319
Boxer, The (Sheridan) 133
boxing
    Aboriginals 161
    and age 7, 8, 60
    corruption 105, 348, 381
    'drying out' 102
    films 132–3, 136, 138, 139
    see also Raging Bull; *Rocky I–V*; *Somebody
    Up There Likes Me*; *When We Were Kings*
    and gambling 150

and left-handedness 229–30
and Olympics 204
and risk 80–1, 358
and violence 9, 439
and women 4, 49
see also Ali, Muhammad; Johnson, Jack;
    King, Don; *Sweet Science, The*; Tyson,
    Mike
Boycott, Geoff 157
Braddock, James L. 209
Bradford 82, 122
Bradford Bulls 410
Brailsford, Dennis 150
brain damage 81, 359
Brasher, Chris 249
Brazil 129, 172
Brazilian National Soccer Federation
    320, 386
Breaking Away (Yates) 135
Brêde 41
Bredemeier, B.J.L. 67
bribery *see* corruption
Briggs, Arnie 400
Brill, A.A. 239
British Athletics Federation (BAF) 274
British Darts Organization (BDO) 33
British Lions 67
British National Party (BNP) 72
British Sports Association for the Disabled
    (BSAD) 90
Brohm, Jean-Marie 195–6, 251
Brooklyn Dodgers 363–4
Broughton, Jack 149
Brown, Bundini 14
Brown, Jim 378
Brown, Kerrith 94
Brown, Pete 449, 452
Brown, Rita Mae 217
Brown *vs.* Board of Education 365, 451
Brown-Sequard, C. 92–3, 96
Brumel, Valery 144
Brundage, Avery 202
Bruno, Frank 220, 291, 407
Brussels 82, 122
Bryant, Kobe 312
BSkyB 63, 198, 290, 291, 293, 407
Budd, Zola 360, 379

Budweiser 386
Buffalo Bills 143, 378
Buhrmann, H.G. 23
bulimia 101–2
Bull Durham (Shelton) 133, 137, 138
bulls/bullfighting 39–41, 42
'bung' inquiry 52, **56–8**, 68, 77
Bunn, Oscar 451
Burke, Glenn 74, 152
burnout 7, **58–61**, 216, 263, 284
Burns, Tommy 1, 207, 208
Burton, David 193
Busby, Matt 287–8
Bush, George 18, 91
Butler, Judith 257
Butt, Dorcas Susan 325, 327

Cablevision 291, 293
Caddyshack (Ramis) 138
caffeine 91, 92, 94
Cagney, James 21, 22
Cairo 173
Calvinism 338
Camp, Walter 313–14
Campbell, Murray 84
Canada 99–100, 306
Canadian Centre for Drug-Free Sport 100
Canal Plus 293
Cancer Research Campaign 414
Cannon, Jimmy 16
Cantona, Eric **62–4**, 110, 191, 295, 439–40
Cantu, R.C. 80
Capello, Fabio 284
capitalism 174–7, 251–2, 299, 301, 339, 341
Capriati, Jennifer 58, 60, 97, 263
Cardus, Neville 75
Carlesimo, P.J. 440
Carling Premiership 385–6
Carlos, John 16, 156, 202, 219, 280
Carlyle, Thomas 338
Carmichael, Stokely 202
Carpenter, Teresa 377
Carr, Antoine 372
Carrigan, T. 255–6
Carrington, Bruce 346
Carruthers, Ed 144
Carter, Jimmy 18

Casals, Rosie 216
Cashmore, E. 284
Castine, Sandra 346
Castle Sport 404
Castro, Humberto Muñoz 81
Catalans 307, 362
cattle wrestling 42
Cauthen, Steve 60
Cayleff, Susan 88
Cayton, Bill 220, 221, 427–8
CBS 202, 315, 316, 424
Cerdan, Marcel 347
Chamberlain, Wilt 312, 329, 376
Champion, Bob 136
Champion (Robson) 133
Champions, The (Irwin) 136
Chandler, Timothy 113
Chapman, Michael 347
chariot racing 25
Chariots of Fire (Hudson) **64–5**, 132, 133,
    203, 283, 323
Charles, Ezzard 398
Charlton, Bobby 288
Chase, Hal 243
cheating **65–8**, 97, 273
Chen Yan 187
chess 82–5
Chicago Bulls 210, 212, 285, 309, 368
Chicago Cubs 293
Chicago Tribune 293
Chicago White Sox 77, 104–5, 127, 134,
    210, 243
Chicago White Stockings 363, 383–4
children
    abuse 58–9, 284
    encouraging 327–8
    of professional athletes 326–7
    see also parenthood
China 68–9, 197
    and Rupert Murdoch 291, 296
    sponsorship 68, 69–70
China Football Association **68–70**, 414
China National Soccer League 69
China National Tobacco Corporation
    (CNTC) 69
Choi, Precilla 297
choking **70–1**, 143

Christianity 48, 64
  and homosexuality 123, 124
  see also muscular Christianity
Christie, Linford 7, 141, 360
Cicotte, Eddie 104, 106
Cincinnati Kid, The (Jewison) 135
Cincinnati Reds 77, 104, 134
Circus Maximus 113
civil rights 2, 16, 202, 412
  see also discrimination; racism
civilizing process 96, 107–8
Clarendon Report (1864) 299
Clark, Charles 438
Clarke, Allan 57
Clay, Cassius *see* Ali, Muhammad
clenbuterol 95
close-up action 30
Clough, Brian 57, 123, 359
Club, The (Beresford) 135
clutch play 71, 143
CNN 424
coaches 234–5, 371–3
  cheating 66–8
  and coercion 286
  and drugs 99
  salaries 313
Coakley, J. Jay 11, 24, 60, 372, 435, 436
Cobb (Shelton) 133, 137, 138
Cobb, Ty 105, 106, 133, 243, 282
Coca-Cola 160, 172, 197, 211, 316
cocaine 91
Cochrane, Jr, Johnny 377
cockfighting 40, 41
Coe, Andrew 403
Coe, Sebastian 192, 214, 360
Coleman, James 22
Coleman, Jim 380
Collins, Steve 141, 355
Colombia 51, 52, 81, 87
Colombian Football Association 51
colonialism 27–8, 306, 306–7
  see also imperialism
Color of Money, The (Scorsese) 135, **187–9**
Comaneci, Nadia **222–3**, 361–2
Combat 18 (C18) **72–3**
combat sports 9, 39
Comcast 293

coming out **73–5**, 215, 218, 233
  see also gays; lesbianism
Comiskey, Charles 104, 105, 106
commercialism 224, 333
  see also marketing
commodification 191, 210–12, 253–4
  see also advertising; endorsements
commonwealth, and cricket 260
Commonwealth (Empire) Games 196, 197,
  247, 332
competition vii–viii, ix, xi, 10
Compton, Dennis 110
computers 82–5
Confédération Africaine de Football 132
configurations 107–8
Connell, Robert 254, 255, 256
Conner, Bart 223, 362
Connors, Dennis 7
Connors, Jimmy 53, 355
conscientious objectors 16
Constantine, Lord Learie **75–6**
consumerism 294
contact sports 3, 4, 7, 10
contraceptive pill 411
contracts 55, 58, 144–7, 226, 242
  see also free agency
Converse 206–7
Cool Runnings (Turteltaub) 137
Cooney, Gerry 367
Cooper, Chuck 364
Cooper, Henry 66–7, 425
Cooper, J. 22
Cooper, Jim 425
Coppell, Steve 56
Coral, Joe 390
Cordobés, El 41
Coren, S. 228
Cornelius, James 18
corrective surgery 95
corrida, la 41
corruption 52, **76–9**
  baseball 243–4
  and endorsements 384
  and gambling 45, 105–6, 134, 149, 150
  in horse racing 95, 186, 321–3
  and IOC (International Olympic Com-
    mittee) 369–71

and Olympics 203, 204
see also Black Sox Scandal; *Blue Chips*;
bung inquiry; cheating
Corsica 173
corticosteroids 95
Cosell, Howard 30
Coubertin, Pierre de 159, 199–200, 204,
352, 371
and women 233, 265, 271–2
Coulthard, David 261
County Championship 260
Courier, Jim 263
Court, Margaret 216, 217, 362
Court-Martial of Jackie Robinson, The
(Peerce) 363
Cowan, Thelma 452
Cowlings, Al 377
Cox, Richard 71, 356
Crabtree, Shirley *see* Big Daddy
Craighill, Frank 336
CrayBlitz 83
Cribb, Tom 209, 443
cricket
and gambling 150
globalization 449
and imperialism 196
and instant replay 198
and left-handedness 230
pitches 165
strikes 392
and technology 404
see also MCC (Marylebone Cricket
Club); Wisden
crime *see* *Angels with Dirty Faces* effect; sex
crimes
critical theory 251–2
reconstructed 253–4
Crosby, A.D.V. 451
Crosset, T.W. 375
Crow, Jim 451
Cruising (Friedkin) 193
Crystal Palace 296
Csikszentmihalyi, Mihaly 140
culture, definition of viii
Cumberland, Duke of 149
Cunningham, Hugh 41
Curley, Jack 77, 209

Curry, E.W. 23
Curry, John 13, 82
Cutting Edge, The (Glazer) 136
cycling
and blood doping 38
and drugs 91–2, 94–5
and EPO 112
films 135
and Olympics 416–19
and technology 404, 416–17
see also Anquetil, Jacques; Tour de
France
Czechoslovakia 335

Dallas Cowboys 119, 146, 153, 309,
313, 323
Dalrymple, James 221
D'Amato, Cus 5, 113–14, 427
danger 98, 286–7
see also death; risk
Daniel, Wayne 165
Darby, Douglas 327
Darke, James 259
darts 33–4
Darwin, Charles 276, 299, 345
Dassler, Horst 172, 370
Datawear 404
Davenport, Lindsay 73, 163
Davidson, Carolyn 317
Davis, E. 22
Dawson, Daniel 321–2
Days of Thunder (Scott) 135
De Boer, Frank and Ronald 425
De Bruin, Michelle 380
de Kruiff, Paul 93, 272
Dean, Dizzy 134
death **80–2**
American football 311
and drugs 28, 91–2, 417–19
and EPO 112
and steroid use 93, 95, 97, 335
wrestling 35
see also disasters; risk
Death Race 2000 (Bartel) 136
Deathsport (Suso and Arkush) 136
Deep Blue **82–5**
Deep Blue Junior 85

Deep Thought 84
Deford, Frank 373
dehydrotesterone 187
Delaphena, Lloyd 'Lindy' 444
Delauney, Henri 129
Dell, Chad 36
Dell, Donald 263, 335–6, 337
democratization 108–9
Demon Internet 387
Dempsey, Jack 105, 130
DeNeui, O.L. 437
Deng Xiaoping 69
Denilson, 55
Dent, Jim 449
Denver Broncos 8
Denver Nuggets 293
derby 5–7
Derrida, Jacques 278
Dershowitz, Alan 375
desegregation 2
Desgranges, Henri 417
Detomidine 95
deviance see Angels with Dirty Faces effect;
    sex crimes
di Canio, Paulo 353
Di Stefano, Alfredo 7, 51, 288
Diadora 111
Dianabol 272
Didrikson, Mildred 'Babe' 88–9, 153,
    217, 232
diet pills 101
diplomacy 332
disability 89–91, 134
    discrimination legislation 91
    and marathon 250
    and medicine 271
    and women 255
disasters 82, 122, 173–4, 287–8
discrimination 90, 216, 224, 400
    see also racism; Title IX; women
disease 48, 134
    see also Aids/HIV
Disney 117, 290, 293, 316, 408, 424
Disneyland 170, 280
Ditka, Mike 359
diuretics 93–4, 101, 102
Dixon, George 443

Dodds, Betty 88
dogs
    and baiting 40
    fighting 41–2, 432
    for hunting 42–3
    racing 25–6, 150
Dokes, Mike 220
D'Oliveira, Basil 155
Dollard, John 10
Dominican Republic, baseball 307
dominoes 34
Donnay 52
Donnie Brasco (Newell) 193
Donohue, Richard 317
Dostoevski, F. 149
Douglas, James 'Buster' 142, 428, 432
Downhill Racer (Ritchie) 135
Draaijer, Johannes 418
Dragon: The Bruce Lee Story (Cohen) 136
dressage 184–5
drugs xi, 273, 334, 421, 441–2
    cartels 81
    and cold remedies 6
    and commercialism 66, 78
    control 92, 97, 272–3
    and death 28, 167, 417–19
    and endorsements 111
    facts 91–5
    and horses 77, 442
    recreational 95
    role of law 225
    testing 92, 274, 419
    and Tour de France 417–19
    values 95–8
    see also blood doping; Dubin Inquiry;
    Johnson, Ben; Modahl case; Reynolds
    case; Slaney case
Drummond, Jon 360
'drying out' 102
Dubin Inquiry 99–100
Dufranc, Michel 41
Dundee, Angelo 14, 15, 67
Dunning, Eric
    blood sports 43
    excitement 107, 388, 433
    hooliganism 178–9, 180
    rugby 282, 409

Duran, Roberto 13, 407
Durkheim, E. 277, 393, 396
Dutton, K. 48
Duva, Lou 359

Eagles 4
Eastham, George 147
Eastman, Susan Tyler 395–6
eating disorders 48, **101–3**, 271, 284, 297
Eaton, Warren 228
Ecclestone , Bernie 414
Eckhardt, Shawn 169
economics
    China 69–70
    and globalization 158–61
    Hoch 176–7
    Marxism 252–4
    of televised sport
    see also free agency; salary caps; sponsorship
Edberg, Stefan 6, 53
Ederle, Gertrude 89
Edward, Harry 444
Edwards, Duncan 287
Edwards, Harry 32, 175, 176, 345, 346
Egan, Pierce 397
Egg, Eleanor 89
Eight Men Out (Sayle) 77–8, **104–6**, 127, 134, 243
Einstein, Albert 148, 276
Elbaum, Don 219
Elder, Lee 449, 452
electroencephalograph (EEG) 141
Elias, Norbert 96, **107–9**, 180
    blood sports 43
    excitement 388, 433, 436
Elliott, Paul 438
Elway, John 8
Embassy 34
empowerment 257
End, The 122
endorphins 297–8
endorsements **109–11**
    and amateur status 89
    and black athletes 378
    Chevrolet/O.J. Simpson 378
    and corruption 384

and FIFA 160
and globalization 197
and homosexuality 111, 153, 206–7, 233
and ideal body 48
Woods, Eldrick 'Tiger' 450
see also Jordan, Michael; Nike
England and Wales Cricket Board 260
Enter the Dragon, The (Clouse) 136
ephedrine 94
EPO (Erythropoietin) 39, 94–5, **111–12**, 186, 419
    see also blood doping
Ereng, Paul 214
eroticism **112–15**
Escape to Victory (Huston) 134
Escobar, Andres 81
Escobar, Pablo 81
ESPN **115–17**, 289, 293, 310, 407, 408
Estrich, Susan 375
ether 91
Eubank, Chris 355
European Court of Justice 54, 55
European Tour Courses (ETC) 263–4
Evans, Lee 345
eventing (horse trials) 27, 185
Evert, Chris 162, 233, 362
Ewald, Mandred 334
Ewing, Patrick 336

FA (Football Association) 57–8, 129, 277, 385–6
    Cup Final 130
fair play *see* cheating; referee
falconry 43
Faldo, Nick 71
Falk, David 210, 212, 310, 336
Familial Benign Essential Tremor 441
Fan, The (Scott) 81, 118–19, 125, 134
fandom **119–21**, 280
    and icons 191–2
    and television 36, 436
    and violence 72
    see also Fever Pitch; hooliganism
fan(s) ix, x, 81, 82, 118–23
    books by 123
    disasters 173
    and identity 125

and ritual 395–6
and spousal abuse 387–8
Fantini, Sergio Santander 370
fanzines 72, **121–23**
Farr, F. 209
Farrakhan, Louis 17
Fashanu, John 58, 77
Fashanu, Justin 74, **123–4**, 152, 376
Fat City (Huston) 133
fear 5, 357–8
Federal Communications Commission (FCC) 116
Federal League 105–6
Fédération Internationale Medico-Sportive et Scientifique 273
Fédération Sportive Féminine Internationale 201
Feinstein, John 371–3
Fellowship of Christian Athletes 218
Felsch, Oscar 106
femininity 49–50, 166, 170–1, 234, 256–7
and lesbianism 151, 218
see also masculinities/femininities; virilism; womanhood
feminism 90, 176, 216, 255–7, 400
and women's bodies 49, 103
see also Title IX; women
Feng-Hsuing Hsu 84
Fenton, Ronnie 56–7
Fentress, Lee 336
Ferguson, Duncan 439
Ferguson, Jesse 429
Ferraro, Chris and Peter 425
Festina team 92, 419
Feuer, Jane 170
Fever Pitch (Hornby) 123, **124–7**, 396
Field of Dreams (Robinson) **127–8**, 137, 301
FIFA (Fédération Internationale de Football Associations) **128–32**, 171–2, 198
and China 68–9
and Colombia 51, 87
and modernity 277
and transfer fees 55
and UEFA 288
and World Cup 159, 160
Fighting Harada 161
figure skating 13, 169–71

Fila 52
films x–xi, 116, **132–9**
comedy/fantasy 136–8
documentaries 138–9
dramatic/biographical 132–6
see also individual titles
Finley, Charlie 146
Fischer, Gloria J. 395
fishing 43
Fist of Fury, The (Lo Wei) 136
Flamengo club, Rio de Janeiro 86
flat racing 27
Fletcher, Sheila 231–2
Flood, Curt 145, 225
Florida 415–16
Florida Marlins 293, 369
Florida Panthers 293
flow **139–40**
Fluosol-DA 38
Fly, The (Cronenburg) 34
focused 10, 53, 71, **140–3**, 432
see also hypnosis; superstition
folk football 85–6
Fonda, Jane 424
football *see* American football; FIFA; soccer
Football Intelligence Unit 178–9
football pools 150–1, 390
'Football Specials' 126
Football Supporters Association (FSA) 122
Forbes, Dave 439
Forbes, Harry 104
Foreman, George 7, 8, 17, 191, 407
and Muhammad Ali 139, 190, 220, 444–6
Formula One 386, 387, 414
Fort, Rodney 145
Fortune magazine x
Fosbury, Dick 143
Fosbury Flop **143–4**
Foster, Michael 43
Foucault, Michel 46, 47, 257, 278, 280
Foul 121
Fouts, Dan 110
Fowler, Robbie 67, 352
Fowles, Jib 111
Fox, Billy 347, 348
Fox Broadcasting 289–90
Fox Entertainment Group 290–1

Fox, Kate 183–4
Fox Network 293, 316
Fox Television 290
foxhunting 26, 27, 42–3, 108, 109
France, and Germany 362
Francis, Bev 49
Francis, Charlie 99
Francophone Games 333
Frank, Thomas 294
Franklin, Benjamin 338
Franklin, Neil 51, 52
Frazier, Jimmy 432, 433
Frazier, Joe 16–17, 116, 219, 326
free agency 51, 77, **144–7**, 224–5, 384
    and commodification 253
    and salary caps 368–9
    see also Bosman case; transfer system
Freeman, Cathy 161, 197
Freidson, Eliot 271
Freud, Sigmund 149, 276–7
Frick, Ford 364
Friedan, Betty 400
Fullerton, Hugh 105
Furedi, Frank 286, 357–8
furosemide 94

Gaines, C. 375
Galaburda, A. 228
Galindo, Rudy 153
gambling 81, **148–51**
    and corruption 45, 77, 104, 105–6, 134
    effects of 225
    and horse racing 27
    sexual dimension 149
    see also nobbling; spread
Gaming Act (1665) 149
Gandl, Chick 104, 106
Gardella, Danny 244
Garnett, Kevin 312–13
Garrincha 172
Garrison, Kelly 59
Garvey, Marcus 208
Gary, Romain 136
Gates, William 182–3
Gatting, Mike 165
Gauld, Jimmy 57
Gavey, N. 49

Gay Games 73–4, 152, 153
gays 13, 113, 123–4, **151–5**, 171
    and endorsements 111, 153, 206–7, 233
    gender-based hierarchy 256
    see also coming out; lesbianism; virilism
Gebrselassie, Haile 386
gender *see* masculinities/femininities;
        medical discourse; Title IX; women
genetics 425–6
genital contact 4
Gennaro, Joseph 219
German Democratic Republic (GDR) 305,
        334–5, 421
Germany
    and France 362
    reunification 306
Geschwind, N. 228
Getty Oil 116
'Ghost Dance' 393
Gibb, Roberta 'Bobbi' 399
Gibson, Althea 452
Gibson, Josh 363
Giddens, Anthony 158
Gillette 30
Gillmore, Al-Tony 207
Giro d'Italia 419
Gitlin, Todd 158
Givens, Robin 427, 428–9, 430
Gladiators 19
Gläser, Rolf 334
Glasgow 86, 173, 362
Gledhill, Christine 190
Gleneagles Agreement **155–8**, 203, 350
globalization **158–61**, 197, 215, 292, 295–6
    cricket 449
    global tournaments 159
    and Nike 321
    satellite communications 159, 405, 435
    sports goods manufacture 159
glycogen 5
Goalkeeper's Fear of the Penalty, The
        (Wender) 135
Goldman, Charlie 142
Goldstein, Jerry 10
golf
    and age 6, 7
    and anxiety 71

black golfers 449–52
films 138
and homosexuality 73
and technology 402–3
and women 237–8
see also McCormack, Mark; Woods,
Eldrick 'Tiger'
Gomez, Julissa 59
Gonzales, Pancho 336
Gooch, Graham 157
Goolagong (Cawley), Evonne 161–2, 197
Gorgeous George 15
Gould, Daniel 58, 60
Grace, W.G. 196, 447, 449
Graf, Peter 162
Graf, Steffi 60, 70, 120, 162–3, 359
Graham, Billy 301
Graham, George 56
Gramsci, Antonio 175, 251
Grand National 26, 81
Grandstand 36, 407
Grant 71
Grant, Horace 212
grass 77, 163–5, 404
Graziano, Rocky 381–2
Greco-Roman games 91
Green Bay Packers 234, 235, 342
Green, Benny 447
Green, Ted 438
Greenblatt, Richard 83–4
Greene, Kevin 240
Greer, Germaine 388
Gregg, Harry 288
Gregory, Anne 452
Gregory's Girl (Forsyth) 134
Gresson, Aaron D. 1
greyhound racing 25–6
Grieg, Dale 399
Griffey, Jr, Ken 364
Griffin, Pat 88, 215, 217, 218, 233, 362
Griffin, Robert 327, 328
Griffith Joyner, Florence 89, 166–7, 256
Grifters, The (Frears) 136
Grobelaar, Bruce 58, 77
Gruneau, Richard 109, 251, 252, 437–8
Guatemala City 173
Gulick, Luther H. 300–1

Gullickson, Tim and Tom 425
Gullit, Ruud 63
Gutman, D. 244
Guttmann, Allen 112–14, 340
Guttmann, Ludwig 89–90

Hackbart, Dale 438
Hackford, Taylor 445
Hagler, Marvin 227
haka 168–9
Halberstam, David 210
Hall, Arsenio 153
Halpern, D. 228
Halupczok, Joachim 418
Hamed, Naseem 221
Hamilton, Charles 202
Hamilton, Linda 115
handicapped see disability
Hao Hai Dong 68
Happily Gilmore (Dugan) 138
Happy Valley racecourse, Hong Kong 27
Hard Road to Glory, A 31
Harder They Fall, The 133, 381
Harder, V.J. 103
Harding, Tonya 169–71, 361
hare, electric 26
Hargreaves, Jennifer 49, 108, 231, 254–5,
257, 270
Hargreaves, John 251, 252, 253, 276
Harlem Globetrotters 308, 312
harness racing 25
Harnisch, Pete 415–16
Harre, Rom 181
Harris, Andre 373
Harris, Lord 260
Harvard-Yale boat race 300
Hase, Dagmar 335
Hashimi, Sam 422
Hastings, Sir Patrick 75
Hauge, Rune 56–7
Hauser, Thomas 14, 16, 17, 18, 445
Havelange, João 160, 171–2
Haven, Herbert 194–5
Hawke, Lord 260
Hawkins, Darryl 312
Hayes, Bruce 153
Hayes, Elvin 312

Haynes, Johnny 58
Haynes, Richard 122
Haywood, Spencer 312
health craze *see* narcissism
Hearns, Thomas 7, 60
Heart Like a Wheel (Kaplan) 135
heart rate monitor 404
Heaton, A.W. 71
Heaven Can Wait (Henry and Beatty)
    136–7
hegemony theory 252–3
Heilborn, Rose 75
Heine, Sonja 61
Heller, Peter 5, 428–9
Hemingway, Ernest 41
Henderson, Edwin 364
Hendry, Stephen 120
Henneberg, Bernd 335
Henrich, Chrysty 59
heroin 91
Hertz Rental Cars 378
heterosexuality, compulsory 257
Heysel stadium, Belgium 122, 173, 178
Hicks, Thomas 424
Higginson, Thomas Wentworth 300
Higgs, Robert 301
high jump 143–4
Hill, Ron 138
Hillsborough 82, 122, 126, **173–4**, 178, 225
Hinault, Bernard 417
Hingis, Martina 7, 73, 261, 403
Hirschbeck, John 353
Hitler, Adolf 201
HIV *see* Aids/HIV
Hoad, Lew 336
Hoberman, John 271, 346
Hoch, Paul **174–7**, 251
hockey 394–5, 437–8
Hodler, Marc 370
Hoffer, Richard 290
Holder, Vanburn 165
Holding, Michael 165
Holm, Eleanor 89
Holmes decision 244
Holmes, Larry 14, 17, 220, 221, 367
Holmes, Oliver Wendell 300
Holyfield, Evander 8, 290, 407

and Mike Tyson 39, 221, 427, 428
Home Box Office (HBO) 116–17, 289,
    407, 424
homophobia/homoeroticism 151–2, 154
homosexuality *see* coming out; gays; les-
    bianism
Hong Kong 68
Hooijdonk, Pierre van 392
hooliganism 9, 122, 125–6, **177–82**
    control of 178–9, 225
    and disasters 82, 173
    psychological and ethological accounts
    180–2
    sociological explanations 179–80
    undercover work 192–3
    see also Combat 18; violence
Hoop Dreams (James, Marx and Gilbert)
    139, **182–3**, 327, 346
Hooper, Carl 392
Hoosiers (Anspaugh) 137
Hope, Bob 89
Hornby, Nick 123, 124–7, 396
horse racing 26–8, 184, 291
    endurance riding 27–8, 185
    and gambling 27, 150
    and risk 81, 358
    see also hunting; nobbling
horses 25, 77, **183–6**
    industrialism 184
    military origins 184–6
Horsman, M. 292
Houston Oilers 143
Howard, Paul 334
Huddlestone, Bishop Trevor 156
Huff, Sam 238
Hughes, Thomas 194, 299
Huizinga, Wayne 293
Hulbert, William 242, 383
Hulk Hogan 19, 35
human growth hormone (hGH) 67, 94,
    112, **186–7**, 335, 419
Hunter, Junior 'Catfish' 146
hunting 41–3, 184, 195
huskies 28
Hustler, The (Rossen) 135, 137, **187–9**
hypnosis 97, 355–6
    see also relaxation

IAAF (International Amateur Athletics Federation) 98, 204, 226, 274, 356, 379–80
IBM 84, 85
Ibrox Park, Glasgow 173
ICC (International (Imperial) Cricket Council (Conference)) 157, 198, 260
ice hockey 138, 290, 437
ice skating 136
Iceland 57
Ichikawa, Kon 138
icons 24, 53, 87, **190–2**, 234
  baseball 242
  and fandom 191–2
  and television commercials 110
ICU (International Cycling Union) 112, 418, 419
i.d. (Davis) 125–6, 135, 179, **192–4**
Iditarod 28
iliac artery 95
Iliad (Homer) 25
illegitimate children *see* paternity
Illich, Ivan 270, 271
Illingworth, Montieth 113, 282–3, 429
IMG (International Management Group) 53, 68, 261–4, 335–6, 450
Imperial London Hotels 75–6
Imperial Tobacco 414
imperialism 27, 34, **194–8**, 299
  and globalization 158
  and national identity 215, 306
incalculability 239–40
Inderol 93, 441, 442
Indiana Hoosiers 371–3
individualism 341, 358
Indurain, Miguel 417, 418
industrialization 108–9, 163, 272, 276
infertility 93
  see also medical discourse
injuries
  and compensation 226
  medical treatment 270
  and painkillers 323
  see also danger; death; risk
instant replay 30, **198–9**, 404, 4336
Institute of Physiology and Performance, Stockholm 37–8

Insulin Growth Factor (IGF1) 186
integrated sports 3–4
International Committee Against Apartheid in Sport 350
International Computer Chess Champion 84
Internet 435
inverted-U theory 70–1
IOC (International Olympic Committee) **199–205**
  and broadcasting rights 159
  and corruption 78, 369–71
  and drugs 92, 99, 167, 418
  and marathon 248
  and modernity 277
  and South Africa 156, 349, 350, 351
  and synthetic tracks 401
Irish Republic, and Tour de France 419
Irish Sweepstakes 30
Irvin, Michael 374
ITV 35, 36, 407

Jacklin, Tony 262
Jackman, Robin 157
Jackson, Bo 320
Jackson, F.S. 260
Jackson, Hurricane 398
Jackson, Jesse 212, 320
Jackson, Joe 106, 127, 128
Jackson, Peter 443
Jackson, Phil 284–5
Jackson, Susan 140
Jacobs, Jimmy 427
Jacopucci, Angelo 439
Jaeger, Andrea 216
Jakobi, Julian 262
James, C.L.R. 75, 160, 196
Jamieson, Katherine 237–8
Japan 160
  J-League 132, 261
Jary, David 122
javelin 88
Jeffries, 'Gentleman Jim' 208
Jefkins, Frank 385
Jenkins, David 99
Jenkins, Henry 119
Jennings, Andrew 371

Jensen, Knut 92, 95, 97, 418
Jenson, J. 120, 191
Jeptha, Andrew 443
Jericho Mile, The (Mann) 133
Jerry Maguire (Crow) 118, 137, 263
Jesus, Esteban de 13, 82
Jiang Zemin 69
Jockey Club 26, 322
Jodzio, Rick 438
Joe Louis – For All Time (Tatum) 139
Johnson, Ben
    and Carl Lewis 360
    drugs case 92, 95, 97, 99, 111, 204, 274
Johnson, Brooks 285
Johnson, Earvin 'Magic'
    Aids/HIV 12, 47, 82, 111, 153, **206–7**
    and Larry Bird 309
    and salary caps 368
    sexual exploits 329, 376
    and violence 353
Johnson, Harold 398
Johnson, Jack 1, 190, **207–10**, 365, 374
    contests against bulls 82
    and fight fixing 77
Johnson, Jeff 318
Johnson, Michael 95, 191, 320, 360
Jones, Jr, Forest 451
Jones, Bobby 352
Jones, Ken 285
Jones, Marion 167
Jordan, Michael x, 8, 116, **210–12**, 368
    commodification of 210–12, 337
    endorsements 111, 336
    focused 8, 140, 143
    as icon 110, 191, 197, 211–12
    motivating others 285
    and Nike 110, 309, 319–20
    and ProServ 336–7
Joseph Bulova School of Watchmaking 90
Joyner-Kersee, Jackie 320

Kaissa 83
Kane, Martin 344–5
Kane, Samantha 422
Kansas City Bomber (Freedman) 19, 136
Karasseva (Kovalenko), Olga 281
Kariuki, Julius 214

Karpov, Anatoly 84
Kasparov, Garry 82, 83, 84–5
Katz, Donald 295, 317
Kay, Tony 52, 57, 58
Keating, James W. 352
Keating, Judith 394–5
Keino, Kip 213
Kenealy, Arabella 231–2
Kentucky Derby 27
Kenyan Athletics Federation 214
Kenyan runners 161, **213–15**, 285
Kerbo, Harry viii
Kerr, Dr Robert 99
Kerr, John 181–2
Kerrigan, Nancy **169–71**, 361
Kestbaum, Ellyn 2, 4, 170, 171
Keter, Joseph 214
Kiatbusaba, Parinya 422
Kid Galahad (Carlson) 138
Kid Galahad (Curtiz) 133
Kidd, Jane 184
Killing, The (Kubrick) 136
Killy, Jean-Claude 262
Kimmage, Paul 418
King, Billie Jean 3, 73, 153, **215–18**, 233
    'Battle of the Sexes' 89, 216–17, 362
    see also coming out; lesbianism
King, Carl 220
King, Don **218–22**, 385
    and Mike Tyson 220–1, 374, 427–8
    and Muhammad Ali 17, 218–20
    and Rupert Murdoch 290
King, John 123
King, Larry 216
King, Samantha 207
Kingsley, Charles 299
Kinsella, Ray 127–8
Kinsella, W.P. 127–8, 301
Kipketer, Wilson 214
Kiptanui, Moses 214
Kirk, Mal 'King Kong' 35
Kitchel, Ted 372
Klein, A. 24, 307, 374–6
Klinsmann, Jürgen 63
Klobkowska, Eva 269, 420–1
Kluge, John 246
Knight, Bob 43, 371–3

Knight, Phil 110, 316, 317–21, 384–5
  and Mary Slaney 380
  and Michael Jordan x, 110, 309, 337
  and Tonya Harding 169–70
  see also Nike
Kodak 200
Komen, Daniel 214, 386
Kopay, David 74, 152
Korbut, Olga 6, **222–3**, 361–2
Kosgei, Mike 214
Koss, 375
Kournikova, Anna 256
Krabbe, Katrin 357, 380
Kramer, Jack 335–6
Krawczyk, B. 425
Krieger, Heidi 335, 421
Kristiansen, Ingrid 249, 280–1
Kuffel, Gene 153
kung fu movies 136
Kwan, Michelle 61

La Motta, Jake 346–8
Ladies Professional Golfers Association
  (LPGA) 452
Lamb, Chris 363
Lambton, George 322
Landis, Kenesaw Mountain 106
Langer, Bernhard 261
Lapchick, Richard 375
Laqueuer, Thomas 265
Lara, Brian 140, 392
Larsson, Magnus 53
Lasch, Christopher 298, 303, 358
Lasix 95
Latinas 237–8
Latinos 246–7
Laver, Rod 7, 227
law **224–7**
  and internal rules 226–7
  and sex discrimination 90
  and violence 437
laxatives 102
Layne, David 52, 57
Le Mans 30
Le Mans (Katzin) 135
League of Their Own, A (Marshall) 137, 245
Lebow, Fred 249

Lee, Bruce 136
Lee, Spike 445
left-handedness **227–30**
Leibnitz, G.W. 148
Leith, 71
Lenskyj, Helen 3, 4, 233, 267, 268, 269, 270
Lenzi, A. 11
Leonard, Ray 407
lesbianism 3, 151, 153, 217–18, **231–4**, 268
  and public opinion 233–4
  and rivalries 362
  see also coming out; King, Billie Jean;
    Navratilova, Martina
Leslie, Lisa 166
Levine, Lawrence 190, 208, 384
Levy, David 84
Levy, J. 228
Lewis, Butch 342–3
Lewis, Carl 167, 360
Liberty Media 290
Liddell, Eric 64–5
Lieberfield, Daniel 429
Lieberman, Nancy 310
Liebling, A.J. 104, 124, 142, 382, **397–9**
Lifestyle 310
'lifestyle enclaves' ix
Liggett Group 415
Lillywhite, Frederick 446
Lindemann, Dieter 334
Lindsay, Lord Andrew 64–5
Lipinski, Tara 6, 61
Lipton, Benjamin 90
Liston, Sonny 15, 190, 342
Livermore, Rev A.A. 300
lockouts *see* strikes
Loda, Nicola 112
Lomax, Lewis 364
Lombardi, Vince 9, **234–5**, 283, 340,
  342, 372
London, Jack 208, 444
London marathon 249
Londres, Albert 418
Loneliness of the Long Distance Runner, The
  (Richardson) 133, **235–7**
Longest Yard, The (*Mean Machine, The*)
  (Aldrich) 137
Lopez, Nancy 89, 233, **237–8**

Lord, Thomas 258
Lord's Cricket Ground 150, 258–9
Loroupe, Tegla 249
Los Angeles Dodgers 290, 292, 293, 295, 424
Los Angeles Lakers 293, 312
Los Angeles Olympics (1984) 98, 203, 204
Louganis, Greg 74, 152, 153
Louis, Joe 15, 139, 209, 452
Louys, Spiridon 247
luck **238–40**, 394
Luckett, Phil 198, 353
Luther, Martin 338
Lutz, Bob 32, 335
Lyotard, Jean-François 278

Mac Hack 83–4
McBride, Willie John 67
McClelland, David 283–4, 325
McColgan, Liz 281
McCormack, Mark 110, **261–4**, 292
    and Björn Borg 53
    and China Football Association 68
    and ProServ 335–6
    and Tiger Woods 450
McCrone, Kathleen 231
MacDonald, Lindsey 59–60
McDonaldization 20
McDonalds 197, 200, 211, 316
Mace, Jem 443
McEnroe, John 6, 10, 52, 53, 295, 320
McGrady, Tracy 312, 313
Machooka, Steve 213
MacIntyre, Alisdair 253
Mackay, Duncan 167
McLeod, Mike 94
McMullin, Fred 106
McNally, Dave 146
McPhail, Billy 359
Maes, H. 425
Maguire, Joseph 158
Mailer, Norman 445
Maiyoro, Nyandika 213
Major League Baseball 118, 160, **241–6**
    and American identity 261
    and black players 1, 364
    exploitation 77, 134, 145
    and homosexuality 74
    industrial unrest 145, 390–1
    and left-handedness 229
    reserve clause 144–6, 147, 225, 242, 245, 384
    and Rupert Murdoch 289
    and salaries 105–6, 369
    and A.G. Spalding 383
    and universities 312
Major League and *Major League II* (Ward) 137
Major League Soccer (MLS) 52, 131, 160, 197, **246–7**
Maki, Wayne 438
Malamud, Bernard 134
Malaysia 77
Malcolm X 15
Malina, Robert 344
Malone, Jeff 328
Malone, Moses 309, 312
managers *see* Carlesimo, P.J.; Clough, Brian; Ferguson, Alex; Jackson, Phil; King, Don; Lombardi, Vince; Poile, David
Manchester United 64, 119, 287–8, 290, 293, 295
Mandela, Nelson 157, 196, 350
Mandell, Richard 42
Maney, Kevin 292
Mangan, J.A. 231
Mann, Terence 127–8
Mao Zedong 69, 332
Maoris 156, 168–9
Maradona, Diego 6, 95
marathon 138, **247–50**
Marciano, Rocky 142, 398
Marichal, Juan 438
marketing 197, 203, 225, 309
    see also commercialism; endorsements; sponsorship
Marlboro 68, 69, 414
Marquee agency 337
Marsh, Peter 181
Marshall, J.D. 103
Martens, James W. 409
martial arts
    films 136

Japanese 140–1
training 24
Marxism 174–7, 180, 195, **250–4**, 276–7
masculinities/femininities 108, 113, 126,
    254–7, 330
    and aggression 11, 180
    hegemonic masculinity 255–6, 257
    and lesbianism 217
    and transvestites 422
    and womanhood 231
    see also sexism; femininity; gays; les-
    bianism; medical discourse; spousal
    abuse; women
Maslow, Abraham 283, 286
Mason, Tony 50, 351
Massachusetts Institute of Technology
    (MIT) 83
Masterkova, Svetlana 281
matadors 41
Mather, Cotton 338
Mathewson, Christy 242
Matthews, Stanley 8
Matza, David 97
Maudsley, Henry 267
Mauresmo, Amélie 73, 218
Maxwell, Robert 289
Maxwell, Vernon 439
Mayne, Judith 171
Mays, Willie 364
MCC (Marylebone Cricket Club) 4, 196,
    258–61, 447
media *see* ESPN; films; Murdochization;
    television; videated
Medical Commission 92
medical discourse 231, 248, **264–70**,
    280, 417
medicalization 38, 49, **270–3**, 405
meditation 285, 355
megamedia 292
Meggyesy, Dave 174
menopause 50
menstruation 266
Merckx, Eddy 417
meritocracy 252–3
Merriwell, Frank 300
Merton, Robert K. 21–2
Messersmith, Andy 146, 423

Messner, M. 255, 256, 257
Metheny, Eleanor 2–3, 88
Mexico City 86–7
Mexico Games (1968) 16, 156, 202, 219, 280
Meynell, Hugo 42
Micheaux, Pierre and Ernest 415
Michel, Henri 62
Mighty Ducks 293, 424
Mighty Ducks, The (*Champions*) (Herek) 117
militarism 194–5, 299
Miller, Charles 129
Miller, Marvin J. 244
Miller, Tom 400
Millionarios, Bogota 51, 87
Mills, Billy 133
Milwaukee Braves 1
Mingxia, Fu 6
Minor Counties Cricket Association 260
minorities *see* racism
minority sports 30
Minter, Alan 439
Mitchell, Dennis 381
Mitten, Charles 51
Moabit trials (1998) 100, 334
Mobutu, President 445
Modahl case 98, **274–5**, 357, 380
modernity/postmodernity 161, **275–80**, 385
Molyneux, Tom 209, 443
Monday Night Football (MNF) 30,
    315, 407
money *see* motivation
Montana, Joe 8, 111, 143
Montreal Olympics (1976) 157, 203, 370
Moorcroft, David 139, 142
Moore, Archie 7, 398
Moore, Bobby 50
Morceli, Noureddine 214, 386
Morgan, Ken 288
Morgan, William 65–6, 78, 251, 253, 254
Morris, Desmond 82, 86
Morris (Philip) tobacco company 68, 197,
    216, 415
Morrison, Tommy 13, 82, 367
Moscow 174, 370
motherhood **280–2**
motivation 112, **282–7**, 326, 373, 426
    money 8, 17, 24

and underdog 432
motor racing 81, 135, 286, 386, 387, 414
Mount Kenya 214
mountain bike racing 419
Mountford, George 51
Mourning, Alonzo 320
Mr Baseball (Schepisi) 137
Mrozek, Donald 88, 232
Mueller, F.O. 80
Muge, Some 214
Muhammad Ali Professional Sports
    (MAPS) 17
Muhammad, Elijah 15, 16, 17
Muhammad, Herbert 17
Muhammad, Murad 221
Muhammad, Wallace D. 17
Munich disaster 82, **287–8**
Munich Olympics (1972) 138, 203
Murdoch, Rupert 74, 117, 279, **288–92**,
    385, 405
    acquiring sports clubs 290, 292, 293,
    408, 424
    BSkyB and football 63, 198
    and Don King 290
    influence of Arledge 31
    and rugby 159, 410
    and salary caps 369
Murdoch, Sir Keith 289
Murdochization **292–7**, 423
muscle dysmorphia 102–3, **297–8**
muscular Christianity 254, **299–301**,
    313, 383
mushin 140–1
Mussabini, Sam 64

Nack, William 298
Nagano Winter Olympics (1998) 370
Naismith, James 300, 308
Naked Gun, The (Zucker) 378
Namath, Joe 315, 329, 432
nandrolone 274–5
narcissism 14, 248, **303–4**, 318, 355, 358
    bodybuilding 114
    and drugs 97
    and eating disorders 103
    and muscle dysmorphia 298
    and women 103, 256, 411

Nastase, Ilie 110
Nation of Islam 15, 16, 17, 18, 219–20, 444
National Association for the Advancement
    of Colored People (NAACP) 364
National Association of Baseball Players
    (NABP) 241–2
National Coursing Club 25, 150
National Darts Association of Great
    Britain 33
National Football League 30
    see also NFL
national identity 304–6, 307, 332
    see also nationalism
National League of Professional Baseball
    Clubs (NL) 242, 277, 383–4
National Socialism 201
National Steeplechase Association 26
National Wheelchair Games 89–90
nationalism 108, 176, 299, **304–7**, 354
    and FIFA 131
    and Olympics 277
    see also Combat 18
Natural, The (Levinson) 134
Naughton, J. 212
Nauright, John 113
Navratilova, Martina 89, 162, 227
    and Chris Evert 362
    coming out 73
    and endorsements 111, 153, 207, 217, 233
NBA (National Basketball Association) xi,
    154, 197, **308–11**, 320
    and college basketball 45, 312
    and globalization 296
    and Olympics 204
    and Rupert Murdoch 291
    and salary caps 368
    strike 391, 424
    and television x, 210–11
    and violence 440
NBC 202, 310, 315, 316, 371
NCAA (National Collegiate Athletic As-
    sociation) 45, 308, **311–13**, 315, 411
NEAT (Nike Environmental Action
    Team) 320
Necessary Roughness (Dragoti) 137
Negro Leagues 104, 363
Nelson club 75

Nelson, Judy 73
Neumann, Uwe 335
neuromuscular stimulation 97
Nevada State Athletic Commission 17
New York Jets 432
New York Knicks 293, 309
New York marathon 249
New York Yankees 242
New Zealand 156, 157, 168–9, 203, 300
Newbery, Piers 86–7
Newbolt, Sir Henry 195
Newborn, Monty 83, 85
Newcastle United 63–4, 147
Newfield, Jack 220
News Corp 289, 292, 293
Newton, Isaac 148, 276
NFL (National Football League) 11, 197,
    313–16
    and AFL merger 406–7
    Europe 160, 290
    role of 391
    and Rupert Murdoch 289, 290, 293
    salary cap 368
    and universities 312
Nguge, John 214
NHL (National Hockey League) 290–1,
    292, 293, 312, 353, 391
Nicklaus, Jack 6, 110–11, 262
Night and the City (Dassin, 1950) 381
Nike x, 197, **316–21**, 333
    and Brazil 386
    criticism of 320–1
    and drugs cases 380
    and icons 295, 317, 320
    and Michael Jordan 210–10, 212, 309, 337
    and rebellious stars 295
    and soccer 247
    television commercials 316–17
    and Tiger Woods 450
    and Tonya Harding 169–70
    see also Jordan, Michael; Knight, Phil
Nike Golf Tour 386
Nike Sports Entertainment (NSE) 263, 320
nitroglycerin 91
Nixon, Richard 332
nobbling 77, 95, 186, **321–23**, 442
Noble, D.F. 402

Nolte, Nick 43
nonicol 92
Noorlander, Eduard 92
Norditropin 187
Norman, Greg 7, 71
North American Soccer League (NASL)
    131, 246
North Dallas Forty (Kotcheff) 134, **323–4**
North Korea 68–9
Northern Ireland 72, 307
Norton, Jr, Ken 326
Norton, Ken 17, 326, 356, 366
notoriety 192
Nottingham Forest 57
Novotna, Jana 70, 143

Oakland Raiders 119, 432
Oates, Joyce Carol 429
O'Brien, Pat 21, 22
Ochoa, Javier 112
O'Connell, Father Colm 214
Off the Ball 122
Ogilvie, Bruce 342
Okikino, Betty 59
oligomenorrhoea 102
Olsen, Jack 345
Olympiad (Riefenstahl) 138, 201
Olympic Games 30, 159, 196, 199–204
    and basketball 309–10
    black power protest 16, 156, 202, 219, 280
    boycotts 203, 213, 312, 331, 332, 370
    and disabled 90
    and drugs 201, 203–4
    and football 129
    hosting 197, 204
    and modernity 277
    political uses of 201–3, 331, 332
    repackaging 203–4
    sponsorship 204, 370–1
    and women 200–1, 265, 271–2, 399
Olympic symbol 370
Olympique Marseilles 78
Onitsuka Co Ltd 317–19
Oosterbosch, Bert 418
Oral Thurinalbol 335
Oriard, Michael 14
Orlygsson, Thorvaldur 57

Orser, Brian 74
O'Sullivan, Sonia 281
Other Side of the Mountain, The (Peerce)
    135–6
Otto, Kristin 335
Oudshoorn, Nelly 265
Out of the Past (Tournier) 134
Over the Top (Golan) 34, 133
Ovett, Steve 360
Owens, Jesse 82, 365

pacifism 15
Paddock, Charley 65
Page, Greg 367
Paige, Satchel 363
painkillers 94
Palacios, Ruben 12
Palmer, Arnold 110–11, 262, 352
Pantini, Marco 112
Paralympic movement 90
Parche, Gunther 359
Pardon, Sydney 448
parenthood 58–9, 162, 284, **325–8**, 426
pari-mutuel betting 26, 27, 150
Paris, Bob 153
Paris St Germain 293
Park, Roberta 231
Parkinson's Syndrome 18
Parr, George 446
Parrish, Bernie 174–5
Parry, Rick 56
Parsons, Ed 116, 277
Pasquel, Jorge 244
paternity **328–31**
    see also sex crimes
Patterson, Floyd 5, 15, 427
pay-per-view (ppv) *see* murdochization;
    television
pedestrianism 150
Peete, Calvin 452
Pelé 172, 246
Penn, Arthur 138
Pepsi 70
peptide hormones 94
Percy, Violet 399
perfectionism 60
perfluorcarbon (pfc) 38–9, 94

performance, analysing 404–5
Perry, Clifton 38
Personal Best (Towne) 133
personal growth 303–4
Peters, Jim 247–8
Peterson, Robert 363
Phar Lap (Winder) 27
pharmaceuticals 272–3
    see also drugs
phencyclidine (PCP) 6
Phenylbutazone 95
Philadelphia 76ers 293
physical appearance 48, 49, 88–9, 101,
    103, 171
    see also eroticism; muscle dysmorphia
physical education 49, 194
physical fitness 46, 47
Pichler, David 153
Picou, Steven 23
pigeon shooting 43
Pilic, Niki 392
Piotrowski, J. 425
Pippig, Uta 275, 380
Planckaert, Eddy 112
Planet Hollywood 450
Player, Gary 262
player power 58, 392
Players' Association 93, 309
Players' League 242
Players' Union 52
Plessy *vs.* Ferguson case 363, 365
Plimpton, George 445
Poa Supina grass 164
Podkopayeva, Yekaterina 7
Poile, David 353
point shaving *see Blue Chips*; bung inquiry
pole vault 138
Polgar, Judit 84
politics 201, 277, **331–4**, 421
Polley, Martin 233
polo 286
Polsky, Ned 188
pool 34, 135, 188–9
    see also snooker
Pope, Harrison G. 297
post-industrial society 278
Postman, Neil 296

postmodernity *see* modernity/post-modernity
Poulidor, Raymond 29, 418
Pound, Richard 99
Povarnitsyn, Rudolf 144
Powell, Renee 452
power 255, 256
pre-menstrual syndrome 50
Prefontaine, Steve 110, 319
pregnancy *see* motherhood
Premiership 63, 198, 291, 407
Press, Irina and Tamara 269, 420
pressure *see* choking; relaxation
Preston, Hubert 448
Preston, Norman 448
Price, Lloyd 219
Price, Nick 402
Pride of St Louis, The (Jones) 134
Pride of the Yankees, The (Woods) 134
Private Eye 121
Pro Athletes Outreach organization 301
probenecid 418
Professional Golf Association (PGA) 263–4, 449, 450, 451–2
professionalism 224–5, 243, 282
Program 1425 **334–5**, 404
Pronger, Brian 152
propaganda 201
Propanolol 442
ProServ 32, 210, 263, 310, **335–7**
Prosser, Elizabeth 181
Protestant ethic 160, 276, 301, **337–41**, 383, 447–8
pseudoephedrene 6
psyching 70, 161, 169, **341–3**, 354
psychology *see* aggression; focused; motivational; psyching
puberty 101–2, 266
public health 48–9
public schools 254, 258, 299
pugilism, and gambling 149
Puglise, M. 101
Puma 317
Pumping Iron (Butler and Fiore) 138
Pumping Iron II: The Women (Butler) 115, 138–9
Puritanism 338, 340

Puskas, Ferenc 87
Quarry, Jerry 16
Quiet Victory: The Charlie Wedemeyer Story (Campanella) 134
Quirk, James 145

race, physical difference 344–5
racehorse stables 26
racism xi, 1–2, 75–6, 212, **344–6**, 450–1
    and Aboriginals 160–1
    and Arthur Ashe 31–2
    discrimination legislation 90–1
    equality of access 333
    of fans 126
    and Maoris 168–9
    and O.J. Simpson 377, 378
    and rugby 196
    South Africa 349–51
    stereotypes 176, 336
    and Titanic 208–9
    see also black power; Combat 18; Robinson, Jackie
radio 130
Radke, Linda 272
Rage on Ice (Lord) 138
Raging Bull (Scorsese) 133, **346–9**
Rainbow Media Holdings 291
Ramsamy, Samba (Sam) 16, 157, **349–51**
Ranatunga, Arjuna 353
Ranjitsinhji, K.S. 196
rape *see* sex crimes
Raskind, Richard 421–2
Rasmussen, Bill 115
Ravanelli, Fabrizio 63
Raymond, Michel 229, 230
Reagan, Ronald 18
Real Betis 55
Real Madrid 55, 288, 362
Reardon, Patsy 443
recreation 338–9
Redhead, Steve 120, 182
Redknapp, Jamie 326
Reebok x, 114, 170, 211, 309
Reece, Gabrielle 166, 233
referee 66, 192, 198, **351–4**, 404
Regen, Richard 221
regulation 224–5

Rehberg, Richard 23
Reid, M. 228
Reid, Robert 56
Reinisch, Rica 335
Reinsdorf, Jerry 212
relaxation 141, 285, 342, **354–6**
religion *see* Christianity; muscular Christianity; superstition
religious conflict 86
Requiem for a Heavyweight (*Blood Money*) 133, 381
Rescher, Nicholas 149, 238–9
reserve clause 144–6, 147, 225, 242, 245, 384
Reynolds case 98, **356–7**, 380, 381
Rhode, Marcus 13
Rhodes, Ted 452
Richards, Renee 421–2
Rickard, Ted 385
Rickey, Branch 363
Rigauer, Bero 251
Riggs, Bobby 89, 216–17, 362
Riggs, Karen E. 395–6
Rimet, Jules 129
Rinehart, Robert 20
Risberg, Swede 106
risk 3, 9, 21, **357–60**
   see also danger; death
Risley, Steve 372
rituals 181, 240, 393–5
   see also superstition
Ritzer, George 20
rivalries **360–2**
   Anquetil-Poulidor 29, 418
   Bird-Johnson 206, 309
   boxing 16–17, 347
   Graziano-Zale 382
   Harding-Kerrigan 169–71
   Korbut-Comaneci 222
   local 86
   Slaney-Budd 379
   tennis 53
Rix, Graham 374
Roberts, Glyn 346
Roberts, Ian 74, 152, 154
Robertson, Oscar 146
Robertson, Roland 158

Robins, David 178
Robinson, Darrell 167
Robinson, Jackie 1–2, 110, 111, **363–5**, 449
Robinson, Sugar Ray 347
Robledo, Luis 51
rock climbing 358
Rocky I–V (Avildsen; Stallone) 132–3, 285, **365–7**, 432
Rodal, Verbjorn 214
Roddy, George 451
rodeo 42, 43, 185
Rodman, Dennis 110, 191, 192, 353, 376
   and cross-dressing 154, 192, 422
Roe *vs.* Wade 411
Rogers, Bill 263
Rogers, Maxwell 5
role models/modeling *see* fandom; icons
Rolex 450
roller derby 19, 136
Rollerball (Jewison) 19, 136
Roman Catholic Church 301
Romifidine 95
Ronaldo 55, 381
Rono, Henry 213–14
Rono, Peter 214
Rooney, Kevin 428
Rose, Lionel 161
Roseborough, John 438
Rosewall, Ken 336
Rothstein, Arnold 104–5
Rous, Sir Stanley 172
Roussel, Bruno 419
Rozelle, Peter 316, 391
RSPCA (Royal Society for the Prevention of Cruelty to Animals) 40
Ruben, Chandra 70, 143
Rubin, Jerry 303
Rudy, Frank 319
rugby 108, 113
   Australian Rules 300
   films 135, 409–10
   and instant replay 198
   and professionalism 311
   ritual 168–9
   rules 311, 313–14
   salary cap 369
   South Africa 156, 157, 196

sponsorship 387
televised 291, 292
Rugby Football League 311
Rugby Football Union (RFU) 129, 311
rules 66, 78, 311–12
Running Brave (Everett) 133
Running Man, The (Glazer) 19–20, 136
Russell, Bill 309
Ruth, Babe 105, 133, 227, 242
   and Babe Didrikson 89
   and Hank Aaron 1, 2
   salary 106, 244, 329
   sexual exploits 329
Ryan, Greg 168
Ryan, Joan 59, 284

Saban, Lou 378
Sabina Park, Jamaica 165
Sabo, D. 255
Sabres, Buffalo 353
Sachau, O.A. 437
sailing 7
St Andrews golf club 262
St Martin, L. 49
salary caps 52, 58, 225, 242–4, **368–9**
   Larry Bird exception 391
Salazar, Alberto 381
Salinger, J.D. 127
Salt Lake City scandal 78, 204, **369–71**
Samaranch, Juan Antonio 203, 370, 371
Sammons, Jeffrey 14
Sampras, Pete 53
Sampson, Kevin 123
Samuelson, Joan 281
San Francisco 49ers 146
SAN-ROC (South African Non-Racial
   Olympic Committee) 156, 349, 350
Sang, Joe 215
Sang, Patrick 214
Santa Fé 51
São Paulo 55, 129
satellites 131, 159, 291, 405
Saunders, Dean 438
Schaap, Dick 152
Schafer, Walter 22–3
Schiebinger, Londa 265, 267
Schlesinger, John 138

Schultz, Jack 65
Schumacher, Toni 355
Schwarzenegger, Arnold 19–20
'scissors' 143
Scott, Jack 93, 175, 323
Scott, Peter 278
Seaman, David 67, 352
Sears, Eleanora Randolph 89, 232
Sears, Robert 325
Season on the Brink, A (Feinstein) 43, 124,
   371–3
Sedin, Daniel and Henrik 425
Seedorf, Clarence 55
Segers, Hans 58, 77
segregation 104, 208, 363–5
Seirawan, Yasser 83
Seldon, Bruce 374
Seles, Monica 47, 120, 263, 359
self, technologies of 47–8
self-actualization 286
self-discipline 21, 47, 48
Selig, Bud 391
Selous, Frederick Courteney 195
Semple, Jock 399, 400
Senna, Ayrton 262
Sennett, Richard 304
Seoul Olympics (1988) 78, 204, 214,
   274, 370
Set-Up, The (Wise) 133, 348
sex
   abstention from 395
   see also eroticism
sex crimes 24, 207, **374–6**
   see also paternity
sex-tests 269, 420
   see also medical discourse; transsexuals
sexism xi, xii, 2–4, 20, 90–1, 176
   see also discrimination
sexual ambiguities 154–5
sexual difference 265–7, 269
sexuality *see* feminism; gays; lesbianism;
   masculinities/femininities; virilism
SFX Entertainment 337
Shankley, Bill 373
Shannon, Claude 83
Shannon, Eddie 91
Shavers, Earnie 219

Sheard, K. 282, 409
Shearer, Alan 55
Sheppard, David 155
Sheringham, Teddy 56–7
Sherman Act 145
Shippen, John 451
Shohat, Ellas 429
showjumping 27, 185
Shriver, Eunice Kennedy 90
Shultz, Johannes 355
Sievers, Jerg 335
Sifford, Charlie 449, 452
Sigall, H. 71
Sillerman, Robert 337
Silva, J.M. 59
Simmons, Roy 152
Simpson, O.J. 376, **377–9**
Simpson, Tommy 28, 91–2, 95, 97, 272–3, 417–18
Singer, Marc 446
Singh, Keith 81, 93
Sixth Man, The (Miller) 137
Ski Bum, The (Clark) 136
skiing, films 135–6
skill 142
Skinner, B.F. 284
Sklad, M. 425
Sky Boxoffice 407
Sky Sport 291, 404
Slaney case 275, 357, **379–81**
Slaney, Mary 360
    see also Slaney case
Slap Shot (Hill) 138, 188
slaves 209, 345, 443
slow-motion 30
Smith, R.E. 59
Smith, Bob 443
Smith, Harold 17
Smith, James 'Bonecrusher' 367
Smith, Michael 436, 439
Smith, Robin 198
Smith, Sam 212
Smith, Stan 32, 335–6
Smith, Steve Hedake 45
Smith, Tommie 16, 156, 202, 219, 280
Sniffin' Glue 121
snooker 34, 93, 386, 441–2

Snyder, Eldon 3, 4, 24, 432, 433
soccer 8, 51, 108, 129
    in America 160
    club ownership 264
    contracts 55, 58
    derbies 85–6
    global game 130–2
    migration of players 50–2
    player power 58
    regulation 225
    and strikes 392
    and technology 404
    transfer systems 51, 54–5, 224, 225
    violence 438, 439
    see also hooliganism
social fragmentation 358–9
Soden, Arthur 144–5
Sofia, Bulgaria 86
solucamphre 418
somatonorm 94, 187
somatotropin 67, 94, 186
Somebody Up There Likes Me (Wise) 105, 133, 188, **381–2**
Soros, George 246
Sotomayor, Javier 144
Sotomayor, Sonia 391
South Africa 155–8, 202, 349–51
South African Council on Sport (SACOS) 350
South African National Olympic Committee 349, 351
South Korea 197
Soweto uprising (1976) 157
Space Jam (Cervone and Pytka) 211
Spady, William 23
Spalding, A.G. 242–3, 363, **383–5**
Special Olympics 90
spectators, and underdog 432–4
Spencer, Herbert 299
Spencer-Devlin, Muffin 73, 233, 234
Spiller, Bill 452
Spinks, Leon 17, 220
Spinks, Michael 342–3
split screens 30
sponsorship 197, **385–7**, 406, 414
    China 68, 69–70
    and cycling 417

and darts 33–4
and FIFA 160, 172
Olympic Games 203, 204, 370–1
tobacco 386–7, 413–14
see also endorsements
sport
  and crime 23–4
  depoliticizing impact 253
  and diplomacy 332
  and economic development 332
  educational benefits of 22–3
  as entertainment ix, 166
  influence of ix–x
  institutionalization 339
  as new opiate 175–7
  rationalization of 339
  and social control 332
  as social institution viii, ix
  state intervention 331–3
Sporting Club Dynamo 334
Sporting Life, The 447
sportization 108–9
sports industry x, 159, 182, 312, 384–5
Sports Medicine Council of Canada 99–100
SportSouth Network 424
spousal abuse 11, 387–9, 408
spread 45, 150, **389–90**
  see also gambling
Spreitzer, Elmer 3, 4
Sprewell, Latrell 328, 440
sprint 138
Spybey, Tony 158
Stacey, J. 190
stadiums 164–5
  and alcohol ban 178
  overcrowding 173–4
  seating 179
stag hunting 42
Stam, Robert 429
Standish, Bert L. 300
Stanley, Edward 85
stanozolol 92
Staples Center, Los Angeles 290
Star Television 117, 291, 293, 295
stars viii, ix, 110
  and physical appearance 48
  superstars 87

see also icons; Jordan, Michael
Stealing Home (Kampmann and Aldiss) 134
steeplechasing 26, 81
Steiner, Troy and Terry 425
Stern, David 116, 310, 368
Stevens, Huub 404
stimulants 94
Stiven, 194
Stockton, John 336
Stoke Mandeville Hospital 89
Stones, Dwight 141, 144
'straddle' 143
Strasser, J.B. 295
stress 107, 354
  see also anxiety; choking; relaxation
strikes 145, 244, 310, 316, **390–2**, 424
Struna, N. 338
strychnine 91
Sulaiman, Jose 220
Sugden, John 171
suicide 53, 74, 81, 123, 152
Sundgrot-Borgen, Jorunn 102
Sundstrom, Patrik and Peter 425
Super Bowl 8, 315, 387, 405, 408
Superstars 19
superstition 126, 139, 169, 240, 377, **392–7**
Surtees, R.S. 42
Sutter, Rich and Ron 425
Swan, Peter 52, 57
Sweeney, John 144
Sweet Science, The (Liebling) 104, 124, 142, 382, **397–9**
Swift, E.M. 78
swimming 69, 186
Switzer, Kathy 248, **399–400**
Swoopes, Sheryl 233
swordplay 149
Sydney, Australia 27
Sydney Olympics (2000) 78
sympathomimetic amine drugs 94
synchronized swimming 204
synthetic materials
  footballs 402
  running tracks 401
synthetic sports 31

T-E ratio 379–380

table tennis 69
taekwondo 24
Taiwan 68
Tanui, William 214
Tapie, Bernard 66, 78
Tarlton, Robert 116
Tatz, Colin 196–7
Taub, Diane 102
Taylor, Ian 179
Taylor, Lord Justice 173
technology 20, 82–5, 116, 276, 286, **401–5**
television 29, 110, 211, **405–8**, 423
    and advertising 294, 333
    and American football 315–16
    building demand 29–30
    cable 115–17, 290–1, 293
    and darts 33–4
    dedicated channels 294
    documentaries 173
    effect of 296, 397–8, 406
    and fandom 120, 125
    and globalization 159, 405, 408, 435
    and golf 450
    and Grand National 81
    growth of 314–15, 405–6
    and IMG 262
    instant replay 198
    and Major League Soccer 246
    and minority sports 30
    and notoriety 192
    and O.J. Simpson 377
    and Olympics 202–3, 370–1
    and player power 392
    power of 294, 313
    and rivalries 222, 360, 361
    and salary caps 369
    and snooker 441
    and soccer 131–2, 385
    subscription 407–8
    subversive potential 251
    and superstars 239, 329–30
    'time-outs' 315
    and women's basketball 310
    and wrestling 35–6
    see also American Gladiators; Arledge,
    Roone; ESPN; Murdochization; Turner,
    Ted; videated

Telstar 131, 159
Tenenbaun, Gershon 8–9, 10
tennis 52–3, 161–2
    and age 6, 7, 8, 53, 58
    and anxiety 70
    and homosexuality 73, 215–18
    injuries 162–3
    and left-handedness 230
    and meditation 355
    professionalism 216
    strikes 392
    and technology 403
    see also ProServ
Terminator 2: Judgement Day
    (Cameron) 115
Terrell, Ernie 16
testosterone 272, 274–5, 379–80
Tevis Cup 185
Tewksbury, Mark 74
Texaco 116
thalidomide 97
This Sporting Life (Anderson) 135, **408–10**
Thomas, Isaiah 182, 371–3
Thompson, Ken 83
Thorpe, Chuck 449
Thorpe, Jim 452
Time Warner 293, 295, 407, 424
Tin Cup (Shelton) 138
Title IX 3, 216, **410–13**
Titleist 450
TNT (Turner Network Television) 424
tobacco 48, **413–16**
    and China 68, 69–70
    and illness 415
    lawsuits 415–16
    sponsorship 34, 216, 386–7, 413–14,
    441–2
    see also Morris (Philip)
Tofler, I. 59
Tokyo Olympics (1964) 156
Tomjanovich, Rudy 438
Tomlinson, Alan 171
Toolson, George 244–5
tote 150
Tour de France **416–19**
    and drugs 28–9, 95, 112, 417–19
    see also cycling

tourism 332
track and field 133
training, overexertion 59, 222, 223, 271
transcendental meditation (TM) 355
transfer fees 54–5, 56, 63, 147, 224, 369
transfer systems 51, 54–5, 144–5, 369
transsexuals 218, 335, **419–22**
    see also gays; masculinities/femininities
transvestites 422
Traver, Bob 443
Tribune Group 424
Trudeau, Pierre 306
Trulson, Michael 24
Trumper, Victor 196
Tubbs, Tony 283
Tunney, Gene 130
turf, artificial 164
Turing, Alan 83
Turner Broadcasting System (TBS) 422
Turner, Robert 'Ted' 279, 292, 293, 385,
    408, **422–5**
Tutko, Thomas 342
Tweedy, Alice 266
TwentyFourSeven (Meadows) 21
twins **425–6**
Tylor, Sir Edward Burnett viii
Tyson, Mike 5, 113–14, 191, 208, 342–3,
    427–30
    comeback 210, 290, 428
    and Don King 220–1
    and endorsements 111, 428
    and Evander Holyfield 39, 221, 427, 428
    fall of 285, 428, 432
    and Frank Bruno 291, 407
    rape 24, 111, 374

UCLA 309
Ueberroth, Peter 203
UEFA (Union de Associans Européenes de
    Football) 132, 178, 224, 288
Uhlir, Ann 412
Ulbricht, Walter 305
Ullrich, Jan 335
Ulster Defence Association (UDA) 72
umpire *see* referee
underdog 15, 221, 366, 428, **431–4**, 445
    and gambling 57, 77

and luck 238
and salary caps 368
Union Cycliste International (UCI) 417
United Golf Association (UGA) 451, 452
United Nations, and South Africa 350
United States Football League (USFL) 316
United States National Organization for
    Women (NOW) 400
United States Tennis Association (USTA)
    421–2
universities *see* NCAA (National Collegiate
    Athletic Association)
US Army Cavalry 185
USA Track and Field (USATF) organiza-
    tion 379–81
USSR
    collapse of 305–6
    medicine and sport 272
    and nationalism 305
    and Olympics 201
USTA (United States Tennis Association)
    215, 216

Vainio, Maarti 37, 94
Valderrama, Carlos 52
Valdes, Nino 398
Vamplew, Wray 186
Van Exel, Nick 353
Van Raalte, Judy 394
Verbruggen, Heinz 112
Verma, Gajendra 327
Vertinsky, Patricia 266, 267
Vicario, Aranxta Sanchez 261
videated 120, 294, **435–6**
Vikelas, Dimitros 199–200
Villeneuve, Jacques 261
Vines, Gail 267
violence 49, 408, **436–40**
    copycat effect 181
    and regulation 225, 437
    and restraint 96, 107–8
    on women 331
    see also aggression; blood sports; Combat
    18; hooliganism; *i.d.*; spousal abuse
Viren, Lasse 38
Virginia Slims tour 216, 386, 413
virilism 89, 187, 231–2, 267–9, 335, 419–21

Visions of Eight (Forman *et al.*) 138
visualization, positive 141
volleyball 69
Volleyball World Championships, Japan
    (1998) 4
vomiting 102
Vorster, John 155, 156
Vuelta de España 419

Waddell, Tom 73–4, 152
Waddington, Ivan 38, 273
Wade, Kirsty 281
Wade, Virginia 422
Wahl, Grant 328, 329
Waitz, Greta 4, 248, 249
Walcott, Jersey Joe 398
Walker, Dougie 274–5
Walker, Moses Fleetwood 363
Walsh, Stella 269
Ward, Colin 195
Warne, Shane 47, 77
Warren, Frank 221
Warrick, Zoe 81
Washington, Booker T. 208
Washington, Desiree 374, 428
Washington, Kermit 438
Water Ski World Cup 261
Watson, Alexander 92
Watson, Curly 443
Waugh, Mark 77
Waugh twins 425
Way of the Dragon, The (Lee) 136
Weaver, Buck 106
Weber, Max 338, 341
Wedemeyer, Charlie 134
Weiden & Kennedy 320
weight, excess 102
weightlifting 28, 69, 138, 186, 272
Wenger, Arsène 67
Wepner, Chuck 366
Werbeniuk, Bill 93, **441–2**
Wertheim, L. Jon 328, 329
Wessig, Gerd 144
West Indies, cricket 306
Whannel, Garry 256, 408
Wharton, Arthur **442–4**
Wheaties 450

When Saturday Comes (fanzine) 122
When Saturday Comes (Geise) 135
When We Were Kings (Gast) 17, 139, 190,
    220, **444–6**
White Conduit Club 258
White Men Can't Jump (Shelton) 137, 138
Whitson, Dave 437–8
Wiegman, Robyn 170
Wiggins, David 18
Wilander, Mats 53
Willard, Jess 77, 209, 397
Williams, Eric 374
Williams, Lefty 105, 106
Williams, Lucy 452
Williams, Montieth 427
Williams, Venus xi
Willoughby, Bill 312
Wills, Thomas W. 300
Wimbledon 261, 262, 406
    boycott 336
winning 97, 234, 282, 283, 340, 352–3
Winning (Goldstone) 135
Wint, Arthur 444
Winter, Lloyd C. 345
Wisden 196, **446–9**
Witherspoon, Tim 220–1, 367
Witt, Katerina 256
Wolffe, Joseph B. 273
womanhood 231–3
    see also femininity
women 50, 103, 256, 257, 267
    acceptable sports 2–4, 88, 200, 231, 232
    and aggression 11, 49
    baseball 245
    basketball 310
    bodybuilding 49, 115
    boxing 4, 49
    cycling 417
    dangers of sport 231–2, 248, 264–70, 420
    equal rights 216, 333–4, 400, 410–12
    marathon 248–9, 399, 400
    and muscular Christianity 300
    Olympic Games 200–1, 265, 271–2, 399
    and physical appearance 49, 88–9, 103,
    114, 256, 257
    repression 268–70, 348
    soccer 132, 172, 246

virilism 89, 187, 231–2, 267–9, 335, 419–21
weakness 266–8, 272
wrestling 36
see also acceptability/nonacceptability; feminism; masculinities/femininities; medical discourse; Title IX
Women's National Basketball Association (WNBA) 310
Women's Olympic Games 200–1
Women's Professional Basketball League 310
Women's Tennis Association (WTA) 215
Woods, Eldrick 'Tiger' xi, 6, 111, 320, 328, **449–52**
Woosnam, Ian 261
working classes 179–80, 235, 282, 299, 300, 328
World Armsport Federation 34
World Athletics Championships 204
World Boxing Council (WBC) 220
World Community of Al-Islam 17
World Cup 129–32, 277, 332
   and television 159, 296, 405
   USA 160, 246
World Health Organization (WHO) 12, 69, 93
World League of American Football 160
World Professional Billiards and Snooker Association (WPBSA) 93, 441, 442
World of Sport 36
World Swimming Championships (1998) 335

Worth, Peter 52
wrestling 19, 35, 99, 407
Wrigley, Philip 232, 245
Wroblewska, A.M. 269
Wu Yanyan 187
WWF (World Wrestling Federation) 35
Wykes, Alan 45, 149

Xylazine 95

Yesterday's Hero (Leifer) 135
Yifter, Miruts 6–7
YMCA (Young Men's Christian Association) 300, 308
Yoga 355
Young, Cy 242
young offenders 20–2, 24, 235–7
Yuan Yuan 67, 187
Yukon Jack World Arm-Wrestling Championships 34
Zaharias, George 'The Weeping Greek' 88

Zale, Tony 382
Zatopek, Emil 248
Zetterling, Mai 138
Zimbalist, Andrew 408
Zivic, Fritzie 347
Zoeller, Fuzzy 450
zone 140–3
Zoth, Oskar 93
Zwinger, Lynda 170
Zworykin, Vladimir 130